CORPVS CHRISTIANORVM

Series Graeca

66

CORPVS CHRISTIANORVM

Series Graeca

66

FLORILEGIVM COISLINIANVM

A

TURNHOUT
BREPOLS ✥ PUBLISHERS
2018

FLORILEGIVM COISLINIANVM
A

EDIDIT

TOMÁS FERNÁNDEZ

TURNHOUT
BREPOLS ❧ PUBLISHERS
2018

CORPVS CHRISTIANORVM

Series Graeca

sub auspiciis
Vniuersitatis Catholicae Louaniensis
KU LEUVEN
in Instituto Studiorum Palaeochristianorum et Byzantinorum
INSTITUUT VOOR VROEGCHRISTELIJKE EN BYZANTIJNSE STUDIES
edita

Editionibus curandis praesunt

Reinhart CEULEMANS
José DECLERCK
Yiannis DEMETRACOPOULOS
Bernard FLUSIN
Carl LAGA
Jacques NORET
Antonio RIGO
Carlos STEEL
Peter VAN DEUN

Huic uolumini parando operam dedit

Johanna MICHELS

D/2018/0095/270
ISBN 978-2-503-40661-9
Printed in the EU on acid-free paper

© 2018, Brepols Publishers n.v., Turnhout, Belgium

All rights reserved. No part of this publication may be reproduced,
stored in a retrieval system, or transmitted, in any form or by any means,
electronic, mechanical, photocopying, recording, or otherwise,
without the prior permission of the publisher.

For my mother and father

Ἐρῶ δὲ ἐμὸν μέν, ὡς ἔφην, οὐδέν [...]. Ἐρῶ τοιγαροῦν ἐμὸν μὲν οὐδέν.

John of Damascus, *Dialectica*

Qu'on ne dise pas que je n'ai rien dit de nouveau: la disposition des matières est nouvelle.

Pascal, *Pensées*

FOREWORD

The aim of this volume is to provide a reliable critical edition of Book Alpha of the *Florilegium Coislinianum*. Since Book Alpha is only about one-fifth of the anthology (72 folios out of 370 in *Par. gr. 924*), this is no more than a humble addition to a much vaster work-in-progress which, under the direction of Peter Van Deun, has been developing since 2006-2007 at KU Leuven. Indeed, most of the research leading to this book was conducted in Leuven between 2007 and 2010. I had arrived at that picturesque and rainy Belgian city thanks to the good offices of Caroline Macé, who informed our research team in Buenos Aires about a PhD position there in the field of Byzantine anthologies. Only with time did I realise how lucky I was. I always enjoyed the undivided support of my supervisor, Peter Van Deun, who read with meticulous attention earlier drafts of this introduction and successive versions of the Greek text, providing thorough and accurate remarks. I profited almost daily from the erudition of Basile Markesinis, to whom Byzantine Greek, no less than Platonic Greek, is a native language, and who would interpret with precision even the most intractable texts I came across. And I shared my office space with Jacques Noret, who did his best to educate me both in the most recent text-critical methods and in the venerable philological tradition of the Bollandists, which he had learned himself from the likes of Bernard Halkin. After all these years, I admire more and more the generosity of these scholars, who invested so much time and energy in me. Jacques in particular was a father for me during those long mornings and afternoons, when I interrupted him constantly to ask about manuscripts and authors and, every day at four o'clock, to offer him a cup of tea before he headed home to Brussels.

I was no less fortunate to meet Reinhart Ceulemans, a most generous friend and also, with time, the severest critic of

VIII   FOREWORD

every text I sent him. From a distance, Pablo Cavallero (who
had taught me Greek for years on end, either in classrooms
or in the tiny office in the Faculty of Arts where we toiled at
Leontius of Neapolis' *Lives*) provided invaluable advice on all
matters, philological or otherwise.

José Declerck allowed me to consult his as-yet-unpublished
collations of many witnesses of the different recensions of the
Sacra Parallela, and always provided me with wise comments.
Paolo Odorico provided precious advice on Byzantine matters. Sever Voicu discussed with me different pseudo-Chrysostomic fragments. Paul Géhin showed me around the IRHT
and put a large number of microfilms at my disposal. The
staff of the IRHT was also extremely helpful. Christian
Förstel made available to me all of the manuscripts of the
Bibliothèque nationale de France that I wished to consult, including one – *Par. Coisl. 294* – in a bad state of conservation.
In the last stage of this book's preparation, José Maksimkzuk
offered unfaltering support and enthusiasm. Johanna Michels
provided invaluable comments on the structure and wording
of this introduction. Bram Roosen advised me on how to up-
grade the Greek text from its penultimate version to the one
I now offer the reader.

It is also a pleasure for me to express my gratitude to FWO
– Flanders, which financed my research between 2007 and
2010, to Conicet (Argentina), which financed it afterwards,
and to various centers where I profited from extraordinary
bibliographical collections and kind advice, especially the
University of Cincinnati (Tytus Fellowship, 2012) and the
Ludwig-Maximilians-Universität in Munich (Humboldt Fellowship, 2016).

A large number of colleagues and friends has been very
helpful in different matters. I am bound to forget many, but
I wish to remember at least some of them: Albrecht Berger,
André Binggeli, Reka Forrai, Niels Gaul, Michael Grünbart,
Martin Hinterberger, Florin Leonte, Katrien Levrie, Karin
Metzler, Elio Montanari, Savvas Neocleous, Paul-Hubert
Poirier, Filippo Ronconi, Elisabeth Schiffer, Erich Trapp,
Dimitrios Zaganas.

SIGLA AND BIBLIOGRAPHICAL ABBREVIATIONS

AB = Analecta Bollandiana.

Amand de Mendieta – Rudberg, *Basilius Caesariensis* = E. Amand de Mendieta – S. Y. Rudberg, *Basilius Caesariensis. Homilien zum Hexaemeron* (*GCS*, N. F., 2), Berlin, 1997.

BA = Byzantinisches Archiv.

Bailly = A. Bailly et al., *Dictionnaire grec-français*, Paris, 1963[26] (repr. 2000).

Barrett, *Euripides* = W. S. Barrett, *Euripides. Hippolytos*, Oxford, 1964.

BBA = Berliner Byzantinistische Arbeiten.

Beck, *Kirche* = H.-G. Beck, *Kirche und theologische Literatur im byzantinischen Reich* (*Handbuch der Altertumswissenschaft* 12, 2, 1. *Byzantinisches Handbuch* 2, 1), München, 1959.

BHG = Bibliotheca Hagiographica Graeca.

Boudignon, *Max. Conf.* = C. Boudignon, *Maximi Confessoris Mystagogia una cum Latina interpretatione Anastasii Bibliothecarii* (*CCSG* 69), Turnhout, 2011.

BSGRT = Bibliotheca Scriptorum Graecorum et Romanorum Teubneriana.

Byz = Byzantion.

BZ = Byzantinische Zeitschrift.

Canart, *Provataris* = P. Canart, *Les manuscrits copiés par Emmanuel Provataris (1546-1570 environ). Essai d'étude codicologique*, in *Mélanges Eugène Tisserant*, 6 (*ST* 236), Città del Vaticano, 1964, p. 173-287.

Cataldi Palau, *Pellicier* = A. Cataldi Palau, *Les vicissitudes de la collection de manuscrits grecs de Guillaume Pellicier*, in *Scriptorium* 40 (1986), p. 32-53.

Catalogue 1848-1853 = Catalogue of Additions to the Manuscripts in the British Museum in the Years 1848-1853, London, 1868.

Catalogue 1888-1893 = Catalogue of Additions to the Manuscripts in the British Museum in the Years 1888-1893, London, 1894.

Catalogue of Greek and Italian Manuscripts = Catalogue of Greek and Italian Manuscripts and English Charters from the Cele-

X   SIGLA AND BIBLIOGRAPHICAL ABBREVIATIONS

brated Collection formed by Sir Thomas Phillipps, Bt. (1792-1872), Auction: 4ᵗʰ July 1972 (*Bibliotheca Phillippica*, N. S. 8), London, 1972.

CCSG = Corpus Christianorum, Series Graeca.

CEULEMANS, *Cosmological* = R. CEULEMANS, *Cosmological Questions Answered through Severian of Gabala in the* Athonensis, Lavras *B 43 (Eustratiadis 163)*, in B. DEMULDER – P. VAN DEUN (eds.), *Questioning the World. Greek Patristic and Byzantine Question and Answer Literature* (*LECTIO Studies on the Transmission of Texts & Ideas*), Turnhout (forthcoming).

CEULEMANS et al., *Eta* = R. CEULEMANS – I. DE VOS – E. GIELEN – P. VAN DEUN, *La continuation de l'exploration du* Florilegium Coislinianum*: la lettre Èta*, in *Byz* 81 (2011), p. 74-126.

CEULEMANS et al., *Psi* = R. CEULEMANS – E. DE RIDDER – K. LEVRIE – P. VAN DEUN, *Sur le mensonge, l'âme de l'homme et les faux prophètes: La lettre Ψ du* Florilège Coislin, in *Byz* 83 (2013), p. 49-82.

CEULEMANS et al., *Theta* = R. CEULEMANS – P. VAN DEUN – S. VAN PEE, *La vision des quatre bêtes, la* Theotokos, *les douze trônes et d'autres thèmes: La lettre Θ du* Florilège Coislin, in *Byz* 86 (2016), p. 91-128.

CEULEMANS et al., *Xi* = R. CEULEMANS – P. VAN DEUN – F. A. WILDENBOER, *Questions sur les deux arbres du Paradis: La lettre Ξ du* Florilège Coislin, in *Byz* 84 (2014), p. 49-79.

CEULEMANS – VAN DEUN, *Réflexions* = R. CEULEMANS – P. VAN DEUN, *Réflexions sur la littérature anthologique de Constantin V à Constantin VII*, in *TM* 21/2 (2017), p. 361-388.

CFHB = Corpus Fontium Historiae Byzantinae.

Cinq années d'acquisitions = *Cinq années d'acquisitions 1969-1973* (*Catalogues des expositions organisées à la Bibliothèque Royale Albert Iᵉʳ*), Bruxelles, 1975.

COHN, *Ueberlieferung* = L. COHN, *Zur indirekten Ueberlieferung Philo's und der älteren Kirchenväter*, in *Jahrbücher für protestantische Theologie* 18 (1892), p. 475-492.

COXE, *Bodleiana* = H. O. COXE, *Catalogi codicum manuscriptorum Bibliothecae Bodleianae pars prima recensionem codicum graecorum continens*, Oxonii, 1853.

COXE, *Canoniciani* = H. O. Coxe, *Catalogi codicum manuscriptorum Bibliothecae Bodleianae pars tertia codices Graecos et Latinos Canonicianos complectens*, Oxonii, 1854.

CPG = M. GEERARD, *Clavis Patrum Graecorum*, 4 vols., Turnhout, 1974-1983; M. GEERARD – F. GLORIE, *Clavis Patrum Grae-*

SIGLA AND BIBLIOGRAPHICAL ABBREVIATIONS   XI

corum, V, Turnhout, 1987; M. GEERARD – J. NORET, *Clavis Patrum Graecorum. Supplementum*, Turnhout, 1998; J. NORET, *Clavis Patrum Graecorum*, III A, editio secunda, anastatica, addendis locupletata, Turnhout, 2003.

DE MONTFAUCON, *Bibliotheca Coisliniana* = B. DE MONTFAUCON, *Bibliotheca Coisliniana, olim Segueriana; siue Manuscriptorum omnium Graecorum, quae in ea continentur, accurata descriptio*, Parisiis, 1715.

DE RIDDER, *Elias Ekdikos* = E. DE RIDDER, *The Fruitful Vineyard of Prayer. A Critical Edition of the* Anthologium gnomicum *by Elias Ekdikos* (CPG *7716)*, Leuven, 2015 (unpublished doctoral dissertation).

DE VOS et al., *Beta* = I. DE VOS – E. GIELEN – C. MACÉ – P. VAN DEUN, *La lettre B du Florilège Coislin: editio princeps*, in *Byz* 80 (2010), p. 72-120.

DE VOS et al., *Gamma* = I. DE VOS – E. GIELEN – C. MACÉ – P. VAN DEUN, *L'art de compiler à Byzance: la lettre Γ du Florilège Coislin*, in *Byz* 78 (2008), p. 159-223.

DECLERCK, *Eust. Ant.* = J. H. DECLERCK, *Eustathii Antiocheni, patris Nicaeni, opera quae supersunt omnia* (*CCSG* 51), Turnhout – Leuven, 2002.

DECLERCK, *Manuscrit* = J. H. DECLERCK, *Un manuscrit peu connu, le* Londinensis, Brit. Libr. Add. 17472, in *Byz* 51 (1981), p. 484-501.

DECLERCK, *Max. Conf.* = J. H. DECLERCK, *Maximi Confessoris Quaestiones et dubia* (*CCSG* 10), Turnhout – Leuven, 1982.

DECLERCK, *Probus* = J. H. DECLERCK, *Probus, l'ex-Jacobite et ses* Ἐπαπορήματα πρὸς Ἰακωβίτας, in *Byz* 53 (1983), p. 213-232.

DECLERCK, *Sacra Parallela* = J. H. DECLERCK, *Les* Sacra Parallela *nettement antérieurs à Jean Damascène: retour à la datation de Michel Le Quien*, in *Byz* 85 (2015), p. 27-65.

DÉROCHE, *Képhalaia* = V. DÉROCHE, *La polémique anti-judaïque au VIe et au VIIe siècle: un mémento inédit, les* Képhalaia, in *TM* 11 (1991), p. 275-311 (repr. in G. DAGRON – V. DÉROCHE, *Juifs et chrétiens en Orient byzantin* [*Bilans de recherche* 5], Paris, 2010, p. 275-311).

DEVREESSE, *Vaticani 330-603* = R. DEVREESSE, *Codices Vaticani graeci*, II. *Codices 330-603* (*Bibliothecae Apostolicae Vaticanae Codices manu scripti recensiti*), Città del Vaticano, 1937.

DEVREESSE, *Vaticani 604-866* = R. DEVREESSE, *Codices Vaticani graeci*, III. *Codices 604-866* (*Bibliothecae Apostolicae Vaticanae Codices manu scripti recensiti*), Città del Vaticano, 1950.

XII   SIGLA AND BIBLIOGRAPHICAL ABBREVIATIONS

DEVREESSE, *Coislin* = R. DEVREESSE, *Catalogue des manuscrits grecs. II: Le fonds Coislin (Bibliothèque nationale. Département des manuscrits)*, Paris, 1945.

DEVREESSE, *Fonds* = R. DEVREESSE, *Le fonds grec de la Bibliothèque Vaticane des origines à Paul V* (*ST* 244), Città del Vaticano, 1965.

DIEKAMP, *Hippolytos* = F. DIEKAMP, *Hippolytos von Theben. Texte und Untersuchungen*, Münster i. W., 1898.

DIEKAMP, *Origenistische Streitigkeiten* = F. DIEKAMP, *Die origenistischen Streitigkeiten im sechsten Jahrhundert und das fünfte allgemeine Concil*, Münster i. W., 1899.

DIMITRAKOPOULOS, *Βιβλιοθήκη* = Ph. A. DIMITRAKOPOULOS, *Ἡ βιβλιοθήκη τῆς Ἱερᾶς Μονῆς Δουσικοῦ*, in *ΕΕΣΜ* 5 (1974-1975), p. 403-426.

DIMITRAKOS = D. DIMITRAKOS, *Μέγα λέξικον τῆς Ἑλληνικῆς γλώσσης*, 9 vols., Athens, 1953.

ΕΕΣΜ = *Ἐπετηρὶς Ἑταιρείας Στερεοελλαδικῶν Μελετῶν*.

EUANGELATOU-NOTARA, *Σημειώματα* = F. EUANGELATOU-NOTARA, *Σημειώματα ἑλληνικῶν κωδίκων ὡς πηγὴ διὰ τὴν ἔρευναν τοῦ οἰκονομικοῦ καὶ κοινωνικοῦ βίου τοῦ Βυζαντίου, ἀπὸ τοῦ 9ου αἰῶνος μέχρι τοῦ ἔτους 1204* (*Βιβλιοθήκη Σοφίας Ν. Σαριπολοῦ* 47), Athens, 1978 (repr. 1982).

FATOUROS, *Theodorus Studita* = G. FATOUROS, *Theodori Studitae Epistulae*, I. *Prolegomena et textum* (*epp. 1-70) continens* (*CFHB* 31), Berolini, 1992.

FC = *Florilegium Coislinianum*.

FERNÁNDEZ, *A Correction* = T. FERNÁNDEZ, *A Correction of the Text of Athanasius of Alexandria's* Epistula ad monachos (*CPG 2108)*, in *JÖB* 62 (2012), p. 1-7.

FERNÁNDEZ, *Anatole* = T. FERNÁNDEZ, *Un fragment inédit attribué à Anatole d'Alexandrie*, in *Byzantion Nea Hellás* 30 (2011), p. 189-202.

FERNÁNDEZ, *Atanasio* = T. FERNÁNDEZ, *Dos fragmentos inéditos atribuidos a Atanasio de Alejandría*, in *Erytheia* 32 (2011), p. 79-93.

FERNÁNDEZ, *Cosmas* = T. FERNÁNDEZ, *Cosmas Vestitor's Ascetic-Physiological Fragment* (*CPG 8163)*, in *BZ* 104 (2012), p. 633-640.

FERNÁNDEZ, *Errores coniunctivi* = T. FERNÁNDEZ, *Errores coniunctivi nec separativi?*, in *Anales de filología clásica* 24 (2011), p. 45-57.

FERNÁNDEZ, *Florilegio* = T. FERNÁNDEZ, *El florilegio de los mss. FH en la letra Alfa del* Florilegium Coislinianum (forthcoming).

SIGLA AND BIBLIOGRAPHICAL ABBREVIATIONS XIII

FERNÁNDEZ, *Hesychius* = T. FERNÁNDEZ, *The Greek Fragment of the* Commentary on Leviticus *by Hesychius of Jerusalem*, in B. CROSTINI – G. PEERS (eds.), *A Book of Psalms from Eleventh-Century Constantinople: The Complex of Texts and Images in Vat. Gr. 752* (*ST* 504), Città del Vaticano, 2016, p. 431-433.

FERNÁNDEZ, *Remarks* = T. FERNÁNDEZ, *Remarks on Editing a Byzantine Anthology*, in *GRBS* 51 (2011), p. 167-179.

FERNÁNDEZ, *Tears* = T. FERNÁNDEZ, *Byzantine Tears. A pseudo-Chrysostomic Fragment on Weeping in the* Florilegium Coislinianum, in P. VAN DEUN – C. MACÉ (eds.), *Encyclopaedic Trends in Byzantium? Proceedings of the International Conference held in Leuven, 6-8 May 2009* (*OLA* 212), Leuven, 2011, p. 125-142.

FERON – BATTAGLINI, *Ottoboniani* = E. FERON – F. BATTAGLINI, *Codices manuscripti graeci Ottoboniani Bibliothecae Vaticanae* (*Bibliothecae Apostolicae Vaticanae Codices manu scripti recensiti*), Romae, 1893, p. 245-248.

FOLLIERI, *Initia hymnorum* = E. FOLLIERI, *Initia hymnorum ecclesiae graecae*, 6 vols. (*ST* 211-215 bis), Città del Vaticano, 1960-1966.

FOUQUERAY, *Histoire* = H. FOUQUERAY, *Histoire de la Compagnie de Jésus en France, des origines à la suppression (1528-1762)*, I. *Les origines et les premières luttes (1528-1575)*, Paris, 1910.

FRANCHI DE' CAVALIERI – MUCCIO, *Index* = P. FRANCHI DE' CAVALIERI – G. MUCCIO, *Index codicum graecorum bibliothecae Angelicae*. Praefatus est Aeneas Piccolomini, in *Studi italiani di filologia classica* 4 (1896), p. 7-184.

GARDTHAUSEN, *Schrift* = V. GARDTHAUSEN, *Die Schrift, Unterschriften und Chronologie im Altertum und im byzantinischen Mittelalter* (*Griechische Palaeographie* 2), Leipzig, 1913.

GCS = *Die griechischen christlichen Schriftsteller der ersten Jahrhunderte*.

GÉHIN, *Kalliandrès* = P. GÉHIN, *Un copiste de Rhodes de la fin du XIIIᵉ siècle: le prêtre Syméon Kalliandrès*, in *Scriptorium* 40 (1986), p. 172-183.

GÉHIN, *Scholia in Prouerbia* = P. GÉHIN, *Évagre le Pontique. Scholies aux Proverbes* (*SC* 340), Paris, 1987.

GIELEN, *Nicephorus* = E. GIELEN, *Nicephori Blemmydae De virtute et ascesi. Iosephi Racendytae De virtute* (*CCSG* 80), Turnhout, 2016.

GIET, *Basile* = S. GIET, *Basile de Césarée. Homélies sur l'Hexaéméron* (*SC* 26 bis), Paris, 1968².

GNO = *Gregorii Nysseni Opera*.

GONNELLI, *Pisidia* = F. GONNELLI, *Giorgio di Pisidia. Esamerone*, Pisa, 1998.

GRBS = *Greek, Roman and Byzantine Studies*.

GUILLAUMONT, *Képhalaia* = A. GUILLAUMONT, *Les "Képhalaia gnostica" d'Évagre le Pontique et l'histoire de l'origénisme chez les Grecs et chez les Syriens* (*Patristica Sorbonensia* 5), Paris, 1962.

HEIMGARTNER, *Pseudojustin* = M. HEIMGARTNER, *Pseudojustin. Über die Auferstehung: Text und Studie* (*PTS* 54), Berlin, 2001.

HILGARD, *Grammatici Graeci* = A. HILGARD, *Grammatici Graeci*, IV/1, Leipzig, 1894, p. 3-42.

HOLL, *Fragmente* = K. HOLL. *Fragmente vornicänischer Kirchenväter aus den* Sacra Parallela (*TU* 20/2), Leipzig, 1899.

HOLL, *Sacra Parallela* = K. HOLL, *Die* Sacra Parallela *des Johannes Damascenus* (*TU*, N. F. 1/1), Leipzig, 1896.

HOSTENS, *Dissertatio* = M. HOSTENS, *Anonymi auctoris Theognosiae (saec. IX/X) Dissertatio contra Iudaeos* (*CCSG* 14), Turnhout, 1986.

JANNARIS, *Grammar* = A. N. JANNARIS, *An Historical Greek Grammar, Chiefly of the Attic Dialect, as Written and Spoken from Classical Antiquity down to the Present Time, Founded upon the Ancient Texts, Inscriptions, Papyri and Present Popular Greek*, London, 1897.

JÖB = *Jahrbuch der Österreichischen Byzantinistik*.

KRETSCHMER, *Wörterbuch* = P. KRETSCHMER, *Ruckläufiges Wörterbuch der griechischen Sprache* (Göttingen, 1944).

LAGA, *Eustratius van Constantinopel* = C. LAGA, *Eustratius van Constantinopel. De mens en zijn werk*, Leuven, 1958 (unpublished doctoral dissertation).

LAGA – STEEL, *Max. Conf.*, I = C. LAGA – C. STEEL, *Maximi Confessoris Quaestiones ad Thalassium*, I. *Quaestiones I-LV una cum latina interpretatione Ioannis Scotti Eriugenae iuxta posita* (*CCSG* 7), Turnhout – Leuven, 1980.

LAGA – STEEL, *Max. Conf.*, II = C. LAGA – C. STEEL, *Maximi Confessoris Quaestiones ad Thalassium*, II. *Quaestiones LVI-LXV una cum latina interpretatione Ioannis Scotti Eriugenae iuxta posita* (*CCSG* 22), Turnhout – Leuven, 1990.

LAKE – LAKE, *Dated Manuscripts* = K. LAKE – S. LAKE, *Dated Greek Minuscule Manuscripts to the Year 1200, III. Manuscripts in the Monasteries of Mount Athos and in Milan* (*Monumenta Palaeographica Vetera. First Series*), Boston, 1935.

LAMBROS, *Athos* = S. P. LAMBROS, Κατάλογος τῶν ἐν ταῖς βιβλιοθήκαις τοῦ Ἁγίου Ὄρους ἑλληνικῶν κωδίκων = *Catalogue*

SIGLA AND BIBLIOGRAPHICAL ABBREVIATIONS   XV

of the Greek manuscripts on Mount Athos, 2 vols., Cambridge, 1895-1900.

Lambros, *Σύμμικτα* = S. P. Lambros, *Σύμμικτα*, in *Νέος Ἑλληνομνήνων* 10 (1913), p. 192-215.

LBG = E. Trapp, *Lexikon zur byzantinischen Gräzität: besonders des 9.-12. Jahrhunderts*, 8 vols., Wien, 1994-2016.

LSJ = H. G. Liddell - R. Scott, *A Greek-English Lexicon, revised and augmented throughout by H.S. Jones with the assistance of R. McKenzie and with the co-operation of many scholars, With a Supplement*, Oxford, 1968.

Maas, *Textkritik* = P. Maas, *Textkritik*, Leipzig, 1960[4].

Mai, *Procopius Gazaeus* = A. Mai, *Procopii Gazaei commentarius in Salomonis proverbia. Eiusdem catena Veterum Patrum in Canticum Canticorum. Scholia minora in Evangelia Lucae et Iohannis. Herennii commentarius ad Metaphysica Aristotelis. Georgii Phrantzae Chronicon parvum rerum sui temporis* (*Classicorum auctorum e vaticanis codicibus editorum* 9), Romae, 1837.

Maksimczuk, *Anthology* = J. Maksimczuk, *The Anthology of* Parisinus gr. *852 and* Vatopediou *36 and its Relation to the* Florilegium Coislinianum, in *REB* (forthcoming).

Martini - Bassi, *Ambrosiana* = E. Martini - D. Bassi, *Catalogus codicum graecorum Bibliothecae Ambrosianae*, 2 vols., Milano, 1906.

Mazzucchi, *Testimone* = C. M. Mazzucchi, *Un testimone della conoscenza del greco negli ordini mendicanti verso la fine del Duecento (Ambr. Q 74 sup.) e un codice appartenuto al Sacro Convento di Assisi (Ambr. E 88 inf.)*, in *Νέα Ῥώμη. Rivista di studi bizantinistici* 3 (2006), p. 355-359 + tav. 1-3.

Michels - Van Deun, *Topaz* = J. Michels - P. Van Deun, *On the Topaz Island: Diodorus of Sicily and the Byzantine* Florilegium Coislinianum, in *Byz* 83 (2013), p. 283-296.

Montanari, *Paul Maas* = E. Montanari, *La critica del testo secondo Paul Maas. Testo e commento* (*Millennio Medievale* 41), Firenze, 2003.

Morani, *Nemesio* = M. Morani, *La tradizione manoscritta del "De natura hominis" di Nemesio* (*Scienze filologiche e letteratura* 18), Milano, 1981.

Munby, *Phillipps* = A. N. L. Munby, *The Formation of the Phillipps Library up to the Year 1840* (*Phillipps Studies* 3), Cambridge, 1954.

Nagel, *Titus von Bostra* = P. Nagel, *Neues griechisches Material zu Titus von Bostra* (Aduersus Manichaeos *III 7-29*), in

XVI SIGLA AND BIBLIOGRAPHICAL ABBREVIATIONS

J. IRMSCHER – P. NAGEL (eds.), *Studia Byzantina*, II. *Beiträge aus der byzantinistischen Forschung der Deutschen Demokratischen Republik zum XIV. internationalen Byzantinistenkongress Bukarest 1971* (*BBA* 44), Berlin, 1973.

NORET, *Accentuation* = J. NORET, *L'accentuation byzantine: en quoi et pourquoi elle diffère de l'accentuation dite "savante" actuelle, parfois absurde*, in M. HINTERBERGER (ed.), *The Language of Byzantine Learned Literature* (*Byzantios. Studies in Byzantine History and Civilization*), Turnhout, 2014, p. 96-146.

NORET, *Catalogues* = J. NORET, *Catalogues récents de manuscrits. Cinquième série* (*Fonds grecs*), in *AB* 91 (1973), p. 419-420.

NORET, *Division* = J. NORET, *Les règles byzantines de la division en syllabes*, in *Byz* 77 (2007), p. 345-348.

NORET, *Indéfinis* = J. NORET, *Quand rendrons-nous à quantité d'indéfinis, prétendument enclitiques, l'accent qui leur revient?*, in *Byz* 57 (1987), p. 191-195.

NORET, *L'accentuation de* τε = J. NORET, *L'accentuation de* τε *en grec byzantin*, in *Byz* 68 (1998), p. 516-518.

NORET – DE VOCHT, *Orthographe* = J. NORET – C. DE VOCHT, *Une orthographe insolite et nuancée, celle de Nicéphore Blemmyde, ou à propos du* δέ *enclitique*, in *Byz* 55 (1985), p. 493-505.

OCT = *Oxford Classical Texts.*

ODORICO, *Cultura* = P. ODORICO, *La cultura della* ΣΥΛΛΟΓΗ. *1) Il cosiddetto enciclopedismo bizantino. 2) Le tavole del sapere di Giovanni Damasceno*, in *BZ* 83 (1990), p. 1-21.

ODORICO, *Prato* = P. ODORICO, *Il prato e l'ape. Il sapere sentenzioso del monaco Giovanni* (*WBS* 17), Wien, 1986.

OLA = *Orientalia Lovaniensia Analecta.*

OLIVIER, *Répertoire* = J.-M. OLIVIER, *Répertoire des bibliothèques et des catalogues de manuscrits grecs de Marcel Richard* (*Corpus Christianorum*), Turnhout, 1995.

OMONT, *Paris* = H. OMONT, *Inventaire sommaire des manuscrits grecs de la Bibliothèque nationale et des autres bibliothèques de Paris et des départements*, 4 vols., Paris, 1898-1888.

PAPADOPOULOS-KERAMEUS, *Jerusalem* = A. PAPADOPOULOS-KERAMEUS, Ἱεροσολυμιτικὴ βιβλιοθήκη ἤτοι κατάλογος τῶν ἐν ταῖς βιβλιοθήκαις τοῦ ἁγιωτάτου ἀποστολικοῦ τε καὶ καθολικοῦ ὀρθοδόξου πατριαρχικοῦ θρόνου τῶν Ἱεροσολύμων καὶ πάσης Παλαιστίνης ἀποκειμένων ἑλληνικῶν κωδίκων, 5 vols., St. Petersburg, 1891-1915.

SIGLA AND BIBLIOGRAPHICAL ABBREVIATIONS   XVII

PAPADOPOULOS-KERAMEUS, *Lesbos* = A. PAPADOPOULOS-KERAMEUS, Κατάλογος τῶν ἐν ταῖς βιβλιοθήκαις τῆς νήσου Λέσβου ἑλληνικῶν χειρογράφων, in Μαυρογορδάτειος βιβλιοθήκη. Παράρτημα τοῦ ιε' τόμου, Constantinople, 1884.

PASINI, *Ambrosiana* = C. PASINI, *Codici e frammenti greci dell'Ambrosiana. Integrazioni al catalogo di Emidio Martini e Domenico Bassi (Testi e studi bizantino-neoellenici* 9), Roma, 1997.

PASINI, *Bibliografia* = C. PASINI, *Bibliografia dei manoscritti greci dell'Ambrosiana (1857-2006) (Bibliotheca erudita: studi e documenti di storia e filologia* 30), Milano, 2007.

PASQUALI, *Gregorius Nyssenus* = G. PASQUALI, *Gregorii Nysseni Epistulae (GNO* 8/2), Leiden, 1959.

PASQUALI, *Storia* = G. PASQUALI, *Storia della tradizione e critica del testo*, Firenze, 1952².

PETIT, *Philon d'Alexandrie* = F. PETIT, *Quaestiones in Genesim et in Exodum: fragmenta Graeca (Les Œuvres de Philon d'Alexandrie* 33), Paris, 1978.

PG = Patrologia Graeca.

PRATO, *Scritture* = G. PRATO, *Scritture librarie arcaizzanti della prima età dei Paleologi e loro modelli*, in *Scrittura e civiltà* 3 (1979), p. 151-193 (repr. in G. PRATO, *Studi di paleografia greca [Centro italiano di studi sull'alto medioevo. Collectanea* 4], Spoleto, 1994, p. 73-114).

PTS = Patristische Texte und Studien.

RAHLFS, *Verzeichnis* = A. RAHLFS, *Verzeichnis der griechischen Handschriften des Alten Testaments, für das Septuaginta-Unternehmen aufgestellt (Akademie der Wissenschaften in Göttingen. Philologisch-historische Klasse. Mitteilungen des Septuaginta-Unternehmens* 2), Berlin, 1914.

REB = Revue des Études Byzantines.

REEVE, *Eliminatio* = M. D. REEVE, Eliminatio Codicum Descriptorum: *A Methodological Problem*, in J. N. GRANT (ed.), *Editing Greek and Latin texts: Papers given at the Twenty-Third Annual Conference on Editorial Problems, University of Toronto, 6–7 November 1987*, New York, 1989, p. 1-35.

RGK = E. GAMILLSCHEG – D. HARLFINGER – H. HUNGER, *Repertorium der griechischen Kopisten 800-1600*. 1. *Handschriften aus Bibliotheken Grossbritanniens*. 2. *Handschriften aus Bibliotheken Frankreichs*. 3. *Handschriften aus Bibliotheken Roms mit dem Vatikan (Österreichische Akademie der Wissenschaften. Philosophisch-historische Klasse. Veröffentlichungen der Kommission für Byzantinistik* 3), Wien, 1981-1997.

XVIII SIGLA AND BIBLIOGRAPHICAL ABBREVIATIONS

RICHARD, *Asterius* = M. RICHARD, *Asterii Sophistae Commentariorum in Psalmos quae supersunt. Accedunt aliquot Homiliae anonymae* (*Symbolae Osloenses, Suppl.* 16), Osloae, 1956.

RICHARD, *British Museum* = M. RICHARD, *Inventaire des manuscrits grecs du British Museum*, I. *Fonds Sloane, Additional, Egerton, Cottonian et Stowe* (*Publications de l'Institut de Recherche et d'Histoire des Textes* 3), Paris, 1952.

RICHARD, *Florilèges* = M. RICHARD, *Florilèges spirituels grecs*, in *Dictionnaire de spiritualité*, 33-34, Paris, 1962, col. 475-512 (repr. in M. RICHARD, *Opera minora*, I, n° 1).

RICHARD, *Opera minora* = M. RICHARD, *Opera minora*, 3 vols., Turnhout – Leuven, 1976-1977.

RICHARD, *Origène* = M. RICHARD, *Les fragments d'Origène sur Prov. XXX, 15-31*, in J. FONTAINE – C. KANNENGIESSER (eds.), *Epektasis. Mélanges patristiques offerts au Cardinal Jean Daniélou*, Paris, 1972, p. 385-394.

RICHARD, *Rapport* = M. RICHARD, *Rapport sur la quatrième mission d'études en Grèce (9 mai - 9 août 1957) (fin)*, in *Bulletin d'information de l'Institut de Recherche et d'Histoire des Textes* 7 (1959), p. 33-45 (repr. in RICHARD, *Opera minora*, III, n° 76).

RIEDINGER, *Pseudo-Kaisarios* = R. RIEDINGER, *Pseudo-Kaisarios. Überlieferungsgeschichte und Verfasserfrage* (*BA* 12), München, 1969.

ROCHAIS, *Florilèges latins* = H.-M. ROCHAIS, *Florilèges spirituels latins*, in *Dictionnaire de spiritualité*, 33-34, Paris, 1962, col. 435-460.

ROMAN et al., *Titus Bostrensis* = A. ROMAN – P.-H. POIRIER – E. CRÉGHEUR – J. DECLERCK, *Titi Bostrensis Contra Manichaeos Libri IV Graece et Syriace* (*CCSG* 82), Turnhout, 2013.

ROOSEN – VAN DEUN, *Ps.-Max.* = B. ROOSEN – P. VAN DEUN (eds.), Ἀρετὴν εἰ ἔχοις πάνθ'ἕξεις. *Byzantine Virtue Speculation: a Case Study*, in G. PARTOENS – G. ROSKAM – T. VAN HOUDT (eds.), *Virtutis Imago: Studies on the Conceptualisation and Transformation of an Ancient Ideal* (*Collection d'Études Classiques* 19), Leuven, 2004, p. 397-422.

Sacr. Par. = *Sacra Parallela*.

SAKKELION, *Athens* = I. SAKKELION – A. I. SAKKELION, Κατάλογος τῶν χειρογράφων τῆς Ἐθνικῆς Βιβλιοθήκης τῆς Ἑλλάδος, Athens, 1892.

SC = *Sources Chrétiennes*.

SE = *Sacris Erudiri*.

SIGLA AND BIBLIOGRAPHICAL ABBREVIATIONS XIX

SMYTH, *Greek Grammar* = H. W. SMYTH, *A Greek Grammar for Colleges*, New York, 1920.

SOPHIANOS – DIMITRAKOPOULOS, Χειρόγραφα = D. Z. SOPHIANOS – Ph. A. DIMITRAKOPOULOS, *Τὰ χειρόγραφα τῆς Μονῆς Δουσικοῦ Ἁγίου Βησσαρίωνος. Κατάλογος περιγραφικός*, Athens, 2004.

SOTIROUDIS, *Iviron* = P. SOTIROUDIS, *Ἱερὰ Μονὴ Ἰβήρων. Κατάλογος ἑλληνικῶν χειρογράφων*, I (1-100), Mount Athos, 1998.

SPYRIDON – EUSTRATIADES, *Laura* = SPYRIDON (Lavriotis) – S. EUSTRATIADES, *Catalogue of the Greek Manuscripts in the Library of the Laura on Mount Athos, With Notices From Other Libraries (Harvard Theological Studies* 12), Cambridge MA, 1925.

ST = *Studi e Testi.*

TLL = *Thesaurus Lingae Latinae.*

TM = *Travaux et mémoires.*

TRAPP et al., *PLP* = E. TRAPP et al., *Prosopographisches Lexikon der Palaiologenzeit*, I (*Österreichische Akademie der Wissenschaften. Philosophisch-historische Klasse. Veröffentlichungen der Kommission für Byzantinistik* 1), Wien, 1976.

TU = *Texte und Untersuchungen zur Geschichte der altchristlichen Literatur.*

UTHEMANN, *Anastasius* = K.-H. UTHEMANN, *Anastasii Sinaitae Viae dux* (*CCSG* 8), Turnhout – Leuven, 1981.

UTHEMANN, Ἄπορα = „*Die Ἄπορα des Gregorius von Nyssa*"? *Ein Beitrag zur Geistmetaphysik in Byzanz mit einer Edition von CPG 1781*, in *Byz* 63 (1993), p. 237-327.

UTHEMANN, *Aporien* = K.-H UTHEMANN, *Antimonophysitische Aporien des Anastasios Sinaites*, in *BZ* 74 (1981), p. 11-26.

UTHEMANN, *Sermones* = K.-H. UTHEMANN, *Anastasii Sinaitae Sermones duo in constitutionem hominis secundum imaginem Dei, necnon Opuscula adversus monotheletas* (*CCSG* 12), Turnhout – Leuven, 1985.

UTHEMANN, *Syllogistik* = K.-H. UTHEMANN, *Syllogistik im Dienst der Orthodoxie. Zwei unedierte Texten byzantinischer Kontroverstheologie des 6. Jahrhunderts*, in *JÖB* 30 (1981), p. 103-112.

VAN DEUN, *Liber Asceticus* = P. VAN DEUN, *Maximi Confessoris Liber Asceticus, adjectis tribus interpretationibus latinis sat antiquis editis a Steven Gysens* (*CCSG* 40), Turnhout – Leuven, 2000.

VAN DEUN, *Eustratius* = P. VAN DEUN, *Eustratii Presbyteri Constantinopolitani De statu animarum post mortem* (*CPG 7522*) (*CCSG* 60), Turnhout – Leuven, 2006.

XX   SIGLA AND BIBLIOGRAPHICAL ABBREVIATIONS

Van Deun, *Opuscula* = P. Van Deun, *Maximi Confessoris Opuscula exegetica duo* (*CCSG* 23), Turnhout – Leuven, 1991.

Vendryès, *Accentuation* = J. Vendryès, *Traité d'accentuation grecque* (*Nouvelle collection à l'usage des classes* 27), Paris, 1904.

Verhelst, *Nicéphore* = M. Verhelst, *Le "Traité de l'âme" de Nicéphore Blemmyde. Histoire du texte, édition critique, traduction et analyse du contenu doctrinal*, 2 vols., Louvain-la-Neuve, 1976 (unpublished doctoral dissertation).

Vogel – Gardthausen, *Griechische Schreiber* = M. Vogel – V. Gardthausen, *Die griechischen Schreiber des Mittelalters und der Renaissance* (*Zentralblatt für Bibliothekswesen. Beiheft* 33), Leipzig, 1909 (repr. 1966).

WBS = Wiener Byzantinistische Studien.

Weiss, *Studia* = G. Weiss. *Studia anastasiana, I: Studien zum Leben, zu den Schriften und zur Theologie des Patriarchen Anastasius I. von Antiochien (559-598)* (*Miscellanea Byzantina Monacensia* 4), München, 1965.

Welz, *Strassburg* = C. Welz, *Descriptio codicum graecorum* (*Katalog der kaiserlichen Universitäts- und Landesbibliothek in Strassburg*), Strassburg, 1913.

Wenger, *Hésychius* = A. Wenger, *Hésychius de Jérusalem. Notes sur les discours inédits et sur le texte grec du commentaire "In Leviticum"*, in *Revue des Études Augustiniennes* 2 (1956), p. 457-470.

Wenger, *Jean Chryostome* = A. Wenger, *Jean Chrysostome. Huit catéchèses baptismales inédites* (*SC* 50 bis), Paris, 1970.

Wilson, *Nicaean and Palaeologan Hands* = N. Wilson, *Nicaean and Palaeologan Hands: Introduction to a Discussion*, in J. Glénisson – J. Bompaire – J. Irigoin (eds.), *La paléographie grecque et byzantine. Actes du Colloque international organisé dans le cadre des Colloques internationaux du Centre National de la Recherche Scientifique à Paris du 21 au 25 octobre 1974* (*Colloques internationaux du Centre national de la recherche scientifique* 559), Paris, 1977, p. 263-267.

Wittek, *Manuscrits* = M. Wittek, *Les manuscrits grecs de la Bibliothèque Royale Albert Ier: vingt années d'acquisitions (1954-1973)*, in J. Bingen – G. Cambier – G. Nachtergael (eds.), *Le monde grec: pensée, littérature, histoire, documents. Hommages à Claire Préaux*, Bruxelles, 1975, p. 245-253.

INTRODUCTION

The *Florilegium Coislinianum* (henceforth *FC*) – or Ἑρμηνεία κατὰ στοιχεῖον τῆς θείας γραφῆς, according to its oldest attested title ([1]) – is an anthology that M. Richard would have called "non-historical" ([2]) and, as such, even some of its most essential features remain indeterminate. Its compiler is anonymous. The date of its composition is as yet undetermined. The latest author cited is Theodore of Stoudios, ([3]) more specifically his epistle 57, which must be dated not before 781, and probably a good deal afterward. ([4]) On the other hand, four of the earliest manuscripts of the florilegium date to the 10th c. Since one of them, *D*, is five steps removed from the archetype, it can be assumed that the *FC* was already in existence in the middle of the 10th c. A reasonable guess would be that the *FC* was composed between 850 and 950, but such a date may well have to be revised in the future. The

---

(1) For the setting and a short account of this title, see below "Manuscript Tradition," description of manuscript *C*.

(2) See Richard, *Opera minora*, I, p. 17: "Jusqu'à la fin de cette époque, fin des années 50, je ne m'étais intéressé qu'à ce que j'appelais les florilèges 'historiques', c'est-à-dire ceux dont nous connaissions les auteurs et qu'il était possible de dater au moins approximativement."

(3) It has been argued that Cosmas Vestitor was active after Theodore, and since there is a fragment in the *FC* attributed to him which might be genuine (Δ 7.1), it is just possible that the *terminus post quem* must be pushed forward in time. All of this, however, is hypothetical, which is why I prefer to leave the Cosmas question aside. Cf. Fernández, *Cosmas*.

(4) Fatouros, *Theodorus Studita*, p. 202*: "Auf jeden Fall fällt er [the epistle 57] zwischen der Tod Platons [the addressee of the epistle] (4. April 814) und den Eintritt des Theodor in Kloster (781)." Fatouros adds that, according to some interpretations, the epistle would have been written either in 797 or in 809-811. At any rate, by definition, only the earliest possible date is strictly relevant for a *terminus post quem*, and that is here, as we have seen, the year 781. Cf. De Vos et al., *Beta*, p. 72, n. 1. Unfortunately, the attribution of this excerpt (E 17.10) is plainly θεοδώρου τοῦ στουδίτου, with no additional words as, for example, τοῦ ἁγίου, which would prove that Theodore was already dead at the time. For further discussion regarding the date of composition (and regarding the relation of the *FC* and Maximus the Confessor's *Diversa capita*, *CPG* 7715), see Ceulemans et al., *Eta*, p. 91-92; Ceulemans et al., *Xi*, p. 57.

XXII INTRODUCTION

place of composition remains unknown. The possibility that it was Southern Italy has been proposed by the editors of Maximus the Confessor's *Quaestiones ad Thalassium* and *Quaestiones et dubia*, yet no definite proof has been found to date. "La présentation des extraits des [*Quaestiones ad Thalassium* in the *FC*] montre que l'auteur du [*FC*] a employé un manuscrit écrit en minuscules avec les textes marginaux en onciales (ou semionciales). Cela signifie que ce modèle avait la même présentation du texte que nos plus anciens *codices*, ceux de l'Italie du Sud." ([5]) For his part, J. Declerck was able to determine that the *FC* is related to the "sélection I" of Maximus the Confessor's *Quaestiones et dubia*, and that this "sélection I," in turn, is related to the hyparchetype α; "cela indiquerait plutôt une origine italo-grecque [of the *FC*]." ([6]) In a footnote, he adds: "[s]ans que nous ayons à apporter d'autres exemples, nous croyons en effet pouvoir affirmer que le lien entre le texte du florilège et celui de nos manuscrits italo-grecs est assez bien établi." ([7]) I can add that, in an anonymous fragment in Π 7.2, a very rare word, φεριάλια, appears. "Son sens doit être celui de 'liste de jours fériés.' Ce mot n'est pas attesté en grec. [...] Le fait que le mot ne soit pas attesté avant le 4ème siècle, et seulement en latin, suggère que le fragment où il se trouve pourrait être tardif [...], et très influencé par un milieu latin. [...] Cela pourrait indiquer que le *FC*, comme l'ont déjà proposé quelques érudits, aurait été composé en Italie du Sud." ([8])

The chapters are called κεφάλαια. Note that in the *Sacr. Par.* and elsewhere they are called τίτλοι. There are 246 of them in manuscripts *CBS* (*AT* stop much before the end of the florilegium), 230 in the short recension (231 in the pinakes of *DEG*). ([9])

Every chapter has a title. Some start in a declarative way, most often with Περί (Α', Ε'-Ϛ', ΙΒ'-ΙΓ', ΙΖ', ΙΘ'- ΚΔ', ΚΖ'-ΚΘ', ΛΑ'-

---

(5) LAGA – STEEL, *Max. Conf.*, I, p. lxxiv.

(6) DECLERCK, *Max. Conf.*, p. ccix.

(7) Ibid., p. ccix, n. 136.

(8) FERNÁNDEZ, *Anatole*, p. 197. See also VAN DEUN, *Opuscula*, p. clvii.; CEULEMANS et al., *Eta*, p. 92-93; CEULEMANS et al., *Xi*, p. 57, n. 30.

(9) The situation of *FH* is more complex; see their relationship below under "Manuscript Tradition." For a more detailed account of the individual manuscripts, see "Manuscript Tradition" below, and cf. now also CEULEMANS – VAN DEUN, *Réflexions*.

INTRODUCTION   XXIII

ΛΕ´, ΛΖ´-ΜΑ´), ([10]) but also with Ἀπόδειξις ὅτι (Γ´-Δ´, ΚΖ´) or
Ὅτι alone (Θ´-ΙΑ´, ΙΗ´). Some other titles begin by an interrogative word: Διατί (Ζ´-Η´), Τί (ΙΔ´-ΙΕ´), Τίνες (Β´, ΚΕ´), Κατὰ
πόσους (ΙΖ´), Πόσαι (ΛΖ´). A special genre of this is the Πῶς
νοητέον, followed by a biblical citation (Λ´). ([11]) These introduc-
tory words are followed by a keyword governing the alphabetical
order of the title. Whereas the formulaic words have a structural
function, keywords are content-related and peculiar to the individual chapters.

The number of excerpts per chapter is variable. There are forty-one chapters in Letter Alpha. In eighteen of them, there is only
one fragment; in nine, two fragments; in five, three fragments; in
four, four fragments; and five chapters, all of them Damascenian
or partly Damascenian, ([12]) have five or more excerpts. The aver-
age number of excerpts per chapter in Letter Alpha is slightly over
2.5 including Damascenian or partly Damascenian chapters, and
1.75 excluding the Damascenian or partly Damascenian chapters
that contain four or more excerpts. ([13]) The length of the excerpts
is also variable, from a single line to many pages. The most strik-
ing examples of this variability in Letter Alpha are fragments Ε´
and ΚΘ´. This is another notable difference with the *Sacr. Par.*: in

---

(10) Note that the titles of the *Sacr. Par.* always start with περί, even
though they are regularly expanded with a declarative ὅτι, for example: Περὶ
αὐτεξουσίου· ὅτι αὐτεξούσιον δέδοται ἡμῖν ὑπὸ θεοῦ κτλ. (Τίτλ. Θ´, *Sacr.
Par.*, PG 95, 1109, 21-23).

(11) Even though it appears only once in Letter Alpha, it is common
elsewhere in the *FC*.

(12) For brevity's sake, I call "Damascenian" fragments or chapters that
are related to the *Sacra Parallela*, even though it is likely that the *Sacr. Par.*
are not by John Damascene; on this see now DECLERCK, *Sacra Parallela, passim.*

(13) Chapters quoting only one excerpt: Β´, Η´-Θ´, ΙΒ´, ΙΕ´, ΙΖ´, ΙΘ´,
ΚΔ´- ΚΖ´, ΚΘ´, ΛΑ´-ΛΔ´, ΛΖ´, ΛΘ´, ΜΑ´; chapters quoting two: Δ´-Ε´, Ζ´, Ι´,
ΙΓ´, ΙΖ´, ΚΓ´, Λ´, Μ´; chapters quoting three: ΙΑ´, ΙΔ´, ΙΗ´, Κ´, ΛΖ´; chapters
quoting four: Α´, Ζ´, ΚΒ´, ΛΗ´; chapters quoting five: ΚΖ´-ΚΗ´; one chapter quotes six: Γ´; one chapter quotes eight: ΚΑ´; one chapter quotes twelve:
ΛΕ´. According to RICHARD, *Florilèges*, col. 485, "[les] chapitres [...] citent
habituellement un seul auteur, plus rarement deux, exceptionnellement trois
ou quatre." As we have seen, this is not exact as far as Letter Alpha is concerned. From another perspective, however, Richard was right: the chapters
with four or more excerpts are all Damascenian or partly Damascenian, and
therefore not purely Coislinian.

XXIV INTRODUCTION

the *FC*, some excerpts are much longer than in any of the extant Damascenian compilations.

Unlike the *Sacr. Par.*, the arrangement of the fragments in the *FC* is often thematic, rather than by author. It often happens that the passage most pertinent to the title in question is quoted first, and afterward those which are of a somewhat derived nature. A paradigmatic case is chapter Ιϛ', Κατὰ πόσους τρόπους ἐξαμαρτάνει ὁ ἄνθρωπος; The first fragment directly answers that question; moreover, the question itself was taken from the same source as its answer. [14] Yet after this, there comes another fragment indirectly related to the title.

Furthermore, if two fragments by different authors deal with the same subject, they may be put together, and after them, another fragment by the first of these authors may come – whereas in the *Sacr. Par.* the general rule is that fragments by the same author occur together. [15] At the same time, excerpts in other chapters appear in a progressive order because the latter comment upon, or correct, those which have come before.

I. Genre and Compiler [16]

The *FC* is not an apologetic or a dogmatic florilegium, although some of its excerpts are indeed dogmatic. [17] It is not a *quaestiones et responsiones* anthology, even though many of the titles are questions which would perfectly suit, say, the Anastasius collection, such as the previously cited chapter Ιϛ' (Κατὰ πόσους τρόπους ἐξαμαρτάνει ὁ ἄνθρωπος;). It is not exegetical, though its oldest attested title points to a compilation of an exegetical nature, and many of its fragments are exegetical. Indeed, some excerpts comment on a specific point of the Bible, as those in chapter Ε' (Περὶ τῶν ἀγγέλων ὧν ἐφιλοξένησεν Ἀβραάμ), chapter ΙΘ' (Περὶ τοῦ ἀστέρος τοῦ ἀνατείλαντος ἐπὶ τῆς Χριστοῦ

---

(14) Max. Conf., *Quaest. Et dub.*, 1, 5, 1-7 (p 140).

(15) This is what happens with the two Chrysostomic fragments (50 and 53 of Letter Alpha), which occur together in the *Sacr. Par.* yet are separated in the *FC*.

(16) For an attempt at classification by genre of spiritual florilegia, see Rochais, *Florilèges latins*.

(17) Such as the earliest attested one, the epistle 57 of Theodore of Stoudios, which is manifestly iconophilic.

γεννήσεως) or chapter Λ' (Πῶς νοητέον τὸ Πᾶν ἄρσεν διανοῖγον μήτραν;); excerpts 76, 97 and 98 have biblical κείμενα which are duly interpreted.

If a clear-cut distinction had to be drawn between edifying and didactic anthologies, the *FC* – and the *Sacr. Par.* – would be didactic. A basic distinction between the *Sacr. Par.* and the *FC* can be noted here: whereas most of the excerpts in the former anthology tend to be moral, and aim at developping the virtue of the reader, those of the *FC* are much more varied in scope. In this regard, it might be argued that the *FC* adopts a more intellectual approach than the *Sacr. Par.* The utilitarian nature of the former is evident in its alphabetical arrangement and in its ambition not to exclude any crucial aspect of theological knowledge. Yet it is less systematic than the *Sacr. Par.*, where the pinakes, for instance, feature cross-references or παραπομπαί, ([18]) which prove that the compiler had in mind what the reader may have sought and took pains to indicate that this information could be found elsewhere. ([19])

Even though the *FC* contains excerpts from many different genres, some exclusions are patent. On the one hand, there is no hagiography. On the other, all autonomous biblical quotations have their immediate source in the *Sacr. Par.*, or in a source related to the *Sacr. Par.*

As for the compiler of the *FC*, all we can say about him is to be gathered from the way he selected and arranged information in the *FC*. ([20]) First of all, he was an *excerptor*, not an *epitomator*

---

(18) Cf. Declerck, *Sacra Parallela*, p. 29, esp. n. 11; and Odorico, *Cultura*, p. 16-17. For instance, Περὶ ἀγαθότητος Θεοῦ· κεῖται ἐνταῦθα ἐν τῷ φ στοιχείῳ τῆς Γ'· οὗ ἡ ἀρχή, περὶ φιλανθρωπίας Θεοῦ (*PG* 95, 1048, 66-68). Most of the cross-references, however, concern titles with more than a keyword (in this example, Περὶ φιλανθρωπίας Θεοῦ, καὶ ἀγαθότητος, καὶ μακροθυμίας, *PG* 96, 392, 34-35) or quasi-synonymous words, as in Περὶ ἀσθενούντων, which is referred to the title, Περὶ νοσούντων (cf. *PG* 95, 1048, 49-50). These cross references fill what otherwise might have seemed to be gaps in the collection's disposition of material. It is clear that an attempt to fill gaps only makes sense in a work aiming at some sort of systematization.

(19) For the very careful disposition of information in a logical way in the *Sacr. Par.*, see Odorico, *Cultura*.

(20) His compilation does not show subjectivity in the same way as the *Sacr. Par.* does, yet the *FC* is far from being entirely impersonal. P. Odorico

XXVI INTRODUCTION

and even less a *metaphrastes*. He rarely added a word, and when he did, it usually seems to be accidental. A notable exception is the material, amounting to a few lines, added before the first fragment of Alpha. Yet, when it comes to slicing and dicing long fragments, he allowed himself a few liberties. A fine example is Chrysostom's *Sermones in Genesim*. Parts of this work are quoted in fr. 19 (2, 47-70 and 2, 79-101), whereas the lines in the middle (2, 70-78), which are relatively autonomous, were conveniently re-arranged in an independent section (fr. 21). This process of slicing long works and distributing the pieces among different chapters is common in the *FC*.[21]

Secondly, the compiler was extremely faithful. Virtually all of the changes introduced in the text were accidental or can be sus-pected to be, in fact, innovations already present in his exemplar. Attributions are also accurate; only rarely are they downright false, and all such cases can be explained as mistakes. Further-more, now and then he writes not only the name of the author of the excerpt, but also the title of the work from which the excerpt is taken;[22] for a few works, this is his usual practice.[23] This inconsistency can probably be explained as due to the intermedi-ate compilations he doubtless used.

This leads us to a vexed question: Does the compiler exhibit a theological tendency? The very fact that this compilation is not a dogmatic florilegium makes it somewhat difficult to situate it in terms of doctrine. I will give only one example to illustrate this issue, even though I am aware that until all of its contents have been studied, it would be hazardous to risk any definite answer. The vast majority of the excerpts in the *FC* are fully orthodox. There are some apparent exceptions, such as the very first excerpt.

---

states that evolution toward indifferentiation took place around the middle of the 10th c., when "le raccolte perdono la loro matrice dotta e personale, per divenire opere più ampie e contemporaneamente meno caratterizzate" (ODORICO, *Prato*, p. 26).

(21) For a very similar example, see FERNÁNDEZ, *Atanasio*.

(22) Or, naturally enough, the *incipit* of the work, as in fr. 79, Τοῦ Χρυσοστόμου Λόγος οὗ ἡ ἀρχή· Πρώην περὶ ἀκαταλήπτου.

(23) For example, the *Fragmenta in Matthaeum* (Βίβλος τῆς ἑρμηνείας τοῦ κατὰ Ματθαῖον εὐαγγελίου or Ἐκ τῆς ἑρμηνείας τοῦ κατὰ Ματθαῖον εὐαγγελίου), ascribed to Athanasius of Alexandria; see excerpts 40 and 77 of Letter Alpha, and elsewhere in the *FC*; cf. however fr. 42, which is prob-ably from the same work, yet lacks a full attribution.

INTRODUCTION

XXVII

It concerns the priority of the creation of the angels, a notoriously thorny subject that may smack of Origenism. Yet it should not be understood that the compiler had any positive sympathy for these doctrines. ([24]) An entire excerpt of Maximus the Confessor (Alpha 73, in chapter ΚΘ', Περὶ ἀποκαταστάσεως) deals precisely with the different senses of *apocatastasis*, setting the term in its proper limits, and stating explicitly that Gregory of Nyssa went too far in accepting what for Maximus is the third and last of its meanings, that which concerns ἡ τῶν ψυχικῶν δυνάμεων τῇ ἁμαρτίᾳ ὑποπεσουσῶν εἰς ὅπερ ἐκτίσθησαν πάλιν ἀποκατάστασις (73.7/9). This is of course the problematic sense of *apocatastasis*, and the only one associated specifically with Origen. According to Maximus, Gregory used the word in this sense abusively – ᾗ καὶ μάλιστα κατακέχρηται ἐν τοῖς ἑαυτοῦ λόγοις ὁ Νύσης Γρηγόριος (73.5/7). Correcting what could have been taken as an Origenist *penchant* in the Cappadocians, this chapter shows that the compiler is by no means positively Origenist. Rather than demonstrating any personal sympathy with Origenism, the compiler's approach is indicative of the huge difference between the time when Origenism was considered a positive risk and the 9th to 10th c., when the compiler of the *FC* was active. ([25]) It is this context that allows him to begin his compilation with an excerpt dealing with what used to be such a disputed issue, and later on to quote an excerpt where the Origenist *apocatastasis* is partly refuted.

II. The *Sacra Parallela*

Different scholars, in particular Holl and Richard, have already investigated the Damascenian material in the *FC*. According to Holl, the titles of eight of the forty-one chapters of Letter Alpha stem from the *Sacr. Par.*, namely Ϛ', ΙΑ', Κ', ΚΑ', ΚΗ', ΛΕ', ΛΖ' and ΛΘ'. He adds, however, that the influence of the *Sacr. Par.*

---

(24) Theodore of Mopsuestia, for example, explicitly criticized Basil for this passage of the *Hexaemeron*; cf. GUILLAUMONT, *Képhalaia*, p. 183-184, and GIET, *Basile*, p. 553.

(25) Cf. BECK, *Kirche*, p. 384-387. For the role played by the fifth General Council (553) in relation to Origenism, see DIEKAMP, *Origenistische Streitigkeiten*, p. 66-98; p. 107-120 contain information about the repercussions of this council in later centuries.

XXVIII INTRODUCTION

on the *FC* is somewhat larger than the chapter titles alone indicate. ([26]) Richard, in turn, considers three chapters as fully Damascenian, namely Κ', ΚΑ' and ΚΗ', all of them already quoted by Holl. To these, Richard adds six partly Damascenian chapters: four already mentioned by Holl (Ϛ', ΙΑ', ΛΕ' and ΛΖ') and two new chapters (Γ' and ΚΖ'). ([27]) This is about all the Damascenian material that can be found in Letter Alpha of the *FC*. ([28]) In what follows, I provide the reader with a list of the Damascenian or partly Damascenian chapters of Letter Alpha of the *FC*, adding the corresponding chapter of the *Sacr. Par.* ([29]) Below these titles, the reader will find those fragments of the *FC* also preserved in the *Sacr. Par.*, along with their attribution in the *FC*.

Γ' Ἀπόδειξις ὅτι ἀγγέλους φύλακας ἡμῖν ἔδωκεν ὁ θεός

Ζ' Περὶ ἀγγέλων· ὅτι ἀγγέλους φύλακας ἐπέστησεν ὁ Θεός
(*Sacr. Par.*, *PG* 95, 1097, 19-20)

    6 Βασιλείου Καισαρείας (= *Sacr. Par.*, *PG* 95, 1160, 21-27)

    8 Διδύμου (= *Sacr. Par.*, *PG* 95, 1097, 35-36)

    9 Εὐαγρίου (= *Sacr. Par.*, *PG* 95, 1097, 38-39)

    10 Γενέσεως (= *Sacr. Par.*, *PG* 95, 1097, 21-25)

Ϛ' Περὶ τῆς τοῦ ἀνθρώπου δημιουργίας καὶ πλάσεως

Η' Περὶ τῆς τοῦ ἀνθρώπου πλάσεως καὶ κατασκευῆς (*Sacr. Par.*, *PG* 95, 1097, 44-45)

    16, 1/20; 23/25 Γρηγορίου τοῦ θεολόγου (= *Sacr. Par.*, *Vat. gr.* 1553, 39ʳ⁻ᵛ, ed. HEIMGARTNER, *Pseudojustin*, p. 249) ([30])

---

(26) HOLL, *Sacra Parallela*, p. 135.

(27) Conversely, Richard did not consider chapter ΛΘ' to be Damascenian.

(28) I was able to find only a minuscule supplementary excerpt in the first fragment of Letter Alpha, whose presence in both the *Sacr. Par.* and the *FC* is surely accidental: 1.23/28 (προηγουμένως – δρόμου) = *Sacr. Par.*, *PG* 95, 1281, 32-38.

(29) I was unable to find the chapter of the *Sacr. Par.* upon which depends, according to Holl, chapter ΛΖ' of the *FC*, Περὶ τοῦ Ἅδου. The fragment present both in the *FC* (93) and the *Sacr. Par.* is the third one of the chapter Περὶ ὥρας θανάτου, in *Sacr. Par.*, *Par. Rupef.* (*PG* 96, 541, 18; cf. also *Sacr. Par.*, ed. HOLL, *Fragmente*, p. 137).

(30) A manuscript related to *Vat. gr.* 1553, viz. *Vatopedi 236*, contains part of this fragment on f. 119ᵛ. Note that this fragment is not included in Mai's partial edition of the *Vat. gr.* 1553 (*PG* 86, 2017-2100).

INTRODUCTION   XXIX

17 Κλήμεντος (= *Sacr. Par.*, ed. HOLL, *Fragmente*, fr. 10,
p. 7)

ΙΑ′ Ὅτι αὐτεξούσιος ὁ ἄνθρωπος

Θ′ Περὶ αὐτεξουσίου· ὅτι αὐτεξούσιον δέδοται ἡμῖν ἀπὸ Θεοῦ,
καὶ ἐν ἡμῖν ἔστι σωθῆναι καὶ ἀπολέσθαι (*Sacr. Par.*, *PG* 95,
1109, 21-23)

26 Κλήμεντος Ῥώμης (= *Sacr. Par.*, ed. HOLL, *Fragmente*,
fr. 26, p. 13-14; fr. 14, p. 8)

Κ′ Περὶ ἀποταξαμένων καὶ πάλιν ἁμαρτανόντων

ΙΔ′ Περὶ ἀποταξαμένων, καὶ ἐξ ὑποστροφῆς ἐκεῖνα πραττόντων
οἷς ἀπετάξαντο (*Sacr. Par.*, *PG* 95, 1172, 27-28)

43 Σολομῶντος (= *Sacr. Par.*, *PG* 95, 1172, 31-33)

44 Βασιλείου Καισαρείας (= *Sacr. Par.*, *PG* 95, 1173, 32-35)

ΚΑ′ Περὶ τῆς ἀστάτου τῶν ἀνθρωπίνων πραγμάτων κατα-στάσεως

Ι′ Περὶ τῆς ἀστάτου καὶ ἀβεβαίου τῶν ἀνθρωπίνων πραγμάτων καταστάσεως· καὶ τίνι ἔοικεν ὁ ἄνθρωπος καὶ ὁ βίος
αὐτοῦ· καὶ ὅτι μάταια τὰ παρόντα, καὶ σκιᾶς ἀδρανέστερα
(*Sacr. Par.*, *PG* 95, 1113, 37-41; 1045, 23-26)

46 Ἰώβ (= *Sacr. Par.*, *PG* 95, 1113, 47-50)

47 Τοῦ Ἐκκλησιαστοῦ (= *Sacr. Par.*, *PG* 95, 1116, 13; 1116,
31-33; 1117, 11-12)

48 Γρηγορίου τοῦ Θεολόγου (= *Sacr. Par.*, *PG* 95, 1124, 14-
22)

49 Βασιλείου Καισαρείας (= *Sacr. Par.*, *PG*, 95, 1117, 40-
49)

50 Τοῦ Χρυσοστόμου (= *Sacr. Par.*, *PG* 95, 1132, 3-25)

51 Γρηγορίου τοῦ Θεολόγου (= *Sacr. Par.*, *PG* 95, 1125, 3-5;
1132, 18-24)

52 Νείλου μοναχοῦ (= *Sacr. Par.*, *PG* 95, 1133, 44 – 1136,
2)

53 Τοῦ Χρυσοστόμου (= *Sacr. Par.*, *PG* 95, 1128, 30-35)

XXX INTRODUCTION

ΚΖ′ Περὶ ἀγάπης καὶ πόσα τὰ τῆς ἀγάπης εἴδη ([31])

ΙΗ′ Περὶ ἀγάπης, καὶ εἰρήνης, καὶ εἰρηνοποιῶν, καὶ πράων ἀνθρώπων (*Sacr. Par.*, *PG* 95, 1193, 25-26; 1045, 43-44)

63 Κλήμεντος Στρωματέων (= *Sacr. Par.*, *PG* 95, 1201, 41-49; *PG* 96, 405, 28-36)

64 Εὐαγρίου (= *Sacr. Par.*, *PG* 95, 1204, 11-15)

66 Τοῦ αὐτοῦ, i.e. τοῦ Χρυσοστόμου (= *Sacr. Par.*, *PG* 95, 1200, 18-24)

ΚΗ′ Περὶ ἀγαθοεργίας καὶ ὅτι οὐ δεῖ ἀποδιδόναι κακὸν ἀντὶ κακοῦ

ΙΑ′ Περὶ ἀγαθοεργίας· καὶ ὅτι χρὴ τὸ ἀγαθὸν πρὸς πάντας ποιεῖν· καὶ ὅτι χρὴ τὰ βάρη τοῦ πλησίον φέρειν, καὶ μὴ μνησικακεῖν, ἀλλὰ ἀντιλαμβάνεσθαι αὐτοῦ, καὶ ἐλέγχειν, μὴ ἀποδιδόναι κακὸν ἀντὶ κακοῦ (*Sacr. Par.*, *PG* 95, 1136, 33-38)

68 Παροιμιῶν (= *Sacr. Par.*, *PG* 95, 1137, 23-26; 1137, 18-20)

69 Ἐκ τῆς πρὸς Ῥωμαίους Παύλου ἐπιστολῆς (= *Sacr. Par.*, *PG* 95, 1141, 3-6)

70 Ἐκ τῆς Πέτρου ἐπιστολῆς (= *Sacr. Par.*, *PG* 95, 1141, 28-30)

71 Ἐκ τοῦ κατὰ Ἰωάννην (= *Sacr. Par.*, *PG* 95, 1141, 31-33)

72 Νείλου (= *Sacr. Par.*, *PG* 95, 1169, 46-48; attributed to Philo)

ΛΕ′ Περὶ ἀνδρῶν ἀσεβῶν καὶ περὶ αἱρετικῶν, ὅτι δεῖ χωρίζεσθαι ἀπ'αὐτῶν

ΙΒ′ Περὶ ἀσεβῶν, καὶ ἁμαρτωλῶν, καὶ κακῶν, καὶ μοχθηρῶν ἀνδρῶν, καὶ ἀδίκων, καὶ παρανόμων (*Sacr. Par.*, *PG* 95, 1148, 38-40)

---

(31) Even if he did not mention it among the Damascenian chapters, Holl was well aware that this title had been influenced by the *Sacr. Par.*: "auch der Titel κζ. Περὶ ἀγάπης καὶ πόσα τὰ τῆς ἀγάπης εἴδη ist aus dem Parallelentitel περὶ ἀγάπης καὶ εἰρήνης καὶ εἰρηνοποιῶν καὶ πράων ἀνθρώπων entstanden. [...] Jedoch, während das Kapitel in der vatikanischen Recension mehrere Seiten füllt, hat der Coisl. 294 [= *A* of *FC*] nur 5 Citate herübergenommen" (HOLL, *Sacra Parallela*, p. 135).

INTRODUCTION XXXI

80 Δαυίδ (= *Sacr. Par.*, *PG* 95, 1233, 40-41; 1585, 10-11; 1129, 57-58)

81 Παροιμιῶν (= *Sacr. Par.*, *PG* 96, 353, 3-13)

82 Ἡσαΐου (= *Sacr. Par.*, *PG* 96, 353, 23-24)

83 Σιράχ (= *Sacr. Par.*, *PG* 96, 353, 25-26)

84 Παύλου τοῦ ἀποστόλου ἐκ τῆς πρὸς Κορινθίους ἐπιστολῆς (= *Sacr. Par.*, *PG* 96, 353, 34-39)

ΛΖ' Περὶ τοῦ Ἅδου

(no corresponding chapter found in *Sacr. Par.*)

93 Ἰωσήππου. Ἐκ τοῦ λόγου τοῦ ἐπιγεγραμμένου κατὰ Πλάτωνος περὶ τῆς τοῦ παντὸς αἰτίας (= *Sacr. Par.*, Ed. Holl, *Fragmente*, fr. 353, 1-35, p. 137-139; also in *Sacr. Par.*, *Par. Rupef.*, *PG* 96, 541, 25 – 544, 32)

ΛΘ' Περὶ τοῦ Ἀντιχρίστου

Δ' Περὶ ἡμέρας ἐσχάτης, καὶ τοῦ Ἀντιχρίστου (*Sacr. Par.*, *Par. Rupef.*, *PG* 96, 525, 27-28)

As previously mentioned, all the excerpts of the *FC* that are fully independent biblical citations are taken from the *Sacr. Par.* ([32]) Yet, as can easily be seen from the list above, the converse is not always true. Indeed, not all the Damascenian or partly Damascenian chapters contain biblical citations.

The excerpts within the Damascenian chapters have sometimes been rearranged in a completely new order. Take the example of chapter ΚΑ', of the *FC* (and Ι' of the *Sacr. Par.*). That chapter has the following excerpts of the *Sacr. Par.*, in this order: 3, 16, 23, 33, 46, 34, 52, 48, 58, 51.

A number of fragments appear in a shorter form in the *FC*; see e.g. fr. 49 of the *FC*, which is four lines longer in the *Sacr. Par.* as printed in the *PG*; or fr. 50, which is thirty-one lines longer in the *Sacr. Par.*; or fr. 49 and 53, which are only a few lines long in the *FC*, whereas in the *Sacr. Par.* they are a small portion of a very long excerpt. At the same time, the text of the *Sacr. Par.* is often

---

(32) By contrast, partly independent biblical citations (as in 103.1/9: the κείμενον of the exegesis that follows) can be found in the non-Damascenian chapters of the *FC*.

superior to that of the *FC*. This is not always visible in the present edition, which only reports the readings of Lequien's edition of the *Sacr. Par.* José Declerck, who is editing the *Sacr. Par.*, has shared his collations with me. On the basis of his work, I have been able to confirm that many of the instances where the *Sacr. Par.* seemed to have an inferior text were, in fact, only mistakes of the manuscript edited by Lequien (*Vat. gr. 1236*) and Mai (*Vat. gr. 1553*), or errors made by the editors themselves. To name but a few, in 44.2, the manuscript *Vlatadon 9* does not omit τὸν ἐπὶ; in 64.1, this same manuscript has the genitive τῶν ἀνθρώπων, not the accusative singular that appears in the *PG*. Other examples could be listed.

Nevertheless, in other instances the text of the *FC* seems superior to the text preserved in the *Sacr. Par.* ([33]) In those instances at least, the text of the *FC* cannot be derived from the *Sacr. Par.* as it is now extant. Although such a conclusion cannot be drawn on the basis of Lequien's or Mai's editions of the *Sacr. Par.*, the collations of Declerck confirm that the extant tradition of the *Sacr. Par.* – we must not forget that the original work is lost – was in all probability not the model of the *FC*. Consequently, such a model has to be looked for in a stage of the *Sacr. Par.* which was closer to the original work; such is the most reasonable possibility, because, as we have seen, the *FC* is clearly dependent on the *Sacr. Par.* in a number of aspects.

---

(33) To quote only one example, the words θηρίον ἐν κόσμῳ, which are present in the *FC* (Γ 14.1) and in the primary source, are omitted in the *Sacr. Par.* The omission also occurs in ms. *Vlatadon 9*.

MANUSCRIPT TRADITION

This chapter presents the manuscripts of the *FC* in the following order: *AT C BPS DEGFH KLQV R IWNOM*. The reason for this arrangement will become apparent in the next chapter, "Relationship of the Manuscripts." I have not attempted to write entries of similar length for each manuscript, since some of them manifestly need a more complete description than others. ([1])

The manuscript tradition of the *FC* has already been accounted for by other scholars, most notably Richard, *Florilèges*, col. 484-486; ([2]) Declerck, *Max. Conf.*, p. cciv-ccxiv; De Vos et al., *Gamma*, p. 160-162. As a rule, these three fundamental works, although they have been consulted in all the pertinent cases, are not quoted for every individual manuscript discussed below. The reader should take them to be implicitly quoted.

Here as elsewhere, I give for unpublished sections of the *FC* the position of the fragment within the chapter, and not that of the fragment within the letter. The reason is that it is relatively easy to find a chapter in the manuscripts, and the chapter numeration is in many cases present in the manuscritpts themselves, whereas fragment numeration is not. Giving the number of the excerpts is therefore only useful for the published parts of this anthology.

I. Main Manuscripts

Ms. **A**, *Parisinus, Coislinianus 294.* ([3]) 11th-12th c. Parchment, 220 folios (227 × 175, written area 190 × 130), one column, 27-28 lines. This manuscript contains the *FC* only; Letter Alpha

---

(1) For the general arrangement of each manuscript description, I have followed the suggestions of Gardthausen, *Schrift*, p. 484-486.

(2) All of the manuscripts are already reported by Richard, with the exception of *MO*, for which see Riedinger, *Pseudo-Kaisarios*, p. 103-104 (and Weiss, *Studia*, p. 116 for *O*); and of *PL*, for which see Declerck, *Max. Conf.*, p. ccix-ccx, and Declerck, *Manuscrit, passim.*

(3) See Holl, *Sacra Parallela*, p. 132-138; Devreesse, *Coislin*, p. 275-276.

XXXIV MANUSCRIPT TRADITION

f. 1-65ᵛ. No title, no pinax; according to Holl, title and pinax were likely also absent from the *Vorlage* of *A*. (⁴)

The manuscript ends abruptly at the ninth chapter of Letter Omicron, (⁵) τί ἐστιν ὀργὴ τοῦ θ(εο)ῦ. This chapter contains only one excerpt, by Maximus Confessor, inc. ὀργὴ θ(εο)ῦ ἐστὶν κατα (*sic*) μίαν ἐπιβολὴν, des. ἑαυτὸν τοῦ παντὸς κατορθώματος ἡγησάμενος αἴτιον τηνικαῦτα... (⁶) The manuscript's peculiar orthography deserves a few words. We read, for instance, μαχίμου (*sic*) instead of μαξίμου (attribution of fr. 58); ψύλλου instead of φύλλου (60.19/20); ἀπολάβειν instead of ἀπολαύειν (67.42; in *A* this kind of mistake is rare, in comparison with other manuscripts such as *L*); φιλεκθρῶν instead of φιλεχθρῶν (77.11); ἀλλ'α (*sic*) instead of ἀλλὰ, *passim*. In addition to these peculiarities, itacism and similar confusions (ο – ω for instance) are extremeley abundant. There are no iota subscripts or adscripts.

Nothing is known about the history of the manuscript. (⁷)

Ms. *T*, *Hierosolymitanus, Sancti Sepulcri 15*. (⁸) 10ᵗʰ c. (⁹) Parchment, 346 folios (319 × 234), (¹⁰) two columns, 41 lines. This manuscript contains the *FC* and three different recensions of the *Sacr. Par.* The *FC* is contained on f. 137-168 (Alpha); f. 189-193ᵛ (Beta); f. 228-232 (Gamma); f. 261ᵛ-271ᵛ (Delta); f. 341ᵛ-345ᵛ (Epsilon); no further books are preserved. No title, no pinax.

---

(4) Holl, *Sacra Parallela*, p. 134.

(5) Ibid., p. 133 and Devreesse, *Coislin*, p. 276 indicate that *A* ends at chapter eight of Letter Omicron. For Devreesse, this last chapter is περὶ ὀργῆς, which is indeed the eighth one. There is, however, yet another chapter in *A*: τί ἐστιν ὀργὴ τοῦ θ(εο)ῦ. Therefore, this manuscript stops at chapter nine of Letter Omicron (chapter 158 in *C*, unnumbered in *A*), and not at the eighth as Holl and Devreesse thought.

(6) Max. Conf., *Quaest. Ad Thal.*, 52, 21-80.

(7) Holl, *Sacra Parallela*, p. 133.

(8) Cf. Papadopoulos-Kerameus, *Jerusalem*, I, p. 65-68; Holl, *Sacra Parallela*, p. 114-132, with Richard's (*Florilèges*, col. 483) caveat: "K. Holl n'a pu utiliser qu'une copie partielle du principal témoin de ce florilège [the *Florilegium Hierosolymitanum*], Jérusalem, Saint-Sépulcre 15 (10ᵉ s.). La notice qu'il a consacrée à celui-ci [...] est donc moins précise et moins exacte que les précédentes."

(9) 11ᵗʰ c. according to Papadopoulos-Kerameus, *Jerusalem*, I, p. 65.

(10) The last folio is numbered 345 because there are two folios 111.

MANUSCRIPT TRADITION
XXXV

There are no marginalia, except for some chapter numbers, ([11]) titles and attributions, additions of words or groups of words accidentally omitted in the text, or indications such as σχόλ(ιον), ἐρώ(τησις), etc. On f. 2ᵛ and 3ᵛ the following words are written in the lower margin: γύρισον φύλ(λ)ον ἔμπροσθεν. This means, in effect, that the correct order of the first folios is 1, 2, 4, 3, 5, 6ff. Nevertheless, between f. 4 and 3 there is at least one missing folio. In the *Sacr. Par.*, as printed in the *PG*, the missing text is almost 11 columns long.

The first numbered quaternion is δ', and it starts on f. 13. This means that some folios must be missing, possibly as many as twelve. These folios may be those of the pinax and title, and/or those missing between f. 4 and 3.

T is consistently composed of quaternions: ϛ' beginning at f. 29, ζ' at f. 37, η' at f. 45, θ' at f. 53, etc. Sometimes the end of the quaternion is numbered in the lower margin to the right (that is, the inner side of a verso-folio), for example ιδ' on f. 100ᵛ.

The order of the folios is seriously disturbed between f. 195 and f. 251. Yet the numeration of the quaternions is right, insofar as it can be read. The correct order of the folios following f. 194 is: f. 243-250 (quaternion κζ'), f. 235-242 (κη'), f. 227-234 (κθ'), f. 219-226 (λ'), f. 211-218 (λα'), f. 203-210 (λβ'), f. 195-202 (λγ'), 251ff. (quaternions λδ' ff.). As can easily be seen, these seven quaternions were bound in the wrong order, from last to first; they were most likely numbered before they were bound, whereas the folios got their numbers only after the binding of the manuscript.

On the outer margin of f. 203, and again at 253ᵛ, are the *essais de plume* of a very unsure hand, which wrote out the whole Greek alphabet in minuscules. On f. 244ᵛ-249ᵛ, parts of hymns have been written in the upper and lower margins of the manuscript. They start with ἦχος α' πρώτιστον ἄσμα τῶ θ(ε)ῶ and are not attested either in Follieri ([12]) or in the *TLG*. On f. 338, there is a monocondylic inscription in the lower margin – it could be a signature, but it is illegible in the microfilm. Finally, on f. 339ʳ⁻ᵛ

---

(11) What most manuscripts of the *FC* refer to as "chapters," κεφάλαια, are usually called τίτλοι by *T* in its first three "books," i.e., in the three recensions of the *Sacr. Par.* This is also the practice of the *Sacr. Par.* and of other anthologies. As for the chapters of the *FC*, they are called κεφάλαια both in *T* and in the other witnesses of this florilegium.

(12) FOLLIERI, *Initia hymnorum.*

XXXVI   MANUSCRIPT TRADITION

the ragged corners of the folio were mended with pieces of paper, and they were written in a cursive script of a much more recent date than the remainder of the manuscript.

To describe the contents of this manuscript, it is useful to quote Richard's account of the *Florilegium Hierosolymitanum* (of which *T* is the most important witness): [13] "L'auteur de ce florilège a entrepris de combiner trois florilèges damascéniens (I. Flor. Vatic. auctum. – II. Ier livre des *Hiera* [= *Sacr. Par.*] recension du Coislin 276. – III. Flor. Thess.) et le Flor. Coislinianum [...], sans mélanger ceux-ci, mais en évitant les doublets. Chaque stoicheion comprend donc quatre livres, dont le premier, le Flor. Vatic. auctum, est reproduit intégralement, les autres avec des coupures qui suppriment les textes déjà cités." [14] The fact that the *FC* was mixed with purely "Damascenian" florilegia shows that the compiler of the *Florilegium Hierosolymitanum* saw no fundamental difference between it and the extant recensions of the *Sacr. Par. T* contains only Letters A-E, and it has not yet been determined whether the rest of the books (or letters) were ever written. [15] In this manuscript, the *FC* is always designated as "Book Four"; thus in Alpha, στοιχεῖον ἄλφα, βιβλίον δ'.

Holl claims that "der Titel, mit dem sie [*T*] abbricht: πῶς νοητέον τὸ προσέχετε τὴν ἐλεημοσύνην ὑμῶν ist ein Titel des βιβλίον δ'," i.e. of the *FC*. [16] This chapter, IE' of Letter Epsilon, is not the last one of *T*. The mistake that Holl makes here was most likely taken over from Papadopoulos-Kerameus. [17] It is true that *T* omits the whole of chapter IϚ', περὶ τῶν ἐλεημοσύνην μὴ ποιούντων ἀλλὰ πλεονεκτούντων, but it does contain chapter IZ', περὶ εἰκόνων προσκυνήσεως (f. 345). Indeed, the last fragment quoted in *T* ends with the words ἀλλ'ὅμως δίκην ἔδοκαν (*sic*) οἱ ταύτην ὑβρίσαντ(ες), [18] which corresponds to Epsilon IZ', 8 of *A*. After the last fragment the following inscription is to be found: τέλος τὸ ε'· τοῦ τετάρτου βιβλίου; the end of f. 345^v

---

(13) RICHARD, *Florilèges*, col. 483-484.

(14) Ibid., col. 483.

(15) According to RICHARD, *Florilèges*, col. 484, only a very careful study of the *Florilegium Laurentianum*, which utilized the *Florilegium Hierosolymitanum* as a source, could possibly allow the scholar to answer this question.

(16) HOLL, *Sacra Parallela*, p. 115.

(17) PAPADOPOULOS-KERAMEUS, *Jerusalem*, I, p. 68.

(18) Io. Chrys., *Ad populum Antiochenum*, PG 49, 57, 21-22.

MANUSCRIPT TRADITION   XXXVII

is also the end of the last quaternion of *T* (με΄, f. 339-345). In *A*, however, Letter Epsilon still has two more fragments, one by a monk named Moschus [19] and another by Theodore of Stoudios. Even if those two fragments were omitted, Letters A-E form a relatively close unity: *T* does not stop abruptly in the middle of a book; no material accident caused the manuscript to end there. This may suggest that the *Florilegium Hierosolymitanum* consisted originally only of Letters A-E. Subsequent letters may have been planned – indeed, the *Atheniensis, Metochion Sancti Sepulcri 274* has a full pinax, up to Letter Omega – but were possibly never executed. [20]

Holl's concluding remark about the *Florilegium Hierosolymitanum* foreshadows Richard's contention that the *FC* is too *sui generis* to be considered a mere recension of the *Sacr. Par.*: "Das βιβλίον δ΄ des Hieros. [= the *FC*] kann kurz abgemacht werden. Cohn [21] hat richtig gesehen, dass es sich mit dem Coisl. 294 [= *A*] deckt, einem codex, dessen Inhalt zwar mit dem Parallelenliteratur zusammenhängt, aber so stark mit anderswoher stammendem Material versetzt ist, dass man ihn nicht mehr als eine Recension der Parallelen rechnen darf." [22]

Ms. *C*, *Parisinus graecus 924*, olim *Reg. 1993*. [23] 10ᵗʰ c. Parchment, 370 folios (330 × 240, written area 225 × 160), two col-

---

(19) On whom see now MAKSIMCZUK, *Anthology.*

(20) Richard apparently believes that *T* ends mutilated; cf. RICHARD, *Opera minora*, I, *appendice*, p. i.

(21) COHN, *Ueberlieferung*, especially p. 482-490; I thank D. Searby for this reference.

(22) HOLL, *Sacra Parallela*, p. 132. Montfaucon was already able to point out a relevant difference between the *Sacr. Par.* and *Parisinus, Coislinianus 294 (= A)*; according to him, this latter manuscript contains "Eclogae seu excerpta Scripturae, Patrum et aliorum in varia Capita argumenta ordine alphabetico digesta, quae a *Parallelis* Joannis Damasceni. Nam hîc Joannes non semel laudatur" (DE MONTFAUCON, *Bibliotheca Coisliniana*, p. 412). John Damascene is mentioned four times in the *FC* – all of them in the second chapter of Letter Omicron – in excerpts with the attribution Ἰωάννου τοῦ Μανσούρ.

(23) OMONT's description (*Paris*, I, p. 177) is exceedingly short: "Loci communes theologici CCXLV., ex SS. Patrum operibus excerpti (Interpretatio sacrae scripturae, ordine alphabetico);" he then adds some codicological remarks. Note that, by stating that there are 245 chapters, Omont shows he was taking into account the text of the manuscript rather than its pinax.

XXXVIII MANUSCRIPT TRADITION

umns, 23 lines. It contains the *FC* only; Letter Alpha f. 6-78. The pinax was written by the same hand as the text. The title, also by the same hand, is: τάδε ἔνεστιν ἐν τῆδε τῇ βίβλωι· [24] ἑρμηνεία κατα στοιχεῖον τῆς θείας γραφῆς, κεφάλ(αια) σμς΄. This is the oldest attested title of the *FC*. It could be translated as: "Alphabetic Interpretation of the Divine Scripture in 246 Chapters."

C is the single most important witness of the *FC*; if only one manuscript had to be chosen on the basis of which to edit the whole anthology, it should be this one. It is true that there are a few cases in which *AT* preserve ampler fragments. [25] Nevertheless, these few cases compensate neither for the lower quality of the text preserved in *AT* (especially in *A*), [26] nor for their more limited extent; both *A* and *T* break off much before the end of the *FC*, as can be seen from their respective descriptions above.

The folios of *C* were on occasion bound in an incorrect order, but happily enough, they had already been numbered. The folios appear in *C* in the following order: 1-45, 78, 47-52, 85, 54-77, 79, 80-84, 53, 86-93, 46, 94-344, 347, 346, 345, 348-370. [27] They are numerated twice: once with Arabic numerals (in the upper right corner of each recto folio), beginning from the pinax; and once with Greek numerals (in the middle of the lower margin of the recto folios), with an α at the beginning of the text of the *FC*, namely at f. 6, after the pinax.

As the title of *C* indicates, there are 246 chapters in the pinax, [28] the last one being περὶ ψευδοπροφητῶν (as in *S*; see below). This proves that letter Omega, not to be found in any manuscript of the *FC*, was also missing in *C*, its best and probably oldest witness. Consequently, it is likely that the florilegium never had it. [29] At the very least, we can be sure that in Δ – the hypar-

---

(24) This is what the first hand (that of the copyist of the whole manuscript) wrote. A second hand took the iota adscript to be a ν, and wrote βίβλων. Another characteristic of this second hand is that it often added tremas on the undiphthonged ι and υ, against the use of the first copyist, who never wrote them.

(25) In Letter Alpha this happens only once, in 16.26/55.

(26) *T* has *prima facie* a correct text, but it exhibits a huge number of *sauts du même au même*.

(27) Cf. Declerck, *Max. Conf.*, p. cciv, n. 122.

(28) As we will see, chapter 246 is missing in the text.

(29) See now Ceulemans – Van Deun, *Réflexions*, p. 376-380.

MANUSCRIPT TRADITION   XXXIX

chetype of *C* and the short recension – it was absent from both
the pinax and the text itself.

Whether *A* or *T* ever had letter Omega is open to speculation,
but it is likely that they did not. The pinax of *Atheniensis, Metochion Sancti Sepulcri 274*, probably an apograph of *T* and at any
rate belonging to the same recension as *AT*, states that there was
nothing in Letter Omega of its fourth book (namely, Letter Omega of the *FC*). See f. 26: στοιχ[εῖον] Ω [...]· βιβλίον δ' οὐδέν. (³⁰)

After this last chapter, there is a dotted line in the pinax of *C*
(f. 5ᵛ), as if to indicate that what comes next does not belong to
the pinax proper. Indeed, the three excerpts that follow lie outside
the alphabetical order of the *FC*: 1. κυρίλλου ἀλεξανδρείας, περὶ
τοῦ λαζάρου· (καὶ) εἰς τὸ ἐνεβριμήσατο τῶ πνεύματι ὁ ἰ(ησοῦ)ς
λέγων ποῦ τεθείκατε αὐτόν. 2. τοῦ ἁγίου ἰωάννου τοῦ χρυσοστόμου ὁμοίως εἰς τὸ ἐνεβριμήσατο καὶ εἰς τὸ ποῦ τεθείκατε αὐτόν. 3. ἱππολύτου ῥώμης, περὶ ἰωσὴφ τοῦ τῆς θ<εοτόκου
μν>ήστορος (³¹) καὶ τῶν υἱῶν καὶ θυγατέρων αὐτοῦ καὶ γενεα-
λογία τῆς ὑπεραγίας θεοτόκου (καὶ) περὶ τῆς πρὸς τὸν κ(ύριο)ν
ἡμῶν ἰ(ησοῦ)ν χ(ριστὸ)ν ἰωάννου τοῦ βαπτιστοῦ συγγενείας.
These three excerpts, according to the usual rules of arrangement
of the *FC*, should have been placed together with the excerpts
about Jesus in Letter Chi.

As we have seen, the last chapter in the pinax is περὶ ψευδοπροφητῶν. In the text itself, by contrast, the manuscript ends
abruptly in the middle of chapter σμε΄, Περὶ ψυχῆς. (³²) The last
words in *C* are ἐφελκόμενοι φέρονται πρὸς αὐτόν (*sic*)· θείαν οὖν
στοργὴν συλλα... (³³) Nevertheless, it can be deduced that not so
much was lost in *C*, probably three or four folios. (³⁴)

---

(30) RICHARD, *Opera minora*, I, *appendice*, p. iii. See now CEULEMANS –
VAN DEUN, *Réflexions*, p. 376-388.

(31) These letters, missing in *C* because of a material accident, were added by CEULEMANS – VAN DEUN, *Réflexions*, p. 378, n. 75, on the basis of *S*.

(32) Cf. DECLERCK, *Max. Conf.*, p. cciv, n. 122. This title appears on the
recto side of the last written folium; in other words, only a folio recto-verso
of the chapter before the last is extant, and the whole last chapter is missing.

(33) Ps.-Clem. Rom., *Homiliae*, 17, 10, 5, 1-2.

(34) The only manuscript of the long recension that has come down to
us unmutilated at the end, namely *S*, has the last words of *C* on f. 186, line 9
(of 30). *S* ends at f. 188ᵛ, line 6, and a folio of *S* has roughly as much text as
a folio and a half of *C*. This means that the portion missing from *C* is about
five pages of *S*, which is roughly equivalent to seven and a half pages of *C*:

XL MANUSCRIPT TRADITION

The following chapter numbers, always preceded by κεφά(λαιον), were written by a second hand: ιβ΄, ιγ΄, ιδ΄ (bis), ις΄, ιζ΄, κ΄, κα΄, κβ΄, κγ΄, κε΄, κς΄, κζ΄, κη΄, κθ΄, λ΄, λα΄, λβ΄, λγ΄, λδ΄, λε΄, λς΄, λζ΄, λη΄, λθ΄, μ΄, μα΄.

A Latin inscription on the first folio indicates that the manuscript was bought for the king of France in June, 1671. ([35]) Below there is another, almost illegible inscription: Ἐκ ὦν τοῦ *αγγίσμου (ut uid.) Νοταρᾶ. In the upper margin of f. 3, the name *Luca Notara* ([36]) is written. In the rest of the manuscript there are a few marginal notes, yet none of them is relevant to establishing the text of the *FC*. See for instance the *essais de plume* at f. 140, 142ᵛ and 188; on the latter folio, a monk gives his name, γεράσιμος (*sic*). This monk is certainly not the scribe of *C*. ([37])

Ms. **B**, *Atheniensis, Bibliothecae Nationalis 464.* ([38]) 10ᵗʰ c. Parchment, 428 pages (290 × 210), one column, 25-26 lines. It contains only the *FC*; Letter Alpha p. 1-76. Sakkelion is very succinct about its contents: περιέχει Ἀδήλου· Παράλληλα ἱερά. Its first twenty-three folios are missing, ([39]) so that the text starts with τῶν ἄλλων ἀρρωστημάτων ἰάσεως. τοιαῦταί τινες εἰσὶν αἱ θηριακαὶ καλούμεναι κατασκευαί [...], numbered as 1 in the manuscript (corresponding to 29.429/431 of the present edition). The manuscript ends, also mutilated, at Letter T 1, 12 (chapter περὶ τῆς ἁγίας καὶ ὁμοουσίου τριάδος). ([40]) In the middle of the manuscript many folios are missing, for example on p. 380, where

_____

four folios, the last of which would not have been written to the end. However, a full quaternion of *C* is missing; its last quaternion, signed as μς΄, comprises f. 363-370, and 370ᵛ is, as we have seen, the last folio of *C*. The last quire must have contained some blank folios, or must have been a binion.

(35) I could not decipher the first name of the inscription: *Vanolib*** emit Nicosio pro Bibl. Regis Chr. Ann. 1671. M. Iunio.*

(36) Or *Nouara*?

(37) The inscription is practically undecipherable. I could make out only part of it: Εγο ταχα γερασιμος· μοναχ(ος)· το επιλην μαρουλ (?) αμαρτολος τιμη εγο **οζος. Note that he never writes breathing marks or accents, and that he always writes omikron instead of omega, even in well-known words.

(38) Cf. Sakkelion, *Athens*, p. 92.

(39) Cf. Ibid., p. 92.

(40) Des. Εἴ τις <διαπεπλάσθαι τὸν>... = Greg. Naz., *Ep.* 101, 17, 1-2. The attribution of this excerpt is τοῦ αὐτοῦ ἐκ τοῦ πρὸς κληδόνιον λόγου in *C* (f. 334), but it is illegible in *B* (p. 428).

MANUSCRIPT TRADITION

B jumps from the last chapter in Letter Omicron to chapter 9 in Letter Pi. [41] In the 16ᵗʰ c., when *S* (an apograph of *B*) was copied, the lacuna after p. 380 already existed, [42] but the first and last folios and the pinax were still present.

As the description of its apographs *P* and *S* will show, *B* must have been in Venice in the 16ᵗʰ c.

Ms. **P**, *Parisinus, graecus 1096* (olim *Colbert. 4942*). [43] 16ᵗʰ c. Paper, 195 folios (145 × 210), 18 lines. The *FC* is contained on f. 5-105 under the title τοῦ μεγάλου μαξίμου, εἰς τὰ ἄπορα τῆς γραφῆς, [44] Letter Alpha on f. 5-93ᵛ; pinax on f. 1-4.

1. F. 5-105. *FC*. The last chapter is the tweltfh of Beta, ἀπόδειξις ὅτι τὰ βρώματα ἡ ψυχὴ ἀναλίσκει (unnumbered in the pinax), [45] and the last words of the *FC* in this manuscript are τὰ καταβαλλόμενα εἰς τὸν λέβητα ἐψεῖ (*sic*). [46] On f. 105, the copyist states "fuerunt et alia plura, sed non possumus ea legere propter vetustate(m) libri." The same copyist also wrote "defuerunt" in the pinax, after the 53ʳᵈ chapter, ἀπόδειξις – ἀναλίσκει. This copyist must be Andreas Darmarios, as we will presently see. Chapters 54-59 are missing both in the pinax and in the text of *P*.

---

(41) The last words of p. 380 are ἐπὶ τῶν ὁδῶν θύουσι· σὺ δὲ ἔμπρο... (Io. Chrys., *Ad populum Antiochenum*, PG 49, 160, 35), and p. 381 begins with: τῶν ἀπελθόντων εἶπε, τίς τῶν ἐρχομένων λέξει... (Io. Chrys., *Paul.*, p. 430, 5-6). For the lacuna between p. 208 and 209, see the description of *S* below.

(42) *S* has the same lacuna as *B* and has left a blank page and a half after ἔμπρο[...], which it completed into ἔμπροσθεν. *P*, another apograph of *B*, ends abruptly in chapter 12 of Letter Beta, thus long before the lacuna in *S*.

(43) Omont, *Paris*, I, p. 219.

(44) This title, manifestly inexact, is found as a heading on f. 5, where the text of the *FC* begins, at the beginning of the pinax and on an unnumbered folio before the pinax. The title was taken at face value by Omont, who wrote in his catalogue "S. Maximi quaestiones et responsiones de variis S* Scripturae dubiis" (Omont, *Paris*, I, p. 219). Cf. Declerck, *Max. Conf.*, p. ccix and Laga – Steel, *Max. Conf.*, II, p. xlii.

(45) This chapter contains an excerpt attributed to Athanasius of Alexandria, but neither the editors of Beta nor I were not able to locate the source of the fragment.

(46) B 24.12.

XLII   MANUSCRIPT TRADITION

2. F. 106-137. (⁴⁷) Here begins a new section, which follows the system of arrangement by title. The chapters, however, no longer follow the alphabetical order of the *FC*. There are nine new chapters, numbered from 60 to 68; they appear also in the pinax. Each chapter contains only one fragment, except for the last one, which can be considered to contain two. The first chapter (⁴⁸) (f. 106-110) is numbered ξ΄. The ensuing chapters are: κε(φάλαι-ον) ξα΄ περὶ τῆς ἀνθρωπήσεως τοῦ μονογενοῦς on f. 110; κε(φά-λαιον) ξβ΄ περὶ τοῦ τίνος λέγομεν εἶναι τὴν ἕνωσιν on f. 112; κε(φάλαιον) ξγ΄ περὶ τοῦ ἄνθρακος on f. 114; κε(φάλαιον) ξδ΄ ὅτι τῆς ἀσωμάτου θεότητος σῶμα γέγονε [...] on f. 115; κε(φάλαιον) ξε΄ ὅτι χ(ριστὸ)ς θ(εο)ῦ καλεῖται γεγονὼς ἄν(θρωπ)ος ὁ τοῦ θ(εο)ῦ λόγος on f. 116; κε(φάλαιον) ξς΄ πῶς ἂν νοοῖτο θ(εο)τόκος ἡ ἁγία παρθένος on f. 119ᵛ; κε(φάλαιον) ξζ΄ περὶ ἁγίων εἰκόνων on f. 124ᵛ; κε(φάλαιον) ξη΄, ἔκθεσις πίστεως· βασιλ(είου) on f. 125ᵛ. There are still two other *titloi*, which can in fact be considered part of this last one: on f. 126ᵛ, σωφρονίου ἱεροσολύμων· περὶ πί-στεως (no number; the title is absent from the pinax), and finally, on f. 134: ἔκθεσις πίστεως τοῦ σοφωτάτου κωνσταντίνου τοῦ ψελλοῦ (= Michael Psellos). Note that the three last chapters are roughly equivalent in meaning; the first and the last one are called ἔκθεσις πίστεως, the second one περὶ πίστεως. This explains why only the first one is numbered, and why they appear under one title in the pinax, as ἔκθεσις πίστεως. The reason is clear enough: the compiler of this part of the manuscript (Darmarios or someone else) allowed only one fragment for each *titlos*; if more than an excerpt was needed, the same title or an analogous one was written. This procedure is yet another difference between the structure of the little compilation found on f. 106-137 and that of the *FC*.

P contains still two more items, listed in the pinax as follows: ἔτι περιέχει τὸ βιβλίον καὶ τάδε· περὶ τῆς συντελείας τοῦ κόσμου λόγος, καὶ περὶ τοῦ ἀντιχρίστου, καὶ εἰς τὴν δευτέραν παρουσίαν. These two items are n. 3 and 4 below.

---

(47) Inc. of the section: καὶ μὴν εἰ ἀπερίγραπτος (Anast. Sin., *Viae dux*, XVI, 4), des. ἀναφέρων τὴν ὁμοιότητα (source not found).

(48) Namely, περὶ τοῦ τί δηλοῖ τὸ ἀποστολικὸν ῥητόν, τὸ, ἐν αὐτῷ κατοικεῖ πᾶν τῷ πλήρωμα τῆς θεότητος σωματικῶς (Col. 2, 9)· σευηριανοῦ ἐπισκόπου γαβάλων.

MANUSCRIPT TRADITION XLIII

3. F. 138-168. Ἱππολίτου τοῦ μακαριωτάτου μάρτυρος λόγος περὶ τῆς συντελείας τοῦ κόσμου, κ(αὶ) περὶ τοῦ ἀντιχρίστου· καὶ εἰς τὴν δευτέραν παρουσίαν τοῦ κ(υρίο)υ ἡμῶν ἰ(ησο)ῦ χ(ριστο)ῦ. Inc. Ἐπειδὴ οἱ μακάριοι προφῆται, des. καὶ τῷ παναγίῳ καὶ ἀγαθῷ, καὶ ζωοποιῷ αὐτοῦ πνεύματι ... ἀμήν = CPG 1910 (= BHG 812z), Ps.-Hippolytus of Rome, *Oratio de consummatione mundi*, from the beginning (including title and attribution) to sect. 44, 8.

4. F. 169-195. τοῦ ἐν ἁγίοις πατρὸς ἡμῶν Γρηγορίου ἐπισκό-που νύσσης, λόγος περὶ τῆς τριημέρου προθε<σ>μίας ([49]) τῆς τοῦ χ(ριστο)ῦ ἀναστάσεως. Inc. Εἴ τις π(ατ)ριαρχῶν εὐλογία, des. ὃν καταγλυκαίνει τὸ κηρίον τῆς ἀγαθῆς ἐλπίδος, ἐν χ(ριστ)ῷ ἰ(ησο)ῦ τῷ κ(υρί)ῳ ἡμῶν ... ἀμήν = Greg. Nyss., *De trid. spat.*, p. 273, 1 – 306, 10.

Both Omont and Vogel-Gardthausen state that *P* was copied by Andreas Darmarios. ([50]) A close examination of the script of *P* shows that they are right. ([51]) The manuscript is not dated, and we do not know where it was copied. Nevertheless, Darmarios is known to have been active in Venice between ca. 1560-1587, with intervals in other cities; his dated manuscripts are from the years 1558 to 1587. ([52]) Furthermore, Darmarios was a friend of Manuel Malaxos, who in turn was a relative of Nikolaos Malaxos. ([53]) Nikolaos knew Ioannes Katelos, the copyist of *S*, who, as we will see, transcribed *B* in Venice in 1542. Both Katelos and Darmarios were active in the circle of the 16th c. Greek *émigrés* in this city. Since *B* is known to have been in Venice by that time, it is almost certain that Darmarios found it there.

One last word about Darmarios: his alteration of the title of the *FC* into τοῦ μεγάλου μαξίμου, εἰς τὰ ἄπορα τῆς γραφῆς was a device to make the manuscript more appealing to its poten-tial buyer and thus exhibits a patent lack of scrupulosity. Indeed, there is no way he could have failed to notice that such a title

---

(49) The σ is missing in the manuscript.

(50) Omont, *Paris*, I, p. 219; Vogel – Gardthausen, *Griechische Schrei-ber*, p. 25.

(51) For samples of his handwriting and an account of his career, see *RGK*, II, § 13; § 21; III, § 22.

(52) Cf. *RGK*, I, § 13, esp. p. 29.

(53) For Manuel Malaxos, see *RGK*, I, § 250; for Nikolaos, *RGK*, I, § 312; II, § 432.

XLIV   MANUSCRIPT TRADITION

is completely unsuited to the actual contents of the manuscript. The statement that after chapter 53 he could no longer decipher the text of his model "due to its old age" is in line with this lack of concern for accuracy; we know that Darmarios' model was *B*, which is perfectly legible to this day.

The manuscript *P* was owned by Jacques-Auguste de Thou (1553-1617), as can still be seen on the folio before the pinax, then by Jean-Baptiste Colbert (1619-1683), to whom it owes its former denomination, and later belonged to the king's library.

Ms. *S*, *Bruxellensis IV, 881* (*olim Phillipps 3080*). [54] 16ᵗʰ c. (*a.* 1542). 192 folios (245 × 345, written area 125 × 230). One column, 30 lines. This manuscript contains only the *FC* (f. 2-188ᵛ); Letter Alpha f. 7-49. The last folios of *S* (f. 189-192) are blank.

The title on f. 1, written by Claude Naulot, [55] runs like this: Ἑρμηνεία κατὰ στοιχεῖα εἰς τὴν θείαν γραφὴν ἐκ πολλῶν τε καὶ ποικίλων θεολόγων. Pinax on f. 2-6ᵛ. Title above the pinax (f. 2): τάδε ἔνεστι ἐν τῆδε τῇ βίβλῳ· ἑρμηνεία κατὰ στοιχεῖον τῆς θεί(ας) γραφῆς, κ(εφά)λ(αια) σμς'. [56] The title of the pinax itself is Πίναξ ἀσφαλής, τῶν θησαυρῶν τῆς βίβλου. As elsewhere in the *FC*, there is no Letter Omega. After the last chapter of Psi, περὶ ψευδοπροφητῶν, we read τέλος τῆς βίβλου ταύτης. [57] It is the only manuscript of the long recension that includes the last chapter of the *FC*, namely περὶ ψευδοπροφητῶν, numbered σμς' in the margin. [58] Since *S* is an apograph of *B* and this latter manuscript, in turn, an apograph of *C*, the presence of this fragment in *S* proves that it was also originally present in *C*.

S notes the lacunae of its model, namely *B*, by leaving blank pages. Examples are f. 95ᵛ and part of f. 95, and f. 152ᵛ and part of

---

(54) See WITTEK, *Manuscrits*, p. 250-251; NORET, *Catalogues*. For the ancient reference numbers of *S*, see CATALDI PALAU, *Pellicier*, p. 38.

(55) Naulot's handwriting appears on f. 1 and f. 188ᵛ. Both instances are partly quoted immediately below. In both cases, Naulot wrote not only in Latin, but also in Greek (and on f. 188ᵛ in French).

(56) Note that this is the same title as in *C*. Manuscript *B*, then, must have had it too – and surely also a pinax.

(57) This and a wealth of other material may be found in CEULEMANS – VAN DEUN, *Réflexions*, p. 376-388.

(58) This chapter contains only one fragment. It is now critically edited in Ceulemans et al., *Psi*, p. 77-78.

MANUSCRIPT TRADITION   XLV

f. 152. ([59]) There are practically no marginalia, apart from chapter numbers and attributions, and only once or twice does a correction appear in the margins.

As we learn from the colophon on f. 188ᵛ, ([60]) Ἰωάννης Κάτελος ([61]) finished copying the manuscript on November 28ᵗʰ, 1542: ͵αφμβʹ νοεμβρ(ίου) κηʹ ἐν τῇ βενετίᾳ διὰ χειρὸς καὶ κόπου ἰωάννου κατέλου τοῦ ναυπλοιώτου. Katelos was a copyist in the service of Guillaume Pellicier (c. 1490-1568) in Venice. ([62]) It is well-known that Pellicier was bishop of Montpellier; between June 1539 and October 1543 ([63]) he was the ambassador of Francis I to Venice, and he also happened to possess a large collection of manuscripts. When Pellicier died, his library – including S – was acquired by Claude Naulot of Avallon. ([64]) As he indicates in a subscription below the aforementioned colophon, he read S in 1573. ([65]) Naulot repeats this information on f. 1: Ἀνέγνωκε

---

(59) After the blank space of f. 95, there follows chapter ριβʹ, Περὶ τῶν τεσσάρων θηρίων ὧν δανϊὴλ τεθέαται (first fragment, no attribution). The last words of f. 95 are οὖσπερ καὶ κέρατα προσηγόρευσεν ἐν οἷς ἀναβήσεται ἕτερον [...]. On f. 96, S jumps from the first fragment of Letter Theta (about the beasts of Daniel; see CEULEMANS, *Theta*, p. 92) to the first fragment of Letter Iota: εἰ ὁ ἠλυμμένος (*sic*), ὃν ὑμεῖς προσδοκᾶτε, for which see DÉROCHE, *Képhalaia*, p. 300, l. 14. (This lacuna takes place in manuscript B between p. 208 and 209.) After the blank on f. 152ᵛ, chapter ρξγʹ, περὶ ὅρκου ἀποχῆς, follows, beginning with a fragment with the attribution τοῦ χρυσοστόμου, ἐκ τῶν ἀνδριάντων. The last words of f. 152 are καὶ οἱ μὲν λησταὶ, ἐπὶ τῶν ὁδῶν θύουσϊ· σὺ δὲ, ἔμπροσθεν.

(60) A reproduction is in WITTEK, *Manuscrits*, pl. II.

(61) *RGK*, II.A, p. 95: "Sohn des Niccolò, aus Nauplion, Herkunftsbezeichnung Naupliotes; datierte Hs. 1542, Zusammenarbeit mit Nikolaos Malaxos [...]." See also VOGEL – GARDTHAUSEN, *Griechische Schreiber*, p. 73. For a description of his writing style, see *RGK*, II.B, p. 85.

(62) *RGK*, II.A, p. 95-96: "[Katelos] kopiert in Venedig im Dienst des Guillaume Pellicier, dort 1553-1563 in der griechischen Gemeinde belegt." For further information on Pellicier, see CATALDI PALAU, *Pellicier*.

(63) CATALDI PALAU, *Pellicier*, p. 32.

(64) The date cannot be determined: À une date incertaine, entre 1567, date de sa mort [Pellicier's], et 1573, une bonne partie de ses manuscrits passa entre les mains de Claude Naulot" (CATALDI PALAU, *Pellicier*, p. 33).

(65) Κλαύδιος ὁ Ναυλῶτος [...] Claudius Naulôtus Claude Naulot [...] L'an de grace 1573 / Ἀνέγνωκε ταῦτα [...] τῷ θεῷ χάρις. "Claude Naulot était sans aucun doute originaire d'Avallon, mais [...] il résidait à Autun en 1573" (CATALDI PALAU, *Pellicier*, p. 33). This author states that the common assumption that Naulot was a scholar is based on a misunderstanding, be-

Ναυλῶτ τάδε· 1573. The next possessors of *S* were the Jesuits of the College of Clermont in Paris. [66] When in the second half of the 18th c. the Jesuits were suppressed and their goods put up for sale, the Dutchman Gerard Meerman (1722-1771) acquired the lot to which *S* belonged. [67] In 1824 Meerman's son, Jan, sold it to Thomas Phillipps (1792-1872), who gave *S* its ancient denomination, *Phillipps 3080*. [68] In 1962, when Richard published his *Florilèges spirituels grecs*, the manuscript was thought to be lost. [69] It was acquired by the Royal Library of Brussels in 1972. [70]

Ms. **D**, *Mediolanensis, Ambrosianus Q 74 sup. (gr. 681)*. [71] 10th c. [72] Parchment, 267 folios (260 × 187, [73] written area

cause he was mereley "greffier de l'Hôtel de Ville [...]. Par un jeu du destin, son travail méticuleux et attentif de clerc sans prétention fut interprété comme des notes des lecture d'érudit; [...] il n'était sans doute qu'un honnête fonctionnaire, accomplissant avec zèle son travail" (ibid., p. 34).

(66) Cf. Cataldi Palau, *Pellicier*, p. 34-35; Fouqueray, *Histoire*, p. 151-152. Thomas Phillipps, whose relation to *S* will presently be discussed, wrote in a letter of 1824 that the lot of manuscripts to which *S* belonged "came originally from the Jesuits' College of Clermont at Paris" (Munby, *Phillipps*, p. 34).

(67) In this lot "les manuscrits grecs étaient au nombre de 341, provenant de différentes bibliothèques: 163 avaient appartenu à Guillaume Pellicier; parmi ceux-ci 104 étaient paraphés par C. Naulot; 4 autres manuscrits avaient appartenu a Naulot (ils en portent le paraphe), mais non à Pellicier" (Cataldi Palau, *Pellicier*, p. 35).

(68) This information can be found in Munby, *Phillipps*, p. 25-26. Munby, who single-handedly wrote the five volumes of the *Phillipps Studies*, has documented in great detail many of the manuscripts owned by Phillipps.

(69) Richard, *Florilèges*, col. 485. Despite not having seen the manuscript Richard was able to determine that *S* was "sans doute" an apograph of *B*.

(70) See *Catalogue of Greek and Italian Manuscripts*, p. 10-11 (§ 1714); *Cinq années d'acquisitions*, p. 124, 126-127 (§ 63).

(71) See Martini – Bassi, *Ambrosiana*, p. 767-780; Diekamp, *Hippolytos*, p. lvi-lviii, n. 1; Uthemann, *Aporien*, especially p. 16-17; id., Ἄπορα. For an extensive bibliography of works concerning *D*, see Pasini, *Bibliografia*, p. 306-307.

(72) "[...] seconda metà del X secolo" (Mazzucchi, *Testimone*, p. 355). As for the geographical setting of *D*, Mazzucchi believes that "l'insieme fa immaginare un'origine siro-palestinese" but does not explain his reasons. Pasini (*Ambrosiana*, p. 85, n. 6) states that the handwriting of *D* belongs to the 10th c.: "La minuscola con cui è vergato, da attribuirsi verosimilmente ad almeno due mani, deve essere collocata tra le grafie corsiveggianti del X secolo e presenta affinità con quella definita *tipo Efrem*."

(73) Or, according to Pasini (*Ambrosiana*, p. 83), 258 × 180; according to Mazzucchi (*Testimone*, p. 355), 255 × 185.

MANUSCRIPT TRADITION   XLVII

170/176 × 125), one column, 30 lines. Miscellaneous manuscript; *FC* on f. 3-131^v; Letter Alpha on f. 3-32^v. The title and part of the pinax are lost. Folios 1-2 and 266-267 were taken from a Latin codex containing a breviary. [74] *D* is mutilated at the beginning; it starts with the word ἀφιπτάμενον (fragment 5.43/44 of the present edition). Another folio was apparently ripped out and is missing after f. 20 (between Οἴα in 47.4 and παθόντας in 55.5 of the present edition). Additionally, four folios that were originally part of *D* have been ripped from it and are now *Mediolanensis, Ambrosianus D 137 suss., 4-7.* [75] The first two folios of *D* contain part of the pinax of the *FC*, between chapters ριθ′ and σλ′, "corrispondenti ai testi vergati ai ff. 74^v-131^v del codice [*D*] (ove figurano con analoga intestazione e con numerazione maggiorata di una o due unità)." [76] Folios 5^v-7^v contain the "*Index in eiusdem codicis partem alteram* (*tit.* Πίναξ σὺν Θεῷ ἕτερος τῆς παρούσης βίβλου, elenco delle intestazioni, numerate da α′ a ρκβ′, corrispondenti ai testi vergati ai ff. 132^r-165^v del codice)." [77] Thus, the miscellaneous treatises of *D* each had their own pinax after that of the *FC*. Pasini indicates that the fragment "è vergato

---

(74) MARTINI – BASSI, *Ambrosiana*, p. 682. For these authors the Latin codex dates from the 14th-15th c. MAZZUCCHI (*Testimone*, p. 357), by contrast, is inclined to place it in the 13th c.: "Scrittura e ornamentazione [...] suggeriscono una datazione alla metà circa del XIII secolo, l'Italia centro-meridionale, e forse influenze francesi". Following the direction his title suggests ("[...] conoscenza del greco negli ordini mendicanti [...]"), Mazzucchi goes as far as to ask whether the Dominicans or the Franciscans owned *D*. He makes a very interesting remark concerning the geographical area where *D* circulated: "più o meno nel periodo in cui fu postillato dal lettore latino, ricevette le attenzioni di quattro mani greche. Doveva quindi trovarsi in un area di tradizione ellenofona" (ibid., p. 358-359). This should be Southern Italy. Mazzucchi's conclusion concerning *D* and another manuscript he examines, the *Ambrosianus E 88 inf.*, is that "nel Due-Trecento, negli ordini mendicanti si poteva acquistare un'adeguata conoscenza della lingua e della 'paleografia' greca" (ibid., p. 359).

(75) See the exhaustive description by PASINI, *Ambrosiana*, p. 83-87.

(76) PASINI, *Ambrosiana*, p. 83. Pasini could not explain this intriguing excess in the numeration of the text in relation to that of the pinax, which also occurs in *EG*: "[...] risultando non facilmente spiegabile il motivo della differente numerazione fra indice e codice [...]" (ibid., n. 3). I can only add that this excess in the numeration – which is peculiar to *DEG*, and does not occur in *C* – is evident only *after* Letter Alpha.

(77) PASINI, *Ambrosiana*, p. 84.

XLVIII   MANUSCRIPT TRADITION

in una scrittura distintiva alessandrina, sospesa al rigo, in cui si sono talora introdotte alcune lettere minuscole. Come [D] di cui doveva far parte sin dall'origine, sembra databile alla fine del X secolo." [78] The pinax was written by the same copyist as the text.

The last chapter of the long recension, Περὶ ψευδοπροφητῶν, appears in D on f. 131, bearing the number σλ´ (σκη´ in the pinax). [79] The short recension as preserved in DEG, however, apparently contained several extra chapters, which are listed in the pinax but are no longer extant. On f. 131^{r-v} D has a chapter numbered σλα´ (σκθ´ in the pinax), Περὶ τοῦ λαζάρου· ἐνεβριμήσατο τῶ πν(εύματ)ι λέγων π(οῦ) τεθείκατε αὐ<τόν> (cf. Io. 11, 34). There follows an attribution, κυρίλλου ἀλεξ(ανδρίνου). [80] On f. 131^v there is a fragment with the attribution τοῦ χρ(υσοστόμου), [81] and yet another one, ἱππολύτ(ου) ῥώμ(ης). [82] These three fragments have been critically edited by Ceulemans and Van Deun. [83]

It is not necessary to list the extremely varied contents of D; this has already been done in great detail, if not always with total accuracy, by Martini and Bassi. [84] There are two excerpts, however, that deserve special mention. They come directly after the FC in D:

(78) Ibid., p. 85.

(79) In EG, this chapter was ΣΛ´ in the text, and ΣΚΘ´ in the pinax. For the contents of this chapter, see the description of E below.

(80) Inc. Ἐπειδὴ οὐ μόνον, des. καὶ τοῦ ὀλοφυρμοῦ συστέλλει τὸ πάθος (no direct source found; the ultimate source is Cyr. Alex., Comm. in Io. [CPG 5208], II, p. 279, 14 – 280, 2).

(81) Inc. ὄχλος παρῆν πολύς, des. πάσης ὑποψίας ἀπαλάσων (sic) αὐτούς (no direct source found). CEULEMANS – VAN DEUN, Réflexions, p. 385, n. 136, identify the ultimate source as Io. Chrys., In Io. homiliae, PG 59, 349, 50 – 350, 11 (CPG 4425); they wonder, however, whether this and the previous chapter were taken from chains.

(82) Inc. Ἰωσὶφ ὁ τῆς παρθ(ένου) μνηστήρ, des. ἐντεῦθεν (οὖν) ὁ βαπτι(στὴς) Ἰ(ω)ά(ννης)· (καὶ) ο κ(ύριο)ς ἡμ(ῶν) ἰ(ησοῦ)ς χ(ριστὸ)ς ἀνεψιοῖ λέγοντ(αι) εἶν(αι). The source is Hippolytus of Thebes (DIEKAMP, Hippolytos, p. 14, 5 – 15, 10); see CEULEMANS – VAN DEUN, Réflexions, p. 386, n. 140.

(83) CEULEMANS – VAN DEUN, Réflexions, p. 382-384. References to these fragments are also extant in the pinakes of CSDEG; their text, on the other hand, is only preserved in DF.

(84) MARTINI – BASSI, Ambrosiana, p. 767-780. The fourteen-page table of contents in D gives an idea of the complexity and variety of the texts in this manuscript.

MANUSCRIPT TRADITION   XLIX

1. F. 132-139ᵛ. Theodore of Stoudios, *Antirrheticus*, ([85]) in two distinct sections. F. 132-137, inc. ἐπειδὴ εἰρχθέντες τοῖς ἐλέγχοις, des. τὸ σαρκίον τῆς θεότητος = Theodore of Stoudios, *Antirrheticus II*, *PG* 99, 353, 13 – 388, 1. F. 137-139ᵛ, inc. οὐκ ἀπερίγραπτον, des. ταῦτα εὐθύνειν οὐ καταγέλαστον([86]) = Theodore of Stoudios, *Antirrheticus I*, *PG* 99, 332, 13 – 349, 11. ([87])

2. F. 139ᵛ-146ᵛ. Theodore Abucara, *Confutatio Iacobitarum* (*PG* 97, 1469, 32 – 1492, 48). Διάκρισις τ(ῶν) φω(νῶν) πε(ρὶ) ἃς οἱ φιλόσοφοι καταγίνονται· καὶ ἔλεγχος σευηρι(ανῶν) καὶ ἰακωβι(τῶν) αἱρέ(σεως). Of the same author, *De unione et incarnatione* (206-208ᵛ; *PG* 97, 1601, 28 –1609, 36).

These two excerpts (or four, depending on how we count them) are so relevant because exactly the same ones, and in the same order, are also present in *F*.

From the pinax of *D* it can be gathered that it once belonged to the library of the cardinal Domenico Grimani (1461-1523). ([88])

Ms. *E*, *Argentoratensis, Bibliothecae Nationalis et Universitatis gr. 12*. ([89]) 13ᵗʰ c. (1285-1286). Parchment, 272 + 4 folios (250 × 175 ([90])), one column, 27-28 lines. It contains the *FC* on f. 7-212, Letter Alpha on f. 7-52ᵛ. Folios 172-177 are missing. ([91]) No title; ([92]) pinax f. 1-4ᵛ. The *FC* begins abruptly on f. 7, with the sev-

---

(85) In *D*, the excerpt from the *Antirrheticus* has the deceptive attribution τοῦ αγίου νικηφόρου αρχϊεπισκόπ(ου) κωνστ(αντινου)πό(λεως) πε(ρὶ) δογμάτ(ων) ἀναγκαίων. Note that, here as elsewhere, many breathing marks are missing in *D*.

(86) Martini – Bassi, *Ambrosiana*, p. 768 wrongly read these last two words as οὐκ ἀκαταγιείαστον (*sic*).

(87) Actually, *PG* 99, 349, 10-11 provides Καὶ πότε τῶν εἰδώλων καθαρθήσεται, καὶ διὰ τίνος; (καὶ τότε τῶν εἰδώλων παύσεται in *D*). After this, both in *D* and in *F* there is a further remark by the heretic, followed by an answer from the orthodoxI was unable to locate the source of this remark. It is four lines long in *D*; inc. εἰ καλὸς ὁμοοῦσιον, des. ταῦτα εὐθύνειν οὐ καταγέλαστον.

(88) I owe this information to the kindness and erudition of P. Géhin.

(89) Welz, *Strassburg*, p. 28-42; Richard, *Rapport*, p. 37-38.

(90) According to Géhin (*Kalliandrès*, p. 175), 240 × 175.

(91) Welz, *Strassburg*, p. 41: "fol. 172-177 desunt vel potius numquam fuerunt. quaternio enim, qui continet fol. 167-180, recte confectus est." See ibid. for an accurate description of the quires of *E*.

(92) Welz, *Strassburg*, p. 28: "Titulus cum quaternione primo deest".

L MANUSCRIPT TRADITION

enth fragment of Letter Alpha. However, this fragment is entirely preserved, including its attribution (γρηγορίου νύσης). The second part of the manuscript, which was originally an independent volume, contains "excerpta Graeca ex scriptis Latinis Ioannis Cassiani abbae" (f. 213-262). ([93])

The pinax is virtually the same as in *G*. The last three chapters, as listed in the pinax, are the same as in *DG* (see their descriptions), namely, σκθ' πε(ρὶ) ψευδοπροφητῶν, σλ' πε(ρὶ) τοῦ λαζάρου ἐνεβριμήσατο τῷ πν(εύματ)ι λέγων· ποῦ τεθείκατε αὐτόν, ([94]) and σλα' πε(ρὶ) τῆς γενεαλογίας τοῦ χ(ριστο)ῦ. The two last chapters are missing in the text. ([95]) *E* does not end mutilated. However, it does not quote to the end the only fragment of chapter περὶ ψευδοπροφητῶν, numbered as σλ' on f. 211ᵛ. Its last words are, as in *G*, ὅτι ἀπὸ παραβατῶν ἔχεις τί ἀγαθὸν ἀκοῦσαι, ἢ ἀπὸ προδοτ(ῶν). ([96]) A few lines of the fragment are missing. In all probability, its model ended here. Even if this last sentence makes sense as it is, there is no reason to believe the scribe of *E* and of *G* would have stopped there if his exemplar had preserved the full fragment.

There is a colophon on f. 212: Ἐγράφη τῷ πανϊηρωτ(ά)τω μ(ητ)ροπο(λί)τ(η) Ῥόδου κρϊτῇ (καὶ) ἐξάρχῳ τῶν Κυκλάδων νή(σων) [(καὶ) ὑπερτίμῳ in mg.] κυρ(ῷ) Θεοδούλῳ ἡ παροῦσα δέλτο(ς), ἐν τῷ ,ϛψϞδ' ἔτει [1285/86]· ἰνδικτιῶνος ιδ'. ([97]) M. Richard thought that only the pinax (f. 1-4ᵛ) and the colophon of this manuscript were written by the same copyist as *G*. ([98]) Géhin has argued that not only the pinax and the colophon, but also the entire *FC* (f. 7-212, written in an archaic script) were cop-

---

(93) Welz, *Strassburg*, p. 41. For a short description of the second work in *E*, see ibid., p. 40-41.

(94) Note that in *F*, the biblical citation ἐνεβριμήσατο – αὐτόν (Io. 11, 33) is part of the excerpt itself, not part of the title.

(95) Cf. Ceulemans – Van Deun, *Réflexions*, p. 379.

(96) Ψ 29.14-15.

(97) Géhin, *Kalliandrès*, p. 175; Declerck, *Max. Conf.*, p. ccv, n. 125; Richard, *Rapport*, p. 38; Welz, *Strassburg*, p. 42.

(98) See Richard, *Rapport*, p. 38: "La comparaison ne laisse aucune place au doute: les colophons [of *E* and *G*] sont de la même main, qui est celle du copiste du cod. Iviron 38 et aussi de l'index, mais seulement de l'index, du manuscrit de Strasbourg." Richard stated the same opinion in a letter to Dom Kotter dated 26 September 1958, quoted by Géhin, *Kalliandrès*, p. 172.

MANUSCRIPT TRADITION   LI

ied by the same scribe, namely, Symeon Kalliandres, [99] already
known to be the copyist of three other manuscripts. [100]

E was offered to Theodule, metropolitan of Rhodes, whereas
G was offered to a monk, also named Theodule. Declerck considers that both manuscripts "furent écrits sur l'ordre d'un certain
Théodule, qui, encore moine en 1281, avait été élevé au rang de
métropolite, juge et exarque en 1286." [101] Géhin, by contrast, believes that the Theodule mentioned in *E* can be identified with a
metropolitan of Rhodes by that name, who was already mentioned
in 1256 and again in 1260, and who, in 1274, "est au nombre des
32 métropolites et 9 archevêques orientaux qui envoient au pape
Grégoire X une lettre en faveur de l'Union, à l'occasion du second
concile de Lyon." [102] *E* and *G*, then, would have been commis-
sioned by two different persons called Theodule. [103]

Wenger mentions *E*, where he found the Greek original of a
homily of Hesychius of Jerusalem which was known hitherto only
in a Latin translation. [104] He also knew that the same homily
was extant in our manuscript *C*. [105] Wenger further discovered
that a fragment of Chrysostom, ἐκ τῶν μυσταγωγικῶν πρὸς τοὺς
φωτισθέντας λόγος γ′ – part of the series of eight Chrysostomic
homilies he had discovered in the Athonite monastery of Stav-
ronikita in 1955 – is also extant in *E*, f. 75ᵛ. [106] His enthusiasm

---

(99) Géhin, *Kalliandrès, passim*. See also *RGK*, II, § 506 *bis*.

(100) The three manuscripts are: *Petropolitanus, Bibliothecae Academiae
Scientiarum 76 + Bibliothecae publicae gr. 311* (formerly *Simopetra 34 =
Athonensis 1302*), year 1281; *Vindobonensis suppl. gr. 107*, year 1283; *Sco-
rialensis Ω. I 16* (= gr. 517). Cf. Géhin, *Kalliandrès*, p. 172-175 and Prato,
Scritture, p. 176-177, with illustrations 17 and 18.

(101) Declerck, *Max. Conf.*, p. ccvi.

(102) Géhin, *Kalliandrès*, p. 178-179. Note that, at the second Council
of Lyon, the name of the metropolitan of Rhodes is not given.

(103) According to Richard, *Rapport*, p. 38, the Theodule mentioned
in *E* was metropolitan of Rhodes already in 1256 – the same opinion as
Géhin – and the two Theodules mentioned in the colophons are in fact two
different persons.

(104) Wenger, *Hésychius*, p. 464. On the Greek text of Hesychius' homily, see now Fernández, *Hesychius*.

(105) Chapter ρνδ′, Τί σημαίνει τὸ· λαμβάνει ὁ ἱερεὺς ὀρνίθια ζῶντα
καθαρά; (f. 150ᵛ-151 ms. *E*). It is a curiosity worth remarking that Wenger,
despite being well aware that the fragment was extant in a much older manuscript (*C*), gave preeminence to *E*.

(106) Wenger, *Jean Chryostome*, p. 35. He notes that the fragment is

LII   MANUSCRIPT TRADITION

about the anthology he found in *E* is characteristic: "[...] florilège peu étudié, et qui m'a déjà réservé plus d'une agréable surprise" (ibidem). Welz indicates that "simile vel potius idem florilegium traditur codice Coislin. 294, codice Athen. 464 [...], tertio ([107]) libro codicis Hieros. 15." ([108])

E was written with great care in an archaizing handwriting. The copyist occasionally wrote some iotas subscript, usually, of course, in the desinence, but at least twice also in the root of a word: ᾅδην in A 97.23; ᾅδου in A 98.25.

Ms. **G**, *Athonensis, Iviron 38.* ([109]) 13th c. (f. 1-148 probably of 1281/1282). Parchment, 256 folios (215/220 × 165/167, written area 170/175 × 115), 23-25 lines (f. 1-148) and 25-27 (f. 149-256). No title; pinax (πίναξ τῆσδε τῆς βίβλου) f. 1-4. ([110]) The *FC* is contained on f. 5-147[v], ([111]) Letter Alpha on f. 5-8[v]; it ends abruptly on the latter folio. The pinax is virtually the same as in *E*. The last three chapters are: σκθ' περὶ ψευδοπροφητῶν, σλ' περὶ τοῦ λαζάρου ἐνεβριμήσατο τῶ πν(εύματ)ι λέγων· ποῦ τεθείκατε αὐτόν, and σλα' περὶ τῆς γενεαλογίας τοῦ χ(ριστο)ῦ. The two last chapters are missing from the text, as also happens in *E*. ([112])

G does not end mutilated, yet, like *E*, it does not copy to the end the final fragment. This fragment, numbered σλ' on f. 147[v], runs up to ὅτι ἀπὸ παραβατῶν ἔχεις τί ἀγαθὸν ἀκοῦσαι, ἢ ἀπὸ προδοτῶν. ([113]) The explanation given for *E* is also valid here: the model of *G* (be it *E* or a common ancestor) probably ended at these words.

---

also extant in the *Sacr. Par.*, *PG* 96, 17, 3-30, but without the title (ibid., n. 3).

(107) Actually it is the fourth book.

(108) WELZ, *Strassburg*, p. 39.

(109) See in the first place SOTIROUDIS, *Iviron*, p. 71-73 (with bibliography); LAMBROS, *Athos*, II, p. 5; RICHARD, *Rapport*, p. 37-38; RAHLFS, *Verzeichnis*, p. 12; RIEDINGER, *Pseudo-Kaisarios*, p. 104 and 106.

(110) This pinax contains, as does the one of *E*, the two extra chapters peculiar to the short recension of the *FC*. Despite its name ([...] τῆσδε τῆς βίβλου), this pinax reports on the *FC* only.

(111) LAMBROS, *Athos*, II, p. 5 called the first part of the manuscript Σειρὰ πατέρων περὶ διαφόρων ἀντικειμένων ἐν κεφ. σλα'.

(112) See CEULEMANS – VAN DEUN, *Réflexions*, p. 379.

(113) Ψ 29.14-15.

MANUSCRIPT TRADITION

LIII

After f. 8ᵛ, where Letter Alpha ends mutilated, ([114]) five quaternions are missing; folio 9 already contains the text of B 1, 1. ([115]) Folios 9-16 were originally the seventh quaternion; the eighth quaternion is found on f. 17-24, the ninth on f. 25-32, and the tenth (which is the first to actually have a number, in the upper righthand corner of the folio) on f. 33-40. ([116])

On f. 149-255, there is the attribution and title προκοπίου χριστιανοῦ σοφιστοῦ, τῶν εἰς τὰς παροιμίας σολομῶντος ἐξηγητικῶν ἐκλογῶν ἐπιτομή. This is Procopius' *Catena in Prouerbia* (*CPG* 7432), ([117]) which remains for the most part unpublished. ([118])

The parchment is not of the highest quality; there are holes that were already present at the time of the copying.

The dating of this manuscript is problematic. According to the colophon, it was written in the year 6790 (1281-1282), in the third indiction: Ἐγράφη ἡ παροῦσα δέλτος τῶ τιμιωτάτω ἐν μοναχοῖς κυρῶ Θεοδούλω ([119]) ἐν τῶ ͵ϛψϞ' ἔτει, ἰνδ. γ'. However, the year 6790 corresponds to the tenth indiction, not to the third. Lambros tried to eliminate the contradiction by changing the number of the year to 6708 (1199-1200), turning thus ͵ϛψϞ' into ͵ϛψη', "seule année exprimée par trois chiffres qui correspon-

---

(114) Ending with Τὰ δὲ δόρατα καὶ τοὺς πέλυκας τὸ τῶν ἀνομοίων διαιρετικόν, = Ps.-Dion., *De coel. hier.*, 15, 5 (p. 55, 7-8); 5.140/141 in the present edition.

(115) Max. Conf. *Quaest. et dubia*, 189, 26: ἐξετάσει τῶν βεβιωμένων.

(116) Sotiroudis, *Iviron*, p. 73.

(117) Cf. Rahlfs, *Verzeichnis*, p. 12. The importance of *G* for this work is great, for only one other witness is extant; see Richard, *Origène*, p. 385: "Le texte original de la chaîne de Procope sur les Proverbes de Salomon s'est conservé dans deux manuscrits du monastère athonite d'Iviron, le cod. 38 (XIIIᵉ siècle) et le cod. 379 (Xᶜ-XIᵉ siècle)."

(118) Sotiroudis, *Iviron*, p. 72: "τὸ πλῆρες κείμενο εἶναι ἀνέκδοτο." Cf. *CPG* 7432, n. b (with bibliography) and Richard, *Origène*, p. 385-394.

(119) Euangelatou-Notara, *Σημειώματα*, p. 82 believes that this Theodule is the scribe of the codex, and takes the wrong dating of *G* (as having been written in 1199-1200) from Lambros. Cf. Sotiroudis, *Iviron*, p. 73. It is, however, impossible that Theodule wrote the previously quoted colophon, for he could hardly speak of himself as τιμιώτατος. Symeon Kalliandres, proposed by Géhin as the copyist of both *E* and *G*, is a far more likely candidate (see Géhin, *Kalliandrès*, *passim*, and the description of *E* above).

LIV   MANUSCRIPT TRADITION

de à une 3ᵉ indiction entre les années du monde 6700 et 6800," as
Richard explains. ([120]) Most scholars, ([121]) however, have followed
Richard in correcting the number of the indiction rather than
that of the year: "Le troisième chiffre de la date du colophon est
indiscutablement un coppa et l'écriture évoque beaucoup plus le
XIIIᵉ-XIVᵉ siècle, que le XIIᵉ-XIIIᵉ." ([122]) At any rate, the fact that
E was written in the decade of 1280, and that it was copied at
least partly by the same scribe as G –Symeon Kalliandres, according to Géhin – ([123]) is the definitive proof that the G cannot date
back to the years 1199-1200.

        Ms. *F*, *Atheniensis, Bibliothecae Nationalis 329.* ([124]) Late 13ᵗʰ
or 14ᵗʰ c. ([125]) Bombycine, 246 folios (240 × 160). ([126]) Miscellaneous manuscript; four different volumes were bound into one.
FC on f. 56-148; Letter Alpha on f. 56-84 ([127]) (order of the folios:
63; 57-62; 56; 64-84; between f. 67 and f. 68 a folio is missing).
No title, no pinax. Its contents are as follows:
        1. F. 1-52. τοῦ ἐν ἁγίοις π(ατ)ρ(ὸ)ς ἡμῶν ἀθανασίου ἀρχιεπισκό-
που ἀλεξανδρεί(ας)· πρ(ὸς) ἀντίοχο(ν) ἄρχοντα [...] Inc. Πιστεύσαντες καὶ βαπτισθέντες, des. ἀναιλεῖ (*sic*) αὐτὸν τῶ πν(εύμα)τι
τοῦ στόματος αὐτοῦ [...] ἀμήν. Ps.-Athanasius of Alexandria,
Quaestiones ad Antiochum ducem, PG 28, 597, 32 – 700, 16.

_____

        (120) Richard, *Rapport*, p. 37.
        (121) Lake – Lake, *Dated Manuscripts*, p. 16 (illustration 209) adopt
Lambros' mistaken date, as indicated by Richard; however, Wilson, *Nicaean
and Palaeologan Hands*, p. 265 believed the numerals of the year ͵ϛψη' to be
merely a misreading of Lake and Lake.
        (122) Richard, *Rapport*, p. 37.
        (123) Géhin, *Kalliandrès, passim*.
        (124) Sakkelion, *Athens*, p. 55; Rahlfs, *Verzeichnis*, p. 7.
        (125) Sakkelion, *Athens*, p. 55 dates it to the 13ᵗʰ c.; Richard, *Florilè-
ges*, col. 485, to the 14ᵗʰ c.; Gonnelli, *Pisidia*, p. 17 states that the part containing George of Pisidia's *Hexaemeron*, on which see immediately below,
"sembra da confermare la datazione alla seconda metà del XIII sec., proposta
dal Sakkelion [...], spostandola forse anche ai primi decenni del XIV."
        (126) Sakkelion and Sakkelion did not seem to be aware that this vol-
ume consisted in fact of two distinct manuscripts of a different format (see
below); it is possible that f. 55-246 were made not of bombycine but of paper.
        (127) Letter Alpha contains some chapters absent from the other recen-
sions of the *FC*. See below, n. 133.

MANUSCRIPT TRADITION LV

2. F. 52ᵛ-55. ἀνθολόγι(ον) γνωμικὸν, φιλοσόφ(ων) σπουδαί(ων)· σπουδασθ(ὲν) καὶ πονηθὲν, ἠλία (sine iot. subsc.) ἐλαχίστῳ πρεσβυτέρῳ καὶ ἐκδίκῳ. πηγὴν νάουσαν ἠθικ(ῶν) δρόσον λόγων, ἐνταῦθ'ἐφεύροις, εἰ μετέλθεις γνησίως. Inc. Ἔξεστι παντὶ χριστιανῷ τῷ ὀρθῶς πιστεύοντι, des. τ(ῶν) συμβεβηκότω(ων) δίχα, ἀτελῆ καθεστήκασι = Elias Ecdicus, *Anthologium Gnomicum* (*CPG* 6080). ([128]) The wording of the attribution to Elias Ecdicus is identical to that in *F*. The same text is attributed elsewhere to Maximus Confessor (see *PG* 90, 1401, 4 – 1412, 37; *CPG* 7716). Since the text of Elias concludes at the end of a fragment, which coincides with the end of a quaternion, it is possible that a larger part of the *Anthologium* was quoted originally and has since been lost. ([129])

3. F. 56-148. *FC*. ([130]) A new quaternion, written by a different hand, starts on f. 56. The penultimate chapter (unnumbered) is περὶ ψευδοπροφητῶν (f. 146ᵛ-147). It contains only one excerpt, with the attribution ἀθανασίου ἀλεξανδρείας (see the description of *D* above for inc. and des.). ([131]) The last chapter is πε(ρὶ) τοῦ λαζάρου, which is also unnumbered (f. 147ʳ·ᵛ). ([132])

The peculiarity of *F* consists both in adding new fragments and chapters ([133]) and in relocating other chapters already present in the *FC*. After περὶ τοῦ λαζάρου, two chapters follow: 1. πε(ρὶ)

---

(128) See Elias Ecdicus, *Capita de ieiunio*. Very recently, De Ridder has stated that *F* "only preserves the first 52 chapters, but must have originally contained the entire *Anthologium*": DE RIDDER, *Elias Ekdikos*, p. 136.

(129) For a critical edition of the chapters, see DE RIDDER, *Elias Ekdikos*, p. 331-348.

(130) This part of the manuscript was given the following title by Sakkelion: Περὶ τῆς νοερᾶς καὶ ἀσωμάτου φύσεως, καὶ ὅτι ἐκ τοῦ μὴ ὄντος εἰς τὸ εἶναι ὑπὸ τοῦ δημιουργοῦ γεγόνασιν (SAKKELION, *Athens*, p. 55). This title, however, only applies to the first chapter of the *FC*, and not to the whole of it.

(131) For the critical edition of the fragment, see now CEULEMANS et al., *Psi*, p. 77-78.

(132) This chapter contains the same three excerpts as in *D*; its last fragment is that of Hippolytus of Rome. Inc. Ἰωσὴφ ὁ τῆς παρθένου μνηστὴρ ὁ τέκτων; des. καὶ ὁ κ(ύριο)ς ἡμῶν ἰ(ησοῦ)ς χ(ριστὸ)ς, ἀνεψιοὶ λέγονται εἶναι. See above the description of *D*, esp. that of f. 132ᵛ, and CEULEMANS – VAN DEUN, *Réflexions*, p. 379-380.

(133) For the additional fragments in Alpha, see now FERNÁNDEZ, *Florilegio*.

LVI　　　　　MANUSCRIPT TRADITION

τῆς ξηρανθήσης (*sic*) συκῆς (not numbered; f. 147ᵛ), (¹³⁴) which is in fact the eighth and last chapter of Letter Sigma of the *FC* and contains only one excerpt, written by Isidore of Pelusium. (¹³⁵) 2. πε(ρὶ) τῶν χερουβίμ, (not numbered, f. 147ᵛ-148), (¹³⁶) which is the third chapter of Letter Chi of the *FC*. It contains only one fragment, by Severian of Gabala. (¹³⁷)

4. F. 148-193ᵛ. These fragments do not belong to the *FC*, which ends at f. 148. In fact, a new collection of quotations seems to begin after the *FC*, or perhaps the compiler of the model of *F* integrated the *FC* into a larger and more comprehensive compilation. The first subsequent excerpt starts with the question διατὶ ὁ θ(εὸ)ς οὐκ εὐθὺς τὰς τιμωρί(ας) ἑκάστῳ πταίοντι ἀπονέμει (f. 148), followed by λ(ύσις)· Ὅτι εἰ μ(ὲν) εὐθὺς ἐγίνοντο αἱ τιμωρίαι – τότε κολασθήσονται (no attribution; source not found for this or any of the following excerpts), followed by ἐρώ(τησις)· εἰ ὡρισμένη ἡ ζωὴ τ(ῶν) ἀν(θρώπ)ων· λ(ύσις)· Ὁ τίς (= Ὅστις) ἐπίσταται ἀναμφιβόλως – τ(οὺς) χρόν(ους) ἡμ(ῶν) ἐπίσταται. At this point f. 148 ends. Another fragment without attribution follows, inc. εἰ πάντα τὰ γενησόμενα, des. ὥρισ(εν) ἑκάστῳ. And yet another one: Πᾶν ὅ ἐστι – καὶ ἄγνωστος.

After this there comes a new chapter, πε(ρὶ) τοῦ ξύλου τῆς ζω(ῆς) (f. 148ᵛ), which *post correctionem* became τῆς γνώσεως, just as the first chapter of Letter Xi in the *FC*. (¹³⁸) The excerpts, however, are not the same as in the *FC*. The first one bears the attribution τίτου μρ, inc. Ξύλον ἐν τ(ῶν) ἐν τῷ παραδείσῳ, des. ἐδιδάσκετο ἀγαθ(όν) τε καὶ κακὸν. Possibly, the attribution

---

(134) Numbered as ρϛ′ in *C*. Its only excerpt (f. 328ʳ⁻ᵛ) has the same attribution, inc. and des. as in *F*.

(135) This short excerpt is on f. 147ᵛ. Attribution ἰσϊδώρου πηλουσιώτου, inc. τὴν συκῆν οὐχ'ἁπλῶς ὁ κ(ύριο)ς κατηράσατο, des. πρὸς δὲ κρίσιν τῶν πεπραγμένων ἑκάστων = Isid. Pel., *Ep.* 1, 51, *PG* 78, 213, 18-35 (cf. *Catena in Matthaeum*, p. 171, 13-26). In *C*, it appears on f. 328ʳ⁻ᵛ, in its correct place at the end of Letter Sigma.

(136) In *C*, the chapter πε(ρὶ) τῶν χερουβίμ bears the number σμβ′; its only excerpt (f. 366-367) has the same attribution, inc. and des. as in *F*.

(137) Attribution σευηρι(α)ν(οῦ) γαβάλ(ων), inc. χερουβὶμ ἑρμηνεύεται, des. καὶ ἐφωτίσθη τὰ πέρατ(α) = Sev. Gab., *De mundi creatione*, *PG* 56, 444, 57 – 446, 23.

(138) Περὶ τοῦ ξύλου τῆς γνώσεως, cf. CEULEMANS et al., *Xi*, p. 70; for an edition of the chapter of *F*, ibid., p. 63-65.

MANUSCRIPT TRADITION   LVII

should be read as μ(ητ)ρ(οπολίτου), as an allusion to Titus of
Bostra, even though Titus of Bostra is usually called "bishop," not
"metropolitan." Richard ([139]) thought that the abbreviation meant
τίτου μ(ά)ρ(τυρος), yet P.-H. Poirier has been so kind as to in-
form me that no source indicates that Titus was a martyr. The
fragment in question is to be found in Titus of Bostra's *Contra
Manichaeos*, 3, 23, 9-24. ([140]) It has recently been critically edited
on the basis of manuscript *F*. ([141]) The second excerpt has the attribution σευηρι(α)ν(οῦ), inc. Ἔστω ἐκώλυ(σε) ὁ θ(εὸ)ς τῶ ἀδὰμ,
des. ὅτι κακ(ὸν) τὸ παραβαίνειν; recently, it has been critically edited on the basis of *F*. ([142]) With this fragment f. 148ᵛ ends. There
follows a large number of usually untitled fragments, including
one attributed to Origen on f. 187ᵛ. The ending of this section
is mutilated, its final words being ἆρα λοιπ(ὸν) συγκεχώρηται =
Anast. Sin., *Quaest. et resp.*, 32, 16-17.

5. F. 194-199ᵛ. Theodore of Stoudios, *Antirrheticus*, in two
distinct sections. F. 194-197ᵛ, where the mutilated text begins
with πώποτε κατὰ τὰ λόγια, des. τὸ σαρκίον τῆς θεότητος =
Theodore of Stoudios, *Antirrheticus II*, PG 99, 356, 2 – 388,
1. F. 197ᵛ-199ᵛ, inc. οὐκ ἀπερίγραπτον, des. ταῦτα εὐθύνειν οὐ
καταγέλαστον = Theodore of Stoudios, *Antirrheticus I*, PG 99,
332, 15 – 349, 11. ([143])

6. F. 199ᵛ-208ᵛ. Theodore Abucara, *Confutatio Iacobitarum*
(f. 199-206; *PG* 97, 1469, 32 – 1492, 48). Διάκρισιν τ(ῶν) φω(νῶν)
πε(ρὶ) ἃς οἱ φιλόσοφοι καταγίνονται· καὶ ἔλεγχος σευηρι(ανῶν)
καὶ ἰακωβι(τῶν) αἱρέ(σεως). In mg. θεοδώρ(ου) τοῦ ἀβουκαρᾶ.
Next is an excerpt from *De unione et incarnatione*, also by Theodore (f. 206-208ᵛ; *PG* 97, 1601, 28 –1609, 36). On f. 201 begins
what seems to be a different manuscript altogether, with more
lines per folio, and written by a different hand; yet the text of the
treatise does not show any rupture.

---

(139) In an unpublished description of the contents of *F*.

(140) P.-H. Poirier located the source for this fragment after I had sent
him a provisional transcription of it, at a time when the *CCSG* edition of
Contra Manichaeos was still unpublished. For an edition of this fragment,
see now Roman et al., *Titus Bostrensis*, p. 279-281. For a previous edition,
see Nagel, *Titus von Bostra*, p. 285-350.

(141) Ceulemans et al., *Xi*, p. 63-64.

(142) Ibid., p. 64-65.

(143) See above, n. 121.

Note that n. 5 and 6 are the same excerpts as contained in *D* after the *FC*.

7. F. 209-232ᵛ. *Siracides*, σοφία ἰησοῦ υἱοῦ σῖράχ, in 3 quaternions; this fragment contains the almost complete text of Sir., from the beginning to 50, 29.

8. F. 233-235ᵛ. *Canticum*, ἄσμα ἀσμάτων; Cant. is quoted from beginning to end. The quaternion starting on f. 233 is written by a different hand.

9. F. 236-240ᵛ. *Sapientia Salomonis*, from 2, 24 to the end. Since there is no attribution and the text starts abruptly with φθόνου [144] δὲ διαβόλου (Sap. 2, 24), it is very likely that a folio is missing. The hand is the same as in the previous fragment.

10. F. 240ᵛ-246ᵛ. George of Pisidia, *Hexaemeron*. This fragment is written in a different hand than the previous fragment. There are 30-32 lines on each folio. The fragment contains the verses 81-1600, written as prose. [145] "Numerossisimi i versi omessi o totalmente alterati; in qualche caso si ha una sorta di parafrasi, in altri goffi adattamenti per dare senso a un contesto che doveva essere già lacunoso nell'antigrafo." [146]

The manuscript's first quaternion (f. 1-7) bears no number; between f. 5 and 6, a folio is missing. The second quaternion (f. 8-15) is numbered only on its last folio, and the third one (f. 16-23) on its first and last folio, as are also f. 24-31; 32-39; 40-47, 48-55. The following quaternion, in which the *FC* begins, has a larger format than the preceding quaternions. There are many more lines on each page (some with 33 lines instead of 28 on f. 1-55), and the hand could be somewhat more recent, and in any case is almost certainly from the 14ᵗʰ c. From f. 56 onwards, quaternions do not seem to be numbered. The order of the folios in the first quaternion (f. 56-63) is disturbed; its first and last folios were placed in inverted positions: f. 56 after 57-62, f. 63 before it. A new hand begins at f. 201, with some 30 lines per folio, but no text is missing. In the quaternion starting at f. 209, another hand takes over, with 33 lines per folio. Another quaternion of the manuscript begins on f. 233 and is written in still another hand. On f. 240ᵛ, another new hand starts writing. There are,

---

(144) Understand: φόβῳ.
(145) GONNELLI, *Pisidia*, p. 17.
(146) Ibid., p. 17.

MANUSCRIPT TRADITION   LIX

consequently, four different manuscripts which were bound together into one volume at an unspecified time. The information
Sakkelion gives about the size and dating of the manuscript seems
to refer only to f. 1-55.

Between f. 55-66, the outer upper corners of the folios are
hardly legible, especially between f. 56 and 65. This was possibly
caused by humidity. The number of the folios, however, is still
legible on the recto side. On a number of folios, for example,
f. 174^v, 224^v, there are *essais de plume* and, on f. 158^v, 208^v, 224^v,
illegible marginalia.

About the history of the manuscript we only know that it was
once in the possession of the monastery of Δουσικόν. ([147])

Ms. **H**, *Vaticanus graecus 491.* ([148]) 13th c. (f. 199-202, 14th-15th
c.). Paper, 202 + 4 folios (240 × 160), 27-33 lines. This witness is
made from two distinct manuscripts: the first one, on f. 1 to 104,
contains works by John Damascene; ([149]) the second one, on f. 105
to 202, contains the *FC* and other texts. *FC* f. 105-198^v; Letter
Alpha f. 105-139 (order of the folios: 105; 111; 107-110; 106; 112-
139). ([150])

H has neither title nor an ancient pinax; it does contain, however, a recent pinax of the whole manuscript, apparently composed
by Winckelmann, ([151]) in which the *FC* is listed as Κεφάλαια ρξ′
θεολογικά, και φυσικα και ήθικά εκ διαφορων συλλεχθεντα. ἡ
ἀρ(χή)· Πάντες σχεδον οἱ κ(α)τ(ὰ) τ(ὴν) οικουμενην (*sic*, several
breathing marks and accents missing). The contents of *H* are as
follows:

1. Works by John Damascene. Firstly, τῷ ὁσϊωτάτω καὶ θεο-
τιμήτω π(ατρ)ὶ κοσμᾶ ἁγιωτάτω ἐπισκόπω τοῦ μαϊμᾶ (*sic*),

---

(147) "Il manoscritto è stato proprietà del monastero di Dusico, vici-
no a Tricca, in Tessaglia, dove potrebbe anche essere stato redatto" (Gon-
NELLI, *Pisidia*, p. 17). For the manuscripts of this monastery, see Lambros,
Σύμμικτα, p. 214; Dimitrakopoulos, *Βιβλιοθήκη*; Sophianos −Dimitra-
kopoulos, *Χειρόγραφα*. For further bibliography, see Olivier, *Répertoire*,
n. 2349-2354.
(148) Devreesse, *Vaticani 330-603*, p. 307-310. See also Devreesse,
Fonds, p. 9, n. 4; 349; 401; 449.
(149) Devreesse, *Vaticani 330-603*, p. 307-308.
(150) Ibid., p. 310.
(151) Ibid., p. 310.

ἰω(άννης) ἐλάχϊστος, inc. τὸ μ(ὲν) στεν(ὸν) τῆς διανοί(ας), des. φϋλλάττον ἀσύγχυτόν τε καὶ ἄτρεπτον = John Damascene, *Dialect.*, proem. 1 – 67, 45. Secondly, τοῦ αὐτοῦ· ὃν οἱ ἀληθεῖς φιλόσοφοι χρυσορρόαν κεκλήκασϊ· περὶ τοῦ ὅτι ἀκατάληπτον τὸ θεῖον· καὶ ὅτι οὐ δεῖ ζητεῖν καὶ περϊεργάζεσθαι τὰ μὴ παραδεδομένα ἡμῖν [...], inc. Θ(εὸ)ν οὐδεὶς ἑώρακε πώποτε, des. τὴν ἀπ'αὐτοῦ εὐφροσύνην καρπούμενοι = Io. Dam., *Exp. fid.* 1, 3 – 100, 131. For a detailed description of this section of *H*, see Devreesse's catalogue. ([152])

2. *FC* on f. 105-198ᵛ. Devreesse states that the beginning of the compilation is mutilated; however, only the Π of the first sentence, Πάντες σχεδὸν οἱ κατὰ τὴν οἰκουμένην κτλ., seems to be missing. ([153]) The last chapter, περὶ τοῦ μὴ κρίνειν (f. 196ᵛ-198ᵛ), has no number (it should have been ριη'). The final fragment, which ends abruptly with καὶ πλουσιωτ(έ)ρ(ω) μὴ κοινώνει· τί κοινήσει, comes from Sir. 13, 2.

In the upper margin of f. 198ᵛ – the last folio containing a portion of the *FC* – "Damasceni philosophica" is written. Devreesse has dated this inscription to the 15ᵗʰ-16ᵗʰ c. In the same period, the manuscript was bound and its quaternions numbered consecutively in Arabic numbers from 1 through 26. ([154]) On f. 199-201 "[s]equuntur alia manu liturgica varia". ([155]) On f. 202 there is a fragment by Chrysostom. ([156])

Devreesse described *H* in sufficient detail. ([157]) The model of *H* was lacunous, as is shown by the numerous *fenestrae*, of different lengths, that *H* contains now and then. ([158]) These *fenestrae* are

---

(152) Ibid., p. 307-308.

(153) Ibid., p. 308. This scholar wrongly reads παντὸς instead of πάντες.

(154) Ibid., p. 310.

(155) Ibid.

(156) Ibid. The fragment is *In Genesim*, PG 53, 164, 45 – 165, 5.

(157) For the first part of *H* (f. 1-104ᵛ), see Ibid., p. 310: "I. (ff. 1-104). Fasciculi quaterniones olim 14, hodie 13, ex exemplari paullo turbato atque fenestris laborante (e.g. ff. 74. 96ᵛ) descripti; fasc. duodecim iam perierat quando superstites in ultima singulorum pagina ima signati sunt (cf. notarum vestigia in ff. 64ᵛ. 72ᵛ. 80ᵛ. 88ᵛ. 92ᵛ). F. 104ᵛ vacuum. Lineae 29-30." It is inexact, however, that all folios have no more than 29-30 lines; some contain as many as 33. As for the second part, he states: "II. (ff. 105-198). Fasciculi 12 quaterniones, excepto nono binione, in prima uniuscuiusque pagina ima signati, ex antigrapho lacunoso (e.g. 106ᵛ. 108. 109ᵛ. 111ᵛ) descripti, humore multum inquinati non sine scripturae damno. Lineae 27-31."

(158) See previous note.

MANUSCRIPT TRADITION LXI

indicated in the critical apparatus of the present edition wherever relevant.

H was possibly already in the Vatican library in 1539; ([159]) "un émissaire, inconnu d'autre part, a inscrit son nom 'Lucianus xama (?) christianus (?), un bref sommaire et souvent un prix d'achat, au début d'une quinzaine de volumes," ([160]) among which *H* is found.

II. FRAGMENTARY MANUSCRIPTS

Ms. **K**, *Athonensis, Koutloumousiou 9.* ([161]) 14th c. Parchment, 570 pages. Letter Alpha p. 336-466. ([162]) The contents of this manuscript are roughly the same as in *L* (see below), and listed by Lambros in this way:

1. Τάξις τῶν μητροπολιτῶν αὐτοκεφάλων καὶ ἀρχιεπισκόπων.

2. Πρόβου Ἐπαπορήματα πρὸς Ἰακωβίτας. ([163])

3. Μιχαὴλ [Κηρυλαρίου] πατριάρχου Ἐπιστολὴ πρὸς Πέτρον Ἀντιοχείας περὶ ἀζύμων.

4. Πέτρου Ἀντιοχείας Ἀντίγραμμα.

5. Ὅρος ἐκτεθεὶς παρὰ Μανουὴλ τοῦ Πορφυρογεννήτου.

6. Κωνσταντίνου τοῦ μεγάλου Πρὸς Σίλβεστρον πάπαν Ῥώμης.

7. Ὁμιλίαι διάφοροι. This is, in fact, the *FC*. Declerck was the first to underline the similarities between *K*, which was already known to M. Richard, and *L*, which Declerck discovered was a witness of the *FC*. ([164]) Since *L* is an apograph of *K*, the exhaustive listing of contents of *L* made by Declerck ([165]) is also valid for *K*, at least partly.

To this this list should be added:

---

(159) See DEVREESSE, *Fonds*, p. 349 and 401 (where the possibility that *H* was present in the Greek catalogues of the years 1539 [with a question mark] and 1548 [also with a question mark] is indicated). See also ibid., p. 449.

(160) Ibid., p. 9, n. 4.

(161) Cf. LAMBROS, *Athos*, I, p. 271.

(162) Unfortunately, I only had access to the last part of *K*, from p. 336 on.

(163) Ed. UTHEMANN, *Syllogistik*, p. 110-112, and DECLERCK, *Probus*, p. 229-231 (only Declerck collated *K*).

(164) DECLERCK, *Manuscrit, passim*. See below, "Relationship of the Manuscripts," I, 5.

(165) DECLERCK, *Manuscrit*, p. 486-492.

LXII   MANUSCRIPT TRADITION

8. Maximus Confessor's *Quaestio* 67 (f. 311-312), overlooked by Lambros and discovered by Declerck. [166]

Ms. **L**, *Londinensis, Brit. Libr. Add. 17472.* [167] 14th c. Parchment, 159 folios (200 × 135), one column, 30-31 lines. [168] *FC* f. 1-73 and 145v-159v, Letter Alpha f. 1-23v.

Declerck suggested that *L* was copied from *K*. [169] Their relationship is discussed below ("Relationship of the Manuscripts," I, 5). Declerck described the titles of *L*, comparing its numeration with that of manuscripts *A CE*. [170] He also described the titles of those fragments present in the manuscript but not part of the *FC* and critically edited one of them. [171]

As to the history of the manuscript, we know only that it was acquired by the British Museum on October 14, 1848. [172] De-

---

(166) Declerck, *Manuscrit*, p. 501, n. 45.

(167) For a detailed study and further bibliography, see Declerck, *Manuscrit*, p. 484. See also *Catalogue 1848-1853*, p. 20, and Richard, *British Museum*, p. 28.

(168) Declerck, *Manuscrit*, p. 499-500: "L'écriture est ronde, droite sur la ligne et jamais entassée; [...] l'écriture appartient au XIVe s., et plutôt à sa première qu'à sa seconde moitié."

(169) Declerck, *Manuscrit*, p. 494-497 stresses the "étroit parallélisme" between *L* and *Par. gr. 1163* (p. 495), and with great prudence states that "rien ne s'oppose [...] à situer le *Londin., Brit. Lib. Add. 17472* dans la descendance du *Par. gr. 1163*" (p. 496). On p. 501 he notes that, when his article was already printed, a microfilm of *K* was made accessible to him, on the basis of which he observes that *K* and not the *Par. gr. 1163* was possibly the forefather of *L*. Two years later, he would think it most likely that *L* was a descendant of *K* (Id. *Probus*, p. 228). Cf. Id., *Max. Conf.*, p. clxii.

(170) Declerck, *Manuscrit*, p. 486-492.

(171) Declerck, *Probus*, p. 229-231. Other manuscripts that contain this fragment, titled Πρόβου ὀρθοδόξου ἀπὸ Ἰακοβιτῶν· ἐπαπορήματα πρὸς Ἰακωβίτας, are the *Oxoniensis, Thomas Roe 22*, "anno scilicet 1286, sumptibus Constantini Maurozumae, manu tamen Jonae Rhacendyti nitide exaratus" (Coxe, *Bodleiana*, col. 480) and the *Vat. gr. 1101*, 13th-14th c. See Declerck, *Probus*, p. 225 and 227 respectively. The *Oxoniensis* and *K* seem to have had a common ancestor; nothing is known about the scribe of the *Oxoniensis*. For Μαυροζώμης Κωνσταντῖνος, see Trapp et al., *PLP*, § 17443. In 1292, this Maurozomes was in Constantinople. The *Oxoniensis* contains the *Historia* of Nicetas Choniates, which no doubt would interest Constantine Maurozomes, since some members of the Maurozomes family are mentioned therein.

(172) *Catalogue 1848-1853*, p. 20 does not provide any further precision, and neither does Richard, *British Museum*, p. 28.

MANUSCRIPT TRADITION   LXIII

clerck states that a second hand has written on f. 80ᵛ τῆς νύσου
πολεως μητιλϋνης. (¹⁷³)

Ms. **Q**, *Atheniensis, Bibliothecae Nationalis 375.* (¹⁷⁴) 13ᵗʰ-15ᵗʰ
c. (¹⁷⁵) Bombycin (?) and paper. (¹⁷⁶) 324 folios (210 × 140). (¹⁷⁷)
FC on f. 197ᵛ-241ᵛ, Letter Alpha on f. 200-210. This volume is in
fact a conflation of different manuscripts. Richard describes it as
"un recueil factice de petits manuscrits écrits par des mains différentes sur des papiers différents." (¹⁷⁸) Some folios are missing
from the beginning, and humidity has damaged large sections of
the manuscript. (¹⁷⁹)
    It comes as no surprise that the contents of this manuscript are
miscellaneous. Sakkelion's description, which is not exhaustive,
quotes seventeen excerpts, mainly of Patristic and Byzantine authors. Five works by Lucian, however, are also contained in *Q*. (¹⁸⁰)
There are four texts by Blemmydes as well: ἐκ τοῦ τρίτου αὐτοῦ
βιβλίου περὶ πίστεως λόγος πρῶτος (f. 110-115), Περὶ ἀρετῆς

---

(173) Declerck, *Manuscrit*, p. 500.

(174) Verhelst, *Nicéphore*, I, p. 51-53; Sakkelion, *Athens*, p. 64; Richard,
Asterius, p. xii-xiv; Gielen, *Nicephorus*, esp. p. xxi, xxxix-xl and xliv-xlvi;
Rahlfs, *Verzeichnis*, p. 7.

(175) Sakkelion, *Athens*, p. 64 and Rahlfs, *Verzeichnis*, p. 7 (probably
following Sakkelion) date it to the 13ᵗʰ c., but Verhelst, *Nicéphore*, I, p. 51
argues that this is a mistake and that all of the manuscripts bound together
are of the 14ᵗʰ or 15ᵗʰ c., though written by different hands. This is a bold
statement for such a heterogenous manuscript as *Q*, and it is doubtful whether
the dating Verhelst advances is valid for the whole manuscript or only for the
part she analyses in more detail. For f. 70-109, and for these only, Richard,
Asterius, p. xiii also favours the late 14ᵗʰ or early 15ᵗʰ c. As we will see, the
part containing *FC* may be dated to the 13ᵗʰ c.

(176) Paper according to Rahlfs, *Verzeichnis*, p. 7 and Richard, *Asterius*, p. xiii; τεῦχος ἐκ χάρτου βαμβακίνου according to Sakkelion, *Athens*,
p. 64.

(177) Sakkelion, *Athens*, p. 64 states that there are 311 folios in this
manuscript.

(178) Richard, *Asterius*, p. xiii.

(179) Sakkelion, *Athens*, p. 64: "ἐλλιπὲς [...] ἐν τῇ ἀρχῇ καὶ ἐν πολλοῖς
ἐκ τῆς νοτίδος ἐξίτηλον."

(180) In f. 280-305ᵛ, written by a different hand in what seems to be paper of a different size. These five works by Lucian are: the dialogue *Charon*,
some letters to Cronos from the *Saturnalia* (sect. 19-36), the *Cataplus*, the
diatribe *De luctu,* and the short novel *Asinus* (by Ps.-Lucian).

LXIV   MANUSCRIPT TRADITION

καὶ ἀσκήσεως (f. 115-123ᵛ), Περὶ ψυχῆς (f. 126-134ᵛ), [181] and chapters 3-7 of the *Epitome logica* (f. 185-195ᵛ). [182] Beginning on f. 309, which is also the beginning of a new quaternion, written by a different hand, there is a letter by Manuel Moschopoulos, which can be dated as late as the 14ᵗʰ c.

In this manuscript, the *FC* has not been preserved as an independent anthology; rather, its contents have been mixed in a very heterogenous compilation of patristic and Byzantine texts. This compilation occupies eleven quaternions (f. 192-279ᵛ), inc. εὔχου γενέσθαι τ(ῶν) ὀλίγ(ων), des. πᾶσα ἀμφιβολία καὶ δισταγμός. [183] Usually only the fragments are given, but occasionally they are arranged under a title, such as περὶ τοῦ ἐν τίνϊ

---

(181) These three treatises were transcribed by the same copyist. VER-HELST, *Nicéphore*, I, p. 52: "Selon M. Richard cette partie du manuscrit se distingue du reste par l'encre très noire et des rubriques vermillon très bien conservées". She is talking about f. 110-135, made up of two quaternions and a quinion. VERHELST (ibid.) adds that "à la fin du cahier précédent (bas du f. 123ᵛ et ff. 124-125) [ont] été rétranscrits des textes étrangers à Blemmyde."

(182) GIELEN, *Nicephorus*, p. xxi. VERHELST, *Nicéphore*, I, p. 51, discovered the chapters of the *Epitome logica* in *Q*.

(183) The first quotation is of Bas. Caes., *Sermo 11*, PG 31, 645, 34; the second one appears in the *Dioptra* of Philip the Solitary, completed – in its original recension – around the year 1097 (VAN DEUN, *Eustratius*, p. xliii). This fragment can also be found in an indirect witness of the *Dioptra*, the *Vaticanus, Palatinus gr. 146* (14ᵗʰ-16ᵗʰ c.), f. 66. The *Palatinus* alters its model freely. For a description of this manuscript, see VAN DEUN, *Eustratius*, p. xli-xlvii, especially p. xlii, n. 53, where part of the text of the present fragment is given. At any rate, the text of *Q* is closer to the *Palatinus* than to the printed edition of the *Dioptra*. The last source of the *Dioptra* is Eustratius of Constantinople's *De statu animarum post mortem* (CPG 7522). I quote the last lines of the fragment of *Q* in full: εἰ δὲ θέλεις μαθεῖν ἀκριβέστερον περὶ <τούτων, ἀνάγνωθι λόγον> ἀνατρεπτικὸν εὐστρατίου πρεσβυτέρου τ(ῆς) ἁγιωτ(ά)τ(ης) <τοῦ θεοῦ μεγάλης ἐκκλησίας> πρὸς τ(οὺς) λέγοντ(ας) μὴ ἐνεργ(εῖν) τὰς τ(ῶν) ἀν(θρώπω)ν ψυ<χὰς μετὰ τὴν διάζευξιν τῶν ἑαυτῶν σωμάτων>, κἀκεῖ εὑρήσεις <πρὸς τὸ ζητούμενον μαρτυρίας> ἀπό τε <τῆς παλαιᾶς καὶ νέας γραφῆς θαυμαστὰς καὶ ἐξαισίας, καὶ λυθήσεταί> σοι πᾶσα ἀμφιβολία καὶ δισταγμός. The sections between triangular brackets (<>), illegible in *Q*, were taken from LAGA, *Eustratius van Constantinopel*, p. 320, where an edition of the fragments from the *Palatinus* concerning Eustratius is given. In the quoted lines the only difference of *Q* and the *Palatinus* is the addition of the σοι before πᾶσα ἀμφιβολία. Note that at least one other manuscript that contains fragments of the *FC*, namely Lesb. *Leim. 268*, also contains the *Dioptra* of Philip the Solitary; cf. PAPADOPOU-LOS-KERAMEUS, *Lesbos*, p. 124-125.

MANUSCRIPT TRADITION   LXV

μέρει τὴν ψυχὴν ὑπάρχειν or περὶ ἀναγνωρϊσμ(ῶν) ψυχ(ῆς) (both on f. 265). The chapters from the *FC* are not numbered. The handwriting of the quaternions that contain the *FC* and other excerpts (f. 192-279ᵛ) seems to be earlier than the late 14th c., even as old as the late 13th c.; it shows some points of contact with the so-called Planudes style. ([184]) However, the reader must be cautious and bear in mind that this earlier dating, though possible, is not entirely sure. Other characteristics of the script are as follows: words are not systematically separated by spaces; non-diphthonged ι and υ always have a trema (ϊ, ϋ); the final ν often looks similar to an υ; abbreviations are abundant; there are no iotas subscript or adscript; itacism and similar confusions are rare, but the manuscript is not free from them; there are very few movable ν's before a consonant. The scribe of *Q* was not concerned about the alphabetical disposition of the chapters. Thus, the title of chapter 27, περὶ ἀγάπης καὶ πόσα τὰ τῆς ἀγάπης εἴδη, was transformed into περὶ φιλίας, losing the keyword starting with alpha.

The scribe alters the text of Letter Alpha freely. In 35.24, for example, he adds in the middle of an excerpt of Cyril of Alexandria a phrase taken from Basil of Ancyra. ([185]) He has a liking for epitomising and paraphrasing. Τῶν ἀνθρώπων τοίνυν οἱ μὲν εἰσὶ δίκαιοι, οἱ δὲ ἁμαρτωλοί. Ἀλλὰ καὶ ἐν τοῖς ἁμαρτωλοῖς καὶ ἐν τοῖς δικαίοις πολλὴ ἡ διαφορά (57.4/6) became in *Q* ὁμοίως (καὶ) ἐπὶ τ(ῶν) ἁμαρτωλ(ῶν) πολλὴ ἡ διαφορά. Displacements and omissions of words or phrases are very frequent. In the case of fragments 74-75, the scribe of *Q* has eliminated the first twenty lines of 75, writing a linking passage of his own to connect the end of 74 ([186]) to the few lines of 75 that survive. Fragment 75 is the last excerpt of Letter Alpha to be quoted in *Q*. Fragments quoted, fully or partially, are: 1, 22-23, 29, 32-37, 39-40, 51, 57, 61-63, 65, 67, 73-75. After these fragments of Letter Alpha, six other excerpts are found:

1. F. 210-212: ἐκ τῶν ἀσκητικῶν τοῦ ἐν ἁγίοις π(α)τρ(ὸ)ς ἡμ(ῶν) βασιλείου τοῦ μεγ(ά)λ(ου), περὶ τ(ῆς) εἰς θ(εὸ)ν ἀγάπης.

---

(184) As Filippo Ronconi kindly pointed out to me.

(185) Bas. of Anc., *De virginitate*, PG 30, 700, 16-18. The phrase the copyist of *Q* adds is: πῦρ γάρ ἐστι καιόμ(ε)ν(ον) ἐπὶ πάντ(ων) τ(ῶν) μελ(ῶν)· οὗ ἂν ἐπέλθῃ, ἐκ ῥιζῶν ἀπώλεσε.

(186) Note that *Q* belongs to the short recension of the *FC*; consequently, its model omitted the last lines of fragment 74.

LXVI MANUSCRIPT TRADITION

Bas. Caes., *Asceticon magnum sive Quaestiones (regulae fusius tractatae)*, PG 31, 908, 27 – 916, 40. Inc. ἀδίδακτος μ(ὲν) ἡ πρὸς θ(εὸν) ἀγάπη, des. ταῖς ψυχαῖς ἐμποιῆσαι.

2. F. 212ʳ⁻ᵛ: Another fragment from Basil's *Asceticon magnum*, with the title πε(ρὶ) τῆς εἰς τὸν πλησίον ἀγάπ(ης), PG 31, 916, 41 – 917, 50. Inc. ἀκόλουθον δ'ἂν εἴη, des. ἔχει ἀπόδειξιν τὰ εἰρημένα.

3. F. 212ᵛ-214: τοῦ χρ(υσοστόμου), ἐκ τ(ῆς) πρὸς κορινθίους πρώτης. Io. Chrys., *In epistulam I ad Corinthios*, PG 61, 31, 5 – 240, 37 (with long omissions). Inc. τὰ τοίνυν ὑπερβαίνοντα λογισμ(ὸν), des. ἐμέρισε μέτρον πίστεως.

4. F. 214ʳ⁻ᵛ. This fragment follows the preceding one without interruption, as if they were both part of the same text. Inc. ὁμοίως δὲ πάλιν (καὶ) ὁ σοφὸς λέγει· χαλεπώτερά σου μὴ ζήτει (= Sir. 3, 21), des. ταλαίπωροι δὲ (καὶ) ἐν κενοῖς αἱ ἐλπίδ(ες) αὐτῶν (cf. Sap. 13, 10).

5. F. 214ᵛ-215: διονυσίου τοῦ ἀρεοπαγίτ(ου). Ps.-Dion., *Epistulae*, 9, 1, 15-47. Inc. χρῆναι γοῦν αὐτῷ, des. τοῦ θεολογικοῦ φωτὸς ἀναπεπλησμένα.

6. F. 215ʳ⁻ᵛ: σχόλιον, inc. γαστέρα θ(εο)ῦ, ([187]) διὰ τὸ ἐκ γαστρὸς, des. σοφῶς ἀναπτύσσοντα τὸ ζητούμενον (source not found).

The first chapter of Letter Beta of the *FC*, Τί ἐστὶν ἡ τοῦ ἁγίου πν(εύματος) βλασφημία, follows this scholion.

The first quaternion bearing a signature in *Q* is f. 46-53. The signature is a number seven. ([188]) The last quaternion to display a signature, f. 272-279, bears the number 35. Nothing is known about the history of the manuscript.

Ms. *V, Vaticanus graecus 728, olim 854.* ([189]) 16ᵗʰ c. Paper, 311 folios (325 × 231). FC f. 270ᵛ-311, Letter Alpha f. 270ᵛ-293. Title of the first fragment of the *FC*: περὶ τῆς νοερᾶς καὶ

---

(187) *Ad* Ps.-Dion., *Epistulae*, 9, 19.

(188) Verhelst, *Nicéphore*, I, p. 51.

(189) For a description of the manuscript, see Devreesse, *Vaticani 604-866*, p. 229-230, esp. p. 230, where he describes the section of the *FC*: "florilegium ordine alphabetico digestum codd. Coisl. 294 atque Vat. 491 ff. 105 ss. proximum; caput primum Περὶ τῆς νοερᾶς καὶ ἀσωμάτου φύσεως, seu de angelis; caput ult. Πῶς ὁ φιλῶν τὴν ψυχὴν αὐτοῦ ἀπολήσει αὐτήν." See also Richard, *Florilèges*, col. 485. Canart (*Provataris*, p. 249 and 268) dates the manuscript to 1542-1572.

MANUSCRIPT TRADITION   LXVII

ἀσωμάτου φύσεως· καὶ ὅτι ἐκ τοῦ μὴ ὄντος εἰς τὸ εἶναι ὑπὸ τοῦ δημιουργοῦ παρήχθησαν (f. 270ᵛ). This manuscript also contains Ps.-Procopius's *Commentarii in Prouerbia* (*CPG* 7445). [190] Mai's edition (reprinted in *PG* 87, 1221-1544) was based on this codex. [191] First title of the manuscript: ἑρμηνεία εἰς τὰς παροιμίας, προκοπίου χριστιανοῦ, inc. Σκοπὸν ἔχων σαλομών, τὸν πόθον ἡμῶν κινῆσαι, des. καὶ τὰ πρακτέα ὑποτιθεὶς καὶ φησὶν ὡς ἐν ἐπιγραφῇ.

The copyist of the codex was Emmanuel Provataris, whereas most of the highly instructive marginal notes belong to Matteo Devaris. [192] On occasion, these notes indicate that something different was written in the primary source, or that the reading transmitted by his exemplar was probably wrong, [193] etc.

Of Letter Alpha, *V* contains fragments 1-5 (f. 270ᵛ-277), 12 (f. 277, attrib. τοῦ αὐτοῦ, i.e. Ps-Dionysius Areopagita), 14 (f. 278ᵛ-279), 16-17 (f. 280ʳ⁻ᵛ), 19-25 (f. 280ᵛ-283ᵛ), 27-28 (f. 283ᵛ-284), 30-32 (f. 284-286), 36-39 (f. 286-287), 43-52 (f. 287-288), 58 (f. 288ʳ⁻ᵛ), 60-61 (f. 288ᵛ-289ᵛ), 63-64 (f. 289ᵛ-290), 73 (f. 290), 80-81 (f. 290-290ᵛ), 83-86 (f. 290ᵛ), 90-94 (f. 291-292), 96-97 (f. 292ʳ⁻ᵛ), 100-101 (f. 292ᵛ-293).

Between fragments 12 and 14, and between fragments 14 and 16, *V* contains a section which is also preserved, in an ampler form, in manuscripts *FH*. [194]

Ms. **R**, *Athonensis, Lavra B 43*. [195] 12ᵗʰ c. Parchment, 216 folios (180 × 120). The compilation where the fragments of the *FC* are inserted begins on f. 153, [196] as Ceulemans has recent-

---

(190) Rahlfs, *Verzeichnis*, p. 254.

(191) Mai, *Procopius Gazaeus*, p. 1-256.

(192) See in particular Canart, *Provataris*, p. 249, and p. 211-212.

(193) In f. 267ᵛ we read πᾶν τὸ μὴ ἐκ τῶν πέντε τούτων. The copyist makes a reference to the μὴ, and writes: *m()t() puto* μιᾷ *loco* μή. His conjecture, μιᾷ, is not embedded in the main text, as if it had been transmitted by his exemplar, but is rather indicated in the margin.

(194) For these additional excerpts, see now Fernández, *Florilegio*.

(195) Cf. Spyridon – Eustratiades, *Laura*, p. 17-18, where a quite thorough description of the contents of *R* can be found. Cf. Richard, *Florilèges*, col. 486, according to whom fragments of the FC were on "f. 160... 195." For a thorough analysis of the florilegium in which the *FC* chapters are integrated, see now Ceulemans, *Cosmological*.

(196) The quaternion is f. 153-160, numbered as ιε′ in the upper

LXVIII MANUSCRIPT TRADITION

ly pointed out,([197]) yet excerpts of the *FC* occur only between f. 177ᵛ and 195; fragments of Letter Alpha occur on f. 177ᵛ-179, 184, 185ʳ⁻ᵛ. The following chapters have been taken, at least partly, from other letters of the *FC*: περὶ θ(εο)ῦ κριμάτων (Κ 9), f. 180ᵛ; πρὸς τοὺς λέγοντ(ας)· εἰ ἔχει ὅρ(ον) ἡ ζωὴ τοῦ ἀν(θρώπ)ου (Ο 7), f. 180ᵛ-181; ἀπόδειξις ὅτι τὰ βρώματα ἡ ψυχὴ ἀναλίσκει (Β 12) f. 182ᵛ-183; περὶ βαπτίσματος (Β 14), f. 187ʳ⁻ᵛ; περὶ ζωῆς αἰωνίου (Ζ 3), f. 187ᵛ-188; φυσιολογία περὶ δακρύων (Δ 8), f. 189; ([198]) περὶ διαφορᾶς ἡλικιῶν (Η 14), f. 191ᵛ-192; περὶ τὸ οὐδεὶς καθαρὸς ἀπὸ ῥύπου (Ρ 2), f. 193ʳ⁻ᵛ; περὶ ψυχῆς (Ψ 2), f. 193ᵛ-195. ([199]) Thanks to the unpublished collations of Ceulemans, I can now add that *R* also contains fragment 4 of Theta, f. 180ᵛ; fragment 24 of Beta, f. 183; fragments 28-29 and 26-27 of Beta, f. 187ʳ⁻ᵛ; Δ 8 (fragments 1 and 2), f. 187ᵛ-189ᵛ; Δ 9 (which consists of only one fragment), f. 189ᵛ; Δ 10 (fragments 1 and 2), f. 189ᵛ; fragments 13-14 of Letter Eta, f. 191ᵛ-192; Λ 4 (fragment 2), f. 192ᵛ-193; fragments 16-18, 23, 25, 27-28 of Letter Psi, f. 193-195. The fragments of Alpha found in *R* are so few that they do not warrant a full description of the manuscript. They occupy only about four pages of text – excerpts 93-97, 99, 98, 100, 12-13, in that order – in *R*. Suffice it to say that occasionally iota subscripts are written, especially in the singular datives, but also in the desinence of contract verbs, e.g. βοᾷ, or in the root of words such as ᾅδης.

III. Minor Fragmentary Manuscripts

Ms. **I**, *Atheniensis, Metochion Sancti Sepulcri 273.* ([200]) 10ᵗʰ c. Parchment, 205 folios (255 × 195). F. 186-205, written on paper, stem from the 14ᵗʰ c. The fragments of the *FC* are found on

---

righthand margin of f. 153, and as κα′ in the lower margin of f. 160ᵛ. This double numeration continues in the following quaternions, up to at least f. 185-192, numbered both as ιθ′ and κε′.

(197) Ceulemans, *Cosmological*, n. 5.

(198) Thereafter follow some excerpts on weeping, including one preserved in the long recension only. For a critical edition, see Fernández, *Tears*.

(199) Note that there is another chapter called περὶ ψυχῆς on f. 174ᵛ.

(200) Papadopoulos-Kerameus, *Jerusalem*, IV, p. 251-252; Boudignon, *Max. Conf.*, p. xvi-xvii.

MANUSCRIPT TRADITION   LXIX

f. 170ᵛ-185ᵛ. Of Letter Alpha, this manuscript contains only fragment 29.1/176 (f. 182ᵛ-185ᵛ).

As for its history, "[I]e manuscrit a [...] appartenu à un monastère Saint-Denys non identifié et il a été envoyé en juillet 1716 pour lecture à Chrysanthe, patriarche de Jérusalem (1707-1731)." [201]

Ms. **W**, *Athonensis, Koutloumousiou 269.* [202] 15ᵗʰ c. Paper, 168 folios. Miscellaneous manuscript. The *FC* is contained on f. 141-149. There is a blank space on the previous page, f. 140ᵛ, as though a new section began there. *W* contains fragment 29 of Letter Alpha.

Ms. **N**, *Londinensis, British Museum, Addit. 34060.* [203] 15ᵗʰ c. (f. 511-557 and 563-579, early 12ᵗʰ c.). Paper, 588 folios (f. 511-557 and 563-579 are parchment). Miscellaneous manuscript. The *FC* is contained on f. 356ᵛ-357.

N contains excerpts 12, 8-9, 36, 61, 94-96 and 101 of Letter Alpha, in that order. On f. 357ʳ⁻ᵛ, there are three other excerpts from the *FC*: 1. τοῦ χρυσοστόμου, περὶ τοῦ κατ᾽εἰκόνα καὶ καθ᾽ὁμοίωσιν, inc. τὸ κατ᾽εἰκόνα, οὐκ ἐν τῷ σώματι νοητέον, des. καὶ τῆς ἀθανασίας τῷ πλάσματι (Κ 2, 1); 2. βασιλείου καισαρείας, inc. κατ᾽εἰκόνα ἔχω, τὸ λογικὸς εἶναι, des. εὐσπλαγχνία ὁμοιωθεὶς θ(ε)ῷ (Κ 2, 2); 3. τοῦ χρυσοστόμου ἐκ τῆς ἑρμηνείας τοῦ ἀποστόλου, inc. Ὦ τῆς ἀνοίας, des. καὶ ἐξώτερον σκότος εἴρηται (Γ 8.1-16). [204] Note that the short recension omits ἐκ – ἀποστόλου in the attribution, whereas *A* omits the ἐκ and *T* has (instead of ἐκ τῆς ἑρμηνείας) εἰς τὴν ἑρμηνείαν.

Immediately after this, still on f. 357ᵛ, there is a fragment not present in the *FC*. Its attribution is μαξίμου τοῦ ὁμολογητοῦ, inc. Τέλειος ἐστὶν, ὁ τοῖς ἑκουσίοις δι᾽ἐγκρατείας μαχομένους, des. εἴτε δια (sic) παραπτωμάτων. A blank space follows. It can be added that "one of the later scribes, Georgius Drazinus, has

———————

(201) Boudignon, *Max. Conf.*, p. xvii; Papadopoulos-Kerameus, *Jerusalem*, IV, p. 251.

(202) Lambros, *Athos*, I, p. 307.

(203) *Catalogue 1888-1893*, p. 168-182.

(204) De Vos et al., *Gamma*, p. 192-193. The manuscript of London also preserves the title that precedes this fragment: ὑπόδειξις (ἀπόδειξις *FC*) περὶ γεέννης, ὅτι ἔξω τοῦ κόσμου ἐστίν.

LXX   MANUSCRIPT TRADITION

added a note (f. 579) that the manuscript was completed by him in July, Indict. 1, 6946 (AD 1438)." [205]

Ms. **O**, *Vaticanus, Ottobonianus graecus 441.* [206] 15ᵗʰ c. (*circa* 1477). Paper, 580 folios (216 × 145), written by Symeon, patriarch of Constantinople. [207] The manuscript contains the following excerpts of Letter Alpha: 54-57 (f. 1ᵛ-3ᵛ), 60.1/48 (f. 3ᵛ-4), 58 (f. 4ʳ⁻ᵛ), 61 (f. 4ᵛ), 6-7 (f. 5ᵛ-6), 27 – 29.1/17 (f. 6ᵛ-7ᵛ), 33.21/28 (f. 7ᵛ), 34 (f. 7ᵛ), 38 (f. 7ᵛ), 32 (f. 7ᵛ-8), 33.1/20 (f. 8ʳ⁻ᵛ), 1-4 (f. 37-38ᵛ). [208]

Ms. **M**, *Lesbiacus, Leimonos 268.* [209] 16ᵗʰ c. (*a.* 1552). Paper, 582 folios. Written by Methodios, son of Ignatios of Methymn. [210] On f. 1-9 there is a pinax of the whole manuscript, containing 179 κεφάλαια. [211] The fragments of the *FC* are on f. 420-576ᵛ. The manuscript contains the following excerpts of Letter Alpha: 61 (f. 420), 75 (f. 420ᵛ-421) 60.1/48 (f. 538ᵛ-539ᵛ), 58 (f. 539ᵛ-540), 61 (f. 540; note that this fragment had already been copied), 6-7 (f. 541ᵛ-542), 27 – 29.1/17 (f. 542ʳ⁻ᵛ); 33.21/28 (f. 542ᵛ-543), 34 (f. 543), 38 (f. 543), 32 (f. 543-544), 33.1/20 (f. 544), 1-4 (f. 574ᵛ-576ᵛ). [212]

IV. OTHER MANUSCRIPTS

After this introduction was written, a number of "new" witnesses to the text of the *FC* – most of them apographs of pre-

---

(205) *Catalogue 1888-1893*, p. 182.

(206) FERON – BATTAGLINI, *Ottoboniani*, p. 245-248; RIEDINGER, *Pseudo-Kaisarios*, p. 102-107; See now CEULEMANS et al., *Psi*, p. 51.

(207) *RGK*, III, § 593.

(208) Originally, I was aware of the presence of excerpts 1-4 only. P. Van Deun has provided the location of the other excerpts. Cf. CEULEMANS et al., *Psi*, p. 52.

(209) PAPADOPOULOS-KERAMEUS, *Lesbos*, p. 124-128; RIEDINGER, *Pseudo-Kaisarios*, p. 102-107; ROOSEN – VAN DEUN, *Ps.-Max.*, p. 405-406; LAGA – STEEL, *Max. Conf.*, II, p. xliii; CEULEMANS et al., *Psi*, p. 51-52.

(210) [...] γραφὲν [...] ὑπὸ Μεθοδίου, υἱοῦ Ἰγνατίου Μεθύμνης (PAPA-DOPOULOS-KERAMEUS, *Lesbos*, p. 124). On f. 38 and elsewhere, the copyist wrote his name: "Ὁμολογῶ ἐγὼ εἰμὶ ὁ γράφων Μεθόδιος" (ibid.).

(211) PAPADOPOULOS-KERAMEUS, *Lesbos*, p. 124.

(212) As is the case with *O*, I was originally aware of the presence of excerpts 1-4 only.

MANUSCRIPT TRADITION   LXXI

served manuscripts or extremely fragmentary – have been collated
and described by the Leuven research team led by P. Van Deun.
Below is presented the information pertinent to the Letter Alpha.

Atheniensis, Metochion Sancti Sepulcri 274. 14ᵗʰ c. Paper, 512
folios, one column, 27-29 lines. (²¹³) Mutilated at the beginning
and at the end. In the 16ᵗʰ c. a πρόλογος τῶν Παραλλήλων was
copied into the manuscript; the prologue is the same as in the
Sacr. Par., PG 95, 1040, 1-31. The manuscript contains the *Florilegium Hierosolymitanum* only (as is the case with *T*, Letters A-E).
Letter Alpha of *FC* is found on f. 229-273ᵛ. The pinax, part of
which was written by a later hand, is found on f. 2ᵛ-26.

This manuscript was inaccessible to Richard in the time of *Florilèges* (1962), to De Vos et al., *Gamma*, and, until recently, to
me; I have not had the opportunity to collate it in full. By 1976
Richard had apparently been able to consult the Metochion manuscript, and he states that "comme le cod. Jérusalem, Saint Sépulcre 15 [= *T*], le cod. Athènes, Metochion du Saint Sépulcre 274
s'achève mutilé au stoicheion E, mais il a l'index presque complet
de la collection toute entière. Une lacune d'un ou deux folios a fait
disparaître celui des stoicheia Υ Livres III-IV. Φ entier, X Livres
I-II. Ceci est regrettable, mais un possesseur de ce manuscrit
nous a rendu un bon service en essayant de combler cette lacune
avec l'index du Flor. Laurentianum (Lᶜ de Holl) pour ces trois
stoicheia. Le stoicheion Z est suivi d'une note du compilateur qui
commence ῞Εως ὧδε κῶδιξ τῶν τῇ πρώτῃ βίβλῳ τεταγμένων
τίτλων...". (²¹⁴) J. Maksimkzuk points out to me that to these
chapters, mentioned by Richard as written by a later hand, the
following must be added: A (first ten titles, f. 2ᵛ), X (books III-IV,
f. 26), all of Ψ (f. 26ʳ), all of Ω (f. 26); these chapters, however, rely
on the original pinax of the *Florilegium Hierosolymitanum* (not
the *Florilegium Laurentianum*). Apparently, this manuscript is an
apograph of *T*. (²¹⁵)

---

(213) Papadopoulos-Kerameus, *Jerusalem*, IV, p. 252-253, according to
whom the manuscript comprises 513 folios. José Maksimkzuk informs me
that the actual number is 512.

(214) Richard, *Opera minora*, I, *appendice*, p. i-ii.

(215) Cf. Petit, *Philon d'Alexandrie*, p. 24, n. 5: "J'incline même à croire
que [the Metochion manuscript] n'est qu'une copie directe de [*T*]. Mais le
temps m'a manqué pour une vérification approfondie.".

Atheniensis, Metochion Santi Sepulchri 405 (*a.* 1717). Apograph of manuscript *I.* It contains fr. 29.1/176 of Letter Alpha on f. 124-125[v].

Ms. **U**, *Oxoniensis, Bodleianus, Baroccianus gr. 91.* [216] 15th c. It contains excerpts 34, 36, 37, 96, 97, 99, 98 and 100 of Letter Alpha.

Ms. **Z**, *Monacensis gr. 551.* 15th c. [217] It contains fragments 35, 3 and 42 of Letter Alpha.

Ms. **Can**, *Oxford Canonic. gr. 56.* [218] 16th c. Related to manuscripts *FH* and especially to *V.* "Aux ff. 179-213[v], joint à une sélection de définitions prises au *Viae dux* d'Anastase le Sinaïte, se trouve un recueil d'extraits patristiques dont la plupart (mais pas tous) sont tirés du *Florilège Coislin.* Il contient le même choix d'extraits que *V* [...]. [L]a première partie de *Can* [...] a été copiée par Michael Myrokephalitès à Venise en 1563, mais sans aucun doute les folios qui nous intéressent datent aussi du XVIe siècle, bien qu'ils aient été copiés d'une autre main, malheureusement non identifiée." [219]

Par. sup. gr. 702, which contains on f. 43[v]-51 what in the present edition is fr. 29, was reported by Morani to be related to the *FC.* [220] I have collated its pertinent folios without finding any of the readings peculiar to our anthology.

A number of manuscripts contain fragments belonging to Maximus or Ps.-Maximus Confessor. The following manuscripts hold A 58 and 60-61: *Londinensis, British Library, Add. 39610* (11th c.), f. 223[r-v]; [221] *Rhenotraiectinus gr. 7* (13th c.), f. 102[v]-104; [222] *Lugdunensis Batavorum, Bibliotheca Publica 67A* (17th c.), f. 13-16, an apograph of the *Rhenotraiectinus* manuscript; [223] *Vaticanus gr. 1084* (14th-15th c.). [224]

---

(216) Ceulemans et al., *Psi*, p. 53-54, with bibliography.

(217) Ibid., p. 53, with full bibliography; Laga – Steel, *Max. Conf.*, II, p. xlix, n. 91.

(218) Ceulemans et al., *Xi*, p. 50; Riedinger, *Pseudo-Kaisarios*, p. 104; Coxe, *Canoniciani*, col. 63-65.

(219) Ceulemans et al., *Xi*, p. 50.

(220) Morani, *Nemesio*, p. 29.

(221) Roosen – Van Deun, *Ps.-Max.*, p. 404-405. For supplementary information on this and the following manuscripts, I thank Prof. Van Deun.

(222) Roosen – Van Deun, *Ps.-Max.*, p. 405-406.

(223) Ibid., p. 405; Declerck, *Max. Conf.*, p. ccxii; Laga – Steel, *Max. Conf.*, II, p. xliii-xliv.

(224) Laga – Steel, *Max. Conf.*, II, p. xliii.

MANUSCRIPT TRADITION   LXXIII

Fragments A 60-61 are present in *Neapolitanus, Bibliotheca Nationalis 56* (II.B.18) (13th c.), f. 78v-79v ([225]) and *Monacensis gr. 56* (year 1547), f. 307r-v and 452r-v. ([226]) In addition to A 60-61, *Vindobonensis, theologicus gr. 325* (16th c.) contains A 51-52. ([227])

Fragments A 60 is present in *Vaticanus, Palatinus gr. 91* (14th c.), f. 144v-145; ([228]) *Monacensis gr. 25* (16th c.), f. 194v-195, apograph of *Vaticanus, Palatinus gr. 91*; ([229]) *Vaticanus gr. 375* (14th c.); ([230]) *Vaticanus gr. 504* (a. 1105); ([231]) *Oxoniensis, Baroccianus 141* (14th c.). ([232])

Fragments A 58 is present in *Athonensis, Vatopedinus 476* (14th c.) ([233]) and in *Mosquensis, Synod. 186 (Vlad. 430)* (12th c.). ([234])

For the sake of completeness, I mention other manuscripts that contain material from the *FC* but not from Letter Alpha: **Ath.**, *Atheniensis, Bibliotheca Nationalis 2429* (14th c.); ([235]) **Y**, *Athonensis, Dionysiou 274* (16th c.); ([236]) *Athonensis, Dionysiou 275* (16th c.); ([237]) *Oxoniensis, Christ Church 47 (16*th c.); ([238]) *Parisinus gr. 852* (10th c.); ([239]) *Athonensis, Vatopedinus 36* (11th c.); ([240]) *Venetus, Marcianus gr. Z 507* (12th c.); ([241]) *Parisi-*

---

(225) ROOSEN – VAN DEUN, *Ps.-Max.*, p. 406; DECLERCK, *Max. Conf.*, p. ccxi.

(226) ROOSEN – VAN DEUN, *Ps.-Max.*, p. 407; DECLERCK, *Max. Conf.*, p. ccxi.

(227) ROOSEN – VAN DEUN, *Ps.-Max.*, p. 407. I thank Prof. Van Deun for supplementary information on this manuscript.

(228) ROOSEN – VAN DEUN, *Ps.-Max.*, p. 406-407.

(229) Ibid., p. 406-407.

(230) Ibid., p. 407.

(231) DECLERCK, *Max. Conf.*, p. ccxi.

(232) Ibid., p. ccxii.

(233) LAGA – STEEL, *Max. Conf.*, II, p. xliii.

(234) Ibid., p. xliv.

(235) CEULEMANS et al., *Theta*, p. 93.

(236) CEULEMANS et al., *Xi*, p. 51; LAMBROS, *Athos*, I, p. 392-396; UTHEMANN, *Anastasius*, p. xlix; LAGA – STEEL, *Max. Conf.*, II, p. xxiv-xxv and p. xlii-xliii.

(237) LAGA – STEEL, *Max. Conf.*, II, p. xxiv-xxv and p. xlii-xliii.

(238) Ibid., p. xliii.

(239) RICHARD, *Florilèges*, col. 486. Prof. Van Deun has established that it has material from the *FC* on f. 116v-128v.

(240) RICHARD, *Florilèges*, col. 486.

(241) Ibid., col. 486.

LXXIV   MANUSCRIPT TRADITION

nus gr. 1555 A (14ᵗʰ c.); (²⁴²) *Romanus, Angelicus gr. 30 (C.3.16)*
(a. 1393-1394); (²⁴³) *Mosquensis, Bibliothecae Synodalis 439*
(Vladimir 425) (14ᵗʰ c.); (²⁴⁴) *Parisinus, Supplementum graecum*
503 (13ᵗʰ c.); (²⁴⁵) *Venetus, Marcianus I, 29* (15ᵗʰ c.); (²⁴⁶) *Vaticanus*
gr. 578 (14ᵗʰ c.). (²⁴⁷)

The highly complicated manuscript tradition of the *FC*, and
in particular the descendants of indirect witnesses, awaits a comprehensive account. This will probably deserve a full-scale mono-
graph. This chapter's discussion of the manuscript tradition is
simply a guide to the witnesses that have been used in the estab-
lishment of the text of Letter Alpha, along with a brief mention
of other manuscripts known to be witnesses of the *FC*. It is perhaps useful to add that, even though many indirect witnesses have
not been collated in full, the text of Letter Alpha would not have
been altered by the addition of their readings. These manuscripts
are usually very low stemmatically, often apographs of preserved
manuscripts, and never representatives of an independent branch
of the text.

---

(242) Ibid., col. 486.
(243) FRANCHI DE' CAVALIERI – MUCCIO, *Index*, p. 64-76.
(244) VAN DEUN, *Liber Asceticus*, p. lxx-lxxi.
(245) DECLERCK, *Eust. Ant.*, p. ccclx.
(246) UTHEMANN, *Sermones*, p. xlv.
(247) Ibid., p. xliv.

RELATIONSHIP OF THE MANUSCRIPTS

The manuscripts of the *FC* can roughly be divided into three groups: *AT*, *C*, and *DEFGH* (= Γ). ([1]) Although they will be analysed in a different section, the fragmentary manuscripts can, for the most part, be safely attached to one of these three groups, with the exception of *R*, which, as we will see, has a peculiar position in the stemma of the *FC*.

Although Richard identifies *AT* as transmitting a "first recension", and *CBS* (he does not mention *P*) as transmitting a "second" one, all these manuscripts can be considered to transmit the original or "long" recension of the *FC*. It is true that *AT* is somewhat longer than *C*, ([2]) but in Letter Alpha this difference only amounts to a few lines. *DEFGH*, in turn, are representatives of the "short" recension (= Γ). This short recension, however, derives from the long one, and *DEFGH* are closely related to *C*; as the stemma will show, *DEFGH* and *C* all have a common hyparchetype. I will call Δ the consensus of the short recension (Γ) and *C*. In a sense, then, we have two major groups: the long recension (*AT C*) and the short recension (Γ). In another sense, more useful for our purposes, we have two groups with textual affinities: *AT* and Δ.

I call "error" or "mistake" any divergence from the model, even if it is an innovation and not an error in the proper sense of the word. ([3])

---

(1) Without taking any of the apographs into consideration.

(2) In their actual states, however, they are shorter, but this may well be coincidental. We have seen that *T* ends in Letter Epsilon and *A* in Letter Omicron of the *FC*. Yet their recension, as Richard pointed out, contains passages absent from all other manuscripts.

(3) For example in 103.59: all of the manuscripts have δόξαν (the reading of the archetype), against *EK*, which have δόξαι together with the source; δόξαι is a good reading, whereas δόξαν is not, but δόξαι must have been found through conjecture.

LXXVI   RELATIONSHIP OF THE MANUSCRIPTS

I. Apographs

1. *B* apograph of *C*

B has innumerable individual readings, ([4]) whereas those of *C* are few and relatively benign. Given the importance of *C* in the stemma, I will dwell longer on the relationship between *B* and *C* than in the case of the other apographs.

Individual readings of *B* include, for example:

29.443 τῶν οἰκείων παθῶν] τῶν παθῶν τῶν οἰκείων *B*

30.15 οὐδὲ τέχναι] καὶ τέχναι *B*

33.5/6 ὥσπερ οὖν καὶ ἐποίησε τοὺς πρώτους χωρίς] ὥσπερ οὖν καὶ ἐποίησε γάμου χωρίς *B*

33.17/18 εἰ τοῖς προστάγμασιν αὐτοῦ πεισθέντες οἱ περὶ τὸν Ἀδάμ] οἱ περὶ τὸν Ἀδάμ εἰ τοῖς προστάγμασιν αὐτοῦ πεισθέντες *B*

42.16 πρὸς σημασίαν] σημασίαν *B*

Fragm. 46] *p. 47.3 trsp. B*

53.1 πραγμάτων σαθρότερον] σαθρότερον πραγμάτων *B*

60.25 μόνους] *om. B*

60.43 γινόμεθα] γεγόναμεν *B*

62.24 τῇ κτήσει τῆς ἀρετῆς] *om. B*

62.130 ἐκκοπὴν] ἐκτομὴν *B*

64.4 δοξάζει] ἀγαπᾷ *B*

65.43 τῆς κοιλίας] *om. B*

Fragm. 72] *om. B, sed attributionem* (νείλου) *seruauit*

74.27 ἀρτίως] *om. B*

76.15 ἔλεγον ἅπαντες] ἅπαντες ἔλεγον *B*

77.2/3 καὶ τὰς ἐπουρανίους μονάς] *om. B*

78.32 σαρκός] τοῦ σώματος *B*

79.31 βασιλεύς] κριτής *B*

79.68 χρηστότητος] πραότητος *B*

92.9 ἀπό] *om. B*

93.32 ὁρωμένη] *om. B*

---

(4) Here as elsewhere, I call them 'individual' even though they might be present in its apographs.

RELATIONSHIP OF THE MANUSCRIPTS LXXVII

97.23/24 κατελθόντος εἰς Ἅδην τοῦ σωτῆρος] κατελθόντα
εἰς ἅδην τὸν σωτῆρα B
98.15 ἐκείνων ψυχαί] ψυχαὶ ἐκείνων B
99.8 τὸν πλοῦτον αὐτοῦ] τὸν πλοῦτον αὐτῶν B
100.17 καὶ ποικίλην] om. B
This list could easily be extended. ([5])

The individual errors of C not present in B, by contrast, are
very few and benign. They are as follows:

29.228 ἀναπνέοντες] ἀναπνέοντος C
29.228 περικεχυμένον] περικεχυμμένον C[a .corr.]
29.316 θνητόν, νοῦ] θνητονοῦ (sic) C
29.388 δι'αὐτὰ] διὰ ταῦτα C (δι'αὐτὸν PS FH, B deest)
47.16 ἔδωκα] ἔδωκεν C
47.32/33 πᾶν ὃ ᾔτησαν] πάντα ὃ ᾔτησαν C
60.32 πηροὶ] πῆροι C
65.3 ἕκαστον] ἕκαστος C
65.33 Παῦλος ἔλεγεν] παῦλον ἔλεγεν C
66.1 ἀλλὰ] ἀλλ' C
76.38 ὁ Χριστὸς ἔρχεται] ἔρχεται ὁ Χριστός C (et fons)
78.38 ὅτου] ὅτε C
99.9 βασιλικά] δεσποτικά C (et DHR)
102.7 ἱερουργίας] ἱερουγίας C

---

(5) As we will see, PS, which are apographs of B, descend independently
from their exemplar. Therefore, when they agree in a reading, this reading
must also have been present in B. In the latter manuscript the first folios
containing the first chapters of Letter Alpha are missing, yet the readings
of B can often be reconstructed with the help of PS. Some examples: 1.11
ὑπερχρόνιος] ὑπερκόσμιος (B)PS; 5.56 κρατητικὸν] κριτικὸν (B)PS; 5.145
ἀναγώγου] ἀναλόγου (B)PS; 5.173 ἡ θεολογία] om. (B)PS; 5.243 τῶν ὁμο-
ταγῶν] τῶν ὁμοτίμων καὶ ὁμοταγῶν (B)PS; 5.263 διακοσμήσεων] δυνάμεων (B)PS; 5.272 ἀκριβοῦς αὐτῶν] om. (B)PS; 16.8 γνώριμος] πρόξενος (B)
PS; 18.24 πάμπαν] πᾶν (B)PS; 19.21 τιμήν] σπουδήν (B)PS; 19.21 τοῦ κό-
σμου] om. (B)PS; 19.27 Οὐ γὰρ δὴ πιστεύουσιν] om. (B)PS; 22.8/9 τὰ κάτω
πάντα σώματα· τὰ ἄνω νοερά, τὰ κάτω αἰσθητά· τὰ ἄνω ἀόρατα] om. (B)
PS; 22.19/20 τὰ κάτω καὶ τὰ ἄνω] τὰ ἄνω καὶ τὰ κάτω (B)PS; 29.53 τῶν
ἀρετῶν] om. (B)PS; 29.141 σωματικῶν] σαρκικῶν (B)PS.

LXXVIII   RELATIONSHIP OF THE MANUSCRIPTS

This list is almost exhaustive ([6]) and also includes trivial errors. In fact, only the examples of 29.388, 76.38 and 78.38 are in a way significant, but even in these cases the reading of the hyparchetype could have easily been found through conjecture. The case of 99.9 is different; here it is almost certain that the reading of *CDHR* was present in the hyparchetype Δ, and that *BEF* independently made the very easy correction into βασιλικά, an adjective which was present in the immediate context. ([7]) Therefore, there are no significant individual mistakes of *C* in Letter Alpha of the *FC,* nor have I found any in the other published letters of the *FC.*

As Pasquali writes, "[è] un pregiudizio credere que la tradizioni degli autori antichi sia sempre meccanica; meccanica è solo dove l'amanuense si rassegna a non intendere." ([8]) This is partly true. The whole truth is that a scribe may not understand and still innovate. As the same author says elsewhere: "Iidem [scribae] scripta patrum, quae vel intellegebant vel se intellegere existimabant, suo arbitrio correxerunt, mutarunt quo speciosiora, ut sibi videbantur, redderent." ([9]) Manuscript *B* has innumerable obvious deviations from his exemplar, most of them for no good reason. The scribe, who takes pleasure in changing πραγμάτων σαθρότερον into σαθρότερον πραγμάτων *B* (53.1) or ἔλεγον ἅπαντες into ἅπαντες ἔλεγον *B* (76.15) will not surprise the reader when he, performing one of these innovations, writes ὁ Χριστὸς ἔρχεται (with the rest of the *FC*) as against the reading ἔρχεται ὁ Χριστός of its probable exemplar, *C* (76.38). Nor will it surprise the reader if our scribe, who changed γινόμεθα into γεγόναμεν (60.43) and χρηστότητος into πραότητος (79.68), gives ὅτου (with the rest of the *FC*) as against ὅτε in *C* (78.38). Now and then the same scribe was also bound to divine an easy reading where his exemplar was corrupt, and in this manner restore the "genuine"

---

(6) It is exhaustive where *B* is extant. In the instances where *B* can be reconstructed from the coincidence of *PS*, individual errors of *C* are also unimportant; to name but one of the typical errors, the title of the tenth chapter has the word ἐπιστημονικὸς in all manuscripts including *PS*, and ἐπιστημονικὸν in *C*.

(7) In 99.5/6, where the same group of words as in 99.9 occurs, namely, ταμιεῖα τὰ βασιλικά.

(8) Pasquali, *Storia*, p. xvii.

(9) Pasquali, *Gregorius Nyssenus*, p. lix; cf. id., *Storia*, p. 137.

RELATIONSHIP OF THE MANUSCRIPTS   LXXIX

text. Not once does the scribe of *B* fill a real gap (an omission) or mend a complex error.

Does this prove that *B* is an apograph of *C*? As a rule, the dependence of a witness upon another cannot be demonstrated directly, but only through the exclusion of its independence. ([10]) The evidence is never fully conclusive. ([11]) In the present case, this means that, to demonstrate that *B* is an apograph of *C*, the possibility of the independence of *B* from *C* must be excluded. This proof would be made by showing that *C*, in a long portion of text, ([12]) has no significant individual mistake. As it happens, this is true of Letter Alpha, yet the possibility that *CB* depend on the same hyparchetype – the copyist of *C* being uncommonly careful – would still remain. *C* has some individual mistakes, which, even if they are never significant, might make the scholar favour the possibility that *CB* derive from a common ancestor. A consideration of the text alone would not enable the editor to demonstrate that *B* is an apograph of *C*.

There is, however, a well-known exception to the rule that the dependence of a manuscript upon another cannot be proven directly. This exception is called "physical evidence" by Reeve, who argues that it is not as much of an exception as had previously been thought. "Physical evidence is any peculiarity of a witness other than its reading that account for an innovation in other witnesses." ([13]) Physical evidence may arise from a variety of accidents (e.g. a speck of straw taken to be punctuation by the apograph), or, as I will argue is the case in *CB*, from "peculiarities of layout" in the exemplar. ([14])

C is written in two columns. Very often the attributions of *C* are written in the inner margin, even if the fragment to which they belong is present in the exterior column, i.e. the first column of a verso page or the second column of a recto page. These attributions

---

(10) See especially MONTANARI, *Paul Maas*, p. 296-299, who explains with admirable clarity this famous rule. See also MAAS, *Textkritik*, p. 26.

(11) See REEVE, *Eliminatio*, p. 1: "establishing the exclusive derivation of one manuscript from another is not merely difficult but impossible." He quickly adds, however, that "probability adequately compensates for certainty" (ibid., p. 2).

(12) Concerning the question of length, see REEVE, *Eliminatio*, p. 3.

(13) REEVE, *Eliminatio*, p. 10.

(14) Ibid., p. 13.

LXXX   RELATIONSHIP OF THE MANUSCRIPTS

confused the copyist of *B*, who seems to have thought that, since the attributions were written close to the inner column, they must belong to the text of that column. ([15]) The first example is on f. 8 of *C*. In the second column, at lines 10-12, the title of the chapter can be read: Τίνες αἱ μορφωτικαὶ τῶν ἀγγελικῶν δυνάμεων εἰκόνες. The following excerpt has the attribution Διονυσίου ἐπισκόπου Ἀθηνῶν, and, in *C*, this attribution stands in the inner margin, thus closer to the first column than to the second one, to which it pertains. Now *B* manifestly thought that this attribution corresponded to the text of lines 10-12 of the *first* column, and consequently wrote the attribution in the middle of the fragment which preceded that of Dionysius. ([16]) *B* thus created a new fragment, beginning with Ὅτε δὲ εἶδε τὸν Ἀδάμ (fragment 4.20). And Ὅτε δὲ εἶδε τὸν Ἀδάμ is present in lines 11-12 of the first column of f. 8 of *C*. The confusion of *B* is manifest, and its reason becomes apparent to anyone who has its model, namely *C*, in sight.

An objection has been made to this hypothesis: "on peut supposer, par exemple, que le modèle de *B* et *C* avait lui aussi divisé le texte en deux colonnes, comme l'avait fait *C*, et que les attributions y étaient placées de la même manière." ([17]) However, this state of affairs would require that this supposed common ancestor of *BC* had exactly the same layout as *C*: same pagination, same lineation, same position of the attributions in the folios. That supposition, though not strictly impossible, is highly unlikely. ([18])

I will give some further examples to make the point clear. The attribution for fragment 30, τοῦ χρυσοστόμου· ἐκ τῆς περὶ παρθένων βίβλου, appears in *C* in the inner column; the attribution is also the first of f. 36. This attribution could easily be thought to pertain to the last few lines of the first column, instead of to the last few lines of the second. Most likely, this is what the copyist of *B* understood. The second-to-last line in the first col-

---

(15) Note that in most cases, when the attribution actually belongs to the text of the inner column, *B* made no mistakes (e.g. fragments 61-62, 63-64, or 86). As for attributions 82-84, even though they are close to the inner columns, *B* copied them correctly, as pertaining to the text in the exterior column (see f. 69ᵛ of *C*, and p. 64 of *B*).

(16) In this case, *B* is absent; but the consensus of its two apographs, *P* and *S*, allows us to know with certainty where its attribution was located.

(17) CEULEMANS et al., *Eta*, p. 81.

(18) Cf. REEVE, *Eliminatio*, p. 15.

umn of f. 36 of *C* has the text εἰδότες οὖν ὅσης κτλ. (29.479). In *B* the attribution is in the margin, precisely next to εἰδότες οὖν ὅσης κτλ. What was ambiguous in *C* has become an obvious mistake in *B*. More interestingly to us, this is a mistake that can easily be explained if *C* is the model of *B*.

C has the attribution of fragment 77 – ἀθανασίου ἀλεξανδρείας· ἐκ τῆς ἑρμηνείας τοῦ κατὰ ματθαῖον εὐαγγελίου – in the second column of f. 65; the attribution is placed as high as lines 18-23 of the text of the columns. In lines 15-23, the first column of *C* has the following text: ἀνέβη δὲ καὶ ἰωσὴφ – καὶ πατρίδος δα(υΐ)δ (76.52/55). Now this is precisely the text to which the scribe of B has applied the attribution – ἀθανασίου ἀλεξανδρείας κτλ. – written in the margin of f. 55. Once again, it is clear that *B* considered the attribution in the inner margin to pertain to the inner column, whereas, in fact, it referred to the outer column.

In the case of the attribution of fragment 42, also present in the first column of *C* (f. 43), the scribe of *B* has simply omitted it, most likely because he overlooked it or could not determine where to place it. ([19])

Such an anomaly in the attribution is very common in *B*; there are more than a dozen examples in Letter Alpha alone. These anomalies are to be found in fragments: 5, 9-12, 30, 33-34, 41, ([20]) 43-45, 47-48, 56, 71, 77. ([21])

These considerations demonstrate beyond reasonable doubt that *B* was copied from *C* or from a descendant of *C*.

2. *P* apograph of *B*

That *P* is an apograph of *B* has already been established with sufficient evidence by other scholars. ([22]) *P* has all the individual mistakes of *B*, and many of its own. As usual, the exceptions are

---

(19) *B* also omits the attribution of *C*, present in the inner margin of fragment 65.

(20) Fr. 41 is visible on the microfilm (f. 42).

(21) Other cases where the attributions of *C* have been placed in the inner margin, and are therefore easy to overlook or to confuse, are those of fragments: 38, 42, 49-50, 54, 58, 61-65, 68-69, 73-74, 82-84, 86, 97. In these cases, *B* has not written the attribution in the wrong place, but either omitted it or located it in the right place.

(22) De Vos et al., *Beta*, p. 76-77.

LXXXII   RELATIONSHIP OF THE MANUSCRIPTS

some minor variants that can easily be explained as insignificant independent readings, e.g., when *P* corrects an obvious mistake of *B*. Some of the individual errors of *P* are:

2.4 ἐννοεῖ] ἐννοεῖν *P*

5.233 ἀλόγων] ἀγγέλων *P*

9.1/2 αὐτῷ – παιδός] *om. P*

29.75 ἀσύμβατα] ἀσύνδετον *P*[a. corr.] ([23])

29.265/266 οὐκ ἰώμενοι] οἰκειούμενοι *P*

29.455/456 κτίσεως – κόσμος] *om. P*

29.459/460 εἰς – διαφεύγοντος] *om. P*

29.463 τοῦ] *om. P*

29.465 κατανοεῖ] κατανοεῖν *P*

29.475 γράφειν] γράφει *P*

29.484 καταπροδόντες] καταπροδότες *P*

29.486 ἀποχῆς] ἐποχῆς *P*

31.2 μήπως] μή τις *P*

33.3 καὶ ὠδίνων] *om. P*

57.64 τὸν μισθόν] τὸ ἀγαθόν *P*

3. *S* apograph of *B*

Katelos, the copyist of *S*, made far fewer innovations than Darmarios, the less faithful copyist of *P*. However, it cannot be doubted that *S*, which has all the mistakes of *B* and a few of its own, is a copy of this latter manuscript. ([24]) Individual readings of *S* include:

1.14/15 καὶ[2] – διακόσμησιν] *om. S*

5.163 ἀνεμιαίαν] ἀνεμίαν *S*

22.12/14 ὁρώμενα – ὄψει] *om. S*

29.131 τὰς φύσεις] τῆς φύσε(ως) *S*

29.241 φολίδας] ὄστρακα *S*

29.248/249 θηρίων] θυρίων *S*

30.12 πηγῆς] ψυχῆς *S*

31.12 ἀνδρός] αὐτῆς *add. S*

---

(23) Suppl. in mg.: γρ ἀσύμβατα.

(24) See also De Vos et al., *Beta*, p. 76-77.

RELATIONSHIP OF THE MANUSCRIPTS LXXXIII

35.53 ἰατρόν] ἄν(θρωπ)ον S

51.1 εἰ] om. S

56.18 οὐδὲ] οὐδὲν S

56.24 Ὅπερ] ὥσπερ S

56.27 σιδήριον] σίδηρον S

57.12 ἐλεήμων – ἐστίν²] om. S.

Since, at the same time, all the errors shared by P and S are also present in B, they are not directly related to each other, but only through B.

4. V apograph of F

As early as the first excerpt of Letter Alpha, it is already apparent that V is related to FH:

1.1/2 τῆς ἐκκλησίας διδάσκαλοι] διδάσκαλοι τῆς ἐκκλησίας F$^{ut\,uid.}$HV

1.11 ἡ αἰωνία om. FHV

1.15 τὴν ἡμετέραν] τε τὴν ἡμετέραν FHV (τὲ FH)

1.17 συμπληροῖ] ἀποπληρεῖ FH, ἀποπληροῖ V

1.22 ἐπεισαχθῆναι] ἐπισυναχθῆναι FHV

The affinity of V with FH is further confirmed by the fact that V preserves some of the "extra" chapters of Letter Alpha, which only FH have. ([25])

Provataris, the copyist of V, was a very careful scribe: his text exhibits practically no variant readings, except for ὄντος instead of ὄντων (1.3) ([26]) or ὑπερκοσμίαις instead of -κοσμίοις (1.10). Matteo Devaris, a later user of manuscript V, had access to a witness of the primary source, and on occasion notes its readings in the margin. Thus in 1.22 where, as we have seen, FHV have ἐπισυναχθῆναι in textu, V has the marginal annotation: ἐπεισαχθῆναι in Bas. codic.; and in 1.31, where all of the manuscripts of the FC have an impossible τῇ, V indicates in the margin that the feminine article in the dative is not present in his Basilian manuscript. Similarly in the first excerpt of Alpha, where the manuscripts of the FC omit a γὰρ (1.17), V notes that the Basilian

---

(25) See FERNÁNDEZ, Florilegio.

(26) However, he duly indicates in the margin that the original had ὄντων.

LXXXIV   RELATIONSHIP OF THE MANUSCRIPTS

manuscript had that particle and also that the source had ὅθεν instead of the ὅτε found in the manuscripts of the *FC* (1.21). ([27])

Further on, it becomes apparent that *V* has all the individual mistakes of *F*, ([28]) but not all those of *H*:

2.21 γοῦν] νῦν *FV*

5.62 διειδεστάτην] διειδέστατον *FV*

5.146 ἐπιστρεπτικῆς] ἐπιτρεπτικῆς *FV*

12.2 κέκληκεν] τάξεις *add. FV*

22.11 καὶ βόες] βόες *FV*

43.1 ἐπέλθῃ] ἔλθῃ *FV*

49.1 καὶ] μοι *FV*

63.4 γὰρ] ἦν *add. FV*

93.24 ὑπὸ] ὑπὲρ *FV*

93.25 κατὰ τόπον ἀγγέλων] ἀγγέλων κατὰ τόπον *FV*, κατὰ τόπον ἀγγέλων κατὰ τόπον (*sic*) *H*

At the same time, *V* does not seem to have been copied directly from *F*, for some information offered by the scribe (or by Devaris) about the exemplar does not appear to correspond to *F*. For example, on f. 280ᵛ (fr. 17.8-9) he has written ἐγκαταλειφθέντος and commented in the margin on the reading of his model: ἐγκαταλειφθεντ (-τ *s.s.*) *abbreuiatus habitur in originali*; yet in *F* there is no possible ambiguity, for it has ἐγκαταλειφθέντο (-ο *s.s.*) (*H* reads ἐγκαταλειφθέντος). ([29]) Another example is on f. 279, where *V* writes in the margin that his model has ξένος (instead of ξένους in the *FC*, including *FH*: fr. 14.14) and ἀπῆρεν (instead of ἐπῆρεν in the *FC*, including *FH*: fr. 14.15), readings which, according to him, should be corrected into ξένοις and ἐπῆρε (*sic*, no ephelcystic ν). Consequently, the model of V was not *F*, but a descendant of *F*.

---

(27) These two variant readings, however, are not present in the critical apparatus of the current critical edition, AMAND DE MENDIETA – RUDBERG, *Basilius Caesariensis*.

(28) It does not literally have *all* of them; some were possibly eliminated by collating other manuscripts.

(29) Sometimes the same formula is utilized to correct a reading present in *F(H)*, for example on f. 278ᵛ (fr. 14.7), where *FHV* have ὧν, *V* has in the margin: *m*()*t*() *puto* ᾧ, which is, indeed, the reading of the other witnesses of the *FC*. The abbreviation *m*()*t*() may mean *mutandum*.

RELATIONSHIP OF THE MANUSCRIPTS   LXXXV

5. *L* apograph of *K* [30]

L has all the mistakes of *K* and a few of its own. All the variant readings of *K* [31] are found in *L*, except, as usual, for some minor variants that can easily be explained as independent corrections, e.g., at 16.22 *EK* have πάσχον, while all the other manuscripts, including *L*, have πάσχων. Rarely, the apograph may also have a variation which can in turn be explained on the basis of the variant reading of its model. See for example 25.6, where *AT C* have an impossible δὴ τοῦ, *EK* τόδε τοῦ, and *L* τόδε; or the attribution of fr. 6, which is βασιλείου καισαρείας in most manuscripts, but βασιλείου in *K*, whereas there is no attribution in *L*.

Some of the individual readings of *L* are:

6.3 καπνὸς] ὁ *praem. L*

7.1 πατρικῆς παραδόσεως] *inuersit L*

7.8 τοῦ ἀνθρώπου] τῶν ἀν(θρώπ)ων *L*

7.9 τῶν δύο τὸν ἄνθρωπον] τῶν (*sic*) ἄν(θρωπ)ον τῶν δύο *L*

13.4 στρατιαὶ] καὶ εἰσὶ καὶ *add. L*

13.11 καὶ] *om. L*

51.2 ὁδεύω] ὁδεύων *L*

52.7 μετακομίζειν τόπους] *inuersit L*

57.28 οὔτε] οὖν *add. L*

57.73 νῦν] *om. L*

67.32 δημιουργήματα] ποιήματα *L*

86.8 ἀπατώμενος] ἀγαπώμενος *L*

To these examples, three cases of confusion between υ and β can be added: 1.28 παυομένη] παβομένη *L*; 2.27 εὐαρμοστίας] ἐβαρμοστίας *L*; 40.7 Εὔας] ἔβας *L*.

---

(30) DECLERCK, *Probus*, p. 228, first suspected that *L* was an apograph of *K*. See further DE VOS et al., *Gamma*, p. 166.

(31) Some examples: the curious iteration of *KL* in 19.12, κτίσεως – τῆς²; 57.24 μικρόν τι ἀγαθόν] τί μικρὸν ἀγαθόν *KL*; 57.31 λέγει] οὖν *add. KL*.

LXXXVI   RELATIONSHIP OF THE MANUSCRIPTS

II. The Short Recension (Γ)

1. Manuscripts *FH*

These two manusripts are the most obviously related, yet each of them has mistakes of its own and, therefore, they must depend upon a common ancestor. Some individual readings of *F* are:

2.21 γοῦν] νῦν *F*
5.144 γεωμετρικὰ] γεωργικὰ *F*
12.2 κέκληκεν] τάξεις *add. F*
22.28 γὰρ] οἱ *add. F*
29.291 μὲν] δὲ *F*
49.1 καὶ] μοι *F*
57.18 ἔχει] *om. F*
98.20 ἐν δεσμοῖς] δεσμοῖς *F*

In turn, individual readings of *H* include:

5.5 ἀπ'εἰκόνων] ἀπείκασται *H*
5.21 ἐμφαίνειν οἶμαι] ἐμφαίνει εἶναι *H*
5.47 Τοῦτο] *om. H*
17.5 λαβεῖν] καὶ *add. H*
35.23 πῦρ ἐν κόλπῳ] ἐν κόλπῳ πῦρ *H*
61.6 χαμευνία] *om. H*
76.38 ἦν] *om. H*
93.10 πυρὸς] *om. H*
101.6 ἐπιφωσκούσῃ] ἐπιφασκούσῃ *H*

The manuscripts *FH* also share innumerable mistakes and innovations that set them apart from the rest of the witnesses of the *FC*:

1.4 ἅγιος] μέγας *FH*
1.11 ἡ αἰωνία] *om. FH*
2.29 δείξῃ μὴ] *inuersit FH*
4.2 ἀεὶ] οὐδὲν *FH*
5.51 ἀνθρωπομόρφους] ἀνθρώπους *FH*
5.139/142 τί τὰ δόρατα – δραστήριον] *post l.* 182 (ἐκκαλουμένην) *trsp. FH*
5.225 λευκοῦ] χαλκοῦ *FH*

RELATIONSHIP OF THE MANUSCRIPTS LXXXVII

16.7 πᾶς] *om. FH*

29.20 τοῦ ἀνθρώπου συντελοῦντα] συντελοῦντα τοῦ ἀνθρώπου *FH*

76.19 ὅστις] ὃς *FH*

77.19 ἀπεγεύετο] ἐγεύετο *FH*

97.24 νοηθῆναι] νοηθέντος *FH*

The examples could easily be multiplied. For the relationship of
FH and *Q*, see below, p. XCV-XCVI.

2. Manuscripts *EG*

For what follows, I take into account only the collations of
other editors of the *FC*, because where *E* starts, the witness *G*,
which has only the first few chapters of Letter Alpha, has already
finished; for this reason, even if one of these manuscripts were
proven to depend upon the other, the text of this edition would
not change. As we have seen, *G* and *E* have possibly been copied by the same scribe, Symeon Kalliandres, who has done his job
with meticulous care. ([32]) The two manuscripts do, however, have
many common mistakes; so one must descend from the other, or
both must have a common ancestor. Some of their common readings are:

Γ 2.18 καὶ] οὗτοι *EG (K deest)*

Γ 2.24 τὸ ἔνδον ἀπεργάζεται] ἀπεργάζεται τὸ ἔνδον *EG*
(K deest)

Γ 4.2 ζητούμενον] ἐπιζητούμενον *EG (K deest)*.

It would seem that *G* is older than *E*, which would require that
the former cannot have been copied from the latter. This conclusion, however, is not certain, since, as we have seen, the dating of
G is problematic. ([33]) Be that as it may, based on internal evidence,
we can confirm that *E* was not copied from *G*, for this latter manuscript has a number of individual mistakes:

Β 9.27 αὐταῖς] αὐτοῖς *G*

Β 23.3-5 *iterauit G*

Β 26.1 ὁ θεὸς] *om. G*

Γ 7.13 νῦν] *om. G*

Γ 8.13 τούτου] *om. G*

---

(32) See above, p. XLIX-LII.

(33) See above, p. LII-LIV.

LXXXVIII RELATIONSHIP OF THE MANUSCRIPTS

On the other hand, there is practically no individual reading of *E*; all those found in Letter Gamma are insignificant: ([34])

Γ 2.7 ἀξίωμα] τὸ *praem. E*

Γ 12.7 οἱ νῦν] νῦν οἱ *E*

The additional individual errors of *E* in Letter Eta are the following: ([35])

Η 10.45 Ἀφρικανὸς] ἀφρικιανὸς (not Ἀφρικίανος) *E*

Η 11.27 (reported as 11.25 in the introduction)] ἐστι *add.*
E KL

Η 12.9 ἐν κύκλῳ] ἐν ἐνκύκλω *E*

In Letters Beta, Theta, Xi and Psi there are no significant mistakes of *E*. ([36]) Any definite conclusion will have to wait until more letters of the *FC* have been edited. For the time being, I will continue to consider *EG* brothers, although it is likely that in the future it will be proven that *G* is an apograph of *E*.

3. Manuscripts *EGK* ([37])

These manuscripts share many mistakes. A few examples from Letter Gamma will suffice:

---

(34) CEULEMANS et al., *Eta*, p. 77 believe that in Γ 7.13 manuscript *E* has δειχθῆναι against all other manuscripts of the *FC*, including *G*. This confusion arises from a faulty collation in DE VOS et al., *Gamma*. Here *G* has the same reading as *E*, namely, δειχθῆναι.

(35) CEULEMANS et al., *Eta*, p. 77. The individual errors of *E* reported for Η 10.19, 12.53 and 16.18, as well as one in 5.8 (which is missing from the introduction), appear to be errors of collation: in all these cases *EG* have indeed the same reading.

(36) Here I am correcting a reading reported in DE VOS et al., *Beta*, for Β 24.30: *E* does not have ἐκφρύγηται, but ἐκφρύγεται, together with the rest of the tradition. In CEULEMANS et al., *Psi*, p. 55 it is stated that in Ψ 13.4 manuscript *E* omits ὑπὲρ πάντα, which is true, but *G* also omits both of these two words (not only ὑπὲρ). In the same publication, it is also stated that in Ψ 28.37 manuscript *E* has ἐπιμιμνησκόμενοι against the rest of the tradition (ibid.), but *G* actually has the same reading as *E*.

(37) Manuscript *K*, although fragmentary, cannot be regarded as an instance of indirect tradition; this impossibility clearly distinguishes *K* from *R*. Indeed, *K* neither rearranges the fragments in a new order nor takes with them any liberty beyond abridgment. Furthermore, *K*, unlike *Q* for example, can easily be given a place in the stemma. This is why *K* is treated here, whereas all other fragmentary manuscripts will be dealt with only after the basic stemmatic facts of the *FC* are well established.

Γ 20.4 ἀδύνατον] οὐ δυνατὸν EGK

Γ 22.2 καὶ ἑορτῇ] om. EGK

K is often in error against EG, as numerous examples in Letters Beta and Gamma demonstrate (such as B 24.37 τοίνυν] om. K). Furthermore, being a fragmentary manuscript, K could not possibly be the model of EG. Nevertheless, K could depend upon the same hyparchetype as EG. This, however, is not the case, since EG occasionally share mistakes against K:

B 9.26 πλανήσωσι λόγοις] trsp. EG

B 9.29 μὲν] om. EG

B 14.7 τυγχάνομεν] om. EG

B 24.28 ὡς] om. EG

Although few, these instances are enough to postulate that K depends on a hyparchetype other than that of EG.

4. Manuscripts DEGK

All of these manuscripts share a number of mistakes. In this section, the demonstration that EG belong to the same group will be indirect because, as we have seen, EG never appear at the same time in Alpha. Nevertheless, wherever DEK share a reading, it can be inferred that G had it as well. ([38])

Examples of mistakes common to DE(G)K in Alpha include:

20.7 τὸ ξύλον] τοῦ ξύλου DEK

21.1 Ὥσπερ] γὰρ add. DEK

39.8 ἐν πυρὶ κατακαυθήσονται] καυθήσονται ἐν πυρὶ DEK (et Q; πυρὶ καυθήσονται FH)

41.11 καὶ] om. DEK

57.31 καὶ] om. DEK (et Q)

57.56 μυρία] om. DEK (et Q)

65.26 Μωϋσῆς] μωσῆς DEK (et Q)

65.33 καὶ] γὰρ add. DEK

79.24/25 εἰς – ἀνάθεμα] om. DEK

79.41 τοῦτον] τοῦτο DEK

85.2 ἢ] φησὶ add. DEK

---

(38) A telling example of a mistake common to DEGK is Γ 22.4 καὶ – εὐτρεπίζει] om. DEGK.

These examples show that *DEGK* form a distinct group within the textual tradition of the *FC*. We have already studied a few individual mistakes of the group *EGK*. Individual mistakes of *D*, which show that manuscript not to be an apograph of any of the aforementioned manuscripts, are frequent.

To quote but a few individual readings of *D*:

    5.56 δὲ] τε *D*
    5.217 καὶ] *om. D*
    24.4 βρώσεως] γνώσεως *D*
    29.437 θεραπείαν] σ(ωτη)ριαν *(sine acc.) D*
    42.30 εἰδωλολατρείας] εἰδωλομανίας *D*
    57.63 ἐνταῦθα] ὧδε *(sic spir.) D*
    60.5 δεινότης] *om. D*
    62.7 ταύτης] τῆς ψυχῆς *D*
    93.18 οἳ] καὶ *praem. D*

These readings show that the hyparchetype of the group *EGK* is related to the model of *D*, whereas none of these manuscripts is derived from one another.

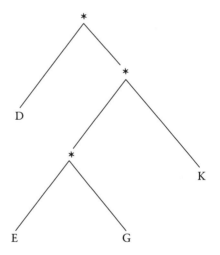

RELATIONSHIP OF THE MANUSCRIPTS XCI

5. Manuscripts DEGK ([39]) and FH

We have already seen that each of these constellations of manuscripts shares a common ancestor. The groups so formed are closely related to one another as against the rest of the manuscripts of the FC, that is, against those of the long recension (AT C). There are innumerable examples:

13.18 δραγμῶν] δραχμῶν DEFHKR; it is clear that, according to the usual rules, this is the only acceptable reading, and no less clear that the archetype had δραγμῶν. ([40])

16.11 τὸ σῶμα λαβών] λαβὼν τὸ σῶμα DEFHK; note that this is also the reading of the source: contamination may be suspected.

22.4 πάντα] om. DEFHK

25.4 δύναμις] om. DEFHK

29.157 τῆς] om. DEFH (et QI)

29.157 τοῦ] om. DEFH (et QI)

41.5/6 μοιχευθεῖσαν τὴν γυναῖκα] τὴν γυναῖκα μοιχευθεῖσαν DEFHK

48.7/9 Ἄνθρωπος – ἐφιλοσόφησεν] om. EFHK (D deest)

Fragm. 50] post fragm. 51 trsp. EFHK (D deest)

Fragm. 52] post fragm. 53 trsp. EFHK (D deest)

56.13 πικρά] μικρά DEFHK

63.5 ἐκ χάριτος] εὐχάριστος DEFHK

65.21/22 εὐπρεπείας ἐκείνης, ἀπὸ τῆς μεγαλοπρεπείας] μεγαλοπρεπείας ἐκείνης DEFHK (et Q)

65.22-26 Καὶ – σου] om. DEFHK (et Q)

67.23/31 καὶ³ – ἐκράτησεν] om. DEFHK (et Q)

80.4/5 καὶ – καθίσω] om. DEFHK

80.6/9 μὴ – ἀποπεσοῦνται] om. DEFHK

93.28/35 καὶ – Ἀβραάμ] om. DEFH (et R)

103.43/44 Οὐδὲ – ἀλλ'] om. DEFHK

---

(39) In most of the following examples, G is missing, but since its position in the group DEGK is well established, it can be taken to be present wherever DEK have the same reading.

(40) Since this orthography can reflect a difference in pronunciation, I have left the reading of the archetype, namely, δραγμῶν, in the edited text.

XCII   RELATIONSHIP OF THE MANUSCRIPTS

The examples could easily be multiplied. The reader will remark that, from about the middle of Letter Alpha on, the peculiarities of the short recension, especially more or less long omissions, become much more frequent.

On occasion, the short recension has the "correct" reading, as
in 29.29 (*DEFHQ*), where it coincides with the source, against
the impossible readings of all other manuscripts. This reading is
clearly a correction of the archetype, and it was found through
conjecture. Similar examples are 79.34, 94.2 and 103.34.

6. *Q* and the short recension (Γ)

The individual readings of *Q* are so many that it is impracti-
cal to quote them all. Besides, the selection of texts present in *Q*
is not found in any other manuscript. It is clear, therefore, that
no extant witness of the *FC* was copied from *Q*. This manuscript
is very peculiar, and for this reason it is dealt with here and not
in its logical position, that is, together with manuscripts *FH* with
which, as we will see, it is closely related.

In particular, *Q* often has an excellent reading against the rest
of the manuscript tradition of the *FC*. ([41]) Some examples:

29.66 νοεροῖς *FC*] νεύροις *Q* (*et fons*);
29.109 ἅ] *deest in Q* (*et in fonte*)
29.117 φωνήσεως] φωνήν, ἕως *Q* (*et fons*)
29.263 ὅταν] οὔτ'ἂν *Q* (*et fons*)
29.413 αὐτοκρατεῖν] αὐτὸ κρατεῖν *Q* (*et fons*)

All of these readings, however, could have been conjectures, ([42])
and the copyist of *Q*, as anyone browsing the critical apparatus of
this edition can see, frequently departed from his model and made

---

(41) Note that in many of the cases where *Q* sides with *E* or with *EK*, the
agreement is likely due to an astute, independent conjecture. The same kind
of conjecture may explain the three variant readings of *EKQ* in B 1.2 αὐτόθι]
αὐτόθεν *EKQ*; B 1.9 Ἐπειδή] γὰρ *add. EKQ*; B 1.17 ἔχομεν] ἐχόμενα *EKQ*.
All of these variant readings improve the text and indeed restore the text of
the primary source. That these manuscripts agree in readings that constitute
material improvements to the text, and not in *adiaphorae lectiones* or mistakes, are enough to make the reader suspect that the improvements have
been arrived at independently; this state of affairs only proves that scribes
were sometimes very clever.

(42) In other words, none of the "mistakes" shared by all the manuscripts
except *Q* is separative.

RELATIONSHIP OF THE MANUSCRIPTS   XCIII

conjectures, most of them wrong. Contamination is another possibility. Nevertheless, in all the cases where the reading of the source could not have been found through conjecture, as in the case of omissions of a group of words, Q does not have the correct reading. [43]

The position of Q in the stemma is difficult to determine. It is clear, however, that it belongs to the short recension, siding with Δ (C and the short recension) against AT where there is disagreement. [44] The following examples will suffice to show that Q belongs to the short recension:

29.29 ἑαυτῆς] ἑαυτοὺς DEFHQ (et fons)

29.157/158 τῆς ψυχῆς καὶ τοῦ σώματος] ψυχῆς καὶ σώματος DEFHQI

29.347 λογικὴν μὲν] μὲν λογικὴν DEFHQ

33.2/3 τούτων ἐκ διαδοχῆς, οὐδὲ] ἐκ διαδοχῆς οὐδὲ τούτων DEFHQ

62.91/134 Κἀκεῖναι – ἐξουσίᾳ] om. DEFHQ

67.15/19 Οὕτω – ἐρᾶν] om. DEFHKQ

67.23/31 καὶ³ – ἐκράτησεν] om. DEFHKQ

74.27/31 κατὰ – πύλαι] om. DEFHQ [45]

The precise position of Q within the short recension is also difficult to determine. Q sides on occasion with D:

22.30 ὁ⁴] om. DQ

29.61 ὁ] om. DQ

29.127 τὸν] om. DQ

29.309 καὶ¹] om. DQ

62.74/75 συντετριμμένα καὶ ὠτότμητα] συντετριμμένον καὶ ὠτότμητον DQ

73.12 ἀποβαλεῖν] ἀπολαβεῖν DQ

Nevertheless, Q is not related to D; when it sides with this manuscript, it is mostly in trivial variant readings. In the more telling instances, such as against a common innovation in E(G)KQ,

---

(43) An example is the omission at 29.424/425, which makes the text incomprehensible. The copyist of Q, however, has not managed to restore the missing text, which would have been impossible through conjecture alone. Yet the copyist of Q probably would have restored the missing text, if he had had access to an independent source.

(44) For cases of mistakes common to CDEFHQ, see below.

(45) Further examples: 62.41/42, 62.64/66, 65.21/22, 65.22/26, 65.27, 65.35/37, 67.10, 67.49/50, 74.9/13, etc.

XCIV   RELATIONSHIP OF THE MANUSCRIPTS

the manuscript *D* has the reading of the hyparchetype of the short recension (Γ), for example in Letter Beta:

B 1.2 αὐτόθι] αὐτόθεν *EKQ*

B 1.10 γὰρ *EKQ*: *om. ceteri*

B.1.17 ἔχομεν] ἐχόμενα *EKQ*

Q also sides with *E*:

29.42 μέν¹] δὲ *EQ*

29.132 οὖν] *om. EQ*

29.227 ἐγκατέστραπται] ἐγκατέσπαρται *EQ (sicut T et fons)*

29.244 οὖν] om. *EQ (et fons)*

29.307 ὅσοι codd.] ὡς οἱ *EQ (et fons)*

32.12 τὸ ἀρχαῖον codd.] εἰς τὸ ἀρχαῖον *EQ (et fons)*

35.39 διακρατεῖ] βία (*intellig.* βίᾳ) κρατεῖ *EQ (*βίᾳ ἐπικρατεῖ *fons*)

74.33 ἠνέῳκτο] ἀνέῳκτο *EQ*

Some of these examples may seem significant variant readings, and in a way they are. Yet in almost of all of the cases they improve the text, something which can hardly impress us in copyists so fond of conjectures. For example, it is not unlikely that two clever copyists have independently corrected διακρατεῖ into βία κρατεῖ, since this is definitely the sense required by the context. This consensus in improvements to the *textus receptus* cannot be significant in the same way as a consensus in *lectiones adiaphorae* or simply in errors, as is the case in the relationship between *Q* and *FH*. ([46])

Because their extant portions rarely coincide, it is difficult to ascertain the relationship between *Q* and *K*. There is, however, a fine example at 1.22, where *GFHK* omit λοιπόν, which is preserved by *Q* and the rest of the manuscripts (*DE desunt*). In 22.29, *EK* have ἦσαν οὗτοι, against the οὗτοι ἦσαν of all other manuscripts, including *Q* (and *D*). At 65.8, *EKQ* have ἐπὶ δὲ τοῦ θεοῦ, against ἐπὶ τοῦ θεοῦ δὲ in the other manuscripts (with the exception of *D*, which omits the δὲ).

67.43 καὶ¹] *om. EKQ (et T)*

73.4 τὸ] τὴν *EKQ*

73.11 καὶ] om. *EKQ*[p.corr.]

---

(46) See below p. XCV-XCVI.

At 22.34, *EK* omit a καὶ present in all other manuscripts including *Q* (and *D*). At 36.5, *DEKQ* have an omission *per homoeoteleuton*.

More often, *Q* sides with *DE(G)*:

29.49 τοῖς²] *om. DEQ*

29.65/66 ὀστοῦν – αἰσθητικοῖς] *om. DEQ (per homoeotel.)*

29.144/145 κατὰ – ἐπουράνιος] *om. DEQ (per homoeotel.)*

29.208 καὶ¹] *om. DEQ*

29.238 οὔτε] *om. DEQ*

29.293 ἐστι τῆς οὐσίας αὐτοῦ] ἐστιν αὐτοῦ τῆς οὐσίας *DEQ (*αὐτοῦ τῆς οὐσίας ἐστὶ *FH)*

29.434 δεδομένας] παραδεδομένας *DEQ*

32.4 προφερόντων] προσφερόντων *DEQ*

All of these mistakes are relatively benign. The transposition of 29.293 might seem somewhat troubling, but *Q* has in fact simply kept the reading of the short recension, which must have been modified independently by the hyparchetype of *FH*. The addition of the prefix at 29.434 is not entirely trivial, but it can be explained through polygenesis, especially if we take into account that *Q* made so many innovations that it was bound to coincide in the mistakes of other manuscripts more often than the faithful scribes of, for example, manuscripts *S* or *EG*. All other coincidences are trivial, such as the omission at 29.49: τοῖς ἀνθρώποις καὶ τοῖς *(*τοῖς *om. DEQ)* ἀλόγοις.

On occasion *Q* sides with *FH*:

23.12 σωματικῶν] τῶν *praem. FHQ*

29.18 συγκατασκευάσθαι] συγκατεσκευάσθαι *FHQ (et fons)*

29.167 αὐτὸν θνητὸν] *inuersit FHQ*

29.328 τὸ] *om. FHQ*[a.corr.]

35.4 ποῦ] που *FHQ*

35.11 αὐτοὶ ἐζήτησαν] αὐτὸς ἐζήτησε *FHQ*

35.49 ἐπεὶ διαρρήσσει] ἐπειδὴ ῥήσει *FH (*ῥήσσει *F*[p.corr.]*),* ἐπειδὴ διαρρήσει *Q*

37.13 ὅτι] *om. FHQ*

39.6 τούτων] φησὶν *add. FHQ*

57.19 δικαιοσύνην] ἐλεημοσύνην *FHQ*

57.24 μικρόν τι] τί μικρὸν *FHQ*

62.6 χημοί] χῆμοι *FHQ (et C)*
65.33 Διατοῦτο] διὰ γὰρ τοῦτο *FHQ*
74.8 πάντως] παντὸς *FHQ (et T)*

At 29.167, 35.11 and 57.19, we have doubtlessly significant variant readings. Moreover, *FHQ* have a text that is in no way superior to that of the hyparchetype of the short recension. Where the text of the exemplar is defective, two copyists can independently arrive at a reasonable reading by conjecture, but they can hardly innovate independently, and in the same way, where the text of the exemplar is unproblematic. This is the greatest difference between the readings shared by *Q* and *DE* on the one hand, and the readings shared by *Q* and *FH* on the other: the former are almost invariably coincidences in better readings, whereas the latter definitely are not. This difference persuades me that *Q* belongs to the same textual branch as *FH*, though it is closer to their hyparchetype than *FH* are themselves. [47]

Stemma of the short recension, including *K* and *Q*:

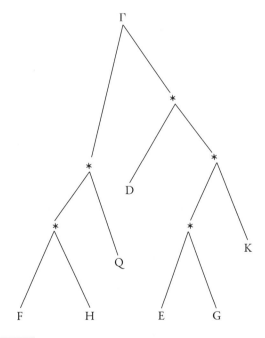

---

[47] There is an instance where *FQ* side against *H* and the rest of the witnesses of the *FC*, namely, 65.40 ὅτι] ὥστε *FQ*. It is clear that *F* and *Q* independently corrected a problematic ὅτι into the more normal ὥστε.

III. C AND Γ (Δ)

C is clearly related to the manuscripts of the short recension; they all depend upon a common hyparchetype (= Δ). In what follows, I include in the short recension not only K but also Q; as for R, representative of a "middle recension," see p. CII-CIV below. Δ has a number of errors not present in the other branch of the manuscript tradition of the FC, namely AT. As usual, I mention not only real errors but also correct readings which seem to be a divergence from the archetype. Errors of Δ against AT include the following:

5.252 ἐκείνων ἱερογραφίαν] εἰκόνα Δ

19.10 καὶ²] om. Δ

19.35/36 προφέρουσι] προσφέρουσι Δ

19.38 ἀρχαγγέλων] τῶν praem. Δ

29.81/82 ἄλλον δι'ἄλλου] δι'ἄλλου ἄλλον Δ

29.217 ἕκαστον] ἕκαστος Δ

29.460/461 κατ'εἰκόνα καὶ ὁμοίωσιν θεοῦ] κατ'εἰκόνα θεοῦ καὶ ὁμοίωσιν Δ

30.3 τὸν ἄνθρωπον ὁ θεὸς] ὁ θεὸς τὸν ἄνθρωπον Δ

31.6 δι'ἐμπαίγματα] δι'ἐμπαίγματος Δ

35.38 καὶ] om. Δ

50.13 ζῶν] om. Δ

56.10/11 κατερχόμενον] κατεχόμενον Δ

57.31 πῶς] om. Δ

57.56/57 κακὰ ποιῶν] κακοποιῶν Δ

63.1 φιλίας] φιλοσοφίας Δ

78.33 ἐστιν] om. Δ

80.1/3 καὶ – ἐκάθισεν] καὶ τὰ λοιπά C, om. Γ

The individual readings of Δ – excluding those that may not be mistakes ([48]) and those in passages absent from the short recension, and which could therefore be individual readings of C – are thus seventeen in number.

---

(48) On these passages, see p. CI-CII below.

XCVIII RELATIONSHIP OF THE MANUSCRIPTS

The passages in which *C* has a mistake that could be individual, since these passages are absent from the short recension, are as follows:

60.97 νομιζόμενα] νομίζομεν *C*

62.89 ἀποκτένων] ἀποκτέννων *C*[p.corr.]

67.17 περιέρχεται] παρέρχεται *C*

67.19 μάθετε] μάθομεν *C*

67.24 ὁρᾶν] ἐρᾶν *C*

79.74/75 ἐμοὶ μαθηταὶ] μαθηταί μου *C*

IV. Manuscripts *AT*

The relationship between *A* and *T* is difficult to establish. They seem to stand out from the rest of the manuscripts, but this could simply be due to their close proximity to the archetype. This is the position defended by De Vos et al., *Gamma* and *Beta*. According to these scholars, *A* and *T* would be two independent branches of the *FC*.

Both *A* and *T* have separative mistakes, so they cannot have been copied from one another. In this regard, omissions of groups of words are especially conspicuous. The manuscript *T* has seventeen of them, of which only one is not *per homoeoteleuton*: 5.199/200. The manuscript *A*, by contrast, has only six omissions, four of which are *sauts du même au même*. *A* and *T* share two of the aforementioned omissions, in both cases *per homoeoteleuton*: the first at 4.8, the second at 24.19/20. Incidentally, the scarcity of omissions in *A* shows that the copyist of *A* was more attentive than its deficient orthography would suggest.

This is the complete list of the mistakes common to *AT* in Letter Alpha: ([49])

1.34 διηγεῖται] διηγητέον *AT*

---

(49) I have excluded trivial orthographic mistakes. I list them here for the sake of comprehensiveness: 5.265 εὑρήσει] εὑρέσει *AT D*; 24.4 Θαρροῦντες] θαροῦντες *AT*; 29.297 προημαρτημένων] προήμαρτημένων *AT*; 40.10 ὑπολειφθῆναι] ὑποληφθῆναι *AT (et D)*; 41.7 πράττων] πράττον *(sic acc.) AT*; 53.5 ἐπίκηρα] ἐπίκαιρα *AT (ἐπίχερα A)*; 60.9 χρεμετίζοντες] χραιμετίζοντες *AT*; 60.26 γηρῶντας] γηροῦντας *AT*; 62.66 ὡδῶν] ὡδῶν *AT (ὁδῶν C)*; 73.11 παρατραπείσας] παρατραπήσας *AT*; 79.71 κέρδησον] κέρδισον *AT*.

RELATIONSHIP OF THE MANUSCRIPTS   XCIX

4.8 καὶ² – σύνοιδε] om. AT
5.35 ὀξύπορον] ὀξυπόρον AT
5.112 τὸ¹] om. AT
5.177 δεύτερα] βαθύτερα AT
5.228 συνάπτον] συνάπτοντος AT
21.5 τῆς] om. AT
24.19/20 καὶ – ἐπεπλήρωτο] om. AT (et Cᵃ·ᶜᵒʳʳ·)
29.75 ἀσύμβατα] ἀσύμβατον AT
29.90 περιέθηκε] παρέθηκε AT (-εν A)
29.126 πρῶτον] πρῶτος AT
29.266 ἐκπέφευγε] ἐκπεφευγῶς (sic acc.) A, ἐκπεφευγότα T
29.372 φύκια καὶ ἄλλα τινὰ] φύκια τινὰ καὶ ἄλλα AT
29.476 καθὰ] καθὼς AT
35.11 λογισμοὺς] λόγους AT
35.17 ἀθεράπευτον] ἀθεράπευτος AT (et FH)
38.3/4 συντετελεσμένη] συντελεσμένη (sic) AT
41.16 ἐλευθερίᾳ] ἐλευθέρας AT
42.26 ὁδηγηθῆναι] ὁδηγηθέντα AT
56.13 καιόμενον, τεμνόμενον] τεμνόμενον· καιόμενον AT
56.13/14 φάρμακα] τραύματα add. AT
57.60/61 καὶ ἀπέλθῃ ἐκεῖ καθαρός] καὶ ἀπελθῶν (sic acc.)
κάθηται A, ἐκεῖ κάθηται ἐλεύθερος πάσης ἁμαρτίας T(⁵⁰)
57.72 ἀπελάμβανες] ἀπέλαβες AT (et Q)
58.12 τῆς] τοὺς AT
62.4 ἀκρωτηριασμοὶ] ἀκροτηρισασμοὶ (sic) AT
65.2 σώματος] σωμάτων AT
79.73 μέγα] μέγιστον AT
81.7 ἐν] om. AT
82.1 φοβηθήσῃ] φοβηθῆς A, φοβηθεὶς T (φοβηθήσει C)
94.2 σκοτεινὰ χωρία] σκοτεινοχωρία AT (-νω- A)
94.3 δύνανται] δύναντος AT
101.4 ἡμέρα] ἡμέραν AT

---

(50) These mistakes, even if they are not identical, can be explained through a corruption in the hyparchetype of AT; this must be the reason why both manuscripts have κάθηται. Both tried to resolve the corruption in their model in different ways.

C RELATIONSHIP OF THE MANUSCRIPTS

The individual readings of *AT* are therefore 32, excluding those passages which are absent from the short recension, namely, 79.73 and 82.1. In Δ there are seventeen individual readings, excluding those sections absent from the short recension. Consequently, of the two branches of the *FC*, Δ gives the correct reading more often than *AT*.

I will now linger on mistakes which are especially significant. They are of different types. The first type comprises impossible readings of *AT*. These errors are for the most part conjunctive, because *A* and *T* could not have committed the mistake independently, and not separative, because the branch having the good reading could have arrived at it by conjecture.[51] An example of this kind of mistake is 5.228 συνάπτον] συνάπτοντος *AT*; Δ could have easily corrected the impossible genitive into the neuter συνάπτον. 29.90 is a similar case. More suggestive is the following example: 35.11 λογισμοὺς] λόγους *AT*. It is most likely that the hyparchetype of *AT* made a mistake while copying, even if the possibility that Δ arrived at λογισμοὺς by conjecture cannot be excluded. The same holds for 41.16: προαιρέσεως ἐλευθερίᾳ] προαιρέσεως ἐλευθέρας *AT*.

An example of the second type of mistake occurs at 1.34 τίς ἡ ἀρχὴ τῆς ὑπάρξεως διηγεῖται] τίς ἡ ἀρχὴ τῆς ὑπάρξεως διηγητέον *AT*. In this case, we can know with certainty that the reading of the archetype was indeed διηγεῖται, because this is also the reading of the primary source and no contamination can be suspected. If the archetype had had διηγητέον, it can hardly be explained why Δ, by mere conjecture, would have corrected a reading perfectly sound in itself, just to reach by accident, as it were, the same reading as the primary source. Examples such as these are numerous. See for instance 29.75 ἀσύμβατα] ἀσύμβατον *AT*. Here again the reading of *AT* is not impossible. Yet the source has the same reading as Δ, and it is unlikely that, if ἀσύμβατον was the reading of the archetype, Δ would have changed it into ἀσύμβατα, recovering the reading of the source. See also 29.337 φύκια καὶ ἄλλα τινὰ] φύκια τινὰ καὶ ἄλλα *AT*. If the archetype did not have the same word order as Δ, it is very unlikely that Δ, by innovating on a correct reading, would have found the reading of the source. Other cases are 29.476: καθὰ] καθὼς *AT*; 65.2:

---

(51) On this problem, see FERNÁNDEZ, *Errores coniunctivi*.

εὐμορφία σώματος] εὐμορφία σωμάτων *AT*; and 79.73: μέγα] μέγιστον *AT*. ([52]) It is impossible that *AT* would coincide so often in readings that are not the one of the archetype, if they did not have a common ancestor.

There is another very telling mistake of *AT* at 5.177: εἰς τὰ δεύτερα δευτεροφανῶς] εἰς τὰ βαθύτερα δευτεροφανῶς *AT*. The reading of *AT* does not need any commentary. This is a conjunctive error, for it is impossible that they both committed the same mistake independently. At the same time, βαθύτερα cannot have been the reading of the archetype, for it is equally impossible that Δ could have conjectured the correct reading of the primary source. This mistake would, even by itself, be a strong hint of the relationship between *A* and *T*.

The cumulative presence of these innovations makes it certain that *A* and *T* are not independent branches of the tradition but belong to the same group of manuscripts.

V. *Adiaphorae lectiones*

Wherever *AT* on the one hand and Δ on the other have different yet acceptable readings, and there is no third party to settle the question (as the primary source often is), there is no way to choose on a stemmatic basis which reading to keep. Equipollent readings in Letter Alpha include the following:

30.17 ζωὴν ζῆν] ζῆν ζωὴν *A*, ἔζων ζωὴν *T* (ζωὴν *fons*)

40.8 οὕτως] καὶ *praem.* Δ

41.22 βία εἰργάσατο ταῦτα] ταῦτα βία εἰργάσατο *AT* (βία ταῦτα εἰργάσατο *fons*)

42.8 ἀπεκρίνοντο] ἀπεκρίναντο Δ

57.20 καθάπερ] καθώσπερ *AT*

62.46 καπνὸς] ἐστιν *add.* Δ

62.88 μοι] *om.* Δ

67.1 ἔθος εστίν] ἐστὶν ἔθος *C*, ἔστι τὸ ἔθος Γ

74.4 ἀφθάρτως] ἀφράστως Δ

In the following cases, the short recension is absent:

---

(52) Another interesting example from Letter Beta is 24.34 τὸ λεχθὲν πρὸς τοῦ κυρίου] παρὰ τοῦ κυρίου *AT* (against the source and all other manuscripts).

CII RELATIONSHIP OF THE MANUSCRIPTS

18.18 ἐφικτὸν] ἐφικτῶς *AT* [53]

60.70 κερατίζοντες] κερατίζοντα *C*

60.78/79 ἀποδιδόντες] ἀποδιδοῦντες *AT*

60.93 κακοποιῆσαι] κακοποιεῖν *C*

62.130/131 παρεδίδετο] παρεδίδοτο *C*[p.corr.]

To these, the readings at 98.5 and 98.7 might be added. However, since it seems clear to me that in the first case the reading of *C* must be favoured and in the second that of *AT*, I have left them off the list.

VI. The Mixed Recension. Manuscript *R*

Despite its fragmentary state and its extreme liberty when handling the text of the *FC*, the manuscript *R* testifies to the existence of a mixed recension, which has some of the omissions and mistakes peculiar to the short recension while still presenting some fragments only preserved in the long recension. Furthermore, as we will presently see, *R* occasionally keeps the good reading, together with *AT*, against all other witnesses of the *FC*.

R very clearly sides with the short recension – *DEFH* – in a number of divergences from the archetype of the *FC* (93.27/28; 98.23/24; 99.1; etc.) and, even more tellingly, in voluntary omissions, for example at 93.28/35 and 98.5/7. The order of the excerpts is also instructive: fragment 98 is placed after fragment 99 in *R*, just as in the short recension. There are occasionally cases of *R* siding with one or another manuscript of the short recension, such as at 97.8 with *D*, at 97.21 with *FH*, [54] and at 97.10 with *E*, but all of these cases are explainable through polygenesis. On the other hand, all of the witnesses of the short recension have mistakes of their own, which shows that *R* does not descend from any of them.

---

(53) The source of this fragment, attributed to Cyril of Alexandria in the *FC*, is unknown. The reading of *AT* is not impossible. That of Δ, however, seems better. Furthermore, Cyril of Alexandria used the word ἐφικτόν a number of times (forty-four are attested in the *TLG*), while the *TLG* does not report even one occurrence of ἐφικτῶς in Cyril's works.

(54) 97.21 δεχόμενοι] δεχομένους *FHR*. Here it is likely that the hyparchetype of *DE(G)* corrected the mistaken accusative to a nominative.

RELATIONSHIP OF THE MANUSCRIPTS   CIII

Yet more interestingly, *R* sides on occasion with the long recension (*AT C*) against the short one, for example at 93.19. ([55])
A telling case is that of 93, 18/24. There, the short recension
has: [...] ἀλλ'οὐκ ἐν τῷ αὐτῷ τόπῳ, ᾧ καὶ οἱ ἄδικοι, ἀλλ'οἱ μὲν
δίκαιοι εἰς δεξιὰ φωταγωγούμενοι κτλ., and *R*: [...] ἀλλ'οὐ τῷ
αὐτῷ τόπῳ, ᾧ καὶ οἱ δίκαιοι· εἰς δεξιὰ φωταγωγούμενοι. The
difference is that the short recension has ἐν before τῷ αὐτῷ τόπῳ
and that, instead of ᾧ καὶ οἱ δίκαιοι, it has ᾧ καὶ οἱ ἄδικοι,
ἀλλ'οἱ μὲν δίκαιοι. The explanation for this last divergence has
to be sought in the long recension. *DEFHR*, unlike *AT C*, omit a
large group of words (93.19/23). It is likely that the hyparchetype
of the short recension had the words: ᾧ καὶ οἱ δίκαιοι, ἀλλ'οἱ μὲν
δίκαιοι εἰς δεξιὰ κτλ. Since this made no sense, *DEFH* corrected
the first δίκαιοι into ἄδικοι, whereas *R* simply omitted ἀλλ'οἱ μὲν
δίκαιοι. Since the reading of *R* cannot be derived from the same
hyparchetype as *DEFH*, ([56]) it must be postulated that it derives
from a hyparchetype higher up in the stemma. In other words,
R is a branch fully independent from Γ, the hyparchetype of the
short recension.

Moreover, *R* occasionally sides with *AT* against *CDEGFH*.
I quote two examples, none of them in Letter Alpha. The first
is fragment 26 of Beta: ἤγουν τοῦ ἰδίου αἵματος *AT*, ἤγουν τοῦ
αἵματος τοῦ ἰδίου *C*, *om. DEGFH*. It is possible that the copyist of *R*, who often modifies the text he copies, has corrected the
exemplar, turning τοῦ αἵματος τοῦ ἰδίου into the roughly syno-
nymical τοῦ ἰδίου αἵματος. The second case is more instructive.
In chapter Θ' of Letter Delta, there is one pseudo-Chrysostomic

---

(55) Some further examples taken from Book Beta of the *FC*: at 24.1,
DEGFHK omit an ἐστι preserved in *R* and *AT C*; at 26.2, *DEGFH* omit
λέγω δή, present in *R* and *AT C*; at 26.3, *DEGFH* omit a τρίτον preserved
in *R* and *AT C*; at 26.4/5, *DEGFH* make a transposition absent from *R* and
AT C; at 26.5/6, *DEGFH* omit τὴν ἄρνησιν ἀπενίψατο, present both in *R*
and in *AT C*.

(56) Another possibility, perhaps less likely, is that the long omission of
93.19/23 was in fact a *saut du même au même* (from οἱ δίκαιοι at l. 19 to οἱ
δίκαιοι at l. 23) of the whole short recension, including *R*. In that case, *R*
would have left the text unchanged, and the hyparchetype of *DEFH* would
have restored by conjecture ἀλλ'οἱ μὲν δίκαιοι, correlated to Οἱ δὲ ἄδικοι on
l. 35. Even if that were true, the position of *R* in the stemma would be the
same.

fragment.([57]) This fragment is absent from the short recension but preserved both in the long recension and in *R*, which further proves the independence of *R* from the short recension. In l. 5-6 of this fragment, we read ἀποπλύνων τὸν μετὰ τὸ βάπτισμα προσγινόμενον ῥύπον τοῦ ἀνθρώπου, which is the reading of *AT*. The manuscript *C*, for its part, omits the προσγινόμενον, while *R* does not omit it, preserving instead the form προσγενόμενον. This shows that *R* is also independent from *C*.

The existence of *R* proves that the short recension extant in *DEFGHK* is only one step in a fairly open textual tradition.

Stemma of the whole *FC*, including *Q* and *R*:

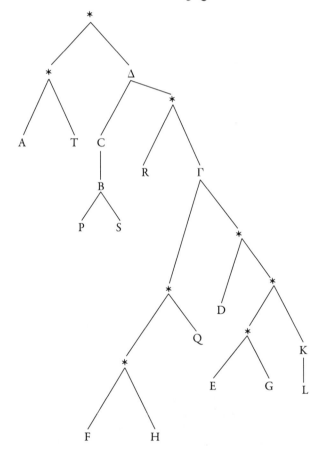

([57]) Critical edition in FERNÁNDEZ, *Tears*.

RELATIONSHIP OF THE MANUSCRIPTS   CV

The extreme bifidity of this stemma is evident; yet I see no other model better able to accommodate the evidence of the manuscripts.

VII. Minor Fragmentary Manuscripts

Ms. **W**, *Athonensis, Koutloumousiou 269* contains fragment 29 of Letter Alpha (Nemesius' excerpt) on f. 141-149. This manuscript contains all the mistakes of *T* and a number of individual mistakes, for example:

29.7 ἀφ'ἑαυτῆς] αὐτῆς *W*

29.9 καὶ Πλωτῖνος] πλωτῖνος *W*

29.54/55 νοητῆς καὶ αἰσθητῆς οὐσίας] νοητῇ καὶ αἰσθητῇ οὐσίᾳ *W*

29.61 τῶν ὄντων] *om. W*

One case is particularly instructive: 29.150/152 οἷον ψυχῆς προσχρωμένης σώματι, ὡς αἱ ἀρεταί, τὰ δὲ τῆς ψυχῆς αὐτῆς καθ'ἑαυτὴν μόνης μὴ προσδεομένης σώματος] οἷον ψυχῆς προσχρωμένης σώματι *W*, οἷον ψυχῆς προσχρωμένης σώματος *T*. It is almost certain that *T* omitted a large group of words by a *saut du même au même*; the scribe of *W* read προσχρωμένης σώματος in his model, and, seeing that this made no sense, corrected σώματος into σώματι.

The possibility that these manuscripts are brothers must be excluded because in a long portion of text, there is no significant mistake of *T* not present in *W* as well. It is unnecessary to list the errors shared by *TW*; the interested reader can consult the critical edition of fragment 29, and deduce that *W* had in most cases the same reading as *T*. There are, however, a few cases of divergence between *T* and *W*. I will quote some of the most important ones:

29.29 ἑαυτοὺς] ἑαυτῆς *AT C*, ἑαυτῶ *W*

29.43 ἀπὸ τῶν τεσσάρων] ἀπὸ τῶν ἀπο *(sic)* τεσσάρων *W*, τῶν ἀπὸ τεσσάρων *T*

29.118 τέλειαν τὴν ἀνθρώπου] τέλειαν τοῦ ἀνθρώπου *T EH*, τέλειαν τὴν τοῦ ἀνθρώπου *F*

29.126 πρῶτον] πρῶτος *AT*, πρώτως *W*

29.312 ὥσπερ] ὡς περι *(sine acc.) A*, ὥσπερϊ *T*, ὥσπερεὶ *W*

CVI   RELATIONSHIP OF THE MANUSCRIPTS

In the very few cases where *W* shares the reading of other manuscripts of the *FC* against *T*, they can easily be explained through the operations of conjecture or polygenesis. It can therefore be stated with confidence that *W* descends from *T*. [58]

Ms. **N**, *Londinensis, British Museum, Addit. 34060*. This manuscript has many mistakes of its own:

Caput Δ' Ἀπόδειξις *(titulum)*] ὑπόδειξις *N*[p.corr.]

12.2 κέκληκεν] (καὶ) δύο οὐσίαι *add. N*

12.4 ἀμέσως] ἀσμένως *N*

12.5 ἡνῶσθαι] ἤνωσθαι *N*

12.5 παραδεδομένην] π(ε)ρϊδεδομένην *N*

12.7 κυριοτήτων] κυριοτάτων *N*

12.8 καὶ ἐξουσιῶν] ἐξουσιῶν *N*

Fragm. 36 Μαξίμου μοναχοῦ *(attributio)*] μαξίμου *N*

36.3 εὐχερῶς] εὐχερεῖς *N*

36.4 ἐπίγνωσιν καὶ μετάνοιαν] μετάνοι(αν) (καὶ) ἐπίγνωσιν *N*

36.5 μήτε τῇ πείρᾳ] μήτε πείρους *N (om. DEKQ)*

36.5 τῷ χρόνῳ] χρόνω *N*

36.6 ἀνήκεστον] ἀνείκαστον *N*

KE' *(titulum) et fragm. 61 (attributio)*] *om. N*

61.3 ἐλεημοσύνη] ἐλεημοσύναι *N*

61.3 σωφροσύνη] *om. N*

61.4 ἀφιλάργυρον] ἀφιλαργυρίαν *N*

94.2 νοούμενον] φαινόμενον *N*

94.2 γὰρ] *om. N*

94.5 σκοτῶδες] σκωτοειδὲς *N*

94. 6 αὐτὸς] *om. N*

LH' *(titulum)*] *om. N*

M', Χριστοῦ *(titulum)*] τοῦ θ(εο)ῦ ἡμῶν *add. N*

101.3/4 Ἡ νὺξ – ἡμέρα] *om. N*

---

(58) As José Maksimkzuk has now shown, *W* is an apograph of *Atheniensis, Metochion Sancti Sepulcri 274* (itself copied from *T*).

RELATIONSHIP OF THE MANUSCRIPTS   CVII

The relationship of *N* to the other extant manuscripts is elusive. I quote the most important variant readings that *N* shares with other witnesses of the *FC*:

36.1 τέσσαρας] τέσσαρεις *(sic) KN*

94.2 σκοτεινὰ χωρία] σκοτινοχωρία *N*, σκοτεινωχωρία *A*, σκοτεινοχωρία *T*

94.2 ὁραθῆναι] *DEFHR (et fons)*, ὁράθη *AN*, ὡράθη *T*

94.3 δύνανται] δύναντος *AT N*

In addition to the fragments of Letter Alpha, I have collated a fragment already edited, namely Γ 8.1/16 (up to εἴρηται). The differences between the text of this fragment of the *FC* and that of the London manuscript are the following:

8.2 βλεπούσης] βλέπουσι *N*

8.3 εἰ βουληθεῖεν] ἡ βουλήθειεν *N*

8.6 αὕτη ἔσται] ἔσται αὕτη *N*

8.7 σοι τούτου μέλλει] σου (= *AD*) τοῦτο (= *T*) μέλλει *N*

8.8 ἐστίν] ἔστιν *N*

8.11 οὐκ] *om. N*

8.12 ἔγωγε] ἐγώγε *N*

τούτου] *om. N* (= *G*)

8.14 διέστηκεν] καθέστηκ(εν) *N*

8.14 δή] *om. N*

8.15 ἔσται] ([59]) ἔσεστω *(sic) N* (ἔσεσται *A*, ἐστὶν *DEFGH*, ὑπάρχει *B, om. C*)

It is clear from this evidence that *N* derives from either *A*, *T*, or their common model. I incline to the possibility that *N* is an apograph of *A*.

Manuscripts **O** (*Vaticanus, Ottobonianus 441*) and **M** (*Lesbiacus, Leimonos 268*) are clearly related. *OM* share a number of variant readings such as:

1.31 τῇ κατὰ πρεσβυγένειαν] τοῦ κατὰ πρεσβυγένειαν *MO*

2.11 βούλομαι μὲν] βούλομαι *MO*

---

(59) ἔσται is the reading of *T* and the source.

CVIII   RELATIONSHIP OF THE MANUSCRIPTS

They also add "εἰς αὐτό" beside the attributions of fragments 2 and 3, and beside βούλομαι (2.11). ([60]) The manuscript *M* has a few individual readings that are absent from *O*:

2.12 ἄτε] ἄ *(sic acc.) M*

3.1 αἱ ἄσαρκοι] καὶ ἄ. *M*

4.1ἐν ἀρχῇ] ἀρχὴ *(sic acc.) M*

The fragment that follows fragm. 4 of the *FC* has the same attribution in *O* and in *M*: τοῦ ἐν ἁγίοις πατρὸς ἡμῶν ἰωάννου ἀρχιεπισκόπου κωνσταντινουπόλεως τοῦ χρυσοστόμου, λόγος ψυχωφελής, καὶ περὶ τῶν θείων καὶ φρικτῶν μυστηρίων, καὶ περὶ ἱερέων καὶ διακόνων. The *incipit* of the fragment is Οὐκ ἀρκὴ *(lege ἀρκεῖ)* τὸ ἁπλῶς καὶ ὡς ἔτυχεν ἀκούειν ἡμᾶς χριστιανούς.

In addition, both manuscripts are closely related to *G*, having all its variant readings in fragments 1-4. Recent research on other sections of the *FC* has confirmed that *OM* derive in all likelihood from *G*, and that *M* is likely an apograph of *O*. ([61])

The stemma of the *FC* is consequently as follows:

---

(60) The manuscript *O* has εἰς αὐτὸ in mg., while *M* has it in the middle of the text: [...] ὑποληπτέον – εἰς αὐτὸ – βούλομαι κτλ.

(61) CEULEMANS et al., *Psi*, p. 57-58; MICHELS – VAN DEUN, *Topaz*, p. 286. GIELEN, *Nicephorus*, p. cxxvii-cxxviii, adduced a line missing in *O* but present in *M*, but J. Maksimczuk has proven that the line, though displaced, is present also in *O*. Consequently, *O* may well be the exemplar of *M*.

RELATIONSHIP OF THE MANUSCRIPTS   CIX

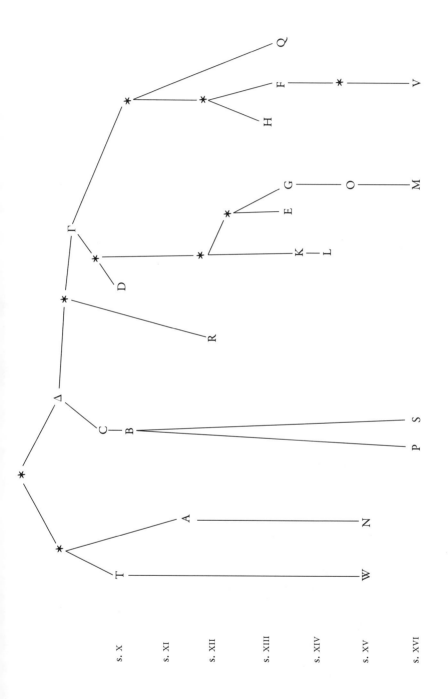

TITLES AND ATTRIBUTIONS

In what follows, only the differences between *AT*, *C* and the short recension will be recorded. In the manuscripts, κεφάλαιον often accompanies the number of the chapter; sometimes the number alone is given. In the following list, only the numbers will be given, unless the indication κεφάλαιον might be significant, as in the attribution of fragment 19 below. A reminder:

Γ = the short recension

Δ = Γ + manuscript *C*

Α′ Περὶ δημιουργίας ἀγγέλων

1 [...] ὁ ... ἅγιος Βασίλειος ἐν τῇ κατ᾽αὐτὸν Ἑξαημέρῳ = Bas. Caes., *Hom. in Hex.*, 1, 5 (p. 8, 17 – 9, 16; p. 10, 4-8)

2 Γρηγορίου τοῦ Θεολόγου ἐκ τοῦ εἰς τὴν Χριστοῦ γένναν = Greg. Naz., *Or.* 38, 9, 1 – 10, 11 (= *Or.* 45, *PG* 36, 629, 7-40)

3 Καισαρίου ἀδελφοῦ Γρηγορίου τοῦ Θεολόγου = Ps.-Caes., *Quaest. et resp.*, 60, 6-7 (p. 53)

4 Ἀναστασίου Ἀντιοχείας = Anast. Sin., *Viae dux*, IV, 8 – 36

Β′ Τίνες αἱ μορφωτικαὶ τῶν ἀγγελικῶν δυνάμεων εἰκόνες;

5 Διονυσίου ἐπισκόπου Ἀθηνῶν = Ps.-Dion., *De coel. hier.*, 15, 1 (p. 50, 13 – 51, 1); 15, 2-9 (p. 51, 22 – 59, 7)

Γ′ Ἀπόδειξις ὅτι ἀγγέλους φύλακας ἡμῖν ἔδωκεν ὁ θεός

6 Βασιλείου Καισαρείας = Bas. Caes., *Hom. super Ps.*, *PG* 29, 364, 15-21

7 Γρηγορίου Νύσης = Greg. Nyss., *Vit. Moys.*, 2, 45, 3 – 46, 8

8 Διδύμου = *Sacr. Par.*, *PG* 95, 1097, 35-36 (Did. Caec.); *T* and Γ omit the fragment.

9 Εὐαγρίου = Euagr., *Schol. in Prou.*, 189, 2-3; *T* and Γ omit the fragment.

TITLES AND ATTRIBUTIONS CXI

10 Γενέσεως = Ex. 23, 20-21; *T* and Γ omit the fragment.

11 Δαυὶδ προφήτου = Ps. 90, 11-13; *T* and Γ omit the fragment.

Δ΄ Ἀπόδειξις ὅτι θ΄ τάγματά εἰσιν οἱ ἄγγελοι

12 Διονυσίου = Io. Dam., *Exp. fidei*, 17, 66-74

13 Ἀθανασίου Ἀλεξανδρείας = Ps.-Athan., *Quaest. ad Ant.*, *PG* 28, 616, 24-41 (= Ps.-Athan., *Test. e script.*, *PG* 28, 77, 19-35); Ps.-Athan., *Quaest. ad Ant.*, *PG* 28, 601, 46-50

Ε΄ Περὶ τῶν ἀγγέλων ὧν ἐφιλοξένησεν Ἀβραάμ
Ε΄] om. Γ

14 Τοῦ Χρυσοστόμου – no source found

15 Εὐσεβίου = *Cat. in Gen.* 1074, ad Gen. 18, 8, l. 1-5 (for the first lines no source was found)

ϛ΄ Περὶ τῆς τοῦ ἀνθρώπου δημιουργίας καὶ πλάσεως
ϛ΄] ε΄ D, om. EFHK

16 Γρηγορίου τοῦ θεολόγου = Greg. Naz., *Or.* 38, 11, 1 – 12, 30 (= *Or.* 45, *PG* 36, 631, 48 – 633, 17); Δ omits 16.26/56.

17 Κλήμεντος = Ps.-Clem. Rom., *Hom.* 10, 3, 3, 2 – 10, 4, 2, 2 (p. 143)

18 Κυρίλλου Ἀλεξανδρείας = Cyr. Alex., *Contra Iul.* 3, 24, 1 – 25, 14; Γ omits the fragment.

19 Τοῦ Χρυσοστόμου = Io. Chrys., *Serm. in Gen.*, 2, 47-70; 2, 79-101; 2, 113-122

Ζ΄ Διατί τελευταῖος ὁ ἄνθρωπος;
Ζ΄] ϛ΄ Γ

20 Γρηγορίου τοῦ Θεολόγου = Greg. Naz., *Or.* 44, *PG* 36, 612, 9-18

21 Τοῦ Χρυσοστόμου = Io. Chrys., *Serm. in Gen.*, 2, 70-78

Η΄ Διατί διπλοῦς ὁ ἄνθρωπος;
Η΄] ζ΄ Γ

22 Τοῦ Χρυσοστόμου = Ps.-Io. Chrys., *Suff. tibi grat.*, *PG* 59, 508, 42 – 509, 19

Θ′ Ὅτι ὀργανικὸν κατεσκευάσθη τοῦ ἀνθρώπου τὸ σχῆμα πρὸς τὴν τοῦ λόγου χρείαν

Θ′] η′ Γ

    23 Γρηρορίου Νύσης = Greg. Nyss., *De hom. opif.*, p. 151, 12 - 152, 13 (= *PG* 44, 149, 23-39)

Ι′ Ὅτι ἐπιστημονικὸς τῆς τοῦ καλοῦ καὶ κακοῦ γνώσεως ὁ ἄνθρωπος

Ι′] θ′ Γ

    24 Τοῦ Χρυσοστόμου = Io. Chrys., *Serm. in Gen.*, 6, 49-66; 6, 77-83

    25 Κυρίλλου Ἀλεξανδρείας = Cyr. Alex., *Contra Iul.* 3, 23, 17-25 (Κυρίλλου Γ)

ΙΑ′ Ὅτι αὐτεξούσιος ὁ ἄνθρωπος

ΙΑ′] ι′ Γ

    26 Κλήμεντος Ῥώμης = *Sacr. Par.*, ed. HOLL, *Fragmente*, fr. 26 (Clem. Rom.); fr. 14 (Clem. Rom.); *T* and Γ omit the fragment.

    27 Κυρίλλου Ἱεροσολύμων = Cyr. Hier., *Cat. ad illum.*, 4, 21, 1-9

    28 Τοῦ αὐτοῦ = Cyr. Hier., *Cat. ad illum.*, 4, 18, 2-9

ΙΒ′ Περὶ φύσεως ἀνθρώπου λόγος κεφαλαιώδης

ΙΒ′] ια′ Γ

    29 Νεμεσίου ἐπισκόπου Ἐμέσης = Nem. Em., *De nat. hom.*, c. 1 (p. 1, 1 - 16, 6)

ΙΓ′ Περὶ τῆς ἐν παραδείσῳ διαγωγῆς Ἀδάμ

ΙΓ′] ιβ′ Γ

    30 Τοῦ Χρυσοστόμου. Ἐκ τῆς περὶ παρθένων βίβλου = Io. Chrys., *De uirg.*, 14, 31-44; 14, 52-67

    31 Τοῦ αὐτοῦ. Ἐκ τοῦ λόγου τοῦ εἰς τὸν πρωτόπλαστον = Ps.-Io. Chrys., *In Ps.* 92, *PG* 55, 615, 29 - 616, 5

ΙΔ′ Τί χρὴ λέγειν πρὸς τοὺς ἐπαποροῦντας, εἰ μετὰ τὴν ἁμαρτίαν ἡ παιδοποιΐα, πῶς ἂν ἐγένετο τὰ τῶν ἀνθρώπων πλήθη, εἰ ἀναμάρτητοι διέμειναν οἱ ἐξ ἀρχῆς;

ΙΔ′] ιγ′ Γ

    32 Γρηγορίου Νύσης = Greg. Nyss., *De hom. opif.*, p. 204, 11 - 205, 21 (= *PG* 44, 188, 28 - 189, 13)

TITLES AND ATTRIBUTIONS CXIII

33 Τοῦ Χρυσοστόμου = Io. Chrys., *De uirg.*, 14, 77-82; 14,
74-75; 15, 2-13; 17, 68-75

34 Ἀθανασίου = Ps-Athan., *Quaest. ad Ant.*, PG 28, 629,
30-36

**ΙΕ′ Τί τὸ τῆς ἁμαρτίας εἶδος; Καὶ ὅτι αὐτοπροαιρέτως
ἁμαρτάνομεν**

ΙΕ′] ιδ′ C (¹) Γ

35 Κυρίλλου Ἱεροσολύμων = Cyr. Hier., *Cat. ad illum.*, 2,
1, 1 – 3, 16; C omits the attribution.

ΙϚ′ Κατὰ πόσους τρόπους ἐξαμαρτάνει ὁ ἄνθρωπος;

ΙΕ′] ιε′ C Γ

36 Μαξίμου μοναχοῦ = Max. Conf., *Quaest. et dub.*, I, 5,
2-7 (p. 140)

37 Μαρκιανοῦ Βηθλεεμίτου = Marc. Bethl., *CPG* 3898. 1

ΙΖ′ Περὶ ἁμαρτίας ἐνθυμηθείσης καὶ μὴ τελεσθείσης

ΙΖ′] ιϚ′ C Γ

38 Ἐκ τῶν λειμώνων, cf. *Quaest. et resp. sen.*, qu. 19

ΙΗ′ Ὅτι οὐ κατὰ ἀστρολογίαν τὰ καθ᾽ἡμᾶς

ΙΗ′] ιζ′ C Γ (ιϚ′ C*a.corr.*)

39 Κυρίλλου Ἱεροσολύμων = Cyr. Hier., *Cat. ad illum.*, 4,
18, 9-17

40 Ἀθανασίου Ἀλεξανδρείας Βίβλος τῆς ἑρμηνείας τοῦ
κατὰ Ματθαῖον εὐαγγελίου – no source was found
(l. 3/5 = Athan., *Fragm. in Matth.*, PG 27, 1364, 15-18
[e *Flor. Coisl.*, ms. C]; cf. Athan., *Fragm. ined.*, II)

41 Τοῦ Χρυσοστόμου = Io. Chrys., *De perf. carit.*, PG 56,
282, 33 – 283, 6

**ΙΘ′ Περὶ τοῦ ἀστέρος τοῦ ἀνατείλαντος ἐπὶ τῆς Χριστοῦ
γεννήσεως**

ΙΘ′] ιη′ Γ (²)

42 Ἀθανασίου Ἀλεξανδρείας – no source was found (cf.
Athan., *Fragm. ined.*, I)

---

(1) C has given both this and the preceding chapter the same number,
namely ιδ′.

(2) C has ιθ′, as do *ATE*; there is no chapter numbered ιη′ in C.

CXIV TITLES AND ATTRIBUTIONS

Κ′ Περὶ ἀποταξαμένων καὶ πάλιν ἁμαρτανόντων
Κ′] ιθ′ Γ

43 Σολομῶντος = Prou. 26, 11; *T* omits the fragment.

44 Βασιλείου Καισαρείας = Bas. Caes., *In ebr.*, *PG* 31, 445, 5-9

45 Τοῦ Χρυσοστόμου = Io. Chrys., *In euang. dict.*, *PG* 64, 39, 58-62

ΚΑ′ Περὶ τῆς ἀστάτου τῶν ἀνθρωπίνων πραγμάτων καταστάσεως
ΚΑ′] κ′ Γ

46 Ἰώβ = Iob 1, 21; *C* omits the attribution.

47 Τοῦ Ἐκκλησιαστοῦ = Eccl. 1, 2; Is. 40, 6-7; Iac. 4, 14; Eccl. 1, 12ss.; Γ omits l. 14/38.

48 Γρηρορίου τοῦ Θεολόγου = Greg. Naz., *Or.* 7, 19, 1-9; *T* omits the fragment; Γ omits l. 7/9.

49 Βασιλείου Καισαρείας = Bas. Caes., *Hom. super Ps.*, *PG* 29, 221, 20-29; *T* omits the fragment.

50 Τοῦ Χρυσοστόμου = Ps.-Io. Chrys., *Ver. frustr. cont.*, *PG* 55, 559, 20-38; *T* omits the fragment.

51 Γρηγορίου τοῦ Θεολόγου = *Sacr. Par.*, *PG* 95, 1125, 3-5; *T* omits the fragment.

52 Νείλου μοναχοῦ = *Sacr. Par.*, *PG* 95, 1133, 44 – 1136, 2 (Nili Anc.); *T* omits the fragment; *CFH* omit the attribution.

53 Τοῦ Χρυσοστόμου = Io. Chrys., *In Eutrop.*, *PG* 52, 393, 12-18; Γ om. the fragment; *CEK* omit the attribution.

ΚΒ′ Περὶ ἀνθρώπων εὐημερούντων καὶ ταλαιπωρούντων, δικαίων καὶ ἁμαρτωλῶν
ΚΒ′] κα′ Γ

54 Τοῦ Χρυσοστόμου = Io. Chry., *De Laz.*, *PG* 48, 997, 51-54; 997, 61 – 998, 3; 998, 46-51; 1003, 59 – 1004, 6

55 Τοῦ αὐτοῦ = Io. Chrys., *De Laz.*, *PG* 48, 1003, 44-59; Δ omits the attribution.

56 Τοῦ αὐτοῦ = Io. Chrys., *De Laz.*, *PG* 48, 1030, 27-54; 1031, 31-32; 1031, 13-35

57 Τοῦ αὐτοῦ = Io. Chrys., *De Laz.*, *PG* 48, 1041, 9-18; 1041, 39 – 1044, 15; *C* omits the attribution.

TITLES AND ATTRIBUTIONS   CXV

ΚΓ′ Περὶ τῶν τεσσάρων ἀπαθειῶν

ΚΓ′] κβ′ Γ

> 58 Μαξίμου μοναχοῦ = Max. Conf., *Quaest. ad Thal.*, 55, 201-218
>
> 59 Ἄλλη θεωρία περὶ τῶν αὐτῶν = *Schol. in Max. Conf.*, 55, 157-169; Γ omits the fragment.

ΚΔ′ Περὶ τῶν τεσσάρων γενικῶν ἀρετῶν

ΚΔ′] κγ′ Γ

> 60 No attribution in *AT C* (τοῦ αὐτοῦ Γ) = Ps.-Max. Conf., *De quat. card. uirt.*; Γ omits l. 49/100.

ΚΕ′ Τίνες ἀρεταὶ ψυχῆς καὶ τίνες σώματος;

ΚΕ′] κδ′ Γ

> 61 Μαξίμου μοναχοῦ = Max. Conf., *Quaest. et dub.*, I, 1, 2-8 (p. 137) (τοῦ αὐτοῦ Γ)

ΚϚ′ Ἀπόδειξις ὅτι οὐδὲν ὄφελος μιᾶς ἀρετῆς, τῶν ἄλλων ἀπόντων

ΚϚ′] κε′ Γ

> 62 Νείλου μοναχοῦ – no source was found (ed. Nil. Anc., *De uirt.*); Γ omits l. 91/134.

ΚΖ′ Περὶ ἀγάπης καὶ πόσα τὰ τῆς ἀγάπης εἴδη

ΚΖ′] κϚ′ Γ

> 63 Κλήμεντος Στρωματέων = Clem. Alex., *Strom.*, 2, 19, 101, 3, 1 – 102, 1, 4
>
> 64 Εὐαγρίου = *Sacr. Par.*, PG 95, 1204, 11-15 (Euag.)
>
> 65 Τοῦ Χρυσοστόμου = Io. Chrys., *Exp. in Ps.*, PG 55, 160, 22 – 161, 14; 161, 26-27
>
> 66 Τοῦ αὐτοῦ = Io. Chrys., *De dec. mil. tal.*, PG 51, 17, 26-32; Γ omits the fragment; *C* omits the attribution.
>
> 67 Τοῦ αὐτοῦ = Io. Chrys., *Exp. in Ps.*, PG 55, 159, 20 – 160, 19

ΚΗ′ Περὶ ἀγαθοεργίας καὶ ὅτι οὐ δεῖ ἀποδιδόναι κακὸν ἀντὶ κακοῦ

T and Γ omit the chapter.

> 68 Παροιμιῶν = Prou. 25, 21-22; 24, 29; 20, 9c

69 Ἐκ τῆς πρὸς Ῥωμαίους Παύλου ἐπιστολῆς = Rom. 12, 17; 12, 21

70 Ἐκ τῆς Πέτρου ἐπιστολῆς = I Pet. 3, 9

71 Ἐκ τοῦ κατὰ Ἰωάννην = III Io. 11

72 Νείλου = *Sacr. Par.*, *PG* 95, 1169, 46-48 (Philonis)

ΚΘ′ Περὶ ἀποκαταστάσεως
ΚΘ′] κη′ *T*, κζ′ Γ

73 Μαξίμου μοναχοῦ = Max. Conf., *Quaest. et dub.*, 19, 5-21 = I, 13, 5-21 (p. 18)

Λ′ Πῶς νοητέον τὸ Πᾶν ἄρσεν διανοῖγον μήτραν;
Λ′] κθ′ *T*, κη′ Γ

74 Ἀμφιλοχίου = Amph., *In occ. dom.*, 49-81

75 Λεοντίου Δαμασκηνοῦ πρεσβυτέρου – no source was found (= Leont. Dam., fr. 1)

ΛΑ′ Περὶ τῆς ἀπογραφῆς τῆς γενομένης ἐπὶ Αὐγούστου Καίσαρος
ΛΑ′] λ′ *T*, κθ′ Γ

76 Τοῦ Χρυσοστόμου = Io. Chrys., *In diem nat.*, *PG* 49, 352, 43-47; 353, 19 – 354, 22; 353, 5-9; *C* omits the attribution.

ΛΒ′ Περὶ τῶν ἀκρίδων ὧν ἤσθιεν ὁ Βαπτιστής
ΛΒ′] λα′ *T*, λ′ Γ

77 Ἀθανασίου Ἀλεξανδρείας ἐκ τῆς ἑρμηνείας τοῦ κατὰ Ματθαῖον εὐαγγελίου – no source was found.

ΛΓ′ Περὶ τοῦ ῍Ισθι εὐνοῶν τῷ ἀντιδίκῳ σου
ΛΓ′] λβ′ *T*, λα′ Γ

78 Τοῦ Χρυσοστόμου = Ps.-Io. Chrys., *De paen.*, *PG* 59, 759, 29-36; 759, 57 – 760, 32; *C* omits the attribution.

ΛΔ′ Περὶ τοῦ μὴ ἀναθεματίζειν ἄνθρωπον πιστόν
ΛΔ′] λγ′ *T*, λβ′ Γ

79 Τοῦ Χρυσοστόμου. Λόγος οὗ ἡ ἀρχή· Πρώην περὶ ἀκαταλήπτου = Io. Chrys., *De anathem.*, *PG* 48, 946, 1-11; 947, 1-9; 948, 10 – 949, 47; Γ omits 79.57/65.

TITLES AND ATTRIBUTIONS CXVII

ΛΕ′ Περὶ ἀνδρῶν ἀσεβῶν καὶ περὶ αἱρετικῶν, ὅτι δεῖ χωρίζεσθαι ἀπ᾽ αὐτῶν

ΛΕ′] λδ′ *AT,* λγ′ Γ

80 Δαυΐδ = Ps. 1, 1; 25, 5; 36, 1-2

81 Παροιμιῶν = Prou. 1, 10; 1, 15-16; 4, 14-15; 22, 5

82 Ἡσαΐου = Is. 54, 14; Γ omits the fragment.

83 Σιράχ = Sir. 13, 1

84 Παύλου τοῦ ἀποστόλου. Ἐκ τῆς πρὸς Κορινθίους ἐπιστολῆς = I Cor. 5, 11; II Thes. 3, 6; Γ omits the attribution.

85 Τοῦ Χρυσοστόμου. Ἐκ τῆς ἑρμηνείας τῆς πρὸς Ἑβραίους = Io. Chrys., *In ep. ad Heb.*, *PG* 63, 231, 50-55; Ἐκ – Ἑβραίους] om. Γ

86 Τοῦ αὐτοῦ = Io. Chrys., *De pseudoproph.*, *PG* 59, 557, 70 – 558, 5; 559, 16-17; 563, 56-62; τοῦ χρυσοστόμου *C*; Γ omits the attribution.

87 Τοῦ ἁγίου Ἰγνατίου. Ἐκ τῆς πρὸς Σμυρναίους ἐπιστολῆς = Ignat., *Ad Smyrn.*, 4, 1, 2-5; Γ omits the fragment.

88 Τοῦ αὐτοῦ. Ἐκ τῆς πρὸς Ἐφεσίους ἐπιστολῆς = Ps.-Ignat., *Ad Philadelph.*, 3, 3 (p. 172, 13-17); ἰγνατίου τοῦ θεοφόρου Γ

89 Ἀθανασίου Ἀλεξανδρείας. Ἐκ τῆς πρὸς μονάζοντας ἐπιστολῆς = Athan., *Ep. ad mon.*, *PG* 26, 1188, 13-30; Γ omits the fragment.

90 Ἐκ τῶν Διατάξεων τῶν ἀποστόλων = *Const. apost.*, 6, 18, 8, 42-45

91 Βασιλείου Καισαρείας = Bas. Caes., *Asc. magn. breu.*, *PG* 31, 1165, 39-46 (= id., *Canon 96*, p. 198, 15 – 199, 1)

ΛϚ′ Πόσαι ἀρεταὶ τοῖς ἄρχουσιν πρέπουσιν;

ΛϚ′] λε′ *T,* λδ′ Γ

92 Ἀθανασίου = Ps.-Athan., *Quaest. ad Ant.*, *PG* 28, 673, 45 – 676, 6; *C* omits the attribution.

ΛΖ′ Περὶ τοῦ Ἅδου

ΛΖ′] λϚ′ *T,* λε′ Γ, *om. A*

93 Ἰωσήππου. Ἐκ τοῦ λόγου τοῦ ἐπιγεγραμμένου κατὰ Πλάτωνος περὶ τῆς τοῦ παντὸς αἰτίας = *Sacr. Par.*,

ed. Holl, *Fragmente*, fr. 353, l. 1-35 (Hippolytus, *De universo*) (= *Sacr. Par.*, *Par. Rupef.*, PG 96, 541, 25 – 544, 32)

94 Τοῦ Χρυσοστόμου = Io. Chrys., *De coem.*, PG 49, 395, 32-39

95 Λεοντίου Δαμασκηνοῦ – no source was found (= Leont. Dam., fr. 2)

ΛΗ′ Περὶ ὧν σέσωκεν ἐν Ἅδῃ Χριστὸς κατελθών

ΛΗ′] λς′ Γ, *om. T*

96 Ἐπιφανίου Κύπρου = Ps.-Epiph., *Hom. in diu.*, PG 43, 440, 53-54

97 Τοῦ ἀποστόλου Πέτρου Καθολικῆς ἐπιστολῆς ... Ἑρμηνεία Μαξίμου μοναχοῦ = Max. Conf., *Quaest. ad Thal.*, 7, 2-3; 7, 5-27; Τοῦ – ἐπιστολῆς] om. C

98 Ἀθανασίου Ἀλεξανδρείας. Ἐκ τῆς ἑρμηνείας τοῦ ψαλτηρίου = Athan., *Fragm. uar.*, PG 26, 1256, 17-18; 19-41; Ἐκ – ψαλτηρίου] om. Γ

99 Τοῦ Χρυσοστόμου = Io. Chrys., *De coem.*, PG 49, 395, 49 – 396, 2; C omits the attribution.

ΛΘ′ Περὶ τοῦ Ἀντιχρίστου

ΛΘ′] λη′ T, λζ′ Γ

100 Κυρίλλου Ἱεροσολύμων = Cyr. Hier., *Cat. ad illum.*, 15, 12, 1-19; C omits the attribution.

Μ′ Περὶ τῆς τριημέρου Χριστοῦ ἀναστάσεως

Μ′] λθ′ T, λη′ Γ

101 No attribution; no source found

102 Γρηγορίου Νύσης = Greg. Nyss., *De trid. spat.*, p. 287, 7 – 288, 6; p. 288, 13 – 289, 3; Γ omits the fragment.

ΜΑ′ Περὶ τοῦ Εὐχόμην ἐγὼ αὐτὸς ἀνάθεμα εἶναι

ΜΑ′] μ′ T, λθ′ Γ

103 Τοῦ ἀποστόλου πρὸς Ῥωμαίους ... Ἑρμηνεία τοῦ Χρυσοστόμου = Rom. 9, 1-5; Io. Chrys., *In ep. ad Rom.*, PG 60, 549, 1-24; Ἑρμηνεία – Χρυσοστόμου] om. Γ

CORRUPTIONS AND DUBIOUS READINGS

What follows is a list of the most important passages in which the archetype was possibly corrupt and which, therefore, require editorial intervention. In addition, the reader will find a selection of dubious cases in which the text has not been corrected, though it might have been. All passages with an editorial intervention of certain importance are preceded by an asterisk; dubious readings or trivial corruptions are not.

*1.31 [τῇ]
The article is deleted because it disrupts the syntax and because it cannot be defended on any ground; it is absent from the source.

*19.26 Μωϋσέως <ᾧ> πιστεύειν φασίν
All manuscripts but *T* omit ᾧ which is present in the source; μωϋσῆ *EK*, μωσέα *FH*.

*19.39/40 οὐκ εἶπεν ἀγγέλῳ καὶ ἀρχαγγέλῳ, ἀλλὰ δι'ἑαυτοῦ παρήγαγεν
The edition adopts ἀγγέλῳ καὶ ἀρχαγγέλῳ with *CDK*; ἀγγέλῳ ἢ ἀρχαγγέλῳ *FH*, ἀγγέλων καὶ ἀρχαγγέλων *AT E*. The archetype probably had the latter reading, and it might have been understood as οὐκ εἶπεν· «ἀγγέλων καὶ ἀρχαγγέλων» κτλ., which is of course rather harsh.

24.9 ἐφιέναι
The source has ἐπιέναι, which is the form that is clearly needed in this context; moreover, ἐφιέναι should be transitive, yet it governs a dative in this fragment. Nevertheless, since ἐφιέναι probably represents only a variation in pronunciation, much like δραχμῶν / δραγμῶν in 13.18, (¹) I have kept it.

26.7/8 Οὐ δυνατόν τινα ἀγαθὸν εἶναι βιαίως, εἰ μὴ κατὰ προαίρεσιν οἰκείαν αὐτεξούσιον

---

(1) Further examples in Noret, *Accentuation*, p. 115, n. 79: καθιδεῖν, ἐφελπίζειν, etc.

CXX   CORRUPTIONS AND DUBIOUS READINGS

The source has: Οὐ δυνατόν τινα ἀγαθὸν εἶναι βεβαίως, εἰ μὴ κατὰ προαίρεσιν οἰκείαν. The εἰ-clause in the FC is strange. Once βιαίως has been stated, it becomes superfluous or, rather, contradictory: it is obvious that if the person has free will, he does good not βιαίως, but out of his own free will.

*29.29 ἵνα τὴν ψυχὴν ἑαυτοὺς εἶναι πιστεύοντες Γ (DEFHQ), ἵνα τὴν ψυχὴν ἑαυτῆς εἶναι πιστεύοντες AT C
The edition adopts the reading of Γ (DEFHQ) and the source. The corruption was already in the archetype; nevertheless, since ἑαυτῆς makes no sense, the logical conjecture of Γ, ἑαυτούς, must be adopted.

*29.66 τοῖς αἰσθητικοῖς νεύροις
Here the edition adopts the reading of Q and the source. All other manuscripts have the untenable reading νοεροῖς.

*29.108/111 οὐδὲ τοῦτο ἀθρόως κατεσκεύασεν, ἀλλὰ πρότερον [ἃ] καὶ τοῖς ἄλλοις ζώοις φυσικὰς τινὰς συνέσεις ... ἐνέθηκεν
Following Q, the edition deletes the pronoun ἃ, which has no antecedent and disrupts the syntax.

*29.113/118 τὸν αὐτὸν δὲ τρόπον καὶ ἐπὶ τῆς φωνῆς ζητῶν, εὑρήσεις ἐξ ἁπλῆς καὶ μονοειδοῦς τῆς ἵππων καὶ βοῶν ἐκφωνήσεως κατὰ μέρος εἰς ποικίλην καὶ διάφορον προαχθῆναι τὴν τῶν κοράκων καὶ μιμηλῶν ὀρνέων φωνήν, ἕως εἰς τὴν ἔναρθρον καὶ τελείαν τὴν ἀνθρώπου κατέληξε
After μιμηλῶν ὀρνέων, most manuscripts have φωνήσεως (φρονήσεως S) instead of φωνήν, ἕως. E has tried to remedy the nonsense by adding ἀλλὰ μὴ ἐκ τῆς τούτων after ὀρνέων, which, however, leaves the τὴν before τῶν κοράκων without a noun. Almost certainly by conjecture, Q wrote φωνήν, ἕως, which is also the reading of the source. This is one of the most peculiar corruptions of Letter Alpha, and it shows the faithfulness of the scribes.

29.226/227 ἐν πᾶσι γὰρ ἢ πλείων ἢ ἐλάττων μοῖρα τοῦ πυρὸς ἐγκατέστραπται
ἐγκατέστραπται A CDH, ἐγκατέσπαρται T EQ and the source. The lectio difficilior ἐγκατέστραπται would not be impossible. As it is recorded, the verb ἐγκαταστρέφω means "zurückwerfen, hinabwerfen" (LBG), "return (a ball in a game)" (LSJ), but it could here be understood as "turn round inside something;"

CORRUPTIONS AND DUBIOUS READINGS CXXI

cf. the definition of Dimitrakos: "ἐντός τινος περιστρέφω." Of course, to our eyes ἐγκατέσπαρται makes better sense. Here it is certain that the archetype had ἐγκατέστραπται; the "corruption" is simple to explain: in reading it was easy to confuse -σπαρ- with -στραπ-. The correction is evident as well: *T EQ*, which are manuscripts that relatively often correct their exemplars, realised that ἐγκατέσπαρται was more adequate to the context. In this case all three manuscripts must have corrected the archetype into the reading of the source independently. Consequently, it is not significant that they and the source have the same reading.

29.241 ὄφισι
ὄφεσι in *EHQ* and the source is the usual dative plural of ὄφις, even if ὄφισι is attested in some grammatical works. ([2]) Since the variation is pretty trivial, there is no risk of misunderstanding and the reading of the archetype possibly reflected an actual pronunciation, the edition retains ὄφισι.

*29.263/264 εἰ γὰρ μὴ προσῆν ἡμῖν αἴσθησις, οὖτ'ἂν ἠλγοῦμεν, οὖτε θεραπείας ἐδεήθημεν μὴ ἀλγοῦντες
All of the manuscripts but *Q* have ὅταν instead of οὖτ'ἂν, which is also the reading of the source. The sense requires the reading of *Q* and the source, and the corruption is easy to explain.

*29.276/280 Δύο δὲ τούτων πρεσβείων ὁ ἄνθρωπος ἐξαιρέτων ἔτυχε – καὶ γὰρ μόνος οὖτος συγγνώμης τυγχάνει μετανοῶν, καὶ τὸ σῶμα τούτου μόνου θνητὸν ὂν ἀπαθανατίζεται –, καὶ τοῦ μὲν σωματικοῦ διὰ τὴν ψυχήν, τοῦ δὲ ψυχικοῦ διὰ τὸ σῶμα
This is a problematic passage. On the one hand, all manuscripts but *Q* have πρεσβειῶν instead of πρεσβείων, ([3]) but this is a relatively unimportant problem that will be dealt with presently. First let us consider the text of this passage as edited by Morani: δύο δὲ τούτων πρεσβείων ὁ ἄνθρωπος ἐξαιρέτων ἔτυχε· καὶ γὰρ μόνος οὖτος συγγνώμης τυγχάνει μετανοῶν καὶ τὸ σῶμα τούτου μόνου θνητὸν ὂν ἀπαθανατίζεται, καὶ τοῦ μὲν σωματικοῦ διὰ τὴν ψυχήν, τοῦ δὲ ψυχικοῦ διὰ τὸ σῶμα <τυγχάνει>. The dif-

---

(2) E.g. Theodosius Alexandrinus, *Canones isagogici de flexione nominum*, p. 11, 2.

(3) From πρεσβεῖον, "gift of honour," though πρεσβεία, meaning "rank, dignity," would in principle be acceptable. I give my reasons for correcting it below.

CXXII   CORRUPTIONS AND DUBIOUS READINGS

ferences between the text of this passage in the edition of Morani and in the present edition are, on the one hand, the punctuation, and on the other, the added τυγχάνει. Both are closely related, as we will see. Morani thought that the constructions τοῦ μὲν σωματικοῦ ... τοῦ δὲ ψυχικοῦ lacked a verb. The copyist of one of the manuscripts of the *FC*, namely *E*, understood the passage in the same way and also added a τυγχάνει (after τὴν ψυχήν). Yet their conjectures stem from a misunderstanding. The statement καὶ γὰρ μόνος οὗτος συγγνώμης τυγχάνει μετανοῶν καὶ τὸ σῶμα τούτου μόνου θνητὸν ὂν ἀπαθανατίζεται is a parenthetical construction, and therefore the phrase καὶ τοῦ μὲν σωματικοῦ διὰ τὴν ψυχήν, τοῦ δὲ ψυχικοῦ διὰ τὸ σῶμα does not lack a verb, for it is governed by the earlier ἔτυχε (l. 277). (⁴) Incidentally, this understanding of the passage also shows that σωματικοῦ and ψυχικοῦ are neuters closely related to πρεσβείων (l. 276), which consequently cannot be the feminine πρεσβειῶν, but indeed the neuter πρεσβείων.

*29.306/309 Δῆλον οὖν ἐκ τούτων <ὡς οἱ> τὴν μετάνοιαν <μὴ> δεχόμενοι τὴν ἐξαίρετον δωρεὰν καὶ τὴν ἰδίαν ἀνθρώπου περιγράφουσιν

The edition follows *EQ* and the source in correcting the ὅσοι of the rest of the manuscripts. This kind of easy corruption (⁵) has generated an unwanted relative sentence. To avoid it, *C* corrects ὅσοι τὴν μετάνοιαν δεχόμενοι, which is the reading of the archetype, to ὅσοι τὴν μετάνοιαν δεχόμεθα, which is difficult to coordinate with the following verb in the third person. A second corruption is no less serious from a semantic point of view: before δεχόμενοι, *E* has μή while the source has οὐ. A negative particle is indispensable for a correct understanding of the sentence. Nemesius is saying that those who do not admit to the possibility of repentance are depriving people of their most valuable gift; if the

---

(4) Furthermore, supplying a τυγχάνει in the text would mean correcting not only the archetype of the *FC*, but also the autograph of its compiler; cf. Fernández, *Remarks*, p. 173-175.

(5) This very corruption also appears elsewhere, for instance in the manuscript *V* (f. 278), where Provataris writes, with his exemplar, δῆλον δὲ ὅσοι ὑπερέχοντες κτλ. but adds in the margin that the source reads ὡς οἱ ὑπερέχοντες (Io. Dam., *Exp. fid.*, 17, 50-51).

CORRUPTIONS AND DUBIOUS READINGS   CXXIII

"not" were suppressed, the idea would plainly become contradictory within the context.

29.365/368 καὶ αὐτὰ δὲ ταῦτα τὰ σαρκοφάγα τροφὴν ποιεῖται τῶν ζώων τὰ τὴν γῆν νεμόμενα, ὡς λύκοι μὲν καὶ λέοντες, καὶ ἄρνας καὶ αἶγας καὶ σῦς καὶ ἐλάφους
The short recension Γ (*DEFHQ*) and the source omit the καί before ἄρνας, thereby making clearer that what follows is the direct object. Since, however, the presence of καί is not problematic, it has been retained in the edition.

29.403/405 Εἰ τοίνυν ὡς ἐν εἰκόνι τῷ ἀνθρώπῳ καὶ τὰ τῶν ἔξωθεν ἐσοπτρίσθημεν, ἐξ αὐτῆς ἂν ἴωμεν τῆς τῶν ζητουμένων οὐσίας τὰς ἀποδείξεις ποιούμενοι
This is one of the more peculiar corruptions in Letter Alpha, showing among other things that optative was becoming less frequent. In the source, there was a perfectly regular conditional period, with ἐσοπτρισθείημεν instead of ἐσοπτρίσθημεν and εἴημεν instead of ἴωμεν. As it stands, ἐσοπτρίσθημεν seems to be an indicative aorist without an augment (*E* actually added the augment, changing the verb to ἐνωπτρίσθημεν), but it might be understood as some kind of optative or a subjunctive (*Q* corrected the verb to ἐσοπτρισθῶμεν). On the other hand, even though ἴωμεν is a subjunctive, it must have been taken to have the same meaning as an optative. *Q* actually corrected it to εἴημεν, which is the reading of the source. The optative of εἶμι sounded just like that of εἰμί, and ἴοιμεν (very rare) like εἴημεν. The subjunctive was ἴωμεν against ὦμεν. One of them was likely to substitute the other, taking, however, a form of the subjunctive which was fairly common and would thus have been familiar to any reader. The meaning of the sentence, however approximately, was surely grasped by the scribes: εἰμί was needed, not εἶμι, and the scribes certainly knew that much. Most likely, ἴωμεν was felt to be some kind of optative form of εἰμί.

*29.422/425 ἰστέον ὡς προηγουμένως τῶν δι᾽ὑπηρεσίαν γενομένων καὶ τὰ ἄλλα πάντα <τὰ ἐνδεχόμενα κατεσκεύασται, ἵνα μηδὲν ἐλλείπῃ τῇ κτίσει τῶν> ἐνδεχομένων γενέσθαι
All manuscripts omit τά ... τῶν. Indicating a lacuna or placing a *crux* would also have been a valid solution. In order to make the

CXXIV   CORRUPTIONS AND DUBIOUS READINGS

task of the reader a little easier, I have chosen to supplement the text of the *FC* with the bracketed words from the source.

32.1/2 Ἀντιλεγόντων ποτὲ τῶν Σαδδουκαίων τῷ κατὰ τὴν ἀνάστασιν λόγῳ
This is the reading of Γ; *A C* have τοῦ ... λόγῳ, whereas *T* has τοῦ ... λόγου. The archetype obviously had the reading of *A C* while *T*, trying to remedy the discordance between the article and the noun, adapted the latter to the case of the former. The scribe of Γ, in turn, found the good reading by noticing that ἀντιλέγω usually governs the dative.

*32.4/5 τίνος μετὰ τὴν ἀνάστασιν ἔσται πυνθανομένων
The edition adopts ἔσται with *FHQ* and the source; *C* has ἐστί, *D* ἔστι, *AT E* ἔσεσθαι. This last reading may have been the reading of the archetype, yet in an indirect interrogative clause such as this, the future indicative must be preferred.

*32.12/13 <εἰς> τὸ ἀρχαῖον ... ἀποκατάστασιν
The preposition is only present in *EQ* and the source, yet ἀποκατάστασις is usually construed with εἰς (or πρὸς) τὸ ἀρχαῖον. Cf. l. 19 of this same fragment: πρὸς τὸ ἀρχαῖον ... ἐπάνοδος.

*32.25/28 Ἀλλ'ὅστις ἐστὶν [ἐν τῷ πλήθει], ἐν τῇ φύσει τῶν ἀγγέλων τοῦ πλεονασμοῦ τρόπος ἄρρητός τε καὶ ἀπερινόητος στοχασμοῖς ἀνθρωπίνοις, πλὴν ἀλλὰ καὶ πιστός ἐστιν
The text of the source is clear: Ἀλλ'ὅστις ἐστὶν ἐν τῇ φύσει τῶν ἀγγέλων τοῦ πλεονασμοῦ τρόπος, ἄρρητος μὲν καὶ ἀνεπινόητος στοχασμοῖς ἀνθρωπίνοις, πλὴν ἀλλὰ πάντως ἐστίν. As it stands, ἐν τῷ πλήθει is very problematic. The whole passage could possibly be understood as, "whatever is the way of procreating among the multitude of angels, in angelical nature." Nevertheless, the addition of ἐν τῷ πλήθει, uncoordinated with the following ἐν-clause, disrupts the understanding of the sentence and is very likely a dittography; any copyist could have rightly copied the ἐν and then have mistakenly thought of πλῆθος, which was present in the context (cf. πληθυσμόν one line above; note that the ending of πλήθει and φύσει is the same), and directly afterwards have added the correct ἐν τῇ φύσει. There is yet another difficulty in this passage: surely considering that the clause πλὴν ... ἐστίν made no sense, *E* has omitted it. If πιστός, however, is understood in

CORRUPTIONS AND DUBIOUS READINGS   CXXV

the sense of "trustworthy" (ἄξιος πίστεως Dimitrakos, s.u., 7),
the clause could mean: "but it is surely trustworthy [the way of
angelic procreation]," i.e., we can be sure that it exists.

33.4/6 οὐκοῦν πολλῷ μᾶλλον ἀνθρώπους ἂν ἐποίησε γάμου
χωρίς, ὥσπερ οὖν καὶ ἐποίησε τοὺς πρώτους χωρίς
The whole sentence could be taken as a question, and the meaning is at any rate clear. Be that as it may, the final χωρίς, with
γάμου understood, is unnecessary. Should it be deleted?

33.10 ὁ τοῦ θεοῦ λόγος ὁ τὴν ἀρχὴν εἰπών
The source has παρὰ τὴν ἀρχήν, but the accusative alone is also
possible. See 35.51, μὴ ῥαθυμήσας τὴν ἀρχήν.

*42.15 μελαμπέπλου
This is the reading of E, which seems to be the best option,
though it is obviously a conjecture of the scribe; μελαμπέλου AT
CFH, μέλαν πέλαου *(sic)* D.

*42.18 παραμυθούμενον
An accusative masculine is needed, but AT DFH have the nominative παραμυθούμενος. The edition follows the reading of CE.

*42.19 ποδηγοῦντα ἐσκοτισμένα ἔθνη TH, ποδηγοῦντα τὰ EF,
ποδηγοῦν τὰ A CD
Since a masculine accusative is needed, the reading of A CD is
hardly acceptable. However, ποδηγοῦντα τά is more likely to derive from ποδηγοῦντα than conversely, and ποδηγοῦντα explains
much more satisfactorily than ποδηγοῦντα τά why some manuscripts have ποδηγοῦν τά.

*50.13 Πλὴν μάτην <ταράσσεται> πᾶς ἄνθρωπος ζῶν
"But in vain is every living person disturbed."

60.12/14 ὡς ἂν τύχοι· ἡ ἔχις χαρακτηρίζει τῇ σμυραίνῃ
συμπλεκομένη, ἑτερογενὴς οὖσα
There are two ways to improve this passage: either to turn ὡς
into οὕς (cf. οὕς added by E after τύχοι) or χαρακτηρίζει into
χαρακτηρίζειν. In both cases the raised dot after τύχοι would
be eliminated. As the text stands, the syntax is very harsh. The
original excerpt, however, does not seem to have had the highest
grammatical standards, so the present edition ventures no improvements.

CXXVI   CORRUPTIONS AND DUBIOUS READINGS

60.68/70 Τὸ δ'αὐτὸ καὶ περὶ τῆς ἀνδρείας καὶ τῶν ἄλλων ἡμῖν ἀρετῶν γενήσεται μικτόν· ὑφ'ᾗ μὲν ἐπαιρόμενοι κριὸς πρὸς κριὸν κερατίζοντες
The previous editors of this fragment suspect both a lacuna after μικτόν and that the antecedent of ᾗ is a word such as θρασύτης. These suspicions are of course possible. The antecedent, however, could also be ἀνδρεία, in which case the ram could be understood as a model of courage when facing another ram. For the concept of θρασύτης, the fragment offers the lion (l. 71) as an example.

60.97/98 Τὰ μὲν οὖν ὅσα δεξιὰ νομιζόμενα φύγωμεν, ὁδῷ δὲ μᾶλλον βασιλικῇ πορευθῶμεν. The editors of the fragment supply <καὶ ὅσα εὐώνυμα> after δεξιά. Cf. Num. 20, 17: ὁδῷ βασιλικῇ πορευσόμεθα, οὐκ ἐκκλινοῦμεν δεξιὰ οὐδὲ εὐώνυμα. The notion that extremes ought to be avoided is clearly enough the import of this statement. Yet since the sentence of the archetype of the FC is not entirely incomprehensible – the idea that we must reject what leans too much to the right ([6]) might imply that the opposite extreme must be equally rejected, – I have not supplied <καὶ ὅσα εὐώνυμα>, although I am well aware that the text would be more natural with the suppletion.

62.5/6 καθάπερ αἱ περιτταὶ ἐπιφύσεις, οἷον ἀκροχορδόνες καὶ χημοί] χυμοὶ T, χῆμοι CFHQ
The word χυμοί is widely attested and could mean here, where context calls for something answering to an excrescence (ἐπίφυσις), the "suppuration d'une blessure" (Bailly). In addition, the corruption of υ into η was very common at the time of the compilation of the FC (9th-10th). Although certainly a conjecture on the part of the scribe of T, χυμοί is a possible reading. The archetype, however, had χημός. This word is not attested, but χήμωσις is "an affection of the eye, when the cornea swells like a cockle-shell (χήμη) so as to impede sight" (LSJ). ([7]) Michael

---

(6) This is the case even if τὰ δεξιά is to be taken as the virtues, as Basile Markesinis has pointed out to me. The sentence would then mean that we must reject even what we consider (νομιζόμενα) to be an excess of virtue: whereas excessive ἀνδρεία would still be considered a virtue by some, it really would fall into the category of θρασύτης. On much stronger grounds, then, it would be understood that vice too must be rejected.

(7) DIMITRAKOS adds that, in modern use, χήμωσις is a φλεγμονώδης ἐξοίδησις τοῦ ἐπιπεφυκότος τοῦ βολβοῦ τοῦ ὀφθαλμοῦ (my italics), and that the χημοί of the fragment must also be some kind of ἐπίφυσις (l. 5).

CORRUPTIONS AND DUBIOUS READINGS CXXVII

Psellos has the variant χήμων: Χήμων δέ ἐστι τῶν βλεφάρων ἡ τάσις, / ὡς μὴ καλύπτειν τοὺς κύκλους τῶν ὀμμάτων. (8) It is possible, then, that χημός / χῆμος (9) also refers to a condition of the eyes. The edition therefore retains, though not without hesitation, χημοί, the reading of the archetype.

62.17 δεθέντα χειρῶν καὶ ποδῶν] δεθέντων χειρῶν καὶ ποδῶν FH, δεθέντα χεῖρας καὶ πόδας Q
Δέω (tie, bind) is only rarely attested with the genitive; yet the combination definitely existed and, moreover, it usually concerns this very passage (Mt. 22, 13): δεθεὶς ποδῶν καὶ χειρῶν and δεθέντες χειρῶν καὶ ποδῶν. (10) It is therefore unnecessary to correct δεθέντα into δεθέντων (with FH), or χειρῶν καὶ ποδῶν into χεῖρας καὶ πόδας (with Q).

62.23/24 ὅταν ἐμποδίζῃ τὸ σκανδαλίζον τῇ κτήσει τῆς ἀρετῆς
T FHQ have κτήσει, A CDE κτίσει, and no source was found. Mistakes of itacism are very common in A and D. Since the reading of T FHQ fits the context better, it has been retained in this edition.

*62.79/81 Τί μοι πλῆθος τῶν θυσιῶν ὑμῶν; <Πλήρης εἰμὶ> ὁλοκαυτωμάτων κριῶν καὶ αἷμα τράγων καὶ ταύρων οὐ βούλομαι. The edition supplies several words from the source text. The only other possibility would have been a crux.

62.118/120 τί ὄφελος ἐγκρατείας προσάγειν κάρπωσιν, ἀνθρωπαρεσκείας πάθει λελωβημένην
T has ἀνθρωπαρεσκίας πάθει, A ἀνθρωπαρεσκίας πάθος, and C ἀνθρωπαρεσκεία (dative) παθῶν. It is impossible to determine stemmatically which of the two branches had the right reading. Since the reading of T makes better sense ("affected by vain-glory"), it has been adopted here.

62.121/125 Ποῖον δὲ θυμίαμα προσευχῆς, ὅταν ὀργῆς καὶ μνησικακίας λογισμὸς τὴν ταύτης εὐωδίαν εἰς ῥυπαρὰν μεταβάλωσιν δυσωδίαν, καὶ γίνονται κατὰ τὴν παροιμίαν πίθος τετριμ-

---

(8) *Poemata* 9, 869-870.
(9) The word χῆμος is listed without further indication in KRETSCHMER, *Wörterbuch*, p. 432.
(10) Orig., *Comm. in Mt.*, 17, 16, 95 and Bas., *in Is.*, 5, 170, 11-12.

CXXVIII CORRUPTIONS AND DUBIOUS READINGS

μένος, τοὺς μισθοὺς μετὰ τῶν πόνων ἐγκαταλιμπάνουσαι; The subject of γίνονται, shown to be feminine by ἐγκαταλιμπάνουσαι, is αἱ ἀρεταί, previously mentioned at l. 115. The subject of μεταβάλωσιν seems at first sight more elusive, at least for a reader who is looking for strict syntactical correspondences. Indeed, the subject cannot be the virtues because they are not responsible for transforming the pleasant smell into a foul one, but rather the λογισμοί. This latter term, however, is singular (λογισμός) in the manuscripts. The verb might agree *ad sensum* with ὀργῆς καὶ μνησικακίας. The subject may also be understood to be ὀργῆς (λογισμὸς) καὶ μνησικακίας λογισμός.

65.27/28 τῷ φίλτρῳ τρωθεὶς τούτῳ, καὶ τῆς δόξης ἐκείνης
The source has ἐρῶν after ἐκείνης. The reading of the source is of course easier to follow, but the genitive could be governed by φίλτρῳ (understand: καὶ τῷ φίλτρῳ τῆς δόξης ἐκείνης). Since the manuscript tradition of the *FC* is practically unanimous, and its reading is not incomprehensible, it has been retained here.

73.9/11 Δεῖ γὰρ ὥσπερ τὴν ὅλην φύσιν ἐν τῇ ἀναστάσει τὴν τῆς σαρκὸς ἀφθαρσίαν χρόνῳ ἐλπιζομένων ἀπολαβεῖν
A CD have ἐλπιζομένων, which is very likely to be the reading of the archetype, while *FH* have the conjecture ἐλπιζομένῳ (together with the source), and *T EKQ* ἐλπιζομένην (together with some witnesses of the source). Since the reading of *A CD* is not impossible *qua* meaning or syntax, it has been retained in the present edition. Indeed, the genitive ἐλπιζομένων could refer to something like ἀγαθῶν, which in this context would yield the meaning, "the time of the good things we hope to attain."

73.12 παραστάσει] παρατάσει *Q*
The latter reading ("extension, continuation") makes better sense in the context, but παραστάσει ("assistance") is not absurd.

74.4 ἀφθάρτως *AT*, ἀφράστως Δ (*DEFH*)
The confusion between these two words is so common that no conclusive decision may be taken.

*76.32/33 κατὰ τὴν ἄνωθεν περὶ αὐτοῦ προφητείαν εἰρημένην ὅτι <οὐκ> ἐκ Ναζαρὲτ ἥξει
I have supplied οὐκ with *FH* and the source, because the whole fragment is about the Messiah *not* coming from Nazareth.

CORRUPTIONS AND DUBIOUS READINGS CXXIX

78.8/9 Ὅμως οὐ δοκεῖ μοι μόνον περὶ χρημάτων ὁ λόγος ἔχειν. Τί τὸ αἴτιον;
This is the punctuation of *AT*. The rest of the manuscripts have: ... ὁ λόγος ἔχειν τί τὸ αἴτιον. In the latter case, τί is indefinite and τί τὸ αἴτιον means "a certain cause," "any cause." Yet another possibility: οὐ δοκεῖ μοι μόνον περὶ χρημάτων ὁ λόγος ἔχειν τί· τὸ αἴτιον ("the speech does not seem to deal with money alone; the cause...") On the other hand, with the punctuation of *AT*, τί becomes interrogative and ἔχω intransitive, governing περὶ χρημάτων and meaning "to be." See *LSJ*, ἔχω B.II, with examples of intransitive ἔχω governing a prepositional complement, including Hdt., 3, 128, περὶ πολλῶν ἔχοντα ([11]) πρηγμάτων. Additionally, since τὸ αἴτιον regularly appears in Chrysostom with questions that have the interrogative τί, the punctuation of *AT* has been preferred.

78.16/18 Οὐ δέδοικε καὶ γραμματείων κλοπήν, καὶ μαρτύρων διαφθοράν, καὶ τὰς <κατὰ τὰς> λεωφόρους ἐπιβουλάς
The source has τὰς κατὰ τὰς λεωφόρους, as would be expected, and *E* conjectures ἐκ τῆς λεωφόρου instead of λεωφόρους. At that time, λεωφόρος was regularly perceived as a noun, despite originally being an adjective (cf. πλατεῖα, which, despite being an adjective, is usually utilized alone, with ὁδός understood ([12])). As is often the case, it is impossible to tell whether this "error" derives from or antedates the archetype.

79.32/35 Τί οὖν τῆς τοσαύτης ἐπελάβου ἀξίας, ἧς τὸ κοινὸν μόνον τῶν ἀποστόλων ἠξίωτο, καὶ οἱ κατὰ πᾶσαν ἀκρίβειαν τούτων ὡς ἀληθῶς γεγονότες διάδοχοι πλήρεις χάριτος καὶ δυνάμεως
AT C have οἳ καὶ after ἠξίωτο. The edition adopts καὶ οἱ with Γ (*DEFHK*) and the source.

81.7 Τρίβολοι καὶ παγίδες ἐν ὁδοῖς σκολιαῖς
All manuscripts have τρίβοι instead of τρίβολοι. In the present edition, the text has been corrected following the source. In conjunction with παγίδες, a reference to "caltrops" can be more

---

(11) Different conjectures have been offered to correct the ἔχοντα of the manuscripts.
(12) Cf. *LSJ* s.u. πλατύς, II.

CXXX   CORRUPTIONS AND DUBIOUS READINGS

easily explained than one to "paths," and the occurrence of ὁδοῖς
shortly afterward also points toward the necessity of the emendation. What would "paths and traps in winding roads" mean?

94.2/3 ἀλλ'ὁραθῆναι πολλάκις δύνανται
The edition adopts ὁραθῆναι with *DEFHR* and the source. The
manuscript *A* has ὁράθη and *T* ὡράθη, both of them impossible;
for its part *C* has ὁρᾶσθαι, which can easily be explained as an
innovation based on the reading of either *A* or *T*, which must in
turn be the reading of the archetype.

96.1/2 Τί οὖν; Πάντας ἁπλῶς ἐν Ἅδῃ σώζει Χριστὸς κατελθών;
Οὔμενουν, ἀλλὰ κἀκεῖ πιστεύσαντας
The manuscripts *T DEFHR* and the source have τοὺς before
πιστεύσαντας, as would be expected in regular Greek. The manuscripts *A C* omit the article; this is the *lectio difficilior*. The article is not absolutely necessary, and the reading of *T DEFH* is
most likely a conjecture.

97.22/24 κατὰ τὸν Ἅδην ὄντες, τῆς θεογνωσίας τὸ κήρυγμα,
διὰ τὸ καὶ νεκροὺς σῶσαι κατελθόντος εἰς Ἅδην τοῦ σωτῆρος
πιστεύσαντας
The source and *EH* have πιστεύσαντες, which would agree with
ὄντες and should therefore be preceded by a comma. In the reading of the archetype of the *FC*, by contrast, πιστεύσαντας agrees
with νεκρούς. Since both possibilities are acceptable, the reading
of the archetype of the *FC* has been retained here.

*102.33/35 Εἶτα ἡ πρὸ τοῦ σαββάτου <νὺξ καὶ μετὰ ταύτην ἡ
τοῦ σαββάτου> ἡμέρα, ἔχεις τὰς τρεῖς νύκτας καὶ τὰς τρεῖς
ἡμέρας
The present edition supplies νὺξ – σαββάτου on the authority of
the source. As for ἔχεις, *A* has ἔχει and *T C* εἰς. A *saut du même
au même* has made the text incomprehensible. Indeed, what follows (ἔχεις τὰς τρεῖς νύκτας καὶ τὰς τρεῖς ἡμέρας) is no longer
true, if νὺξ – σαββάτου is not present: we would not have three
nights and three days, but only *two* nights and three days. If the
omission *per homoeoteleuton* is kept, the passage does not make
sense for various other reasons which the interested reader will remark at once. In particular, the combination ἡ πρὸ τοῦ σαββάτου
ἡμέρα is exceedingly infelicitous, because the day before *Shabbat*,

CORRUPTIONS AND DUBIOUS READINGS   CXXXI

that is, the time between sunrise and sunset on Friday, has already been accounted for in the previous lines. Both *T* and *C* tried to ameliorate the nonsense by correcting ἔχεις (or ἔχει?) to εἰς, yet either ἔχεις or ἔχει was present in the archetype, as proven by the presence of the latter in *A*.

103.34/35 Εἰ δὲ θορυβεῖ σε ἅτε ἀσθενέστερον ὄντα ταῦτα λεγόμενα
Adopted here is the reading θορυβεῖ σε on the authority of the source and Γ (*DEFHK*); *AT C* have θορυβῆσαι, which must have been the reading of the archetype of the *FC*.

*103.40/42 καὶ πολλὰ ἄτοπα ὁ μὴ τοῦτον τηρῶν τὸν κανόνα ὑποπτεύσειε
This is the reading of *EK* and the source, which has been retained in this edition; the rest of the manuscripts have the impossible plural ὑποπτεύσοιεν.

*103.59 δόξαι
This is the reading of *EK* and the source. All other manuscripts have δόξαν. The infinitive is needed, whereas the accusative makes no sense.

RATIO EDENDI

By and large, this edition follows the general rules of the *CCSG*, including, wherever possible, a strict adherence to the readings of the manuscripts, even when they contradict the usual grammatical rules.

Since in many fragments, especially those for which a source could not be found, it remains impossible to know which parts of the text originate with the compiler and which do not, the text of all fragments has been printed in bold. The number of each fragment preserved only or predominantly in the *FC* is preceded by an asterisk.

I. APPARATUSES

1. *Apparatus fontium*

As a rule, in this apparatus only the direct sources of the *FC* are indicated. There are, however, a number of exceptions. The most conspicuous is that of biblical citations, which are always indicated. In cases where the source of the source might be relevant, it has been indicated. For example, in excerpt 12, which is attributed to Ps.-Dionysius in the *FC*, the immediate source is actually John of Damascus, but since John was himself quoting Ps.-Dionysius, a reference to the latter has been provided in the *apparatus fontium*. Wherever no direct source has been found, all identified sources are indicated. If more than one critical edition is available, all of them are consulted and all relevant variant readings indicated.

2. *Apparatus siglorum*

The sigla of all available manuscripts are indicated for each fragment. Omissions within the same fragment are indicated in this apparatus only when they are substantially long.

3. *Apparatus criticus*

The apparatus is negative in the vast majority of the cases. However, when an emendation is made, the reading of all the

RATIO EDENDI

manuscripts is indicated, including those – if they exist – which have the same reading as the text. Emendations are introduced by *scripsi*, deletions by *seclusi*.

If a *uaria lectio* would alter the accentuation of the text in an obvious way, this has not been indicated. For instance, if the text has ἄνθρωπός τις and a given manuscript – say, *A* – omits τις, only "τις] om. *A*" is indicated, and not, as would be more precise: "ἄνθρωπός τις] ἄνθρωπος *A*". The same is true for the apparatus of comparison with the sources. If the *FC* has Ὅπερ οὖν ἐστι νόσος (56.3), whereas in the source οὖν is not present, the apparatus simply reports "οὖν non hab. Chrys.," even though, as can easily be surmised, the source has ἐστὶ with an accent.

If the same word appears more than once on the same line, but with a different accent (for example: χορὸς περὶ αὐτόν; Αὐτὸν θρήνει ... in 56.21), no indication is given as to which instance of the word is meant (thus αὐτόν and not αὐτόν¹, αὐτὸν and not αὐτὸν²).

4. *Traditio directa*

Unimportant typos in the text of the sources are tacitly corrected, e.g., μάκρον instead of μακρόν in Cyr. Hier., *Cat. illum.* 2, 3, 6 (*FC* 35.42). Minor differences concerning orthography or enclitics are as a rule not recorded. Consequently, no indication is given that the source has κατ'εὐθύ instead of κατευθύ (5.219); διὰ τοῦτο instead of διατοῦτο, *passim*; τις instead of τίς (indefinite), *passim*; οὐκ ἔτι instead of οὐκέτι (78.39); movable -ν, or final -ς in οὕτω / οὕτως (e.g. 79.37); etc.

When the *FC* omits words contained in the source, the comparative apparatus marks the alteration in the following way: "*post* X] Y *hab*. Chrys.," and not "X] Y *add*. Chrys." This formulation may seem clumsier, and it is less concise, but it has the advantage of not suggesting that it is the quoted author who is at fault.

5. *Traditio indirecta*

Information about other florilegia is given here. If, as in 50.7/12, the *Sacr. Par.* quotes a fragment or part of that fragment more than once, an indication will be given in the comparative apparatus if and only if there is a textual difference between the instances of citation.

CXXXIV　　　　*RATIO EDENDI*

II. Grammar and Orthography

1. Specific words

- γεμήν in one word, if γε is not enclitic: e.g., at 18.13 only
  T has σῶμά γε μήν, while the other manuscripts have σῶμα
  γεμήν (or γε μήν). [13]
- κατευθύ, 5.219.
- ἐπίσης, e.g., at 62.12/13.
- διατί, e.g., in the titles of chapters Ζ' and Η'.
- διατοῦτο, *passim*. [14] This is a special case. In this edition, the expression is written as one word when it fulfils
  the grammatical function of a connective particle, similar
  in meaning and use to ὅθεν or to *quare*. When the expression preserves its full anaphorical force, however, it is written as two words. Examples: 41.24/25 Ἐπειδὴ δὲ ἴσμεν ὅτι
  οὐκ ἔστιν ἀνάγκης, διὰ τοῦτο οὐ συγγινώσκομεν (τοῦτο =
  what we know, ἴσμεν); 54.9/11: διὰ τοῦτο μᾶλλον θρήνησον,
  ὅτι νοσήματι κατεχόμενος καὶ σηπεδόνι χαλεπωτάτῃ, τὴν
  ἀρρωστίαν ἐπιτείνει (τοῦτο refers to the following ὅτι-
  clause); 56.38/39 οὐ διὰ τοῦτο μόνον ὅτι βελτίων γίνεται,
  ἀλλ'ὅτι πολλὰ τῶν ἁμαρτημάτων αὐτοῦ (τοῦτο refers to
  the ὅτι-clauses). This distinction has been kept even when
  διατοῦτο and διὰ τοῦτο are so close that there seems to
  be an inconsistency. See for example 57.58/65: Οὕτως
  οὖν κἂν δίκαιος τίς ἐστι καὶ πάσχει τί δεινόν, διὰ τοῦτο
  ἀπολαμβάνει ὧδε ... διὰ τοῦτο ἀπολαμβάνει ἐνταῦθα
  εὐημερίας, ἵνα μὴ ἐκεῖ ἀπαιτήσῃ τὸν μισθόν. Διατοῦτο καὶ
  Ἀβραάμ, ἐπειδὴ συνέβαινε καὶ τὸν Λάζαρον ἔχειν τινὰς
  ἁμαρτίας κτλ. Although the distinction between διατοῦτο
  and διὰ τοῦτο is often observed in the manuscripts, divergences are not recorded in the apparatus.

---

(13) Noret, *Accentuation*, p. 122. The modest title of Noret's contribu-
tion should not deceive the interested reader. Besides offering an account of
Byzantine accentuation, the article tackles a number of other orthographical
matters.

(14) For this word, ἐπίσης, and many others, see Noret, *Accentuation*,
p. 113, n. 70.

RATIO EDENDI   CXXXV

– μὴ δέ is written as two words when it so appears in the manuscripts, e.g., at 29.354. ([15])
– οὐχ’ is written with an apostrophe, following the manuscripts, which usually do not have simply οὐχ. ([16])

2. Differences in accentuation

Differences in accentuation are recorded wherever they could
be significant:
  – 16.5 μίξις *codd.*] μῖξις editor of Gregory of Nazianzus.
  – 29.22 κομιδή *scripsi cum codd.* Only *DE* have κομιδῆ.
    This use has already been recorded by, among others, M.
    Hostens, ([17]) who remarks that in the manuscript he edited
    "l'adverbe κομιδῆ est toujours écrit κομιδή." Since there is
    only one appearance of the word κομιδή in Letter Alpha
    of the *FC*, it is impossible to determine whether the manu-
    scripts consistently followed this orthography or not.
  – 29.255 καταψύξαι *codd.*] καταψῦξαι *scripsi*.

Variations in the position of accents is normally indicated (e.g.
29.414, where *Q* has a strange τετάκται). There are similar examples in *D*. The latter manuscript often utilizes (e.g., at 29.462) τὶς
instead of τίς (interrogative); this is also recorded.

Accents are written as acute before a sign of punctuation, re-
gardless of the reading of the manuscripts. ([18])

3. Itacism and analogous cases (αι-ε, ο-ω)

These are never indicated, except when the variant reading
has a different meaning (for example, indicative/subjunctive) or
when practically all manuscripts have the variant, as in 18.39
(ἀπειρημένων *A*[p. corr.], ἀπηρημένων *A*[a. corr.] *T C*). Such differences
are also indicated when they could be relevant for any other reason, especially if the word in question is a less common one (e.g.,
60.9 χρεμετίζοντες] χραιμετίζοντες *AT*). The instances of second person βούλει, written on occasion as βούλη or βούλῃ (in

_____

(15) Noret, *Accentuation*, p. 113.
(16) Ibid., p. 118-119.
(17) Hostens, *Dissertatio*, p. xlix.
(18) Cf. Noret, *Accentuation*, p. 111-112.

CXXXVI   *RATIO EDENDI*

65.32, by *A E*; in 65.41 by *E* alone), are recorded in order to show that some of the copyists did not respect the traditional rule. Nevertheless, when it is the modern editor who does not respect the rule, ([19]) this is not indicated.

4. Iota subscript

In the text, no iota subscript is added to the root of the word, for example δαδουχία (42.19) or ἄδοντας καὶ ἀδούσας (47.31). If, as very exceptionally happens, a given manuscript has an iota subscript (or adscript) in the root of a word, this is recorded in the apparatus, e.g. ᾄδην in 97.23; ᾄδου in 98.25, both in manuscript *E*. Iota subscripts or adscripts not of the root but required by morphology are not recorded (e.g. 18.15 γελῶιεν *C*). On the other hand, in the main text, in order to facilitate the task of the reader, iota subscripts are always added whenever morphology requires them, e.g., in the dative singluar of certain nouns.

  – πάντη is written without a iota subscript (29.72; 29.75).
  – κοινῇ (29.437) is spelled this way because it was originally a feminine dative.

The critical apparatus quotes the forms exactly as they are found in the manuscripts. Consequently, iota subscripts are never added there. However, whenever the manuscripts quoted do have them, they are kept. This is the case for instance in 31.1, "παρθένον ἀγνὴν παραστῆσαι τῷ χριστῷ *add. E*," where *E* actually has an iota subscript both in the article and in the noun.

5. Ephelcystic ν and analogous cases (οὕτω / οὕτως)

The manuscripts *A* and *C* often write unnecessary ephelcystic ν. When other manuscripts follow them, the ν is retained in the main text. In all other cases, instances of the unnecessary ephelcystic ν are eliminated. Divergence with regard to the ephelcystic ν is not indicated in the apparatus. Neither the main text nor the apparatus indicates the presence or absence of final sigma in οὕτως / οὕτω (e.g., at 29.69, where all manuscripts have οὕτω except *TQ*, which add a final -ς).

In a very few cases, some manuscripts have ἕνεκε instead of ἕνεκεν, although this -ν was perceived virtually as ephelcystic;

---

(19) This happens only once in Letter Alpha (65.32).

RATIO EDENDI   CXXXVII

these cases are indicated in the apparatus, precisely because of
their rarity.

6. Orthographical / morphological incoherence

The manuscripts are followed as closely as possible, and when
no decision can be reached from an examination of the manuscripts, the orthography of *C* is preferred. In accordance with the
practice of the *CCSG*, orthographical or morphological inconsistencies are preserved whenever possible. See for instance 5.12/13
οὐρανίους οὐσίας as against 5.185 οὐρανίαις οὐσίαις or 5.189
οὐρανίαν αἴγλην, or 29.171 δέεται (δεῖται *E* and the source) but
further on in the same fragment (l. 342) δεῖται (all of the manuscripts). Some instances of orthographical inconsistency may con-
vey a difference in meaning, even if there is no apparent reason
for this. For example, at 27.5 we have ἡτοίμασεν ὁ θεός while
at 27.7 we have ἡτοίμαζεν ὁ θεός (the source has ἡτοίμασεν in
both cases). Since the manuscripts provide these readings, they are
retained in this edition.

The same is true for numerals; for example, I have not hesitat-
ed to put δ′ instead of τετάρτη, even if some lines before πρώτη,
δευτέρα, τρίτη (58.1/8) was printed. In all cases, the present edition follows the manuscripts, duly indicating in the critical apparatus the different readings.

7. Word division

I follow the usual rule: "Any group of consonants that can begin a word, and a group formed by a stop with μ or ν, and by
μν, belongs with the second vowel: τύ-πτω, ὄ-γδοος, ἄ-στρον,
ἔ-χθος." [20] Traditionally, there is an exception to this rule, namely, that "[c]ompounds divide at the point of union: εἰσ-φέρω,
προσ-φέρω". [21] J. Noret, however, has shown that Byzantine
manuscripts are unaware of this pretended exception. [22] They
write εἰ-σφέρω, προ-σφέρω, etc. As elsewhere, the present edition
follows the practice of the manuscripts.

---

(20) SMYTH, *Greek Grammar*, § 140.
(21) Ibid.
(22) NORET, *Division*.

CXXXVIII   *RATIO EDENDI*

8. Geminated letters

They are always indicated.

9. Enclitics: τις, τι

No standardization has been made. Nevertheless to prevent the critical apparatus from becoming crowded, discrepancies in the accentuation of enclitics are usually not indicated.

Τίς often has an accent even when it is not interrogative. This is indicated in the apparatus in order to avoid confusion, e.g. 1.9 τίς] *sic acc. codd., etsi indefinitum*. This annotation means that, despite being indefinite, τίς is accentuated in all the manuscripts. [23]

By contrast, when the accented particle is, e.g., τινά or τινές, instances in which no confusion with the interrogative definite pronoun is possible, no indication is given in the apparatus, despite not following the rules of traditional grammar. See for example 29.110 φυσικὰς τινὰς, 29.474/475 δόξωμεν τισὶν, 35.19 κατέχειν ἐν χειρὶ τινὰ or 60.95 φύρσιν τινὰ (φύρσίν τινα *T*). In these cases, it is clear enough that τινάς, τισίν or τινά, being oxytone and not paroxytone, must be indefinite.

Not indicated are, among many others, the following cases: 2.9 εἴτέ τινα (εἴτέ τινα *T*), 2.28 (and 31.8) ἄλλό τι, 5.42 καθάπέρ τινι, 23.7 ὥσπέρ τις, 29.129 γενέσθαί τινα, 29.208 ἄπέρ ἐστι (ἄπερ ἐστὶ *CDF*), 29.326 ἄλλά τινα.

According to some classical rules, εἴτέ τινα or ἄλλό τι are regular, [24] whereas λόγός τις is not, [25] even if in both cases there is a paroxytone word followed by an enclitic pronoun. Since this rule is not so widely known, it is worthwhile to quote Vendryès, [26] who explains very adequately that "les paroxytons trochaïques dont la première syllabe est longue de position" get an enclitic accent – φύλλά τε, Λάμπέ τε – they were felt to be equivalent to σῆμά τε. In principle, this is true only of a short syllable followed by a liquid or a nasal, but the rule was extended "au-delà de ses limites naturelles" to groups such as ὅσσά τε, ὄφρά

---

(23) Cf. NORET, *Indéfinis, passim*, and id., *Accentuation*, p. 133.
(24) NORET, *Accentuation*, p. 137.
(25) Ibid., p. 141-143.
(26) VENDRYÈS, *Accentuation*, § 92.

σοι, ἐστί τις. This would explain ἄλλό τι but not εἴτέ τινα, ([27]) "Quand un groupe *proclitique* + *enclitique* est lui-même suivi d'enclitique, il semble que le premiers des enclitiques ait porté l'accent aigu. De là l'accentuation μήτέ τι Φ 288 dans le Venetus A [...]."

It is true that, in the time of the *FC* but also much earlier, the difference between a properispomenon and a paroxytone word was no longer heard and existed only orthographically. This explains the phenomenon of the Byzantine enclisis better than the classical rules, which had probably already been forgotten. Thus, it is almost certain that a 9th-c. copyist wrote ἔνθά τε not because of the ancient rule but because σῆμά τε seemed to him to be its precise equivalent. This explains why he could also write λόγός τε, which the classical rule would not allow. ([28])

On the other hand, when the manuscripts do follow the classical rules, such readings are preserved in the present edition, e.g., 18.15 γελῷέν τινες (where *C* has γελῶιεν τινὲς), 19.7 ἕτερόν τινα (ἕτερον τινὰ *C*), or 48.4 φάσμα τι. No attempt has been made to ameliorate the possible inconsistency between these and other seemingly equivalent cases where the usual rules are disregarded.

10. Enclitics: ἐστί or ἔστι?

Here too the present edition follows the practice of the manuscripts, where orthotone ἔστι is found only in the beginning of a sentence, after οὐκ and in similar cases. ([29]) The rule according to which ἔστι must be so accentuated if it is existential, or when accompanying an infinitive, etc., is not based on historical evidence, ([30]) as has also been recognised by classical philologists, and not only by those concerned with later Greek. ([31]) See for example

----

(27) VENDRYÈS, *Accentuation*, § 98.

(28) An additional, more sophisticated explanation can be found in NORET, *Accentuation*, p. 141-143.

(29) Ibid., p. 132.

(30) "Quant à la pseudo-règle qui voudrait qu'on accentue ἔστι chaque fois que le verbe équivaut à ἔξεστι ou chaque fois qu'il correspond à 'exister' dans les langues modernes, elle n'est ni attestée chez les anciens grammairiens ni confirmée par les manuscrits" (NORET, *Accentuation*, p. 133, n. 194).

(31) For the statement of a classical philologist, cf. BARRETT, *Euripides*, p. 425-426: "Whether ἐστι is orthotone (ἔστι) or enclitic depends solely on its position: ἔστι when initial (or quasi-initial [...]), otherwise ἐστι. This is both stated by ancient grammarians and confirmed by linguistic theory; the

RATIO EDENDI

29.394/395 Λοιπόν ἐστιν ἐπιδιασκέψασθαι (D is the only manuscript which has ἔστιν). On the other hand, ἔστι is orthotone when preceded by οὐκ, καί, εἰ, ὡς (e.g. 4.2, 41.24/25, etc.); on this point, the manuscripts of the FC follow the usual rules. ([32])

Ἐστί is very often not enclitic, e.g., 19.9 Ἄνθρωπος ἐστί or 29.159 ἡμῶν ἐστὶν. In such cases, the apparatus of the present edition does not record whether other manuscripts have ἄνθρωπός ἐστί. ([33]) The variation ἐστί / ἔστι, however, is always reported; for example, at 19.9 A has ἔστι, as can be seen in the apparatus.

Very often, on the other hand, ἐστι is enclitic, e.g., 29.148 Τῶν δὲ καλῶν τὰ μέν ἐστι or 29.155 Τίνα δέ ἐστι. These inconsistencies between orthotone and enclitic ἐστι have never been suppressed in this edition, because even the best manuscripts have them, often in exactly the same way.

11. Enclitics: particles

Enclitic δέ appears, ([34]) though very rarely and only in Q:
- 29.113 αὐτόν δε Q
- 29.368 ἀετοί δε Q

---

modern differentiation between ἐστι copula, ἔστι to affirm existence of possibility, is mistaken." In a note (ibid., p. 426, n. 2), however, he concedes that this differentiation has its roots in the Byzantine era: "I say 'modern' (it was propounded by Hermann, *De em. rat. Gr. gramm.* [1801], 82ff.) but it seems to have its root in antiquity;" he goes on to quote Eustathius (on *Il.*, p. 880, 22) and Photius (*s.u.* ἔστι), who "record a view that the accent varies with the meaning." Barrett's conclusion: "There seem to have been divergent practices; but we shall do well to prefer that which linguistic theory shows to have been original" (ibid.). Some scholars, on the other hand, defend the rule of the classical grammars; cf. JANNARIS, *Grammar,* § 983, "[t]he 3rd person singular is paroxytone, ἔστι – [...] *b.* when it means *there exists, there is; c.* when it stands for ἔξεστι, *it is permitted* [...]." This is also the solution adopted by most modern editors of classical texts.

(32) Even though these rules were not always respected in Byzantium. Cf. NORET, *Accentuation,* p. 132: after οὐκ and ἀλλ', ἔστι is always orthotone; yet after εἰ, καί, ὡς, ἀλλά, τοῦτο there might be fluctuations.

(33) In 19.9 this is the case for *CK*; since ἐστί was not enclitic in all other manuscripts, the accent is retained in the present edition, following the usual rules.

(34) Parallels are, for example, in Nicephorus Blemmydes. Cf. most the recent account in GIELEN, *Nicephorus,* p. lxvii-lxviii; see also NORET – DE VOCHT, *Orthographe, passim* and NORET, *Accentuation,* p. 124.

RATIO EDENDI CXLI

The edition has τε or τέ in accordance with the practice of the manuscripts, e.g., 16.9/10 ἀοράτου τὲ (τε CF) λέγω but 93.8-9 τάς τε [...] κολάσεις, without attempting to achieve consistency. [35] If the manuscripts disagree, no indication of this disagreement is given in the critical apparatus. [36]

12. Combination of enclitics [37]

E.g., 63.7 ἡ μὲν τίς ἐστι. The phrase is printed this way in the present edition in accordance with the manuscripts, although the editor is not unaware that in analogous cases ἐστι may have retained its accent, e.g., 29.430 Τοιαῦταί τινες εἰσίν. Traditional grammar would of course recommend ἡ μέν τίς ἐστι and τοιαῦταί τινές εἰσιν.

---

(35) NORET, *L'accentuation de* τε; id., *Accentuation*, p. 129.

(36) Here as elsewhere it is possible that the inconsistencies, or apparent inconsistencies, reflect the accentuation of the different *Vorlagen* of the compiler.

(37) NORET, *Accentuation*, p. 138-140.

FLORILEGIVM COISLINIANVM

ALPHA

CONSPECTVS SIGLORVM

A   Parisinus, Coislinianus 294 (s. XI-XII), f. 1-65^v

T   Hierosolymitanus, Sancti Sepulcri 15 (s. X), f. 137-168

C   Parisinus gr. 924 (s. X), f. 6-78

D   Mediolanensis, Ambrosianus Q 74 sup. (s. X), f. 3-32^v

E   Argentoratensis, Bibliothecae Nationalis et Universitatis gr. 12 (s. XIII, a. 1285-1286), f. 7-52^v

G   Athonensis, Iviron 38 (s. XIII, a. 1281-1282), f. 5-8^v

F   Atheniensis, Bibliothecae Nationalis 329 (s. XIII-XIV), f. 56-84

H   Vaticanus gr. 491 (s. XIII), f. 105-139

K   Athonensis, Koutloumousiou 9 (s. XIV), p. 336-466

Q   Atheniensis, Bibliothecae Nationalis 375 (s. XIII-XV), f. 200-210

R   Athonensis, Lavra B 43 (s. XII), f. 177^v-179, 184, 185^{r-v}

I   Atheniensis, Metochion Sancti Sepulcri 273 (s. X), f. 182^v-185^v

Α'

Περὶ δημιουργίας ἀγγέλων

1 Πάντες σχεδὸν οἱ κατὰ τὴν οἰκουμένην τῆς ἐκκλησίας
διδάσκαλοι πᾶσαν τὴν νοερὰν καὶ ἀγγελικὴν φύσιν ἐκ
μὴ ὄντων ὑπὸ τοῦ πάντων δημιουργοῦ προϋφεστάναι
τοῦδε τοῦ κόσμου διδάσκουσι. Καὶ ὁ μὲν ἅγιος Βασίλει-
5 ος ἐν τῇ κατ'αὐτὸν Ἑξαημέρῳ φησὶν οὕτως· Ἦν γάρ τι
φῶς ὡς ἔοικε πρὸ τοῦ κόσμου τούτου, ὃ τῇ μὲν διανοίᾳ
ἡμῶν ἐστι θεωρητόν, ἀνιστόρητον δὲ κατελείφθη διὰ τὸ
τοῖς εἰσαγομένοις ἔτι καὶ νηπίοις κατὰ τὴν γνῶσιν ἀνε-
πιτήδειον. Ἦν τίς πρεσβυτέρα τῆς τοῦ κόσμου γενέσε-
10 ως κατάστασις ταῖς ὑπερκοσμίοις δυνάμεσι πρέπουσα,
ἡ ὑπερχρόνιος, ἡ αἰωνία, ἡ ἀΐδιος. Δημιουργήματα δὲ
ἐν αὐτῇ ὁ τῶν ὅλων κτίστης καὶ δημιουργὸς ἀπετέλεσε,
φῶς νοητὸν πρέπον τῇ μακαριότητι τῶν φιλούντων
τὸν κύριον, τὰς λογικὰς καὶ ἀοράτους φύσεις καὶ πᾶσαν
15 τὴν τῶν νοητῶν διακόσμησιν, ὅσα τὴν ἡμετέραν διάνοιαν ὑπερβαίνει, ὧν οὐδὲ τὰς ὀνομασίας ἐξευρεῖν δυνατόν. Ταῦτα τοῦ ἀοράτου κόσμου συμπληροῖ τὴν οὐσίαν,
ὡς διδάσκει ἡμᾶς Παῦλος λέγων· Ὅτι ἐν αὐτῷ ἐκτίσθη
τὰ πάντα, εἴτε ὁρατά, εἴτε ἀόρατα, εἴτε θρόνοι, εἴτε κυ-
20 ριότητες, εἴτε ἀρχαί, εἴτε ἐξουσίαι, εἴτε δυνάμεις, εἴτε

Font. **1.5/28** = Bas. Caes., Hom. in Hex., 1, 5 (p. 8, 17 – 9, 16)   **18/20** Col. 1, 16
cf. Eph. 1, 21

Mss.   **1** *AT CGFHK*

Tit.   **Α'** Περὶ – ἀγγέλων] *om. GH*

Crit.   **1.1/2** διδάσκαλοι τῆς εκκλησίας *Fut uid.*H   **4** μὲν ἅγιος] μὲν μέγας *FH*, μέγας μὲν *C*   **4/5** Βασίλειος] βασιλ(είου) add. *Cin marg.*   **9** τίς] *sic acc. codd.,*
etsi indefinitum   τῆς] *om. K*   **11** ἡ αἰωνία] *om. FH*   **13** μακαριότη
(sic) A   **15** τὴν²] τὲ *(sic) praem. FH*   **17** ἀποπληρεῖ *FH*   **18** ἡμᾶς]
om. C

Comp.   **1.6** φῶς] *non hab. Bas.*   *ante* πρὸ] καὶ *hab. Bas.*   **11** ὑπέρχρονος *Bas.*
(A1 G2 = Coisl.)   **18** *ante* Παῦλος] ὁ *hab. Bas.*

4 FLORILEGIVM COISLINIANVM

ἀγγέλων στρατιαί, εἴτε ἀρχαγγέλων ἐπιστασίαι. Ὅτε
δὲ ἔδει λοιπὸν καὶ τὸν κόσμον τοῦτον ἐπεισαχθῆναι τοῖς
οὖσι, προηγουμένως μὲν διδασκαλεῖον καὶ παιδευτήριον
τῶν ἀνθρωπίνων ψυχῶν, ἔπειτα μέντοι καὶ ἀπαξαπλῶς
25 πάντων τῶν ἐν γενέσει καὶ φθορᾷ ἐπιτήδειον ἐνδιαίτη-
μα, συμφυὲς ἄρα τῷ κόσμῳ καὶ τοῖς ἐν αὐτῷ ζώοις τε
καὶ φυτοῖς, ἡ χρόνου διέξοδος ὑπέστη, ἐπειγομένη ἀεὶ
καὶ παραρρέουσα καὶ μηδαμοῦ παυομένη τοῦ δρόμου.
Καὶ μετ'ὀλίγον. Ἐν ἀρχῇ ἐποίησεν ὁ θεὸς τὸν οὐρανόν,
30 τουτέστιν ἐν ἀρχῇ ταύτῃ τῇ κατὰ χρόνον. Οὐ γὰρ δὴ
[τῇ] κατὰ πρεσβυγένειαν πάντων τῶν γενομένων προ-
έχειν αὐτὸν μαρτυρῶν λέγει ἐν ἀρχῇ γεγονέναι, ἀλλὰ
μετὰ τὰ ἀόρατα καὶ νοούμενα, τῶν ὁρατῶν τούτων καὶ
αἰσθήσει ληπτῶν τίς ἡ ἀρχὴ τῆς ὑπάρξεως διηγεῖται.

Font.   **29** Gen. 1, 1   **29/34** = Bas. Caes., Hom. in Hex., 1, 5 (p. 10, 4-8)

Mss.   *AT CGFHK* (*Q* inde a Ὅτε usque ad δρόμου, 1.21/28)

Crit.   **21** Ὅτε] τοῦ μεγ(άλου) βασϊλείου· ἐκ τοῦ ἑξαημέρου *praem. Q*   **22** λοιπὸν]
om. GFHK   ἐπισυναχθῆναι *FH*   **23** διδασκάλιον (*sic acc.) T*, διδασκα-
λεῖα *H*   **24** μέντοι] δὲ *Q*   **26** τῷ κόσμῳ] *om. Q*   **29** Καὶ μετ'ὀλίγον]
καὶ μετ'ὀλίγα *GFHK*, καὶ μετ'ὀλίγον *uel* ὀλίγα *A*, καὶ μετὰ ταῦτα *C*   τὸν
οὐρανόν] καὶ τὴν γῆν *add. K*   **30** χρόνον] τὸν *praem. GK*   **31** τῇ] *seclusi
cum fonte, habent codd. omnes*   **34** διηγητέον *AT*

Comp.   **24** *post* ψυχῶν] ἐστιν *hab. Sacr. Par.*   **25** πάντων] *non hab. Sacr. Par.*
26 συμφυὴς *Bas. et Sacr. Par.*   **27** *ante* χρόνου] τοῦ *hab. Bas.* (*B1 B2 G2
= Coisl.*)   ὑπέστη] ἐπέστη *Sacr. Par.*   **29** ὁ – οὐρανόν] *non hab. Bas.*
34 τίς – ἀρχὴ] τὴν ἀρχὴν *Bas.*

Ind.   **23/28** προηγουμένως – δρόμου = Sacr. Par., PG 95, 1281, 32-38

ALPHA 1-2

2

Γρηγορίου τοῦ Θεολόγου
Ἐκ τοῦ εἰς τὴν Χριστοῦ γένναν

Ἐπεὶ δὲ οὐκ ἤρκει τῇ ἀγαθότητι τοῦτο, τὸ κινεῖσθαι μόνον τῇ ἑαυτῆς θεωρίᾳ, ἀλλ'ἔδει χεθῆναι τὸ ἀγαθὸν καὶ
ὁδεῦσαι, ὡς πλείονα εἶναι τὰ εὐεργετούμενα – τοῦτο
γὰρ τῆς ἄκρας ἦν ἀγαθότητος –, πρῶτον μὲν ἐννοεῖ τὰς
5 ἀγγελικὰς δυνάμεις καὶ οὐρανίους, καὶ τὸ ἐννόημα ἔργον ἦν, λόγῳ συμπληρούμενον καὶ πνεύματι τελειού-
μενον. Καὶ οὕτως ὑπέστησαν λαμπρότητες δεύτεραι,
λειτουργοὶ τῆς πρώτης λαμπρότητος, εἴτε νοερὰ πνεύ-
ματα, εἴτε πῦρ οἷον ἄϋλον καὶ ἀσώματον, εἴτέ τινα φύ-
10 σιν ἄλλην, ὅτι ἐγγυτάτω τῶν εἰρημένων, ταύτας ὑποληπτέον. Βούλομαι μὲν εἰπεῖν ὅτι ἀκινήτους πρὸς τὸ
κακὸν καὶ μόνην ἐχούσας τὴν τοῦ καλοῦ κίνησιν, ἅτε
περὶ θεὸν οὔσας καὶ τὰ πρῶτα ἐκ θεοῦ λαμπομένας·
τὰ γὰρ ἐνταῦθα, δευτέρας ἐλλάμψεως. Πείθει δέ με μὴ
15 ἀκινήτους ἀλλὰ δυσκινήτους καὶ ὑπολαμβάνειν ταύτας καὶ λέγειν ὁ διὰ τὴν λαμπρότητα Ἑωσφόρος, σκότος διὰ τὴν ἔπαρσιν καὶ γενόμενος καὶ λεγόμενος, αἵ τε
ὑπ'αὐτὸν ἀποστατικαὶ δυνάμεις, δημιουργοὶ τῆς κακίας
τῇ τοῦ καλοῦ φυγῇ, καὶ ἡμῖν πρόξενοι.
20 Οὕτω μὲν οὖν ὁ νοητὸς αὐτῷ καὶ διὰ ταῦτα ὑπέστη
κόσμος, ὡς ἐμὲ γοῦν περὶ τούτων φιλοσοφῆσαι, μικρῷ λόγῳ τὰ μεγάλα σταθμώμενον. Ἐπεὶ δὲ τὰ πρῶτα
καλῶς εἶχεν αὐτῷ, δεύτερον ἐννοεῖ κόσμον ὑλικὸν καὶ
ὁρώμενον, καὶ οὗτός ἐστι τὸ ἐξ οὐρανοῦ καὶ γῆς καὶ

---

ont. **2.2/31** = Greg. Naz., Or. 38, 9, 1 – 10, 11 (= Or. 45, PG 36, 629, 7-40)
16 cf. Is. 14, 12-15

---

ss. **2** *AT CGFHK*

---

it. **2** Γρηγορίου – Θεολόγου] τοῦ ἁγίου γρηγορίου τοῦ θεολόγου *T, om.* H
Ἐκ – γένναν] εἰς τὴν χριστοῦ γένναν *T*, λόγου τοῦ εἰς τὴν χριστοῦ γένναν *A,*
om. GHK, illeg. F

---

rit. **2.1** ἀγαθότι *(sic)* C   **9** οἷον] *om.* H, *illeg.* F   **15** καὶ] *om.* FH
21 γοῦν] νῦν *F*   **22** σταθμούμενον *T, illeg. A*

6   FLORILEGIVM COISLINIANVM

25 τῶν ἐν μέσῳ σύστημά τε καὶ σύγκριμα, ἐπαινετὸν μὲν
    τῆς καθ'ἕκαστον εὐφυΐας, ἀξιεπαινετώτερον δὲ τῆς
    ἐξ ἁπάντων εὐαρμοστίας καὶ συμφωνίας, ἄλλου πρὸς
    ἄλλό τι καλῶς ἔχοντος καὶ πάντων πρὸς ἅπαντα, εἰς
    ἑνὸς κόσμου συμπλήρωσιν, ἵνα δείξῃ μὴ μόνον οἰκείαν
30 ἑαυτῷ φύσιν ἀλλὰ καὶ πάντῃ ξένην ὑποστήσασθαι δυ-
    νατὸς ὤν.

3   Καισαρίου ἀδελφοῦ Γρηγορίου τοῦ Θεολόγου

     Πᾶσαι γὰρ ἐν φωτὶ διῆγον αἱ ἄσαρκοι τῶν ἀγγέλων χο-
     ρεῖαι καὶ πρὸ τοῦ γενέσθαι τὸν κόσμον.

4   Ἀναστασίου Ἀντιοχείας

     Ἐν ἀρχῇ ἦν ὁ θεός, καὶ ὁ θεὸς ἦν ἐν ἀρχῇ καὶ πρὸ ἀνάρ-
     χου ἀρχῆς· ἦν ἀεὶ καὶ ἔστι καὶ ἔσται ὁ θεός. Θεὸν δὲ
     λέγω τὴν ἁγίαν καὶ ὁμοούσιον καὶ ἄκτιστον τριάδα πα-
     τρὸς καὶ υἱοῦ καὶ ἁγίου πνεύματος. Οὗτος ὁ θεὸς ἡμῶν,
5   ὁ ἀεὶ ὢν καὶ προὼν καὶ πρὸ πάντων προών, ταῖς προ-
     αναρχικαῖς αὐτοῦ καὶ παναδήλοις θεοβουλίαις πρῶτον
     πάσης κτίσεως ἐννοεῖ καὶ ποιεῖ τὰς ἁγίας καὶ ἀγγελι-
     κὰς δυνάμεις, ὅτε οἶδε καὶ ὅπου οἶδε καὶ ὡς ἂν σύνοιδε
     καὶ ὡς μόνος αὐτὸς οἶδεν· ὧν τὴν οὐσίαν καὶ τὴν τάξιν
10   καὶ τὸν ἀριθμὸν καὶ τὴν διαγωγὴν καὶ τὴν ἰδέαν μόνος

Font.   **3.**1/2 = Ps.-Caes., Quaest. et resp., 60, 6-7 (p. 53)   **4.**1/29 = Anast. Sin.,
        Viae dux, IV, 8 – 36 (p. 82-83)   **1** Io. 1, 1   **4** Bar. 3, 36

Mss.   *AT CGFHK*   3 *AT CGFHK*   4 *AT CGFHK*

Tit.   **3** Καισαρίου – Θεολόγου] *om. H*   Γρηγορίου] *om. GFK*   **4** Ἀναστασίου
        Ἀντιοχείας] *post* πνεύματος *(l. 4) trsp. GK*   Ἀντιοχείας] ἀντιόχου *C*

Crit.   **29** μὴ δείξῃ *FH*   **30** ὑποστήσεσθαι *T*   **4.1** προανάρχου *A^{a.corr.}T GF*
        2 ἀεὶ] οὐδὲν *FH*   **4** καὶ¹] *om. GFHK*   **7** ἁγίας καὶ] *om. GFHK*
        8 οἶδε¹] εἶδε *G*   ὅπου] ὅπως *GK*   οἶδε²] εἶδε *G*   καὶ² – σύνοιδε]
        om. AT   σύνειδε *G*

ALPHA 2 – 4   7

αὐτὸς ὁ τούτων ποιητὴς γινώσκει θεός. Ἐκ τούτων δὴ
τῶν ἀσωμάτων καταγγελμάτων ταξίαρχος εἷς ἀλαζο-
νευθεὶς κατὰ τοῦ δημιουργοῦ, ὥς φησιν Ἡσαΐας καὶ
Ἰεζεκιὴλ οἱ προφῆται, ἀπερρίφη καὶ ἔπεσε σὺν τῷ τάγ-
15 ματι αὐτοῦ, ὁ καλούμενος νῦν διάβολος καὶ οἱ δαίμονες
οἱ σὺν αὐτῷ. Δημιουργοῦντος οὖν τοῦ θεοῦ τὸν ὁρώμενον κόσμον – λέγω δὴ τὸν οὐρανὸν καὶ τὴν γῆν καὶ τὰ
ἐν αὐτῇ – ἐνόμιζεν ὁ διάβολος, ὥς φησι τίς τῶν διδα-
σκάλων, ὅτι αὐτὸν μέλλει καθιστᾶν ὁ θεὸς βασιλέα καὶ
20 κύριον τῆς ὁρατῆς κτίσεως. Ὅτε δὲ εἶδε τὸν Ἀδὰμ γε-
γονότα καὶ κατασταθέντα ὑπὸ τοῦ θεοῦ δεσπόζειν τῶν
ἐπὶ τῆς γῆς, διαπονηθεὶς καὶ φθονήσας τῷ ἀνθρώπῳ ὁ
πονηρὸς ἠπάτησεν αὐτὸν διὰ τῆς Εὔας καὶ τοῦ ξύλου,
εἴτε κατὰ παραχώρησιν θεοῦ, εἴτε καθ'ἕτερόν τινα μυ-
25 στικώτερον τρόπον, τῷ θεῷ ἔγνωσται· οὐ γὰρ δεῖ ἡμᾶς
περιεργάζεσθαι τὰ σεσιωπημένα τῇ θείᾳ γραφῇ, λέγω
δὴ τὰ περὶ Παραδείσου καὶ τοῦ ξύλου τῆς γνώσεως καὶ
τῶν χιτώνων καὶ ἑτέρων τινῶν τοιούτων μὴ σαφῶς δε-
δηλωμένων ἡμῖν ἐν ταῖς βίβλοις ταῖς ἱεραῖς.

'ont.   **11/16** cf. Is. 14, 12-15; Ez. 28, 17-18   **18/20** locum non inueni; cf. Anast.
Sin., Quaest. et resp., 80, 8-13   **22/23** cf. Gen. 3, 1-6

Ass.   *AT CGFHK*

'rit.   **12** καταγγελμάτων] *om. T GFHK*   **18** αὐτῇ] αὐτοῖς *GK*, αὐτῷ *H, illeg.*
F   τίς] *sic acc. codd., etsi indefinitum*   **20** εἶδε] οἶδε *FHK*   **22** τῆς]
om. T GFH   **25** ἔγνωται *T^{ut uid.}*   γὰρ δεῖ] γὰρ δὴ *A*, δεῖ γὰρ *GK*
27 γνώσεως] γυμνώσεως *A*   **29** ἐν ταῖς ἱεραῖς βίβλοις *GFHK*

'omp.   **12** καταγγελμάτων] στρατευμάτων καὶ ταγμάτων *Anast. (BCEHKNXYΔ =*
Coisl.)   **27** τῆς γνώσεως] καὶ τῆς γυμνώσεως *Anast. (ΝΘΣ = Coisl.)*

8 FLORILEGIVM COISLINIANVM

Β'

Τίνες αἱ μορφωτικαὶ τῶν ἀγγελικῶν δυνάμεων εἰκόνες;

5 Διονυσίου ἐπισκόπου Ἀθηνῶν

Φέρε δὴ λοιπὸν ἀναπαύοντες ἡμῶν εἰ δοκεῖ τὸ νοερὸν
ὄμμα τῆς περὶ τὰς ἑνικὰς ὑψηλὰς θεωρίας ἀγγελοπρεποῦς
συντονίας, ἐπὶ τὸ διαιρετὸν καὶ πολυμερὲς πλάτος τῆς
πολυειδοῦς τῶν ἀγγελικῶν μορφοποιῶν ποικιλίας κα-
5 ταβάντες, πάλιν ἀπ'αὐτῶν ὡς ἀπ'εἰκόνων ἐπὶ τὴν ἁπλότητα τῶν οὐρανίων νοῶν ἀναλυτικῶς ἀνακάμπτωμεν.
Ἀρκτέον δὲ τοῦ λόγου καὶ ζητητέον ἐν πρώτῃ τῶν
τύπων ἀνακαθάρσει δι'ἣν αἰτίαν ἡ θεολογία σχεδὸν
παρὰ πάντας εὑρίσκεται τιμῶσα τὴν ἐμπύριον ἱερογρα-
10 φίαν. Εὑρήσεις γοῦν αὐτὴν οὐ μόνον τροχοὺς πυρώδεις
διαπλάττουσαν, ἀλλὰ καὶ ζῶα πεπυρωμένα καὶ ἄνδρας
ὡς πῦρ ἐξαστράπτοντας καὶ περὶ αὐτὰς τὰς οὐρανίους

Font. **5.1/6** = Ps.-Dion., De coel. hier., 15, 1 (p. 50, 13 – 51, 1) **7/247** = Ps.-
Dion., De coel. hier., 15, 2-9 (p. 51, 22 – 59, 7) **10** cf. Ez. 1, 15; 10, 2. 6. 9;
Dan. θ' 7, 9 **11** cf. Ez. 1, 14 **11/12** cf. Mt. 28, 3

Mss. **5** *AT CGFH*

Tit. **Β'** Τίνες – εἰκόνες] = *Ps.-Dion. mss.* PaRcPtPnPb Τίνες] περὶ τοῦ *praem.* F
ἀγγελικῶν] ἀγγέλων *A* **5** Διονυσίου – Ἀθηνῶν] *om.* H

Crit. **5.3** ἐπὶ] καὶ *praem.* C αἱρετὸν *FH* **5** ἀπ'εἰκόνων] ἀπείκασται *H*
6 ἀνακάμψωμεν *C* **10** πυρώδεις *FH* **11** πεπυρρωμένα *A*

Comp. **Β'.3** *post* εἰκόνες] καὶ τὰ ἑξῆς *hab. Ps.-Dion. mss.* PaRcPtPnPb, καὶ τάξεις *hab.*
VvFaLc, τί τὸ πυρῶδες, τί τὸ ἀνθρωποειδές, τίνες οἱ ὀφθαλμοί, τίνες αἱ ῥῖνες,
τίνα τὰ ὦτα, τίνα τὰ στόματα καὶ τὰ λοιπὰ τοῦ κεφαλαίου *hab.* Fb, τί τὸ πυρῶδες, τί τὸ ἀνθρωποειδές, τίνες οἱ ὀφθαλμοί, τίνες αἱ χεῖρες, τίνα τὰ ὦτα,
τίνες αἱ ῥῖνες καὶ τὰ λοιπὰ τοῦ κεφαλαίου ὁμοίως *hab. VcKa (cf. infra* 5.20,
5.49, 5.58, 5.64, 5.69, 5.72, 5.76, 5.79, 5.82, 5.85, etc.) **5.2** *post* ἑνικὰς] καὶ
hab. Ps.-Dion. (FbFa = Coisl.) **4** μορφοποιῶν *Ps.-Dion. (FbVv = Coisl.)*
9 πάντας] πάσας *scripsit Heil cum* Ka^{p.corr.} *(cett. = Coisl.)*

ALPHA 5   9

οὐσίας σωροὺς ἀνθράκων πυρὸς περιτιθεῖσαν καὶ ποταμοὺς ἀσχέτῳ ῥοίζῳ πυριφλεγέθοντας. Ἀλλὰ καὶ τοὺς
15 θρόνους φησὶ πυρίνους εἶναι, καὶ αὐτοὺς δὲ τοὺς ὑπερ-
τάτους σεραφὶμ ἐμπρηστὰς ὄντας ἐκ τῆς ἐπωνυμίας
ἐμφαίνει καὶ τὴν πυρὸς ἰδιότητα καὶ ἐνέργειαν αὐτοῖς
ἀπονέμει καὶ ὅλως ἄνω καὶ κάτω τὴν ἐμπύριον τιμᾷ
ἐγκρίτως τυποπλαστίαν.

20   Τί τὸ πυρῶδες;

Τὸ μὲν οὖν πυρῶδες ἐμφαίνειν οἶμαι τὸ τῶν οὐρανίων νοῶν θεοειδέστατον. Οἱ γὰρ ἱεροὶ θεολόγοι τὴν
ὑπερούσιον καὶ ἀμόρφωτον οὐσίαν ἐν πυρὶ πολλαχῇ
διαγράφουσι ὡς ἔχοντι πολλὰς τῆς θεαρχικῆς, εἰ θέμις
25 εἰπεῖν, ἰδιότητος ὡς ἐν ὁρατοῖς εἰκόνας. Τὸ γὰρ αἰσθητὸν
πῦρ ἐστὶ μὲν ὡς εἰπεῖν ἐν πᾶσι, καὶ διὰ πάντων ἀμιγῶς
φοιτᾷ, καὶ ἐξήρηται πάντων, καὶ παμφαὲς ὂν ἅμα καὶ
ὡς κρύφιον, ἄγνωστον αὐτὸ καθ᾽αὑτό, μὴ προκειμένης
ὕλης εἰς ἣν ἀναφάνοι τὴν οἰκείαν ἐνέργειαν, ἄσχετόν τε
30 καὶ ἀθεώρητον, αὐτοκρατητικὸν ἁπάντων καὶ τὰ ἐν οἷς
ἂν ἐγγένηται πρὸς τὴν οἰκείαν ἐνέργειαν ἀλλοιωτικόν,
μεταδοτικὸν ἑαυτοῦ πᾶσι τοῖς ὁπωσοῦν πλησιάζουσιν,
ἀνανεωτικὸν τῇ ζωπύρῳ θερμότητι, φωτιστικὸν ταῖς
ἀπερικαλύπτοις ἐλλάμψεσιν, ἀκράτητον, ἀμιγές, δια-

Font.   **13** cf. Ez. 1, 13; 10, 2   **13/14** cf. Dan. 7, 10   **15** cf. Dan. θ′ 7, 9
22/23 cf. Ex. 3, 2-6; 14, 24; 19, 18; Deut. 4, 24

Mss.   *AT CGFH*

Crit.   **13** οὐσίας] δυνάμεις *T*   παρατιθεῖσαν *CFH*   **14** περιφλεγέθοντας *T*
20 πυρρῶδες *FH*   **21** πυρρῶδες *FH*   ἐμφαίνειν οἶμαι] ἐμφαίνειν οἴομαι *G*, ἐμφαίνει εἶναι *H*   **22** νόων *T FH*   θεολόγοι] λόγοι *H*
24 πολλὰς] πολλάκις *C*, *om. G*   **25** εἰκόνα *FH*   **26** ἔστι *C*   **29** ἀνα-
φαίνει *FH*   **29/31** ἄσχετόν – ἐνέργειαν] *om. T*   **30** αὐτοκρατικὸν (*sic*) *A*
31 ἂν] *om. H, illeg. F*   ἐγγίνηται *H, illeg. F*   **32** μεταδοτικὸν] καὶ
praem. H   **34** ἐλάμψεσιν *Aᵃ·ᶜᵒʳʳ·*

Comp.   **15** πυρίους *Ps.-Dion.* (*Fbᵖ·ᶜᵒʳʳ·Lc = Coisl.*)   **19** ἐκκρίτως *Ps.-Dion.*
21 οἴομαι *Ps.-Dion.* (*Vv = Coisl.*)   **29** ἀναφαίνοι *Ps.-Dion.* (*RcPtPnᵃ·ᶜᵒʳʳ·*
PbVvLcVcKa = Coisl., ἂν φάναι *Fa*)

10 FLORILEGIVM COISLINIANVM

35 κριτικόν, ἀναλλοίωτον, ἀνώφορον, ὀξύπορον, ὑψηλόν,
οὐδεμιᾶς ἀνεχόμενον ὑποπεζίας ὑφέσεως, ἀεικίνητον,
ταυτοκίνητον, κινητικὸν ἑτέρων, περιληπτικόν, ἀπε-
ρίληπτον, ἀπροσδεὲς ἑτέρου, λανθανόντως αὐξητικὸν
ἑαυτοῦ καὶ πρὸς τὰς ὑποδεχομένας ὕλας ἐμφαῖνον
40 τὴν ἑαυτοῦ μεγαλειότητα, δραστήριον, δυνατόν, ἅπασι παρὸν ἀοράτως, ἀμελούμενον οὐκ εἶναι δοκοῦν, τῇ
τρίψει δὲ καθάπέρ τινι ζητήσει συμφυῶς καὶ οἰκείως
ἐξαίφνης ἀναφαινόμενον καὶ αὖθις ἀκαταλήπτως ἀφιπτάμενον, ἀμείωτον ἐν πᾶσι ταῖς πανολβίοις αὐτοῦ με-
45 ταδόσεσι. Καὶ πολλὰς ἄν τις εὕροι τοῦ πυρὸς ἰδιότητας
οἰκείας ὡς ἐν αἰσθηταῖς εἰκόσι θεαρχικῆς ἐνεργείας.
Τοῦτο γοῦν εἰδότες οἱ θεόσοφοι, τὰς οὐρανίους οὐσίας
ἐκ πυρὸς διαπλάττουσιν, ἐμφαίνοντες αὐτῶν τὸ θεοειδὲς καὶ ὡς ἐφικτὸν θεομίμητον.

50 Τί τὸ ἀνθρωποειδές;

Ἀλλὰ καὶ ὡς ἀνθρωπομόρφους αὐτοὺς ἀναγράφου-
σι, διὰ τὸ νοερὸν καὶ πρὸς τὸ ἄναντες ἔχειν τὰς ὀπτικὰς δυνάμεις καὶ τὸ τοῦ σχήματος εὐθὺ καὶ ὄρθιον καὶ
τὸ κατὰ φύσιν ἀρχικὸν καὶ ἡγεμονικόν, καὶ τὸ κατ'αἴ-
55 σθησιν μὲν ἐλάχιστον ὡς πρὸς τὰς λοιπὰς τῶν ἀλόγων

Font.   51 cf. Ez. 1, 10; Apoc. 4, 7

Mss.   AT CGFH (D inde a ἀφιπτάμενον, 5.43/44)

Crit.   35 ὀξυπόρον AT   36 ἀνεχόμενον] iter. A^{a.corr.} (erasit)   ὑφέσεως] ἢ
praem. C   ἀεικινητικὸν T   37 ταυτοκίνητον] αὐτοκίνητον GF,
om. T H   κινητικὸν] om. T   37/38 ἀπερίληπτον] ἀπαράληπτον C
38 λανθάνοντος T   39 πρὸς] κατὰ G   ἐκφαῖνον CG   40 μεγα-
λιότητα A^{a.corr.}   δραστήριον] om. FH   44 πανολβίαις G   47 Τοῦτο]
om. H   48 ἐμφαίροντες (sic) T   50 Τί] τοῦ αὐτοῦ praem. F   51 ἀν-
θρωπομόρφους] ἀνθρώπους FH   54 καὶ ἡγεμονικόν] om. H

Comp.   39 ἐκφαῖνον Ps.-Dion.   44 πάσαις Ps.-Dion. (PaRcPt^{a.corr.}PnFaLc = Coisl.)
πανολβίαις Ps.-Dion.   ἑαυτοῦ Ps.-Dion. (Vv = Coisl.)   46 αἰσθητοῖς
Ps.-Dion. (RcPtVvFaVcKa = Coisl.)   εἰκόνας scripsit Heil   47 οὐρανίας
Ps.-Dion.   51 ὡς] non hab. Ps.-Dion.   52 post καὶ] τὸ hab. Ps.-Dion. (Pb
= Coisl.)

ALPHA 5

ζώων δυνάμεις, κρατητικὸν δὲ πάντων τῇ τοῦ νοῦ κατὰ
περιουσίαν δυνάμει καὶ τῇ κατὰ λογικὴν ἐπιστήμην
ἐπικρατείᾳ καὶ κατὰ τὸ φύσει τῆς ψυχῆς ἀδούλωτον
καὶ ἀκράτητον.

60   Τί οἱ ὀφθαλμοί;

Τὰς δὲ ὀπτικὰς δυνάμεις ἐμφαίνειν φασὶ τὴν πρὸς
τὰ θεῖα φῶτα διειδεστάτην ἀνάνευσιν, καὶ αὖθις τὴν
ἁπλῆν καὶ ὑγρὰν καὶ οὐκ ἀντίτυπον, ἀλλ᾽ὀξυκίνητον
καὶ καθαρὰν καὶ ἀναπεπταμένην ἀπαθῶς ὑποδοχὴν τῶν
65 θεαρχικῶν ἐλλάμψεων.

Τί αἱ ῥῖνες;

Τὰς δὲ τῶν ὀσφραντῶν διακριτικὰς δυνάμεις, τὸ τῆς
ὑπὲρ νοῦν εὐώδους διαδόσεως ὡς ἐφικτὸν ἀντιληπτι-
κὸν καὶ τῶν μὴ τοιούτων ἐν ἐπιστήμῃ διακριτικὸν καὶ
70 ὁλικῶς ἀποφευκτικόν.

Τί τὰ ὦτα;

Τὰς δὲ τῶν ὤτων δυνάμεις, τὸ μετοχικὸν καὶ γνω-
στικῶς ὑποδεκτικὸν τῆς θεαρχικῆς ἐπιπνοίας.

Τί τὰ στόματα;

75   Τὰς δὲ γευστικάς, τὴν τῶν νοητῶν τροφῶν ἀποπλή-
ρωσιν καὶ τὸ τῶν θείων καὶ τροφίμων ὀχετῶν ὑποδε-
κτικόν.

'ont.   **56** cf. Gen. 1, 26

/ss.   *AT CDGFH*

:rit.   **56** δὲ] τε D   **62** φῶτα – ἀνάνευσιν] *om.* H *(30 litt. spat.)*   διειδέστατον F
69/73 καὶ² – ὑποδεκτικὸν] *om.* A   **75** τῶν τροφῶν τῶν νοητῶν G

:omp.   **59** *post* ἀκράτητον] Ἔστι δὲ καὶ καθ᾽ἕκαστον ὡς οἶμαι τῆς σωματικῆς ἡμῶν
πολυμερείας εἰκόνας ἐναρμονίους ἐξευρεῖν τῶν οὐρανίων δυνάμεων φάσκον-
τας *hab.* Ps.-Dion.   **61** δὲ] μὲν Ps.-Dion.   ἐμφαίνειν δυνάμεις Ps. Dion.
φασὶ] *non hab.* Ps.-Dion.   **63** ἀπαλὴν Ps.-Dion. *(RcPtFbFa = Coisl.)*

12 FLORILEGIVM COISLINIANVM

Τίς ἡ ἀφή;

Τὰς ἁπτικὰς δὲ δυνάμεις, τὸ τοῦ προσφυοῦς ἢ τοῦ
80 βλάπτοντος ἐν ἐπιστήμῃ διαγνωστικόν.

Τί τὰ βλέφαρα;

Τὰ βλέφαρα δὲ καὶ τὰς ὀφρύας, τὸ τῶν θεοπτικῶν
νοήσεων φρουρητικόν.

Τίς ἡ ἀκμή;

85 Τὴν ἡβῶσαν δὲ καὶ νεανικὴν ἡλικίαν, τὸ τῆς ἐπακμα-
ζούσης ἀεὶ ζωτικῆς δυνάμεως.

Τί οἱ ὀδόντες;

Τοὺς ὀδόντας δέ, τὸ διαιρετικὸν τῆς ἐνδιδομένης
τροφίμου τελειότητος· ἑκάστη γὰρ οὐσία νοερὰ τὴν
90 δωρουμένην αὐτῇ πρὸς τῆς θειοτέρας ἐνοειδῆ νόησιν
προνοητικῇ δυνάμει διαιρεῖ καὶ πληθύνει πρὸς τὴν τῆς
καταδεεστέρας ἀναγωγικὴν ἀναλογίαν.

Τί οἱ ὦμοι;

Τοὺς ὤμους δὲ καὶ τὰς ὠλένας καὶ αὖθις τὰς χεῖρας,
95 τὸ ποιητικὸν καὶ ἐνεργητικὸν καὶ δραστήριον.

Τίς ἡ καρδία;

Τὴν δ' αὖ καρδίαν σύμβολον εἶναι τῆς θεοειδοῦς ζωῆς
τῆς τὴν οἰκείαν ζωτικὴν δύναμιν ἀγαθοειδῶς εἰς τὰ
προνοούμενα διασπειρούσης.

Mss.   *AT CDGFH*

Crit.   **78** Τίς – ἀφή] *om.* G   **79** δυνάμεις δὲ H   **82** τὰς] τοὺς *T*   **88** οἱ
ὀδόντες *FH*   **97** δὲ *FH*

Comp.   **79** δυνάμεις] *non hab. Ps.-Dion.*   **91** πληθύει *Ps.-Dion. (PbFa = Coisl.)*

ALPHA 5

100 Τί τὰ στήθη;

Τὰ στέρνα δὲ αὖθις ἐμφαίνειν τὸ ἀδάμαστον καὶ τὸ φρουρητικόν, ὡς ἐπὶ τῆς ὑποκειμένης καρδίας, τῆς ζωτικῆς διαδόσεως.

Τί τὰ νῶτα;

105 Τὰ δὲ νῶτα, τὸ συνεκτικὸν τῶν ζωογόνων ἁπασῶν δυνάμεων.

Τί οἱ πόδες;

Τοὺς πόδας δέ, τὸ κινητικὸν καὶ ὀξὺ καὶ ἐντρεχὲς τῆς ἐπὶ τὰ θεῖα πορευτικῆς ἀεικινησίας. Διὸ καὶ πτερωτοὺς
110 ἡ θεολογία τοὺς τῶν ἁγίων νοῶν ἐσχημάτισε πόδας· τὸ γὰρ πτερὸν ἐμφαίνει τὴν ἀναγωγικὴν ὀξύτητα καὶ τὸ οὐράνιον καὶ τὸ πρὸς τὸ ἄναντες ὁδοποιητικὸν καὶ τὸ παντὸς χαμαιζήλου διὰ τὸ ἀνώφορον ἐξῃρημένον.

Τί τὰ πτερά;

115 Ἡ δὲ τῶν πτερῶν ἐλαφρία, τὸ κατὰ μηδὲν πρόσγειον, ἀλλ'ὅλον ἀμιγῶς καὶ ἀβαρῶς ἐπὶ τὸ ὑψηλὸν ἀναγόμενον.

Τί ἡ γυμνότης;

Τὸ δὲ γυμνὸν καὶ ἀνυπόδετον, τὸ ἄφετον καὶ εὔλυτον
120 καὶ ἄσχετον καὶ καθαρεῦον τῆς τῶν ἐκτὸς προσθήκης

Font.   105 cf. Ez. 1, 18   110/111 cf. Ez. 1, 7

Mss.   *AT CDGFH*

Crit.   102 ἐπὶ τῆς] ὑπὸ τῆς *T CD*, ἀπὸ τῆς *G, om. FH*   καρδίας] τῆς *praem. FH*
109 τῇ θείᾳ *DFH*   110 νόων *T FH*   111 πτερωτὸν *T*   τὸ] τὸν *A*
112 τὸ¹] om. *AT*   114 τὰ] περὶ ἄνω (*sic*) add. *G*   115 πτερῶν] ποδῶν
CD   116/117 μεταγόμενον *D*   118 Τί] τίς *Gᵃ·ᶜᵒʳʳ·*   119 ἀφετὸν *D*

Comp.   102/103 ζωτικῆς] ζωοποιοῦ *Ps.-Dion.*   109 πτερωτοὺς] ὑποπτέρους
Ps.-Dion. (RcPtPnVvLc = Coisl.)

14 FLORILEGIVM COISLINIANVM

καὶ τὸ πρὸς τὴν ἁπλότητα τὴν θείαν ὡς ἐφικτὸν ἀφο-
μοιωτικόν.

Τί ἡ λαμπρὰ ἐσθής;

Τὴν δὲ φανὴν ἐσθῆτα καὶ τὴν πυρώδη σημαίνειν οἴο-
125 μαι τὸ θεοειδὲς κατὰ τὴν πυρὸς εἰκόνα καὶ τὸ φωτιστικὸν διὰ τὰς ἐν οὐρανῷ λήξεις, ὅπου τὸ φῶς καὶ τὸ καθόλου νοητῶς ἐλλάμπον ἢ νοερῶς ἐλλαμπόμενον.

Τί ἡ ἱερατική;

Τὴν δὲ ἱερατικήν, τὸ πρὸς τὰ θεῖα καὶ μυστικὰ θεάμα-
130 τα προσαγωγικὸν καὶ τὸ τῆς ὅλης ζωῆς ἀφιερωμένον.

Τί αἱ ζῶναι;

Τὰς δὲ ζώνας, τὸ τῶν γονίμων αὐτῶν δυνάμεων
φρουρητικὸν καὶ τὸ τὴν συνάγωγον αὐτῶν ἕξιν εἰς
ἑαυτὴν ἑνιαίως συνεστράφθαι κύκλῳ μετ'εὐκοσμίας τῇ
135 ἀμεταπτώτῳ ταυτότητι περὶ ἑαυτὴν συνελίσσεσθαι.

Τί αἱ ῥάβδοι;

Τὰς δ'αὖ ῥάβδους, τὸ βασιλικὸν καὶ ἡγεμονικὸν καὶ
εὐθεῖα τὰ πάντα περαῖνον.

Font.   124 cf. Lc. 24, 4   129 cf. Ez. 9, 2; 10, 6   132 cf. Ez. 9, 2; Dan. 10, 5;
Apoc. 15, 6   137 cf. Iud. 6, 21

Mss.   AT CDGFH

Crit.   124 φαεινὴν C   126 διὰ] καὶ D   127 ἐκλάμπον D   νοητῶς
H, illeg. F   128 ἡ] om. FH   130 ζῆς (sic) F   ἀφιερομένος D
133 συνάγωγον] sic acc. AT D^{a.corr.}H, συναγωγὸν CD^{p.corr.}G, illeg. F   134 συνε-
στράφθαι] καὶ add. G, ut expectaueris   135 ταυτότι, τι A   137 δὲ D
138 εὐθεία DF^{p.corr.}, εὐθέα CG^{p.corr.}, εὐθ(') H

Comp.   121/122 post ἀφομοιωτικόν] Ἀλλ'ἐπειδὴ αὖθις ἡ ἁπλῆ καὶ «Πολυποίκιλος σοφία» καὶ τοὺς ἀσκεπεῖς ἀμφιέννυσι καὶ σκεύη τινὰ δίδωσι περιφέρειν αὐτοῖς,
φέρε καὶ τὰ τῶν οὐρανίων νοῶν ἱερὰ περιβλήματα καὶ ὄργανα κατὰ τὸ ἡμῖν
δυνατὸν ἀναπτύξωμεν hab. Ps.-Dion.   124 δὲ] μὲν γὰρ Ps.-Dion.
133 συναγωγὸν Ps.-Dion.   134 post συνεστράφθαι] καὶ hab. Ps.-Dion.
137 δὲ Ps.-Dion.   138 εὐθείᾳ Ps.-Dion. (RcPtPbFaLc = Coisl.)

ALPHA 5   15

Τί τὰ δόρατα;

140   Τὰ δὲ δόρατα καὶ τοὺς πέλυκας, τὸ τῶν ἀνομοίων
διαιρετικὸν καὶ τὸ τῶν διακριτικῶν δυνάμεων ὀξὺ καὶ
ἐνεργὲς καὶ δραστήριον.

Τί τὰ σχοινία;

Τὰ δὲ γεωμετρικὰ καὶ τεκτονικὰ σκεύη, τὸ θεμελιω-
145   τικὸν καὶ οἰκοδομητικὸν καὶ ὅσα ἄλλα τῆς ἀναγώγου
καὶ ἐπιστρεπτικῆς ἐστι τῶν δευτέρων προνοίας.
῎Εστι δὲ ὅτε καὶ τῶν εἰς ἡμᾶς θεοκρισιῶν ἐστι σύμ-
βολα τὰ πλαττόμενα τῶν ἁγίων ἀγγέλων ὄργανα, τῶν
μὲν δηλούντων ἐπανορθωτικὴν παιδείαν ἢ τιμωρὸν δι-
150   καιοσύνην, τῶν δὲ περιστάσεως ἐλευθερίαν ἢ παιδείας
τέλος ἢ προτέρας εὐπαθείας ἐπανάληψιν ἢ προσθήκην
ἑτέρων δωρεῶν, μικρῶν ἢ μεγάλων, αἰσθητῶν ἢ νοητῶν, καὶ ὅλως οὐκ ἂν ἀπορήσειεν ὁ διορατικὸς νοῦς
οἰκείως ἁρμόσαι τοῖς ἀφανέσι τὰ φαινόμενα.

155   Τί οἱ ἄνεμοι;

Τὸ δὲ καὶ ἀνέμους αὐτοὺς ὀνομάζεσθαι τὴν ὀξεῖαν
αὐτῶν ἐμφαίνει καὶ ἐπὶ πάντα σχεδὸν ἀχρόνως διήκου-
σαν ποίησιν καὶ τὴν ἄνωθεν ἐπὶ τὰ κάτω καὶ αὖθις ἐκ
τῶν κάτω πρὸς τὸ ἄναντες διαπορθμευτικὴν κίνησιν,
160   τὴν ἀνατείνουσαν μὲν τὰ δεύτερα πρὸς τὸ ὑπέρτερον

Font.   **140** cf. II Mac. 5, 2   cf. Ez. 9, 2   **143/144** Zach. 2, 5; Ez. 40, 3; 47, 3;
Apoc. 21, 15   **156** cf. Ps. 103, 4; Zach. 6, 5; Ez. 1, 4; 3, 14; Dan. 7, 2

Mss.   *AT CDGFH* (*G* usque ad διαιρετικὸν, 5.141)

Crit.   **139/142** Τί – δραστήριον] *post* ἐκκαλουμένην (*l.* 182) *trsp. FH*   **139** δόρα-
τα] δῶρα *A^{p.corr.}* (δώρα *A^{a.corr.}*)   **142** ἐνεργὸν *T*, ἐναργὲς *F*   **144** γεωμετ-
ρικὰ] γεωργικὰ *F*   **146** ἐπιτρεπτικῆς *FH^{a.corr.}*   ἐστι] εἶναι *FH*
147 ἐστι] εἰσὶ *A^{p.corr.} H*   **151** ἀνάληψιν *T*   **159** πρὸς – ἄναντες] καὶ τὰ
ἄνω τες *D^{p.corr. ut uid.}* (πρὸς τὸ ἄναντες *V^{a.corr.}*)

Comp.   **140** πελέκεις *Ps.-Dion.* (*PaRcPtLc = Coisl.*)   **145** *post* οἰκοδομητικὸν] καὶ
τελειωτικὸν *hab. Ps.-Dion.*   ἀναγωγοῦ *Ps.-Dion.*   **158** πτῆσιν *scripsit*
Heil cum VcKa (*cett. = Coisl.*)

16 FLORILEGIVM COISLINIANVM

ὕψος, κινοῦσαν δὲ τὰ πρῶτα πρὸς κοινωνικὴν καὶ προνοητικὴν τῶν ὑφειμένων πρόοδον. Εἴποι δ'ἄν τις τὴν τοῦ ἀερίου πνεύματος ἀνεμιαίαν ἐπωνυμίαν καὶ τὸ θεοειδὲς τῶν οὐρανίων νοῶν ἐμφαίνειν· ἔχει γὰρ καὶ τοῦτο
165 θεαρχικῆς ἐνεργείας εἰκόνα καὶ τύπον – ὡς ἐν τῇ Συμβολικῇ Θεολογίᾳ κατὰ τὴν τετράστοιχον ἀνακάθαρσιν ἡμῖν διὰ πλειόνων ἀποδέδεικται – κατὰ τὸ τῆς φύσεως κινητικὸν καὶ ζωογόνον καὶ τὴν ὀξεῖαν καὶ ἀκράτητον χώρησιν καὶ τὴν ἄγνωστον ἡμῖν καὶ ἀόρατον κρυφιό-
170 τητα τῶν κινητικῶν ἀρχῶν καὶ ἀποπερατώσεων· Οὐ γὰρ οἶδας φησὶ πόθεν ἔρχεται καὶ ποῦ ὑπάγει.

Τί αἱ νεφέλαι;

Ἀλλὰ καὶ νεφέλης αὐτοῖς ἰδέαν ἡ θεολογία περιπλάττει, σημαίνουσα διὰ τούτου τοὺς ἱεροὺς νόας τοῦ μὲν
175 κρυφίου φωτὸς ὑπερκοσμίως ἀποπληρουμένους, τὴν πρωτοφαῆ δὲ φωτοφάνειαν ἀνεκπομπεύτως εἰσδεχομένους, καὶ ταύτην ἀφθόνως εἰς τὰ δεύτερα δευτεροφανῶς καὶ ἀναλόγως διαπορθμεύοντας, καὶ μὴν ὅτι τὸ γόνιμον αὐτοῖς καὶ ζωοποιὸν καὶ αὐξητικὸν καὶ τελειω-
180 τικὸν ἐνυπάρχει κατὰ τὴν νοητὴν ὀμβροτοκίαν, τὴν τὸν ἐκδόχιον κόλπον πιαλέοις ὑετοῖς ἐπὶ ζωτικὰς ὠδῖνας ἐκκαλουμένην.

Font.   170/171 Io. 3, 8   173 cf. Ez. 1, 4; 10, 3-4; Apoc. 10, 1

Mss.   AT CDFH

Crit.   164 νόων T FH   167 ἀναδέδικται Aᵃ·ᶜᵒʳʳ·, ἀναδέδεικται Aᵖ·ᶜᵒʳʳ·
168 ζωογονητικόν C   173 αὐτῆς F, αὐταῖς H   175 ἀποπληρωμένους FH
176 ἀνεκπομπευτῶς T   177 δεύτερα] δευτέραν FH, βαθύτερα AT
180 ἐν ὑπάρχει Aᵖ·ᶜᵒʳʳ· T CD

Comp.   176 πρωτοφανῆ Ps.-Dion. (FbVvVcKa = Coisl.)

ALPHA 5 17

Τί ὁ χαλκός;

Εἰ δὲ χαλκοῦ καὶ ἠλέκτρου καὶ λίθων πολυχρωμά-
185 των εἶδος ἡ θεολογία ταῖς οὐρανίαις οὐσίαις περιτίθη-
σι, τὸ μὲν ἤλεκτρον ὡς χρυσοειδὲς ἅμα καὶ ἀργυροειδὲς
ἐμφαίνει τὴν ἄσηπτον ὡς ἐν χρυσῷ καὶ ἀδάπανον καὶ
ἀμείωτον καὶ ἄχραντον διαύγειαν, καὶ τὴν φανὴν ὡς ἐν
ἀργύρῳ καὶ φωτοειδῆ καὶ οὐρανίαν αἴγλην, τῷ δὲ χαλ-
190 κῷ κατὰ τοὺς ἀποδοθέντας λόγους ἢ τὸ πυρῶδες ἢ τὸ
χρυσοειδὲς ἀπονεμητέον.

Τί αἱ χροαὶ τῶν λίθων;

Τὰς δὲ τῶν λίθων πολυχρωμάτους ἰδέας ἐμφαίνειν
οἰητέον ἢ ὡς λευκὰς τὸ φωτοειδές, ἢ ὡς ἐρυθρὰς τὸ
195 πυροειδές, ἢ ὡς ξανθὰς τὸ χρυσοειδές, ἢ ὡς χλωρὰς τὸ
νεανικὸν καὶ ἀκμαῖον, καὶ καθ᾽ἕκαστον εἶδος εὑρήσεις
ἀναγωγικὴν τῶν τυπικῶν εἰκόνων ἀνακάθαρσιν. Ἀλλ᾽ἐ-
πειδὴ ταῦτα κατὰ δύναμιν ἀρκούντως εἰρῆσθαι νομίζω,
μετιτέον ἐπὶ τὴν ἱερὰν ἀνάπτυξιν τῆς τῶν οὐρανίων
200 νοῶν ἱεροτύπου θηρομορφίας.

---

ont. **184** cf. Ez. 1, 7; 40, 3; Dan. 10, 6   cf. Ez. 1, 4; 8, 2   **192** cf. Ez. 1, 26;
10, 1; Apoc. 4, 3

Ass. *AT CDFH*

:rit. **184/185** πολυχρωμάτων] ἀπὸ χρομάτων *T*   **185** οὐρανίοις *A* *C*^p.corr.·*D*
185/186 παρατίθησι *A, illeg. D*   **186** τὸ] τὸν *C*   ἠλέκτρινον *FH*
187 ἀδαπάνητον *C*   **188** φαεινὴν *T* *C*^p.corr.   **189** οὐράνιον *DFH*
189/190 τὸ δὲ χαλκὸν *FH*   **190** πυρρῶδες *FH*   τὸ²] *om. H*
192 χρόαι *C*, χροιαί *T*   **193** εἰδέας *A DFH*^a. uel p.corr.   **195** πυρροειδὲς *FH*
χλοερὰς *A*, χλορὰς *T, illeg. D*   **197** ἀναγωγικῶς *C*   **199/200** τὴν –
νοῶν] *om. T*   **200** νόων *FH*

:omp. **184** *post* δὲ] καὶ *hab. Ps.-Dion.*   **195** πυρῶδες *Ps.-Dion.* (πυρωειδὲς *Lc*)
χλοερὰς *Ps.-Dion. (VcKa = Coisl.)*   **197** τυπωτικῶν *Ps.-Dion. (PaVvFaLc =*
Coisl.)   **198** *post* δύναμιν] ἡμῖν *hab. Ps.-Dion.*

18 FLORILEGIVM COISLINIANVM

Τί τὸ λεοντοειδές;

Λέοντα μὲν γὰρ ἐμφαίνειν οἰητέον τὸ ἡγεμονικὸν καὶ
ῥωμαλέον καὶ ἀδάμαστον καὶ τὸ πρὸς τὴν κρυφιότητα
τῆς ἀφθέγμονος θεαρχίας ὅση δύναμις ἀφομοιωματι-
205 κὸν τῇ τῶν νοερῶν ἰχνῶν περικαλύψει καὶ τῇ μυστι-
κῶς ἀνεκπομπεύτῳ περιστολῇ τῆς κατὰ θείαν ἔλλαμ-
ψιν ἐπ'αὐτὴν ἀνατατικῆς πορείας.

Τί τὸ βοοειδές;

Τὴν δὲ τοῦ βοός, τὸ ἰσχυρὸν καὶ ἀκμαῖον καὶ τοὺς νο-
210 εροὺς αὔλακας ἀνευρῦνον εἰς ὑποδοχὴν τῶν οὐρανίων
καὶ γονιμοποιῶν ὄμβρων, καὶ τὰ κέρατα τὸ φρουρητικὸν καὶ ἀκράτητον.

Τί τὸ ἀετοειδές;

Τὴν δὲ τοῦ ἀετοῦ, τὸ βασιλικὸν καὶ ὑψηφόρον καὶ
215 ταχυπετές, καὶ τὸ πρὸς τὴν δυναμοποιὸν τροφὴν ὀξὺ
καὶ νῆφον καὶ ἐντρεχὲς καὶ εὐμήχανον, καὶ τὸ πρὸς τὴν
ἄφθονον καὶ πολύφωτον ἀκτῖνα τῆς θεαρχικῆς ἡλιοβο-
λίας ἐν ταῖς τῶν ὀπτικῶν δυνάμεων εὐρώστοις ἀνατά-
σεσιν ἀνεμποδίστως κατευθὺ καὶ ἀκλινῶς θεωρητικόν.

Font.   **202** cf. Ez. 1, 10; Apoc. 4, 7   **209** cf. Ez. 1, 10; Apoc. 4, 7   **214** cf. Ez. 1, 10;
Apoc. 4, 7

Mss.   *AT CDFH*

Crit.   **202/203** τὸ – πρὸς] *om. DFH*   **205** νοερῶν] ἱερῶν *FH*   **206** περιβολῇ *T*
207 ἀναστατικῆς *T*, ἀνατακῆς *(sic) A*   **215** τὸ] τὴν *FH*   **217** καὶ]
om. D   **218** εὐρρώστοις *CF*

Comp.   **202** Λέοντα – γὰρ] καὶ τὴν μὲν λέοντος μορφὴν *Ps.-Dion.* (λέοντα γὰρ *PaRc*,
καὶ τὴν μὲν λέοντος μορφὴν λέοντα γὰρ *Pt*[a.corr.]*PnLc*)   **204/205** ἀφομοι-
ωτικὸν *Ps.-Dion.* *(Pb = Coisl.)*   **214** ὑψίφορον *Ps.-Dion. (VcKa = Coisl.,*
ὑψιπόρον *VvFa)*

ALPHA 5

220

Τί οἱ ἵπποι;

Τὴν δὲ τῶν ἵππων, τὸ εὐπειθὲς καὶ εὐήνιον, καὶ λευ-
κῶν μὲν ὄντων τὸ λαμπρὸν καὶ ὡς μάλιστα τοῦ θείου
φωτὸς συγγενές, κυανῶν δὲ ὄντων τὸ κρύφιον, ἐρυ-
θρῶν δὲ τὸ πυρῶδες καὶ δραστήριον, συμμίκτων δὲ
225 πρὸς λευκοῦ καὶ μέλανος τὸ τῇ διαπορθμευτικῇ δυνάμει τῶν ἄκρων συνδετικὸν καὶ τὰ πρῶτα τοῖς δευτέροις
καὶ τὰ δεύτερα τοῖς πρώτοις ἐπιστρεπτικῶς ἢ προνοη-
τικῶς συνάπτον.

Τί τὸ θυμοειδές;

230 Τὸ μὲν θυμοειδὲς αὐτῶν εἰς τὴν νοερὰν ἀνδρείαν, ἧς
ἐστιν ἔσχατον ὁ θυμὸς ἀπήχημα, τὴν δ'αὖ ἐπιθυμίαν
εἰς τὸν θεῖον ἔρωτα, καὶ συλλήβδην εἰπεῖν, ἁπάσας τὰς
τῶν ἀλόγων ζώων αἰσθήσεις τε καὶ πολυμερείας εἰς τὰς
ἀΰλους τῶν οὐρανίων οὐσιῶν νοήσεις καὶ ἑνοειδεῖς δυ-
235 νάμεις ἀνάγοντες.

Font. **221** cf. IV Reg. 2, 11; Ioel 2, 4; Zach. 1, 8; 6, 2.3; Apoc. 6, 2; 19, 11

Mss. *AT CDFH*

Crit. **221** εὐπειθὲς] εὐθὲς *FH* καὶ²] *om. FH* **223/224** ἐρρυθρῶν *F*
224 πυροειδὲς *T,* πυρρῶδες *F* **225** λευκοῦ] χαλκοῦ *FH* **227** δεύτερα – πρώτοις] πρῶτα τοῖς δευτέροις *A^{a.corr.}* (δευτέροις *cancell. p. corr.*)
228 συνάπτοντος *AT* **231** ὁ θυμὸς] *ante* ἔσχατον *trsp. FH* **233** πολ-
λυμερίας *D* **235** ἀνάγοντες] ἐνάγοντες *C*

Comp. **230** *ante* Τὸ] Ἀλλ'εἰ μὴ τῆς τοῦ λόγου κατεστοχαζόμεθα συμμετρίας, καὶ τὰς
κατὰ μέρος τῶν εἰρημένων ζώων ἰδιότητας καὶ πάσας τὰς σωματικὰς αὐτῶν
διαπλάσεις ἐφηρμόσαμεν ἂν οὐκ ἀπεικότως ταῖς οὐρανίαις δυνάμεσι κατὰ
τὰς ἀνομοίους ὁμοιότητας *hab. Ps.-Dion.* **231** δὲ *Ps.-Dion.* (*VcKAFa^{p.corr.}* =
Coisl.) **232** πάσας *Ps.-Dion.* (*PaRcPtPnVvFaLc = Coisl.*)

20 FLORILEGIVM COISLINIANVM

Τί οἱ ποταμοί;

Ἐπισκεπτέον δὲ καὶ τὸ ποταμοὺς εἰρῆσθαι καὶ τροχοὺς καὶ ἅρματα συνημμένα ταῖς οὐρανίοις οὐσίαις. Οἱ
μὲν γὰρ ἐμπύριοι ποταμοὶ σημαίνουσι τοὺς θεαρχικοὺς
240 ὀχετούς, ἄφθονον αὐτοῖς καὶ ἀνέκλειπτον ἐπίρροιαν
χορηγοῦντας καὶ ζωοποιοῦ θρεπτικῆς γονιμότητος.

Τί τὰ ἅρματα;

Τὰ δὲ ἅρματα, τὴν συζευκτικὴν τῶν ὁμοταγῶν κοινωνίαν.

245   Τί οἱ τροχοί;

Οἱ δὲ τροχοὶ πτερωτοὶ μὲν ὄντες, ἐπὶ δὲ τὰ πρόσθεν
ἀνεπιστρόφως καὶ ἀκλινῶς πορευόμενοι τὴν κατ'εὐθεῖαν
καὶ ὄρθιον ὁδὸν τῆς πορευτικῆς αὐτῶν ἐνεργείας δύναμιν, ἐπὶ τὸν αὐτὸν ἀκλινῆ καὶ ἰθύτομον οἶμον ἁπάσης
250 αὐτῶν τῆς νοερᾶς τροχιᾶς ὑπερκοσμίως ἰθυνομένης.

Ἔστι δὲ καὶ κατ'ἄλλην ἀναγωγὴν ἀνακαθᾶραι τὴν
τῶν νοερῶν τροχῶν ἐκείνων ἱερογραφίαν· Ἐπεκλήθη
γὰρ αὐτοῖς, ὥς φησιν ὁ θεολόγος, Γελγέλ· ἐμφαίνει δὲ
τοῦτο κατ'Ἑβραϊκὴν φωνὴν ἀνακυκλισμοὺς καὶ ἀνα-

Font.   237 cf. Ez. 47, 1-12; Dan. 7, 10; Apoc. 22, 1   237/238 cf. supra l. 10
         242 cf. Zach. 6, 1-5   252/253 cf. Ez. 10, 13

Mss.   AT CDFH

Crit.   238 οὐρανίαις DFH   239 ἐμπύριοι] ἐν πυρὶ οἱ D^{ut uid.}   243 Τὰ – ἄρ-
         ματα] om. FH   συζευτικὴν D   249 ὕμνον A^{p.corr.} (οἶμον A^{a. corr. ut uid.})
         251 κατὰ ἄλλην FH   252 ἐκείνων ἱερογραφίαν] εἰκόνα CDFH
         253 γέλ· γέλ T FH   254 κατ'Ἑβραϊκὴν] (sic uel κατεβραϊκὴν A CDFH)
         κατὰ ἑβραϊκὴν T   καὶ] iter. A^{a.corr.}

Comp.   237 ante Ἐπισκεπτέον] Ἀρκεῖ δὲ τοῖς ἐχέφροσιν οὐ ταῦτα μόνον, ἀλλὰ
         καὶ μιᾶς ἀπεμφαινούσης εἰκόνος ἀνακάθαρσις εἰς τὴν τῶν παραπλησί-
         ων ὁμοιότροπον διασάφησιν hab. Ps.-Dion.   238 οὐρανίαις Ps.-Dion.
         240 αὐταῖς Ps.-Dion. (FaLc = Coisl.)   241 θρεπτικοὺς Ps.-Dion.
         252 ἐκείνων ἱερογραφίαν] εἰκονογραφίαν Ps.-Dion.   254 καθ'Ἑβραϊ-
         κὴν scripsit Heil (PaRcPt^{a.corr.}PnPbFa = Coisl.)   ἀνακυλισμοὺς Ps.-Dion.
         (FaPtPa^{a. corr.}Pb = Coisl.)

ALPHA 5

255 καλύψεις. Οἱ γὰρ ἐμπύριοι καὶ θεοειδεῖς τροχοὶ τοὺς
μὲν ἀνακυκλισμοὺς ἔχουσι τῇ περὶ τὸ ταὐτὸν ἀγαθὸν
ἀειδινήτῳ κινήσει· τὰς ἀνακαλύψεις δέ, τῇ τῶν κρυφί-
ων ἐκφαντορίᾳ καὶ τῇ τῶν περιπεζίων ἀναγωγῇ καὶ τῇ
τῶν ὑψηλῶν ἐλλάμψεων εἰς τὰ ὑφειμένα καταγωγικῇ
260 διαπορθμεύσει.

Τίς ἡ λεγομένη χαρὰ τῶν ἀγγέλων;

Λοιπὸς ἡμῖν εἰς διασάφησιν ὁ περὶ τῆς χαρᾶς τῶν
οὐρανίων διακοσμήσεων λόγος· καὶ γὰρ ἄδεκτοι παντελῶς εἰσὶ τῆς καθ'ἡμᾶς ἐμπαθοῦς ἡδονῆς, συγχαίρειν
265 δὲ θεῷ λέγονται τῇ τῶν ἀπολωλότων εὑρέσει κατὰ τὴν
θεοειδῆ ῥᾳστώνην καὶ τὴν ἐπὶ τῇ προνοίᾳ καὶ σωτηρίᾳ
τῶν ἐπὶ θεὸν ἐπιστρεφόντων ἀγαθοειδῆ καὶ ἄφθονον
εὐφροσύνην καὶ τὴν εὐπάθειαν ἐκείνην τὴν ἄρρητον ἧς
ἐν μεθέξει πολλάκις γεγόνασι καὶ ἄνδρες ἱεροὶ κατὰ τὰς
270 θεουργοὺς τῶν θείων ἐλλάμψεων ἐπιφοιτήσεις.

Τοσαῦτά μοι περὶ τῶν ἱερῶν ἀναπλάσεων εἰρήσθω,
τῆς μὲν ἀκριβοῦς αὐτῶν ἐκφαντορίας ἀπολειπόμενα,
συντελοῦντα δὲ ὡς οἶμαι πρὸς τὸ μὴ ταπεινῶς ἡμᾶς
ἐναπομεῖναι ταῖς τυπωτικαῖς φαντασίαις.

---

ont. **262/263** cf. Lc. 15, 10

Ass. *AT CDFH*

Crit. **256** περὶ] παρὰ *C*   **265** εὑρήσει *AT D*   **267** τῶν] *iter. D*
270 ελάμψεων *FH*

Comp. **256** ἀνακυλισμοὺς *Ps.-Dion. (Fa^{p.corr.} PtPn^{p.corr.} Pb^{a.corr.}* = *Coisl.)*   **267** ἐπι-
στρεφομένων *Ps.-Dion.*   **271** *post* μοι] καὶ *hab. Ps.-Dion.*

22 FLORILEGIVM COISLINIANVM

Γ'

Ἀπόδειξις ὅτι ἀγγέλους φύλακας ἡμῖν ἔδωκεν ὁ θεός

6   Βασιλείου Καισαρείας

Παντὶ ἀνθρώπῳ πεπιστευκότι εἰς τὸν κύριον ἄγγελος παρεδρεύει, ἐὰν μήποτε αὐτὸν ἡμεῖς ἐκ τῶν πονη-
ρῶν ἔργων ἀποδιώξωμεν· ὡς γὰρ τὰς μελίσσας καπνὸς
φυγαδεύει, καὶ τὰς περιστερὰς ἐλαύνει δυσωδία, οὕτως
5 καὶ τὸν φύλακα τῆς ζωῆς ἡμῶν ἄγγελον ἡ πολύδακρυς
καὶ δυσώδης ἀφίστησιν ἁμαρτία.

7   Γρηγορίου Νύσης

Λόγος τίς ἐστιν, ἐκ πατρικῆς παραδόσεως τὸ πιστὸν
ἔχων, ὅς φησι, πεσούσης ἡμῶν εἰς ἁμαρτίαν τῆς φύσεως, μὴ παριδεῖν τὸν θεὸν τὴν πτῶσιν ἡμῶν ἀπρονόητον,
ἀλλ'ἄγγελόν τινα τῶν τὴν ἀσώματον εἰληχότων φύσιν
5 παρακαθιστᾶν εἰς συμμαχίαν τῇ ἑκάστου ζωῇ, ἐκ δὲ

Font.   **6.1/6** = Bas. Caes., Hom. super Ps., PG 29, 364, 15-21   **7.1/16** = Greg.
Nyss., Vit. Moys., 2, 45, 3 – 46, 8

Mss.   **6** *AT CDK*   **7** *AT CDEK*

Tit.   **Γ'**] *om.* K   Ἀπόδειξις – θεός] ἀπόδειξις ὅτι ἄγγελοι παρέπονται τοῖς
πιστοῖς K; *cf.* Sacr. Par., PG 95, 1097, 19-20 (Περὶ ἀγγέλων· ὅτι ἀγγέλους φύλακας ἐπέστησεν ὁ Θεός)   **6** Καισαρείας] *om.* K

Crit.   **7.2** ὅς] ὥς CD   φασιν C   **4** τὴν τῶν ἀσωμάτων E

Comp.   **6.1** *ante* Παντὶ] Παρεμβαλεῖ ἄγελλος Κυρίου *hab.* Sacr. Par.   ἀνθρώπῳ]
non hab. Bas. *et* Sacr. Par.   **4** ἐξελαύνει δυσωδία Sacr. Par., Loc. comm.
et Corp. Par. (P = Coisl.), δυσωδία ἐξελαύνει Bas.   **7.3** περιϊδεῖν Greg.
(EKSin330 = Coisl.)

Ind.   **6.1/6** = Sacr. Par., PG 95, 1160, 21-27   **3/6** = Ps.-Max., Loc. comm. 26, 8, /8
(p. 573); Corp. Par. 1, 38

ALPHA 6 – 9   23

τοῦ ἐναντίου τὸν φθορέα τῆς φύσεως ἀντιμηχανᾶσθαι
τὸ ἴσον, διὰ πονηροῦ τινὸς καὶ κακοποιοῦ δαίμονος τὴν
τοῦ ἀνθρώπου ζωὴν λυμαινόμενον, ἐν μέσῳ δὲ ὄντα
τῶν δύο τὸν ἄνθρωπον, ἑκατέρου τῶν παρεπομένων
10 σκοπόν, ὑπεναντίως πρὸς τὸν ἕτερον ἔχοντα· δι᾽ἑαυ-
τοῦ ποιεῖ κατὰ τοῦ ἄλλου ὁ νενικηκὼς ἐπικρατέστερον,
προδεικνύντος τοῖς λογισμοῖς τοῦ μὲν ἀγαθοῦ τὰ τῆς
ἀρετῆς ἀγαθά, ὅσα δι᾽ἐλπίδος τοῖς κατορθοῦσιν ὁρᾶται,
τοῦ δὲ πονηροῦ τὰς ὑλώδεις ἡδονάς, ἀφ᾽ὧν ἐλπὶς μὲν
15 οὐδεμία ἀγαθῶν, τὸ δὲ παρὸν καὶ μετεχόμενον καὶ ὁρώμενον τὰς αἰσθήσεις τῶν ἀνοητοτέρων ἀνδραποδίζεται.

8   Διδύμου

Τοὺς μὲν ἁγίους φωταγωγοὶ φυλάττουσιν ἄγγελοι, τοὺς δὲ φαύλους σκοτεινοί.

9   Εὐαγρίου

Ὁ ἀκάθαρτος ἄνθρωπος καὶ ἀπὸ τοῦ δοθέντος αὐτῷ
ἐκ παιδὸς ἀγγέλου χωρίζεται.

---

ont.   **8.1/2** locum non inueni nisi in flor.; cf. Did. Caec., Comm. in Iob, 375, 1-3 et
        ibid. 375, 28-31   **9.1/2** = Euagr., Schol. in Prou., 189, 2-3

Iss.   *AT CDEK*   **8** *AC*   **9** *AC*

---

rit.   **9** ἐκκατέρου *(sic spir.)* T

---

omp.   **7/8** τῇ τοῦ ἀνθρώπου ζωῇ *Greg. (Sin330 = Coisl.)*   **9** *post* ἄνθρωπον] τὸν
        hab. Greg. (KSin330 = Coisl.)   **11** ποιεῖν *Greg.*   ὁ νενικηκὼς] *non hab.*
        Greg.   **13** τοῖς κατορθοῦσιν δι᾽ἐλπίδος *Vat. gr. 1907 et ed. Greg. Daniélou;*
        ed. Musurillo = Coisl.   **14** πονηροῦ] ἑτέρου *Greg.*   **15** ἀγαθῶν οὐδεμία
        Greg.   **16** ἀνοήτων *Greg. (E = Coisl.)*   **8.1** φυλάσσουσιν *Ps.-Antonius*
        9.1 *post* Ὁ] δὲ *hab. Euagr., Ps.-Antonius et Corp. Par.*   *post* ἄνθρωπος] ὃν
        πένητά φησι *hab. Sacr. Par.*

---

d.   **8.1/2** = Sacr. Par., PG 95, 1097, 35-36; Ps.-Ant. Mel., Loc. comm., PG 136,
       1084, 14-15   **9.1/2** = Sacr. Par., PG 95, 1097, 38-39; Ms. Athen. Bib. Nat.
       1070, f. 137ᵛ (cit. Géhin, *Scholia in Prouerbia*, p. 76); Ps.-Ant. Mel., Loc. comm.,
       PG 136, 1084, 17-18; Corp. Par., 1, 265

24 FLORILEGIVM COISLINIANVM

10 Γενέσεως

Ἰδοὺ ἐγὼ ἀποστέλλω τὸν ἄγγελόν μου πρὸ προσώπου σου, ἵνα φυλάξῃ σε ἐν τῇ ὁδῷ, ὅπως εἰσαγάγῃ σε
εἰς γῆν ἣν ἡτοίμασά σοι. Πρόσεχε σεαυτῷ καὶ εἰσάκουε
αὐτοῦ καὶ μὴ ἀπειθήσῃς αὐτῷ· οὐ γὰρ μὴ ὑποστελεῖταί
5 σε. Τὸ γὰρ ὄνομά μου ἐστὶν ἐπ'αὐτῷ· ὁ ἄγγελός μου ὁ
ῥυόμενός σε.

11 Δαυῒδ προφήτου

Ὅτι τοῖς ἀγγέλοις αὐτοῦ ἐντελεῖται περὶ σοῦ τοῦ δια-
φυλάξαί σε ἐν πάσαις ταῖς ὁδοῖς σου· ἐπὶ χειρῶν ἀροῦ-
σί σε, μήποτε προσκόψῃς πρὸς λίθον τὸν πόδα σου· ἐπὶ
ἀσπίδα καὶ βασιλίσκον ἐπιβήσῃ καὶ καταπατήσεις λέον-
5 τα καὶ δράκοντα.

Font.   **10.1/5** immo = Ex. 23, 20-21   **5/6** = Gen. 48, 16   **11.1/5** = Ps. 90,
11-13

Mss.   **10** AC   **11** AC

Tit.   **11** προφήτου] om. C

Crit.   **10.5/6** ὁ¹ – σε] om. C   **11.2/5** ἐπὶ – δράκοντα] om. C

Comp.   **10.3** ante γῆν] τὴν hab. Sacr. Par. et Ex. (707, 527 = Coisl.)   4 ἀπειθή-
σῃ Sacr. Par., ἀπείθει Ex.   ὑποστείληταί Ex.   5 ἐν αὐτῷ Sacr. Par.
μου²] non hab. Gen.   6 σε] με Gen.   **11.3** ἐπὶ] ἐπ' Ps.

Ind·   **10.1/5** (usque ad ἐπ'αὐτῷ) = Sacr. Par., PG 95, 1097, 21-25

ALPHA 10 – 13

Δ′

Ἀπόδειξις ὅτι θ′ τάγματά εἰσιν οἱ ἄγγελοι

12   Διονυσίου

Πᾶσα ἡ θεολογία, ἤγουν ἡ θεία γραφή, τὰς οὐρανίους οὐσίας ἐννέα κέκληκεν, ταύτας δὲ εἰς τρεῖς ἀφο-
ρίζει τριαδικὰς διακοσμήσεις. Καὶ πρώτην μὲν εἶναι
φησὶ τὴν περὶ θεὸν οὖσαν ἀεὶ καὶ προσεχῶς καὶ ἀμέσως
5 ἡνῶσθαι παραδεδομένην, τὴν τῶν ἑξαπτερύγων σεραφὶμ καὶ τῶν πολυομμάτων χερουβὶμ καὶ τῶν ἁγιωτά-
των θρόνων, δευτέραν δὲ τὴν τῶν κυριοτήτων καὶ τῶν
δυνάμεων καὶ ἐξουσιῶν, τρίτην δὲ καὶ τελευταίαν τὴν
τῶν ἀρχῶν καὶ ἀρχαγγέλων καὶ ἀγγέλων.

13   Ἀθανασίου Ἀλεξανδρείας

Ἔργον τῶν ἐπουρανίων δυνάμεων, ὕμνος ἄληκτος

Font.   **12.1/9** Ps.-Dion., De coel. hier. 6, 2 (p. 26, 11 – 27, 3), ut cit. est a Io. Dam., Exp.
fid., 17, 66-74 (Καθὼς δὲ ὁ ἁγιώτατος καὶ ἱερώτατος καὶ θεολογικώτατός
φησι Διονύσιος ὁ Ἀρεοπαγίτης· «Πᾶσα ἡ θεολογία ἤγουν ἡ θεία γραφὴ κτλ.)
13.1/15 = Ps.-Athan., Quaest. ad Ant., PG 28, 616, 24-41; Ps.-Athan., Test. e
script., PG 28, 77, 19-35

Mss.   **12** *AT CDEFHKR*   **13** *AT CDEFHKR*

Tit.   **Δ′**] *om. EFHK*, ξϛ′ *R*   Ἀπόδειξις – ἄγγελοι] περὶ ἀγγέλων ὅτι ἐννέα
τάγματα εἰσίν *R*   θ′] ἐννέα *E*   **12** Διονυσίου] τοῦ αὐτοῦ *F, om. EHR*
13 Ἀλεξανδρείας] *om. T R*

Crit.   **12.2** ἐννέα *A*, θ′ *FH*   κέκληκεν] τάξεις *add. F*   ταύτας] *om. H (10 litt.
spat.)*   **3** πρώτην] α′ *D*   **4** περὶ] παρὰ *C*   οὐσίαν *T*   **5/6** σεραφὶμ *D*   **6** πολυομάτων *T D*   **7** δευτέραν] β′ *add. C^(in marg.) D^(in marg.)*
7/8 τὴν – ἐξουσιῶν] καὶ τελευταίαν τὴν ἀρχῶν, καὶ ἀρχαγγέλων· καὶ ἀγγέλων *R*   **8** τρίτην] γ′ *add. C^(in marg.) D^(in marg.)*

Comp.   **12.2** δὲ] ὁ θεῖος ἱεροτελεστὴς *Io. Dam.*   **8** *post* καὶ¹] τῶν *hab. Io. Dam.*
13.1 *ante* Ἔργον] Τί δὲ *hab. Ps.-Athan. Test.*, Τί δὲ τὸ *Ps.-Athan. Quaest.*
post δυνάμεων] ἐν οὐρανοῖς ὑπάρχει *hab. Ps.-Athan. Quaest.*, ὑπάρχει *hab.
Ps.-Athan. Test.*

26 FLORILEGIVM COISLINIANVM

καὶ ἔρως ἄπαυστος τῆς μεγαλοπρεπείας τοῦ θεοῦ· τάχα
δὲ καὶ εὐχὴ ἐπίμονος ὑπὲρ σωτηρίας ἡμῶν. Ἐπειδὴ δὲ
καὶ τάξεις καὶ στρατιαὶ λέγονται, δεῖ λοιπὸν ἐννοεῖν τά-
5 ξιν διδασκαλικήν, τάξιν ἐπιστρεπτικήν, τάξιν προνοη-
τικήν, τάξιν φυλακτικήν, τάξιν διακονητικήν, τάξιν τιμωρητικήν, τάξιν ψυχῶν χωριστικήν, τάξιν πολεμικήν,
τάξιν ἐν ἀνθρώποις παραμονητικήν. Ὥσπερ δὲ τάξεων
διαφοραί, οὕτω καὶ στάσεως καὶ γνώσεως. Οἱ μὲν οὖν
10 θρόνοι καὶ τὰ χερουβὶμ καὶ τὰ σεραφὶμ ἀμέσως παρὰ
θεοῦ μανθάνουσιν, ὡς πάντων ἀνώτερα καὶ θεῷ πλησιώτερα τυγχάνοντα· τὰ δὲ σεραφὶμ διδάσκει τὰ κατώτε-
ρα τάγματα, καὶ οὕτως ἐφεξῆς τὰ ἀνώτερα διδάσκει τὰ
κατώτερα· τὸ δὲ κατώτερον τάγμα εἰσὶν οἱ ἅγιοι ἄγγε-
15 λοι, οἱ καὶ τῶν ἀνθρώπων ὄντες διδάσκαλοι.

Mss.   *AT CDEFHKR*

Crit.   **2** ἔρως] ὅρος *A CFHR*, ὅρος *D*ᵃᶜᵒʳʳ·   **4** καὶ¹] *om. R*   **5** διδασκαλικήν] τάξιν
πολημικὴν *add. FH*   ἐπιτρεπτικὴν *DFH*   **5/6** τάξιν προνοητικήν] *om.*
FH   **6** φυλακτὶν *(sic) T*   **6/8** τιμωρητικήν – παραμονητικήν] ψυχωχω-
ριστικὴν *(sic) R*   **7** τάξιν πολεμικήν] *om. FH (uid. l. 5)*   **9/14** Οἱ – δὲ]
om. R   **11/12** πλησιώτερα τυγχάνοντα] πλησιώτερα τυγχάννοντα *D*,
πλησιέστερα τυγχάνοντα *C*ᵖᶜᵒʳʳ· *(πλησιώτερα τυγχάνοντα C*ᵃᶜᵒʳʳ·*)*, πλησιέστερα τυγχανουσα *(sine acc.) H*, πλησιέστεραι τυγχάνουσι *F*, πλησιάζοντα *EK*
14 τάγμα] τῶν ἄλλων *praem. FH*   ἅγιοι] *om. A R*

Comp.   **2** ἔρως] αἶνος *Ps.-Athan. Quaest.*   **3** ἔμμονος *Ps.-Athan. Quaest. et Ps.-Athan.*
Test.   ante σωτηρίας] τῆς *hab. Ps.-Athan. Quaest.*   **4** *ante* τάξεις] αὗται
αἱ *hab. Ps.-Athan. Quaest. et Ps.-Athan. Test.*   στρατιαὶ] στρατιῶται
Ps.-Athan. Test.   **5** ἐπιστρεπτικήν] *sic Ps.-Athan. Quaest. in nota (ms. Reg. 3)*,
ἐπιτρεπτικήν *Ps.-Athan. Quaest. in textu et Ps.-Athan. Test.*   **5/6** τά-
ξιν³ – διακονητικήν] *non hab. Ps.-Athan. Test.*   **6** φυλακτικήν τάξιν] *sic in*
nota Ps.-Athan. Quaest. (ms. Reg. 3); deest in textu   διακονικὴν *Ps.-Athan.*
Quaest.   **7** ψυχοχωριστικὴν *Ps.-Athan. Quaest.*   **7/8** πολεμικὴν τάξιν]
sic in nota Ps.-Athan Quaest. (ms. Palat. 1); deest in textu Ps.-Athan. Quaest. et
Ps.-Athan. Test.   **8** ἀνθρώποις] *sic in nota Ps.-Athan. Quaest. (Palat. 1),*
ἄλλοις *in textu*   **8/9** τάξεων διαφοραί] τάξεων διαφορὰς ἐν ταῖς ἄνω
δυνάμεσιν ἔγνωμεν *Ps.-Athan. Quaest.*, καὶ τάξεως διαφορὰν ἐν ταῖς ἄνω
δυνάμεσιν ἔγνωμεν *Ps.-Athan. Test.*   **9** οὖν] *non hab. Ps.-Athan. Test.*
10 καὶ¹ – χερουβὶμ] *post* σεραφὶμ *hab. Ps.-Athan. Test.*   **11** *ante* θεοῦ] τοῦ
hab. Ps.-Athan. Quaest.   **11/12** πλησιώτερα τυγχάνοντα] πλησιάζοντα
Ps.-Athan. Quaest. (πλησιέστερα τυγχάνοντα Reg. 3) et Ps.-Athan. Test.
12 τὰ¹ – σεραφὶμ] ταῦτα δὲ *Ps.-Athan. Quaest. et Ps.-Athan. Test.*   **14** *post*
κατώτερον] πάντων *hab. Ps.-Athan. Quaest.*   ἅγιοι] *non hab. Ps.-Athan. Test.*

ALPHA 13 – 14

Ϟθ′ δὲ μέρη εἰσὶ πρὸς τὸν ἀριθμὸν τῆς ἀνθρωπότητος,
κατὰ τὴν παραβολὴν τοῦ κυρίου τῶν ἑκατὸν προβάτων
καὶ τῶν δέκα δραγμῶν.

Ε′

Περὶ τῶν ἀγγέλων ὧν ἐφιλοξένησεν Ἀβραάμ

* 14

Τοῦ Χρυσοστόμου

Οὐκ ἐκάθευδεν ὡς ἔθος τισὶν ἐν μεσημβρίᾳ Ἀβραάμ,
ἀλλ' ἐγρηγόρει περισκοπῶν θήραν ξένων. Οὐ καθέζεται
ἐπὶ σκηνήν, ἀλλ' εἱστήκει περιβλεπόμενος μήποτε ξένος παρελθὼν ζημιώσῃ τὸν μὴ ὑποδεξάμενον. Εἶδεν ὁ
5 θεὸς τὴν προθυμίαν αὐτοῦ, καὶ πέμπει τρεῖς· μυστικὸς
ὁ ἀριθμός, ἱκανὸς ἀναπαῦσαι ψυχὴν τοῦ ποθοῦντος·
τριπλᾶ τῷ Ἀβραὰμ τὰ ἀγαθά, ᾧ τὸ ἀναλίσκειν εἰς τοὺς
ξένους κέρδος ἦν, τὸ δὲ μὴ ἀναλίσκειν ζημία. Βλέπει
οὖν τρεῖς· ὅτι δὲ οἱ μὲν δύο ἄγγελοι ἦσαν, τοῦτο δῆλον.
10 Τίς δὲ ὁ τρίτος, ὑπὲρ ἐμὲ τὸ ἑρμηνεῦσαι· ὅμως δὲ φαίνον-
ται οἱ τρεῖς, οὐδὲ οἱ ἄγγελοι ὡς ἄγγελοι, οὐδὲ ὁ τρίτος
ὅστις ἦν, ἀλλ' ὡς ἄγγελος· εἰ γὰρ ᾔδει τοὺς ἀγγέλους ἢ

Font. 16/18 = Ps.-Athan., Quaest. ad Ant., PG 28, 601, 46-50; cf. Lc. 15, 4-9; Mt.
18, 12   **14.1/24** locum non inueni   **1/2** cf. I Thess. 5, 6   **1** Gen. 18, 1
3 Gen. 18, 1   **5** Gen. 18, 2

Mss.   *AT CDEFHKR*   **14** *AT CDEFH*

Tit.   **Ε′**] *om. DEFH*   Ἀβραάμ] *praem.* ὁ *C*   **14** Τοῦ Χρυσοστόμου] *om. E*

Crit.   **16** Ϟθ′] ἐνενήκοντα ἐννέα *EHKR* (ἐνενίκοντα *R,* ἐνέα *H),* Ϟε′ *T, illeg. F*
πρὸς τὸν] κατὰ *R*   τῆς ἀνθρωπότητος] καὶ ἐν τῶν ἀνθρώπων *R*
17 ἑκατὸν] ρ′ *CDHR*   **18** δέκα] ι′ *CD,* ιβ′ *E*   δραχμῶν *DEFHKR*
14.2 ξένων] ξένην *E*   **4** οἶδεν *FH*   **7** ᾧ] ὧν *FH*   **11** οὐδὲ¹] *om. A*
12 ὅστις] ὅτι *A^{a.corr.}*   εἰ] ἢ *C^{a.corr. ut uid.}*   ᾔδει] εἴδη *C^{a.corr.}* *D*

Comp.   **16** Ϟθ′ δὲ μέρη εἰσὶ] Οἱ μέν φασιν ἐνενήκοντα ἐννέα μέρη εἶναι τοὺς ἀγγέλους *Ps.-Athan.*   **18** καὶ] ἄλλοι δὲ ἐννέα κατὰ τὴν παραβολὴν *Ps.-Athan.*
δραχμῶν *Ps.-Athan.*

28 FLORILEGIVM COISLINIANVM

τὴν ἀξίαν τοῦ παρόντος, ἔλαττον ἦν τὸ θαῦμα· τὴν γὰρ
ἀξίαν ἐφαίνετο τιμῶν, καὶ οὐχὶ ξένους δεξιούμενος.
15 Ἐπῆρεν οὖν φησὶν Ἀβραὰμ τοὺς ὀφθαλμοὺς αὐτοῦ καὶ
εἶδε καὶ ἰδοὺ τρεῖς ἄνδρες οὐχ'ὅτι ἄνδρες ἦσαν, ἀλλ'ὅτι
ἄνδρες ἐνομίσθησαν· οὐ γὰρ μετάπτωσις τῆς φύσεως
γέγονεν, ἀλλὰ τὴν ὑπόνοιαν τοῦ θεασαμένου φησὶν ἡ
γραφή.
20 Μετὰ ταῦτα. Καὶ αὐτοὺς μὲν εἰσάγει τοὺς δύο ἀγγέλους καὶ τὸν τρίτον· ἐν καιρῷ δὲ ἰδίῳ ἐροῦμεν τὰ
περὶ τοῦ τρίτου, ἑρμηνεύειν καὶ τότε δεδιότες· τὸ γὰρ
περὶ θεοῦ λέγειν, φοβερὸν καὶ ἐπικίνδυνον.
Καὶ παρέθηκεν αὐτοῖς φησὶν Ἀβραὰμ καὶ ἔφαγον.

15   Εὐσεβίου

Πῶς ἐνδέχεται τὴν ἀσώματον οὐσίαν σῶμα φαγεῖν,
εἰ μή τις εἴποι ὅτι τὸ Ἀνηλῶσθαι αὐτὰ φαγεῖν εἶπεν ἡ
γραφή; Εἰ οἱ ἄγγελοι ἔφαγον παρὰ τῷ Ἀβραάμ; Οὐκ
ἔφαγον, ἀλλ'ἐνέργεια κατηνάλωσε τὰ παρακείμενα,
5 προσποιήσει τοῦ φαγεῖν. Καὶ γὰρ ὅτε πρὸς Γεδεὼν ἦλ-
θεν ὁ ἄγγελος, παρέθηκεν αὐτῷ κρέα καὶ ἀζύμους, καὶ
ἐξῆλθε πῦρ ἐκ τῆς πέτρας, καὶ κατέφαγεν αὐτά.

Font.   15/16 Gen. 18, 2   16/17 τρεῖς – ἐνομίσθησαν] cf. Cat. in Gen. 1070, ad
        Gen. 18, 8, l. 3-4   24 Gen. 18, 8; cf. Cat. in Gen. 1069, ad Gen. 18, 8, l. 4
        15.2/3 cf. Cat. in Gen. 1069, ad Gen. 18, 8, l. 4-5; Gen. 18, 8   3/7 Cat. in
        Gen. 1074, ad Gen. 18, 8, l. 1-5   6/7 Iud. 6, 21

Mss.   AT CDEFH   15 AT CDE

Crit.   13 τὴν γὰρ] οὐ γὰρ τὴν F^{ut uid.}H   14 καὶ οὐχὶ] ἀλλὰ F^{ut uid.}H   20 Μετὰ
        ταῦτα] om. T, μετ'ὀλίγα DE, καὶ μετ'ὀλίγα FH, μ(ε)τ(α) A   Καὶ] om. E
        μὲν] οὖν add. E   21 δὲ] om. T   22/24 τὸ – ἔφαγον] om. FH
        15.3 Εἰ] om. T   οἱ] om. E   4 ἐνέργεια (sine acc.) C, ἐνεργεία T D (-εῖα
        D), ἐνεργεία (sic acc.) τις θειοτέρα E   κατανάλωσαν C^{p.corr.}   6 ἄζυμα E

Comp.   15.4 ἐνέργεια κατηνάλωσε] ἐνεργείᾳ ἀοράτῳ κατανάλωσαν (sic) Cat.
        5 γὰρ] non hab. Cat.   6 κρέας Cat.

ALPHA 14 – 16   29

ς'

Περὶ τῆς τοῦ ἀνθρώπου δημιουργίας καὶ πλάσεως

16   Γρηγορίου τοῦ θεολόγου

Νοῦς μὲν οὖν ἤδη καὶ αἴσθησις οὕτως ἀπ'ἀλλήλων δια-
κριθέντα, τῶν ἰδίων ὅρων ἐντὸς εἱστήκεισαν καὶ τὸ
τοῦ δημιουργοῦ μεγαλεῖον ἐν ἑαυτοῖς ἔφερον, σιγῶντες
ἐπαινέται τῆς μεγαλουργίας καὶ διαπρύσιοι κήρυκες.
5 Οὔπω δὲ ἦν κρᾶμα ἐξ ἀμφοτέρων, οὐδέ τις μίξις τῶν
ἐναντίων, σοφίας μείζονος γνώρισμα καὶ τῆς περὶ τὰς
φύσεις πολυτελείας, οὐδ'ὁ πᾶς πλοῦτος τῆς ἀγαθότητος γνώριμος. Τοῦτο δὴ βουληθεὶς ὁ τεχνίτης ἐπιδείξασθαι Λόγος καὶ ζῶον ἓν ἐξ ἀμφοτέρων, ἀοράτου τὲ
10 λέγω καὶ ὁρατῆς φύσεως, δημιουργεῖ τὸν ἄνθρωπον.
Καὶ παρὰ μὲν τῆς ὕλης τὸ σῶμα λαβὼν ἤδη προϋπο-
στάσης, παρ'ἑαυτοῦ δὲ πνοὴν ἐνθείς – ὃ δὴ νοερὰν ψυχὴν καὶ εἰκόνα θεοῦ οἶδεν ὁ λόγος –, οἷόν τινα κόσμον
δεύτερον, ἐν μικρῷ μέγαν, ἐπὶ τῆς γῆς ἵστησιν, ἄγγε-
15 λον ἄλλον, προσκυνητὴν μικτόν, ἐπόπτην τῆς ὁρατῆς

Font.   **16.1/56** = Greg. Naz., Or. 38, 11, 1 – 12, 30 (= Or. 45, PG 36, 631, 48 – 633,
17)   **13** cf. Gen. 1, 26-27

Mss.   **16** *AT CDEFHK*

Tit.   **ς'**] ε' *D*, *om. EFHK*   Περὶ – πλάσεως] *cf. Sacr. Par., PG 95, 1097, 44-45*
(Περὶ τῆς τοῦ ἀνθρώπου πλάσεως καὶ κατασκευῆς)

Crit.   **16.1** οὖν] *om. CF*   οὕτως] *om. DFH*   **1/2** διακριθέντες *E*   **3** τοῦ]
om. A   δημιουργοῦ] λόγου *add. EK*   αὐτοῖς *FH*   **4** ἐπαινεταὶ *D*
5 δὲ] δ' *A DH*, γὰρ *F*   τῶν] *iter. D*   **6** τῆς] τὰς *E*, *om. FH*   **7** οὐδὲ *C*
πᾶς] *om. FH*   **11** λαβὼν τὸ σῶμα *DEFHK*   **12** ἑαυτῷ *Cᵖ·ᶜᵒʳʳ·DK, illeg. F*
13 οἶδεν] εἶδεν *T*   **15/16** ἐπόπτην – κτίσεως] *om. Eᵃ·ᶜᵒʳʳ· (suppl. in marg.)*

Comp.   **16.3** *post* δημιουργοῦ] Λόγου *hab. Greg.*   **5** μῖξις *in editione Greg.*
7 οὐδὲ *Greg.*   **11** λαβὼν τὸ σῶμα *Greg.*

Ind.   **16.1/20** = Sacr. Par., Vat. gr. 1553, 39ʳ⁻ᵛ, cf. HEIMGARTNER, *Pseudojustin*, p. 249

30 FLORILEGIVM COISLINIANVM

κτίσεως, μύστην τῆς νοουμένης, βασιλέα τῶν ἐπὶ γῆς,
βασιλευόμενον ἄνωθεν, ἐπίγειον καὶ οὐράνιον, πρόσ-
καιρον καὶ ἀθάνατον, ὁρατὸν καὶ νοούμενον, μέσον με-
γέθους καὶ ταπεινότητος· τὸν αὐτὸν πνεῦμα καὶ σάρκα,
20 πνεῦμα διὰ τὴν χάριν, σάρκα διὰ τὴν ἔπαρσιν· τὸ μέν,
ἵνα μένῃ καὶ δοξάζῃ τὸν εὐεργέτην· τὸ δέ, ἵνα πάσχῃ,
καὶ πάσχων ὑπομιμνήσκηται καὶ παιδεύηται τῷ μεγέ-
θει φιλοτιμούμενος· ζῷον ἐνταῦθα οἰκονομούμενον καὶ
ἀλλαχοῦ μεθιστάμενον, καὶ πέρας τοῦ μυστηρίου, τῇ
25 πρὸς θεὸν νεύσει θεούμενον.

Καὶ μετ'ὀλίγα. Τοῦτον ἔθετο μὲν ἐν τῷ παραδείσῳ,
ὅστίς ποτε ἦν ὁ παράδεισος οὗτος, τῷ αὐτεξουσίῳ τι-
μήσας, ἵν'ᾖ τοῦ ἑλομένου τὸ ἀγαθὸν οὐχ'ἧττον ἢ τοῦ
παρασχόντος τὰ σπέρματα, φυτῶν ἀθανάτων γεωργόν,
30 θείων ἐννοιῶν ἴσως, τῶν τε ἁπλουστέρων καὶ τῶν τε-
λειοτέρων, γυμνὸν τῇ ἁπλότητι καὶ ζωῇ τῇ ἀτέχνῳ καὶ
δίχα παντὸς ἐπικαλύμματος καὶ προβλήματος· τοιοῦτον
γὰρ ἔπρεπεν εἶναι τὸν ἀπ'ἀρχῆς. Καὶ δίδωσι νόμον, ὕλην
τῷ αὐτεξουσίῳ. Ὁ δὲ νόμος ἦν ἐντολὴ ὧν τε μεταλη-
35 πτέον αὐτῷ φυτῶν, καὶ οὗ μὴ προσαπτέον· τὸ δὲ ἦν τὸ
ξύλον τῆς γνώσεως, οὔτε φυτευθὲν ἀπ'ἀρχῆς κακῶς,
οὔτε ἀπαγορευθὲν φθονερῶς – μὴ πεμπέτωσαν ἐκεῖ τὰς
γλώσσας οἱ θεομάχοι, μὴ δὲ τὸν ὄφιν μιμείσθωσαν –,
ἀλλὰ καλὸν μὲν εὐκαίρως μεταλαμβανόμενον – θεωρία

Font. 26 Gen. 2, (8) 15   31 cf. Gen. 2, 25   34/36 cf. Gen. 2, 16-17
38 cf. Gen. 3, 1-3

Mss. *AT CDEFHK* (*CDEFHK* usque ad θεούμενον, 16.25)

Crit. 21 δέ] δ' *FH*   22 πάσχον *EK*   23 φιλοτιμούμενον *EK*   24 πέρα
T CFH   26 μετ'ὀλίγα] μ(ε)τ(α) (*sic*) *A*   τῷ] τὸ (*sic*) *T, om. A*
30/31 τελεωτέρων *A^{p.corr.}*   39 θεωρίαν *T*

Comp. 25 *post* θεούμενον] Εἰς τοῦτο γὰρ ἐμοὶ φέρει τὸ μέτριον ἐνταῦθα φέγγος τῆς
ἀληθείας, λαμπρότητα Θεοῦ καὶ ἰδεῖν καὶ παθεῖν, ἀξίαν τοῦ καὶ συνδήσαντος,
καὶ λύσοντος καὶ αὖθις συνδήσοντος ὑψηλότερον *hab. Greg.*   30/31 τελεωτέρων *Greg. (S PPd Vb Vp Dmg. = Coisl.)*

Ind. 23/25 = Sacr. Par., Vat. gr. 1553, 39^v, cf. HEIMGARTNER, *Pseudojustin*, p. 249

ALPHA 16 – 17

40 γὰρ ἦν τὸ φυτὸν ὡς ἡ ἐμὴ θεωρία, ἧς μόνης ἐπιβαίνειν
ἀσφαλὲς τοῖς τὴν ἕξιν τελειοτέροις –, οὐ καλὸν δὲ τοῖς
ἁπλουστέροις ἔτι καὶ τὴν ἔφεσιν λιχνοτέροις, ὥσπερ
οὐδὲ τροφὴ τελεία λυσιτελὴς τοῖς ἁπαλοῖς ἔτι καὶ δεο-
μένοις γάλακτος. Ἐπεὶ δὲ φθόνῳ διαβόλου καὶ γυναι-
45 κὸς ἐπηρείᾳ, ἣν τὲ ἔπαθεν ὡς ἁπαλωτέρα, ἣν προσήγαγεν ὡς πιθανωτέρα – φεῦ τῆς ἐμῆς ἀσθενείας· ἐμὴ γὰρ
ἡ τοῦ προπάτορος –, τῆς μὲν ἐντολῆς ἐπελάθετο τῆς δοθείσης καὶ ἡττήθη τῆς πικρᾶς γεύσεως, ὁμοῦ δὲ τοῦ τῆς
ζωῆς ξύλου καὶ τοῦ παραδείσου καὶ τοῦ θεοῦ διὰ τὴν
50 κακίαν ἐξόριστος γίνεται καὶ τοὺς δερματίνους ἀμφιέν-
νυται χιτῶνας, ἴσως τὴν παχυτέραν σάρκα καὶ θνητὴν
καὶ ἀντίτυπον, καὶ τοῦτο πρῶτον γινώσκει, τὴν ἰδίαν
αἰσχύνην, καὶ ἀπὸ θεοῦ κρύπτεται. Κερδαίνει μὲν τί κἀν-
ταῦθα, τὸν θάνατον καὶ τὸ διακοπῆναι τὴν ἁμαρτίαν,
55 ἵνα μὴ ἀθάνατον ᾖ τὸ κακόν, καὶ γίνεται φιλανθρωπία
ἡ τιμωρία. Οὕτω γὰρ πείθομαι κολάζειν θεόν.

17 Κλήμεντος

Ὁ ἄνθρωπος κατ'εἰκόνα καὶ καθ'ὁμοίωσιν θεοῦ θείαν

Font. 42/44 cf. I Cor. 3, 2; I Petr. 2, 2   47/48 cf. Gen. 3, 6   48/49 cf. Gen.
3, 23-24   50/51 cf. Gen. 3, 21   52/53 cf. Gen. 3, 7-8   17.1/9 = Ps.-
Clem. Rom., Hom. 10, 3, 3, 2 – 10, 4, 2, 2 (p. 143)   1 Gen. 1, 26

Mss. *AT*   17 *AT CDEFHK*

Tit. 17 Κλήμεντος] *om. D*

Crit. 40 ἡ] *om. T*   μόνης] μόνοις *T*ᵃ·ᶜᵒʳʳ·   41 τελεωτέροις *A*ᵖ·ᶜᵒʳʳ·   42 λυχνο-
τέροις *T*   43 ἔτι τοῖς ἁπαλοῖς *A*ᵃ·ᶜᵒʳʳ·   45 ἥν τε *A*ᵃ·ᶜᵒʳʳ·   53 μὲν τί] *sic acc. A*,
μέντοι *T*   56 θεῶ *A*   17.1 Ὁ] *om. FH*   θεοῦ] *om. FH*   θείαν]
post εἰκόνα *trsp. FH*

Comp. 41 τοῖς – τελειοτέροις] τοὺς τελεωτέρους *Greg.* (τοῖς τελεωτέροις *TVZ O² P²*
Pb Ald. Maur.)   45 *post* ἁπαλωτέρα] καὶ *hab. Greg.*   17.1 θεοῦ θείαν]
θείαν *Sacr. Par., non hab. Ps.-Clem.*

nd. 17.1/9 = Sacr. Par., ed. HOLL, *Fragmente*, fr. 10, p. 7

32 FLORILEGIVM COISLINIANVM

γεγονὼς ἄρχειν καὶ κυριεύειν κατεστάθη. Ὅτε μέντοι
δίκαιος ἐτύγχανε, πάντων τῶν παθημάτων ἀνώτατος
ἦν καὶ ἀθάνατος, σώματι κατὰ θείαν μεγαλοδωρεὰν τοῦ
5 κτίσαντος τοῦ ἀλγεῖν πεῖραν λαβεῖν μὴ δυνάμενος. Ὅτε
δὲ ἥμαρτεν, ὡς δοῦλος γεγονὼς ἁμαρτίας πᾶσιν ὑπέ-
πεσε τοῖς παθήμασι, πάντων τῶν καλῶν δικαίᾳ κρίσει
στερηθείς· οὐ γὰρ εὔλογον ἦν τοῦ δεδωκότος ἐγκαταλειφθέντος τὰ δοθέντα παραμένειν τοῖς ἀγνώμοσιν.

18 Κυρίλλου Ἀλεξανδρείας

Ἔκτισε μὲν ὁ τῶν ὅλων θεὸς τὸν ἄνθρωπον ἐπὶ ἔργοις
ἀγαθοῖς, καθὰ γέγραπται, ἀπροσδεᾶ παντὸς καλοῦ καὶ
ἀρτίως ἔχοντα κατά γε τοὺς ἐνόντας τῇ φύσει λόγους,
τοὺς ἐν ψυχῇ τέ φημι καὶ σώματι. Ἐπεποίητο μὲν γὰρ
5 ὁ νοῦς τοιοῦτος αὐτῷ ὡς οἷός τε εἶναι καθορᾶν θεὸν καὶ
τὰ αὐτοῦ, κατά γε φημὶ τὸ ἐκνεμηθὲν τῇ φύσει μέτρον
– Βλέπομεν γὰρ δι’ ἐσόπτρου καὶ αἰνίγματος, κατὰ τὸ
γεγραμμένον –, ἐφέσεως δὲ τῆς εἰς πᾶν ὁτιοῦν τῶν τε-
θαυμασμένων ἐπίμεστος ὤν, καὶ οἱονεί πως ἁπλῆν ἔτι
10 καὶ μονοειδῆ τὴν ἀγαθοῦ παντὸς λαχὼν ἐπιστήμην,
καὶ εἰς αὐτὸ βλέπων ἀπερισπάστως ὡς μόνον ὁρῶν

Font.   6 cf. Rom. 6, 17. 20   18.1/45 Cyr. Alex., Contra Iul. 3, 24, 1 – 25, 14
1/2 cf. Eph. 2, 10   7 I Cor. 13, 12

Mss.   AT CDEFHK   18 AT C

Tit.   18 Κυρίλλου] κυρίλου A^{a.corr.}

Crit.   3 ἀνώτερος F   4 θείαν] τὴν praem. EK   5 λαβεῖν] καὶ add. H
6/7 ἐπέπεσε T   8 στερρηθείς F   18.4 τε φημὶ C   6 αὐτοῦ] αὐτὰ T
11 βλέπον T

Comp.   2 post ἄρχειν] τε hab. Ps.-Clem.   post κατεστάθη] complura hab. Ps.-Clem.
3 πάντων τῶν] πάντων Sacr. Par., καὶ πάντων Ps.-Clem.   4 καὶ] ὡς
Ps.-Clem.   ἀθανάτῳ Ps.-Clem. et Sacr. Par.   4/5 κατὰ – κτίσαντος]
non hab. Ps.-Clem.   6 post ἥμαρτεν] ὡς ἐχθὲς καὶ τῇ πρὸ αὐτῆς ἐδείξαμεν
hab. Ps.-Clem.   ante ἁμαρτίας] τῆς hab. Ps.-Clem.   7 τῶν] non hab.
Ps.-Clem.   18.1 τῶν ὅλων] om. Cyr. (V = Coisl.) ἐπ’ Cyr.   5 post θεὸν]
τε hab. Cyr. (F = Coisl.)

ALPHA 17 – 18   33

αὐτό, καὶ ὁλοκλήροις θελημάτων ῥοπαῖς ἀπονενευκώς,
καὶ ἐθελουργῶς εὖ μάλα πρὸς τοῦτο ἰών. Σῶμα γεμὴν
αὐτῷ πεποίηται μὲν ἐκ γῆς, ἄμεινον δὲ θανάτου καὶ
15 φθορᾶς, κἂν εἰ γελῷέν τινες τῶν ἀπίστων τὸ εἰρημένον,
ἀκουόντων ὅτι θεοῦ γε ἐθέλοντος ἦν, οὗ τοῖς νεύμασιν
ἡ τῶν πραγμάτων ἕπεται φύσις, παντί τε καὶ πάντως
τὸ αὐτῷ δοκοῦν ἀρρήτοις τισὶν ἐνεργείαις ἐφικτὸν ἀπο-
φαίνοντος, ὅτι τὸ κατὰ γνώμην αὐτῷ, τοῦτο καὶ τῶν
20 γεγονότων ἑκάστῳ φύσις. Οὐ γὰρ δήπου Πλάτωνι μὲν
ἔξεστι λέγειν ὡς ἐκ προσώπου θεοῦ τοῖς παρ'αὐτοῦ γε-
γονόσιν, ἤγουν οὐρανῷ καὶ ἡλίῳ καὶ ἄστροις, ἃ δὴ καὶ
αἰσθητοὺς ὀνομάζει θεούς· Διὸ ἐπείπερ γεγένησθε, οὐκ
ἀθάνατοι μὲν ἐστὲ οὐδὲ ἄλυτοι τὸ πάμπαν, οὔτι γεμὴν
25 λυθήσεσθε οὐδὲ τεύξεσθε θανάτου μοίρας, τῆς ἐμῆς
βουλήσεως μείζονος ἔτι δεσμοῦ καὶ κυριωτέρου λαχόν-
τες ἐκείνων οἷς ὅτε ἐγίνεσθε ξυνεδεῖσθε. Ἀπιστήσομεν
τοῖς Μωσέως γράμμασιν εἰ πέρα τοῦ φθείρεσθαι τεθεῖ-
σθαι λέγοι θεοῦ γε ἐθέλοντος τὸ φθείρεσθαι πεφυκός;
30 Ἦν οὖν ἄρα θανάτου τὸ σῶμα κρεῖττον· ἐνεφύτευσε
γὰρ αὐτῷ τὴν ζωὴν ὁ πάντων δημιουργός. Ἐπειδὴ δὲ
ἦν τοῦ φθείρεσθαι πέρα, ἐμφύτους μὲν τὰς ἐφέσεις

'ont.   **23/27** = Plat., Tim., 41 b 2-7   **27/30** cf. Gen. 3, 19

Iss.   *AT C*

'rit.   **12** αὐτὸς *T*   **18** ἐφικτῶς *AT*   **19** αὐτὸ *T*   **20** γὰρ] *om. A*
24 ἔστε *Aᵃ·ᶜᵒʳʳ·T*   ἄλλυτοι *A*   **27** ἐγγίνεσθε *A*   ξυνεδήσθε *A*, ξυνεδῆ-
σθε *T*   ἀπιστήσωμεν *T*   **29** πεφυκὼς *A*   **30** ἐνεφύσησε *A*

'omp.   **16** ἀκούοντες *Cyr. (V = Coisl.)*   **17** παντί] πάντη *Cyr.*   **21** ἔξεσται *Cyr.*
24 γεμὴν] μήν γε *Cyr.*, μὲν δὴ *Plat.*   **27** *post* Ἀπιστήσομεν] δὲ hab. *Cyr.*

34 FLORILEGIVM COISLINIANVM

διεκληρώσατο, τὰς ἐπί γε τοῖς ἐδωδίμοις καὶ παιδο-
γονίαις, ἀτυράννευτον δὲ ταῖς εἰς τοῦτο ῥοπαῖς τὸν
35 νοῦν ἔχων ἐθαυμάζετο· ἕδρα γὰρ ἐλευθέρως τὸ δοκοῦν,
οὔπω τῆς σαρκὸς τοῖς ἐκ τῆς φθορᾶς πάθεσιν ὑπενη-
νεγμένης. Ἐπειδὴ δὲ προσκέκρουκε τῷ τεκτηναμένῳ
θεῷ, τῆς δοθείσης ἀλογήσας ἐντολῆς, καὶ ἀρχὴ γέγονεν
ἀκρασίας αὐτῷ τῶν ἀπειρημένων ἡ βρῶσις, νενίκηται
40 τὸ ἐντεῦθεν ταῖς εἰς τὸ φαῦλον ἡδοναῖς, καὶ τὴν τοῦ
σώματος φύσιν ὁ τῆς ἁμαρτίας εἰσέδυ νόμος, καὶ καθάπερ ἐξ ἀνοσίου ῥίζης τῆς φθορᾶς τὰ τῶν ἐκτόπων
ἐπιθυμιῶν ἐβλάστησε πάθη, καὶ οἷα τί τῶν ἀτιθάσσων
θηρίων ἀγριαίνει λοιπὸν ἐν ἡμῖν τὸ φιλήδονον, ταῖς εἰς
45 πᾶν ὁτιοῦν τῶν ἀρίστων προθυμίαις ἀντανιστάμενον.

19 Τοῦ Χρυσοστόμου

Καὶ εἶπεν ὁ θεὸς φησὶ *Ποιήσωμεν ἄνθρωπον κατ᾽εἰκό-*
να καὶ καθ᾽ὁμοίωσιν ἡμετέραν. Ἕν τοῦτο πρῶτον ἄξιον
ἐπιζητῆσαι, τί δήποτε, ὅτε μὲν οὐρανὸς ἐγένετο, οὐδα-
μοῦ τὸ *Ποιήσωμεν* εἴρηται, ἀλλὰ *Γενηθήτω* οὐρανὸς
5 καὶ *Γενηθήτω φῶς,* καὶ καθ᾽ἕκαστον μέρος τῆς κτίσεως
οὕτως, ἐνταῦθα δὲ τὸ *Ποιήσωμεν* μόνον, καὶ βουλὴ καὶ

Font.   **41** cf. Rom. 8, 2   **19.1/23** = Io. Chrys., Serm. in Gen., 2, 47-70
1/2 Gen. 1, 26   **3/4** cf. Gen. 1, 1   **5** Gen. 1, 3   **6** cf. supra l. 1/2

Mss.   **19** *AT CDEFHK*

Tit.   **19** Τοῦ Χρυσοστόμου] *om. D*

Crit.   **34** ἀτυράνευτον *A*   **39** ἀπηρημένων *(sic) A*[a.corr.]*T C*   **43** ἐβλάτησε
A   οἷά τι *T*   ἀτιθάσων *C*   **44** ταῖς] τοὺς *T*   **19.1** Καὶ] *om.*
FH   φησὶ] *om. K*   **2** ἡμετέραν] *post* εἰκόνα *trsp. K*   πρῶτον] *om. E*
3 ἐπιζητεῖν *H*   οὐρανὸς] ὁ *praem. K*   **4/5** Γενηθήτω – καὶ[1]] γεννηθήτω
οὐρανὸς καὶ *D*, *om. A FH*   **5** Γενηθήτω[2]] γεννηθήτω *A*[a.corr.]*D*   φῶς]
καὶ ἐγένετο φῶς *add. FH*   καθ᾽] κα᾽ *A*

Comp.   **33** *post* γε] φημι *hab. Cyr.* (*V = Coisl.*)   **19.2** καθ᾽] *non hab. Chrys.* (*PV =*
Coisl.)   πρῶτον τοῦτο *Chrys.*   **3** ζητῆσαι *Chrys.* (*P = Coisl.*)   *ante*
οὐρανὸς] ὁ *hab. Chrys.* (*P = Coisl.*)   ἐγίνετο *Chrys.* (*P = Coisl.*)   **5** τῆς
κτίσεως μέρος (*P = Coisl.*)

ALPHA 18 – 19   35

σκέψις καὶ πρὸς ἕτερόν τινα ὁμότιμον ἀνακοίνωσις. Τίς
ποτε ἄρα ἐστὶν ὁ δημιουργεῖσθαι μέλλων, ὅτι τοσαύτης
ἀπολαύει τῆς τιμῆς; Ἄνθρωπος ἐστί, τὸ μέγα ζῶον καὶ
10 θαυμαστόν, καὶ τῆς κτίσεως ἁπάσης τῷ θεῷ τιμιώτερον, δι'ὃν οὐρανὸς καὶ γῆ καὶ θάλαττα καὶ τὸ λοιπὸν
ἅπαν τῆς κτίσεως σῶμα· ἄνθρωπος, οὗ τῆς σωτηρίας
οὕτως ἡράσθη θεὸς ὡς μὴ δὲ τοῦ μονογενοῦς φείσασθαι
δι'αὐτόν· οὐ γὰρ ἀπέστη πάντα ποιῶν καὶ πραγματευό-
15 μενος ὁ θεὸς ἕως αὐτὸν ἀναγαγὼν ἐκάθισεν ἄνω ἐν
δεξιᾷ αὐτοῦ. Καὶ βοᾷ Παῦλος λέγων· Συνήγειρε καὶ
συνεκάθισεν ἡμᾶς ἐν τοῖς ἐπουρανίοις ἐν Χριστῷ. Διὰ
τοῦτο βουλὴ καὶ σκέψις καὶ πρὸς ἕτερόν τινα ὁμότιμον
ἀνακοίνωσις, οὐκ ἐπειδὴ ὁ θεὸς βουλῆς δεῖται – μὴ γέ-
20 νοιτο –, ἀλλὰ τῷ σχήματι τῶν ῥημάτων τὴν γενομένην
ἡμῖν ἐνδείκνυται τιμήν. Καὶ πῶς φησὶν εἰ τοῦ κόσμου
τιμιώτερός ἐστι, πάντων ὕστερος παράγεται; Δι'αὐτὸ
τοῦτο, ἐπειδὴ τοῦ κόσμου τιμιώτερός ἐστι.
     Ποιήσωμεν ἄνθρωπον φησὶ *κατ'εἰκόνα.* Ἀκουέτω
25 Ἰουδαῖος. Πρὸς τίνα φησὶν ὁ θεὸς *Ποιήσωμεν;* Μωϋσέ-

Font.   **13** cf. Rom. 8, 32   **15/16** Eph. 1, 20 et loc. par.   **16/17** Eph. 2, 6
         24/46 = Io. Chrys., Serm. in Gen., 2, 79-101   **24/25** cf. supra l. 1/2

Mss.   *AT CDEFHK*

Crit.   **7** Τίς] τί *T DEK*   **8** ἄρα *A*^{a.corr.} *CE*   ὅτι] *om. H (15 litt. spat.)*
         9 ἐστι *A*   **10** καὶ] *om. CDEFHK*   **10/12** κτίσεως – τῆς¹] *iter. K*
         11 θάλασσα *DEFHK*   **12** σωτηρίας] *om. H (5 litt. spat.)*   **13** οὕτως]
         οὗτος *D, om. FH*   **15** ἀναγαγὼν – ἄνω] ἄνω ἀναγαγὼν ἐκάθισεν ἄνω
         C, ἄνω ἀναγαγὼν ἐκάθισεν *DEFHK*   **16** Συνήγειρε] καὶ *praem. EFHK*
         17 οὐρανίοις *EK*   **18** τοῦτον *H*   **22** ὕστερον *C*   Δι'αὐτὸ] διατί
         DEK (διατὶ D)   **25** Ἰουδαῖος] ὁ *praem. EFH*   ὁ θεὸς] *om. FH*
         25/26 μωϋσέος *C,* μωσέως *H, illeg. F*

Comp.   **9** τῆς] *non hab. Chrys.*   **13** ὁ θεὸς ἡράσθη *Chrys.*   **15** ἄνω] *non hab.*
         Chrys. (P = Coisl.)   **16** ἑαυτοῦ *Chrys.*   *ante* Συνήγειρε] καὶ *hab. Chrys.*
         (TSPR = Coisl.)   **17** *post* ἡμᾶς] ἐν δεξιᾷ ἑαυτοῦ *hab. Chrys. (P = Coisl.)*
         post Χριστῷ] Ἰησοῦ *(cf. Eph. 2, 6) hab. Chrys. (P = Coisl.)*   **18** πρὸς – ὁμότι-
         μον] *non hab. Chrys. (P = Coisl.)*   **20** τὴν γενομένην] τὴν εἰς τὸν γενόμενον
         Chrys. (τὴν εἰς τὴν γενομένην *P)*   **22** παντὸς *Chrys.*   *post* ὕστερος] τοῦ
         κόσμου *hab. Chrys.*   **24** φησὶ] *non hab. Chrys.*   **25** *ante* Ἰουδαῖος] ὁ *hab.*
         Chrys. (P = Coisl.)   *post* φησὶν] εἶπεν *hab. Chrys. (MPV = Coisl.)*

36   FLORILEGIVM COISLINIANVM

ὡς εἰσὶ τὰ γράμματα, Μωϋσέως <ᾧ> πιστεύειν φασίν.
Οὐ γὰρ δὴ πιστεύουσιν· εἰ γὰρ ἐπιστεύετε φησὶ Μωϋσεῖ, ἐπιστεύετε ἂν ἐμοί. Νῦν δὲ παρ'ἐκείνοις μὲν τὰ βι-
βλία, παρ'ἡμῖν δὲ τῶν βιβλίων ὁ θησαυρός· παρ'ἐκείνοις
30 τὰ γράμματα, παρ'ἡμῖν δὲ καὶ τὰ γράμματα καὶ τὰ νοήματα. Πρὸς τίνα οὖν φησὶ Ποιήσωμεν ἄνθρωπον; Πρὸς
ἄγγελον φησὶν ἢ ἀρχάγγελον. Ἁπλῶς τὸ ἐπιὸν φθέγγεσθε, ὦ Ἰουδαῖοι· καθάπερ γὰρ οἱ μαστιγίαι τῶν οἰκετῶν
οἱ παρὰ τῶν δεσποτῶν ἐγκαλούμενοι καὶ ἐξ εὐθείας
35 οὐκ ἔχοντες ἀποκρίνεσθαι, τὸ ἐπελθὸν ἅπαν προφέρου-
σι, οὕτω δὴ καὶ ὑμεῖς. Πρὸς ἄγγελον καὶ ἀρχάγγελον
εἶπε; Ποῖον ἄγγελον; Οὐ γὰρ ἀγγέλων ἐστὶ τὸ δημιουρ-
γεῖν, οὐδὲ ἀρχαγγέλων τὸ ἐργάζεσθαι ταῦτα. Τίνος δὲ
ἕνεκεν, ὅτε μὲν τὸν οὐρανὸν ἐποίησεν, οὐκ εἶπεν ἀγ-
40 γέλῳ καὶ ἀρχαγγέλῳ, ἀλλὰ δι'ἑαυτοῦ παρήγαγεν, ὅτε
δὲ τὸ τιμιώτερον οὐρανοῦ καὶ παντὸς τοῦ κόσμου πα-
ρήγαγε ζῷον, τὸν ἄνθρωπον, τότε τοὺς δούλους κοινωνοὺς λαμβάνει τῆς δημιουργίας; Οὐκ ἔστι τοῦτο, οὐκ

Font.   27/28 Io. 5, 46   31 cf. supra l. 1/2   39 cf. Gen. 1, 1

Mss.   *AT CDEFHK*

Crit.   26 μωϋσέος *C*, μωϋσῇ *EK*, μωσέα *FH*   ᾧ] *scripsi cum T et fonte, om. cett.*
27 Οὐ – πιστεύουσιν] ἀλλ'οὐ πιστεύουσιν *EK*   28 νυνὶ *FH*   29 ὁ τῶν
βιβλίων θησαυρός *FH*   30 καὶ¹] *om. T*   32 φησὶν] *om. K*
32/33 φθέγγεσθε τὸ ἐπιὸν *EK*   32/33 φθέγγεσθε] φθέγγεσθαι *D*
33 αἱ μάστιγες *A C^{p.corr.}D*   34 οἱ] αἱ *A C^{p.corr.}D, om. FH*   ἐγκαλούμε-
ναι *(sic acc.) D*   35 ἀποκρίνασθαι *FH*   35/36 προσφέρουσι *CDEFK*
36 ὑμεῖς] φατὲ *add. EK*   καὶ²] ἢ *DEFHK*   38 ἀρχαγγέλων] τῶν
praem. CDEFHK   τὸ] *om. T*   39/40 ἀγγέλῳ – ἀρχαγγέλῳ] *scripsi cum*
CDK, ἀγγέλῳ ἢ ἀρχαγγέλῳ *FH*, ἀγγέλων καὶ ἀρχαγγέλων *ATE*   40 ἑαυ-
τοῦ] αὐτοῦ *TFH*   41 οὐρανοῦ] τοῦ *praem. E^{a.corr.} (expunx.)*   τοῦ] *om. T*

Comp.   26 ἐστὶ *Chrys.*   27/28 φησὶ – ἐπιστεύετε] Μωϋσεῖ ἐπιστεύετέ φησιν
Chrys.   30 δὲ] *non hab. Chrys. (R = Coisl.)*   32 *post* ἢ] πρὸς *hab. Chrys.*
(SR = Coisl.)   τὸ ἐπιὸν] *non hab. Chrys. (P = Coisl.)*   32/33 φθέγγε-
ται *Chrys. (sic SMR, cett.* φθέγγεσθαι)   33 ὦ Ἰουδαῖοι] *non hab. Chrys.*
34 οἱ] *non hab. Chrys.*   35 ἀποκρίνασθαι *Chrys.*   36 *post* ἄγγελον] φησὶ
hab. Chrys. (P = Coisl.)   37 *post* ἄγγελον] ποῖον ἀρχάγγελον *hab. Chrys.*
(P = Coisl.)   41 τοῦ] *non hab. Chrys.*   43 τοῦτο] ταῦτα *Chrys. (P = Coisl.)*

ALPHA 19 – 20

ἔστιν· ἀγγέλων γὰρ τὸ παρεστάναι, οὐ τὸ δημιουργεῖν·
45 ἀρχαγγέλων τὸ λειτουργεῖν, οὐ τὸ γνώμης κοινωνεῖν
καὶ βουλῆς. Ἀλλὰ τίς ἐστι πρὸς ὅν φησι Ποιήσωμεν ἄνθρωπον; Ὁ θαυμαστὸς σύμβουλος, ὁ ἐξουσιαστὴς καὶ
θεὸς ἰσχυρός, ὁ ἄρχων τῆς εἰρήνης, ὁ πατὴρ τοῦ μέλλοντος αἰῶνος, αὐτὸς ὁ τοῦ θεοῦ μονογενὴς παῖς. Πρὸς
50 ἐκεῖνον φησὶ καὶ τὸ πνεῦμα Ποιήσωμεν ἄνθρωπον
κατ'εἰκόνα ἡμετέραν. Οὐδὲ γὰρ εἶπε τὴν ἐμὴν καὶ τὴν
σήν, ἀλλὰ κατ'εἰκόνα ἡμετέραν, μίαν δηλῶν τὴν συμ-
φωνίαν καὶ μίαν τὴν ὁμοίωσιν. Θεοῦ δὲ καὶ ἀγγέλων
οὐκ ἔστιν εἰκὼν μία οὐδὲ ὁμοίωσις μία.

Ζ'

Διατί τελευταῖος ὁ ἄνθρωπος;

20   Γρηγορίου τοῦ Θεολόγου

Εἰ δὲ τελευταῖος ὁ ἄνθρωπος ἀνεδείχθη, καὶ ταῦτα χειρὶ θεοῦ καὶ εἰκόνι τετιμημένος, θαυμαστὸν οὐδέν· ἔδει
γάρ, ὥσπερ βασιλεῖ, προϋποστῆναι τὰ βασίλεια, καὶ

---

ont.   **46/54** = Io. Chrys., Serm. in Gen., 2, 113-122   **46/47** cf. supra l. 1/2
47/49 Is. 9, 5   **50/51** cf. supra l. 1/2   **52/53** cf. supra l. 1/2   **54** cf.
supra l. 1/2   **20.1/8** = Greg. Naz., Or. 44, PG 36, 612, 9-18

---

ss.   *AT CDEFHK*   **20** *AT CDEFHK*

---

it.   **Ζ'**] ς' *DH, illeg. F, om. A EK*   ἄνθρωπος] τῆς δημιουργίας *add. DEK*
20 Γρηγορίου τοῦ Θεολόγου] γρηγορίου θεολόγου *A K, om. DE*

---

rit.   **46** τίς] τί *A*, τὶς *D*   **47** ὁ] καὶ *T CDFH*   **51/52** Οὐδὲ – ἡμετέραν] *om.*
D^(a.corr.) *(suppl. in marg.)*   **53** ἀγγέλου *FH*   **20.1** τελευταῖος] τῆς δημιουργίας *add. C*   ἄνθρωπος] τῆς δημιουργίας *add. DEFHK*   **3** βασι-
λεῖ] βασιλέα *F,* βασιλ() *(sine acc.) H*   προϋφεστάναι *FH*

---

omp.   **47/48** καὶ θεὸς] ὁ Θεὸς ὁ *Chrys.*   **49** τοῦ – παῖς] μονογενὴς τοῦ Θεοῦ
Ὑιός *Chrys.*   **50** καὶ – πνεῦμα] *non hab. Chrys.*   **50/51** *post* εἰκόνα] καὶ
καθ'ὁμοίωσιν *hab. Chrys.*   **51** *post* σήν] ἢ «τὴν ἐμὴν καὶ τὴν ὑμῶν» *hab.*
Chrys.   **52/53** συμφωνίαν] εἰκόνα *Chrys. (P = Coisl.)*

38 FLORILEGIVM COISLINIANVM

οὕτως εἰσαχθῆναι τὸν βασιλέα πᾶσιν ἤδη δορυφορού-
5 μενον. Εἰ μὲν οὖν ἐμείναμεν ὅπερ ἦμεν καὶ τὴν ἐντολὴν
ἐφυλάξαμεν, ἐγενόμεθα ἂν ὅπερ οὐκ ἦμεν, τῷ ξύλῳ τῆς
ζωῆς προσελθόντες, μετὰ τὸ ξύλον τῆς γνώσεως. Καὶ τί
γεγονότες; Ἀπαθανατισθέντες καὶ θεῷ πλησιάσαντες.

21 Τοῦ Χρυσοστόμου

Ὥσπερ βασιλέως εἰς πόλιν εἰσέρχεσθαι μέλλοντος,
στρατηγοὶ καὶ ὕπαρχοι καὶ δορυφόροι καὶ δοῦλοι καὶ
πάντες προτρέχουσιν, ἵνα τὰ βασίλεια παρασκευάσαν-
τες, καὶ πᾶσαν τὴν ἄλλην εὐτρεπίσαντες θεραπείαν,
5 μετὰ πολλῆς τῆς τιμῆς ὑποδέξωνται τὸν βασιλέα, οὕτω
δὴ καὶ ἐνταῦθα, καθάπερ βασιλέως εἰσάγεσθαι μέλλοντος, προέφθασεν ἥλιος, προέδραμεν οὐρανός, προεισῆλ-
θε τὸ φῶς, ἅπαντα γέγονε καὶ εὐτρεπίσθη, καὶ τότε ὁ
ἄνθρωπος μετὰ πολλῆς ὕστερον εἰσάγεται τῆς τιμῆς.

Font. 6/7 cf. Gen. 2, 9   21.1/9 = Io. Chrys., Serm. in Gen., 2, 70-78

Mss. AT CDEFHK   21 AT CDEFHK

Tit. 21 Τοῦ Χρυσοστόμου] τοῦ ἁγίου ἰωάννου praem. F, om. D

Crit. 7 τὸ ξύλον] τοῦ ξύλου DEK   τὶ D   21.1 Ὥσπερ] γὰρ add. DEK
2 δορυφόροι] πάντες add. E   2/3 καὶ πάντες] om. E, πάντες FHK
5 τῆς] om. AT   7/8 προεισῆλθε] προοσῆλθε A^{ut uid.}, προῆλθε T
8 ηὐτρεπίσθη K, προηυτρεπίσθη H, illeg. F   9 εἰσάγεται μετὰ πολλῆς
τῆς τιμῆς ὕστερον FH

Comp. 21.1 post Ὥσπερ] γὰρ hab. Chrys. (P = Coisl.)   εἰς – εἰσέρχεσθαι] εἰσε-
λαύνειν Chrys. (εἴς τινα πόλιν ἐλαύνειν SR)   2/3 καὶ³ – προτρέχουσιν] καὶ
πάντες οἱ δοῦλοι προφθάνουσιν Chrys. (οἱ δοῦλοι πάντες προτρέχουσιν C)
7 ante ἥλιος] ὁ hab. Chrys (sic R, cett. = Coisl.)   ante οὐρανός] ὁ hab. Chrys.
(PR = Coisl.)

Ind. 5/6 Εἰ – ἦμεν = Ps.-Max., Loc. comm. 51, -, /58, -, /6a (p. 832)

ALPHA 20 – 22

H'

Διατί διπλοῦς ὁ ἄνθρωπος;

22   Τοῦ Χρυσοστόμου

Ὅτε τὸν παναρμόνιον τουτονὶ κόσμον εἰργάζετο ὁ θεός,
τὰ μὲν ἄλλα πάντα ἀπὸ μοναδικῆς ἐποίησεν οὐσίας.
Κἂν ἀσαφὴς ᾖ ὁ λόγος, ποιήσω αὐτὸν σαφέστερον· τὰ
μὲν ἄλλα πάντα ἀπὸ μοναδικῆς ἐποίησεν οὐσίας, τὰ
5 ἄνω καὶ τὰ κάτω – καὶ γὰρ κόσμος ἐκεῖνος καὶ κόσμος
οὗτος, δύο οὗτοι κόσμοι –, ἀλλ'ἕκαστος τῶν γενομένων
ἀπὸ μοναδικῆς ἦν οὐσίας. Οἷόν τι λέγω· τὰ ἄνω πάντα
ἀσώματα, τὰ κάτω πάντα σώματα· τὰ ἄνω νοερά, τὰ
κάτω αἰσθητά· τὰ ἄνω ἀόρατα, τὰ κάτω ὁρατά. Πάντα
10 σώματα τὰ κάτω, καὶ οὐρανός, καὶ ἥλιος, καὶ σελήνη,
καὶ γῆ, καὶ θάλασσα, καὶ δένδρα, καὶ φυτά, καὶ βόες,
καὶ πρόβατα, καὶ ἵπποι· πάντα ὁρώμενα, πάντα αἰ-
σθητά, πάντα σώματα, πάντα ἀφῇ ὑποβαλλόμενα καὶ
ὄψει ὁρώμενα. Τὰ ἄνω πάντα ἀόρατα, νοερά, ἄγγελοι,
15 ἀρχάγγελοι, θρόνοι, κυριότητες, ἀρχαί, ἐξουσίαι, δυνάμεις, τὰ χερουβίμ, τὰ σεραφίμ. Οὔτε ἐκεῖνα ὁρατά, οὔτε

---

ont.   **22.1/39** = Ps.-Io. Chrys., Suff. tibi grat., PG 59, 508, 42 – 509, 19

---

ss.   **22** *AT CDEFHK*

---

it.   **H'**] ζ' *DH, illeg. EF, om. A K*

---

rit.   **22.1** τοῦτον *T*, τουτονὶ *(sic acc.) D*   **3** ποιήσομεν *F*ᵃ·ᶜᵒʳʳ·*H (*ποιήσωμεν
*F*ᵖ·ᶜᵒʳʳ·*)*   **3/4** τὰ – οὐσίας] *om. T*   **4** πάντα] *om. DEFHK*   **5** τὰ
om. T   **7** οὐσίας ἦν *E*   οἷον τί *(sic acc.) A FH*   **10** σώματα] τὰ
ἄνω καὶ *EK*   οὐρανός] ὁ *praem. E*   ἥλιος] ὁ *praem. E*   **11** καὶ γῆ]
om. T   θάλαττα *A DK*   καὶ⁵] *om. F*   βόας *D*   **12/13** πάντα
αἰσθητά] *om. D*ᵃ·ᶜᵒʳʳ· *(suppl. in marg.)*   **14** νοερά] *om. K*ᵃ·ᶜᵒʳʳ· *(suppl. in marg.)*
16 χερουβίμ] καὶ *add. E*   ὁρατά] ἀόρατα *EK ut expectaueris*

---

omp.   **22.1** *post* Ὅτε] δὲ *hab. Ps.-Chrys.*   ὁ θεός] *non hab. Ps.-Chrys.*   **3** *post*
σαφέστερον] ἐὰν προσέχητε *hab. Ps.-Chrys.*   **7** ἦν] οὖν *in textu Ps.-Chrys.*
In nota autem: "legendum videtur cum Savilio ἦν*"*

40   FLORILEGIVM COISLINIANVM

ταῦτα ἀόρατα· οὔτε ἐκεῖνα σώματα, ἀλλ'εἰ καὶ ταῦτα
σώματα, πάντα ἐκ μοναδικῆς ἐγένετο οὐσίας, καὶ τὰ
κάτω καὶ τὰ ἄνω· καὶ τὰ μὲν ἀπὸ σωμάτων, τὰ δὲ ἐξ
20 ἀσωμάτων· τὰ μὲν σώματα, τὰ δὲ ἀσώματα. Μόνος ὁ
ἄνθρωπος ἀπὸ διπλῆς ἐγένετο οὐσίας, τῆς μὲν βελτίο-
νος, τῆς δὲ χείρονος, ψυχῆς τε καὶ σώματος. Ἡ μὲν γὰρ
ἀόρατος καὶ νοερά, ἡ ψυχή· τὸ δὲ σῶμα, αἰσθητὸν καὶ
ὁρατόν. Τίνος οὖν ἕνεκεν οἱ μὲν δύο κόσμοι οὗτοι ἀπὸ
25 μοναδικῆς ἐγένοντο οὐσίας, καὶ οὔτε ἄνω σώματα, οὔτε
κάτω ἀσώματα, ἄνθρωπος δὲ μόνος ἀπὸ ἀσωμάτου καὶ
σώματος συνέστηκεν; Ἀκούσατε τὴν αἰτίαν, καὶ μάθετε
τοῦ ἐργασαμένου τὴν σοφίαν. Ἐπειδὴ γὰρ δύο κόσμοι
οὗτοι ἦσαν τῇ οὐσίᾳ διεστηκότες, ὁ μὲν ἀσώματος, ὁ δὲ
30 σωματικός, ὁ μὲν ἀόρατος, ὁ δὲ ὁρατός, ὁ μὲν νοερὸς ὁ
ἄνω, ὁ δὲ αἰσθητὸς ὁ κάτω, ἵνα μὴ ἡ διαφορὰ τῶν ἔργων διαφόρους δημιουργοὺς εἰσαγάγῃ, καὶ μὴ λέγηται
Ἄλλος τὰ ἄνω ἐποίησε καὶ ἄλλος τὰ κάτω, διπλοῦν
ζῶον ἐν τῷ κόσμῳ τέθεικεν ἀνακηρύττειν καὶ τῶν ἄνω
35 καὶ τῶν κάτω τὴν δημιουργίαν. Διπλοῦς κόσμος ὁ ἄνθρωπος, καὶ τῶν ἄνω τὸ συγγενὲς ἔχων τὴν ψυχήν, καὶ
τῶν κάτω τὸ σῶμα, σύνδεσμός τις καὶ γέφυρα, ἕνα δη-

Mss.   *AT CDEFHK* (*Q* inde a Τίνος, 22.24)

Crit.   **17** ἀόρατα] ὁρατά *EK ut expectaueris*   σώματα – καὶ] ἀσώματα, οὔτε
EK   **18** πάντα] οὖν *add. EK*   ἐγένοντο *K*   καὶ] *om.* D^{p.corr. ut uid.}
19 ἀπὸ σωμάτων] ἀσωμάτων *T*^{a.corr.}   **20** ὁ] *om. T*   **24** Τίνος] τοῦ χρυσοστόμου *praem. Q*   οὖν] *om. Q*   **28** γὰρ] οἱ *add. F*   **29** ἦσαν οὗτοι
EK   τὴν οὐσίαν *FH*   **30** ὁ⁴] *om. DQ*   **31** ὁ²] *om. Q*   **32** μὴ]
om. Q   **33** ἐποίησε] ποιεῖν *Q*   **34** τέθηκεν *Q*   ἀνακηρύττον *T*
καὶ] *om. EK*   **35** τῶν] τα (*sine acc.*) *D*   τὴν] *om. H*

Comp.   **17/18** ἀλλ' – σώματα] οὔτε ταῦτα ἀσώματα, ἀλλὰ καὶ ταῦτα σώματα, καὶ
ἐκεῖνα ἀσώματα *Ps.-Chrys.*   **21** ἀπὸ] ἐκ *Ps.-Chrys.*   **22** *post* γὰρ] ἐστιν
hab. Ps.-Chrys.   **28** ἐργαζομένου *Ps.-Chrys.*   **29** ἦσαν οὗτοι *Ps.-Chrys.*
30 σωματικός] ἐνσώματος *Ps.-Chrys.*   **32** *post* λέγηται] ὅτι *hab. Ps.-Chrys.*
34 τέθεικεν] ἔθηκεν *Ps.-Chrys.*   **35** ὁ] *non hab. Ps.-Chrys.*   **37/38** *post*
δημιουργὸν] ἔχων *hab. Ps.-Chrys.*

ALPHA 22 – 23

μιουργὸν τὸν τὰ ἄνω καὶ κάτω ἐργασάμενον κηρύττων
διὰ τὸ σύνθετον τῆς πλάσεως.

Θ'

Ὅτι ὀργανικὸν κατεσκευάσθη τοῦ ἀνθρώπου τὸ
σχῆμα πρὸς τὴν τοῦ λόγου χρείαν

23   Γρηγορίου Νύσης

Ἐπεὶ οὖν νοερόν τι χρῆμα καὶ ἀσώματόν ἐστιν ὁ νοῦς
καὶ ἀκοινώνητον ἔσχε τὴν χάριν καὶ ἄμικτον, διά τινος
ἐπινοίας φανερουμένης αὐτοῦ τῆς κινήσεως, τούτου
χάριν τῆς ὀργανικῆς ταύτης προσεδεήθη κατασκευῆς,
5 ἵνα πλήκτρου δίκην τῶν φωνητικῶν μορίων ἁπτόμενος, διὰ τῆς ποιᾶς τῶν φθόγγων τυπώσεως ἑρμηνεύῃ
τὴν ἔνδοθεν κίνησιν. Καὶ ὥσπέρ τις μουσικῆς ἔμπει-
ρος ὢν ἰδίαν ἐκ πάθους μὴ ἔχοι φωνήν, βουλόμενος δὲ
φανεροποιῆσαι τὴν ἐπίκτησιν, ἀλλοτρίαις ἐμμελῳδοίη
10 φωναῖς, δι'αὐλῶν ἢ λύρας δημοσιεύων τὴν τέχνην,

Font.   **23.1/16** = Greg. Nyss., De hom. opif., ed. Sels, p. 151, 12 – 152, 13 (= PG 44,
149, 23-39)

Mss.   *AT CDEFHKQ*   **23** *AT CDEFHKQ*

Tit.   **Θ'**] η' *DH, illeg. EF, om. KQ*   Ὅτι – χρείαν] = Greg. Nyss., De hom. opif.,
ed. Sels, p. 151, 1-3; PG 44, 149, 15-16   σχῆμα] σῶμα *Q*   **23** Γρηγορίου
Νύσης] Γρηγορίου νύσσης *A^{p.corr.} Q (νύσ A^{a.corr.}), om. EF*

Crit.   **38** κάτω] τὰ *praem. EF^{ut uid.}Q*   **23.1** χρῆμα] σχῆμα *F*   ἔστιν *Q*
5 τῶν] *om. K*   **6** διὰ τῆς] διά τινος *Q*   ἑρμηνεύει *T CDFH*   **7** ὥσπέρ
τις] ὥσπερ εἴ τις *Q*   **8** ἔχῃ *EH,* ἐχ() *F*   **9** ἐπίκτησιν] ἐπιστήμην *Q*
ἀλλοτρίοις *T*   ἐμμελῳδοίη *C,* ἐνμελῳδοίη *D,* ἐκ μελῶν δοίη *E,* ἐνμελω-
δήσει *FH,* ἐμμελωδεῖ *Q*   **10/11** τὴν – οὕτω] αὐτὴν *Q*

Comp.   **38** *ante* κάτω] τὰ *hab. Ps.-Chrys.*   **38/39** κηρύττων – πλάσεως] *non hab.*
Ps.-Chrys.   **23.2** καὶ¹] *non hab. Greg.*   *post* ἀκοινώνητον] ἂν *hab. Greg.*
ante διά] μὴ *hab. Greg.*   **6** ἑρμηνεύῃ *Greg.*   **9** φανεροποιῆσαι – ἐπί-
κτησιν] φανερὰν ποιῆσαι τὴν ἐπιστήμην *Greg.*

42 FLORILEGIVM COISLINIANVM

οὕτω καὶ ὁ ἀνθρώπινος νοῦς, παντοδαπῶν νοημάτων
εὑρετὴς ὤν, τῷ μὴ δύνασθαι τοῖς διὰ σωματικῶν αἰσθή-
σεων ἐπαΐουσιν γυμνῇ τῇ ψυχῇ δεικνύειν τὰς τῆς διανοίας ὁρμάς, καθάπερ τις ἁρμοστὴς ἔντεχνος, τῶν ἐμ-
15 ψύχων τούτων ὀργάνων ἁπτόμενος, διὰ τῆς ἐν τούτοις
ἠχῆς φανεροποιεῖ τὰ κεκρυμμένα νοήματα.

Ι′

Ὅτι ἐπιστημονικὸς τῆς τοῦ καλοῦ καὶ κακοῦ
γνώσεως ὁ ἄνθρωπος

24 Τοῦ Χρυσοστόμου

Ὑπεσχόμεθα ὑμῖν εἰπεῖν περὶ τοῦ ξύλου, πότερον ἐξ
ἐκείνου γέγονεν ἡ γνῶσις τοῦ καλοῦ καὶ πονηροῦ τῷ
Ἀδάμ, ἢ πρὸ τῆς βρώσεως εἶχε τὴν διάγνωσιν ταύτην.
Θαρροῦντες οὖν λέγομεν νῦν ὅτι πρὸ τῆς βρώσεως τὴν
5 διάγνωσιν εἶχε ταύτην. Εἰ μὴ γὰρ ᾔδει τί μὲν καλόν,

Font. **24.1/16** = Io. Chrys., Serm. in Gen., 6, 49-66   **1/3** cf. Gen. 2, 16-17

Mss. *AT CDEFHKQ*   **24** *AT CDEFHK*

Tit. **Ι′**] θ′ *DH, om. EFK*   ἐπιστημονικὸν *C*   ὁ ἄνθρωπος] ὑπῆρχεν ὁ ἄνθρωπος πρὸ τῆς παραβάσεως *C*   **24** Τοῦ Χρυσοστόμου] *om. CE*

Crit. **12** δύνασθαι] δηλοποιεῖσθαι *add. Q*   σωματικῶν] τῶν *praem.* FHQ
13/14 γυμνῇ – ὁρμάς] διὰ τῶν φανερῶν ἀπηχήσεων τὴν τῆς διανοίας φανεροποιεῖ κρυφιότητα *Q*   **14** τις] αὐλητὴς *add. Q*   **14/15** ἐμψύχων] φωνητικῶν *Q*   **15** ἁπτόμενος] καὶ *add. Q*   τῆς] ἐμπνευστης (*sic*) *add. Q*
15/16 ἐν – φανεροποιεῖ] ἐνάρθρου ἠχοῦς εἰς φῶς τιθῶν *Q*   **16** φανεροπίει
(*sic*) *T*   νοήματα] μυστήρια *Q*   **24.1** ὑμῖν] ἡμῖν *F*ᵃ·ᶜᵒʳʳ·*H*   περὶ]
παρὰ *C*   **4** θαρροῦντες *AT*   οὖν] *om. FH*   λέγωμεν *A D*   βρώσε-
ως] γνώσεως *D*   **5** εἶχε] *post* βρώσεως *trsp. DEFH*   μὲν] *om. D*

Comp. **16** φανεροποιεῖ] φανερὰ ποιεῖ *Greg.*   **24.1** ὑμῖν εἰπεῖν] γὰρ ἐρεῖν *Chrys.*
πότερον] πρότερον εἰ *Chrys.* (πότερον εἰ *MV*)   **2** *ante* πονηροῦ] τοῦ *hab.*
Chrys.   **3** *post* ἢ] καὶ *hab. Chrys.* (*TS* = *Coisl.*)   **4** λέγομεν] ἂν εἴποι-
μεν *Chrys.*   *post* ὅτι] καὶ *hab. Chrys.*   **4/5** ταύτην εἶχε τὴν διάγνωσιν
Chrys.   **5** γὰρ μὴ *Chrys.*

ALPHA 23 – 24   43

τί δὲ πονηρόν, καὶ αὐτῶν τῶν ἀλόγων ἀλογώτερος ἦν.
Πῶς γὰρ οὐκ ἄτοπον αἶγας μὲν καὶ πρόβατα εἰδέναι
ποία μὲν αὐτοῖς βοτάνη χρήσιμος, ποία δὲ ὀλέθριος,
καὶ μὴ πάσαις αὐταῖς ἐφιέναι ταῖς φαινομέναις, ἀλλ᾽ἔ-
10 χειν τὴν διάγνωσιν καὶ εἰδέναι σαφῶς τί μὲν ἐπιβλα-
βές, τί δὲ ὠφέλιμον, τὸν δὲ ἄνθρωπον ταύτης ἀποστε-
ρεῖσθαι τῆς ἀσφαλείας; Εἰ μὴ γὰρ τοῦτο εἶχεν, οὐδενὸς
ἄξιος ἦν, ἀλλὰ καὶ εὐτελέστερος πάντων ὑπῆρχε. Πολλῷ γὰρ αἱρετώτερον ἦν αὐτῷ ἐν σκότει διάγειν καὶ
15 τοὺς ὀφθαλμοὺς ἐκκεκόφθαι καὶ τοῦ φωτὸς ἀποστε-
ρεῖσθαι, ἢ μὴ εἰδέναι τί μὲν καλόν, τί δὲ πονηρόν· τὸ γὰρ
καλὸν καὶ πονηρὸν ἐκεῖνοι μόνοι ἀγνοοῦσιν ὅσοι τῶν
κατὰ φύσιν εἰσὶν ἐστερημένοι φρενῶν. Ὁ δὲ Ἀδὰμ σοφίας πολλῆς ἐπεπλήρωτο καὶ διαγνωστικὸς ἑκατέρων
20 τούτων ἦν· καὶ ὅτι σοφίας πολλῆς ἐπεπλήρωτο, ἄκουσον αὐτῆς τὴν ἀπόδειξιν· Ἤγαγε τὰ θηρία πρὸς αὐτὸν
ὁ θεός, ἰδεῖν τί καλέσει αὐτά, καὶ εἴ τι ἐκάλεσεν αὐτὰ
Ἀδάμ, τοῦτο ὄνομα αὐτοῖς.

Font.   **16/23** = Io. Chrys., Serm. in Gen., 6, 77-83   **21/23** Gen. 2, 19

Mss.   *AT CDEFHK*

Crit.   **6** ἦν ἀλογώτερος *DFHK*   **7** Πῶς] μὲν *add. FH*   αἶγας] αἴγες *(sic) A*
μὲν] *om. E*   **8** ὀλεθρία *F*, ὀλεθρ() *(sine acc.) H*   **9** ἑαυταῖς *T*   ἐφιέ-
ναι] *sic codd. omnes, intellige* ἐπιέναι   **11** δὲ¹] δὴ *H*   τὸν – ἄνθρωπον]
om. H   **15** τοῦ] *om. E*   **15/16** ἀπεστερεῖσθαι *E*   **17** μόνον *DFH*
19/20 καὶ– ἐπεπλήρωτο] *om. AT C^{a.corr.} (suppl. in marg. C)*   **19** ἑκατέρων]
ἑκάστω *F^{ut uid.}H*   **23** Ἀδάμ] ὁ *praem. D*

Comp.   **6** *post* ἦν] καὶ τοῦ δούλου ὁ δεσπότης ἀνοητότερος *hab. Chrys.*   **8** ὀλεθρία
Chrys.   **9** πάσαις – φαινομέναις] πᾶσιν αὐτὰ ἐπιέναι τοῖς φαινομένοις
Chrys.   **10** *post* μὲν] αὐτοῖς *hab. Chrys. (MV = Coisl.)*   **11** ταύτης] το-
σαύτης *Chrys.*   **12** γὰρ μὴ *Chrys.*   **14** σκότω *Chrys. (GPM = Coisl.)*
15/16 ἀπεστερῆσθαι *Chrys. (sic MV, cett. = Coisl.)*   **18** ἀπεστερημένοι
Chrys.   **20** πολλῆς ἐπεπλήρωτο] ἐπεπλήρωτο πνευματικῆς *Chrys.*
21 τὰ – αὐτὸν] πρὸς αὐτὸν τὰ θηρία *Chrys.*   **22** ὁ θεός] *non hab. Chrys.*
(M = Coisl.)

44 FLORILEGIVM COISLINIANVM

25 Κυρίλλου Ἀλεξανδρείας

Τὸ μὲν γὰρ ὁλοτρόπως ἀγνοεῖν τί μέν ἐστιν τὸ ἀγαθόν, τί δὲ τὸ ἔμπαλιν, κτηνοπρεπὲς ἂν εἴη καὶ λίθῳ μᾶλλον ἢ ξύλῳ προσπεφυκός· λογικῆς δὲ οἶμαι ψυχῆς ἀλλότριον παντελῶς. Ἡ δέ γε τῆς λέξεως δύναμις – τοῦ εἰδέναι
5 φημὶ καλόν τε καὶ φαῦλον – κατασημήνειεν ἂν παρά γε ταῖς θεοπνεύστοις γραφαῖς, οὐχὶ δήπου πάντως τὸ ὡς ἐν ψιλῇ καὶ μόνῃ δέχεσθαι γνώσει τῶν πραγμάτων τὴν ἐπιστήμην, ἀλλ᾽ὡς ἐν δυνάμει καὶ πείρᾳ.

ΙΑ′

Ὅτι αὐτεξούσιος ὁ ἄνθρωπος

26 Κλήμεντος Ῥώμης

Ὁ μεγαλόδωρος θεός, πρόνοιαν ποιούμενος τοῦ κατὰ θείαν εἰκόνα τετιμημένου ἀνθρώπου, καὶ ἀμοιβὰς ἀρετῶν παρασχεῖν βουλόμενος, αὐτεξούσιον κατεσκεύασε

Font. **25.1/8** Cyr. Alex., Contra Iul., 3, 23, 17-25   **4/5** cf. Gen. 2, 9   **26.1/6** locum non inueni nisi in flor.

Mss. **25** *AT CDEFHK*   **26** *AC*

Tit. **25** Κυρίλλου Ἀλεξανδρείας] Κυρίλλου *EF*ᵘᵗ ᵘⁱᵈ·*HK, om. D*   **ΙΑ′**] ι′ *DH, om. EFK*   Ὅτι – ἄνθρωπος] *cf. Sacr. Par., PG 95, 1109, 21-23 (*Περὶ αὐτεξουσίου· ὅτι αὐτεξούσιον δέδοται ἡμῖν ἀπὸ Θεοῦ, καὶ ἐν ἡμῖν ἔστι σωθῆναι καὶ ἀπολέσθαι*)*

Crit. **25.3** προσπεφυκὼς *AT*ᵃ·ᶜᵒʳʳ· (-ὼς *A*), προσεοικώς *E*, προσεεικώς *K*   **4** γε] *om. D*ᵃ·ᶜᵒʳʳ· (γε *sup. l.*)   δύναμις] *om. DEFHK*   **5** φαῦλον] χρῆσις *add. EK*   γε] τε *FH*   **6** δήπου] *scripsi cum fonte,* δὴ τοῦ *AT C,* δὲ τοῦ *D,* διὰ τοῦ *FH,* τόδε τοῦ *EK*   ὡς] *om. E*

Comp. **25.2** *post* δὲ] καὶ *add. Cyr.*   **4** *ante* τοῦ] τῆς *hab. Cyr.*   **26.3** κατεσκεύασε] κατέστησε *Sacr. Par.*

Ind. **26.1/6** = Sacr. Par., ed. HOLL, *Fragmente*, fr. 26 (Clem. Rom.), p. 13-14

ALPHA 25 – 27

τοῦτον, τοῦ κρείττονος καὶ τοῦ χείρονος παρασχὼν τὰς
5 αἱρέσεις, ὅπως ἐν γνώσει καὶ διακρίσει τῶν μὲν ἀγαθῶν ἐραστής, τῶν δὲ ἐναντίων δυσμενὴς ἀναφανῇ.
Οὐ δυνατόν τινα ἀγαθὸν εἶναι βιαίως, εἰ μὴ κατὰ
προαίρεσιν οἰκείαν αὐτεξούσιον· ὁ γὰρ ὑφ'ἑτέρου ἀνάγκης ἀγαθὸς γενόμενος, οὐκ ἀγαθός, ὅτι μὴ ἰδίᾳ προαι-
10 ρέσει ἐστὶν ὅ ἐστιν· τὸ γὰρ ἑκάστου ἐλεύθερον ἀποτελεῖ
τὸ ὄντως ἀγαθόν, καὶ δεικνύει τὸ ὄντως κακόν· ὅθεν διὰ
τῶν ὑποθέσεων τούτων ἐμηχανήσατο ὁ θεὸς φανερῶ-
σαι τὴν ἑκάστου διάθεσιν.

27   Κυρίλλου Ἱεροσολύμων

Αὐτεξούσιος ἐστὶ πᾶς ἄνθρωπος. Καὶ ὁ μὲν διάβολος τὸ
ὑποβάλλειν δύναται, τὸ δὲ ἀναγκάσαι παρὰ προαίρεσιν
οὐκ ἔχει τὴν ἐξουσίαν. Ὑπογράφει πορνείας λογισμόν·
ἐὰν θέλῃς, ἐδέξω. Εἰ γὰρ κατὰ ἀνάγκην ἐπόρνευες, τί-
5 νος ἕνεκεν τὴν γέενναν ἡτοίμασεν ὁ θεός; Εἰ κατὰ φύ-

Font.   7/13 locum non inueni nisi in flor.   **27**.1/10 = Cyr. Hier., Cat. ad illum.,
4, 21, 1-9

Mss.   *AC*   27 *AT CDEFHK*

Tit.   27 Κυρίλλου] κυρίλου *A*

Crit.   **4** τοῦτον] τὸν ἄνθρωπον *C*   **7** Οὐ] τοῦ αὐτοῦ *add. C*ⁱⁿ ᵐᵃʳᵍ·   **8** οἰκείαν] ὡς
add. C   **27.2** τὸ] τοῦ *EK*   **3** Ὑπογράφει] ὑποβάλλει *F*   **4** ἐπόρνευ-
σας *D*   **5** ἕνεκε *TFH*   **5/7** Εἰ – θεός] *om. D*ᵃ·ᶜᵒʳʳ· *(suppl. in marg.)*

Comp.   **4** παρασχὼν] παραχωρήσας *Sacr. Par.*   **6** ἀναφανείη *Sacr. Par. (M = Coisl.)*
7 βιαίως] βεβαίως *Sacr. Par. (RLᵃ = Coisl.) et Loc. comm.*   **8** αὐτεξούσι-
ον] *non hab. Sacr. Par. et Loc. comm.*   **27.1** πᾶς ἄνθρωπος] ἡ ψυχή *Cyr.*
μὲν] *post* τὸ *hab. Cyr.*   **2** *post* δὲ] καὶ *hab. Cyr.*   **3** *post* Ὑπογράφει] σοι
hab. Cyr.   **4** *post* ἐδέξω] ἐὰν μὴ θέλῃς οὐκ ἐδέξω *hab. Cyr.*   κατ' *Cyr.*
4/5 *ante* τίνος] καὶ *hab. Cyr.*   **5** ἕνεκα *Cyr.*

Ind.   7/13 = Sacr. Par., ed. HOLL, *Fragmente*, fr. 14 (Clem. Rom.), p. 8; Ps.-Max., Loc.
comm. 48, -, /55, 18 (p. 807)

46 FLORILEGIVM COISLINIANVM

σιν καὶ οὐ κατὰ προαίρεσιν ἐδικαιοπράγεις, τίνος ἔνε-
κεν στεφάνους ἀνεκδιηγήτους ἡτοίμαζεν ὁ θεός; Πρᾶον
ἐστὶ τὸ πρόβατον, ἀλλ'οὐδέποτε τοῦτο διὰ τὴν πραότη-
τα ἐστεφανώθη, ἐπειδὴ τὸ πρᾶον οὐκ ἐκ προαιρέσεως,
10 ἀλλ'ἐκ φύσεως αὐτῷ πρόσεστι.

28   Τοῦ αὐτοῦ

Γνῶθι σαυτὸν τίς εἶ – διπλοῦς ἄνθρωπος καθέστηκας, ἐκ ψυχῆς καὶ σώματος συγκείμενος –, καὶ ὅτι,
καθὼς καὶ πρὸ βραχέως εἴρηται, ὁ αὐτὸς θεὸς καὶ ψυχῆς καὶ σώματός ἐστι δημιουργός. Καὶ γίνωσκε ψυχὴν
5 ἔχειν αὐτεξούσιον, ἔργον θεοῦ κάλλιστον, κατ'εἰκόνα
τοῦ πεποιηκότος· ἀθάνατον, διὰ τὸν ἀπαθανατίσαντα·
ζῷον λογικὸν καὶ ἄφθαρτον, διὰ τὸν ταῦτα χαρισάμε-
νον· ἐξουσίαν ἔχον ποιεῖν ὃ βούλεται.

Font.   **28.1/8** = Cyr. Hier., Cat. ad illum., 4, 18, 2-9

Mss.   *AT CDEFHK*   28 *AT CDEFHK*

Tit.   **28** Τοῦ αὐτοῦ] *om. A D*

Crit.   **6** ἐδικαιοπράγης *AT D*   **6/7** ἔνεκε *FH*   **7** ἡτοίμασεν *T D^{ut uid.}*
        28.1/2 καθέστηκας] *post* σώματος *trsp. FH*   **3** καθὰ *DEFHK*   βρα-
        χέος *FH*   αὐτὸς ὁ *FH*   **4** ἐστι] *post* θεὸς *trsp. FH (hab.* ἐστὶ)
        6 ἀπαθανατήσαντα *A F,* ἀθανατήσαντα *T^{p.corr.} (*ἀθάνατα *T^{a.corr.})*   **8** ἔχοντα *A,*
        ἔχων *T F^{a. uel p.corr.},* ἔχειν *E*

Comp.   **6** καὶ] ἀλλ᾽ *Cyr.*   **7** ἡτοίμασεν *Cyr.*   **28.1** Γνῶθι – τίς] καὶ σεαυτὸν
        γνῶθι λοιπὸν ὅστις *Cyr. (RE. Casaub.* τίς *loco* ὅστις)   *ante* διπλοῦς] ὅτι
        hab. Cyr. (RE. Casaub. = *Coisl.)*   **2** *post* ψυχῇς] τε *hab. Cyr.*   **3** καὶ¹]
        non hab. Cyr.   βράχεος *Cyr.*   **3/4** *ante* ψυχῆς] τῆς *hab. Cyr.*   **4** *ante*
        σώματός] τοῦ *hab. Cyr.*   **6** ἀπαθανατίσαντα] ἀπαθανατίζοντα θεόν *Cyr.*
        7 καὶ] *non hab. Cyr.*   **8** ὃ] ἃ *Cyr.*

ALPHA 27 – 29

IB'

Περὶ φύσεως ἀνθρώπου λόγος κεφαλαιώδης

29   Νεμεσίου ἐπισκόπου Ἐμέσης

Τὸν ἄνθρωπον ἐκ ψυχῆς νοερᾶς καὶ σώματος ἄριστα   p. 1 (ed. Morani)
κατεσκευασμένον, καὶ οὕτω καλῶς ὡς οὐκ ἐνεδέχετο
ἄλλως γενέσθαι ἢ συνεστάναι, πολλοῖς καὶ ἀγαθοῖς ἀνδράσιν ἔδοξεν. Ἐκ τοῦ δὲ νοερὰν λέγεσθαι τὴν ψυχήν,
5 ἀμφιβολίαν ἔχοντος πότερον προσελθὼν ὁ νοῦς τῇ
ψυχῇ ὡς ἄλλος ἄλλῃ νοερὰν αὐτὴν ἐποίησεν, ἢ τὸ νοερὸν ἀφ'ἑαυτῆς ἡ ψυχὴ καὶ φύσει κέκτηται καὶ τοῦτό
ἐστιν αὐτῆς τὸ κάλλιστον μέρος, ὡς ὀφθαλμὸς ἐν σώματι, τινὲς μὲν οὖν, ὧν ἐστι καὶ Πλωτῖνος, ἄλλην εἶναι
10 τὴν ψυχὴν καὶ ἄλλον τὸν νοῦν δογματίσαντες, ἐκ τριῶν
τὸν ἄνθρωπον συνεστάναι βούλονται, σώματος καὶ ψυχῆς καὶ νοῦ. Οἷς ἠκολούθησε καὶ Ἀπολινάριος ὁ τῆς Λα-
οδικείας γενόμενος ἐπίσκοπος· τοῦτον γὰρ πηξάμενος
τὸν θεμέλιον τῆς ἰδίας δόξης, καὶ τὰ λοιπὰ προσῳκο-
15 δόμησε κατὰ τὸ οἰκεῖον δόγμα. Τινὲς δὲ οὐ διεστείλαντο
ἀπὸ τῆς ψυχῆς τὸν νοῦν, ἀλλὰ τῆς οὐσίας αὐτῆς ἡγε-

Font.   **29.1/488** = Nem. Em., De nat. hom., c. 1 (p. 1, 1 – 16, 6)

Mss.   **29** *AT CDEFHQI*

Tit.   **IB'**] ια' *DH* (*H hab.* ιβ' *ante fr. 31, cf. infra*), *om. FQI*   Περὶ – κεφαλαι-
ώδης] = *Nem. mss. ΠΗ*

Crit.   **29.1** νοερᾶς] *om. Q*   2 οὐκ ἐνεδέχετο] οὐ...*(15 litt. spat.) H*   ἐνεδέχετο *Q*
3 καὶ] *om. H*   4 τοῦ δὲ] τούτου *D*   5 ἔχοντες *FH*   6 ἄλλος] ἄλλως *Q*
7 καὶ¹] *om. E*   8 τὸ κάλλιστον αὐτῆς *FH*   9 ὧν] *om. A*   ἔστι *A*
10 δογματίσαντες] *om. H (15 litt. spat.)*   11 καὶ] *om. H*   12 Ἀπολι-
νάριος] ὁ ἄνους *praem. Q*   13 πηξάμενον *FH*   14 ἰδίας] οἰκείας *E*
15 κατὰ] πρὸς *D*

Comp.   **29.2** *post* ἐνεδέχετο] καλῶς *hab. Nem.* (*B H KF Alf. Arm. = Coisl.*)   **9** οὖν]
non hab. Nem.   **15** διέστειλαν *Nem.* (*B H = Coisl.*)

48 FLORILEGIVM COISLINIANVM

μονικὸν εἶναι τὸ νοερὸν ἡγοῦνται. Ἀριστοτέλης δὲ τὸν
μὲν δυνάμει νοῦν συγκατασκευάσθαι τῷ ἀνθρώπῳ, τὸν
δὲ ἐνεργείᾳ θύραθεν ἡμῖν ἐπεισιέναι δοξάζει, οὐκ εἰς τὸ
20 εἶναι καὶ τὴν ὕπαρξιν τοῦ ἀνθρώπου συντελοῦντα,
ἀλλ'εἰς προκοπὴν τῆς τῶν φυσικῶν γνώσεως καὶ θεωρίας
συμβαλλόμενον· κομιδῇ γοῦν ὀλίγους τῶν ἀνθρώπων,
καὶ μόνους τοὺς | φιλοσοφήσαντας, τὸν ἐνεργείᾳ νοῦν   p. 2
ἔχειν διαβεβαιοῦται. Πλάτων δὲ οὐ δοκεῖ λέγειν τὸν ἄν-
25 θρωπον εἶναι τὸ συναμφότερον, ψυχὴν καὶ σῶμα, ἀλλὰ
ψυχὴν σώματι τοιῷδε χρωμένην, ἀξιοπρεπέστερον φαν-
ταζόμενος τὰ κατὰ τὸν ἄνθρωπον, καὶ αὐτόθεν ἡμᾶς
ἐπιστρέφων ἐπὶ τὴν τῆς ψυχῆς μόνης θειότητα καὶ ἐπι-
μέλειαν, ἵνα τὴν ψυχὴν ἑαυτοὺς εἶναι πιστεύοντες, τὰ
30 τῆς ψυχῆς ἀγαθὰ μόνα μεταδιώκωμεν, τὰς ἀρετὰς καὶ
τὴν εὐσέβειαν, καὶ μὴ τὰς τοῦ σώματος ἐπιθυμίας ἀγα-
πήσωμεν, ὡς οὐκ οὔσας ἀνθρώπου ἢ ἄνθρωπον, ἀλλὰ
ζώου μὲν προηγουμένως, ἀνθρώπου δὲ ἑπομένως, ἐπειδὴ καὶ ζῶον ὁ ἄνθρωπος. Καὶ ἄλλως δὲ κυριώτερον τοῦ
35 σώματος ἡ ψυχὴ πᾶσιν ἀνθρώποις εἶναι καθωμολόγη-
ται· ἀπὸ ταύτης γὰρ ὡς ὄργανον κινεῖται τὸ σῶμα. Δηλοῖ δὲ ὁ θάνατος· χωρισθείσης γὰρ τῆς ψυχῆς, ἀκίνητον
μένει τὸ σῶμα παντελῶς καὶ ἀνενέργητον, ὡς τεχνίτου
χωρισθέντος ἀκίνητα μένει τὰ ὄργανα.
40   Γνώριμον δὲ ὅτι καὶ τοῖς ἀψύχοις κοινωνεῖ καὶ τῆς
τῶν ἀλόγων ζώων μετέχει ζωῆς καὶ τῆς τῶν λογικῶν

Mss.   AT CDEFHQI

Crit.   18 συγκατεσκευάσθαι T FHQ, ut expectaueris   19 ἡμῖν] om. E   ὑπει-
σιέναι Q   20 συντελοῦντα τοῦ ἀνθρώπου FH   21 τῆς] τὴν I   22 κο-
μιδὴ] sic acc. codd, κομιδῆ DE   24 ἔχει C   διαβεβαιοῦνται FH   δὲ]
ἰδὲ Q   28 μόνης] μόνην DE, om. Q   29 ἑαυτοὺς] scripsi cum DEFHQ
et fonte, ἑαυτῆς AT C   30 διώκωμεν Q   τὰς ἀρετὰς] τὴν ἀρετὴν I
32 οὐκ οὔσας] ἤκουσαν E   ἢ ἄνθρωπον] ἢ ἀνθρώπου Q   33/34 ἐπειδὴ]
ἐπεὶ FH   34 ἄλλος A D   39 ὄργανα] καὶ ἀνενέργητα add. FH
40 τῆς] τοῖς T

Comp.   18 συγκατεσκευάσθαι Nem.   32 ἢ ἄνθρωπον] ἢ ἄνθρωπος Nem. (H K F P
= Coisl.)   34 κυριωτέρα Nem.

ALPHA 29 49

μετείληφε νοήσεως. Κοινωνεῖ μέν, τοῖς μὲν ἀψύχοις
κατὰ τὸ σῶμα καὶ τὴν ἀπὸ τῶν τεσσάρων στοιχείων
κρᾶσιν, τοῖς δὲ φυτοῖς κατά τε ταῦτα καὶ τὴν θρεπτι-
45 κὴν καὶ σπερματικὴν δύναμιν, τοῖς δὲ ἀλόγοις καὶ ἐν
τούτοις μέν, ἐξ ἐπιμέτρου δὲ κατά τε τὴν καθ'ὁρμὴν κίνησιν καὶ κατὰ τὴν ὄρεξιν καὶ τὸν θυμὸν καὶ τὴν αἰσθητικὴν καὶ ἀναπνευστικὴν δύναμιν· ταῦτα γὰρ ἅπαντα κοινὰ τοῖς ἀνθρώποις καὶ τοῖς ἀλόγοις ἐστίν, εἰ καὶ
50 μὴ πᾶσι πάντα. Συνάπτεται δὲ διὰ μὲν τοῦ λογικοῦ
ταῖς ἀσωμάτοις καὶ νοεραῖς φύσεσι, λογιζόμενος καὶ
νοῶν καὶ κρίνων ἕκαστα, καὶ τὰς ἀρετὰς μεταδιώκων,
καὶ τῶν ἀρετῶν τὸν κολοφῶνα, τὴν εὐσέβειαν, ἀσπα-
ζόμενος. Διὸ καὶ ὥσπερ ἐν μεθορίοις ἐστὶν νοητῆς καὶ
55 αἰσθητῆς οὐσίας, συναπτόμε|νος κατὰ μὲν τὸ σῶμα   p. 3
καὶ τὰς σωματικὰς δυνάμεις τοῖς ἄλλοις ζώοις τε καὶ
ἀψύχοις, κατὰ δὲ τὸ λογικὸν ταῖς ἀσωμάτοις οὐσίαις,
ὡς εἴρηται. Ὁ γὰρ δημιουργὸς ἐκ τοῦ κατ'ὀλίγον ἔοικεν
ἐπισυνάπτειν ἀλλήλαις τὰς διαφόρους φύσεις, ὥστε
60 μίαν εἶναι καὶ συγγενῆ τὴν πᾶσαν κτίσιν, ἐξ οὗ μάλιστα δείκνυται εἷς ὢν ὁ πάντων τῶν ὄντων δημιουργός·
οὐ γὰρ μόνον ἥνωσε τὴν ὕπαρξιν τῶν κατὰ μέρος ἀτό-
μων, ἀλλὰ καὶ ἕκαστα πρὸς ἄλληλα συνήρμοσεν οἰκείως. Ὥσπερ γὰρ ἐν ἑκάστῳ τῶν ζώων ἥνωσε τὰ ἀναί-
65 σθητα τοῖς αἰσθητικοῖς, ὀστοῦν καὶ πιμελὴν καὶ τρίχας,
καὶ τὰ ἄλλα τὰ ἀναίσθητα τοῖς αἰσθητικοῖς νεύροις, καὶ

Mss.   AT CDEFHQI

Crit.   **42** μέν¹] δὲ EQ   μὲν²] om. FI   **43** τῶν ἀπὸ T   τεσσάρων] δ' EFH, om.
D (4 litt. spat.)   **44** ταῦτα καὶ] om. FH   **49** κοινὰ] καὶ add. Q   τοῖς²]
om. DEQ   εἰσίν Q   **51** λογιζόμενον C   **52** κρῖνον A   ἕκαστον E   **54** ἔστι D   **55/56** τὸ - τὰς] τὰς I (τῶ a. corr. ut uid.)
56 ἄλλοις] ἀλόγοις EFH   **60** μίαν] φύσιν add. Aᵃ·ᶜᵒʳʳ· (cancell.)   **61** ὁ]
om. DQ   **63** ἥρμοσεν FH   **64** γὰρ] om. T   **65** αἰσθητοῖς E
65/66 ὀστοῦν - αἰσθητικοῖς] om. DEQ   **66** τὰ ἀναίσθητα] om. T
νεύροις] scripsi cum Q et fonte, νοεροῖς cett., καὶ praem. EF

Comp.   **42** μέν] γὰρ Nem.   **50** μὲν] non hab. Nem. (D P = Coisl.)   **56** ἄλλοις]
ἀλόγοις Nem. (Π HSGQF = Coisl.)   **58** post εἴρηται] πρότερον hab. Nem.

50 FLORILEGIVM COISLINIANVM

ἐποίησεν ἐξ ἀναισθήτων καὶ αἰσθητικῶν συγκείμενον
τὸ ζῶον, καὶ οὐ μόνον συγκείμενον, ἀλλὰ καὶ ἓν ἀπέδειξεν, οὕτω καὶ ἐπὶ τῆς ἄλλης κατ'εἶδος κτίσεως πε-
70 ποίηκε, συνάπτων ἄλληλα τῇ κατ'ὀλίγον οἰκειότητι καὶ
παραλλαγῇ τῆς φύσεως, ὡς μὴ κατὰ πολὺ διεστάναι
τὰ πάντη ἄψυχα τῶν ἐχόντων φυτῶν τὴν θρεπτικὴν
δύναμιν, μὴ δ'αὖ ταῦτα τῶν ἀλόγων καὶ αἰσθητικῶν
ζώων, μήτε μὴν τὰ ἄλογα τῶν λογικῶν ἀπηλλοτριῶ-
75 σθαι πάντη καὶ ἀσύμβατα καὶ ἄνευ δεσμοῦ τινὸς εἶναι
συμφυοῦς καὶ φυσικοῦ. Διαλλάττει μὲν γὰρ καὶ λίθος
λίθου δυνάμει τινί, ἀλλ'ἡ μαγνῆτις λίθος ἐξεληλυθέναι
δοκεῖ τὴν τῶν ἄλλων λίθων φύσιν τε καὶ δύναμιν ἐν τῷ
προφανῶς ἕλκειν πρὸς ἑαυτὴν καὶ κατέχειν τὸν σίδη-
80 ρον, ὥσπερ τροφὴν αὐτὸν ποιήσασθαι βουλομένη, καὶ
μὴ μόνον ἐφ'ἑνὸς σιδήρου τοῦτο ποιεῖν, ἀλλὰ καὶ ἄλλον δι'ἄλλου κατέχειν τῷ μεταδιδόναι τοῖς ἐχομένοις
πᾶσι τῆς δυνάμεως ἑαυτῆς· κατέχει γοῦν καὶ ὁ σίδηρος
σίδηρον, ὅταν ὑπὸ τῆς μαγνήτιδος ἔχηται. Εἶτα πάλιν
85 ἀπὸ τῶν φυτῶν ἐπὶ τὰ ζῶα μετιών, οὐκ ἀθρόως ἐπὶ
τὴν μεταβατικὴν καὶ αἰσθητικὴν ὥρμησε φύσιν, ἀλλ'ἐκ
τοῦ κατ'ὀλίγον ἐπὶ ταύτην ἐμμελῶς προῆλθε· τὰς γὰρ
πίννας καὶ τὰς ἀκαλήφας ὥσπερ αἰσθητικὰ δένδρα κα-
τεσκεύασεν· ἐρρίζωσε μὲν γὰρ αὐτὰς ἐν τῇ θαλάσσῃ δί-
90 κην φυτῶν καὶ ὥσπερ ξύλα τὰ ὄστρακα περιέθηκε καὶ

Mss. *AT CDEFHQI*

Crit. **67** αἰσθητῶν *FH* **68** τὸ – συγκείμενον] *om. E^{a.corr.} (suppl. in marg.)*
ἀλλὰ] *om. C^{a.corr.} (suppl. in marg.)* **69** τῆς] τοῖς *T* **72** τὰ – ἄψυχα] *om.*
FH πάντη] πάντα *D^{a.corr.}E* **75** ἀσύμβατον *AT* **76** συμφυῶς *D*
λίθος] ὁ *praem. FH* **77** ἀλλ'] ὡς *FH* ἐληλακέναι *FH* **78** λίθων]
om. T **80** τρυφὴν *Q* **81/82** δι'ἄλλου ἄλλον *CDEFHQI* **82** τῷ]
τὸ *DE* **83** ἑαυτῆς] τῆς *praem. Q* γοῦν] γὰρ *Q* **84** πάλιν] *om. Q*
85 τὰ] *om. FH* **87** τοῦ κατ'ὀλίγον] τῶν κατ'ὀλίγων *E* **88** ἀκαλίφας
AT F^{ut uid.}HI αἰσθητὰ *FH* **89** μὲν] *om. T* ἐν – θαλάσσῃ] *post* φυτῶν *trsp. FH* **90** παρέθηκε *AT* (-εν *A*)

Comp. **68** *post* ἓν] ὃν *hab. Nem.* **84** *post* πάλιν] ἐξῆς *hab. Nem.*

ALPHA 29   51

ἔστησεν ὡς φυτά, αἴσθησιν δὲ αὐταῖς ἐνέθηκε τὴν ἁπτι-
κὴν | καὶ κοινὴν πάντων τῶν ζώων αἴσθησιν, ὡς κοι-   p. 4
νωνεῖν τοῖς μὲν φυτοῖς κατὰ τὸ ἐρριζῶσθαι καὶ ἑστά-
ναι, τοῖς δὲ ζώοις κατὰ τὴν ἀφήν. Τὸν γοῦν σπόγγον,
95 καίτοι προσπεφυκότα ταῖς πέτραις, καὶ συστέλλεσθαι
καὶ ἀμύνεσθαι ὅταν προσιόντος αἴσθηταί τινος, Ἀριστοτέλης ἱστόρησε. Διὸ τὰ τοιαῦτα πάντα ζωόφυτα καλεῖν
ἔθος ἔχουσιν οἱ παλαιοὶ τῶν σοφῶν. Πάλιν δὲ ταῖς πίν-
ναις καὶ τοῖς τοιούτοις συνῆψε τὴν τῶν μεταβατικῶν
100 μὲν ζώων γένεσιν, μακρὰν δὲ προελθεῖν μὴ δυναμένων,
ἀλλ'αὐτόθεν αὐτοῦ που κινουμένων· τοιαῦτα δέ ἐστι
τὰ πλεῖστα τῶν ὀστρακοδέρμων καὶ τὰ καλούμενα γῆς
ἔντερα. Εἶθ'οὕτω κατὰ μέρος προστιθεὶς τοῖς μὲν αἰσθήσεις πλείους, τοῖς δὲ τὸ μεταβατικὸν ἐπὶ πλεῖστον,
105 εἰς τὰ τελειότερα τῶν ἀλόγων ζώων κατήντησε· λέγω
δὴ τὰ τελειότερα τὰ πάσας ἔχοντα τὰς αἰσθήσεις καὶ
προϊέναι μακρὰν δυνάμενα. Πάλιν δὲ μεταβαίνων ἀπὸ
τῶν ἀλόγων ἐπὶ τὸ λογικὸν ζῶον τὸν ἄνθρωπον, οὐδὲ
τοῦτο ἀθρόως κατεσκεύασεν, ἀλλὰ πρότερον [ἃ] καὶ
110 τοῖς ἄλλοις ζώοις φυσικάς τινας συνέσεις καὶ μηχανὰς
καὶ πανουργίας πρὸς σωτηρίαν ἐνέθηκεν, ὡς ἐγγὺς λογικῶν αὐτὰ φαίνεσθαι, καὶ οὕτως τὸ ἀληθῶς λογικὸν
ζῶον τὸν ἄνθρωπον προεβάλετο· τὸν αὐτὸν δὲ τρόπον

Mss.   *AT CDEFHQI*

Crit.   **91/92** ἀναπτικὴν *A*   **92** αἴσθησιν] *om. E*   ὡς] καὶ *F, om. H*
95 καίτοι] καὶ τοῖς *A*, ἔτι *FH*   **97** Διὸ] om. *Q*   ζώφυτα *A D*ᵃ·ᶜᵒʳʳ·   **100** δὲ]
μὲν *F*   δυναμένη *E*   **101** κινουμένη *E*   **101/102** τοιαῦτα – ὀστρα-
κοδέρμων] *om. T*   **102** γῆς] τῆς *praem. Q*   **103** προσθεὶς *DEFHQ*
τοῖς μὲν] *post* οὕτω *trsp. FH*   **105** ἀλόγων] *om. FH*   κατήντησε] τῶν
ἀλόγων *add. FH*   **106** δὴ] δὲ *E*   τὰ τελειότερα] τελειότερα *EFH,*
om. Q   τὰ²] τοῦ *F*   **107** δυνάμενος *A,* δυναμένας *D*   μεταβαίνον
(sic acc.) A   ἀπὸ] ἐπὶ *A*   **109** κατεσκευάσθη *C*   ἃ] *seclusi cum Q et*
fonte, hab. cett.   **111** σωτηρίαν] καὶ σύστασιν τῆς ἑαυτῶν φύσεως *add. I*
112 αὐτὰ] αὐτὴν *FH,* ταῦτα αὐτὰ *(*αὐτὰ *sup. l.) Q*   **113** προεβάλλετο *TFH*
αὐτὸν δὲ] αὐτόν δε *(sic acc.) Q*

Comp.   **91** ἐνέθηκε] ἐνέδωκε *Nem. (F D P = Coisl.)*   **92** καὶ] τὴν *Nem.*   τῶν]
non hab. Nem.   **106** δὴ τὰ] δὲ *Nem.*   **109** ἃ] *non hab. Nem.*

52 FLORILEGIVM COISLINIANVM

καὶ ἐπὶ τῆς φωνῆς ζητῶν, εὑρήσεις ἐξ ἁπλῆς καὶ μονο-
115 ειδοῦς τῆς ἵππων καὶ βοῶν ἐκφωνήσεως κατὰ μέρος εἰς
ποικίλην καὶ διάφορον προαχθῆναι τὴν τῶν κοράκων
καὶ μιμηλῶν ὀρνέων φωνήν, ἕως εἰς τὴν ἔναρθρον καὶ
τελείαν τὴν ἀνθρώπου κατέληξε. Πάλιν δὲ τὴν ἔναρθρον διάλεκτον ἐξῆψε τῆς διανοίας καὶ τοῦ λογισμοῦ,
120 ἐξάγγελον ποιήσας αὐτὴν τῶν κατὰ νοῦν κινημάτων,
καὶ οὕτως πᾶσι πάντα μουσικῶς συνήρμοσε καὶ εἰς ἓν
συνήγαγε τά τε νοητὰ καὶ τὰ ὁρατὰ διὰ μέσης τῆς τῶν
ἀνθρώπων γενέσεως. Διὸ καὶ καλῶς ὁ Μωϋσῆς τὴν δη-
μιουργίαν | ἐκτιθέμενος, τελευταῖον ἔφησε τὸν ἄνθρω- p. 5
125 πον γεγενῆσθαι, οὐ μόνον ὅτι πάντων δι'αὐτὸν γενομένων ἀκόλουθον ἦν πρῶτον τὰ πρὸς τὴν χρῆσιν αὐτοῦ
παρασκευασθῆναι καὶ οὕτως αὐτὸν τὸν χρησόμενον πα-
ραχθῆναι, ἀλλ'ὅτι νοητῆς γενομένης οὐσίας καὶ πάλιν
ὁρατῆς ἔδει γενέσθαί τινα σύνδεσμον ἀμφοτέρων, ἵνα
130 ἓν ᾖ τὸ πᾶν καὶ συμπαθὲς ἑαυτῷ καὶ μὴ ἀλλότριον αὐτὸ
ἑαυτοῦ· ἐγένετο οὖν τὸ συνδέον ἀμφοτέρας τὰς φύσεις
ζῶον ὁ ἄνθρωπος. Τὰ μὲν οὖν τῆς σοφίας τοῦ δημιουργοῦ, συντόμως εἰπεῖν, τοιαῦτα.
    Ἐν μεθορίοις οὖν τῆς ἀλόγου καὶ λογικῆς φύσεως ὁ
135 ἄνθρωπος ταχθείς, ἐὰν μὲν ἐπὶ τὸ σῶμα ῥέψῃ καὶ τὰ
τοῦ σώματος πλέον ἀγαπήσῃ, τὸν τῶν ἀλόγων ἀσπάζε-

Mss.   *AT CDEFHQI*

Crit.   **115** τῆς – βοῶν] τῆς τῶν βόων *F* (τῆς *a. uel p. corr.*), καὶ βόων *H*   τῆς] τῶν
add. *E*   **116** προαχθῆσαν *I*^*a.corr.* (προαχθεῖσαν *p. corr.*)   **117** ὀρνέων]
ἀλλὰ μὴ ἐκ τῆς τούτων add. *E*   φωνήν, ἕως] scripsi cum Q et fonte, φωνήσεως cett.   **118** τὴν¹] τοῦ *T EH*, τὴν τοῦ *F*   **120** ἐξάγγελ(ων) *F*, ἐξαγ-
γέλ(ειν) *H*   νοῦν] τὸν praem. *FH*   **121** συνήρμοσε] καὶ συνέδησε add. *I*
122 νοητὰ ... ὁρατὰ] ὁρατὰ ... νοητὰ *FH*   **123** γενέσεως] γενέσθαι *C*   **125** δι'αὐτὸν] δι'αὐτοῦ *T CD*   **126** πρῶτος *AT*   **127** τὸν]
om. *DQ*   χρησάμενον *C*   **128** γεναμένης *DF*   **129** τινα] καὶ add. *I*
132 οὖν] om. *EQ*   **134** οὖν] δὲ *Q*   **135** μὲν] om. *FH*   ῥέψῃ] ῥίψῃ *H*
136 ἀγαπήσει *E*   **136/137** ἀσπάσηται *FH*

Comp.   **116** προαχθεῖσαν *Nem.*   **117** ὄρνεων *Nem.*   **121** post συνήρμοσε] καὶ
συνέδησε hab. *Nem.*   **129** post τινα] καὶ hab. *Nem.*

ALPHA 29   53

ται βίον, καὶ τούτοις συναριθμηθήσεται, καὶ χοϊκὸς κληθήσεται κατὰ Παῦλον, καὶ ἀκούσεται Γῆ εἶ καὶ εἰς γῆν
ἀπελεύσῃ, καὶ Παρασυνεβλήθη τοῖς κτήνεσι τοῖς ἀνοή-
140   τοις καὶ ὡμοιώθη αὐτοῖς· ἐὰν δὲ ἐπὶ τὸ λογικὸν χωρήσῃ καταφρονήσας τῶν σωματικῶν πασῶν ἡδονῶν, τὴν
θείαν τε καὶ θεοφιλεστάτην ζωὴν μετέρχεται καὶ τὴν
ὡς ἀνθρώπου προηγουμένως. Ἔσται οἷος ὁ ἐπουράνιος,
κατὰ τὸ εἰρημένον· Οἷος ὁ χοϊκός, τοιοῦτοι καὶ οἱ χοϊ-
145   κοί, καὶ οἷος ὁ ἐπουράνιος, τοιοῦτοι καὶ οἱ ἐπουράνιοι.
Τῆς δὲ λογικῆς φύσεως τὸ κεφάλαιόν ἐστι φεύγειν μὲν
καὶ ἀποστρέφεσθαι τὰ κακά, μετιέναι δὲ καὶ αἱρεῖσθαι
τὰ καλά. Τῶν δὲ καλῶν τὰ μέν ἐστι κατὰ κοινωνίαν
ψυχῆς καὶ σώματος, ἐχόντων καὶ τούτων ἐπὶ τὴν ψυ-
150   χὴν τὴν ἀναφορὰν οἷον ψυχῆς προσχρωμένης σώματι,
ὡς αἱ ἀρεταί, τὰ δὲ τῆς ψυχῆς αὐτῆς καθ᾿ἑαυτὴν μόνης
μὴ προσδεομένης σώματος, ὡς ἡ εὐσέβεια καὶ ἡ τῶν
ὄντων θεωρία. Ὅσοι τοίνυν τὸν ἀνθρώπου βίον ὡς ἀνθρώπου προαιροῦνται ζῆν καὶ μὴ ὡς ζώου μόνου, τὰς
155 | ἀρετὰς μετέρχονται καὶ τὴν εὐσέβειαν. Τίνα δέ ἐστι   p. 6
τὰ τῶν ἀρετῶν καὶ τίνα τὰ τῆς εὐσεβείας, ἐν τοῖς ἑξῆς

---

ont.   **137** cf. I Cor. 15, 47   **138/139** Gen. 3, 19   **139/140** Ps. 48, 13. 21
144/145 I Cor. 15, 48

ss.   *AT CDEFHQI*

rit.   **137/138** καὶ² – κληθήσεται] ...θήσεται *H (20 litt. spat.), om. Q*
138 Παῦλον] τὸν *praem. FH*   **139** παρεσυνεβλήθη *FH,* παρασυνελήφθη
C   **140** τὸ λογικὸν] τῶν λογικῶν *D*   **142** καὶ¹] *om. FH*   **143** ὡς]
om. E   ἄνθρωπος *T*   Ἔσται] καὶ *praem. CDQI,* καὶ ἀκούσεται *E*
144/145 κατὰ – ἐπουράνιος] *om. DEQ*   **144** κατὰ – εἰρημένον] καταπει-
ρημένων *(sic) T*   **145** καὶ¹] *om. H*   **150** προσχρησαμένης *FH*   σώμα-
τι] τῶ *praem. F*   **150/152** σώματι – προσδεομένης] *om. T*   **151** τῆς] *om.*
DEFHQI   ψυχῆς] μόνω *add. I*   ἑαυτὴν] ἑαυτῆς *CDEFHI*   μόνης]
om. I   **152** ἡ²] *om. FH*   **153** ἀνθρώπου¹] ἄν(θρωπ)ον *D,* ἀν(θρώπ)ινον
EFHQ   **154** ζῆν προαιροῦνται *I*   προαιροῦν *A*   ζῆν] ζωὴν *D*
μόνου] καὶ *add. FH*   **155/156** Τίνα – εὐσεβείας] *om. T*

omp.   **139** παρεσυνεβλήθη *Nem.*   **143** *ante* Ἔσται] καὶ *hab. Nem. (B = Coisl.)*
154 ζῆν προαιροῦνται *Nem.*

54 FLORILEGIVM COISLINIANVM

διακριθήσεται, ὅταν τὸν περὶ τῆς ψυχῆς καὶ τοῦ σώματος ἀποδῶμεν λόγον· οὐδέπω γὰρ ἐγνωσμένου τίποτε ἡμῶν ἐστὶν ἡ ψυχὴ κατ'οὐσίαν, οὐκ ἔστιν ἀκόλουθον
160 περὶ τῆς ἐνεργείας αὐτῆς διαλαβεῖν. Ἑβραίων δόξα περὶ ἀνθρώπων. Ἑβραῖοι δὲ τὸν ἄνθρωπον ἐξ ἀρχῆς οὔτε θνητὸν ὁμολογουμένως οὔτε ἀθάνατον γεγενῆσθαι φασίν, ἀλλ'ἐν μεθορίῳ ἑκατέρας φύσεως, ἵνα, ἂν μὲν τοῖς σωματικοῖς ἀκολουθήσῃ πά-
165 θεσι, περιπέσῃ καὶ ταῖς σωματικαῖς μεταβολαῖς, ἂν δὲ τὰ τῆς ψυχῆς προτιμήσῃ καλά, τῆς ἀθανασίας ἀξιωθῇ. Εἰ γὰρ ἐξ ἀρχῆς αὐτὸν θνητὸν ἐποίησέ φησιν ὁ θεός, οὐκ ἂν ἁμαρτόντα θανάτῳ κατεδίκασε· τοῦ γὰρ θνητοῦ θνητότητα οὐδεὶς καταδικάζει· εἰ δ'αὖ πάλιν ἀθάνατον,
170 οὐδ'ἂν τροφῆς αὐτὸν ἐνδεᾶ κατεσκεύασεν – οὐδὲν γὰρ τῶν ἀθανάτων τροφῆς σωματικῆς δέεται – οὐδ'ἂν οὕτω ῥᾳδίως μετενόησε καὶ τὸν γενόμενον ἀθάνατον θνητὸν εὐθέως ἐποίει· οὐδὲ γὰρ ἐπὶ τῶν ἁμαρτησάντων ἀγγέλων τοῦτο φαίνεται πεποιηκώς, ἀλλὰ κατὰ τὴν ἐξ
175 ἀρχῆς φύσιν ἀθάνατοι διέμειναν, ἄλλην τῶν ἡμαρτημένων ἐκδεχόμενοι δίκην, ἀλλ'οὐ τὸν θάνατον. Βέλτι-

Mss.   *AT CDEFHQI* (*I* usque ad ἐκδεχόμενοι, 29.176)

Crit.   **157** τῆς] *om. DEFHQI*   τοῦ] *om. DEFHQI*   **158** οὐδέποτε *FH*
159 οὐκ ἔστιν] ἢ τί ἐστιν *F*, ἔστιν *H*   **160** αὐτῆς] αὐτ(ῶν) *D*
161 Ἑβραίων – ἀνθρώπων] *in textu C, in marg. A E*, φίλωνος ἕως ὧδε
(*sine acc.*) *Q^{in marg}, om. T DFHQI*   ἀνθρώπων] ἀνθρώπου *A*, *illeg. E*
161/163 Ἑβραῖοι – γεγενῆσθαι] *iter. D^{in marg}* (*om.* ὁμολογουμένως)   δὲ]
γοῦν *E*   **161/162** ἐξ ἀρχῆς τὸν ἄνθρωπον *Q*   **165** καὶ ταῖς σωματικαῖς περιπέσῃ *I*   περιπέσει *A CD*   **166** τὰ] τὴν *H*   ἀθανασί-
ας] ἀθανάτου *H*   **167** θνητὸν αὐτὸν *FHQ*   φησιν] *post* ἀρχῆς *trsp. Q*,
om. I   **168** ἁμαρτῶντα *T FQ*   **170** οὐδ'] οὐκ *E*   ἂν] πάλιν *add.*
FH   τροφῆς αὐτὸν] προφήτης αὐτός (*sic acc.*) *A*   ἐνδεᾶ κατεσκεύασεν]
κατέστησεν ἐνδεᾶ *Q*   **171** σωματικῆς τροφῆς *E*   δεῖται σωματικῆς *I*
δεῖται *E*   **173** ἐποίησεν *T*   οὐδὲ] οὐ *FH*   **176** ἀπεκδεχόμε (*mutilus*) *I*
δίκην ἐκδεχομένοι *FH*

Comp.   **160** διαλαμβάνειν *Nem.* (*F D P = Coisl.*)   **161** Ἑβραίων – ἀνθρώπων] *non*
hab. Nem.   **163** μεθορίῳ] μεθορίοις *Nem.*   **167** φησιν] *non hab. Nem.*
171 δεῖται *Nem.*   **173** ἐποίησεν *Nem.* (*B H K D P = Coisl.*)   **176** ἀπεκ-
δεχόμενοι *Nem.*

ALPHA 29   55

ον οὖν ἢ τοῦτον τὸν τρόπον νοεῖν τὸ προκείμενον ἢ ὅτι
θνητὸς μὲν κατεσκευάσθη, δυνάμενος δὲ ἐκ προκοπῆς
τελειούμενος ἀθάνατος γενέσθαι, τουτέστιν δυνάμει
180 ἀθάνατος.

Ἐπειδὴ δὲ οὐ συνέφερεν αὐτῷ πρὸ τῆς τελειώσεως
γνῶναι τὴν φύσιν ἑαυτοῦ, ἀπηγόρευσεν αὐτῷ μὴ γεύ-
σασθαι τοῦ ξύλου τῆς γνώσεως· ἦσαν γάρ, μᾶλλον δὲ
εἰσὶν ἔτι καὶ νῦν, δυνάμεις ἐν τοῖς φυτοῖς μέγισται·
185 τότε δέ, ὡς ἐν ἀρχῇ τῆς κοσμοποιΐας ἀκραιφνεῖς οὖσαι,
ἰσχυροτάτην εἶχον τὴν ἐνέργειαν. Ἦν οὖν καὶ ἀπόγευ-
σις τινὸς καρποῦ γνῶσιν ἐμποιοῦσα τῆς οἰκείας φύσεως. Οὐκ ἐβούλετο δὲ αὐτὸν ὁ θεὸς πρὸ τῆς τελειώσεως
| γνῶναι τὴν οἰκείαν φύσιν, ἵνα μή, γνοὺς ἑαυτὸν ἐν-   p. 7
190 δεᾶ πολλῶν ὄντα, τῆς σωματικῆς ἐπιμεληθῇ χρείας,
καταλιπὼν τὴν τῆς ψυχῆς πρόνοιαν, καὶ διὰ ταύτην
τὴν αἰτίαν ἐκώλυσεν αὐτὸν μεταλαβεῖν τοῦ καρποῦ τῆς
γνώσεως. Παρακούσας δὲ καὶ γνοὺς ἑαυτόν, τῆς μὲν
τελειώσεως ἐξέπεσε, τῆς δὲ σωματικῆς χρείας ἐντὸς
195 ἐγένετο. Σκέπασμα γοῦν εὐθέως ἐπιζητεῖ· φησὶ γὰρ ὁ
Μωϋσῆς ὅτι Γυμνὸς ὢν ἔγνω. Πρότερον δὲ ἐν ἐκστάσει
αὐτὸν ἐποίησε καὶ ἐν ἀγνωσίᾳ ἑαυτοῦ· ἐκπεσὼν οὖν
τῆς τελειώσεως ἐξέπεσεν ὁμοίως καὶ τῆς ἀθανασίας,
ἣν ὕστερον ἀπολήψεται χάριτι τοῦ ποιήσαντος αὐτόν.
200 Μετὰ δὲ τὴν ἔκπτωσιν, καὶ ἡ τῶν κρεῶν ἀπόλαυσις

---

ont.   **182/183** cf. Gen. 2, 16-17   **192/193** cf. ibid.   **196** Gen. 3, 7

ss.   *AT CDEFHQ (F* usque ad φησὶ, 29.195)

rit.   **178** μὲν] *om. Q*   **179** τελειούμενος] *om. Q*   ἀθανάτους *D*
179/180 τουτέστιν – ἀθάνατος] τοῦτο π(αρὰ) λόγον κεῖ(ται) *add. A*ⁱⁿ ᵐᵃʳᵍ·,
π(αρὰ) λόγ(ον) κεῖ(ται) *add. E*ⁱⁿ ᵐᵃʳᵍ·   **179/199** τουτέστιν – αὐτόν] *om. Q*
181 δὲ] *om. E*   **182** ἑαυτοῦ] αὐτοῦ *DE*   **183** γνώσεως] βρώσεως *D*
186 καὶ] *om. FH*   **194** τελειώσεως] γνώσεως *FH*   **196** ὢν] *om. H*
199 ὕστερον] οὖν *D*

omp.   **194** ἐντὸς] *non hab. Nem.*   **195** ἐπεζήτησεν *Nem.*   **196** ὅτι – ἔγνω]
"ἔγνω ὅτι γυμνὸς ἦν" *Nem.*   **199** ἀναλήψεται *Nem.*

56   FLORILEGIVM COISLINIANVM

αὐτῷ συνεχωρήθη· πρότερον μὲν γὰρ τοῖς ἀπὸ γῆς μόνοις ἐκέλευσεν αὐτὸν ἀρκεῖσθαι – ταῦτα γὰρ ἦν ἐν τῷ
παραδείσῳ –, ἀπεγνωσμένης δὲ τῆς τελειώσεως, τῇ συγ-
καταβάσει λοιπὸν συνεχωρήθη τὰ τῆς ἀπολαύσεως.

205   Ἐπειδὴ δὲ ἐκ σώματός ἐστιν ὁ ἄνθρωπος, πᾶν δὲ
σῶμα ἐκ τεσσάρων στοιχείων συνέστηκεν, ἀνάγκη
τούτοις τοῖς πάθεσι περιπίπτειν αὐτόν, οἷς καὶ τὰ στοιχεῖα, τομῇ καὶ μεταβολῇ καὶ ῥεύσει, ἅπέρ ἐστι μόνου
τοῦ σώματος· μεταβολῇ μὲν τῇ κατὰ ποιότητα, ῥεύσει
210   δὲ τῇ κατὰ κενώσει· κενοῦται γὰρ ἀεὶ τὸ ζῷον διά τε
τῶν προδήλων πόρων καὶ τῶν ἀδήλων. Ἀνάγκη τοίνυν
τοῖς κενουμένοις ἀντεισφέρεσθαι τὰ ἴσα, ἢ διαλύεσθαι
τὸ ζῷον ἐνδείᾳ τῶν ἐπεισιόντων. Ξηρῶν δὲ ὄντων καὶ
ὑγρῶν καὶ πνεύματος τῶν κενουμένων, ἀνάγκη καὶ ξη-
215   ρᾶς καὶ ὑγρᾶς τροφῆς δεῖσθαι τὸ ζῷον, καὶ πνεύματος.
Ἔστι δὲ ἡμῖν ἡ τροφὴ καὶ τὸ ποτὸν | διὰ τῶν στοιχεί-   p. 8
ων ἐξ ὧν καὶ συνετέθημεν· ἕκαστον γὰρ τῷ μὲν οἰκείῳ
καὶ ὁμοίῳ τρέφεται, τῷ δὲ ἐναντίῳ θεραπεύεται. Τῶν
δὲ στοιχείων τὰ μὲν προσεχῶς τε ἅμα, τὰ δὲ διὰ μέσων
220   τινῶν προσφερόμεθα, ὡς ὕδωρ ποτὲ μὲν καθ᾽αὑτό, ποτὲ

Mss.   *AT CDEHQ*

Crit.   **201** πρότερον] πρῶτον *Q*   **205** ἐπεὶ *Q*   **206** τεσσάρων] δ' *H*   στοι-
χείων] στυχείω (sic) *A*   **207** παραπίπτειν *CH*   **208** καὶ¹] om. *DEQ*
ἅπέρ ἐστι] ἅπερ ἐστὶ *CDF*, ἃ πάντα ἐστὶ *Q*   **209** σώματος] τῇ θερ-
μασίᾳ καὶ ψύξει καὶ τὰ τοιαῦτα add. *Qⁱⁿ ᵐᵃʳᵍ*   μὲν] δὲ *Q*   ποιότητι *T*
210 κένωσιν *Q*   **210/213** διά – ζῷον] om. *H*   **213** ἐνδείᾳ] ἐν praem. *T*
214 πνεύματος] ἐνδεῶν add. *E*   **215** καὶ¹ – δεῖσθαι] δεῖσθαι τροφῆς *E*
217 συνετέθημεν] τομῇ μ(ὲν), τῇ ἀπὸ τῆς ζωῆς εἰς θάνατον τεμνούσῃ αὐτό·
τοῖς ἀπὸ τῶν στοιχείων ἑνώσεως δι'ὧν συνετέθ(η), καὶ εἰς φθορὰν ἀπολυού-
σῃ, μετὰ τὴν τοῦ πνεύματος ὑποχώρησιν add. *Qⁱⁿ ᵐᵃʳᵍ*   ἕκαστος *CDEHQ*
219 ἅμα – διὰ] om. *H (20 litt. spat.)*   **220** αὐτό] ἑαυτὸ *T*

Comp.   **201** ante γῆς] τῆς hab. *Nem.* (*F D P = Coisl.*)   **206** ante τεσσάρων] τῶν
hab. *Nem.* (*Π = Coisl.*)   **210** κενώσει] κένωσιν *Nem.*   **211** post καὶ]
διὰ hab. *Nem. (H D = Coisl.)*   post ἀδήλων] περὶ ὧν ὕστερον ἐροῦμεν hab.
Nem.   post τοίνυν] ἢ hab. *Nem. (H D = Coisl.)*   **219** post δὲ²] καὶ hab.
Nem.   **220** ἑαυτό *Nem.*

ALPHA 29   57

δὲ καὶ διὰ μέσου τοῦ οἴνου καὶ τοῦ ἐλαίου καὶ πάντων
τῶν καλουμένων ὑγρῶν καρπῶν· οὐδὲν γὰρ ἕτερόν
ἐστιν οἶνος ἢ ὕδωρ ὑπ'ἀμπέλου πεποιωμένον. Ὁμοίως δὲ καὶ πυρὸς μεταλαμβάνομεν, ποτὲ μὲν προσεχῶς
225   ὑπ'αὐτοῦ θαλπόμενοι, ποτὲ δὲ διὰ μέσων ὧν ἐσθίομεν
ἢ πίνομεν· ἐν πᾶσι γὰρ ἢ πλείων ἢ ἐλάττων μοῖρα τοῦ
πυρὸς ἐγκατέστραπται. Τὸν αὐτὸν τρόπον καὶ τοῦ ἀέ-
ρος· προσεχῶς μὲν ἀναπνέοντες καὶ περικεχυμένον
ἡμῖν ἔχοντες καὶ ἐν τῷ ἐσθίειν καὶ πίνειν ἕλκοντες, διὰ
230   μέσων δὲ τῶν ἄλλων πάντων ὧν προσφερόμεθα. Τὴν
δὲ γῆν προσεχῶς μὲν ἡμεῖς οὐδαμῶς, διὰ μέσων δέ τι-
νων· γῆ μὲν γὰρ σῖτος γίνεται, σῖτον δὲ ἡμεῖς ἐσθίομεν·
κορυδοὶ μὲν γὰρ καὶ περιστεραὶ πολλάκις καὶ πέρδικες
τὴν γῆν σιτοῦνται, ἄνθρωπος δὲ διὰ μέσων τῶν σπερ-
235   μάτων καὶ τῶν ἀκροδρύων καὶ τῶν σαρκῶν. Ἐπειδὴ δὲ
οὐ μόνον δι'εὐπρέπειαν, ἀλλὰ καὶ δι'εὐαισθησίαν τὴν
κατὰ τὴν ἀφήν, ᾗ μάλιστα πλεονεκτεῖ πάντα τὰ ζῷα ὁ
ἄνθρωπος, οὐ περιέθηκεν ἡμῖν οὔτε δέρμα παχὺ ὡς τοῖς
βουσὶ καὶ τοῖς ἄλλοις τοῖς παχυδέρμοις, οὔτε τρίχας
240   μεγάλας καὶ πυκνὰς ὡς ταῖς αἰξὶ καὶ τοῖς προβάτοις

Mss.   *AT CDEHQ*

Crit.   **221** καὶ¹] *om. E*   μέσου] μέσω *H*   **224** καὶ – μεταλαμβάνομεν]
...λαμβάνομεν *(15 litt. spat.) H*   **225** δὲ] καὶ *add. H*   μέσων] μέσου *H*
226 πίνομεν] ἢ λουόμεθα *add. Q*   ἢ³] ἡ *add. Cᵖ·ᶜᵒʳʳ·*   **227** ἐγκατέστραπται
A CDH; an legendum ἐγκατέσπαρται *cum T EQ et fonte?*   αὐτὸν] δὲ *add.*
H   **228** ἀναπνέοντος *C*   περικεχυμμένον *Cᵃ·ᶜᵒʳʳ·*, (παρα)κεχυμένον *H*
229 ἡμῖν] αὐτὸν *add. E*   ἕλκοντες] ἔχοντες *Aᵃ·ᶜᵒʳʳ·*   διὰ] καὶ *praem. T E*
230 μέσου *H*   δὲ] καὶ *add. H, om. E*   πάντων] *post* προσφερόμεθα
trsp. H   **233** κόρυδοι *Q*, κορῶναι *T*, κολοιοὶ *H*   καὶ πέρδικες]
post σιτοῦνται *trsp. E*   **234** ἄνθρωπος] μὲν γὰρ *add. Aᵃ·ᶜᵒʳʳ·* *(cancell.)*
235 ἀκροδύων *D*   σαρκῶν] καρπῶν *H*   ἐπεὶ *H*   **236** οὐ – καὶ]
om. H   εὐσθησίαν *(sic) A*, ἐσθησίαν *(sic) D*   τὴν] *om. D*   **237** πάντα – ζῷα] πάντων τῶν ζώων *E*   **238** περιέθηκεν – ὡς] *om. A*   οὔτε]
om. DEQ   παχὺν *DE*   **240** ταῖς] τοῖς *H*

Comp.   **226** ἢ¹] καὶ *Nem.* (β *D P = Coisl.*)   **227** ἐγκατέσπαρται *Nem.*
233 κόρυδοι *Nem.*

58 FLORILEGIVM COISLINIANVM

καὶ λαγωοῖς, οὔτε φολίδας ὡς τοῖς ὄφισι καὶ τοῖς ἰχθύσιν, οὔτε ὄστρακα ὡς ταῖς χελώναις καὶ τοῖς ὀστρέοις,
οὔτε ἀπαλόστρακα ὡς τοῖς καράβοις, οὔτε πτέρυγας
ὡς τοῖς ὀρνέοις, ἀναγκαίως οὖν ἐσθῆτος ἐδεήθημεν τῆς
245 ἀναπληρούσης ἐν ἡμῖν ὅπερ ἡ φύσις τοῖς ἄλλοις ἐδωρή-
σατο. Διὰ ταῦτα μὲν οὖν τροφῆς καὶ ἐσθῆτος δεόμεθα,
οἰκήσεως δὲ | καὶ διὰ ταῦτα μὲν δι'ἃ καὶ ἐσθῆτος καὶ   p. 9
τροφῆς ἐδεήθημεν, οὐχ'ἥκιστα δὲ καὶ διὰ τὰς τῶν θηρίων ἀποφυγάς. Διὰ δὲ τὰς δυσκρασίας τῶν ποιοτήτων
250 καὶ τὴν λύσιν τῆς συνεχείας τοῦ σώματος ἰατρῶν καὶ
θεραπείας ἐν χρείᾳ κατέστημεν. Τῆς δὲ μεταβολῆς κατὰ
ποιότητα γινομένης, ἀνάγκη διὰ τῆς ἀντικειμένης ποι-
ότητος εἰς τὸ σύμμετρον ἀγαγεῖν τὴν κατάστασιν τοῦ
σώματος· οὐ γάρ, ὡς οἴονταί τινες, τὸ θερμανθὲν σῶμα
255 καταψῦξαι πρόκειται τοῖς ἰατροῖς, ἀλλ'εἰς τὸ εὔκρατον
μεταποιῆσαι· εἰ γὰρ καταψύξειαν, εἰς τὴν ἐναντίαν πε-
ριΐσταται νόσον ἡ διάθεσις. Χρεία τοίνυν ἀνθρώπῳ τροφῆς μὲν καὶ ποτοῦ διὰ τὰς κενώσεις καὶ διαφορήσεις,
ἐσθῆτος δὲ διὰ τὸ μηδεμίαν ἔχειν ἐκ φύσεως ἰσχυρὰν
260 περιβολήν, οἴκου δὲ διά τε τὰς δυσκρασίας τοῦ περιέχον-

Mss.   AT CDEHQ

Crit.   241 λαγωοῖς] τοῖς praem. EH   ὄφεσι EHQ   241/242 ἰχθύσιν – τοῖς]
om. T E   242 ὀστρέοις] ὀστέοις T   243 ἀπαλόσαρκα DEH
244 οὖν] om. EQ   246 μὲν] om. H   καὶ] ... (3 litt. spat.) τὸ τρ°στοιχ(ον)
... (1 litt. spat.) τὸ σῶμα, τέσσαρας δυνάμεις ἔχεις· ἑλκτικ(ὴν), καθεκτικὴν, ἀλ-
λοιωτικ(ὴν), διαβατικήν. τριχ(η) δέ ἐστι διαβατόν· κατά τε μῆκος, καὶ πλάτος,
καὶ βάθος, καὶ ... (5 litt. spat.) καὶ παρακμὴν καὶ ἡ μ(ὲν) αὔξησις, μέχρι τ(οῦ)
γὰρ μέθη ... (10 litt. spat.) τ(οῦ) θερμοῦ καὶ ὑγροῦ· ἐπὶ δὲ τ(ῶν) θηλει(ῶν) add.
Qin marg. inf.   δεόμεθα] δεήθημεν H   247/248 οἰκήσεως – τροφῆς] om. Q
247 δι'ἃ] διὰ A D   248 καὶ] om. A   τῶν] om. H   248/249 θη-
λίων T H   251 κατέστημεν] δι'ἣν αἰτίαν γίνονται αἱ ὀδύναι add. Qin marg.
254 θερμαθὲν (sic) H   255 καταψύξαι AT DEH   257 νόσος H
Χρεία] μὲν add. DHQ   259 ἰσχυρὰν] om. T   260 τε] om. Q

Comp.   241 ante λαγωοῖς] τοῖς hab. Nem. (B H K D Pm = Coisl.)   ὄφεσι Nem.
244 οὖν] non hab. Nem.   247/248 δι' – ἐδεήθημεν] secl. Morani cum parte
trad. indir. (Alf. arm. An.), codd. = Coisl.   256 μεταποιῆσαι] μεταστῆσαι
Nem.

ALPHA 29   59

τος καὶ διὰ τὰ θηρία, θεραπείας δὲ διὰ τὰς μεταβολὰς
τῶν ποιοτήτων καὶ τὴν αἴσθησιν τὴν ἐνδοθεῖσαν τῷ
σώματι· εἰ γὰρ μὴ προσῆν ἡμῖν αἴσθησις, οὖτ'ἄν ἠλγοῦμεν, οὖτε θεραπείας ἐδεήθημεν μὴ ἀλγοῦντες, καὶ διε-
265 φθάρημεν ἄν ἐν ἀγνωσίᾳ τοῦ κακοῦ, τὸ πάθος οὐκ ἰώ-
μενοι. Διά τε τὰς τέχνας καὶ τὰς ἐπιστήμας καὶ τὰς ἀπὸ
τούτων χρείας, ἀλλήλων δεόμεθα. Διὰ δὲ τὸ δεῖσθαι
ἀλλήλων, εἰς ταὐτὸ πολλοὶ συνελθόντες κοινωνοῦμεν
ἀλλήλοις κατὰ τὰς τοῦ βίου χρείας ἐν τοῖς συναλλάγ-
270 μασιν – ἥντινα σύνοδον καὶ συνοικίαν πόλιν ὠνόμασαν –,
ἵν'ἐγγύθεν καὶ μὴ πόρρωθεν τὰς παρ'ἀλλήλων ὠφε-
λείας καρπώμεθα· φύσει γὰρ συναγελαστικὸν καὶ πολι-
τικὸν ζῶον γέγονεν ὁ ἄνθρωπος· εἷς γὰρ οὐδεὶς αὐτάρ-
κης ἑαυτῷ πρὸς ἅπαντα. Δῆλον οὖν ὡς αἱ πόλεις διὰ τὰ
275 συναλλάγματα καὶ τὰ μαθήματα συνέστησαν.
   Δύο δὲ τούτων πρεσβείων ὁ ἄνθρωπος ἐξαιρέτων
ἔτυχε – καὶ γὰρ μόνος οὗτος συγγνώμης τυγχάνει μετανοῶν, καὶ τὸ σῶμα τούτου μόνου θνητὸν ὂν ἀπαθανατίζεται –, καὶ τοῦ μὲν σωματικοῦ διὰ τὴν ψυχήν,
280 τοῦ δὲ ψυχικοῦ διὰ τὸ σῶμα. Μόνος γὰρ ὁ ἄνθρωπος
τῶν λογικῶν ἐξαίρετον ἔσχε τὸ συγγνώμης ἐν τῷ | με-   p. 10
τανοεῖν ἀξιοῦσθαι· οὔτε γὰρ οἱ δαίμονες οὔτε ἄγγελοι

Mss. *AT CDEHQ*

Crit. **261** διὰ¹] *om. E*   **262** ἐνδεθεῖσαν *E*   **263** οὖτ'ἄν] *scripsi cum Q et
fonte,* ὅταν *cett.*   **263/264** ἠλγῶμεν *T,* ἀλγῶμεν *H,* ηγοῦμεν *(sine spir.)*
D   **266** Διά] πάλιν *praem. E*   τε] δὲ *H,* μὲν οὖν *Q*   **267** δὲ] *om. Q*
268/269 εἰς – ἀλλήλοις] *om. T*   **269/270** συναλλάγμασιν *A*   **272** καρ-
πούμεθα *A* $C^{a.corr.}D$ **273** γέγονεν] *om. T*   εἷς] εἰ *D,* ἢν *E*   **275** συ-
ναλάγματα *A*   **276** τούτων] ἐξαιρέτως *add. H*   πρεσβείων] *scripsi
cum Q,* πρεσβειῶν *cett.*   ὁ – ἐξαιρέτων] ὁ ἄνθρωπος ἐξαιρέτως *CDQ,*
ἐξαιρέτως ὁ ἄνθρωπος *E*   **277** συγγνώμης *C*   **279** ψυχήν] τυγχάνει
add. E   **281/282** μετανοεῖν] π(ερι) *(sine acc.)* τοῦ μετανοεῖν τοῦ ἀνθρώπου
καὶ ἀγγελ() *(sine acc.)* οὐχὶ *hab.* $D^{in\,marg.}$ **282** ἄγγελοι] οἱ *praem. H*

Comp. **264** οὔτε] οὔτ'ἄν *Nem.*   **266** τε] δὲ *Nem.*   **280** *post* σῶμα] <τυγχάνει>
scripsit Morani   **282** οἱ] *non hab. Nem.*

60 FLORILEGIVM COISLINIANVM

μετανοήσαντες συγγνώμης ἀξιοῦνται· καὶ ἐν τούτῳ
μάλιστα δίκαιος καὶ ἐλεήμων ὁ θεὸς δείκνυται· τοῖς
285 γὰρ ἀγγέλοις μηδὲν ἔχουσιν ἐπανάγκασμα περιέλκον
εἰς ἁμαρτίαν, ἀλλ'ἐλευθέροις οὖσιν ἐκ φύσεως τῶν σωματικῶν παθῶν τε καὶ χρειῶν καὶ ἡδονῶν, εἰκότως οὐδεμία δίδοται συγγνώμη μετανοοῦσιν. Ὁ δὲ ἄνθρωπος
οὐ μόνον ἐστὶ λογικόν, ἀλλὰ καὶ ζῶον· αἱ δὲ χρεῖαι τοῦ
290 ζώου καὶ τὰ πάθη πολλάκις περιέλκουσι τὸν λογισμόν.
Ὅταν οὖν ἀνανήψας ἀποφύγῃ μὲν ταῦτα, χωρήσῃ δὲ
ἐπὶ τὰς ἀρετάς, ἐλέου δικαίου τυγχάνει τῆς συγγνώμης. Καὶ ὥσπερ ἴδιόν ἐστι τῆς οὐσίας αὐτοῦ τὸ γελα-
στικόν, ἐπειδὴ καὶ μόνῳ τούτῳ πρόσεστι καὶ παντὶ καὶ
295 ἀεί, οὕτως ἐν τοῖς κατὰ χάριν ἴδιον ἀνθρώπου παρὰ
πᾶσαν τὴν λογικὴν κτίσιν τὸ διὰ τῆς μετανοίας ἀπολύ-
εσθαι τῶν προημαρτημένων τὰς αἰτίας· καὶ γὰρ μόνῳ
ἀνθρώπῳ τοῦτο δεδώρηται καὶ παντὶ καὶ ἀεὶ παρὰ τὸν
καιρὸν τῆς ἐγκοσμίου ζωῆς, μετὰ δὲ τὸν θάνατον οὐκέ-
300 τι. Οὕτω δέ τινες καὶ τοὺς ἀγγέλους βούλονται μηκέτι
μετὰ τὴν ἔκπτωσιν τυγχάνειν τῆς ἐκ μετανοίας συγ-
γνώμης· θάνατος γὰρ τούτων ἡ ἔκπτωσις, πρὸ δὲ τῆς
ἐκπτώσεως καθ'ὁμοιότητα τῆς ζωῆς τῆς τῶν ἀνθρώπων καὶ αὐτοὺς ἀξιοῦσθαι συγγνώμης, ὅπερ μὴ ποιή-
305 σαντες ἀσύγγνωστον καὶ διαιωνίζουσαν ἔχουσι τὸ λοιπὸν τῆς τιμωρίας τὴν προσήκουσαν δίκην. Δῆλον οὖν

Mss. *AT CDEHQ* (*F* inde a τὸν, 29.290)

Crit. **283** συγνώμης *C* **287/288** οὐδεμία εἰκότως *Q* **288** συγνώμη *C*
291 Ὅταν] μὲν *add. FH* μὲν] δὲ *F* χωρήσει *AT D,* χωρήσ() *FH*
292 ἐλέου] ἐλαίου *A D,* ἐλέω *T,* καὶ *add. E* δικαίω *T* **292/293** συγνώμης *C* **293** αὐτοῦ τῆς οὐσίας ἐστὶ *FH,* ἐστιν αὐτοῦ τῆς οὐσίας *DEQ*
294 ἐπεὶ *H* καὶ¹] *om. Q* μόνῳ] τῷ ἀνθρώπῳ *add. E* τούτῳ μόνῳ *Q*
τούτῳ] τοῦτο *A DE* πάντι *T* **298** πάντι *T* παρὰ] περὶ *F*
299 ἐγκοσμίου] ἐν κόσμῳ *FH* **301/302** συγνώμης *C* **302/304** θάνατος – συγγνώμης] *om. D^{a.corr.} (suppl. in marg.)* **303** τῆς¹] *om. E* τῆς²]
om. E **305** διαιωνίζουσαν] ἔχουσαν *(sic) add. D* τὸ] *om. EFH*

Comp. **283** μετανοοῦντες *Nem.* (*K F D = Coisl.*) **284** *post* μάλιστα] καὶ *hab.*
Nem. *post* δείκνυται] τε καὶ λέγεται *hab. Nem.* *post* τοῖς] μὲν *hab.*
Nem. **296/297** ἀποδύεσθαι *Nem.* (*D = Coisl.*)

ALPHA 29   61

ἐκ τούτων <ὡς οἱ> τὴν μετάνοιαν <μὴ> δεχόμενοι τὴν
ἐξαίρετον δωρεὰν καὶ τὴν ἰδίαν ἀνθρώπου περιγράφουσιν. Ἴδιον αὐτοῦ καὶ ἐξαίρετον καὶ τὸ μόνον τῶν ἄλ-
310 λων ζῴων, τὸ τούτου σῶμα μετὰ τὸν θάνατον ἀνίστασθαι καὶ εἰς ἀθανασίαν χωρεῖν· τυγχάνει δὲ τούτου διὰ
τὴν τῆς ψυχῆς ἀθανα|σίαν, ὥσπερ ἐκείνου διὰ τὴν τοῦ   p. 11
σώματος ἀσθένειάν τε καὶ πολυπάθειαν. Ἴδια δὲ αὐτοῦ
καὶ τὰ τῶν τεχνῶν τε καὶ ἐπιστημῶν μαθήματα καὶ αἱ
315 κατὰ τὰς τέχνας ταύτας ἐνέργειαι. Διὸ καὶ τὸν ἄνθρωπον ὁρίζονται ζῷον λογικόν, θνητόν, νοῦ καὶ ἐπιστήμης
δεκτικόν· ζῷον μέν, ὅτι ἄνθρωπος οὐσία ἐστὶν ἔμψυχος
αἰσθητική – οὗτος γὰρ ὁ τοῦ ζῴου ὅρος –· λογικὸν δέ,
ἵνα χωρισθῇ τῶν ἀλόγων, καὶ θνητόν, ἵνα χωρισθῇ τῶν
320 ἀθανάτων λογικῶν· τὸ δὲ νοῦ καὶ ἐπιστήμης δεκτικόν,
ὅτι διὰ μαθήσεως προσγίνονται ἡμῖν αἱ τέχναι καὶ αἱ
ἐπιστῆμαι, ἔχουσι μὲν δύναμιν δεκτικὴν καὶ τοῦ νοῦ
καὶ τῶν τεχνῶν, τὴν δὲ ἐνέργειαν κτωμένοις ἐκ τῶν
μαθημάτων. Λέγουσι δὲ τοῦτον τὸν ὅρον προστεθῆναι
325 ὕστερον· ἐρρῶσθαι μὲν γὰρ καὶ χωρὶς τούτου τὸν ὅρον,
ἀλλ᾽ἐπειδὴ νύμφας καὶ ἄλλά τινα γένη δαιμόνων τινὲς

Mss.   *AT CDEFHQ*

Crit.   **307** ὡς οἱ] *scripsi cum EQ et fonte,* ὅσοι *cett.*   μὴ] *scripsi cum E, om. cett.*
δεχόμεθα C   **308** τὴν] *om.* FH   τὴν ἰδίαν] τὸ ἴδιον E   **309** Ἴδι-
ον] δὲ *add.* E   καὶ¹] *om.* DQ   τὸ] *om.* E   **310** τούτου σῶμα] *om.*
E   τὸν] τοῦ σώματος *add.* E   **312** ὥσπερ] ὡς περι *(sine acc.)* A, ὡς περϊ
(sine acc.) T   **313** τε] *om.* T   τε καὶ] *om.* Q   πολυπαθεῖαν D   δὲ]
om. H   **315** ταύτας] *om.* Q   **316** θνητόν, νοῦ] θνητὸνοῦ *(sic)* C
317/320 ζῷον – δεκτικόν] *om.* Q   **317** ἄνθρωπος] ὁ *praem.* E   ἐστὶν]
δὲ FH   **318** οὕτως *AT* C   **319** χωριστῇ *(sic)* H   **321** διὰ] ἀπὸ Q
ἡμῖν] *post* μαθήσεως *trsp.* FH   αἱ²] *om.* A   **322** μὲν] γὰρ *add.* FH
δεκτικὴν] οἱ ἄνθρωποι *add.* Q   **323** δὲ ἐνέργειαν] ἐνέργειαν F, *om.* H (20
litt. spat.)   κτωμένοις] κτῶνται Q   **324/325** τοῦτον – ὕστερον] τοῦτο
ὕστερον προστεθῆναι τῷ ὅρῳ Q   **325** ἔρρωσθαι A   **326** ἐπεὶ Q

Comp.   **307** *ante* δεχόμενοι] οὐ *hab. Nem.*   **309** *post* Ἴδιον] δὲ *hab. Nem.*
317 *ante* ἄνθρωπος] καὶ ὁ *hab. Nem.*   **318** ὁ – ὅρος] ὅρος ζῴου *Nem.*
324 τοῦτον – ὅρον] τοῦτο τῷ ὅρῳ *Nem.*   **325** μὲν] *non hab. Nem. (ΠΒΗ =*
Coisl.)   **326** *post* ἐπειδὴ] καὶ *hab. Nem.*

62 FLORILEGIVM COISLINIANVM

εἰσάγουσι πολυχρόνια μέν, οὐ μὴν ἀθάνατα, ἵνα καὶ ἀπὸ
τούτων διαστείλωσι τὸν ἄνθρωπον, προσέθηκαν τὸ νοῦ
καὶ ἐπιστήμης δεκτικόν· οὐδὲν γὰρ ἐκείνων μανθάνει,
330 ἀλλὰ φύσει οἶδεν ἃ οἶδεν.
Ἑβραίων δὲ δόγμα, τὸ πᾶν τοῦτο διὰ τὸν ἄνθρωπον
γεγενῆσθαι· προσεχῶς μὲν δι'αὐτόν, οἷον νωτοφόρα καὶ
βόας πρὸς γεωργίαν, χόρτον δὲ διὰ ταῦτα. Τῶν γὰρ γενομένων, τὰ μὲν δι'ἑαυτὰ γέγονε, τὰ δὲ δι'ἄλλα· δι'ἑαυ-
335 τὰ μὲν τὰ λογικὰ πάντα, δι'ἕτερα δὲ τά τε ἄλογα καὶ
τὰ ἄψυχα. Εἰ δὲ ταῦτα δι'ἄλλα γέγονε, διὰ ποῖα γέγονε
σκοπήσωμεν. Ἆρ'οὖν δι'ἀγγέλους; Οὐκ ἄν τις εὖ φρο-
νῶν εἴποι δι'ἀγγέλους αὐτὰ γεγενῆσθαι· τὰ γὰρ δι'ἄλλα γενόμενα, πρὸς σύστασιν ἐκείνων καὶ διαμονὴν καὶ
340 ἄνεσιν γέγονεν, ἢ γὰρ τῆς διαδοχῆς τοῦ γένους ἕνεκεν ἢ
τροφῆς ἢ σκέπης ἢ θεραπείας ἢ διαγωγῆς καὶ ἀναπαύ-
σεως. Ἄγγελος δὲ τούτων οὐδενὸς δεῖται· οὔτε γὰρ δια-
δοχὴν ἔχει γένους, οὔτε τροφῆς ἐνδεής ἐστι σωματικῆς
οὔτε σκέπης οὔτε τῶν ἄλλων. Εἰ δὲ μὴ ἄγγελος, δῆλον
345 ὡς οὐδὲ ἄλλη τίς φύσις ὑπεραναβεβηκυῖα τῶν ἀγ-
γέλων· ὅσῳ γὰρ ὑπέρκειται, τοσούτῳ μᾶλλον αὐτῇ καὶ
τὸ ἀνενδεὲς πρόσεστι. Ζητητέον δὲ φύσιν λογικὴν μέν, |
ἐνδεᾶ δὲ τῶν προειρημένων. Τίς οὖν ἑτέρα τοιαύτη φα- p. 12

Mss.   AT CDEFHQ

Crit.   **328** τὸ] om. *FHQ*ᵃ·ᶜᵒʳʳ·   **332** προσαχῶς *(sic) F*   οἷον] ζῷα *add. T*
333 βόες *T*   χόρτος *T*   **334** ἑαυτὰ] αὐτὰ *FH*   **334/335** ἑαυτὰ]
αὐτὰ *T*   **336/337** διὰ – σκοπήσωμεν] διὰ – σκοπήσ(ου)μεν *D*, σκοπήσωμεν διὰ ποῖα *E*, σκοπήσωμεν διὰ ποῖα ἄλλα *FH*   **337** Ἆρ'] ἆρα *EH*,
ἄρα *F*   **338** αὐτὰ] ταυτὰ *(sic) Q*   **339** πρὸς σύστασιν] προσύστασιν *C*
340 ἢ γὰρ] ἤγουν *Q*   γένους] *iter D*ᵃ·ᶜᵒʳʳ· *(expunx.)*   **342** οὐδενὸς τούτων
EFH   **344** δὲ] *om. A*   ἀγγέλους *D*   **345** ὡς] *om. Q*   τίς] *sic acc.*
codd., etsi indefinitum   τῶν] τὴν *praem. Q*   **345/346** τὸν ἄγγελον *E*
346 ὅσον *FH*   τοσοῦτον *FH*   αὐτῇ] *post* ἀνενδεὲς *trsp. E*, αὐτ(ῆς) *H*,
αὐτ() *(sine acc.) F*   **347** δὲ] οὖν *E*   λογικὴν μέν] μὲν λογικὴν *DEFHQ*
348 δὲ] *om. E*   τῶν] τῶ *(sic) T*   **348/349** φανείη τοιαῦτα *FH*

Comp.   **333** *post* βόας] τοὺς *hab. Nem.*   **337** *ante* Οὐκ] ἀλλ' *hab. Nem.*
345/346 τῶν ἀγγέλων] τὸν ἄγγελον *Nem. (B K Alf. = Coisl.)*   **347** δὲ]
οὖν *Nem.*

ALPHA 29   63

νείη παραλιπόντων ἡμῶν τὸν ἄνθρωπον; Οὐκοῦν συνά-
350 γεται διὰ τοῦτον τά τε ἄλογα καὶ τὰ ἄψυχα γεγενῆσθαι.
Ἐπειδὴ τοίνυν δι'αὐτὸν, ὡς ἐδείχθη, γέγονε, διατοῦτο
καὶ ἄρχων αὐτῶν κατέστη. Ἄρχοντος δὲ ἔργον πρὸς
μέτρον χρείας τοῖς ἀρχομένοις κεχρῆσθαι, καὶ μὴ πρὸς
ἡδυπάθειαν ἀκολάστως ἐξυβρίζειν, μὴ δὲ φορτικῶς καὶ
355 ἐπαχθῶς προσφέρεσθαι τοῖς ἀρχομένοις. Ἁμαρτάνουσιν ὅσοι τοῖς ἀλόγοις οὐκ εὖ κέχρηνται· οὐ γὰρ ποιοῦσιν ἄρχοντος ἔργον, οὐδὲ δικαίου κατὰ τὸ γεγραμμένον·
Δίκαιος οἰκτείρει ψυχὰς κτηνῶν αὐτοῦ. Ἀλλ'ἴσως ἐρεῖ
τίς ὡς οὐδὲν δι'ἄλλο, ἀλλ'ἕκαστον δι'ἑαυτὸ γέγονεν.
360 Οὐκοῦν χωρίσαντες πρῶτον τὰ ἔμψυχα ἀπὸ τῶν ἀψύ-
χων, ἴδωμεν εἰ δύναται τὰ ἄψυχα δι'ἑαυτὰ γεγενῆσθαι.
Εἰ γὰρ ταῦτα δι'ἑαυτά, πῶς ἢ πόθεν τραφήσεται τὰ
ζῶα; Ὁρῶμεν γὰρ τὴν φύσιν ἐπιχορηγοῦσαν τοῖς ζώοις
τροφὰς ἐκ τῆς γῆς καρπῶν τε καὶ φυτῶν, πλὴν ἐλαχί-
365 στων τῶν σαρκοφάγων, καὶ αὐτὰ δὲ ταῦτα τὰ σαρκοφάγα τροφὴν ποιεῖται τῶν ζώων τὰ τὴν γῆν νεμόμενα,
ὡς λύκοι μὲν καὶ λέοντες, καὶ ἄρνας καὶ αἶγας καὶ σῦς
καὶ ἐλάφους, ἀετοὶ δὲ πέρδικας καὶ φάσσας καὶ λαγω-
οὺς καὶ τὰ ὅμοια, ἅτινα τοὺς καρποὺς τῆς γῆς νέμεται.
370 Καὶ γὰρ τῶν ἰχθύων ἡ φύσις ἀλληλοφάγος οὖσα, οὐ
μέχρι πάντων διήκει σαρκοφαγοῦσα, ἀλλὰ κατέληξεν

Font.   **358** Prou. 12, 10

AT CDEFHQ

Mss.

Crit.   **349** παραλειπόντων *C*^(a.corr.)   **351** δι'αὐτὸν] *post* ἐδείχθη *trsp.* *FH*^(a.corr.)   δια-
τοῦτο] διὰ τούτων *A*   **352** αὐτὸν *F*   κατέστησε *F*   **353** μέτρων
χρείαν *FH*   χρῆσθαι *Q*   **354** ἐνυβρίζειν *FH*   **355/356** Ἁμαρτάνου-
σιν] τοίνυν *add.* *E*, οὖν *add.* *Q*   **356** ἀλόγοις] ἁμαρτάνουσιν *FH*
359 τίς] *sic acc. codd., etsi indefinitum*   **361** εἴδωμεν *D*, εἴδομεν *E*
δύνανται *FH*   **365** αὐτά δε *Q*   **366** τοῖς ζώοις *FH*   τὰ – γῆν]
om. *D*^(a.corr.) *(suppl. in marg.)*   **367** λέοντας *T*   καὶ²] *an secludendum cum*
DEFHQ et fonte?   καὶ⁴] *om.* *FH*   **368** ἀετοὶ δὲ] ἀετοί δε *(sic acc.)* *Q*
371 κατέλληξεν *F*

Comp.   **355/356** *post* Ἁμαρτάνουσιν] τοίνυν *hab. Nem.*   **367** καὶ²] *non hab. Nem.*

64 FLORILEGIVM COISLINIANVM

ἐν τοῖς νεμομένοις φύκια καὶ ἄλλα τινὰ ἐν τῷ ὕδατι
φυόμενα. Εἰ γὰρ ἦν πάντα τὰ γένη τῶν ἰχθύων σαρκοφάγα καὶ μηδὲν ἦν ἐκφεῦγον τὴν τῆς σαρκὸς σίτησιν,
375 οὐκ ἂν οὐδ'ἐπ'ὀλίγον ἐπήρκεσεν, ἀλλὰ διεφθάρη τὰ μὲν
ὑπ'ἀλλήλων, τὰ δὲ διὰ τροφῆς ἔνδειαν. Ἵνα δὲ μὴ τοῦτο
γένηται, τινὲς τῶν ἰχθύων κατεσκευάσθησαν σαρκῶν
ἀπεχόμενοι, τὴν δέ, ὡς ἄν τις εἴποι, θαλασσίαν βοτάνην
νεμόμενοι, ἵν'ἐκ τούτων καὶ τ'ἄλλα διασώζηται· γίνεται
380 γὰρ βορὰ μὲν τούτων τὰ φύκια, ἐκεῖνα δὲ τῶν ἄλλων,
καὶ πάλιν ταῦτα τῶν ἄλλων, ὡς διὰ τὴν τῶν τελευταί-
ων τροφὴν ἀδιαλείπτως ἐκ τοῦ γεώδους τοῦ κατὰ τὴν
θάλασσαν παρεχομένην καὶ τὴν τῶν | ἄλλων ὑπόστασιν   p. 13
σώζεσθαι. Ἀπέδειξεν οὖν ὁ λόγος τὴν τῶν φυτῶν γένε-
385 σιν μὴ δι'ἑαυτήν, ἀλλ'εἰς τροφὴν καὶ σύστασιν ἀνθρώπων καὶ τῶν ἄλλων ζώων γεγενημένην. Εἰ δὲ ταῦτα διὰ
τὸν ἄνθρωπον καὶ τὰ ζῶα, δῆλον ὡς καὶ τὰ τῆς τούτων
αὐξήσεως καὶ γενέσεως αἴτια δι'αὐτὰ γέγονεν. Οὐκοῦν
ἀστέρων κίνησις καὶ οὐρανὸς καὶ ὧραι καὶ ὄμβροι καὶ
390 πάντα τὰ τοιαῦτα διὰ ταῦτα γέγονεν, ἵνα τῶν τροφῶν
ὡς ἐν κύκλῳ διηνεκῶς χορηγουμένων, ἀνελλιπὴς καὶ ἡ
τῶν προσφερομένων τοὺς καρποὺς διαμείνη φύσις, ὡς
εὑρίσκεσθαι ταῦτα μὲν διὰ τοὺς καρπούς, τοὺς δὲ καρποὺς διὰ τὰ ζῶα καὶ τὸν ἄνθρωπον. Λοιπόν ἐστιν ἐπι-
395 διασκέψασθαι πότερον καὶ ἡ τῶν ἀλόγων φύσις δι'ἑαυ-

Mss.   *AT CDEFHQ*

Crit.   **372** φυκία *E*   τινὰ] *post* φύκια *trsp. AT*   τῷ ὕδατι] τοῖς ὕδασι *FH*
373 φυσόμενα *T,* νεμόμενα *FH*   **377** τινὲς] τινὰ *FH*   κατεσκευάσθη
FH   **378** ἀπεχόμενα *DFH,* ἀπέχονται *Q*   δέ] *om. F*   εἴπη *FQ*
379 νεμόμενα *FH*   **380** γὰρ] δὲ *FH*   βορρὰ *CF (-ᾶ F)*   μὲν] *post*
γίνεται *trsp. Q*   φυκία *T*   **381** καὶ – ἄλλων] *om. A*   διὰ] δὴ *FH*
381/382 τελευταίων] λευταίων *(sic) A*   **388** δι'αὐτὰ] διὰ ταῦτα *C,*
δι'αὐτὸν *FH*   γέγονεν] γεγονέναι *FH*   **388/390** Οὐκοῦν – γέγονεν]
om. T   **389** καὶ²] *om. FH*   ὄμβροι καὶ ὧραι *E*   **392** προφερομένων
T   διαμένει *FH*   **393/394** καρποὺς δὲ *FH*   **394** ἔστιν *D*

Comp.   **377** *post* σαρκῶν] μὲν *hab. Nem.*   **379** τ'ἄλλα] τὰ ἄλλα *Nem.*
385/386 *ante* ἀνθρώπων] τῶν *hab. Nem. (KDP = Coisl.)*   **388** δι'αὐτὰ] διὰ
ταῦτα *Nem.*   **389** κίνησις] κινήσεις *Nem. (B K F = Coisl.)*

ALPHA 29   65

τὴν γέγονεν ἢ διὰ τὸν ἄνθρωπον. Ἀλλ᾽ἴσως ἄτοπον, τὰ
φρονήσεως ἄμοιρα καὶ καθ᾽ὁρμὴν φυσικὴν μόνην ζῶντα καὶ πρὸς γῆν κάτω κεκυφότα καὶ τὴν δουλείαν διὰ
τοῦ σχήματος ἐνδεικνύμενα λέγειν δι᾽ἑαυτὰ παρῆχθαι.

400 Πολλῶν δὲ ὄντων τῶν ἐνδεχομένων εἰς τοῦτο ῥηθῆναι,
καὶ σχεδὸν ἰδίας συγγραφῆς διὰ τὸ πλῆθος δεομένων,
ἐπὶ τὰ σύντομα μέν, καίρια δὲ καταντῆσαι προσήκει.
Εἰ τοίνυν ὡς ἐν εἰκόνι τῷ ἀνθρώπῳ καὶ τὰ τῶν ἔξωθεν ἐσοπτρίσθημεν, ἐξ αὐτῆς ἂν ἴωμεν τῆς τῶν ζητου-

405 μένων οὐσίας τὰς ἀποδείξεις ποιούμενοι. Ὁρῶμεν οὖν
ἐν τῇ καθ᾽ἡμᾶς ψυχῇ τὴν ἀλογίαν καὶ τὰ ταύτης μέρη
– λέγω δὲ τὴν ὄρεξιν καὶ τὸν θυμόν – πρὸς ὑπηρεσίαν
δεδομένα τῷ λογικῷ, καὶ τὸ μὲν ἄρχον, τὰ δὲ ἀρχόμενα,
καὶ τὸ μὲν κελεῦον, τὰ δὲ κελευόμενα καὶ ὑπηρετούμε-

410 να ταῖς χρείαις αἷς ἂν ὁ λόγος ὑποβάλῃ, ὅταν σῴζῃ τὸ
κατὰ φύσιν ὁ ἄνθρωπος. Εἰ δὲ τῶν ἐν ἡμῖν ἀλόγων τὸ
ἐν ἡμῖν ἄρχει λογιστικόν, πῶς οὐκ εἰκὸς καὶ τῶν ἔξωθεν ἀλόγων αὐτοκρατεῖν καὶ πρὸς τὰς χρείας αὐτῶν
ἐκδεδόσθαι; Ὑπηρετεῖσθαι γὰρ φύσει τέτακται τὸ ἄλο-

415 γον τῷ λογικῷ, ὡς ἐν τοῖς καθ᾽ἡμᾶς ἐδείχθη. Δηλοῖ δὲ
τοῦτο καὶ ἡ τῶν | πολλῶν ζώων κατασκευὴ πρὸς ὑπη-   p. 14
ρεσίαν τῶν ἀνθρώπων ἐπιτήδειος γενομένη, βόες μὲν
καὶ πάντα τὰ νωτοφόρα πρὸς γεωργίαν καὶ ἀχθοφορί-
αν, τὰ πολλὰ δὲ τῶν πτηνῶν καὶ τῶν ἐνύδρων καὶ τῶν

---

ss.   *AT CDEFHQ*

---

rit.   **399** ἐπιδεικνύμενα *FH*   ἑαυτὴν *FH*   **404** ἐνωπτρίσθημεν *E,* ἐσοπτρισθῶμεν *Q*   αὐτῆς] αὐτῶν *FH*   ἴωμεν] εἴημεν *Q*   τῆς] τὰς *F*
406 ἀναλογίαν *T*   **407** δὲ] δὴ *T DFHQ*   **408** λογιστικῶ *Q*
409 κελευόμενα] ἑπόμενα *Q*   **410** ὑποβάλει *A,* ὑποβάλλη *T DF*[p. corr.]
HQ   σώζει *A*   **411** τὸ] *iter. H*   **413** αὐτὸ κρατεῖν *Q*   χρείας]
αὐτοκρατορίας *FH*[ut uid.]   αὐτῶν] αὐτοῦ *FH*   **414** τετάκται *(sic acc.) Q*
415 τῷ λογικῷ] τῶν λογικῶν *E*   **417** ἐπιτήδειον *C,* ἐπιτήδ() *FH*
γεγενημένη *FH*   **419** τῶν¹– καὶ¹] *om. F*[a. corr.] *(suppl. in marg.)*

---

omp.   **401** *post* δεομένων] μὴ χωρούσης τῆς προκειμένης ὑποθέσεως τὸ μῆκος τῶν
λόγων *hab. Nem.*   **404** ἐσοπτρισθείημεν *Nem.*   ἴωμεν] εἴημεν *Nem.*
412 λογικόν *Nem.*   **413** αὐτὸ κρατεῖν *Nem.*   αὐτῷ *Nem.*   **414** δε-
δόσθαι *Nem.*   **417** τῷ ἀνθρώπῳ *Nem. (K D P Alf. = Coisl.)*

66 FLORILEGIVM COISLINIANVM

420 χερσαίων πρὸς ἀπόλαυσιν, τὰ δὲ μιμηλὰ πρὸς τέρψιν
καὶ ἄνεσιν. Εἰ δὲ μὴ πάντα τὰ τοιαῦτα ταῖς χρείαις ὑπη-
ρετεῖται, ἀλλ'ἔνια καὶ λυμαίνεται τὸν ἄνθρωπον, ἰστέον
ὡς προηγουμένως τῶν δι'ὑπηρεσίαν γενομένων καὶ τὰ
ἄλλα πάντα <τὰ ἐνδεχόμενα κατεσκεύασται, ἵνα μηδὲν
425 ἐλλείπῃ τῇ κτίσει τῶν> ἐνδεχομένων γενέσθαι. Οὐδὲ
ταῦτα δὲ παντάπασιν ἐκπέφευγε τὴν τῶν ἀνθρώπων
ὄνησιν, ἀλλὰ καὶ τὰ δηλητηριώδη πρὸς οἰκείαν ὠφέλειαν ὁμολόγως καρποῦται· κατακέχρηται γὰρ αὐτοῖς πρὸς
θεραπείαν τῆς ἐξ αὐτῶν ἐκείνων βλάβης καὶ τῆς τῶν
430 ἄλλων ἀρρωστημάτων ἰάσεως. Τοιαῦταί τινες εἰσὶν αἱ
θηριακαὶ καλούμεναι κατασκευαὶ ἃς ὁ λόγος ἐπενόη-
σεν, ἵνα καὶ τούτων κρατῇ δι'αὐτῶν, καὶ ὡς παρὰ τῶν
πολεμίων κρατηθέντων ὠφελοῖτο. Ἔχει δὲ μυρίας ὁ
ἄνθρωπος ἀντιπαθεῖς τούτων δυνάμεις δεδομένας παρὰ
435 τοῦ δημιουργοῦ, εἴργειν καὶ ἀμύνεσθαι καὶ διορθοῦσθαι
τὰς ἐπιβουλὰς αὐτῶν δυνάμενος· ἄλλα μὲν γὰρ ἄλλαις
ἁρμόζει χρείαις, κοινῇ δὲ πάντα πρὸς θεραπείαν ἀνθρώπου συντελεῖν πέφυκε, καὶ τὰ μὴ ταῖς ἄλλαις χρείαις
χρήσιμα. Καὶ ταῦτα μὲν ὡς πρὸς τὴν νῦν κατάστασιν
440 τοῦ καθ'ἡμᾶς βίου λεγέσθω, ἐπεὶ τό γε ἀρχαῖον οὐδὲν

Mss.   *AT CDEFHQ*

Crit.   **420** δὲ] μὴ *add. A*   **421** τὰ] *om. T*   **424/425** τὰ – τῶν] *scripsi cum*
fonte, om. codd.   **425** ἐνδεχομένων] ἐνδεχομένως *T*   Οὐδὲ] ἀλλὰ μὴν
praem. E, ἂν δὲ *F*   **426** ταῦτα δὲ] τὰ λυμαίνεσθαι λεγόμενα *E*   δὲ] *om.*
T F   ἐκπέφευγε] ἐκπεφευγῶς *(sic acc.) A,* ἐκπεφευγότα *T*   **427** ἀλλὰ]
om. A   **428** ὁμολογουμένως *FH*   καρποῦται] *om. H (10 litt. spat.)*
432 τούτων] τοῦτον *E*   κρατῇ – ὡς] κρα... *H (20 litt. spat.)*   **433** ὠφε-
λεῖτο *E*   **434** δεδομένα *T,* δεδόμενας *CH,* παραδεδομένας *DEQ*
436 δυνάμενα *D,* δυναμένας *E*   **436/437** ἄλλαις ἁρμόζει] ἄλλαι *(sic)* ἁρμόζει *A, om. H (15 litt. spat.)*   **437** θεραπείαν] σ(ωτη)ριαν *(sine acc.) D*
440 γε] *om. FH*

Comp.   **421** τὰ – ταῖς] ταῖς τοιαύταις *Nem.*   **428** ὁμολόγως] ὁ λόγος *Nem.*
429 τῆς²] πρὸς *scripsit Morani cum parte trad. indir. (Alf. arm.), codd. = Coisl.*
430 ἰάσεως] ἴασιν *scripsit Morani cum parte trad. indir. (Alf. arm.), codd. =*
Coisl.   **432** τῶν] *non hab. Nem. (Π H = Coisl.)*   **436** δυναμένας *Nem.*

ALPHA 29   67

τῶν ἄλλων ζώων ἐτόλμα καταβλάπτειν τὸν ἄνθρωπον,
ἀλλ'ἦν αὐτῷ πάντα δοῦλα καὶ ὑποτεταγμένα καὶ πει-
θήνια, ἕως ἐκράτει τῶν οἰκείων παθῶν καὶ τῆς ἀλογί-
ας τῆς ἐν αὐτῷ. Μὴ κρατῶν δὲ τῶν ἰδίων παθῶν, ἀλλὰ
445 κρατούμενος ὑπ'αὐτῶν, ἐκρατήθη καὶ παρὰ τῶν ἔξωθεν εὐλόγως θηρίων· συνεισῆλθε γὰρ τῇ ἁμαρτίᾳ καὶ ἡ
παρὰ τούτων βλάβη. Ὅτι δὲ τοῦτό ἐστιν ἀληθές, δῆλον
ἐκ | τῶν τὸν ἄριστον μετελθόντων βίον· κρείττους γὰρ   p. 15
ἀριδήλως ὤφθησαν οὗτοι τῆς τῶν θηρίων ἐπιβουλῆς,
450 ὡς λεόντων μὲν ὁ Δανιήλ, Παῦλος δὲ τοῦ δήγματος
τῆς ἐχίδνης.

Τίς οὖν ἀξίως θαυμάσειε τὴν εὐγένειαν τούτου τοῦ
ζώου, τοῦ συνδέοντος ἐν ἑαυτῷ τὰ θνητὰ τοῖς ἀθα-
νάτοις καὶ τὰ λογικὰ τοῖς ἀλόγοις συνάπτοντος, τοῦ
455 φέροντος ἐν τῇ καθ'ἑαυτὸν φύσει πάσης κτίσεως τὴν
εἰκόνα – διὸ καὶ μικρὸς κόσμος εἴρηται –, τοῦ τοσαύτης
ἠξιωμένου παρὰ τοῦ θεοῦ προνοίας, δι'ὃν πάντα καὶ τὰ
νῦν καὶ τὰ μέλλοντα, δι'ὃν καὶ θεὸς ἄνθρωπος γέγονε,
τοῦ λήγοντος εἰς ἀφθαρσίαν καὶ τὸ θνητὸν διαφεύγον-
460 τος; Ἀνθρώπων βασιλεύει, κατ'εἰκόνα καὶ ὁμοίωσιν
θεοῦ γεγονώς, Χριστῷ συνδιάγει, θεοῦ τέκνον ἐστί, πάσης ἀρχῆς καὶ ἐξουσίας προκάθηται. Τίς δ'ἂν ἐξειπεῖν
δύναιτο τὰ τούτου τοῦ ζώου πλεονεκτήματα; Πελάγη

ont.   450 cf. Dan. 6, 6   450/451 cf. Act. 28, 3   460 Gen. 1, 26

Ass.   AT CDEFHQ

Crit.   441 ἄλλων – ἐτόλμα] ἄλλων ἐτόλμα ζώων E, ἀλλ.....τόλμα H (5 litt. spat.)
444 ἰδίων] οἰκείων E   446 συνῆλθε E   447 ἐστιν] ἢ (sic acc.) H
δῆλον] δῆλον ὅτι CD   450 παῦλον C   452 θαυμάσει Q   457 ἠξι-
ωμένου] post θεοῦ trsp. Q   τοῦ] om. FH   προνοίας] τῆς praem. FH
457/458 δι' – μέλλοντα] om. Eᵃ·ᶜᵒʳʳ· (suppl. in marg.)   460 ἄνθρωπος FH
460/461 κατ'εἰκόνα θεοῦ καὶ ὁμοίωσιν CDEFHQ   462 τὶς D   463 δύ-
ναιτο] δύναται E   τούτου] post ζώου trsp. Q

Comp.   449 ἀριδήλως] ἀδηρίτως Nem.   455 ante πάσης] τῆς hab. Nem.
456 διὸ] δι'ἃ Nem. (D P = Coisl.)   457 ὃν] ὃ scripsit Morani cum D², codd. =
Coisl.   458 ὃν] ὃ scripsit Morani cum D², codd. = Coisl.   460 Ἀνθρώπων]
οὐρανῶν Nem.   461 γεγονὸς scripsit Morani cum D² Ell., codd. = Coisl.

68 FLORILEGIVM COISLINIANVM

διαβαίνει, οὐρανὸν ἐμβατεύει τῇ θεωρίᾳ, ἀστέρων κίνη-
465 σιν καὶ διαστήματα καὶ μέτρα κατανοεῖ, γῆν καρποῦται
καὶ θάλασσαν, θηρίων καὶ κητῶν καταφρονεῖ, πᾶσαν
ἐπιστήμην καὶ τέχνην καὶ μέθοδον κατορθοῖ, ὑπερόριον
διὰ τῶν γραμμάτων οἷς βούλεται προσομιλεῖ, μηδὲν ὑπὸ
τοῦ σώματος ἐμποδιζόμενος προφητεύει τὰ μέλλοντα,
470 πάντων ἄρχει, πάντων κρατεῖ, πάντων ἀπολαύει, ἀγγέλοις καὶ θεῷ διαλέγεται, τῇ κτίσει κελεύει, δαίμοσιν
ἐπιτάττει, τὴν τῶν ὄντων φύσιν ἐρευνᾷ, θεὸν περιεργά-
ζεται, οἶκος καὶ ναὸς γίνεται θεοῦ, καὶ ταῦτα πάντα διὰ
τῶν ἀρετῶν νοεῖται καὶ τῆς εὐσεβείας. Ἀλλ'ἵνα μὴ δό-
475 ξωμεν τισὶν ἀπειροκάλως ἀνθρώπου γράφειν ἐγκώμιον
καὶ μὴ μόνον τὴν φύσιν ἐκτίθεσθαι καθὰ προεθέμεθα,
αὐτοῦ που καταπαύσωμεν τὸν λόγον, εἰ καὶ τὰ μάλιστα
τῆς φύσεως πλεονεκτήματα λέγοντες τὴν φύσιν αὐτὴν
διηγούμεθα. Εἰδότες οὖν ὅσης εὐγενείας μετειλήφα-
480 μεν καὶ ὅτι φυτὸν | ἐσμὲν οὐράνιον, μὴ καταισχύνωμεν   p. 16
τὴν φύσιν, μὴ δὲ τῶν τοσούτων δωρεῶν ἀποφανθῶμεν
ἀνάξιοι, μὴ δὲ ἑαυτοὺς τοσαύτης ἐξουσίας καὶ δόξης
καὶ μακαριότητος ἀποστερήσωμεν – ὀλίγου καιροῦ καὶ
βραχείας ἡδονῆς, πάντων τῶν αἰωνίων καταπροδόντες
485 τὴν ἀπόλαυσιν –, ἀλλὰ διὰ τῶν καλῶν ἔργων καὶ διὰ
τῆς ἀποχῆς τῶν φαύλων καὶ τοῦ ὀρθοῦ σκοποῦ ᾧ μάλιστα τὸ θεῖον συνεργεῖν εἴωθε, διὰ τῶν εὐχῶν τὴν εὐγένειαν διασώσωμεν.

Mss.   AT CDEFHQ

Crit.   **469** ἐμποδιζόμενον Q   προφητεύει] πρόσεχ() φιλότ(ης) add. T^{in marg.}
475 γραφεὶν (sic acc.) D   ἐγκώμια F   **476** καθὼς AT   **477** που] om.
D^{a.corr.} (που sup. l.)   καταπαύσομεν CD   μάλιστα] τὰ add. E
478 αὐτὴν] αὐτοῦ Q   **480** οὐράνιον] τ(οῦ) χρ(υσοστόμου) ἐκ τ(οῦ)
π(ερὶ) παρθ(ενίας) add. Q^{in marg.}   **481** δὲ] δὴ Q   **482** δὲ] δὴ Q
487 εἰώθαμεν FH

Comp.   **464/465** κινήσεις scripsit Morani cum parte trad. indir. (Alf. arm. ar. An.),
codd. = Coisl.   **469** ἐμποδιζόμενον Nem. (P = Coisl.)   **473** διὰ] non
hab. Nem. (P = Coisl.)   **474** νοεῖται] ὠνεῖται Nem.   **477** post μάλι-
στα] τὰ hab. Nem. (B D = Coisl.)   **485** διὰ²] non hab. Nem. (K F = Coisl.)
487 ante διὰ] καὶ hab. Nem.

ALPHA 29 – 30

ΙΓ'

Περὶ τῆς ἐν παραδείσῳ διαγωγῆς Ἀδάμ

30   Τοῦ Χρυσοστόμου
       Ἐκ τῆς περὶ παρθένων βίβλου

Ἐπειδὴ γὰρ ὁ σύμπας κόσμος οὗτος ἀπήρτιστο καὶ
πάντα ηὐτρέπιστο τὰ πρὸς ἀνάπαυσιν καὶ χρῆσιν τὴν
ἡμετέραν, ἔπλασεν τὸν ἄνθρωπον ὁ θεὸς δι'ὃν καὶ τὸν
κόσμον ἐποίησε. Πλασθεὶς δὲ ἐκεῖνος, ἔμενεν ἐν παρα-
5 δείσῳ, καὶ γάμου λόγος οὐδεὶς ἦν. Ἐδέησεν αὐτῷ καὶ
βοηθὸν γενέσθαι, καὶ ἐγένετο, καὶ οὐδὲ οὕτως ὁ γάμος
ἀναγκαῖον εἶναι ἐδόκει, ἀλλ'οὐδὲ ἐφαίνετό που· ἀλλ'ἔ-
μενον ἐκεῖνοι τούτου χωρίς, καθάπερ ἐν οὐρανῷ, τῷ
παραδείσῳ διαιτώμενοι καὶ ἐντρυφῶντες τῇ πρὸς θεὸν
10 ὁμιλίᾳ. Μίξεως δὲ ἐπιθυμία καὶ σύλληψις καὶ ὠδῖνες
καὶ τόκοι καὶ πᾶν εἶδος φθορᾶς ἐξώριστο τῆς ἐκείνων
ψυχῆς. Ὥσπερ δὲ ῥεῖθρον διειδὲς καὶ ἐκ καθαρᾶς πηγῆς
προϊόν, οὕτως ἦσαν ἐν ἐκείνῳ τῷ χωρίῳ, τῇ παρθενίᾳ
κοσμούμενοι. Καὶ πᾶσα τότε ἡ γῆ ἔρημος ἦν ἀνθρώπων·

---

ont.   **30.1/14** = Io. Chrys., De uirg., 14, 31-44   **1/4** cf. Gen. 1, 1-30

Ass.   **30** *AT CDEFH*

it.   **ΙΓ'**] κεφάλαιον ιβ' *D*, ια' *H^ut uid.*, *om. EF*   Ἀδάμ] τοῦ *praem. T CDFE*
    30 Ἐκ – βίβλου] *om. DEFH*

rit.   **30.1** γὰρ] *om. A*   **2** τὰ] *om. E*   **3** ἡμέτεραν *(sic acc.) D*   ἔπλασεν]
    πλάσας *FH*   ὁ θεὸς τὸν ἄνθρωπον *CDEFH*   **4** ἔμεινεν *EFH*   ἐν] ἐμ *D*
    5 αὐτῷ] *post* βοηθὸν *trsp. FH*   καὶ²] *om. E*   **6** οὕτως] οὗτος *CD*
    7 ἀναγκαίως *A*   που] ποῦ ποῦ *(sic) D*   **8** ἐκεῖνοι τούτου] ἐκείνου τότε *E*
    9 παραδείσσω *D*   διαιττώμενοι *A*   **10** δὲ] *om. T*

omp.   **30.1** οὗτος κόσμος *Chrys.*   **4** ἔμεινεν *Chrys.*   **5/6** καὶ βοηθὸν γενέ-
    σθαι] γενέσθαι καὶ βοηθόν *Chrys.*   **7** ἀναγκαῖος *Chrys.*   **12** καὶ] *non*
    hab. Chrys.

70 FLORILEGIVM COISLINIANVM

15 οὐκ ἦσαν τότε πόλεις οὐδὲ τέχναι, οὐκ οἰκίαι – καὶ γὰρ
τούτων ἡμῖν οὐχ ὡς ἔτυχε μέλει, ἀλλ'οὐκ ἦν ποτὲ ταῦτα –,
ἀλλ'ὅμως τὴν μακαρίαν ζωὴν ζῆν καὶ πολλῷ ταύτης
ἀμείνω οὐδὲν οὔτε ἐνεπόδιζεν οὔτε ἐνέκοπτεν. Ἐπειδὴ
δὲ παρήκουσαν τοῦ θεοῦ καὶ ἐγένοντο γῆ καὶ σποδός,
20 ἀπώλεσαν μετὰ τῆς μακαρίας διαγωγῆς καὶ τὸ τῆς παρθενίας καλόν, καὶ μετὰ τοῦ θεοῦ καὶ αὕτη καταλιποῦσα
αὐτοὺς ἀνεχώρησεν. Ἕως μὲν γὰρ ἦσαν ἀνάλωτοι τῷ
διαβόλῳ καὶ τὸν δεσπότην ἡδοῦντο τὸν αὐτῶν, παρέ-
μενε καὶ ἡ παρθενία κοσμοῦσα αὐτοὺς μᾶλλον ἢ τοὺς
25 βασιλεῖς τὸ διάδημα καὶ τὰ ἱμάτια τὰ χρυσᾶ. Ἐπειδὴ δὲ
αἰχμάλωτοι γενόμενοι, τὴν βασιλικὴν ταύτην ἀπεκδύ-
σαντο στολὴν καὶ τὸν οὐράνιον ἀπέθεντο κόσμον, ἐδέ-
ξαντο δὲ καὶ τὴν ἀπὸ τοῦ θανάτου φθορὰν καὶ τὴν ἀρὰν
καὶ τὴν ὀδύνην καὶ τὸν ἐπίμοχθον βίον, τότε καὶ ὁ γά-
30 μος ἐπεισέρχεται μετὰ τοῦτον καὶ τὸ θνητὸν τοῦτο καὶ
δουλικὸν ἱμάτιον· Ὁ γὰρ γαμήσας φησὶ μεριμνᾷ τὰ τοῦ
κόσμου.

Font. **15/32** = Io. Chrys., De uirg., 14, 52-67 **19** Gen. 18, 27 **31/32** I Cor.
7, 33

Mss. *AT CDEFH*

Crit. **15** οὐδὲ] οὔδε *(sic acc.) D* **16** ἡμῖν] *om. D* μέλλει *CFH* πότε
D^*a.corr.*, τότε *EFH*, πω *T* **17** ζωὴν ζῆν] ζῆν ζωὴν *A*, ἔζων ζωὴν *T*
21 καταλειποῦσα *(sic acc.) T D* **22** γὰρ] *om. FH* **23** τὸν²] *om. T*
αὐτῶν] ἑαυτῶν *H* **24** ἢ μᾶλλον *FH* **26/27** ἀπεκδύσαντο] *sic AT*
C (ἀπεξεδύσαντο *expectaueris*), ἀπεδύσαντο *DEFH* **28** καὶ¹] *om. FH*
τοῦ] *om. T* καὶ² – ἀρὰν] *om. E* **30** εἰσέρχεται *E* μετὰ] καὶ
praem. T **31** δουλικὸν] βασιλικὸν *H*^*a.corr.* (δουλικὸν *sup. l.*)

Comp. **15** οὐκ²] οὐδὲ *Chrys.* **16** ποτὲ] τότε *Chrys.* **17** ἀλλ'] καὶ *Chrys.*
post μακαρίαν] ἐκείνην *hab. Chrys.* ζῆν] *non hab. Chrys.* **19** ἐγένον-
το] ἐγένετο *codd. Chrys.* **20** *post* μακαρίας] ἐκείνης *hab. Chrys.*
21 κάλλος *Chrys. (XM = Coisl.)* αὐτὴ *Chrys.* **23** τὸν¹] *non hab. Chrys.*
26/27 ἀπεδύσαντο *Chrys.* **28** καὶ¹] *non hab. Chrys.* **29** ἐπίμοχθον]
ἐπίπονον *Chrys.* **30** τοῦτον καὶ] τούτων *Chrys.*

ALPHA 30 – 31

31 Τοῦ αὐτοῦ

Ἐκ τοῦ λόγου τοῦ εἰς τὸν πρωτόπλαστον

Ἡρμοσάμην ὑμᾶς ἑνὶ ἀνδρί, φησὶν ὁ Παῦλος· Φοβοῦμαι
δὲ μήπως ὡς ὄφις ἐξηπάτησεν Εὔαν ἐν τῇ πανουργίᾳ
αὐτοῦ, καὶ τὰ ἑξῆς. Ὁρᾷς ὅτι οὐχ ὁ ἀνὴρ ἐσκελίσθη,
ἀλλ᾽ ἡ γυνὴ ἠπατήθη; Καὶ τίς ἡ ἀπατηθεῖσα, καὶ τίς ἡ τῷ
5 ὄφει προσπαίξασα; Ἡ ὀφιόστομος καὶ ἰοβόλος γυνή.
Τίς προσέπαιξε τῷ ὄφει; Ἡ δι᾽ἐμπαίγματα μελετῶσα.
Οὐδεὶς ἦν ἐν τῷ παραδείσῳ πλὴν αὐτῆς καὶ τοῦ ἀνδρὸς
αὐτῆς, καὶ μήτε τὴν μόνωσιν μήτε ἄλλό τι φοβηθεῖσα
περιήρχετο πλανωμένη, ῥεμβομένη ποῦ παρακοίτην
10 εὕρῃ, πρὸ τῆς συναφείας τοῦ γάμου τὴν μοιχοσπορί-
αν μελετῶσα. Εἰ προσῆν τῷ ἀνδρί, οὐκ ἂν ἐπλησίασεν
ὁ ὄφις. Ἔξω τοῦ ἀνδρὸς αὐτὴν εὗρε, καὶ ἐδελέασεν

---

ont.   **31.1/16** = Ps.-Io. Chrys., In Ps. 92, PG 55, 615, 29 – 616, 5   **1/3** II Cor. 11,
2-3   **1/13** cf. Gen. 3, 1-7

Iss.   **31** *AT CDEFH*

it.   **31** Τοῦ αὐτοῦ] *om. FH*   Ἐκ τοῦ λόγου τοῦ] ἐκ τοῦ αὐτοῦ λόγου τοῦ *FH*,
λόγου *A*, λόγου τοῦ *CDE*   πρωτόπλαστον] ἀδάμ *add. F*, κεφάλαιον ιβ´
add. H

rit.   **31.1** ἀνδρί] παρθένον ἁγνὴν παραστῆσαι τῷ χριστῷ (*cf. II Cor. 11, 2*) *add. E*
Παῦλος] ἀπόστολος *add. F*   **2** ὡς] *om. T C*   ὄφις] ὁ (*cf. II Cor. 11, 2*)
praem. T D   εὔα *(sine spir.) D*   **3** καὶ – ἑξῆς] *om. DEFH*   ἐσκελ-
λίσθη *A D*   **5** ὀφιοστόμος *A^{a.corr.} C*   **6** δι᾽ἐμπαίγματος *CDEFH*
8 ἄλλό τι] ἄλλ᾽ὅτι *(sic) E*   **10** εὕρει *A DH*, εὕροι *EF*   **11** ἐπλησίαζεν
DEFH

omp.   **31.1** *post* Ἡρμοσάμην] γὰρ *hab.* Ps.-Chrys.   φησὶν ὁ Παῦλος] παρθένον
ἁγνὴν παραστῆσαι τῷ Χριστῷ (*cf. II Cor. 11, 2*) Ps.-Chrys.   **2** δὲ] δὴ
Ps.-Chrys.   *ante* ὄφις] ὁ (*cf. II Cor. 11, 2*) *hab.* Ps.-Chrys.   **2/3** ἐν –
ἑξῆς] καὶ ὑμᾶς ἀπατήσῃ Ps.-Chrys.   **4** Καὶ] *non hab.* Ps.-Chrys.   καὶ]
non hab. Ps.-Chrys.   **9** πλανωμένη] πλαζομένη Ps.-Chrys.   παράκοιτον
Ps.-Chrys.   **10** εὕροι Ps.-Chrys.   συναφῆς Ps.-Chrys.   **11** ἐπλησίαζεν Ps.-Chrys.   **12** *post* ὄφις] τῷ ὄφει *hab.* Ps.-Chrys.

72 FLORILEGIVM COISLINIANVM

αὐτήν· γυνὴ γὰρ μόνῳ ἀνδρὶ συνοῦσα ἀεὶ καὶ διαπαν-
τός, φθορὰν οὐχ'ὑπομένει, ἧτταν οὐ δέξεται, χωρι-
15 σθεῖσα δὲ τοῦ ἀνδρός, κἂν μετὰ ἀγγέλων ᾖ συνδιατρί-
βουσα, εὐεπηρέαστος γίνεται.

ΙΔ'

Τί χρὴ λέγειν πρὸς τοὺς ἐπαποροῦντας, εἰ μετὰ
τὴν ἁμαρτίαν ἡ παιδοποιΐα, πῶς ἂν ἐγένετο τὰ
τῶν ἀνθρώπων πλήθη, εἰ ἀναμάρτητοι
διέμειναν οἱ ἐξ ἀρχῆς;

32 Γρηγορίου Νύσης

Ἀντιλεγόντων ποτὲ τῶν Σαδδουκαίων τῷ κατὰ τὴν
ἀνάστασιν λόγῳ, καὶ τὴν πολύγαμον γυναῖκα τὴν τοῖς
ἑπτὰ γεγενημένην ἀδελφοῖς εἰς σύστασιν τοῦ καθ'ἑαυτῶν δόγματος προφερόντων, εἶτα τίνος μετὰ τὴν ἀνά-
5 στασιν ἔσται πυνθανομένων, ἀποκρίνεται πρὸς τὸν λόγον ὁ Κύριος, οὐ μόνον τοὺς Σαδδουκαίους παιδεύων,

Font.   **32.1/31** = Greg. Nyss., De hom. opif., ed. Sels, p. 204, 11 – 205, 21 (= PG 44,
188, 28 – 189, 13)   **1/10** cf. Mt. 22, 23-30

Mss.   **32** *AT CDEFHQ*

Tit.   **ΙΔ'**] ιγ' *DH*, τρισκαιδέκατον *F, om. E*   ἡ] *om. T*   παιδοποιΐα] περὶ
τοὺς ἐπαποροῦντας εἰ μετὰ τὴν ἁμαρτίαν ἡ παιδοποιεία (*sic*) *add. D*^in marg.
πῶς] καὶ *praem. F*   τὰ ... πλήθη] τὸ ... πλῆθος *CDEQ*, τὸ ... γένος *FH*
διέμειναν] ἔμειναν *Q*   οἱ] *om. FH*

Crit.   **14** δέξηται *A D*   **15** μετ' *DE*   **32.1/2** τῷ ... λόγῳ] τοῦ ... λόγω (*sic*) *A*
C, τοῦ ... λόγου *T*   **3** ἑπτὰ] ζ' *A C*   γεγαμένην *E*   **4** προσφερόντων
DEQ   **5** ἔσται] *scripsi cum FHQ et fonte*, ἐστὶ *C*, ἔστι *D*, ἔσεσθαι *AT E*

Comp.   **13** αὐτήν] *non hab. Ps.-Chrys.*   μόνῳ] νομίμῳ *Ps.-Chrys.*   ἀεὶ συνοῦσα *Ps.-Chrys.*   καὶ] *non hab. Ps.-Chrys.*   **14** δέξεται] δέχεται, μοιχείαν
οὐκ εἰσπράττεται *hab. Ps.-Chrys.*   **14/15** χωρισθέντος *Ps.-Chrys.*
15 μετὰ] μετ' *Ps.-Chrys.*   **32.2** *post* πολύγαμον] ἐκείνην *hab. Greg.*
3 γενομένην *Greg.*   **3/4** ἑαυτοὺς *Greg.*

ALPHA 31 – 32   73

ἀλλὰ καὶ πᾶσι τοῖς μετὰ ταῦτα τῆς ἐν τῇ ἀναστάσει
ζωῆς φανερῶν τὸ μυστήριον· Ἐν γὰρ τῇ ἀναστάσει
φησὶν οὔτε γαμοῦσιν οὔτε γαμίσκονται, οὔτε γὰρ ἀπο-
10 θανεῖν ἔτι δύνανται· Ἰσάγγελοι γάρ εἰσι, καὶ υἱοὶ θεοῦ
εἰσι, τῆς ἀναστάσεως υἱοὶ ὄντες. Ἡ δὲ τῆς ἀναστάσεως
χάρις οὐδὲν ἕτερον ἡμῖν ἐπαγγέλλεται ἢ τὴν <εἰς> τὸ
ἀρχαῖον τῶν ἐκπεπτωκότων ἀποκατάστασιν· ἐπάνοδος γάρ τις ἐστὶν ἐπὶ τὴν προτέραν ζωὴν ἡ προσδοκω-
15 μένη χάρις, τὸν ἀποβληθέντα τοῦ παραδείσου πάλιν
ἐπ'αὐτὸν ἐπανάγουσα. Εἰ τοίνυν ἡ τῶν ἀποκαθισταμέ-
νων ζωὴ πρὸς τὴν τῶν ἀγγέλων οἰκείως ἔχει, δηλονότι
ὁ πρὸ τῆς παραβάσεως βίος ἀγγελικός τις ἦν· διὸ καὶ ἡ
πρὸς τὸ ἀρχαῖον τῆς ζωῆς ἡμῶν ἐπάνοδος τοῖς ἀγγέλοις
20 ὡμοίωται. Ἀλλὰ μήν, καθὼς προείρηται, γάμου παντὸς
παρ'αὐτοῖς οὐκ ὄντος, ἐν μυριάσιν ἀπείροις αἱ στρατιαὶ
τῶν ἀγγέλων εἰσίν. Οὐκοῦν κατὰ τὸν αὐτὸν τρόπον, εἴπερ μηδεμία παρατροπὴ καὶ ἔκστασις ἀπὸ τῆς ἀγγελικῆς ὁμοτιμίας ἐξ ἁμαρτίας ἡμῖν ἐγένετο, οὐκ ἂν οὐδὲ
25 ἡμεῖς τοῦ γάμου πρὸς τὸν πληθυσμὸν ἐδεήθημεν.
Ἀλλ'ὅστις ἐστὶν [ἐν τῷ πλήθει], ἐν τῇ φύσει τῶν ἀγγέλων
τοῦ πλεονασμοῦ τρόπος ἄρρητός τε καὶ ἀπερινόητος
στοχασμοῖς ἀνθρωπίνοις, πλὴν ἀλλὰ καὶ πιστός ἐστιν·

Font. 8/9 Mt. 22, 30; cf. Mc. 12, 25, Lc. 20, 35   10/11 Lc. 20, 36

Mss. *AT CDEFHQ*

Crit. **8** ζωῆς – ἀναστάσει] *om. T*   **10** ἔτι δύνανται] ἐστιν ἔτι *Q*   **11** εἰσι]
om. Q   ὄντες] γεγονότες *Q*   **12** εἰς] *scripsi cum EQ et fonte, om. cett.*
12/13 τὸ ἀρχαῖον] τῶν ἀρχεῖων *(sic) D*   **17** οἰκείωσιν *C*   **25/29** Ἀλλ' –
τόν] οἱ *Q*   **26** ἐν¹ – πλήθει] *seclusi cum fonte, hab. codd. omnes*
27 πλεονασμοῦ] πλατυσμοῦ *FH*   **28** ἀνθρωπίνοις] ἀνθρώποις *A D*, ἀνθρώπων *E*   πλὴν – ἐστιν] *om. E*

Comp. **13** πεπτωκότων *Greg.*   **14** προτέραν] πρώτην *Greg.*   **16** ἐπ'] εἰς *Greg.*
20 εἴρηται *Greg.*   παντὸς] *non hab. Greg.*   **22** *post* εἰσίν] οὕτω γὰρ ἐν
ταῖς ὀπτασίαις ὁ Δανιὴλ διηγήσατο *hab. Greg.*   **23** *post* παρατροπὴ] τε
hab. Greg.   **26** ἐν τῷ πλήθει] *non hab. Greg.*   **27** τε] μὲν *Greg.*   ἀπε-
ρινόητος] ἀνεπινόητος *Greg.*   **28** καὶ πιστός] πάντως *Greg.*

74 FLORILEGIVM COISLINIANVM

οὗτος ἂν καὶ ἐπὶ τὸν βραχύ τι παρ'ἀγγέλους ἠλαττω-
30 μένον ἐνήργησεν, εἰς τὸ ὡρισμένον ὑπὸ τῆς βουλῆς τοῦ
πεποιηκότος μέτρον τὸ ἀνθρώπινον αὔξων.

33 Τοῦ Χρυσοστόμου

Μυρίαι μυριάδες ἀγγέλων λειτουργοῦσι τῷ θεῷ, καὶ
χίλιαι χιλιάδες παρεστήκεισαν αὐτῷ, καὶ οὐδεὶς τούτων ἐκ διαδοχῆς, οὐδὲ ἐκ τόκων καὶ ὠδίνων καὶ συλ-
λήψεων· οὐκοῦν πολλῷ μᾶλλον ἀνθρώπους ἂν ἐποίη-
5 σε γάμου χωρίς, ὥσπερ οὖν καὶ ἐποίησε τοὺς πρώτους
χωρίς.
Ποῖος γὰρ εἰπέ μοι γάμος ἀπέτεκε τὸν Ἀδάμ; Ποῖαι
τὴν Εὔαν ὠδῖνες; Ἀλλ'οὐκ ἂν ἔχοις εἰπεῖν. Καὶ νῦν δὲ
οὐχ'ἡ τοῦ γάμου δύναμις συγκροτεῖ τὸ γένος τὸ ἡμέ-
10 τερον, ἀλλ'ὁ τοῦ θεοῦ λόγος ὁ τὴν ἀρχὴν εἰπών· Αὐξά-
νεσθε καὶ πληθύνεσθε καὶ πληρώσατε τὴν γῆν. Τί γὰρ

Font.   29/30 Ps. 8, 6   33.1/6 = Io. Chrys., De uirg., 14, 77-82   1/2 cf. Dan.
7, 10   7/8 = Io. Chrys., De uirg., 14, 74-75   8/20 = Io. Chrys., De uirg.,
15, 2-13   10/11 Gen. 1, 28

Mss.   AT CDEFHQ   33 AT CDEFHQ

Tit.   33 Τοῦ Χρυσοστόμου] om. DEQ

Crit.   29 οὕτως T C   ἂν] ὁ λόγος ὃς FH   ἀγγέλους] αὐτοὺς Q
30/31 ἐνήργησεν – αὔξων] om. Q   31 πεποιηκότος] πεπιστευ-
κότος D   33.2 παρεστήκεσαν A, παρειστήκεισαν E, παρεστήκασιν Q
2/3 τούτων] post οὐδὲ (l. 3) trsp. DEFHQ   3 ἐκ¹] ἐ (sic) A   3/4 συλλήψεως DEFH   5/6 ὥσπερ – χωρίς] om. FH   6 χωρίς] an secludendum
cum Q et fonte?   8 οὐκ ἂν] οὐκ κἂν E

Comp.   29 τὸν] τῶν Greg.   29/30 ἠλαττωμένον] ἠλαττωμένων ἀνθρώπων
Greg.   33.1 καὶ] non hab. Chrys.   2 post χιλιάδες] ἀρχαγγέλων hab.
Chrys.   παρεστήκεισαν] παρεστᾶσιν Chrys.   2/3 post τούτων] γέγονεν hab. Chrys.   3 οὐδὲ] οὐδεὶς Chrys.   3/4 συλλήψεως Chrys.
4 οὐκοῦν] οὔκουν scripsit Musurillo   4/5 ἐποίησεν ἂν Chrys.   6 χω-
ρίς] ὅθεν ἅπαντες ἄνθρωποι Chrys.   7 τὸν] non hab. Chrys.   8 Ἀλλ']
non hab. Chrys.   9 τὸ γένος συγκροτεῖ Chrys.   10 θεοῦ] κυρίου Chrys.
ante τὴν] παρὰ hab. Chrys.

ALPHA 32 – 34

εἰπέ μοι τὸν Ἀβραὰμ εἰς παιδοποιΐαν ὁ γάμος ὤνησεν;
Οὐκ ἐπὶ τοσούτοις αὐτῷ χρησάμενος ἔτεσι ταύτην
ὕστερον ἀφῆκε τὴν φωνήν· Δέσποτα, τί μοι δώσεις;
15 Ἐγὼ δὲ ἀπόλλυμαι ἄτεκνος; Ὥσπερ οὖν τότε ἀπὸ νε-
κρῶν σωμάτων τοσαύταις μυριάσι δέδωκε τὴν ὑπόθε-
σιν καὶ ῥίζαν ὁ θεός, οὕτω καὶ παρὰ τὴν ἀρχὴν εἰ τοῖς
προστάγμασιν αὐτοῦ πεισθέντες οἱ περὶ τὸν Ἀδὰμ τῆς
ἡδονῆς ἐκράτησαν τοῦ ξύλου, οὐκ ἂν ἠπόρησεν ὁδοῦ
20 δι’ ἧς τὸ τῶν ἀνθρώπων αὐξήσει γένος.

Καὶ πῶς ἂν φησὶν αἱ τοσαῦται μυριάδες τῶν ἀνθρώπων ἐγένοντο; Ἐγὼ δέ σε πάλιν ἐρωτῶ, ἐπειδή σε σφόδρα παρέμεινε κατασείων οὗτος ὁ φόβος· πῶς ὁ Ἀδάμ,
πῶς δὲ ἡ Εὖα, μὴ μεσιτεύοντος γάμου; Τί οὖν; Οὕτως
25 φησὶν ἔμελλον ἅπαντες ἄνθρωποι γίνεσθαι; Εἴτε οὕτως
εἴτε ἑτέρως, οὐκ ἔχω λέγειν· τὸ γὰρ ζητούμενον νῦν,
ὅτι γάμου οὐκ ἔδει τῷ θεῷ πρὸς τὸ πολλοὺς ποιῆσαι
τοὺς ἐπὶ γῆς ἀνθρώπους.

34 Ἀθανασίου

Ἠδύνατο ὁ θεὸς ὁ λόγῳ συστησάμενος τὰ πλήθη τῶν
ἀγγέλων, τιμίῳ τινὶ καὶ καθαρῷ τρόπῳ συστήσασθαι

ont. **14/15** Gen. 15, 2   **21/28** = Io. Chrys., De uirg., 17, 68-75   **34.1/7** =
Ps-Athan., Quaest. ad Ant., PG 28, 629, 30-36

Ass. *AT CDEFHQ*   **34** *AT CDEFHQ*

Crit. **13** ταύτην] ταῦτα *CD*   **16/17** ὑπόθεσιν] ὑπόσχεσιν *FH*   **20** αὐξῆσαι *C*
21 Καὶ] ἐρώτησις *praem.* *A*$^{in\ marg}$*T E*   **22** Ἐγὼ] ἀπόκρισις *praem.*
A$^{in\ marg}$*T DE (E iter. in marg.)*   **23** κατέμεινε *Q*   οὗτος] *post* φόβος
trsp. FH   **24** δὲ] *om. DEFHQ*   μεσιτεύσαντος *FH*   Τί] ἐρώτησις *praem.* *A*$^{in\ marg}$*T DE (E iter. in marg.)*   οὗτος *T DE*   **24/25** φησὶν
οὕτως *FH*   **25** Εἴτε] *praem.* ἀπόκρισις *A*$^{in\ marg}$*T DE*   **34.1** ἐδύνατο *H*
(rubricat.)   **2** συστήσασθαι τρόπῳ *Q*

Comp. **12** ὁ γάμος] τὸ πρᾶγμα *Chrys.*   **15** ἀπόλλυμαι] ἀπολύομαι *Chrys.*
16 τὴν] *non hab. Chrys.*   **20** γένος αὐξήσει *Chrys.*   **21/22** τῶν ἀνθρώ-
πων] *non hab. Chrys.*   **28** *ante* γῆς] τῆς *hab. Chrys.*   **34.1** ὁ θεὸς] *non*
hab. Athan.   τὸ πλῆθος *Athan.*

76 FLORILEGIVM COISLINIANVM

καὶ πλῆθος γένους ἀνθρώπων. Τινὲς δὲ φασὶν ὅτι τοῦ
θεοῦ ἄρσεν καὶ θῆλυ ποιήσαντος, εὔδηλον ὅτι διὰ σπερ-
5 μογονίας ἠβουλήθη τὸ γένος τῶν ἀνθρώπων συστήσασθαι. Ὅμως δὲ οὐκ ἠβούλετο διὰ παρακοῆς, ἀλλὰ μετὰ
τιμῆς γενέσθαι τοῦτο.

IE'

Τί τὸ τῆς ἁμαρτίας εἶδος; Καὶ ὅτι αὐτοπροαιρέτως
ἁμαρτάνομεν

35 Κυρίλλου Ἱεροσολύμων

Δεινὸν ἡ ἁμαρτία, καὶ νόσος χαλεπωτάτη ψυχῆς ἡ πα-
ρανομία, ὑποτέμνουσα τὰ νεῦρα ταύτης καὶ πυρὸς αἰωνίου γινομένη παραίτιος. Καὶ ὅτι γε αὐτοπροαιρέτως
ἁμαρτάνομεν λέγει ποῦ σαφῶς ὁ προφήτης· Ἐγὼ δὲ
5 ἐφύτευσά σε ἄμπελον καρποφόρον πᾶσαν ἀληθινήν·
πῶς ἐστράφης εἰς πικρίαν ἡ ἄμπελος ἡ ἀλλοτρία; Ἡ
φυτεία καλή, ὁ καρπὸς ἐκ προαιρέσεως κακός, καὶ διατοῦτο ὁ φυτεύσας μὲν ἀναίτιος, ἡ δὲ ἄμπελος καυθήσε-
ται, ἐπειδὴ εἰς ἀγαθὸν ἐφυτεύθη καὶ εἰς κακὸν ἐκαρπο-

Font.   3/4 cf. Gen. 1, 27   35.1/53 = Cyr. Hier., Cat. ad illum., 2, 1, 1 – 3, 16
4/6 Ier. 2, 21

Mss.   *AT CDEFHQ*   35 *AT CDEFHQ*

Tit.   **IE'**] ιδ' *CDFH, om. EQ*   35 Κυρίλλου Ἱεροσολύμων] *om. C*

Crit.   6 ἠβούλετο] ἐβούλετο *CE, post* τῶν ἀνθρώπων *trsp. Q*   35.4 που *FHQ,* ποῦ
cett., etsi indefinitum   5 σε] *om. F*   καρποφόρον] *om. FH*   6 ἀλλο-
τρία] ἀληθινή *E*

Comp.   3 καὶ] *non hab. Athan.*   5 ἠβουλήθη] ἐβουλήθη ὁ θεὸς *Athan.*   35.2 τὰ
νεῦρα ταύτης] μὲν αὐτῆς τὰ νεῦρα *Cyr. (C. M. = Coisl.)*   *post* πυρὸς] δὲ
hab. Cyr. (RE. Cas. = Coisl.)   3 *post* παραίτιος] Κακὸν αὐτεξούσιον, βλάστημα προαιρέσεως *hab. Cyr.*   4 που *Cyr.*   δ' *Cyr.*   7 *post* ὁ] δὲ *hab.*
Cyr.   8 φυτεύσας μὲν] φυτουργὸς *Cyr.*   8/9 καυθήσεται] κατακαυ-
θήσεται πυρὶ *Cyr.*   9/10 *post* ἐκαρποφόρησεν] ἐκ προαιρέσεως *hab. Cyr.*

ALPHA 34 – 35   77

10 φόρησεν. Ἐποίησε γὰρ ὁ θεὸς τὸν ἄνθρωπον εὐθῆ, κατὰ
τὸν Ἐκκλησιαστήν, καὶ αὐτοὶ ἐζήτησαν λογισμοὺς πολ-
λούς. Καὶ ὁ Ἀπόστολος φησίν· Αὐτοῦ γὰρ ἐσμὲν ποίη-
μα, κτισθέντες ἐπ'ἔργοις ἀγαθοῖς, οἷς προητοίμασεν ὁ
θεός, ἵνα ἐν αὐτοῖς περιπατήσωμεν. Ὁ μὲν οὖν κτίστης
15 ἀγαθὸς ὤν, ἐπ'ἀγαθοῖς ἔκτισε, τὸ δὲ κτισθέν, ἐξ οἰκείας προαιρέσεως εἰς πονηρίαν ἐτράπη. Δεινὸν μὲν οὖν
κακόν, ὡς εἴρηται, ἡ ἁμαρτία, ἀλλ'οὐκ ἀθεράπευτον·
δεινὸν τῷ κατέχοντι, εὐΐατον δὲ τῷ διὰ μετανοίας ἀπο-
θεμένῳ. Ὑπόθου μοι γὰρ κατέχειν ἐν χειρὶ τινὰ πῦρ·
20 ἕως ὅτου κατέχει τὸν ἄνθρακα, φλέγεται πάντως· εἰ
δὲ ἀποθοῖτο τοῦτον, συναπέβαλε καὶ τὸ φλέγον· εἰ δέ
τις ἁμαρτάνων νομίζει μὴ κατακαίεσθαι, τούτῳ λέγει
ἡ Γραφή· Ἀποδήσει τίς πῦρ ἐν κόλπῳ, τὰ δὲ ἱμάτια οὐ
κατακαύσει; Καίει γὰρ ἡ ἁμαρτία, ὑποτέμνει τὰ νεῦρα
25 τῆς ψυχῆς καὶ συντρίβει τὰ νοήματα τῆς διανοίας, καὶ
σκοτοῖ τὸ φωτεινὸν τῆς καρδίας.

Font. 10/12 Eccl. 7, 29   12/14 Eph. 2, 10   23/24 Prou. 6, 27

AT CDEFHQ

Mss.

Crit. 10 εὐθὺ E   11 αὐτοὶ ἐζήτησαν] αὐτὸς ἐζήτησε FHQ   λογισμοὺς] λόγους AT   13 προητίμασεν Q   15 ἔκτισε] ἐποίησε FQ   17 κακόν]
om. Q   ἀθεράπευτος AT FH   18 εὐΐατον H   19 μοι] με FH
τινὰ] ante ἐν trsp. FH   20 ὅτου] οὗ EFH   φλέγηται H   21 δὲ] δ᾽
EFHQ   ἀπόθηται E   συναπέβαλλε F   22 κατακαίεσθαι] κα-
τέεσθαι F   τοῦτο AT DE   23 ἀποδύσει E   τίς] sic acc. codd., etsi
indefinitum   πῦρ] om. D, post κόλπῳ trsp. H   ἱμάτια] αὐτοῦ add. FQ
24 κατακαύσει] πῦρ γάρ ἐστι καιόμ(ε)ν(ον) ἐπὶ πάντ(ων) τ(ῶν) μελ(ῶν)· οὗ
ἂν ἐπέλθῃ, ἐκ ῥιζῶν ἀπώλεσε add. Q   ἁμαρτία] καὶ add. FH   26 σκο-
τεῖ EFH

Comp. 12 Καὶ – φησίν] φησὶν ὁ Ἀπόστολος, post ἀγαθοῖς hab. Cyr.   13 ἐπ᾽] ἐπὶ
Cyr.   13/14 οἷς – περιπατήσωμεν] non hab. Cyr. (lib. Mon. et Ottob. 2
= Coisl.)   15 post ἀγαθοῖς] ἔργοις hab. Cyr. (C. M. Coisl. RE. Ottob. 2. =
Coisl.)   18/19 ἀποτιθεμένῳ Cyr.   19 γάρ μοι Cyr.   ante πῦρ] τὸ
hab. Cyr.   21 τοῦτον] τὸν ἄνθρακα Cyr.   post συναπέβαλε] ἂν hab. Cyr.
22 ἁμαρτάνων] post κατακαίεσθαι hab. Cyr.   24/25 ὑποτέμνει – ψυχῆς]
τὰ νεῦρα τῆς ψυχῆς ὑποτέμνεται Cyr.   25 τὰ νοήματα τῆς διανοίας] τὰ
νοητὰ τῆς διανοίας ὀστέα Cyr. (Ottob. 1 RE. Casaub. Coisl. = Coisl.)

78 FLORILEGIVM COISLINIANVM

Ἀλλ'ἐρεῖ τίς· τί ποτε ἄρα ἐστὶν ἡ ἁμαρτία; Ζῷόν ἐστιν,
ἄγγελός ἐστι, δαίμων ἐστί; Τί ἐστι τοῦτο τὸ ἐνεργοῦν;
Οὐκ ἔστιν ἐχθρός, ἄνθρωπε, ἔξωθεν καταγωνιζόμενος,
30 ἀλλὰ βλάστημα κακὸν αὐτοπροαιρέτως αὖξάνον ἀπὸ
σοῦ. Ὀρθοῖς βλέπε σοῖς ὄμμασι, καὶ οὐκ ἔστιν ἐπιθυμία.
Μὴ ἅρπαζε τὰ ἀλλότρια, καὶ ἁρπαγὴ κεκοίμηται. Μνη-
μόνευε τῆς κρίσεως, καὶ οὔτε πορνεία, οὔτε μοιχεία,
οὔτε φόνος, οὔτέ τι τῶν παρανομημάτων ἰσχύει παρὰ
35 σοί. Ὅταν δὲ ἐπιλάθῃ τοῦ θεοῦ, τότε λοιπὸν ἄρχῃ λογί-
ζεσθαι πονηρὰ καὶ συντελεῖν παράνομα.

Οὐ μόνος δὲ σὺ καθέστηκας τοῦ πράγματος ἀρχηγός,
ἀλλὰ γὰρ καὶ ἄλλος κάκιστός ἐστιν ὁ ὑποβολεὺς διάβολος. Ὑποβάλλει μὲν οὖν ἐκεῖνος, οὐ μὴν διακρατεῖ τῶν
40 μὴ πειθομένων. Διατοῦτο λέγει ὁ Ἐκκλησιαστής· Ἐὰν
πνεῦμα τοῦ ἐξουσιάζοντος ἀναβῇ ἐπὶ σέ, τόπον σου μὴ
ἀφῇς· ἐὰν ἀποκλείσῃς τὴν θύραν μακράν σου τυγχά-
νων, οὐ βλάψει σε· ἐὰν δὲ ἀδιαφόρως δέξῃ τὴν ἐνθύμη-
σιν τῆς ἐπιθυμίας, διὰ τῶν λογισμῶν ῥίζας ἐν σοὶ κα-
45 ταβάλλεται καὶ καταδεσμεύει σου τὴν διάνοιαν καὶ εἰς

Font. 31 Prou. 4, 25   40/42 Eccl. 10, 4

Mss. *AT CDEFHQ*

Crit. **27** τίς] *sic. acc. codd., etsi indefinitum*   τί] τίς *D*, ἐρώτ(ησις) π(ερὶ) ἁμαρ-
τ(ίας) τὶ (ἐστὶ)· ἀγγελ(ος) (ἐστὶ) δαίμον *(sic)* (ἐστὶ) *add. D in marg.*   ἄρα]
ἄρα *C, om. Q*   **29** ἔξωθεν] *om. Q*   **31** ὀρθὰ *T*   ὄμμασι] ὀφθαλμοῖς
FH   **33** καὶ – μοιχεία] καὶ οὔτε μοιχεία καὶ οὔτε πορνεία *F*   **34** φθό-
νος *T*   **34/35** παρὰ σοί] κατὰ σοῦ *Q,* παρὰ σοῦ *A CD*   **37** τοῦ – ἀρχη-
γός] *om. H*   **38** καὶ] *om. CDEFH*   ὁ] *ante* διάβολος *trsp. FH*
39 διακρατεῖ] διακρατῶν *F,* διακρατ(~) *H,* βία κρατεῖ *EQ*   **40** Ἐὰν] ἂν *F*
41/42 τόπον – ἀποκλείσῃς] *om. H*   **41** σου] σὺ *CD*   **44** ἐν σοὶ] *om. A*
44/45 κατεβάλλετο *F,* κατεβάλετο *H*   **45** καταδεσμεύσει *E,* δε-
σμεύει *FH*   σου] *om. FH*   τὴν διάνοιαν] τὸν λογισμὸν *H*

Comp. **29** ἔξωθεν ἄνθρωπε *Cyr.*   **31** σοῖς ὄμμασι] τοῖς ὄμμασί σου *Cyr.*
34 οὔτέ] οὐδέ *Cyr.*   ἰσχύσει *Cyr.*   **38/39** γὰρ – διάβολος] καὶ ἄλλος
τίς ἐστι κάκιστος ὑποβολεύς, ὁ διάβολος *Cyr.*   **39** διακρατεῖ] βία ἐπικρατεῖ *Cyr.*   **42** μακράν σου] σου, καὶ μακρὸν σοῦ *Cyr.*   **44** τῆς] *non
hab. Cyr.*   **45** καταδεσμεῖ *Cyr.*   **45/46** εἰς βόρβορόν σε κατασπᾷ]
κατασπᾷ σε εἰς βόθρον *Cyr.*

ALPHA 35 – 36   79

βόρβορόν σε κατασπᾷ κακῶν. Ἀλλ'ἴσως ἐρεῖ τίς· πιστός
εἰμι, καὶ οὐ περιγίνεταί μου ἐπιθυμία, κἂν ἐπιθυμήσω
πυκνότερον. Ἀγνοεῖς ὅτι καὶ πέτραν ἔρρηξε ῥίζα πολλάκις παραμένουσα; Μὴ δέξῃ τὸν σπόρον, ἐπεὶ διαρρήσσει
50 σου τὴν πίστιν. Πρὶν ἀνθήσει, πρὸ καιροῦ ἔξελε τὸ κακόν, μὴ ῥαθυμήσας τὴν ἀρχήν, πέλυκας ὕστερον καὶ πῦρ
πολυπραγμόνει· ἀρχόμενος ὀφθαλμιᾶν ἰατρεύου κατὰ
καιρόν, ἀλλὰ μὴ τυφλωθεὶς, τότε ζήτει τὸν ἰατρόν.

ΙϚ'

Κατὰ πόσους τρόπους ἐξαμαρτάνει ὁ ἄνθρωπος;

36   Μαξίμου μοναχοῦ

Οἶμαι κατὰ τέσσαρας τρόπους ἁμαρτάνειν τὸν ἄνθρωπον, κατὰ συναρπαγήν, κατὰ ἀπάτην, κατὰ ἄγνοιαν,
κατὰ διάθεσιν. Καὶ οἱ μὲν πρῶτοι τρεῖς εὐχερῶς εἰς
ἐπίγνωσιν καὶ μετάνοιαν ἔρχονται, ὁ δὲ ἐκ διαθέσεως

Font.   **36 .1/6** = Max. Conf., Quaest. et dub., I, 5, 2-7 (p. 140)

Mss.   **36** *AT CDEFHKQ*

Tit.   **ΙϚ'**] ιε' *CDFH*, λβ' *K, om. Q*   Κατὰ – ἄνθρωπος] *om. Q, = Max. Conf.,*
Quaest. et dub., 1, 5, 1   **36** Μαξίμου μοναχοῦ] μαξίμου βηθλεεμίτου *F,*
μαξίμου (μον)αχ(οῦ) βηθλεημίτου *H*

Crit.   **46** κατασπᾷ] κατάγει *H*   ἴσως] *om. F*   τίς] *sic acc. codd., etsi inde-*
finitum   **47** καὶ] *om. FH*   παραγίνεταί *CH*ᵃ·ᶜᵒʳʳ· *(περι- sup. l. H)*
48 Ἀγνοεῖς] οὐκ ἀκούεις *F,* ἀκούεις *H*   **49** ἐπεὶ διαρρήσσει] ἐπειδὴ
ῥήσει *FH,* ἐπειδὴ διαρρήσει *Q*   **51** πέλεκας *Q*   **52** πολυπραγμονεῖς *E*
36.1 τέσσαρεις *(sic) K*   ἐξαμαρτάνειν *Q*   **3** πρῶτοι] *om. C*

Comp.   **46** ἐρεῖ τίς] λέγεις *Cyr.*   **47** ἐπιθυμήσω] ἐνθυμήσω *Cyr.*   **48/49** παραμένουσα πολλάκις *Cyr.*   **49** διαρρήσσει] διαρρήξει *Cyr.*   **50** ἀνθή-
σει] [ἢ] ἀνθήσῃ *Cyr.*   πρὸ καιροῦ] πρόρριζον *Cyr.*   **51** τὴν ἀρχήν] ἐξ
ἀρχῆς *Cyr.*   **52** πολυπραγμονήσῃς *Cyr.*   ἰατρεύου] θεραπεύου *Cyr.*
53 ἀλλά] ἵνα *Cyr.*   ζητήσῃς *Cyr.*   **36.3** οἱ] αἱ *Max. (Z BLD = Coisl.)*
πρῶται *Max. (Z = Coisl., om. BLD)*

80 FLORILEGIVM COISLINIANVM

5 ἁμαρτάνων, καὶ μήτε τῇ πείρᾳ μήτε τῷ χρόνῳ εἰς μετάνοιαν ἐρχόμενος ἀνήκεστον ἔχει τὴν κόλασιν.

37 Μαρκιανοῦ Βηθλεεμίτου

Ὥσπερ τὰ σωματικὰ πάθη, τὰ μὲν ἐπιπόλαια καὶ
εὐθεώρητα καὶ τὴν θεραπείαν εὐαίρετον ἐπιδέχεται καὶ
τῷ θεραπεύοντι οὐ παρέχει ἀδηλότητα, τὰ δὲ ἐνδομυ-
χούμενα ἀλγεινότερα καὶ χαλεπώτερα καὶ δυσθεράπευ-
5 τα, οὕτω καὶ ἐπὶ τῶν ἁμαρτητικῶν παθημάτων. Τὰ τῆς
σαρκὸς ἡττήματα καὶ τὴν αἰσχύνην πρόδηλον ἔχοντα
καὶ διακοπὴν λαμβάνοντα, εὔλυτα μᾶλλον καὶ εὐσυγ-
χώρητα γινώσκεται καὶ μετανοίας τόπον ἔχοντα, τὰ
δὲ φρονητικὰ βαρύτερα καὶ δυσαπάλλακτα καὶ ὥσπερ
10 προαιρετικὰ κατασκευάζεται καὶ οὔτε ἐξομολογήσε-
ως μέθοδον ἐπιδέχεται. Τίς γὰρ ἑαυτοῦ κατηγορεῖ ὅτι
πονηρός ἐστιν, ἢ ὅτι φθονερός, ἢ δόλιος, ἢ φιλόδοξος,
ἢ ὅτι ἐπηρμένος; Καὶ διατοῦτο τὰ μὲν φανερὰ διὰ τοῦ
γράμματος κεκώλυνται· Οὐ φονεύσεις, καὶ τὰ λοιπά·
15 τὰ δὲ ἄλλα διὰ τοῦ Πνεύματος ἐν τῷ λέγειν· Λούσασθε,

Font.   **37.1/26** = Marc. Bethl., CPG 3898.1   **14** Ex. 20, 15; Deut. 5, 18 et loc.
par.   **15/17** Is. 1, 16

Mss.   *AT CDEFHKQ*   37 *AT CDEFHKQ*

Tit.   37 Βηθλεεμίτου] βηθλεμίτου *T D (βι- T), om. FH*

Crit.   **5** μήτε¹ – πείρᾳ] *om. DEKQ*   μήτε²] μὴ *EK*   **37.2** αὐθαίρετον *C,* εὐία-
τον *T,* εὔκολον *FH*   ἐπιδέχονται *Q*   **3** ἀδηλότητι *F*   **3/4** ἐνδομυ-
χόμενα *Dᵖ·ᶜᵒʳʳ·* (ἐνδον μυχόμενα *a. corr.*), ἔνδον μυχόμενα *A EK* (μυχούμενα *E*),
ἔνδον σμυχόμενα *T Q*   **5** ἁμαρτικῶν *D,* ἁμαρτηματικῶν *FH*   **8** ἔχον-
τα] ἐπιδέχεται *FH*   **9** δυσσαπάλακτα *A*   **11** Τίς] τί *T FH*
12 δόλιος] δόλος *D*   **13** ὅτι] *om. FHQ*   **15** δὲ] δ᾽ *FH*   ἐν – λέγειν]
om. T   Λούσασθε] καὶ *add. EF*

Comp.   **37.1** Βηθλεεμίτου] Βηθλεμίτου *scripsit* Kohlbacher *(Ps m = Coisl.)*
2 εὐαίρετον] εὔκολον *Marc. (L JaMoPsVi m = Coisl.)*   **6** καὶ] *non hab.*
Marc.   **14** *post* κεκώλυνται] τὸ *hab. Marc. (HLN JaMoPsVi m = Coisl.)*

ALPHA 36 – 38   81

καθαροὶ γένεσθε, ἀφέλετε τὰς πονηρίας ἀπὸ τῶν ψυχῶν. Τρεῖς γὰρ τρόποι εἰσὶν ἁμαρτητικοί· ἐν τοῖς βιω-
τικοῖς, οἱ τελῶναι· ἐν τοῖς σαρκικοῖς, οἱ πόρνοι· ἐν τοῖς
φρονητικοῖς, οἱ Φαρισαῖοι καὶ οἱ πονηρευόμενοι. Καὶ
20 διατοῦτο χαλεπώτεραι αἱ φρονητικαὶ ἁμαρτίαι. Αἱ μὲν
γὰρ βιωτικαὶ καὶ σαρκικαί, ἔξωθεν προσγίνονται καὶ
διακοπὴν λαμβάνουσι, διὸ καὶ μετανοίας ἐπιδέχονται
τρόπον· αἱ φρονητικαὶ δὲ ἔσωθεν ἐκ τῆς καρδίας ἐξέρ-
χονται καὶ διατοῦτο δυσίατοι ἢ ἀνίατοι γίνονται, ὅτι
25 φθαρτικαί εἰσι τῆς φρονήσεως ὥσπερ ἀπὸ ῥίζης τινὸς
προϊοῦσαι.

IZ'

Περὶ ἁμαρτίας ἐνθυμηθείσης καὶ μὴ τελεσθείσης

38   Ἐκ τῶν λειμώνων

Τὴν πέτραν οὐ μὴ ἀδικήσουσι τὰ κύματα· οὕτω καὶ ἡ
προσβολὴ ἄπρακτος μένουσα οὐ μὴ ἀδικήσει τὸν ἄν-
θρωπον· γέγραπται γὰρ ὅτι πᾶσα ἁμαρτία μὴ συντετε-
λεσμένη οὐκ ἔστιν ἁμαρτία.

'ont.   **38.1/4** cf. Quaest. et resp. sen., qu. 19

Ass.   *AT CDEFHKQ*   **38** *AT CDEFHK*

'it.   **IZ'**] ις' *CDFH*, λγ' *K*   Περὶ – τελεσθείσης] *om. FH*   **38** Ἐκ – λει-
μώνων] ἀπὸ τῶν λειμώνων *H*, κυρίλλου ἱεροσολύμων ἀπὸ τοῦ λειμῶνος *F*

:rit.   **16** γίνεσθε *DEF*^(p.corr.) *K* (γένεσθαι *F*^(a.corr.))   ἀφέλεσθε *FH*   **16/17** ψυχῶν]
ὑμῶν *add. T EFHK*, ἡμῶν *add. D*   **17** τρόποι] τόποι *F*   ἁμαρτηκοί
(*sic*) *C*   **19/20** διατοῦτο καὶ *Q*   **23** τρόπους *C*   **24** ἢ] καὶ *add. FH*
γένονται (*sic*) *T*   **38.1** ἀδικήσωσι *CFH*   **2** ἀδικήση *T CE*
3/4 συντελεσμένη (*sic*) *AT*

:omp.   **16** γίνεσθε *Marc. (F JaMo = Coisl.)*   **16/17** *post* ψυχῶν] ὑμῶν (*cf. Is. 1, 16*)
hab. Marc.   **38.1** οὕτω] ὡσαύτως *Quaest.* (οὕτως *TKM*)   **3/4** συντετε-
λεσμένη] ἀποτελεσθεῖσα *Quaest. (TKR = Coisl.)*

82 FLORILEGIVM COISLINIANVM

IH'

"Ότι οὐ κατὰ ἀστρολογίαν τὰ καθ'ἡμᾶς

39 Κυρίλλου Ἱεροσολύμων

Οὐ γὰρ κατὰ γένεσιν ἁμαρτάνεις, οὐδὲ κατὰ τύχην πορνεύεις, οὐδέ, καθὼς ληροῦσί τινες, αἱ τῶν ἀστέρων πλοκαὶ ταῖς ἀσελγείαις σε προσέχειν ἀναγκάζουσι. Τί φεύγων ὁμολογῆσαι τὰ ἑαυτοῦ κακά, τοῖς ἀναιτίοις
5 ἄστροις ἐπιγράφεις τὴν αἰτίαν; Μή μοι πρόσεχε λοιπὸν ἀστρολόγοις· περὶ γὰρ τούτων ἡ θεία γραφή· *Στήτωσαν καὶ σωσάτωσάν σε οἱ ἀστρολόγοι τοῦ οὐρανοῦ· ἰδοὺ ὡς φρύγανα ἐν πυρὶ κατακαυθήσονται, καὶ οὐ μὴ ἐξέλωνται τὴν ψυχὴν αὐτῶν ἐκ φλογός.*

Font.   **39.**1/9 = Cyr. Hier., Cat. ad illum., 4, 18, 9-17   6/9 Is. 47, 13-14

Mss.   39 *AT CDEFHKQ*

Tit.   **IH'**] ιζ' *CDFH (*ις' *C^{a.corr. ut uid.}*), *om. EKQ*   ἡμᾶς] οὔτε κατὰ εἱμαρμένην διοικούμεθα *add. EK*

Crit.   **39.**1 Οὐ] οὐδὲ *FH*   γὰρ] *om. Q*   2 ἄστρων *FH*   3 ἀναγκάζουσι] κατ'ἀνάγκουσι *F,* ἀνέχουσι *H*   4 ἑαυτοῦ] σεαυτοῦ *FH*   6 τούτων] φησὶν *add. FHQ*   θεία] φησὶ *add. E*   γραφή] φησὶ *add. K*   7 σε] *om. FH*   8 ἐν – κατακαυθήσονται] καυθήσονται ἐν πυρὶ *DEKQ,* πυρὶ καυθήσονται *FH*   9 αὐτῶν] αὐτοῦ *T*

Comp.   **39.**1 οὐδὲ] οὔτε *Cyr.*   2 οὐδέ] οὔτε *Cyr.*   ἄστρων *Cyr.*   4 ἑαυτοῦ] σεαυτοῦ *Cyr.*   5 προσγράφεις *Cyr.*   6 post τούτων] λέγει *hab. Cyr.*   7 post οὐρανοῦ] καὶ ἑξῆς *hab. Cyr.*   post ἰδοὺ] πάντες *hab. Cyr.*   8 φρύγανα ἐν] φρύγανον ἐπὶ *Cyr.*   9 αὐτῶν *Cyr.*

ALPHA 39 – 40   83

*40   Ἀθανασίου Ἀλεξανδρείας
Βίβλος τῆς ἑρμηνείας τοῦ κατὰ
Ματθαῖον εὐαγγελίου

Εἰ δὲ ἦν καθ'ἕκαστον ἄνθρωπον ἀστὴρ ἐν τῷ οὐρανῷ,
πῶς τῇ τρίτῃ ἡμέρᾳ ὁ οὐρανὸς κατέγεμε τῶν ἀπείρων
καὶ ἀναριθμήτων ἄστρων, τοῦ Ἀδὰμ πλασθέντος τῇ
ἕκτῃ ἡμέρᾳ; Εἰ δὲ καὶ ἦν ἐν τῷ γεννᾶσθαι ἄνθρωπον
5   κτιζόμενος ἀστὴρ ἐν τῷ οὐρανῷ, ἐχρῆν ἐν ἀρχῇ τῆς
κοσμοποιΐας μόνον δύο ἀστέρας κατασκευασθῆναι ἐν
τῷ οὐρανῷ, τοῦ τε Ἀδὰμ καὶ τῆς Εὔας. Εἰ δὲ καὶ θνή-
σκοντός τινος πίπτει ἀστὴρ ἐκ τοῦ οὐρανοῦ, οὕτως ἔδει
καὶ ἐν τῷ καιρῷ τοῦ κατακλυσμοῦ μόνον ὀκτὼ ἀστέρας
10   ὑπολειφθῆναι ἐν τῷ οὐρανῷ τῆς γενεᾶς τοῦ Νῶε· το-
σοῦτοι γὰρ τὸν ἀριθμὸν εἰσῆλθον εἰς τὴν ἀναυάγητον
κιβωτόν, τῶν ἄλλων ἁπάντων ἀνθρώπων ἄρδην ἐξα-
λειφθέντων.

Font.   **40.1/13** locum non inueni; ed. Athan., Fragm. ined., II   1/4 Athan.,
Fragm. in Matth., PG 27, 1364, 15-18   2/3 cf. Gen. 1, 13-18   3/4 cf.
Gen. 1, 26-27 (31)   9/13 cf. Gen. (6, 9-10) 7, 6-7.

Ass.   **40** *AT CDEFHKQ*

Fit.   **40** Βίβλος – εὐαγγελίου] βιβλιου *(sine acc.)* τῆς ἑρμηνείας τοῦ κατὰ ματθαῖον
εὐαγγελίου *D*, ἐκ τοῦ β(ίβλου) τοῦ κατὰ ματθαῖον εὐαγγελίου *E*, ἐκ τῆς ἑρμηνείας τοῦ κατὰ ματθαῖον εὐαγγελίου *F*, βίβλου τῆς ἑρμηνείας τοῦ κατὰ
ματθαῖον εὐαγγελίου *H*, ἐκ τοῦ β(ίβλου) τῆς ἑρμηνείας τοῦ κατὰ ματθαῖον
εὐαγγελίου *K, om. T Q*

Crit.   **40.1** δὲ] δέ γε *FH*   ἕκαστον ἄνθρωπον] ἑκάστου ἀνθρώπου *FH*   τῷ]
om. T   2 τῇ] ἐν praem. *FH*   2/3 ὁ – ἄστρων] κατέγεμε τῶν ἄστρων ὁ
οὐρανὸς ἀπείρων καὶ ἀναριθμήτων *FH*   4 ἕκτῃ] ς' *CQ*   5 ἀστὴρ κτιζόμενος *D* κτιζόμενον *CE*   6 μόνους *F*   δύο] β' *H*   8 ἀστέρα (-α sup.
l.) *F*   οὕτως] καὶ praem. *CDEFHKQ*   9 καὶ] *om. EK*   μόνους *H*
ὀκτὼ] η' *A CDQ, post* ὑπολειφθῆναι *trsp. F, om. H*   10 ὑποληφθῆναι *AT D*
γενεᾶς] γενέσεως *FH*   12/13 ἐξαλειφθέντων] ἀπολωλότων *FH*

84 FLORILEGIVM COISLINIANVM

41 Τοῦ Χρυσοστόμου

Ὅτι γὰρ οὔτε εἱμαρμένη, οὔτε γένεσις, οὔτε δρόμος
ἀστέρων τὰ καθ'ἡμᾶς διοικεῖ, ἐντεῦθεν δῆλον· εἰ γὰρ
ἐκεῖθεν ἤρτηται τὰ γινόμενα πάντα, καὶ οὐ τῆς προαιρέσεως τῶν ἀνθρώπων, τίνος ἕνεκεν μαστιγοῖς τὸν
5 οἰκέτην κεκλοφότα; Τίνος ἕνεκεν μοιχευθεῖσαν τὴν
γυναῖκα εἰς δικαστήριον ἕλκεις; Τίνος ἕνεκεν αἰσχύνῃ
πονηρὰ πράττων; Τίνος ἕνεκεν οὐδὲ τὰ ῥήματα φέρεις
ὀνειδιζόμενος, ἀλλ'ἐάν τίς σε καλέσῃ μοιχόν, ἢ πόρνον,
ἢ μέθυσον, ἢ τί τοιοῦτον, ὕβριν τὸ πρᾶγμα καλεῖς; Εἰ
10 γὰρ μὴ τῆς σῆς γνώμης τὸ ἁμαρτάνειν, οὔτε ἔγκλημα
τὸ γινόμενον, οὔτε ὕβρις τὸ λεγόμενον. Νῦν δὲ καὶ δι'ὧν
τοῖς ἁμαρτάνουσιν οὐ συγγινώσκεις, καὶ δι'ὧν αὐτὸς
αἰσχύνῃ τὰ κακὰ πράττων καὶ λανθάνειν σπουδάζεις,
καὶ δι'ὧν τοὺς ταῦτά σοι προφέροντας ὑβριστὰς νομί-
15 ζεις, διὰ πάντων ὁμολογεῖς ὅτι οὐκ ἀνάγκῃ δέδεται τὰ
ἡμέτερα, ἀλλὰ προαιρέσεως ἐλευθερίᾳ τετίμηται. Τοῖς
γοῦν ἀνάγκῃ συνεχομένοις συγγινώσκειν οἴδαμεν· κἂν
ὑπὸ δαίμονός τινος ὀχλούμενός τις τὸν χιτῶνα διαρ-

Font.   **41.1/32** = Io. Chrys., De perf. carit., PG 56, 282, 33 – 283, 6

Mss.   **41** *AT CDEFHK*

Tit.   **41** Τοῦ Χρυσοστόμου] *om. E*

Crit.   **41.1** Ὅτι] μὲν *add. H*   γὰρ] *om. F*   **2** ἡμᾶς] ἡμῶν D   **3** ἤρτητο
FH   **5/6** τὴν γυναῖκα μοιχευθεῖσαν DEFHK   **7** πράττον *(sic acc.) AT*
8 ὀνειδιζόμενα C   **9** τί] *sic acc. codd., etsi indefinitum*   τοιοῦτον] τῶν
τοιούτων F *(τῶν sup. l.)*   **10** γὰρ μὴ] μὴ γὰρ FH   **11** καὶ] *om. DEK*
12/13 αἰσχύνῃ αὐτὸς FH   **16** ἐλευθέρας AT   **17** γοῦν] οὖν E
18 τινος – τις] τινος ἐνοχλούμενός τις C, τινος ὀχλούμενος DFH *(ὀχλούμενος om. F*ᵃ·ᶜᵒʳʳ·*, suppl. in marg.)*, τις ὀχλούμενος EK

Comp.   **41.1/2** Ὅτι γὰρ – ἐντεῦθεν δῆλον] Οὐκ ἐκ τούτων δὲ μόνον, ἀλλὰ καὶ ἐξ ὧν
ἡμεῖς αὐτοὶ ποιοῦμεν δῆλον ὅτι οὔτε εἱμαρμένη, οὔτε τύχη, οὔτε γένεσις, οὔτε
δρόμος ἀστέρων τὰ καθ'ἡμᾶς διοικεῖ *Chrys.*   **1** *post* εἱμαρμένη] οὔτε τύχη
hab. Chrys.   **7** πονηρὰ πράττων] πράττων τὰ ἄτοπα *Chrys.*   **17** συνε-
χομένοις] κατεχομένοις *Chrys.*   **18** τινος – τις] τις ὀχλούμενος ἢ *Chrys.*

ALPHA 41 – 42

ῥήξῃ τὸν ἡμέτερον, ἢ πληγὰς ἐπενέγκῃ, οὐ μόνον οὐκ
20 ὀνειδίζομεν, ἀλλὰ καὶ ἐλεοῦμεν καὶ συγγινώσκομεν. Τί
δήποτε; Ὅτι οὐχ ἡ τῆς προαιρέσεως ἐλευθερία, ἀλλ' ἡ
τοῦ δαίμονος βία εἰργάσατο ταῦτα, ὥστε εἰ καὶ τὰ ἄλλα
ἁμαρτήματα ἀπὸ τῆς ἀνάγκης τῆς κατὰ τὴν εἱμαρμένην ἐγίνοντο, συνέγνωμεν ἄν. Ἐπειδὴ δὲ ἴσμεν ὅτι οὐκ
25 ἔστιν ἀνάγκης, διὰ τοῦτο οὐ συγγινώσκομεν, οὔτε δε-
σπόται οἰκέταις, οὔτε ἄνδρες γυναιξίν, οὔτε γυναῖκες
ἀνδράσιν, οὔτε διδάσκαλοι μαθηταῖς, οὔτε πατέρες
παισίν, οὔτε ἄρχοντες ἀρχομένοις, ἀλλὰ πικροὶ τῶν
τετολμημένων ἐξετασταὶ καὶ τιμωροὶ γινόμεθα, καὶ δι-
30 καστήρια καταλαμβάνομεν, καὶ πληγαῖς ὑποβάλλομεν,
καὶ ἐπιτιμήσεσι χρώμεθα, καὶ πάντα πράττομεν, ὅπως
ἀπαλλάξωμεν αὐτοὺς τῶν κακῶν.

ΙΘ'
Περὶ τοῦ ἀστέρος τοῦ ἀνατείλαντος ἐπὶ τῆς
Χριστοῦ γεννήσεως

*42   Ἀθανασίου Ἀλεξανδρείας

*Τοῦ δὲ Ἰησοῦ γεννηθέντος ἐν Βηθλεὲμ τῆς Ἰουδαίας ἐν
ἡμέραις Ἡρώδου τοῦ βασιλέως, ἰδοὺ μάγοι ἀπὸ ἀνατο-*

---

ont. **42.1/12** locum non inueni; ed. Athan., Fragm. ined., I   1/3 Mt. 2, 1

---

lss. *AT CDEFHK*   **42** *AT CDEFH*

---

it. **ΙΘ'**] ιη' *DFH*   Χριστοῦ] τοῦ *praem. F*

---

rit. **19** οὐ μόνον] *iter. H*   **21** οὐχ'ἡ] οὐχὶ *T CDFH* (οὐχὴ *T*), οὐχη *(sine acc.) A*
ἐλευθερία] ἡ *praem. FH*   **22** ταῦτα βία εἰργάσατο *AT*   **24** δὲ] *om. H*
26 οἰκέτας *T*   **26/27** οὔτε² – μαθηταῖς] *om. T*   **28** ἄρχοντες] ἄρχουσιν *FH*   **29** γινόμενοι *E*   **42.1** δὲ] *om. E*   **1/2** ἐν² – βασιλέως] *om.*
FH   **2** βασιλέως] τὰ ὀνόμ(ατα) τῶν μ(άγων) *A^{in marg.}*

---

omp. **19/20** οὐκ ὀνειδίζομεν] οὐ κολάζομεν αὐτὸν *Chrys.*   **22** ταῦτα εἰργάσατο
Chrys.   **24** ἐγίνετο *Chrys.*   **27/28** οὔτε¹ – παισίν] οὔτε πατέρες παι-
σὶν, οὔτε διδάσκαλοι μαθηταῖς *Chrys.*

86 FLORILEGIVM COISLINIANVM

λῶν παρεγένοντο – ἐκαλεῖτο δὲ ὁ μὲν πρῶτος αὐτῶν
Βαθισαρσαί, ὁ δεύτερος Μελιχιώρ, ὁ δε τρίτος Γαθα-
5 σπᾶ –, ζητοῦντες τὸ ἄληκτον καὶ ἀδιάδοχον φῶς, τὸν ἥλιον τῆς δικαιοσύνης, εἰς Ἱερουσαλὴμ λέγοντες· Ποῦ ἐστὶν
ὁ τεχθεὶς βασιλεὺς τῶν Ἰουδαίων; Οἱ δὲ ἐρωτώμενοι
ἀπεκρίνοντο· Τί γὰρ τοιοῦτον τεκμήριον ἐθεάσασθε ἵνα
ταῦτα φάσκητε; Οἱ δὲ μάγοι· Εἴδομεν αὐτοῦ τὸν ἀστέρα
10 ἐν τῇ ἀνατολῇ καὶ ἤλθομεν προσκυνῆσαι αὐτῷ· οὐ γὰρ
ὑβρίσαι ἢ ἐπιβουλεῦσαι, ἀλλὰ τιμῆσαι καὶ δοξάσαι.
Οἵτινες ἐθεάσαντο ἀστέρα ἐν τῇ ἀνατολῇ, οὐκ αἰσθητὸν
ἢ ἕνα τῶν πολλῶν – οὔτε μὴν ἐξ ἐκείνων τῶν ἄστρων
εἶδον τῶν κατασκευασθέντων ἐν ἀρχῇ τῆς κοσμοποιΐας
15 πρὸς παραμυθίαν τῆς μελαμπέπλου καὶ βαθυσκίου νυ-
κτὸς ἢ πρὸς σημασίαν διαφόρων καιρῶν καὶ χρόνων –,
ἀλλὰ λογικὸν καὶ νοητὸν καὶ τῇ ὁράσει ὄντα καινοπρεπῆ
καὶ ἐπίδοξον, παραμυθούμενον δὲ οὐ βαθύσκιον νύκτα,
ἀλλὰ ποδηγοῦντα ἐσκοτισμένα ἔθνη τῇ δαδουχίᾳ τοῦ
20 φωτὸς εἰς ὁδὸν τῆς θεογνωσίας. Οὔτε δὲ οὗτος ὁ νοητὸς
καὶ λογικὸς ἀστὴρ βεβαιοῖ τὰς φωνὰς τῶν διϊσχυριζο-
μένων ἕκαστον ἄνθρωπον ἔχειν ἀστέρα ἐν τῷ οὐρανῷ.
Καὶ μετὰ ταῦτα. Χειραγωγοῦνται οὖν οἱ μάγοι εἰς ἐπίγνωσιν τοῦ Χριστοῦ παρὰ λογικοῦ καὶ νοητοῦ ἀστέρος
25 κατὰ πολλοὺς τοὺς τρόπους· πρῶτον μέν, διὰ τὸ καὶ τὸν
Ἰσραὴλ ἐξελθόντα ἐκ γῆς Αἰγύπτου ὁδηγηθῆναι ὑπὸ

Font. **5/6** Mal. 3, 20   **6/7** Mt. 2, 1-2   **9/10** Mt. 2, 2   **12** cf. supra l. 9/10
26 cf. Ex. 3, 10. 11, etc.   **26/27** cf. Ex. 13, 21-22

Mss.   *AT CDEFH*

Crit.   **4** βαθισαρσέ *E*^{ut uid.}, βαθησαρσαί *D*   ὁ¹] δὲ *add. F*   τρίτος] γ′ *D*   γα-
θασπά *T E*   **7** τεχθεὶς] γεννηθεὶς *FH*   **8** ἀπεκρίναντο *CDEFH*
τεκμήριον τοιοῦτον *E*   **9** φάσκεται *A*   Εἴδομεν] γὰρ *add. FH*
10 αὐτῷ] αὐτὸν *DFH*   **12** Οἵτινες] οὗτοι μὲν οὖν *E*   **13** ἄστρων]
ἀστέρων *F*   **15** μελαμπέπλου] *scripsi cum E,* μελαμπέλου *AT CFH,* μέλαν
πέλαου *(sic) D*   **16** προσημασίαν *(sic) A*   **18** παραμυθούμενος *AT*
DFH   δὲ] *om. FH*   **19** ποδηγοῦντα] ποδηγοῦν τὰ *A CD,* ποδηγοῦντα
τὰ *EF*   **20** θεογνωσίας] δικαιοσύνης *E*   **20/21** λογικὸς καὶ νοητὸς *FH*
23 μετὰ ταῦτα] μετ'ὀλίγα *T DEFH,* μ(ε)τ(ά) *A*   **24** λογικοῦ] τοῦ *praem. F*
λογικοῦ – νοητοῦ] τοῦ νοητοῦ καὶ λογικοῦ *E*   **25** τοὺς] *om. FH*   διὰ]
καὶ *praem. FH*   **26** γῆς] τῆς *FH*   ὁδηγηθέντα *AT*

ALPHA 42 – 43

τοῦ πυροειδοῦς στύλου· ἔπειτα διὰ τὸ γεγράφθαι ἐν
τοῖς Ἀριθμοῖς· Ἀνατελεῖ ἄστρον ἐξ Ἰακώβ, καὶ ἀναστή-
σεται ἄνθρωπος καὶ θραύσει τοὺς ἀρχηγοὺς Μωάβ, ἤτοι
30 τοὺς δαίμονας τῆς εἰδωλολατρείας· πρὸς τούτοις δέ, ἵνα
καὶ τοῦ Ἡρώδου ταραχθέντος ὅτι ἐγεννήθη ὁ μέλλων
αὐτοῦ καταλύειν τὴν βασιλείαν, οἱ ἀρχιερεῖς καὶ οἱ νο-
μοδιδάσκαλοι καὶ ἄκοντες ὁμολογήσουσι γεννᾶσθαι τὸν
Χριστὸν ἐν Βηθλεὲμ τῆς Ἰουδαίας· οὓς μάγους καλέσας
35 Ἡρώδης, ἐπύθετο παρ'αὐτῶν τὸν χρόνον τοῦ φαινο-
μένου ἀστέρος, εἰπὼν αὐτοῖς· Πορευθέντες, ἀκριβῶς
ἐξετάσετε τὰ περὶ τοῦ παιδίου· ἐπὰν δὲ εὕρητε, ἀπαγ-
γείλατέ μοι, ὅπως κἀγὼ ἐλθὼν προσκυνήσω αὐτῷ.

K'

Περὶ ἀποταξαμένων καὶ πάλιν ἁμαρτανόντων

43   Σολομῶντος

Ὥσπερ κύων ὅταν ἐπέλθῃ ἐπὶ τὸν ἑαυτοῦ ἔμετον καὶ

---

ont. 28/29 Num. 24, 17   31 Mt. 2, 3-4   32/34 cf. Mt. 2, 4-5
34/38 cf. Mt. 2, 4-8   43.1/3 Prou. 26, 11

Ass. AT CDEFH   43 A CDEFH

---

it. K'] ιθ' DFH   Περὶ – ἁμαρτανόντων] cf. Sacr. Par., PG 95, 1171, 27-28
(Περὶ ἀποταξαμένων, καὶ ἐξ ὑποστροφῆς ἐκεῖνα πραττόντων οἷς ἀπετάξαντο)   43 Σολομῶντος] om. H

---

rit. 27 διὰ – γεγράφθαι] διαγεγράφθαι FH   29 ἄνθρωπος] add. ἐξ ἰούδα T, add. ἐξ ἰσραηλ (sine acc.) (cf. Num. 24, 17) D   30 εἰδωλομανίας D
τούτοις δέ] τοῖσδε FH   31/32 αὐτοῦ ὁ μέλλων DEFH   32 αὐτῷ T
33 ὁμολογήσωσι E   34 μάγους] γάμους H   35 Ἡρώδης] ὁ praem. F
36 Πορευθέντες] Πορεύθητη (sic) F   37 ἐξετάσατε T DEF   τὰ] om.
T EF^{p.corr.}   παιδὸς C   38 αὐτῷ] αὐτὸ FH, αὐτὸν A   43 .1 ὅταν] στρα-
φεὶς E   ἐπέλθῃ] om. E, ἔλθη F   ἑαυτοῦ] ἴδιον E   ἐμετὸν (sic acc.) F

---

nd. 43.1/3 = Sacr. Par., PG 95, 1172, 31-33; Ps.-Max., Loc. comm. 25, 4, /4 (p. 557);
Corp. Par. 1, 429

88 FLORILEGIVM COISLINIANVM

μισητὸς γένηται, οὕτως ἄφρων τῇ ἑαυτοῦ κακίᾳ ἀναστρέψας ἐπὶ τὴν ἁμαρτίαν αὐτοῦ.

44 Βασιλείου Καισαρείας

Ὁ ἐν προκοπῇ γενόμενος ἀγαθῶν ἔργων, εἶτα παλινδρομήσας εἰς τὴν ἀρχαίαν συνήθειαν, οὐ μόνον τὸν ἐπὶ τοῖς πεπονημένοις μισθὸν ἐζημιώθη, ἀλλὰ καὶ βαρυτέρας ἀξιοῦται τῆς κατακρίσεως.

45 Τοῦ Χρυσοστόμου

Οἱ γὰρ τῷ ἁγίῳ ἁγίως προσελθεῖν βουληθέντες, ἐὰν μὲν κατορθώσωσιν ἐνταῦθα, μεγάλων καὶ λαμπρῶν στεφάνων τυγχάνουσιν· οἵτινες δὲ προθέμενοι οὐκ ἐτελείωσαν, ἐξαίσιον αὐτοῖς τὸ πτῶμα γενήσεται.

Font.   44.1/4 = Bas. Caes., In ebr., PG 31, 445, 5-9   45.1/4 = Io. Chrys., In euang. dict., PG 64, 39, 58-62   4 cf. Iob 18, 12; 20, 5

Mss.   ACDEFH   44 AT CDEFH   45 AT CDEFH

Tit.   44 Βασιλείου Καισαρείας] τοῦ ἀθα(νασίου) F

Crit.   3 ἁμαρτίαν αὐτοῦ] ἁμαρτίαν τὴν ἑαυτοῦ E, ἑαυτοῦ ἁμαρτίαν FH
44.1 γενάμενος A   45.1 Οἱ] Εἰ (rubricat.) F   ἁγίως] om. C^{a.corr.}   προελθεῖν A   2 μὲν] γὰρ add. H   κατορθώσιν DH (-ῶσιν H), κατορθωθῶσιν (sic acc.) E   3 ἐπιτυγχάνουσιν FH

Comp.   2 αὐτοῦ Sacr. Par.   3 ἁμαρτίαν αὐτοῦ] ἑαυτοῦ ἁμαρτίαν Prou., Loc. comm. et Corp. Par., ἁμαρτίαν Sacr. Par.   44.1 post Ὁ] γὰρ hab. Bas.   2 εἰς] πρὸς Bas., Sacr. Par., Loc. comm. et Corp. Par.   τὸν ἐπὶ] non hab. Sacr. Par.
45.1 βουλόμενοι Chrys.   4 γίνεται Chrys.

Ind.   44.1/4 = Sacr. Par., PG 95, 1173, 32-35; Ps.-Max., Loc. comm. 25, 6, /6 (p. 558); Corp. Par. 1, 40

ALPHA 43 – 47

ΚΑ΄

Περὶ τῆς ἀστάτου τῶν ἀνθρωπίνων πραγμάτων καταστάσεως

46 **Ἰώβ**

Γυμνὸς ἐξῆλθον ἐκ κοιλίας μητρός μου, γυμνὸς καὶ ἀπελεύσομαι ἐκεῖ. Σκιὰ γάρ ἐστιν ὁ βίος ἡμῶν.

47 **Τοῦ Ἐκκλησιαστοῦ**

Ματαιότης ματαιοτήτων, τὰ πάντα ματαιότης. Πᾶσα σὰρξ χόρτος, καὶ πᾶσα δόξα ἀνθρώπου ὡς ἄνθος χόρτου· ἐξηράνθη ὁ χόρτος καὶ τὸ ἄνθος ἐξέπεσε. Οἷα ἐστὶν ἡ ζωὴ ἡμῶν· ἀτμὶς γάρ ἐστιν ἡ πρὸς ὀλίγον
5 φαινομένη, ἔπειτα καὶ ἀφανιζομένη.

Font.   **46.1/2** = Iob 1, 21   **2** = Iob 8, 9   **47.1** = Eccl. 1, 2   **2/3** = Is. 40, 6-7   **4/5** = Iac. 4, 14

Mss.   **46** *AT CDEFHK*   **47** *AT CDEFHK (D* usque ad ἐξέπεσε, 47.3)

Tit.   **ΚΑ΄]** κ΄ *DFH,* λδ΄ *K*   Περὶ – καταστάσεως] *cf. Sacr. Par., PG 95, 1113, 37-41; 1041, 23-26 (*Περὶ τῆς ἀστάτου καὶ ἀβεβαίου τῶν ἀνθρωπίνων πραγμάτων καταστάσεως· καὶ τίνι ἔοικεν ὁ ἄνθρωπος καὶ ὁ βίος αὐτοῦ· καὶ ὅτι μάταια τὰ παρόντα, καὶ σκιᾶς ἀδρανέστερα*)*   τῆς] *om. DEFHK*   ἀνθρωπίνων] ἀνθρώπων *DH*   καταστάσεως] καταστάσεων *C*   **46** Ἰώβ] τοῦ *praem. FH, om. C*   **47** Τοῦ] *om. EH*   Τοῦ Ἐκκλησιαστοῦ] *suppl. ante* Πᾶσα σάρξ *(fr. 47.2)* K, ἐκκλησιαστοῦ *EH*

Crit.   **47.4** ἐστὶν] ἔστιν *K*   ἀτμὶς] ἔστιν *praem. C*   ἡ²] ἤ *F,* ἤ *H*

Comp.   **46.1** *ante* μητρός] τῆς *hab. Sacr. Par.*   **2** *post* ἐκεῖ] Ὁ βίος μου ἐστὶν ἐλαφρότερος λαλιᾶς *(Iob 7, 6) hab. Sacr. Par.*   ὁ βίος ἡμῶν] ἡμῶν ἐπὶ τῆς γῆς ὁ βίος Iob, ὁ βίος ἡμῶν ἐπὶ τῆς γῆς *Sacr. Par.*   **47.2** πᾶσα²] *non hab. Sacr. Par.*   **3** *post* ἄνθος²] αὐτοῦ *hab. Sacr. Par.*   **4** Οἷα ἐστὶν] ποία *Iac., Sacr. Par.*   *post* ἡμῶν] ἐστιν *hab. Sacr. Par.*   ἀτμὴ *Sacr. Par.*   ἐστιν] ἐστε *Iac.*

Ind.   **46.1/2** = Sacr. Par., PG 95, 1113, 47-50   **47.1** = Sacr. Par., PG 95, 1116, 13   **2/3** = Sacr. Par., PG 95, 1116, 31-33   **4/5** = Sacr. Par., PG 95, 1117, 11-12

90 FLORILEGIVM COISLINIANVM

Ἐγὼ Ἐκκλησιαστὴς ἐμεγαλύνθην καὶ προσέθηκα·
ἐγενόμην βασιλεὺς ἐπὶ Ἰσραὴλ ἐν Ἰερουσαλήμ, καὶ
ἔδωκα τὴν καρδίαν μου τοῦ ἐκζητῆσαι καὶ κατασκέψα-
σθαι ἐν τῇ σοφίᾳ περὶ πάντων τῶν γενομένων ὑπὸ τὸν
10 οὐρανόν· ὅτι περισπασμὸν πονηρὸν ἔδωκεν ὁ θεὸς τοῖς
υἱοῖς τῶν ἀνθρώπων τοῦ περισπᾶσθαι ἐν αὐτῷ. Καὶ
εἶδον πάντα τὰ πεποιημένα ὑπὸ τὸν ἥλιον, καὶ ἰδοὺ τὰ
πάντα ματαιότης καὶ προαίρεσις πνεύματος.
Ἰδοὺ ἐγὼ ἐμεγαλύνθην καὶ προσέθηκα σοφίαν ἐπὶ
15 πᾶσιν οἳ ἐγένοντο ἔμπροσθέν μου ἐπὶ Ἰερουσαλήμ. Καὶ
ἔδωκα τὴν καρδίαν μου γνῶναι σοφίαν καὶ γνῶσιν· πα-
ραβολὰς καὶ ἐπιστήμην ἔγνων, ὅτι καί γε τοῦτό ἐστι
προαίρεσις πνεύματος, ὅτι ἐν πλήθει σοφίας πλῆθος
γνώσεως, καὶ ὁ προστιθεὶς γνῶσιν προστίθησιν ἄλγη-
20 μα. Τῷ γέλωτι εἶπα περιφοράν, καὶ τῇ εὐφροσύνῃ· τί
τοῦτο ποιεῖς; Ἐμεγάλυνα ποίημά μου, ᾠκοδόμησά μοι
οἴκους, ἐφύτευσά μοι ἀμπελῶνας, ἐποίησά μοι κή-
πους καὶ παραδείσους καὶ ἐφύτευσα ἐν αὐτοῖς ξύλον
πάγκαρπον· ἐποίησά μοι κολυμβήθρας ὑδάτων τοῦ πο-
25 τίσαι ἀπ᾽αὐτῶν, δρυμῶν βλαστῶν καὶ τὰ ξύλα. Ἐκτη-
σάμην δούλους καὶ παιδίσκας, καὶ οἰκογενεῖς ἐγένοντό
μοι, καί γε κτήσεις βουκολίου καὶ ποιμνίου πολλαὶ ἐγέ-

Font.   6/13 Eccl. 1, 12-14   6 ἐμεγαλύνθην – προσέθηκα = Eccl. 1, 16; 2, 9
        14/20 = Eccl. 1, 16-18   20/21 = Eccl. 2, 2   21/24 = Eccl. 2, 4-8

Mss.   AT CEFHK (EFHK usque ad πνεύματος, 47.13)

Crit.   7 ἐπὶ Ἰσραὴλ] om. FH, ἐν Ἰσραὴλ K   ἐν Ἰερουσαλήμ] om. EK
        9/10 τῶν οὐρανῶν Fp.corr.   10 πονηροῦ C   16 ἔδωκεν C   21 μου
        om. T   27 μοι] om. AC

Comp.   8/9 ante κατασκέψασθαι] τοῦ hab. Eccl.   9 γινομένων Eccl.   11 τοῦ
        ἀνθρώπου Eccl.   Καὶ] non hab. Eccl.   12 post εἶδον] σὺν hab. Eccl.
        post τὰ¹] ποιήματα τὰ hab. Eccl.   14 Ἐγὼ ἰδοὺ Eccl. (S = Coisl.)
        15 ἐπὶ] ἐν Eccl.   post Ἰερουσαλήμ] καὶ καρδία μου εἶδεν πολλά, σοφίαν καὶ
        γνῶσιν hab. Eccl.   16 τὴν] non hab. Eccl.   ante γνῶναι] τοῦ hab. Eccl.
        17 τοῦτ᾽ἔστιν Eccl.   19 προσθήσει Eccl.   24 πάγκαρπον] πᾶν καρποῦ
        Eccl. (πάγκαρπον Procopii Catena in Eccl. ch. 2, 4-8, 3 et alii)   25 δρυμῶν –
        τὰ] δρυμὸν βλαστῶντα Eccl.   27 κτῆσις Eccl.   27/28 πολλαὶ ἐγένον-
        τό] πολλὴ ἐγένετό Eccl.

ALPHA 47 – 48   91

νοντό μοι ὑπὲρ πάντας τοὺς γενομένους ἔμπροσθέν μου
ἐν Ἱερουσαλήμ. Συνήγαγόν μοι καί γε ἀργύριον καί
30 γε χρυσίον καὶ περιουσιασμοὺς βασιλέων καὶ χωρῶν.
Ἐποίησά μοι ᾄδοντας καὶ ᾀδούσας, καὶ ἐντρυφήματα
υἱῶν τοῦ ἀνθρώπου, οἰνοχόους καὶ οἰνοχόας· καὶ πᾶν
ὃ ᾔτησαν οἱ ὀφθαλμοί μου οὐκ ἀφεῖλον ἀπ᾽αὐτῶν, οὐκ
ἀπεκώλυσα τὴν καρδίαν μου ἀπὸ πάσης εὐφροσύνης,
35 ὅτι καρδία μου εὐφράνθη ἐν παντὶ μόχθῳ μου. Καὶ ἐπέ-
βλεψα ἐγὼ ἐν πᾶσι ποιήμασί μου οἷς ἐποίησαν αἱ χεῖρές
μου, καὶ ἐν μόχθῳ ᾧ ἐμόχθησα τοῦ ποιεῖν, καὶ ἰδοὺ τὰ
πάντα ματαιότης καὶ προαίρεσις πνεύματος.

48   Γρηγορίου τοῦ Θεολόγου

Τοιοῦτος ὁ βίος ἡμῶν, ἀδελφοί, τῶν ζώντων πρόσκαι-
ρα· τοῦτο τὸ ἐπὶ γῆς παίγνιον· οὐκ ὄντας γενέσθαι, καὶ
γενομένους ἀναλυθῆναι. Ὄναρ ἐσμὲν οὐχ᾽ἱστάμενον,
φάσμα τι μὴ κρατούμενον, πτῆσις ὀρνέου παρερχομέ-
5 νου, ναῦς ἐπὶ θαλάσσης ἴχνος οὐκ ἔχουσα, κόνις, ἀτμίς,
ἑωθινὴ δρόσος, ἄνθος καιρῷ φυόμενον καὶ καιρῷ λυό-

Font. **32/38** = Eccl. 2, 10-11 **48.1/9** = Greg. Naz., Or. 7, 19, 1-9 **3/4** cf. Iob
20, 8   **4/5** cf. Sap. 5, 11   **5** cf. Sap. 5, 10   **5/6** cf. Os. 13, 3

Mss. *AT C*   **48** *A CEFHK*

Tit. **48** Γρηγορίου τοῦ Θεολόγου] τοῦ θεολόγου *F*, θεολόγου *H*

Crit. **32** πάντα *C*   **35** εὐφράνθην *A*   **38** προαιρέσεως *T*   **48.1** ἡμῶν ὁ
βίος *E*   **2** τοῦτο] τοιοῦτον *EK*   **4/5** παρερχομένη *EK*   **5** ναῦς]
νηὸς *H*   οὐκ] μὴ *EK^{a.corr.}*

Comp. **30** γε] *non hab. Eccl. (BA = Coisl.)*   *ante* χωρῶν] τῶν *hab. Eccl.*   **32** οἰ-
νοχόον *Eccl. (AS^c = Coisl.)*   **33** οὐκ ἀφεῖλον] οὐχ ὑφεῖλον *Eccl. (BS = Coisl.)*
35 *post* μου²] καὶ τοῦτο ἐγένετο μερίς μου ἀπὸ παντὸς μόχθου μου *hab. Eccl.*
48.1/2 τῶν – πρόσκαιρα] *non hab. Sacr. Par.*   **2** τοῦτο] τοιοῦτο *Greg.*,
τοιοῦτον *Sacr. Par.*   ὄντα *Sacr. Par.*

nd. **48.1/9** = Sacr. Par., PG 95, 1124, 14-22

92   FLORILEGIVM COISLINIANVM

μενον. Ἄνθρωπος, ὡσεὶ χόρτος αἱ ἡμέραι αὐτοῦ· ὡσεὶ ἄνθος τοῦ ἀγροῦ, οὕτως ἐξανθήσει, καλῶς ὁ θεῖος Δαυῒδ περὶ τῆς ἀσθενείας ἡμῶν ἐφιλοσόφησεν.

49   Βασιλείου Καισαρείας

Σκόπει δὲ καὶ τὰ τοῦ βίου εἰ μὴ παραπλήσια. Σήμερον τὴν γῆν σὺ ἐγεώργησας, καὶ αὔριον ἄλλος, καὶ μετ'ἐκεῖνον ἕτερος· τοῦ δεῖνος ἐλέγετο, εἶτα νῦν ἄλλου λέγεται. Μακάριος οὖν ὅς ἐπὶ τῆς ὁδοῦ τῶν ἁμαρτωλῶν οὐκ ἔστη.

50   Τοῦ Χρυσοστόμου

Ταράσσεται ἄνθρωπος, καὶ τὸ τέλος ἀπόλλυται. Ταράσσεται, καὶ ὡς μὴ γενόμενος ἀφανίζεται, ὡς πῦρ ἀνα-

---

Font.   7/8 Ps. 102, 15   49.1/4 = Bas. Caes., Hom. super Ps., PG 29, 221, 20-29
    4 Ps. 1, 1   50.1/13 = Ps.-Io. Chrys., Ver. frustr. cont., PG 55, 559, 20-38

Mss.   49 *A CEFHK*   50 *A CEFHK*

Tit.   50 Τοῦ Χρυσοστόμου] *om. EK*

Crit.   7/9 Ἄνθρωπος – ἐφιλοσόφησεν] *om. EFHK*   49.1 καὶ] μοι *F*   τὰ – μὴ]
εἰ μὴ τὰ τοῦ βίου *H*, τὰ τοῦ βίου *F*   3 εἶτα] *om. EFH*   νῦν] *add.* δὲ
EFHK   4 ἔστη] ἔστι *H*   50.1/13 *fr. 50 post fr. 51 trsp. EFHK*

Comp.   9 τῆς] *non hab. Sacr. Par.*   49.1 εἰ μὴ καὶ τὰ τοῦ βίου παραπλήσια *Sacr.*
Par.   1/2 Τὴν γῆν σήμερον *Sacr. Par.*   3 *post* ἕτερος] Ὁρᾷς τοὺς ἀγροὺς
τούτους καὶ τὰς πολυτελεῖς οἰκίας; Πόσα ἤδη (εἴδη *Sacr. Par.*) ὀνόματα (-των
Sacr. Par.) ἀφ'οῦ γέγονε (ἀφ'οῦ γ. *non hab. Sacr. Par.*) τούτων ἕκαστον ἤμειψε (ἤμειψεν; *Sacr. Par.*) *hab. Bas. et Sacr. Par.*   *post* εἶτα] μετωνομάσθη
πρὸς ἕτερον· πρὸς τὸν δεῖνα μετῆλθεν, εἶτα *hab. Bas. et Sacr. Par.*   *post*
λέγεται] Ἄρ' (Ἄρα *Sacr. Par.*) οὖν οὐχ ὁδὸς ἡμῶν (*non hab. Sacr. Par.*) ὁ βίος,
ἄλλοτε ἄλλον (ἄλλου *Sacr. Par.*) μεταλαμβάνων, καὶ πάντας ἔχων ἀλλήλοις
ἐφεπομένους; *hab. Bas. et Sacr. Par.*   50.1 ἄνθρωπος] *non hab. Ps.-Chrys.*
2 καὶ] *non hab. Sacr. Par.*   ὡς μὴ γενόμενος ἀφανίζεται] πρὶν καταστῆναι καταποθεῖται *Ps.-Chrys.*   *post* ἀφανίζεται] ταράσσεται, καὶ πρὶν καταστῆναι καταποντίζεται *hab. Sacr. Par.*

Ind.   49.1/4 = Sacr. Par., PG, 95, 1117, 40-49   50.1/13 = Sacr. Par., PG 95, 1132,
3-25

ALPHA 48 – 51 93

καίεται, καὶ ὡς καλάμη ἀποτεφροῦται· ὡς ἄνθος ὡρα-
ΐζεται, καὶ ὡς χόρτος ξηραίνεται. Αὐτοῦ αἱ ταραχαί,
5 καὶ ἄλλων αἱ τρυφαί· αὐτοῦ οἱ πόνοι, καὶ ἄλλων οἱ θη-
σαυροί· αὐτοῦ αἱ φροντίδες, καὶ ἄλλων αἱ εὐφροσύναι·
αὐτοῦ αἱ θλίψεις, καὶ ἄλλων αἱ ἀπολαύσεις· αὐτοῦ αἱ
ἁρπαγαί, καὶ ἄλλων αἱ ἡδοναί· αὐτοῦ αἱ περιστάσεις,
καὶ ἄλλων αἱ θεραπεῖαι· κατ'αὐτοῦ οἱ στεναγμοί, καὶ
10 παρ'ἑτέροις οἱ πλεονασμοί· κατ'αὐτοῦ τὰ δάκρυα, καὶ
παρ'ἑτέροις τὰ χρήματα· αὐτὸς ἐν Ἅδῃ κολάζεται, καὶ
ἄλλοι πολλάκις ἐν τοῖς αὐτοῦ τρυφῶντες ψάλλουσι.
Πλὴν μάτην <ταράσσεται> πᾶς ἄνθρωπος ζῶν.

51   Γρηγορίου τοῦ Θεολόγου

Τίς βίος, ποία ζωή, εἰ ἐκ τάφου πηδήσας ἐπὶ τάφον

Font.   **13** Ps. 38, 12   **51.1/3** locum non inueni nisi in flor.; cf. Greg. Naz., Carm.
mor., 15, 133-134 (PG 37, 775, 13 – 776, 1)

Mss.   **51** *A CEFHKQ*

Tit.   **51** Γρηγορίου τοῦ Θεολόγου] τοῦ θεολόγου *HQ,* θεολόγου *H, om. CEK*

Crit.   **3** τεφροῦται *FHK*   **4/5** Αὐτοῦ – καὶ¹] *om. H (15 litt. spat.)*   **6** φροντί-
δες] πόνοι *FH*   **9** αἱ θεραπεῖαι] *om. H (10 litt. spat.)*   **9/10** κατ'αὐτοῦ –
πλεονασμοί] *om. F*   **13** Πλὴν – ζῶν] *om. H (20 litt. spat.),* πλὴν μάτην πᾶς
ἄνθρωπος *CEFKQ,* πλὴν μάτην πᾶς ἄνθρωπος ζῶν *AT,* ταράσσεται *scripsi*
cum Psalm., Ps.-Chrys. et Sacr. Par.   **51.1** εἰ] ἢ *C,* ἡ *A*

Comp.   **3** *post* ἀποτεφροῦται] ὡς θύελλα ἐπαίρεται (ὑπεραίρεται *Sacr. Par.),* καὶ ὡς
κόνις ἐδαφίζεται (ἐξαφανίζεται *Sacr. Par.)* ὡς φλὸξ ἀναρριπίζεται, καὶ ὡς
καπνὸς διαλύεται hab. *Ps.-Chrys. et Sacr. Par.*   **4** *post* ξηραίνεται] complura
hab. *Ps.-Chrys.* (l. 25-29) *et Sacr. Par.* (l. 14-20)   **7/8** αὐτοῦ αἱ ἁρπαγαὶ
καὶ ἄλλων αἱ ἡδοναί] *post* θεραπεῖαι hab. *Ps.-Chrys.*   **8** περιστάσεις] κα-
τάραι *Ps.-Chrys., Sacr. Par. et Loci communes*   **9** κατ'αὐτοῦ οἱ στεναγμοί]
παρ'αὐτῷ ὁ στεναγμὸς *Ps.-Chrys.*   **10** κατ'αὐτοῦ] παρ'αὐτῷ *Ps.-Chrys.*
12 πολλάκις] πάλιν *Ps.-Chrys.*   τρυφῶντες ψάλλουσι] ἐντρυφῶσι ψάλ-
λοντες *Ps.-Chrys.*   **13** ζῶν] *non hab. Psalm.*   **51.1** εἰ] *non hab. Sacr. Par.*

Ind.   **7/12** = Sacr. Par., PG 95, 1509, 10-15; Ps-Max., Loc. comm. 7*, 17, ms. F (p. 183)
51.1/3 = Sacr. Par., PG 95, 1125, 3-5

94 FLORILEGIVM COISLINIANVM

πάλιν ὁδεύω, ἐκ δὲ τοῦ τάφου πάλιν ἐν πυρὶ θάπτομαι
ἀποτόμως;

52 Νείλου μοναχοῦ

Θρὶξ λελευκασμένη τὴν ἐντεῦθεν τῆς ψυχῆς ἀποδημί-
αν βοᾷ καὶ διαμαρτύρεται. Ὅθεν κατὰ τὸ γεγραμμένον,
Ἑτοίμαζε εἰς τὴν ἔξοδον τὰ ἔργα σου· θεατέον γὰρ τὴν
χώραν τῆς κεφαλῆς καὶ τοῦ πώγωνος ὅτι λευκή ὑπάρ-
5 χει πρὸς θερισμόν, καὶ μέλλει ὁ δρεπανιστὴς διὰ θανάτου ἐκτέμνειν τὴν ψυχὴν ἐκ τοῦ σώματος, καὶ εἰς ξένους τινὰς καὶ ἀγνοουμένους μετακομίζειν τόπους τῇ
τοῦ Κυρίου διατάξει, μέχρι τῆς κοινῆς ἀναστάσεως.

53 Τοῦ Χρυσοστόμου

Οὐδὲν τῶν ἀνθρωπίνων πραγμάτων σαθρότερον· διὸ
ὅπερ ἂν εἴποι τίς ὄνομα τῆς εὐτελείας αὐτῶν, ἔλαττον

Font. **52.1/8** locum non inueni nisi in flor. **3** Prou. 24, 27 **4/5** Io. 4, 35
53.1/6 = Io. Chrys., In Eutrop., PG 52, 393, 12-18

Mss. *A CEFHKQ* **52** *A CEFHK* **53** *AT CEFHK*

Tit. **52** Νείλου μοναχοῦ] *om. CFH* **53** Τοῦ Χρυσοστόμου] *om. CEK*

Crit. **2** πάλιν[1]] *ante* ἐπὶ *trsp.* H **3** ἀποτόμῳ *EK* **52.1/8** *fr. 52 post fr. 53*
trsp. EFHK **1** λελευκαμμένη *A EK,* λελευκαμένη *C* **3/4** τὴν χώραν]
om. FH **6** ἐκ] ἀπὸ *FH* **7** ἀγνουμένους *H* **53.2** τίς] *sic acc. codd.,*
etsi indefinitum

Comp. **2** ὁδεύω] ὁδεύων *Sacr. Par.* **52.3** εἰς τὴν ἔξοδον] *post* σου *hab. Sacr. Par.*
5 ὁ δρεπανιστὴς] δρεπάνη τις νοητὴ *Sacr. Par.* **6** *post* ψυχὴν] σου *hab.*
Sacr. Par. **7** *post* καὶ] πάμπαν *hab. Sacr. Par.* **8** μέχρι τῆς κοινῆς ἀνα-
στάσεως] *non hab. Sacr. Par.* **53.1** *post* Οὐδὲν] γὰρ *hab. Chrys.* σα-
θρότερον] ἀσθενέστερον *Chrys.* **1/2** διὸ ὅπερ] διόπερ οἷον *Chrys.*

Ind. **52.1/8** = Sacr. Par., PG 95, 1133, 44 – 1136, 2 **1/2** = Ps.-Max., Loc.
comm. 70, 19, /41, 21 (p. 1028) **53.1/6** = Sacr. Par., PG 95, 1128, 30-35

ALPHA 51 – 54

τῆς ἀληθείας ἐρεῖ, κἂν σκιάν, κἂν χόρτον, κἂν ὄναρ,
κἂν ἄνθη ἐαρινά, κἂν εἴ τι οὖν ἕτερον ὀνομάσῃ· οὕτω
5 γὰρ ταχέως ἀφίπταται, οὕτως ἐστὶν ἐπίκηρα καὶ τῶν
οὐδὲν ὄντων οὐδαμινέστερα.

ΚΒ'

Περὶ ἀνθρώπων εὐημερούντων καὶ
ταλαιπωρούντων, δικαίων καὶ ἁμαρτωλῶν

54   Τοῦ Χρυσοστόμου

Τῶν ἀνθρώπων οἱ μὲν ἐνταῦθα τιμωροῦνται μόνον,
οἱ δὲ ἐνταῦθα μὲν οὐδὲν πάσχουσι τοιοῦτον, πᾶσαν δὲ
ἐκεῖ τὴν τιμωρίαν ἀπολαμβάνουσιν, οἱ δὲ καὶ ἐνταῦθα
κἀκεῖ κολάζονται. Ὁ μὲν γὰρ ἐνταῦθα τιμωρίαν διδούς,
5 κουφοτέρας αἰσθάνεται τῆς ἐκεῖ κολάσεως, ὁ δὲ πᾶσαν
ἀναγκαζόμενος ἐκεῖ τὴν κόλασιν ὑπομεῖναι, ἀπαραίτη-
τον ἕξει τὴν δίκην, καθάπερ ὁ πάλαι πλούσιος. Ὅταν
οὖν ἴδῃς ἄνθρωπον ἐν πονηρίᾳ ζῶντα καὶ πολλῆς ἀπο-

Font. **54.1/4** = Io. Chrys., De Laz., PG 48, 997, 51-54   **4/7** = ibid., 997, 61 –
998, 3   **7** cf. Lc. 16, 19-25   **7/12** = Io. Chrys., De Laz., PG 48, 998,
46-51

Mss. *AT CEFHK*   **54** *AT CEFHK*

Tit. **ΚΒ'**] κα' *FH,* λε' *K*   ταλαιπωρουμένων *CEFHK*

Crit. **4** εἰτιοῦν *H,* ὁτιοῦν *F*   **5** ἀφιπτᾶται *(sic acc.) F*   ἐπίκαιρα *AT* (ἐπίκερα
A)   **54.4** κἀκεῖ] καὶ ἐκεὶ *FH*   **5** ἐκεῖ] *post* κουφοτέρας *trsp. F, om.*
EHK   **6** ἀναγκαζόμενος] *post* κόλασιν *trsp. FH*   **7** δίκην] καταδίκην
EK   πάλαι] *om. E*

Comp. **3** κἂν σκιάν] κἂν καπνὸν αὐτὰ *Chrys.,* κἂν καπνὸν κἂν σκιὰν *Sacr. Par.*
4 εἴ – ἕτερον] ὁτιοῦν *Chrys.,* ὁτιοῦν ἕτερον *Sacr. Par.*   **4/5** οὕτω – ἀφίπτα-
ται] *non hab. Chrys. et Sacr. Par.*   **5** οὕτως – ἐπίκηρα] *non hab. Sacr. Par.*
6 οὐδαμινώτερα *Chrys. et Sacr. Par.*   **54.1** *post* Τῶν] γὰρ *hab. Chrys.*
2 τοιοῦτον] δεινὸν *Chrys.*   **4** κἀκεῖ] καὶ ἐκεῖ *Chrys.*   δοὺς *Chrys.*
5 αἰσθήσεται *Chrys.*   **7** ὁ πάλαι] καὶ οὗτος ὁ *Chrys.*   **8** οὖν] *non hab.*
Chrys.   ἐν πονηρίᾳ ζῶντα] πονηρίᾳ συζῶντα *Chrys.*

96 FLORILEGIVM COISLINIANVM

λαύοντα τῆς εὐημερίας καὶ οὐδὲν πάσχοντα δεινόν, διὰ
10 τοῦτο μᾶλλον θρήνησον, ὅτι νοσήματι κατεχόμενος καὶ
σηπεδόνι χαλεπωτάτῃ, τὴν ἀρρωστίαν ἐπιτείνει, διὰ
τῆς τρυφῆς καὶ τῆς ἀνέσεως χείρω γενόμενος. Πάλιν
ἐὰν ἴδῃς δίκαιον θλιβόμενον ἢ τὰ προειρημένα πάσχοντα, μὴ καταπέσῃς· καὶ γὰρ ἐκείνῳ μᾶλλον λαμπροτέ-
15 ρους τοὺς στεφάνους ἐργάζεται τὰ δεινά. Καὶ τιμωρία
δὲ πᾶσα, ἂν μὲν ἐπὶ τῶν ἁμαρτωλῶν γίνηται, ὑποτέμνεται τὸ τῆς πονηρίας φορτίον· ἂν δὲ ἐπὶ τῶν δικαίων,
φαιδροτέραν αὐτῷ ἐργάζεται τὴν ψυχήν, καὶ μέγιστον
ἑκατέροις τὸ κέρδος διὰ τῆς θλίψεως συμβαίνει, μόνον
20 ἐὰν εὐχαρίστως φέρωμεν.

55 Τοῦ αὐτοῦ

Ὅταν ἴδῃς τινὰς ναυαγίῳ περιπεσόντας, ἢ ὑπὸ οἰκίας
καταχωσθέντας, ἢ ἐμπρησμῷ παραπολλυμένους, ἢ ὑπὸ
ποταμῶν παρασυρέντας, ἢ ἑτέρῳ τινὶ τρόπῳ βιαίῳ τὴν
ζωὴν καταλύσαντας, εἶτα ἑτέρους τὰ αὐτὰ αὐτοῖς ἢ καὶ

Font. **12/20** = Io. Chrys., De Laz., PG 48, 1003, 59 – 1004, 6   **55.1/14** = Io.
Chrys., De Laz., PG 48, 1003, 44-59

Mss. **55** *AT CEFHK*

Tit. **55** Τοῦ αὐτοῦ] *om. CEFHK*

Crit. **12** χείρων *K*   **14** ἐκείνῳ] ἐκεῖ *T*   **16** γίνεται *T* *H*^(ut uid.)   **17** πονηρί-
ας] πανουργίας *EK*   **18** αὐτῷ] αὐτῶν *T* *EK*   **55.1** ναυγίῳ *(sic) A*
3 παρασυρρέντας *F*   τρόπῳ τινὶ *FH*   **4** αὐτοῖς] αὐτοὺς *T*

Comp. **12** χείρων γινόμενος *Chrys.*   **13** ἐὰν] ἂν *Chrys.*   *post* προειρημένα]
ἅπαντα *hab. Chrys.*   **14** ἐκείνῳ] κἀκείνῳ *Chrys.*   μᾶλλον] *non hab.*
Chrys.   **15/16** Καὶ – πᾶσα] Καὶ ἁπλῶς πᾶσα κόλασις *in textu Chrys.*,
sed in nota: "Alii δεινά· καὶ γὰρ τιμωρία πᾶσα, ἂν μέν."   **16** τῶν] *non hab.*
Chrys.   **17** πονηρίας] ἁμαρτίας *Chrys.*   τῶν] *non hab. Chrys.*
18 αὐτῷ] αὐτῶν *Chrys.*   **19** διὰ] ἀπὸ *Chrys.*   **55.1** *post* Ὅταν] οὖν *hab.*
Chrys.   *post* τινὰς] ἢ *hab. Chrys.*   **2** ἐμπρησμῷ] ὑπὸ ἐμπρησμοῦ *Chrys.*
3 ἑτέρῳ] ἄλλῳ *Chrys.*   *post* τρόπῳ] τοιούτῳ *hab. Chrys.*

ALPHA 54 – 56

5 τὰ χείρονα ἁμαρτάνοντας καὶ μηδὲν παθόντας τοιοῦτον,
μὴ θορυβηθῇς λέγων· Τί δήποτε τὰ αὐτὰ ἁμαρτάνοντες
οὐ τὰ αὐτὰ πεπόνθασιν; Ἀλλ᾽ἐκεῖνο λογίζου, ὅτι τὸν μὲν
εἴασεν ἀναιρεθῆναι ἢ ἀποπνιγῆναι, ἡμερωτέραν αὐτῷ
παρασκευάζων τὴν ἐκεῖ τιμωρίαν, ἢ καὶ τέλεον αὐτὸν
10 ἀπαλλάττων· τὸν δὲ οὐδὲν τοιοῦτον ἀφῆκε παθεῖν, ἵνα
τῇ τούτου τιμωρίᾳ σωφρονισθείς, ἐπιεικέστερος γένηται, ἂν δὲ ἐπιμείνῃ τοῖς αὐτοῖς, ἀπαραμύθητον ἑαυτῷ
παρὰ τῆς ἑαυτοῦ ῥαθυμίας σωρεύσει τὴν τιμωρίαν· καὶ
ὁ θεὸς οὐκ αἴτιος τῆς αὐτοῦ κολάσεως.

56   Τοῦ αὐτοῦ

Ἐπὶ τῶν νοσημάτων τῶν ἐπὶ τὰ σώματα, οὐκ ἐκείνους
θρηνοῦμεν τοὺς θεραπευομένους, ἀλλ᾽ἐκείνους τοὺς τὰ
ἀνίατα νοσοῦντας. Ὅπερ οὖν ἐστι νόσος καὶ τραῦμα,
τοῦτό ἐστιν ἁμαρτία· ὅπερ ἐστὶ τομὴ καὶ φάρμακον,
5 τοῦτό ἐστι τιμωρία. Συνήκατε τί λέγω; Προσέχετε·
φιλόσοφον γὰρ ὑμᾶς παιδεῦσαι βούλομαι λόγον. Διὰ
τί τοὺς κολαζομένους θρηνοῦμεν, ἀλλὰ μὴ τοὺς ἁμαρτάνοντας; Οὐ γὰρ οὕτω χαλεπὸν κόλασις, ὡς χαλεπὸν
ἁμαρτία. Ἐὰν τοίνυν ἴδῃς τινὰ σηπεδόνα ἔχοντα, καὶ

ont.   **56.1/22** = Io. Chrys., De Laz., PG 48, 1030, 27-54

Ass.   *AT CEFHK (D* inde a παθόντας, 55.5)   **56** *AT CDEFHK*

Crit.   **5** τὰ] *om. EFHK*   ἁμαρτόντας *EK* (ἁμαρτῶντας *E*)   καὶ] *om. F*
τοιοῦτο *A C*   **9** ἐκεῖ τὴν *T*   **10** ἀπαλλάττων] ταύτης *add. EK*
11 σωφρισθῇς *(sic) H*   **56.1** τὰ σώματα] τοῦ σώματος *FH*   **4** τομὴ] τὸ
μη *(sic) D*   **8** κόλασις] ἡ *praem. DEFHK*   **9** τοίνυν] οὖν *EK, om. FH*
σηπεδόνας *EK*

Comp.   **7** Ἀλλ᾽ἐκεῖνο] ἀλλὰ τοῦτο *Chrys.*   **8** ἢ] καὶ *Chrys.*   **10** τὸν] τοῦτον
Chrys.   ἀφῆκε τοιοῦτον *Chrys.*   **12** ἐπιμένῃ *Chrys.*   **13** τῆς] τοῖς
Chrys.   **14** αὐτοῦ] ἀφορήτου *Chrys.*   **56.1** τῶν ἐπὶ τὰ σώματα] καὶ τῶν
τραυμάτων *Chrys.*   **2** ἀλλ᾽] ἀλλὰ *Chrys.*   **3** οὖν] *non hab. Chrys.*
4 *post* ἐστιν] καὶ *hab. Chrys.*   **5** *post* ἐστι] καὶ *hab. Chrys.*   **6** βούλομαι
παιδεῦσαι *Chrys.*   **7** ἀλλὰ μὴ] ἀλλ᾽οὐ *Chrys.*   **9** ἁμαρτία] ἡ ἁμαρτία·
τῆς γὰρ κολάσεως ὑπόθεσις ἡ ἁμαρτία *Chrys.*

98 FLORILEGIVM COISLINIANVM

10 σκώληκας καὶ ἰχῶρα περὶ τὸ σῶμα αὐτοῦ κατερχό-
μενον, καὶ ἀμελοῦντα τοῦ ἕλκους καὶ τῆς σηπεδόνος,
ἕτερον δὲ τὰ αὐτὰ πάσχοντα ἰατρικῶν ἀπολαύοντα χειρῶν, καιόμενον, τεμνόμενον, πικρὰ ὑπομένοντα φάρ-
μακα, τίνα θρηνεῖς; Τὸν νοσοῦντα καὶ μὴ θεραπευόμε-
15 νον, εὔδηλον. Οὕτως ἔστωσαν δύο ἁμαρτωλοί, ὁ μὲν
κολαζόμενος, ὁ δὲ μὴ κολαζόμενος. Μὴ λέγε· Μακάριος
ἐκεῖνος· πλουτεῖ, ὀρφανοὺς ἀποδύει, χήρας βιάζεται·
καὶ τί οὐδὲ νοσεῖ, ἀλλὰ ἁρπάζων εὐδοκιμεῖ, ἀπολαύει
τιμῆς δυναστείας πολλῆς, οὐδὲ τὰ ἀνθρώπινα ὑπομέ-
20 νει, πυρετὸν οὐχ᾽ὑπέμεινεν, εἰς γῆρας ἦλθε μακρὸν καὶ
λιπαρόν, παιδίων χορὸς περὶ αὐτόν; Αὐτὸν θρήνει μᾶλλον, ὅτι καὶ νοσεῖ καὶ οὐ θεραπεύεται· δύο γὰρ κακά,
καὶ νόσος καὶ ἀθεράπευτον. Ὅπερ γάρ ἐστι τὸ φάρμα-

Font. 22/23 = Io. Chrys., De Laz., PG 48, 1031, 31-32 (cf. infra l. 39/40)
23/43 = Io. Chrys., De Laz., PG 48, 1031, 13-35

Mss. *AT CDEFHK*

Crit. **10** ἰχώρας *T,* ἰχῶρι *EK*   περὶ] παρὰ *D, om. EK*   αὐτοῦ] *add.* ἅπαν *EK*
10/11 κατεχόμενον *CDEFHK*   **12** ἀπολάβοντα *K*   **13** τεμνόμενον·
καιόμενον *AT*   πικρὰ] μικρὰ *DEFHK*   **13/14** φάρμακα] *add.* τραύματα *AT*   **14** Τὸν] οὐ *praem. EK*   **14/15** θεραπευόμενον] ἢ τὸν νοσοῦντα
καὶ θεραπευόμενον *add. T*   **15** εὔδηλον] ὅτι τὸν μὴ θεραπευόμενον *add. T*
(μὴ *om. a. corr.*)   Οὕτως] ὄντως *EK*   δύο] β' *H*   **18** ἀλλὰ] ἀλλ' *DE*
ἀπολάβει *K*   **19** οὐδὲ – ἀνθρώπινα] οὐδέν τι τῶν ἀνθρωπίνων κακῶν *FH*
20 πυρετὸν οὐχ᾽ὑπέμεινεν] *om. FH*   **21** παίδων *FH*   αὐτόν] αὐτῶν *D*
23 ἀθεράπευτον] τὸ *praem. EK*   γάρ] *om. FH*

Comp. **10** ἰχῶρας *Chrys.*   **10/11** περὶ – κατερχόμενον] ἀπὸ τοῦ σώματος κατερ-
χομένους *Chrys.*   **13** *ante* τεμνόμενον] καὶ *hab. Chrys.*   *ante* πικρὰ] καὶ
hab. Chrys.   ὑπομένοντα] πίνοντα *Chrys.*   **14** θρηνεῖς] θρηνήσεις; εἰπέ
μοι· τὸν νοσοῦντα, καὶ μὴ θεραπευόμενον, ἢ τὸν νοσοῦντα, καὶ θεραπευόμενον; Δῆλον ὅτι *Chrys.*   **15** εὔδηλον] *non hab. Chrys.*   **17** ἐκεῖνος] οὗτος,
ὅτι *Chrys.*   **18** καὶ τί οὐδὲ] Καίτοι οὐ *Chrys.*   **18/19** ἀπολαύει – πολλῆς]
τιμῆς ἀπολαύει καὶ δυναστείας *Chrys.*   **19** οὐδὲ τὰ ἀνθρώπινα] οὐδὲν τῶν
ἀνθρωπίνων *Chrys.*   **20/21** πυρετὸν – αὐτόν] οὐ πυρετόν, οὐ κάκωσιν,
οὐκ ἄλλην τινὰ νόσον· παίδων χορὸς περὶ αὐτόν, γῆρας λιπαρόν *Chrys.*
21/22 Αὐτὸν θρήνει μᾶλλον] ἀλλὰ τοῦτον μάλιστα θρήνει *Chrys.*   **23** ἀθε-
ράπευτον] τὸ ἀνίατον *Chrys.*

ALPHA 56

κον τὸ πικρὸν τὸ παρὰ τοῦ ἰατροῦ, καὶ ἡ τομή, καὶ τὸ
25 πῦρ, τοῦτό ἐστιν ἡ τιμωρία ἡ παρὰ τοῦ θεοῦ. Ὥσπερ τὸ
πῦρ πολλάκις ἐπέρχεται καῖον, καὶ τὴν νομὴν κωλύει,
καὶ τὸ σιδήριον ἀφαιρεῖ τὴν σηπεδόνα, οὕτω καὶ τιμωρία, καὶ λοιμός, καὶ λιμός, καὶ ὅσα τοιαῦτα δοκοῦντα
εἶναι δεινά, ἀντὶ σιδήρου καὶ πυρὸς ἐπάγεται τῇ ψυχῇ,
30 ἵνα τὴν νομὴν τῶν νοσημάτων κωλύσῃ, καὶ βελτίονα
ἐργάσηται. Ἔστωσαν οὖν δύο πόρνοι, καὶ ὑποκείσθω
τῷ λόγῳ ἡ εἰκών· οἱ δύο πόρνοι, ὁ μὲν πλούσιος, ὁ δὲ
πένης. Τίς μᾶλλον ἐλπίδα σωτηρίας ἔχει; Ὡμολόγηται
ὅτι ὁ πένης. Μὴ τοίνυν ἴδῃς ὅτι πορνεύει καὶ πλουτεῖ,
35 καὶ διατοῦτο μακαρίσεις αὐτόν; Μᾶλλον γὰρ ἔδει σε
μακαρίζειν αὐτὸν εἰ πορνεύων ἐπένετο, εἰ πορνεύων
ἐλίμωττεν· εἶχε γὰρ διδάσκαλον κατηναγκασμένον
τῆς φιλοσοφίας τὴν πενίαν. Ὅταν οὖν ἴδῃς κακὸν ἄνθρωπον εὐημεροῦντα, δάκρυε· δύο γὰρ κακά, καὶ νόσος
40 καὶ ἀνίατον. Ὅταν δὲ ἴδῃς κακὸν ἄνθρωπον ἐν συμφο-

Mss.   *AT CDEFHK*

Crit.   **24** τὸ²] τοῦ *Aᵃ·ᶜᵒʳʳ·*   τοῖς ἰατροῖς *FH*   **25** τουτέστιν *(sic acc.) F*   τοῦ]
om. H   Ὥσπερ] γὰρ *add. FH*   **27** σίδηρον *T*   ἀφαιρεῖται *FH*
28 λιμὸς καὶ λοιμὸς *T (καὶ λιμὸς a. corr.)*   **28/29** δοκοῦντα – δεινά] κακὰ
εἶναι *FH,* δοκοῦντα εἶναι κακὰ *DEK*   **30/31** βελτίονα ἐργάσηται] βέλτιον ἀπεργάσηται *E*   **31/32** καὶ – πόρνοι] *om. T*   **31** ὑποκείσθωσαν *H*
32 τῆς εἰκόνος *FH*   **34** πένης] πόρνος *Fᵃ·ᶜᵒʳʳ·*   ἴδῃς] τὸν πρότερον *add. EK*   ὅτι²] ὁ πλούσιος *add. FH*   **35** μακαρίσῃς *DEFᵃ·ᶜᵒʳʳ·H*
39 νόσσος *D*   **40** ἀνίατον] τὸ *praem. EK*   κακὸν] καλὸν *EK*

Comp.   **24** πικρὸν τὸ] *non hab. Chrys.*   **25** *post* Ὥσπερ] γὰρ *hab. Chrys.*
26 ἐπέρχεται καῖον] ἐπαγόμενον καίει *Chrys.*   **27** ἀφαιρεῖται *Chrys.*
post σηπεδόνα] ἔχον μὲν ὀδύνην, παρέχον δὲ ὠφέλειαν *hab. Chrys.*
27/28 τιμωρία – λιμός] λιμὸς καὶ λοιμοὶ *Chrys.*   **28** τοιαῦτα] κακὰ *Chrys.*
29 δεινά] *non hab. Chrys.*   ἐπάγονται *Chrys.*   **30** *post* νοσημάτων] κατὰ
τὴν εἰκόνα τῶν σωμάτων *hab. Chrys.*   **31** Ἔστωσαν οὖν] Πάλιν ἔστωσαν
Chrys.   **32** οἱ] *non hab. Chrys.*   *ante* οἱ] ἀλλ' *hab. Chrys.*   **33** ἐλπί-
δας *Chrys.*   **34** ὅτι¹] δηλονότι *Chrys.*   ἴδῃς] εἴπῃς *Chrys.*   *post* ὅτι²]
ὁ πλούσιος *hab. Chrys.*   **35** μακαρίζω *Chrys.*   γὰρ] *non hab. Chrys.*
38 οὖν] *non hab. Chrys.*   **38/39** ἄνθρωπον] *non hab. Chrys.*   **39** δάκρυ-
σον *Chrys.*   **40** *ante* ἀνίατον] τὸ *hab. Chrys.*   δὲ] *non hab. Chrys.*
ἄνθρωπον] *non hab. Chrys.*   **40/41** *post* συμφοραῖς] ὄντα *hab. Chrys.*

100 FLORILEGIVM COISLINIANVM

ραῖς, τότε παραμυθοῦ, οὐ διὰ τοῦτο μόνον ὅτι βελτίων γίνεται, ἀλλ'ὅτι πολλὰ τῶν ἁμαρτημάτων αὐτοῦ καὶ ἐνταῦθα διαλύεται.

57   Τοῦ αὐτοῦ

Τῶν ἀνθρώπων ἁπάντων οἱ μὲν εἰσὶν ἁμαρτωλοί, οἱ δὲ δίκαιοι. Πάλιν ἐν τοῖς δικαίοις πολλὴ ἡ διαφορά· ὁ μὲν γὰρ δίκαιος, ὁ δὲ ἐπὶ πλεῖον δίκαιος, ὁ δὲ ὑψηλότερος, ὁ δὲ μείζων. Τῶν ἀνθρώπων τοίνυν οἱ μὲν εἰσὶ δίκαι-
5 οι, οἱ δὲ ἁμαρτωλοί. Ἀλλὰ καὶ ἐν τοῖς ἁμαρτωλοῖς καὶ ἐν τοῖς δικαίοις πολλὴ ἡ διαφορά, πολλὴ καὶ ἄπειρος. Ἀλλὰ προσέχετε· κἂν οὖν δίκαιός τις οὕτως εὑρίσκοιτο, κἂν μυριάκις ἐστὶ δίκαιος, ἀλλ'ἄνθρωπός ἐστι. Τίς γὰρ καυχήσεται ἀγνὴν ἔχειν τὴν καρδίαν; Ἢ τίς παρ-
10 ρησιάσεται καθαρὸς εἶναι ἀπὸ ἁμαρτίας; Ἀμήχανον τοίνυν εἶναι ἄνθρωπόν τινα ἀναμάρτητον. Τί γὰρ λέγεις; Δίκαιος ἐστίν, ἐλεήμων ἐστί, φιλόπτωχος ἐστίν;

Font.   **57.1/10** = Io. Chrys., De Laz., PG 48, 1041, 9-18   **8/10** Prou. 20, 9
       10/44 = Io. Chrys., De Laz., PG 48, 1041, 39 – 1042, 27

Mss.   **57** *AT CDEFHKQ*

Tit.   **57** Τοῦ αὐτοῦ] *om. H,* τοῦ χρυσοστόμου *CQ*

Crit.   **41** βελτίον *TD,* βέλτιον *E*   **42** ὅτι] καὶ *add. FH*   πολλὰ] τὰ *praem. EK,*
κ*αὶ praem. FH*   **57.1** ἁπάντων] *om. FH*   **2** ἐν] *om. Q*   **4/6** Τῶν –
δικαίοις] ὁμοίως καὶ ἐπὶ τῶν ἁμαρτωλῶν. *Q*   **6** πολλὴ¹ – διαφορά] *post*
ἁμαρτωλοῖς *(l. 5) trsp. E*   πολλὴ¹] πολλοὶ *H*   **7** Ἀλλὰ προσέχετε]
om. DEFHKQ   οὕτως *om. T*   **7/8** κἂν – εὑρίσκοιτο] *om. A*
7/8 οὕτως – δίκαιος] μυριάκις ἐστὶν *Q*   **8** ἀλλὰ *DEFHK*   **10** ἁμαρ-
τίας] ῥύπου *praem. Q*   **11** ἄνθρωπόν – ἀναμάρτητον] τινὰ ἄνθρωπο
ἀναμάρτητον *FH,* ἄνθρωπον ἀναμάρτητον τινά *Q*

Comp.   **41** τότε] *non hab. Chrys.*   οὐ] μὴ *Chrys.*   **42** καὶ] *non hab. Chrys.*
57.1/6 Τῶν – ἄπειρος] Τῶν ἀνθρώπων τοίνυν οἱ μὲν εἰσὶ δίκαιοι, οἱ δὲ ἁμαρ-
τωλοί· ἀλλὰ καὶ ἐν τοῖς δικαίοις πολλὴ διαφορά, καὶ ἐν τοῖς ἁμαρτωλοῖς
πολλὴ καὶ ἄπειρος *Chrys.*   **7** πρόσεχε *Chrys.*   κἂν οὖν] Εἰ καὶ *Chrys.*
post δίκαιός] ᾖ *hab. Chrys.*   **7/8** οὕτως εὑρίσκοιτο] *non hab. Chrys.*
8 ἐστὶ] ᾖ *Chrys.*   *post* δίκαιος] complura *hab. Chrys. (l. 13-15)*

ALPHA 56 – 57 101

Ἀλλ'ἔχει τί ἐλάττωμα· ἢ ὑβρίζει ἀκαίρως, ἢ κενοδοξεῖ,
ἢ ἄλλό τι τοιοῦτον ποιεῖ· οὐ γὰρ δεῖ πάντα καταλέγειν.
15 Ὁ μὲν ἐλεήμων, ἀλλ'οὐ σώφρων· πολλάκις σώφρων,
ἀλλ'οὐκ ἐλεήμων· ὁ μὲν ἐν ταύτῃ τῇ ἀρετῇ, ὁ δὲ ἐν ἄλλῃ
ὀνομάζεται. Ἔστω δέ τις καὶ δίκαιος, καὶ πολλάκις μὲν
δίκαιός ἐστι, καὶ ἔχει πάντα τὰ ἀγαθά, ἔσχε δὲ καὶ ἀπό-
νοιαν διὰ τὴν δικαιοσύνην, καὶ ἐλυμήνατο αὐτοῦ τὴν
20 δικαιοσύνην ἡ ἀπόνοια, καθάπερ ἐπὶ τοῦ Φαρισαίου
ἀκούομεν. Οὐκ ἔστιν οὖν ἄνθρωπον καθόλου οὕτως εἶναι δίκαιον ὡς καθαρὸν εἶναι ἀπὸ ἁμαρτίας, καὶ πάλιν
οὐκ ἔστιν ἄνθρωπον οὐδένα καὶ θαρρῶ καὶ λέγω οὕτως
εἶναι κακόν, ὡς μὴ ἔχειν μικρόν τι ἀγαθόν, οἷον· ὁ δεῖνα
25 ἁρπάζει, λυμαίνεται, πλεονεκτεῖ, ἀλλ'ἐνίοτε ἐλεημοσύνην δίδωσιν, ἢ σώφρων ἐστίν, ἢ λόγον ἔχει χρηστόν,
ἢ κἂν ἑνί τινι ἐβοήθησεν. Οὔτε οὖν δίκαιός ἐστι χωρὶς
ἁμαρτίας, οὔτε ἐστὶν ἁμαρτωλὸς χωρὶς δικαιοσύνης ἢ

Font. 20/21 cf. Lc. 18, 10-14

Mss. AT CDEFHKQ

Crit. 13 τί] sic acc. codd., etsi indefinitum   ἀκαίρρος (sic) D   14 δεῖ] δὴ AT
CFH   15/16 ἀλλ' – ἐλεήμων] om. T   16 μὲν] δὲ T   17 καὶ¹]
om. FH   17/18 μὲν – ἐστι] om. Q   18 ἐστι] om. FH   ἔχει] om.
F   καὶ²] om. F   19 δικαιοσύνην] ἐλεημοσύνην FHQ   20 δικαιο-
σύνην] ἐλεημοσύνην· ἐλυμήνατο αὐτοῦ τὴν δικαιοσύνην FH   καθώσπερ
AT   21 ἀκούομεν] καὶ πιστεύομεν add. FH   21/22 Οὐκ – ἁμαρτί-
ας] om. Q   22 εἶναι²] om. E   23 θαρρῶ – λέγω] θαρρῶν καὶ λέγων K
24 μικρόν – ἀγαθόν] τί μικρὸν ἀγαθόν FHQ, τί ἀγαθὸν μικρόν K   ὁ δεῖνα]
om. FH   27 κἂν ἑνί] καὶ πένητι T   28 ἐστίν] om. E, ἔστιν KQ   δι-
καιοσύνης] τινὸς praem. Q   ἢ] καὶ Q

Comp. 15 σώφρων – σώφρων] σώφρων πολλάκις· ὁ δὲ σώφρων μὲν Chrys.
16 ἄλλῃ] ἐκείνῃ Chrys.   17 ὀνομάζεται] post ἀρετῇ hab. Chrys.   δέ –
καὶ¹] τις Chrys.   18 ἔσχε – καὶ²] καὶ ἔσχεν Chrys.   19 αὐτοῦ] αὐτῷ Chrys.
20/21 καθάπερ – ἀκούομεν] loco horum verborum complura hab. Chrys. (l. 50-
55)   21 ἔστιν οὖν] ἐστὶ γοῦν Chrys.   23/24 καὶ¹ – κακόν] κακὸν εἶναι Chrys.   24 μικρόν τι] τι κἂν μικρὸν Chrys.   post οἷον] τι λέγω hab.
Chrys.   25 λυμαίνεται πλεονεκτεῖ] καὶ πλεονεκτεῖ καὶ λυμαίνεται Chrys.
26 ἢ¹] ἀλλ'ἐνίοτε Chrys.   ἢ²] ἀλλ'ἐνίοτε Chrys.   27 ἢ] ἀλλ'ἐνίοτε Chrys.
τινι] ἀνδρὶ Chrys.   post ἐβοήθησεν] ἀλλ'ἐνίοτε ἔκλαυσεν, ἀλλ'ἐνίοτε ἐστύ-
γνασεν hab. Chrys.   28 χωρὶς – ἢ] non hab. Chrys.

102 FLORILEGIVM COISLINIANVM

καθόλου ἔρημος ἀγαθοῦ. Τί τοῦ Ἀχαὰβ χαλεπώτερον;
30 Ἥρπασε καὶ ἐφόνευσεν, ἀλλ'ὅμως ἐπειδὴ ἤκουσε τοῦ
θεοῦ καὶ ἐστύγνασε, λέγει τῷ Ἡλίᾳ ὁ θεός· Εἶδες πῶς
κατενύγη Ἀχαάβ; Τί τοῦ Ἰούδα χεῖρον τοῦ προδότου;
Ἀλλ'ὅμως καὶ αὐτὸς ἐποίησέ τι ἀγαθὸν μικρόν. Ἥμαρ-
τον γάρ φησιν παραδοὺς αἷμα ἀθῶον. Ὅπερ οὖν ἔφην·
35 οὔτε ἀγαθός τις οὕτως ἐστὶν ὡς μὴ ἔχειν μικρὰν κη-
λῖδα, οὔτε πονηρός τις οὕτως ὡς μὴ ἔχειν κἂν μικρὸν
ἀγαθόν.

Ἐπεὶ οὖν πάντων ἐστὶν ἀντίδοσις, καὶ πάντων ἐστὶν
ἀμοιβή, κἂν φονεύσῃ τίς, κἂν πορνεύσῃ, κἂν πλεονε-
40 κτήσῃ, ποιήσει δέ τι καλόν, μένει αὐτῷ τοῦ καλοῦ ἡ
ἀντίδοσις· οὐδὲ γὰρ διὰ τὰ κακὰ ἃ ἐποίησεν ἄμισθον γίνεται τὸ καλόν. Καὶ πάλιν, κἂν μυρία ἐργάζηται ἀγαθὰ
τίς, ποιήσει δέ τι φαῦλον μικρόν, μένει αὐτῷ τοῦ φαύ-
λου ἡ ἀντίδοσις. Τί οὖν γίνεται; Ὁ ἁμαρτωλὸς ἀπολαμ-

Font. 29 cf. III Reg., 16, 29-34   31/32 cf. III Reg., 20, 28-29   33/34 Mt. 27, 4
44/83 = Io. Chrys., De Laz., PG 48, 1042, 51 – 1044, 15

Mss. *AT CDEFHKQ*

Crit. 31 καὶ] *om. DEKQ*   λέγει] οὖν *add. K*   πῶς] *om. CDFHQ*   32 κα-
τηνύγη *AT (-ει A)*   33 καὶ αὐτὸς] *post* τι *trsp. DEFHK, post* ἐποίησέ
trsp. Q   ἀγαθὸν τι *Q*   34/37 Ὅπερ – ἀγαθόν] *om. Q*   36 κἂν]
om. EFH   39 ἀμοιβή] ἀμειβῆ *F*   φονεύσῃ – πορνεύσῃ] μοιχεύσῃ – φονεύσῃ *F^{p.corr.}H* (φονεύσῃ – μοιχεύσῃ *F^{a.corr.}*)   40 ποιήσῃ *E*   αὐτῷ] οὕτω
F^{a.corr.}H (τούτω *F^{p.corr.}*)   ἡ] *ante* τοῦ *trsp. FH*   41 οὐδὲ] οὐ *EFHKQ*
43 ποιήσῃ *F*   44 ἡ] *ante* τοῦ *trsp. FH*

Comp. 30/31 ἤκουσε – καὶ] *non hab. Chrys.*   32 *post* Ἀχαάβ] εἶδες ἐν τοσούτῳ
βυθῷ κακῶν πῶς εὑρέθη τι μικρὸν ἀγαθόν *hab. Chrys.*   τοῦ¹] *non hab.
Chrys.*   *post* προδότου] τοῦ αἰχμαλωτισθέντος ὑπὸ τῆς φιλαργυρίας *hab.
Chrys.*   33 τι – μικρόν] κἂν μικρόν τι μετὰ ταῦτα ἀγαθόν *Chrys.*
34 *post* ἀθῶον] *complura hab. Chrys. (l. 9-18)*   ἔφην] εἶπον *Chrys.*   36 *post*
οὕτως] ἐστὶν *hab. Chrys.*   38 ἀντίδοσίς ἐστι *Chrys.*   39 *post* κἂν¹] γὰρ
hab. Chrys.   39/40 φονεύσῃ – πλεονεκτήσῃ] φονεὺς ᾖ τις, κἂν πονηρός
τις ᾖ, κἂν πλεονέκτης *Chrys. (Vatic. = Coisl.)*   40 ποιήσῃ *Chrys.*   τι]
non hab. Chrys.   41 ἀνταπόδοσις *Chrys.*   οὐδὲ γὰρ] καὶ οὐ *Chrys.*
43 τίς] *post* μυρία *hab. Chrys. (τις)*   ποιήσῃ *Chrys.*   μικρόν] *non hab.
Chrys.*   44 ἀνταπόδοσις *Chrys.*   οὖν] *non hab. Chrys.*

ALPHA 57

45 βάνει τῶν ἀγαθῶν αὐτοῦ τὸ ἰσόρροπον, τὴν ἀντίδοσιν,
ἐάν τι ἔχῃ ἀγαθὸν μικρόν, καὶ ὁ δίκαιος τῆς ἁμαρτίας
αὐτοῦ ἀπολαμβάνει τὸ ἰσόρροπον κἂν μικρόν τι ποιήσῃ
κακόν. Τί οὖν ποιεῖ ὁ θεός; Δύο ὥρισε, νόσον καὶ ἁμαρτίαν, βίον καὶ τὸν μέλλοντα αἰῶνα. Ἐὰν οὖν ᾖ τίς δί-
50 καιος, καὶ ἐργάσηταί τι φαῦλον, καὶ νοσήσῃ ὧδε, καὶ
τῇ ἁμαρτίᾳ παραδοθῇ, μὴ θορυβηθῇς, ἀλλ’ἐννόησον
καθ’ἑαυτὸν καὶ εἰπὲ ὅτι οὗτος ὁ δίκαιος πάντως κακὸν
ἐποίησέ τι μικρόν, καὶ ἀπολαμβάνει ὧδε, ἵνα ἐκεῖ μὴ
κολασθῇ. Πάλιν ἐὰν ἴδῃς ἁμαρτωλὸν ἁρπάζοντα, πλεο-
55 νεκτοῦντα, μυρία ποιοῦντα κακά, καὶ εὐθηνούμενον, μὴ
θορυβηθῇς, ἀλλ’εἰπέ· οὗτος ὁ ἁμαρτωλὸς ὁ μυρία κακὰ
ποιῶν, τί ποτε ἐποίησεν ἀγαθόν, καὶ ἀπολαμβάνει ὧδε
τὸ ἀγαθόν, ἵνα μὴ ἐκεῖ ἀπαιτήσῃ τὸν μισθόν. Οὕτως οὖν
κἂν δίκαιος τίς ἐστι καὶ πάσχει τί δεινόν, διὰ τοῦτο ἀπο-
60 λαμβάνει ὧδε, ἵνα τὴν ἁμαρτίαν ἀποθῆται καὶ ἀπέλθῃ
ἐκεῖ καθαρός· κἂν ἁμαρτωλός τις ᾖ, γέμων κακῶν καὶ

Mss. *AT CDEFHKQ*

Crit. **45/47** τῶν– ἀπολαμβάνει] *om. A*   **45/47** τὸ – ἀπολαμβάνει] *om. T D*
45 τὸ] *om. EK*   **47** κἂν] καὶ *Q*   ποιήσας *Q*   **48/49** ἁμαρτίαν]
τιμωρίαν *FH*   **49** τίς] *sic acc. codd., etsi indefinitum*   **51** ἁμαρτίᾳ] παι-
δεία *T*   **53** μὴ ἐκεῖ *EK*   **55** εὐθυνούμενον *DEHKQ*   **56** μυρία]
om. DEKQ   **56/57** κακὰ ποιῶν] κακοποιῶν *CDEFHKQ*   **57/58** καὶ –
ἀγαθόν] *om. A*   **58** τὸ ἀγαθόν] τὸν μισθὸν *FH*   ἐκεῖθεν *FH*
58/64 Οὕτως – μισθόν] *om. Q*   οὖν] *om. FH*   **59** κἂν] καὶ *C* τίς] *sic
acc. codd., etsi indefinitum*   πάσχῃ *T EF* τί] *sic acc. codd., etsi indefinitum*
59/60 ἀπολαμβάνει] ἀπολαύει *E*   **60** ἀποθεῖται *A*, ἀπωθῆται *C*, ἀπο-
θηται *(sine acc.) D*, ἀπώθηται *EF*, ἀπόθηται *HK*   **60/61** καὶ – καθαρός]
καὶ ἀπελθῶν *(sic acc.)* κάθηται *A*, ἐκεῖ κάθηται ἐλεύθερος πάσης ἁμαρτίας *T*
61 γέμων] μυρίων *add. T*

Comp. **45** τὸ] *non hab. Chrys.*   **46** ἀγαθὸν μικρόν] κἂν μικρὸν ἀγαθόν *Chrys.*
47 ἀπολαμβάνει] *post* δίκαιος *hab. Chrys.*   τὸ ἰσόρροπον] τὴν ἰσόρροπον
κρίσιν *Chrys.*   **48** *post* οὖν] γίνεται, καὶ τί *hab. Chrys.*   **48/49** Δύο –
ἁμαρτίαν] Ἀφώρισε νόσον τῇ ἁμαρτίᾳ, τὸν παρόντα *(δύο ὥρισεν, νόσον καί
ἁμαρτίαν Vatic.) Chrys.*   **51** τῇ ἁμαρτίᾳ] τιμωρίᾳ *Chrys.*   **52** καθ’]
πρὸς *Chrys.*   **52/53** πάντως – μικρόν] πώποτε μικρόν τι κακὸν ἐποίησε
Chrys.   **53** μὴ ἐκεῖ *Chrys.*   **55** καὶ εὐθηνούμενον] κἂν εὐθυνῇ *Chrys.*
55/57 μὴ – ἀγαθόν] ἐννόησον ὅτι ἐποίησέ ποτε ἀγαθόν τι *Chrys.*   **58** τὰ
ἀγαθά *Chrys.*   Οὕτως οὖν] οὕτω *Chrys.*   **59** τίς ἐστι] ᾖ τις *Chrys.*
πάσχῃ δεινόν τι *Chrys.*   **60** τὴν – ἀποθῆται] ὧδε ἀπόθηται τὴν ἁμαρτίαν
Chrys.

104 FLORILEGIVM COISLINIANVM

μυρία ἀνίατα νοσῶν, ἁρπάζων, πλεονεκτῶν, διὰ τοῦτο
ἀπολαμβάνει ἐνταῦθα εὐημερίας, ἵνα μὴ ἐκεῖ ἀπαιτήσῃ
τὸν μισθόν. Διατοῦτο καὶ Ἀβραάμ, ἐπειδὴ συνέβαινε
65 καὶ τὸν Λάζαρον ἔχειν τινὰς ἁμαρτίας, καὶ τὸν πλούσι-
ον ἔχειν τί ἀγαθόν, λέγει· Μηδὲν ὧδε ζήτει· Ἀπέλαβες
τὰ ἀγαθά σου ἐκεῖ, καὶ Λάζαρος τὰ κακά. Ἀπέλαβες τὰ
ἀγαθά σου. Ποῖα; Ἐποίησάς τι ἀγαθόν; Ἀπέλαβές σου
τὸν πλοῦτον, τὴν ὑγείαν, τὴν τρυφήν, τὴν δυναστείαν·
70 ὧδε οὐδέν σοι κεχρεώστηται. Ἀπέλαβες τὰ ἀγαθά σου
ἐκεῖ. Τί οὖν; Λάζαρος οὐδὲν ἥμαρτε; Ναί, ἀλλ'ὅταν σὺ
ἀπελάμβανες τὰ ἀγαθά σου, τότε καὶ Λάζαρος τὰ κακά.
Διατοῦτο οὗτος νῦν παρακαλεῖται, σὺ δὲ ὀδυνᾶσαι.
Ὥστε ὅταν ἴδῃς δίκαιον κολαζόμενον ὧδε, μακάριζε
75 καὶ λέγε· Οὗτος ὁ δίκαιος ἁμαρτίαν ἔχει καὶ ἤδη ἀπέλα-
βεν αὐτήν, καὶ ἀπέρχεται ἐκεῖ καθαρός. Εἰ δὲ πλέον
τῶν ἁμαρτημάτων κολάζεται, προσθήκη ἁγιωσύνης

Font.   64/66 cf. Lc. 16, 19-24   66/67 Lc. 16, 25   67/68 cf. supra l. 66/67
68 cf. supra l. 66   70 cf. supra l. 66/67   72/73 Lc. 16, 25

Mss.   *AT CDEFHKQ*

Crit.   **62** πλεονεκτῶν] καὶ *add. FH*   **63** ἀπολαμβάνει] ἀπολαύει *EK*   ἐνταῦθα]
ὧδε *(sic spir.) D, om. T*   **64** ἀβραάμ *T C*$^{a. \, uel \, p.corr.}$ *EHQ,* αβρααμ *(sine spir.) A*
65 καὶ¹] *om. FHQ*   **66** ἔχειν] *om. F*   τί] *sic acc. codd., etsi indefinitum*
67/68 ἐκεῖ – σου¹] *om. T*   **68** τι] *om. T*   σου²] *om. EK*   **70/71** Ἀπέλαβες – ἐκεῖ] *om. Q*   **71** Λάζαρος] ὁ *praem. T*   ὅτε *DEFHQ*
72 ἀπέλαβες *AT Q*   Λάζαρος] ὁ *praem. T*   **75** καὶ¹] *om. Q*   ἔχει]
εἶχε *F*

Comp.   **63** ἀπολαμβάνει] ἀπολαύει *Chrys.*   **64** τὸν] *non hab. Chrys.*   Διατοῦτο – Ἀβραάμ] διὰ τοῦτο ὁ Ἀβραάμ *ante* λέγει *(l. 66) hab. Chrys.*   *post*
ἐπειδὴ] οὖν *hab. Chrys.*   **65** τινὰς ἁμαρτίας] τινὰ ἁμαρτήματα *Chrys.*
66 Μηδὲν ὧδε] Ὧδε μηδὲν *Chrys.*   **67** *ante* Λάζαρος] ὁ *hab. Chrys.*   *post*
κακά] αὐτοῦ. Καὶ ἵνα μάθῃς ὅτι οὐχ ἁπλῶς λέγω ταῦτα, ἀλλ'οὕτως ἐστί, λέγει *hab. Chrys.*   **69** *post* δυναστείαν] τὴν τιμήν *hab. Chrys.*   **70** ὧδε]
non hab. Chrys.   **71** ἐκεῖ] *non hab. Chrys.*   *ante* Λάζαρος] ὁ *hab. Chrys.*
ἀλλ'ὅταν] καὶ Λάζαρος τὰ κακὰ αὐτοῦ. Ὅτε *Chrys.*   **72** σου] *non hab. Chrys.*
73 νῦν οὗτος *Chrys.*   **74** *post* μακάριζε] αὐτὸν *hab. Chrys.*   **75** *post*
δίκαιος] ἢ *hab. Chrys.*   **75/76** ἤδη ἀπέλαβεν] ἀπολαμβάνει *Chrys.*
76 Εἰ δὲ] ἢ *Chrys.*   **77** *ante* προσθήκη] καὶ *hab. Chrys.*   ἁγιωσύνης]
δικαιοσύνης *Chrys.*

ALPHA 57 – 58   105

αὐτῷ λογίζεται. Τί οὖν ποιεῖ ὁ θεός; Λόγος γὰρ γίνεται
ἐκεῖ, καὶ λέγει ὁ θεὸς τῷ δικαίῳ· "Ἔχεις μου τόσον καὶ
80 ἔχω σου τόσον· ὁ θεὸς πιστεύει δέκα ὀβολούς, καὶ ποιεῖ
αὐτῷ λόγον τῶν δέκα ὀβολῶν· ἐὰν πένης ᾖ ἔχων ἑξή-
κοντα ὀβολούς, λέγει αὐτῷ ὁ θεός· Τοὺς δέκα ὀβολοὺς
λογίζομαί σοι εἰς ἁμαρτίαν, καὶ τοὺς ν' εἰς δικαιοσύνην.

ΚΓ'
Περὶ τῶν τεσσάρων ἀπαθειῶν

58   Μαξίμου μοναχοῦ

Πρώτη ἐστὶν ἀπάθεια ἡ παντελὴς ἀποχὴ τῶν κατ'ἐ-
νέργειαν κακῶν, ἐν τοῖς εἰσαγομένοις θεωρουμένη·
δευτέρα ἐστὶν ἀπάθεια ἡ παντελὴς κατὰ διάνοιαν περὶ
τὴν τῶν κακῶν συγκατάθεσιν ἀποβολὴ λογισμῶν, ἐν
5 τοῖς μετὰ λόγου τὴν ἀρετὴν μετιοῦσι γινομένη· τρίτη
δέ, ἡ κατ'ἐπιθυμίαν περὶ τὰ πάθη παντελὴς ἀκινησία,
ἐν τοῖς διὰ τῶν σχημάτων τοὺς λόγους νοητῶς θεωμέ-

Font.   **58.1/18** = Max. Conf., Quaest. ad Thal., 55, 201-218

Mss.   *AT CDEFHKQ*   **58** *AT CDEFH*

Tit.   **ΚΓ'**] κβ' *DFH*   τεσσάρων] δ' *D*   ἀπαθειῶν] περὶ τῶν δ' γενικῶν ἀρετῶν *E indic. Welz (illeg. in ms.)*   **58** Μαξίμου μοναχοῦ] μαχίμου *(sic)* μοναχοῦ *A*, μαξίμου *FH*

Crit.   **78** λογίζεται] γίνεται *FH*   **78/83** Τί – δικαιοσύνην] *om. Q*   **79** μου]
μοι *C*   **80** ἐμπιστεύει *FH*   **81** πένης] *om. E*   **81/82** ἑξήκοντα] ξ'
CDFH   **83** ν'] πεντήκοντα *DEFHK*   **58.2** ἀγομένοις *T*   **3** δευτέ-
ρα] β' *D*   ἐστὶν] *om. FH*   περὶ] παρὰ *C*   **4** λογισμοῦ *E*   **6** περὶ]
ἡ *praem. FH*

Comp.   **78** Τί – θεός] *non hab. Chrys.*   **79/80** καὶ² – θεὸς] τυχὸν δὲ *Chrys.*
80 *post* πιστεύει] αὐτῷ *hab. Chrys.*   **81** πένης – ἔχων] δὲ δαπανήσῃ *Chrys.*
83 ν'] πεντήκοντα *Chrys.*   **58.1** *post* Πρώτη] γάρ *hab. Max.*   **3** ἐστὶν
ἀπάθεια] δὲ *Max.*   **6** δέ] *non hab. Max.*

106   FLORILEGIVM COISLINIANVM

νοις τῶν ὁρωμένων· δ' ἀπάθεια ἡ καὶ αὐτῆς τῆς ψιλῆς
τῶν παθῶν φαντασίας παντελὴς κάθαρσις, ἐν τοῖς διὰ
10 γνώσεως καὶ θεωρίας καθαρὸν καὶ διειδὲς ἔσοπτρον τοῦ
θεοῦ ποιησαμένοις τὸ ἡγεμονικὸν συνισταμένη. Ὁ τοίνυν καθάρας ἑαυτὸν ἐνεργείας παθῶν, καὶ τῆς ἐπ'αὐτοῖς
κατὰ διάνοιαν συγκαταθέσεως ἐλευθερώσας, καὶ τῆς
περὶ αὐτὰ κατ'ἐπιθυμίαν κινήσεως στάσιν λαβών, καὶ
15 τῆς αὐτῶν ψιλῆς φαντασίας τὸν νοῦν καταστήσας ἀμό-
λυντον, τὰς τέσσαρας γενικὰς ἀπαθείας ἔχων, ἐξέρχε-
ται τῆς ὕλης καὶ τῶν ὑλικῶν, καὶ πρὸς τὴν θείαν καὶ
εἰρηνικὴν τῶν νοητῶν ἐπείγεται λῆξιν.

59   Ἄλλη θεωρία περὶ τῶν αὐτῶν

     Πρώτην ἀπάθειαν λέγει τὴν πρὸς ἁμαρτίαν τοῦ
σώματος κατ'ἐνέργειαν ἀνέπαφον κίνησιν· δευτέραν δὲ
τὴν κατὰ ψυχὴν τῶν ἐμπαθῶν λογισμῶν τελείαν ἀπο-
βολήν, δι'ἧς ἡ τῶν παθῶν ἀπομαραίνεται κατὰ τὴν πρώ-
5   την ἀπάθειαν κίνησις, ἐξάπτοντας αὐτὴν πρὸς ἐνέργειαν, οὐκ ἔχουσα τοὺς ἐμπαθεῖς λογισμούς· τρίτην πάλιν
ἀπάθειαν λέγει τὴν περὶ τὰ πάθη τελείαν τῆς ἐπιθυμίας
ἀκινησίαν, δι'ἣν καὶ ἡ δευτέρα γίνεσθαι πέφυκε, τῇ τῶν
λογισμῶν καθαρότητι συνισταμένη· τετάρτην ἀπάθει-
10 αν λέγει τὴν κατὰ διάνοιαν πασῶν τῶν αἰσθητῶν φαν-
τασιῶν τελείαν ἀπόθεσιν, καθ'ἣν ἡ τρίτη τὴν γένεσιν

Font.   **59.1/13** = Schol. in Max. Conf., 55, 157-169

Mss.   *AT CDEFH*   **59** *AT C*

Crit.   **8** δ'] τετάρτη *CEFH*   ἡ] εἰ *D*   **9** φαντασία *C*   **12** τῆς] τοὺς *AT,*
         τοῖς *DFH*   **13** τῆς] τοῖς *FH*   **15/16** ἀμόλυντον] *om.* H *(10 litt. spat.)*
         16 τέσσαρας] δ' *DH*   **17** ὑλικῶν] παθῶν *add. FH*   **59.3** κατὰ] *om. A*
         5 ἐξάπτοντος *T*   **6** οὐκ' *C*

Comp.   **8** δ'] τετάρτη *Max.*   **16** γενικὰς ἀπαθείας] μυρίαδας *Max.*   **59.2** δὲ]
         ἀπάθειαν λέγει *Schol.*   **6** ἔχουσα] ἔχουσαν *Schol. (B Va = Coisl.)*   πάλιν]
         non hab. Schol.

ALPHA 58 – 60

εἴληφεν, οὐκ ἔχουσα τὰς φαντασίας τῶν αἰσθητῶν εἰδοποιούσας αὐτῇ τῶν παθῶν τὰς εἰκόνας.

ΚΔ΄

Περὶ τῶν τεσσάρων γενικῶν ἀρετῶν

*60 Τέσσαρες εἰσὶ γενικαὶ ἀρεταί, αἷς παρέπονται ἑκάστῃ αὐτῶν δύο κακίαι. Εἰσὶ δὲ αὗται σωφροσύνη, ἀνδρεία, δικαιοσύνη καὶ φρόνησις. Κακίαι δὲ ὀκτώ, ἀκολασία, μισαλληλία, θρασύτης, δειλία, ἀδικία, 5 ἀνισότης, δεινότης καὶ ἡ ἀφροσύνη.

Διαίρεσις

α΄ Σωφροσύνη· ἀντίκειται αὐτῇ ἀκολασία. Ταύτῃ ἡττῶνται οἱ θηλυμανεῖς, ἵπποι θηλυμανεῖς γινόμενοι καὶ ἀκρατῶς πρὸς τὰς ἀτάκτους ἡδονὰς χρεμετίζοντες. 10 Ἀντίκειται αὐτῇ μισαλληλία. Ταύτῃ ἡττῶνται Μανιχεῖς καὶ Βορβορῖται, τὸν μὲν τίμιον βδελυττόμενοι γάμον, πρὸς δὲ τὰς αἰσχρὰς ἡδονὰς ἀκρατεῖς ὄντες ὡς ἂν τύχοι· ἡ ἔχις χαρακτηρίζει τῇ σμυραίνῃ συμπλεκομένη, ἑτερογενὴς οὖσα.

Font. **60.1/100** = Ps.-Max. Conf., De quat. card. uirt.   **8/9** cf. Ier. 5, 8
11/12 cf. Heb. 13, 4

Mss. **60** *AT CDEFH*

Tit. **ΚΔ΄**] κγ΄ *DFH, om. E*   Περὶ – ἀρετῶν] *om. E*   τεσσάρων] δ΄ *A DH*
post ἀρετῶν] τοῦ αὐτοῦ *add. DEFH*

Crit. **60.1** γενικαὶ] γινικαὶ *(sic)* αἰ *(sic spir.) A^{a.corr.}*, γινικαὶ *A^{p.corr.}*   αἷς παρέπονται] αἷς παρέσονται *T, om. H (10 litt. spat.)*   **2** δύο] β΄ *H*   **3** κακία *D*
ὀκτώ] η΄ *A DH* (ἡ *D*)   **5** δεινότης] *om. D*   καὶ – ἀφροσύνη] καὶ ἀφροσύνη *T*, ἀφροσύνη *E*, καὶ *H (15 litt. spat.)*   **7** α΄] post σωφροσύνη *in marg. trsp. D, om. T FH*   σωφροσύνης *CDEFH (D hab. σωφροσύνη in marg., E hab. σωφροσύνης in marg.)*   αὐτῇ] αὕτη *FH*   **9** χραιμετίζοντες *AT*
10 αὐτῇ] αὕτη *H*, αὖ ταύτηι *F, om. T*   **10/11** μανιχαῖοι *T E*   **11** βορβορῖται *E*   βδελυσσάμενοι *T*   **13** τύχοι] τύχη *FH*, οὓς *add. E*   ἐχὶς
FH   σμυραίνῃ] μυραίνη *F*, μυρρένη *H^{a.corr.}* (-αί- *p. corr.*)

108 FLORILEGIVM COISLINIANVM

15 β΄ Ἀνδρεία· ἀντίκειται αὐτῇ θρασύτης, ὥσπερ ὁ λέων·
τοιοῦτοί εἰσιν οἱ ἀλόγιστοι, ὡς οὐ κατὰ μόνης τῆς ἁμαρτίας κινούμενοι, ἀλλὰ κατὰ τῶν ἀσθενεστέρων διε-
γειρόμενοι. Ἀντίκειται αὐτῇ δειλία, ὥσπερ οἱ λαγωοί·
τοιοῦτοί εἰσιν οἱ ἄνανδροι, οὓς θορυβεῖ καὶ ἦχος φύλ-
20 λου· τὸν γὰρ ἀνδρεῖον, οὐδὲ ὁρμαὶ ἀσεβῶν θρυλλοῦσιν,
οὐδὲ πτόησις ἐπερχομένη.

γ΄ Δικαιοσύνη· ἀντίκειται αὐτῇ ἀδικία, ὥσπερ ὁ πέρ-
διξ· τοιοῦτοί εἰσιν οἱ τὸ δίκαιον τοῦ δικαίου ἀποστεροῦντες, ὥσπερ ὁ πέρδιξ συνάγων ἃ οὐκ ἔτεκεν. Ἀντίκειται
25 αὐτῇ ἀνισότης, ὡς ὁ πελαργός, μόνους τοὺς γονεῖς δια-
τρέφων γηρῶντας· τοιοῦτοί εἰσιν οἱ μὴ πρὸς πάντας
ἀνοίγοντες σπλάγχνα.

δ΄ Φρόνησις· ἀντίκειται αὐτῇ δεινότης, ὡς ἀλώπηξ
νεκρὰν προσποιουμένη ἑαυτὴν καὶ θηρῶσα ἑαυτῇ τρο-
30 φὴν ἐκ τῶν πετεινῶν· τοιοῦτοί εἰσιν οἱ εἰς τὸ κακοποιῆσαι μόνον σοφοί. Ἀντίκειται αὐτῇ ἀφροσύνη, ὡς ὁ
ἀσφάλαξ· τοιοῦτοί εἰσιν οἱ πηροὶ τὸν νοῦν, οἳ καὶ ἀπε-
ρισκέπτως ἐν τῷ βίῳ κινούμενοι, φθείρουσι καὶ συγ-
χέουσιν, ὥσπερ ὁ ἀσφάλαξ.

Font. 20/21 cf. Prou. 3, 25 23/24 cf. Is. 5, 23 24 Ier. 17, 11
30/31 cf. Ier. 4, 22

Mss. *AT CDEFH*

Crit. **15** β΄] *post* ἀνδρεία *trsp. D, om.* T CFH ἀνδρείας E θρασύτης] ἡ
praem. E **16** ἀλόγιστοι] ἀκόλαστοι FH οὐ] *om.* T **17/18** ἀλλὰ –
διεγειρόμενοι] *om.* D*ᵃ.ᶜᵒʳʳ.* (*suppl. in marg.*) **17** ἀλλὰ] καὶ *add.* F
17/18 ἐγειρόμενοι T **19/20** ψύλλου *A* **20** ορμαῖς (*sic*) *A* θρυ-
λοῦσιν C, θρηλοῦσιν FH **21** πτῶσις FH **22** γ΄] *post* δικαιοσύνη
trsp. D, om. T FH δικαιοσύνης E **25** πελιαργός CFH μόνος F
26 γηροῦντας *AT* μὴ] *om.* T πάντα F*ᵃ.ᶜᵒʳʳ.*H **28** δ΄] *post* φρόνησις *trsp. D, om.* T FH φρονήσεως E ἀλώπηξ] ὁ *praem. A,* ἡ *praem.* T
29 νεκρὸν *A* θηρῶσαν T ἑαυτῇ] ἑαυτὴν C **30** οἱ] *om.* T F
31 ἀντίκεινται D ὡς] ὥσπερ T ὁ] *om.* F*ᵃ.ᶜᵒʳʳ.* **32** ἀσπάλαξ EFH
πειροὶ D, πῆροι C, ἄπειροι *A,* πονηροὶ T E **33/34** συγχέουσιν] τὰ πάντα
add. E **34** ἀσπάλαξ EFH

ALPHA 60   109

35 Αἱ μὲν οὖν χαρακτηρίζουσαι τοὺς λογικοὺς καὶ
θείους ἄνδρας, αἱ τέσσαρες αὗται δηλονότι εἰσὶν ἀρεταί, αἱ δὲ μετὰ τὴν παράβασιν ὑπεισελθοῦσαι τῷ βίῳ,
αἱ ταύταις ἑπόμεναι ὀκτὼ κακίαι τυγχάνουσιν, ἃς καὶ
τὰ ἄλογα ζῶα φυσικῶς ἔχοντα, ὑφ'ἑαυτῶν ἀναλίσκον-
40 ται· προγινώσκων γὰρ παρεκτροπήν, τοῖς μὲν ἀλόγοις
ταῦτα ἀπένειμεν, ἵνα ὅταν παραβαίνωμεν τὰ ἐφ'οἷς
γεγόναμεν ἀγαθὰ ἔργα, γνῶμεν ἑαυτοὺς οἷοι ἀνθ'οἵων
γινόμεθα, καὶ τίνα μιμούμεθα οἱ κατ'εἰκόνα θεοῦ ἐπ'ἔργοις ἀγαθοῖς κτισθέντες· Ἄνθρωπος γὰρ ἐν τιμῇ ὢν οὐ
45 συνῆκεν· παρασυνεβλήθη τοῖς κτήνεσι τοῖς ἀνοήτοις
καὶ ὡμοιώθη αὐτοῖς. Διατοῦτο τιμήσωμεν τὸν τιμήσαν-
τα ἡμᾶς, αἰδούμενοι τὴν εἰκόνα, ἵνα μᾶλλον τῷ κτίστῃ
καθὸ δυνατὸν ὁμοιωθῶμεν, καὶ μὴ τοῖς κτήνεσι.
Καὶ οἷς μὲν ὁ τίμιος γάμος ποθεῖται καὶ σπουδάζε-
50 ται, τὸ σεμνὸν πλέον σπουδασθείη, μὴ πρὸς ἡδονήν,
ἀλλὰ πρὸς διαμονὴν τοῦ γένους ὁρῶσιν· συνδημιουρ-
γοὶ γὰρ τρόπον τινὰ τῷ δημιουργῷ γενήσονται, οὐκ ἐξ
οὐκ ὄντων, ἀλλ'ἐξ ἑαυτῶν τὸ γένος διακρατοῦντες, τῷ
νόμῳ πειθόμενοι, ἄχρις ἂν μετασκευάσῃ ἐπὶ τὸ κρεῖτ-
55 τον τὴν φύσιν ὁ πανσόφως τὰ πάντα δημιουργήσας
θεός. Μὴ βδελυττέσθωσαν δὲ τὸν ἱερὸν γάμον, μὴ δὲ
χωριζέτωσαν ἑαυτοὺς εὐλαβείας ἕνεκεν, εἰ μήπω κατὰ
τὸν ἀποστολικὸν κανόνα τοῦτο κρίνοι, ἵνα μὴ εἰς ἀκα-
θέκτους καὶ μυσαρὰς περιπέσοι βδελλυρίας, οὐ φύσε-

Font.   **41/42** cf. infra l. 43/44   **43** Gen. 1, 26-27; 5, 1   **43/44** Eph. 2, 10
44/46 Ps. 48, 13   **49** cf. supra l. 11/12   **56/58** cf. Const. apost. 8, 47,
17-19 (cf. Ps.-Max. Conf., De quat. cad. uirt., p. 420, n. 117)

Mss.   *AT CDEFH* (*DEFH* usque ad κτήνεσι, 60.48)

Crit.   **36** τέσσαρες] δ' *A DH*   δηλονότι (*sic*) *A,* δῆλον ὅτι *T CD*   **37** ἐπεισελ-
θοῦσαι *F*ᵃ· ᵘᵉˡ ᵖ·ᶜᵒʳʳ·*H*   **38** ὀκτὼ] η' *DH*   **40** παρεκτροπήν] ὁ δημιουργὸς
add. *E*   **41/42** ἵνα – γεγόναμεν] om. *T*   **41** ἵνα] ἰν' *CE*   παρα-
βαίνομεν *D*   **42** ἑαυτοῖς *T*   οἷοι] οἷον *A*   **44** ὢν ἐν τιμῇ *E*
45/46 παρασυνεβλήθη – αὐτοῖς] om. *DEFH*   **45** παρεσυνεβλήθη *A*
45 τοῖς κτήνεσι] *iter. C*   **58/59** ἀκαθέκτας *T*   **59** περιπέσοιεν *C*ᵖ·ᶜᵒʳʳ·

110 FLORILEGIVM COISLINIANVM

60 ὡς δὲ μόνης, ἀλλ᾽ἡδονῆς ἕνεκα ἐξελκόμενος κατὰ τοὺς
ἐχιδνώδεις καὶ ἀνοσίους αἱρετικούς, μήποτε πειράσῃ
ὑμᾶς ὁ Σατανᾶς φησὶ διὰ τὴν ἀκρασίαν ὑμῶν. Εἰ δέ τις
τὸ παρθενίας θηρᾶται δῶρον, τῆς ἀγγελικῆς πολιτείας
ἴδιον τοῦτο· εἰ δὲ καὶ ἀπολέλυταί τις τοῦ τῆς ἰδιογαμίας
65 ζυγοῦ, προσμένοι καρτερικῶς τῇ δεήσει καὶ τῇ ἁγνείᾳ,
οὐχ᾽ἧττον κατὰ τὴν ἐμὴν γνώμην τῶν ἀπειρογάμων
εὑρεθήσεται οὗτος.

Τὸ δ᾽αὐτὸ καὶ περὶ τῆς ἀνδρείας καὶ τῶν ἄλλων ἡμῖν
ἀρετῶν γενήσεται μικτόν· ὑφ᾽ᾗ μὲν ἐπαιρόμενοι κριὸς
70 πρὸς κριὸν κερατίζοντες, ᾗ φησὶν ἡ προφητεία, ἵνα μὴ
τῷ ὠμοτάτῳ καὶ ἀγριωτάτῳ ἀφομοιωθῶμεν λέοντι,
ἀλλὰ μὴ δὲ πέρα τοῦ μέτρου συσταλῶμεν, πτήσσοντες
ἃ μὴ δεῖ· *Οὐ γὰρ ἔδωκεν ἡμῖν ὁ θεὸς πνεῦμα δειλίας εἰς*
φόβον, ἀλλὰ πνεῦμα υἱοθεσίας· ἀνδρισώμεθα τοίνυν
75 κατὰ πάσης ἁμαρτίας, ἐξαιρέτως δὲ ὑπὲρ τῆς εἰς Χριστὸν τὸν θεὸν ἡμῶν ὀρθῆς ὁμολογίας.

Τὴν δὲ δικαιοσύνην ἐπ᾽ἴσης μετέρχεσθαι, μὴ δὲ
τοὺς ὅρους αὐτῆς ὑπερβαίνειν, τὰ ἄλλων ἄλλοις ἀποδιδόντες, καὶ τὸ δίκαιον τοῦ δικαίου ἀποστεροῦντες.
80 Μήτε δὲ ὑπερβολῇ ἰδιοπαθείας ἤγουν φιλαυτίας ταῖς
ἑαυτῶν ἐναγώμεθα θέλξεσι· τὸ γὰρ προΐστασθαι
τῶν οἰκείων ἐν ἅπασι καλόν, τὸ δὲ καὶ τοῖς ἄλλοις
ἀνοίγειν τὰ σπλάγχνα ὡς οἰκείοις τὴν φύσιν, χρι-
στιανοῖς ἡμῖν πρέπει, οἵ γε καὶ τοὺς ἐχθροὺς εὐεργε-

Font.   **61/62** I Cor. 7, 5   **65** cf. I Tim. 5, 5   **66** I Cor. 7, 40   **70** cf. Dan. 8, 4
73 II Tim. 1, 7   **74** Rom. 8, 15   **78/79** cf. Ps.-Dion., De diu. nom.,
8, 7 (p. 204, 14)   **79** cf. supra l. 23/24   **81/82** cf. I Tim. 3, 4. 12
84/85 cf. Mt. 5, 44 et loc. par.

Mss.   *AT CDEFH*

Crit.   **62** σατανᾶς *T*   **63** παρθενείας *AT*   **69** μικτῶν *A; lacunam post* μικτὸν
indic. Roosen – Van Deun   ὑφ᾽ᾗ μὲν] ὑφῆμεν *A,* ὑφῆμὲν *C,* ὑφ᾽ᾗ μὲν *T*
ἐπαιρόμενος *C*   **70** κερατίζοντα *C*   ᾗ] *om. A^{a.corr.}*   **72** συσταλλῶμεν
A   **73/74** πνεῦμα – ἀλλά] *om. C^{a.corr.}*   **77** ἐφ᾽ἴσης *A*   μετέρχεσθε *T*
78/79 ἀποδιδοῦντες *AT (et* Roosen – Van Deun*)*   **81** ἐναγόμεθα *C*
82 τοὺς ἄλλους *T*

ALPHA 60 – 61

85 τεῖν κελευόμεθα ὡς Χριστοῦ μαθηταί, τοῦ καταλλά-
ξαντος ἡμᾶς ἑαυτῷ, ἐχθροὺς ὑπάρχοντας πρότερον.
Καὶ φρονήσεως δὲ πρὸ πάντων ἐπιμελησώμεθα, ἵνα
καὶ τὰς ἄλλας λογικῶς καὶ ἐπιστημόνως ἀσκῶμεν ἀρετάς, γινώσκοντες καιρῶν καὶ βίων μεταλλαγὰς καὶ συ-
90 στάσεις, καὶ μὴ πρὸς τὰ ἥδοντα καὶ θέλγοντα ἡμᾶς τὰς
αἰσθήσεις ἀποβλέπωμεν, μήτε δὲ δεινοὶ κατὰ τῶν λυ-
πούντων γινώμεθα, πανουργίαις καὶ δόλοις χρώμενοι
εἰς τὸ κακοποιῆσαι καὶ ἀμύνεσθαι· οἵ γε καὶ νηπιάζειν
τῇ κακίᾳ κελευόμεθα· ἀλλὰ μὴ δὲ ἀφρόνως καὶ εἰκῆ τοῖς
95 πράγμασιν ἐγχειρῶμεν, ἵνα μὴ φύρσιν τινὰ καὶ φθορὰν
περιεργαζόμενοι τῷ τυφλῷ ἑρπετῷ ἀφομοιωθῶμεν.
Τὰ μὲν οὖν ὅσα δεξιὰ νομιζόμενα φύγωμεν, ὁδῷ δὲ
μᾶλλον βασιλικῇ πορευθῶμεν, δι'ἧς τῆς ἄνω πόλεως ἐν
αὐτῷ τῷ Χριστῷ τῇ ἀπλανεῖ ἡμῶν ὁδῷ, τυχεῖν δυνη-
100 θείημεν.

ΚΕ'

Τίνες ἀρεταὶ ψυχῆς καὶ τίνες σώματος;

61 Μαξίμου μοναχοῦ

Ἀρεταὶ ψυχῆς εἰσὶν αὗται· ἀγάπη, ταπείνωσις, πραό-

Font. **85/86** II Cor. 5, 18   **86** cf. Col. 1, 21   **93** cf. supra l. 30/31
93/94 I Cor. 14, 20   **97/98** cf. Num. 20, 17   **99** cf. Io. 14, 6   **61.1/7** Max.
Conf., Quaest. et dub., I, 1, 2-8 (p. 137)

Mss. **61** *AT CDEFHQ*

Tit. **ΚΕ'**] κδ' *FH,* ιβ' *(sic) E, illeg. D, om. Q*   Τίνες – σώματος] *Max. Conf.,*
Quaest. et dub., I, 1, 1 (p. 137)   **61** Μαξίμου μοναχοῦ] τοῦ αὐτοῦ *DEFH*

Crit. **87** ἐπιμελησόμεθα *A*   **93** κακοποιεῖν *C*   ἀμύνασθαι *T*   **97** δεξιὰ]
<καὶ ὅσα εὐώνυμα> add. *Roosen – Van Deun "on the basis of Num. 20, 17",*
forsan recte   νομίζομεν *C*

112 FLORILEGIVM COISLINIANVM

της, μακροθυμία, ἀνεξικακία, ἀοργησία, ἄθυμον, ἄφθονον, ἄκριτον, ἀκενόδοξον, ἐλεημοσύνη, σωφροσύνη,
ἀφιλάργυρον, ἀπάθεια, ἄτυφον, ἀνυπερήφανον, ἀμνη-
5 σίκακον, κατανυκτικόν. Ἀρεταὶ δὲ σώματος εἰσὶν αὗται·
χαμευνία, ἀγρυπνία, ἀκτημοσύνη, ἐγκράτεια καὶ τὸ
ἀπερίσπαστον.

ΚϚ'

Ἀπόδειξις ὅτι οὐδὲν ὄφελος μιᾶς ἀρετῆς, τῶν
ἄλλων ἀπόντων

*62 Νείλου μοναχοῦ

Οὕτω τῆς κατὰ ψυχὴν εὐμορφίας φρόντιζε, ὡς ἂν
φροντίσαιεν οἱ λίαν κομψοὶ καὶ φιλοσώματοι τῆς τῶν
μελῶν ἀρτιότητος· καὶ γὰρ ἡ λείπουσα ἀρετή, καθάπερ
οἱ ἀκρωτηριασμοὶ καὶ τὰ κολοβώματα τῷ σώματι, καὶ
5 ἡ κακία, καθάπερ αἱ περιτταὶ ἐπιφύσεις, οἷον ἀκροχορδόνες καὶ χημοί, ἀπρέπειαν περιάπτουσι τῇ ψυχῇ, τῷ
φυσικῷ ταύτης λυμαινόμεναι κάλλει καὶ τὸ τῶν ἄλ-

Font. 62.1/135 locum non inueni; ed. Nil. Anc., De uirt.

Mss. *AT CDEFHQ*   62 *AT CDEFHQ*

Tit. **ΚϚ'**] κε' *DEFH*, om. *Q*

Crit. 4 ἀπάθειαν *A*, ἀπαθῆ *C*   5 σωμάτων *CE*   6 χαμευνία] om. *H*
62.4 ἀκροτηρισασμοὶ (sic) *AT*   5 ἐκφύσεις *Q*   οἷον om. *T*   6 χημοί]
χυμοὶ *T*, χῆμοι *CFHQ*   προσάπτουσι *F*, προσάπτουσαι *H*   7 ταύτης]
τῆς ψυχῆς *D*   λομαινόμεναι (sic) *A*   7/8 ἄλλων] om. *F*

Comp. 2 post ἀνεξικακία] ἀμνησικακία hab. Max.   ante ἄθυμον] τὸ hab. Max.
2/3 ante ἄφθονον] τὸ hab. Max.   3 ante ἄκριτον] τὸ hab. Max.   ante
ἀκενόδοξον] τὸ hab. Max.   4 ἀπάθεια] συμπάθεια Max.   ante ἄτυφον]
τὸ hab. Max.   ante ἀνυπερήφανον] τὸ hab. Max.   4/5 ἀμνησίκακον]
non hab. Max.   6 ante χαμευνία] νηστεία hab. Max.   ἐγκράτεια, ἀκτημοσύνη Max.   καὶ] non hab. Max.

ALPHA 61 – 62   113

λων ἀρετῶν ἀφανίζουσαι καὶ ἀχρειοῦσαι φαιδρόν. Μὴ
τοίνυν τίς ἀπατάσθω, μίαν περιέπων καὶ φιλοκαλῶν
10 ἀρετήν, ὡς δι'αὐτῆς μόνης εἰσελευσόμενος εἰς τὴν βασιλείαν τοῦ θεοῦ, μὴ δ'αὖ τὴν παρθενίαν δίχα τῶν ἄλλων
πρὸς σωτηρίαν ἱκανὴν νομιζέτω. Δεῖ γὰρ πάσας ἐπίσης κατορθωθῆναι τὰς ἀρετάς, ἵνα τίς ἄξιος κληθῇ τῆς
βασιλείας τῶν οὐρανῶν, καθάπερ ὁλοκλήρῳ καὶ ἀρτίῳ
15 σώματι ἐγκρινόμενος στρατιωτικῷ καταλόγῳ. Εἰ γὰρ
τὸν οὐκ ἐνδεδυμένον ἔνδυμα γάμου τοῦ δείπνου ἐξέβαλε καὶ δεθέντα χειρῶν καὶ ποδῶν, οἷς πάντως ἤργησε
πρὸς τὸ πλῦναι τὴν ῥυπωθεῖσαν ἐσθῆτα, εἰς ἐξώτερον
ἀπενεχθῆναι παρεσκεύασε σκότος, πῶς οὐκ ἐκβαλεῖ
20 τῆς βασιλείας, καθάπερ μέλους πήρωσις, ἡ λείπουσα
τῷ κάλλει τῆς ψυχῆς ἀρετή, μᾶλλον μέλους παντὸς
οὖσα πρὸς σωτηρίαν χρησίμη; Ὀφθαλμοῦ μὲν γὰρ καὶ
χειρὸς καὶ ποδὸς ἄνευ, ὅταν ἐμποδίζῃ τὸ σκανδαλίζον
τῇ κτήσει τῆς ἀρετῆς, εἰς τὴν βασιλείαν εἰσελθεῖν δυ-
25 νατόν, ἀρετὴ δὲ παρημελημένη, καὶ ταῖς λοιπαῖς ποιεῖν τὸν πόνον ἀνόνητον εἴωθεν, σκάζειν καὶ χωλεύειν
ποιοῦσα περὶ τὴν εἴσοδον, καὶ μένειν ἔξω παρασκευά-

Font.   10/11 cf. Mt. 19, 24 et loc. par.   11/12 cf. Nil. Anc., Ep. 3, 298, PG 79,
532, 4-17   13/14 cf. Mt. 5, 19 et loc. par.   16/19 cf. Mt. 22, 11-13
22/25 cf. Mc. 9, 43-47

Ass.   AT CDEFHQ

Crit.   8 ἀχριοῦσαι A, ἀγριοῦσαι T, ἀχρειοῦσι FH   9 τίς] sic acc. codd., etsi
indefinitum; om. T   10 εἰσελευσόμεθα C   11 παρθενίαν A, παρθένον C   12 ἱκανὴν πρὸς σωτηρίαν E   12/13 ἐφίσης (sic) AC^{a. uel p.corr.}
13 κατορθῆναι (sic) A   τίς] sic acc. codd., etsi indefinitum   15 στρατικῶ
A   16/17 ἐξέβαλε τοῦ δείπνου FH   17 καὶ¹ – ποδῶν] post ἐσθῆτα trsp.
Q   δεθέντων FH   χειρῶν – ποδῶν] om. D^{a.corr.} (suppl. in marg.), χεῖρας
καὶ πόδας Q   ἤργασε T, εἴργησε E^{p.corr.}F   19 ἀπενεχθῆναι – σκότος]
om. A   ἐκβάλλει Q   22 γὰρ] om. Q   23 ὅταν] μὴ add. FH   τὸ
σκανδαλίζον] ...δαλίζον F (10 litt. spat.)   24 κτίσει A CDE   25 δὲ]
om. Q   παραμελημένη A D   26 ἀνόνητον] om. Q   σκάζειν] καὶ
σκανδαλίζειν FH   27 ποιοῦσα – εἴσοδον] περὶ τῆς ἀρετῆς τὴν εἴσοδον
ποιοῦσα FH   περὶ] παρὰ Q

Comp.   16/17 ἐξέβαλε – ποδῶν] δήσαντες αὐτοῦ πόδας καὶ χεῖρας ἐκβάλετε Mt.

114 FLORILEGIVM COISLINIANVM

ζουσα. Τί γὰρ ὄφελος τινὰς μὲν ἢ τὰς πλείστας ἔχειν
δοκεῖν ἀρετάς, διὰ δὲ τὴν λείπουσαν ἀποτυγχάνειν τοῦ
30 σπουδαζομένου, τῆς γραφῆς σαφῶς λεγούσης ὃς ἂν
ὅλον τὸν νόμον πληρώσῃ, πταίσῃ δὲ ἐν ἑνί, γέγονε πάντων ἔνοχος; Τί τὰς πέντε παρθένους ὁ τοσοῦτος τῆς
παρθενίας ὤνησε κάματος, διὰ τὸ ἀσυμπαθὲς καὶ ἀφι-
λάλληλον ἔξω τοῦ νυμφῶνος ἀποκλεισθείσας; Τί δὲ
35 τὸν Φαρισαῖον ὠφέλησεν ἡ τῶν κτωμένων διαπαντὸς
ἀποδεκάτωσις καὶ ἡ συνεχὴς νηστεία, δι'ὑπερηφανίαν
κατακριθέντα; Τί δὲ τὸν Ἰούδαν ἡ ἀποστολὴ καὶ τὰ λοιπὰ κατορθώματα, διὰ φιλαργυρίαν εἰς τὸ τῆς προδοσίας βάραθρον καταπεσόντα;
40 Ἐλεημοσύνη ὑπερηφάνου, κυνὸς ἐστιν κάρπωσις,
καὶ εὐποιΐα ἀκολάστου, μίσθωμα πόρνης ἐστίν, ἀπρόσδεκτα καὶ ἀνίερα θύματα· θυμώδης παρθένος ναός ἐστι
δαίμονος, καὶ ὀργίλου προσευχή, ἐβδελυγμένον θυμία-
μα· πλεονέκτου δῶρον, θυσία ἀκάθαρτος καὶ αἷμα ὕει-
45 ον· δάκρυον ἀνθρωπαρέσκου, ψαλμῳδία μνησικάκου,
ἦχος ἐστὶν ἀηδής, καὶ νηστεία κενοδόξου, καπνὸς εἰς
ἀέρα διαλυόμενος.

Font.   31/32 Iac. 2, 10   32/34 cf. Mt. 25, 1-12   34/37 cf. Mt. 23, 23, Lc. 11, 42
37/39 cf. Mt. 26, 47 – 27, 10, Mc. 14, 43-46, Lc. 22, 47-48, Io. 18, 1-9
40/41 Deut. 23, 19   42/46 cf. Euag. (sub nomine Nili Ancyrani), De oct.
spir. mal., PG 79, 1156, 12-15   44/45 Is. 66, 3

Mss.   AT CDEFHQ

Crit.   28 ἢ] οἳ F   28/29 δοκεῖν ἔχειν FH   29 ἀπολείπουσαν E   31 τὸν
νόμον ὅλον Q   32 πέντε] ε' D   32/33 τῆς παρθενείας A, τῆς παρθένων C,
τὴν παρθενίαν H   33/34 ἀφιλάλιλον (sic) A   35 ὠφέλησεν] ὤνησεν F
36/37 δι'– κατακριθέντα] ὑπερηφανίᾳ κρατηθέντα F, ὑπερηφανίας κρατηθέντα H   38 κατορθῶμαται (sic acc.) A   41 πόρνης] πορνείας F
41/42 ἀπρόσδεκτα – θύματα] om. DEFHQ   42 παρθενία DE   43 ὀρ-
γίλλου F   44 θυσία] sequitur 10 litt. spat. F   45 ἀθρωπρέσκου (sic) A,
μόλυσμα add. Q   ψαλμῳδία] καὶ praem. DEFH   46 καὶ] om. DEFHQ
καπνὸς] ἐστιν add. CDEFHQ, forsan recte   47 λυόμενος Q

Comp.   42/46 θυμώδης – ἀηδής] Θυμώδους προσευχὴ ἐβδελυγμένον θυμίαμα· καὶ
ψαλμῳδία ὀργίλου ἦχος ἀηδής. Δῶρον μνησικάκου μυρμηκιῶσα θυσία Euag.

ALPHA 62   115

Θέλεις ἰδεῖν καὶ νηστείαν ἀπρόσδεκτον; Ἄκουσον
ἐγκαλοῦντος τισὶ τοῦ θεοῦ καὶ λέγοντος· "Ἵνα τί νη-
50 στεύητέ μοι σήμερον ἀκουσθῆναι τὴν φωνὴν ὑμῶν; Οὐ
ταύτην τὴν νηστείαν ἐξελεξάμην, λέγει Κύριος. Θέλεις
καὶ δάκρυον ἰδεῖν μισούμενον; Καὶ ταῦτα φησὶν ἃ ἐμί-
σουν ἐποιεῖτε· ἐκαλύπτετε δάκρυσι τὸ θυσιαστήριόν
μου. Καὶ μισεῖ δάκρυον ἄρα θεός, ὁ πανταχοῦ τοῦτο καὶ
55 πάντοτε παρὰ τῶν ἀνθρώπων δῶρον καταλλαγῆς ἀπαι-
τῶν καὶ τῶν ἡμαρτημένων αἰώνιον φάρμακον; Ναί.
Μισεῖ δάκρυον τῶν ἐν μὲν τῇ προσευχῇ δοκούντων
θρηνεῖν, μετὰ δὲ τὴν προσευχὴν ἐπιλανθανομένων τῆς
καταστάσεως ἐκείνης τῆς συντετριμμένης, καὶ πάν-
60 τα ποιούντων καὶ λεγόντων ἀδιαφόρως λοιπόν, ὅσα
πληροῦν οἶδε θυμὸν καὶ ἐπιθυμίαν καὶ ἡδονὴν καὶ πᾶν
πάθος κινούμενον, καὶ τὴν τὸ γλυκὺ βρύουσαν νᾶμα
πηγὴν πικραῖς ἐκταραττόντων καὶ αἰσχραῖς λοιδορίαις.
Ἀλλὰ καὶ τῷ ψάλλοντι μετὰ τοῦ μνησικακεῖν τὸ πλη-
65 σίον ἐπιπληκτικῶς ἐμβοᾷ· Μετάστησον ἀπ'ἐμοῦ ἦχον
ᾠδῶν σου, καὶ ψαλμὸν ὀργάνων σου οὐκ ἀκούσομαι.
    Καὶ μετὰ ταῦτα. Τί τῶν Ἰουδαϊκῶν θυσιῶν ὡς πρὸς
τὸν καιρὸν ἐκεῖνον ἦν τῷ θεῷ τιμιώτερον; Καὶ μετὰ
πόσης ἀκριβείας καὶ προσοχῆς διετάξατο, τέλεια καὶ
70 ὁλόκληρα καὶ παντὸς ἀπηλλαγμένα μώμου κελεύσας

Font.   **49/51** Is. 58, 4-5   **52/54** Mal. 2, 13   **65/66** Am. 5, 23

Mss.   *AT CDEFHQ*

Crit.   **49** τισὶ – θεοῦ] τοῦ θεοῦ τισὶ *FH*   **50** ἀκουσθῆναι] ὥστε praem. *T*
52 καὶ – ἰδεῖν] ἰδεῖν καὶ δάκρυον *DE*, δάκρυον ἰδεῖν *T*   **53** ἐκαλύπτεται
A *F*^{a.corr.}*H*^{a.corr.}   δάκρυσι] δάκρυον *A*   **54** Καὶ] ἐρώτησις praem. *AT E*
δάκρυον – θεός] δάκρυον ἄρα ὁ θεὸς *E*, δάκρυον ὁ θεὸς ἄρα *FH* (ἄρα *F*), ἄρα
δάκρυον θεὸς *Q*   **56** Ναί] ἀπόκρισις praem. *AT E*   **61** οἶδε πληροῦν *FH*
καὶ¹] om. *FH*   **63** πηγὴν] om. *F*   **64/66** Ἀλλὰ – ἀκούσομαι] om.
DEFHQ   **64** τὸ] τῷ *C*, τὸν *T*   **65** ἐμβοῶν *T*   **66** ᾠδῶν *AT*, ὁδῶν
C, ψαθμῶν *T*   **67** Καὶ – ταῦτα] καὶ μετ'ὀλίγα *T*, om. *DEFHQ*   **68** τῷ
θεῷ] om. *F*   τιμιώτατος *E*   Καὶ] πῶς add. *E*   **69** πόσης] πάσης *FH*

Comp.   **49/50** νηστεύητέ μοι] μοι νηστεύητε ὡς *Is.*   **50** post ἀκουσθῆναι] ἐν κραυ-
γῇ hab. *Is.*

116 FLORILEGIVM COISLINIANVM

προσάγειν αὐτὰ τῷ βωμῷ, καὶ ὀσμὴν εὐωδίας ἑαυτῷ
λέγων τὴν ἐκ τούτων ἀναπέμπεσθαι κνῖσαν. Ἀλλ'ὅτε
ῥαθύμως καὶ ἠμελημένως ἔγνω αὐτοὺς προσάγοντας
καὶ ἀντὶ ὁλοκλήρων, ἀσθενῆ καὶ συντετριμμένα καὶ
75 ὠτότμητα καὶ μυρμηκιῶντα προσφέροντας – ἀπειρημέ-
νον τοῦτο πάλαι σπουδαίως –, καὶ οὐ λύτρον ἁμαρτημάτων, ἀλλὰ μισθὸν μὲν τῶν ἐπταισμένων ἤδη, ἀρραβῶ-
να δὲ τῶν αὖθις ἁμαρτηθησομένων διδόντας τὰ ἱερεῖα,
πῶς ἐβδελύξατο καὶ ἀπεστράφη λέγων· Τί μοι πλῆθος
80 τῶν θυσιῶν ὑμῶν; <Πλήρης εἰμὶ> ὁλοκαυτωμάτων
κριῶν καὶ αἷμα τράγων καὶ ταύρων οὐ βούλομαι. Κα-
θαρῶς μὲν καὶ εὐαγῶς γινόμενα ταῦτα, καλὰ καὶ προαιρέσεως εὐχαρίστου σύμβολα· ἀνάγνως δὲ καὶ βεβήλως,
μυσαρὰ καὶ τοῦ βδελύττεσθαι ἄξια. Παρ'ὃ καὶ τοῖς οὕτω
85 προσφέρουσιν ὁ θεός· Ἐὰν προσφέρητέ μοι σεμίδαλιν,
μάταιον· θυμίαμα βδέλυγμά μοι ἐστί. Καὶ πάλιν περὶ
τινος περὶ τὰς θυσίας μὲν φιλοτιμουμένου, ἀμελοῦντος
δὲ τῶν ἠθικῶν ἀρετῶν· Ὁ δὲ ἄνομος φησίν, ὁ θύων μοι
μόσχον, ὡς ὁ ἀποκτένων κύνα· ὁ δὲ ἀναφέρων σεμίδα-
90 λιν, ὡς αἷμα ὕειον· ὁ διδοὺς λίβανον, ὡς βλάσφημος.

Κἀκεῖναι μὲν αἱ θυσίαι, μικραὶ καὶ νηπίοις πρέπουσαι
τισί, πρὸς τὴν ἀθυρματώδη τῶν Ἰουδαίων ἡρμοσμένην
κατάστασιν· αἱ δὲ νῦν, μεγάλαι καὶ τελείοις ἁρμόζουσαι

Font.   71 cf. Gen. 8, 21; Leu. 2, 12; et loc. par.   73/75 cf. Leu. 22, 22-23
79/81 Is. 1, 11   85/86 Is. 1, 13   88/90 Is. 66, 3

Mss.   AT CDEFHQ (DEFHQ usque ad βλάσφημος, 62.90)

Crit.   72 ἀντιπέμπεσθαι T   74/75 συντετριμμένα καὶ ὠττότμητα A, συντετριμμένα καὶ ἄτμητα H^{ut uid.}, συντετριμμένον καὶ ὠτότμητον DQ
76 πάλαι] om. FH   79 ἐβεδελλύξατο D, ἐβδελύγξατο E^{ut uid.}   80 Πλήρης
εἰμὶ] scripsi cum fonte, om. cett.   80/81 ὁλοκαυτωμάτων – βούλομαι]
om. Q   82 μὲν] γὰρ add. E   83 σύμβουλα T   84 Παρ'ὃ] παραγγέλ-
λων FH   οὕτω] οὕτο (sic) D   85 προσφέρουσιν] φησὶν E   87 περὶ]
πρὸς Q   μὲν] om. T   φιλοτιμωμένου A   88 τῶν] περὶ praem. Q
μοι] om. CDEFHQ   89 ὁ¹] om. HQ   ἀποκτέννων C^{p.corr.}   91 πρέπουσι C
92 ἡρμοσμένην] sic codd., an ἡρμοσμέναι corrigendum?

Comp.   80 post ὑμῶν] hab. λέγει κύριος Is.   89 ἀποκτένων] ἀποκτέννων Is.
90 post λίβανον] εἰς μνημόσυνον hab. Is.

ALPHA 62 117

ἀνδράσιν. Τοσοῦτον γὰρ τῶν Ἰουδαϊκῶν διαφέρουσιν,
95 ὡς τὸν Δαυΐδ μὴ δυνηθέντα ταῖς νομικαῖς θυσίαις περὶ
τῆς μοιχείας καὶ τοῦ φόνου τὸν θεὸν ἱλεώσασθαι, ταῖς
ἡμετέραις τοῦτον ἑαυτῷ καταλλάξαι. Καίτοι, βασιλεὺς
ὤν, ἠδύνατο τὰ πρῶτα καὶ τιμιώτερα προσενεγκεῖν
δι'εὐπορίαν, καὶ τὴν λεγομένην ἑκατόμβην καταθῦσαι
100 φιλοτίμῳ δαψιλείᾳ, ἀλλ'εἰδὼς τὰς ἐν γνώμῃ διὰ τοῦ
σώματος ἐπιτελουμένας εὐαγεῖς τε εἶναι καὶ καθαράς,
καὶ μᾶλλον εὐπροσδέκτους θεῷ, φησίν· Ὅτι εἰ ἠθέλη-
σας θυσίαν, ἔδωκα ἄν· ὁλοκαυτώματα οὐκ εὐδοκήσεις,
κἀκείνας ἀθετήσας ταῖς νῦν πολιτευομέναις ἐχρήσατο
105 λέγων· Θυσία τῷ θεῷ πνεῦμα συντετριμμένον, ἵνα μὴ
ἡ φιλοτιμία τῆς περιουσίας, ἀλλ'ἡ τῆς ψυχῆς προθυ-
μία θυσία κρίνηται ἀληθής, πᾶσιν ὁμοῦ κατ'ἐξουσίαν
προκειμένη, πλουσίοις καὶ πένησιν, ἀρχομένοις καὶ ἄρχουσι, βασιλεῦσι καὶ ὑπηκόοις, ἐν τῷ ἀδαπάνῳ τὰς τῆς
110 ἀδυναμίας προφάσεις περικόπτουσα· πάλιν γὰρ τοῦτο
φησί· Θυσίαν καὶ προσφορὰν οὐκ ἠθέλησας· σῶμα δὲ
κατηρτίσω μοι, τὰς δι'αὐτοῦ γινομένας ἐκ προαιρέσεως πράξεις πρέπουσαν προσφορὰν εἶναι λέγων. Ἀλλ'ὡς
ἐκεῖ ἄμωμα εἰσφέρειν προσετέτακτο τὰ ἱερά, οὕτω καὶ
115 παρ'ἡμῖν. Τὰ μὲν γὰρ θύματα ἡμῶν εἰσὶν αἱ ἀρεταί, τὸ δὲ
ἄμωμον αὐτῶν, τὸ μηδαμῶς μηδὲν λελωβῆσθαι πάθει.
Τί γὰρ ὄφελος σωφροσύνης ἀναφέρειν θυσίαν, ἀπο-
νοίᾳ καὶ τύφῳ μεμωκημένην, ἢ τί ὄφελος ἐγκρατείας
προσάγειν κάρπωσιν, ἀνθρωπαρεσκείας πάθει λελωβη-
120 μένην; Ποῖον δὲ κέρδος ἐλεημοσύνης, πρὸς ἐπίδειξιν γινομένης; Ποῖον δὲ θυμίαμα προσευχῆς, ὅταν ὀργῆς καὶ

Font. **95/96** cf. II Reg. 12, 16-18   **102** cf. I Petr. 2, 5   **102/103** Ps. 50, 18
105 Ps. 50, 19   **111/112** Ps. 39, 7; Heb. 10, 5   **114** cf. Leu. 9, 2. 3

Mss. *AT C*

Crit. **94** τῶν] τω (sic) T   **98** πρῶτα] πρώβατα T   **110** προφάσεις] om. T
112/113 προαιρέσεω (sic) A   **114** ἱερά] ἱερεῖα T   **115** αἱ] om. A
119 ἀνθρωπαρεσκείας πάθει] scripsi cum T (-σκίας), ἀνθρωπαρεσκίας πάθος
A, ἀνθρωπαρεσκεία παθῶν C

118 FLORILEGIVM COISLINIANVM

μνησικακίας λογισμὸς τὴν ταύτης εὐωδίαν εἰς ῥυπαρὰν
μεταβάλωσιν δυσωδίαν, καὶ γίνονται κατὰ τὴν παροιμίαν πίθος τετριμμένος, τοὺς μισθοὺς μετὰ τῶν πόνων
125 ἐγκαταλιμπάνουσαι; Ὅσον γὰρ τὸ μὴ ποιεῖν τὸ καλόν,
τὸ μοχθηρᾷ διαθέσει τοῦτο ποιεῖν· ἀγέραστον ὁμοίως
ἑκάτερον καὶ πρὸς ἀμοιβὴν οὐκ ἐπιτήδειον, εἴ γε κατὰ
τὴν δεσποτικὴν φωνὴν Πᾶν δένδρον μὴ ποιοῦν καρπὸν
καλόν, ἐκκόπτεται καὶ εἰς πῦρ ἐμβάλλεται. Οὐ γὰρ ὅτι
130 ἄκαρπον ἦν κατεδικάζετο τὴν ἐκκοπὴν καὶ πυρὶ παρε-
δίδετο, ἀλλ᾽ὅτι ὃν εἶχε φύσεως φέρειν καρπόν, τοῦτον
γνώμῃ διέφθειρε, δύναμιν μὲν καρποφορίας ἔχον ἐκ
φύσεως, τὴν δε ποιότητα τοῦ καρποῦ πρὸς τὸ πονη-
ρότερον ἀμεῖψαν προαιρέσεως ἐξουσίᾳ.

ΚΖ'
Περὶ ἀγάπης καὶ πόσα τὰ τῆς ἀγάπης εἴδη

63 Κλήμεντος Στρωματέων

Τρισσὰ εἴδη φιλίας διδασκόμεθα, καὶ τούτων τὸ μὲν

Font. 124 cf. Prou. 23, 27 128/129 Mt. 3, 10; 7, 19; Lc. 3, 9 63.1/8 Clem.
Alex., Strom., 2, 19, 101, 3, 1 – 102, 1, 4

Mss. *AT C* 63 *A CDEFHKQ*

Tit. **ΚΖ'**] κς' *DEFH*, λς' *K om. Q* Περὶ – εἴδη] περὶ ἀγάπης καὶ πόσα τὰ εἴδη
τῆς ἀγάπης *FH*, περὶ φιλίας *Q; cf. Sacr. Par.*, PG 95, 1193, 25-26; 1045, 43-
44 (Περὶ ἀγάπης, καὶ εἰρήνης, καὶ εἰρηνοποιῶν, καὶ πράων ἀνθρώπων)
63 Κλήμεντος Στρωματέων] κλήμεντος *Q*

Crit. *122* λογισμὸς] sic codd., λογισμοί expectaueris *124* τετριμμένος] sic codd.,
intellige τετρημένος (cf. Prou. 23, 27); uid. autem Sacr. Par., PG 95, 1337,
14-16 *126* τὸ] sic codd., τοσοῦτον expectaueris ποιεῖ *A* *129* πῦρ]
τὸ praem. *T C* βάλλεται *A* *130/131* παρεδίδοτο *C^{p.corr.}* *134* ἐξουσίαν *C* *63.1* φιλίας] φιλοσοφίας *CDEFHK*

Comp. *124* τετρημένος Prou. *63.1* Τρισσὰ] Τριττὰ δὲ *Clem.*

Ind. *63.1/8* = Sacr. Par., PG 95, 1201, 41-49; PG 96, 405, 28-36

ALPHA 62 – 64

πρῶτον, ἄριστον, τὸ κατ'ἀρετήν· στερρὰ γὰρ ἡ ἐκ λόγου
ἀγάπη. Τὸ δεύτερον καὶ μέσον, τὸ κατ'ἀμοιβήν· κοινω-
νικὸν τοῦτο καὶ μεταδοτικὸν καὶ βιωφελές· κοινὴ γὰρ
5 ἡ ἐκ χάριτος φιλία. Τὸ δὲ ὕστατον καὶ τρίτον, ἡμεῖς τὸ
ἐκ συνηθείας φαμέν· οἱ δὲ Ἕλληνες φασὶ τὸ καθ'ἡδονὴν τρεπτὸν καὶ μεταβλητόν. Οὐκοῦν ἡ μὲν τίς ἐστι φι-
λοσόφου φιλία, ἡ δὲ ἀνθρώπου, ἡ δὲ ζώου.

64   Εὐαγρίου

Ἡ τῶν ἀνθρώπων ἀγάπη εἰς τρία μερίζεται πρόσωπα· ὁ
μὲν διὰ θεὸν ἀγαπᾷ ὃν ἀγαπᾷ, ὁ δὲ ἐπεὶ πλούσιος ἐστὶν,
χάριν λήψεως δώρων, ὁ δὲ ἐμπαθῶς. Καὶ ὁ μὲν εἰλικρι-
νῶς δοξάζει ὃν ἀγαπᾷ, ὁ δὲ διὰ πλεονεξίαν, ὁ δὲ χάριν
5 ἡδονῆς.

Font.   **64.1/5** locum non inueni nisi in flor.

Mss.   *ACDEFHKQ*   **64** *A CDEFHK*

Crit.   2 πρῶτον] καὶ *add. EK*   λόγου] καὶ ἀρετῆς *Q*   3 κατ'] κατὰ *C*
4 γὰρ] ἦν *add. F*   5 ἐκ χάριτος] εὐχάριστος *DEFHKQ*   6/7 κατὰ ἡδονὴν *A*, κατ'ἡδονὴν *FH*   7 τρεπτὸν] τερπνὸν *H*   7/8 φιλοσόφου] φιλοσοφίας *F*, φιλοσόφ() *aut* φιλοσοφ(') *H*   **64.1** τρία] γ' *D*   2 ὃν ἀγαπᾷ]
om. A

Comp.   2 *post* πρῶτον] καὶ *hab. Clem. et Sacr. Par.*   3 *post* Τὸ] δὲ *hab. Clem. et*
Sacr. Par.   τὸ] *non hab. Clem.*   3/4 *post* κοινωνικὸν] δὲ *hab. Clem.*
5 ἐκ χάριτος] εὐχάριστος *Sacr. Par.*   *post* ἡμεῖς] μὲν *hab. Clem. et Sacr. Par.*
(PG 95)   5/6 ἡμεῖς – φασί] τὸ ἐκ συνηθείας φαμέν, πρὸς Ἕλληνας. Οἶδα,
φησὶ *Sacr. Par. (PG 96)*   6 οἱ – φασί] οἳ δὲ *Clem.*   7 *post* μεταβλητόν]
complura (102, 1, 1-3) hab. Clem.   **64.1** Ἡ ἀγάπη τὸν ἄνθρωπον *Sacr. Par.*,
Ἡ ἀγάπη τῶν ἀνθρώπων *Loc. comm.*   ὁ] ὃς *Loc. comm.*   2/3 ὃν –
δώρων] *non hab. Loc. comm.*   3 ὁ¹] ὃς *Loc. comm.*   ὁ²] ὃς *Loc. comm.*
4 ὁ¹] ὃς *Loc. comm.*   ὁ²] ὃς *Loc. comm.*

---

ad.   **64.1/5** = Sacr. Par., PG 95, 1204, 11-15; Ps.-Max., Loc. comm. 66, -, /37, 9c, ms.
F (p. 973)

120 FLORILEGIVM COISLINIANVM

65 Τοῦ Χρυσοστόμου

Τὸν ἔρωτα τὸν παρ'ἡμῖν, τρία ταῦτα ποιεῖν εἴωθεν, ἢ
εὐμορφία σώματος, ἢ εὐεργεσίας μέγεθος, ἢ τὸ φιλεῖ-
σθαι παρά τινος. Τούτων γὰρ ἕκαστον αὐτὸ καθ'αὑτὸ
δύναται ἐμποιῆσαι φίλτρον ἡμῖν. Κἂν γὰρ μηδὲν ὦμεν
5 εὖ παθόντες παρά τινος, ἀκούομεν δὲ μόνον ὅτι φιλῶν
ἡμᾶς διατελεῖ, ἐπαινῶν ἡμᾶς καὶ θαυμάζων, εὐθέως
αὐτῷ συγκολλώμεθα καὶ στέργομεν ὡς εὐεργέτην· ἐπὶ
τοῦ θεοῦ δὲ οὐχὶ τοῦτο μόνον, ἀλλὰ τὰ τρία ταῦτα ἐστὶν
ἰδεῖν μεθ'ὑπερβολῆς συνελθόντα, καὶ μεθ'ὑπερβολῆς το-
10 σαύτης, ὅσην οὐδὲ λόγος παραστῆσαι δυνήσεται. Καὶ
πρῶτον, τὸ κάλλος τῆς μακαρίας ἐκείνης καὶ ἀκηρά-
του φύσεως ἀμήχανον πῶς ἐστὶ καὶ ἄμαχον, καὶ πάντα
ὑπερβαῖνον λόγον, πᾶσαν ἐκφεῦγον διάνοιαν. Κάλλος
δὲ ὅταν ἀκούσῃς, μηδὲν σωματικὸν ὑποπτεύσῃς, ἀγα-
15 πητέ, ἀλλὰ ἀσώματόν τινα δόξαν καὶ μεγαλοπρέπειαν
ἄφραστον. Ταύτην γοῦν ἐμφαίνων ὁ προφήτης, οὕτως
ἔλεγεν· *Καὶ τὰ σεραφὶμ εἰστήκεισαν κύκλῳ αὐτοῦ,
καὶ ταῖς μὲν δυσὶ πτέρυξι κατεκάλυπτον τὸ πρόσωπον,*

Font. **65.**1/45 = Io. Chrys., Exp. in Ps., PG 55, 160, 22 – 161, 14   **17**/20 Is.
6, 2-3

Mss. **65** *AT CDEFHKQ*

Crit. **65.**1 ταῦτα] *om. Q*   2 σωμάτων *AT*   3 ἕκαστος *C*   4 ἐμποῆ-
σαι *D*   Κἂν] καὶ *D*   5 μόνον] *om. F*   6 ἡμᾶς²] τε *EK*   7 ὡς]
ὦ (*sic*) *A*   8 δὲ] *post* ἐπὶ *trsp. EKQ, om. D*   ἔστιν *A Q*   9 συνελθόντα – ὑπερβολῆς] *om. A*   καὶ] *om. Q*   10 δύναται *FH*   Καὶ] α'
praem. E^{in marg.}   11 ἐκείνης] *post* φύσεως *trsp. Q*   12 πῶς] *sic acc. codd., etsi*
indefinitum   καὶ¹] *om. T*   12/13 καὶ² – λόγον] *om. T*   13 λόγον]
καὶ *add. FH*   ἐκφεῦγον] ἐκπίπτων *F*   15 ἀλλ' *EK*   16 γοῦν] οὖν
FH   ἐμφαινὼς (*sic*) *T*

Comp. **65.**3 παρά τινος] παρ'αὐτοῦ *Chrys.*   αὐτὸ] ἑαυτὸ *Chrys.*   4 ἐμποιεῖν
Chrys.   5 ἀκούωμεν *Chrys.*   μόνον] *non hab. Chrys.*   8 ταῦτα *Chrys.*
post ἀλλὰ] καὶ *hab. Chrys.*   ἔστιν *Chrys.*   9 συνελθόντα – ὑπερβολῆς]
non hab. Chrys.   12 *post* φύσεως] ὅτι *hab. Chrys.*   πῶς ἐστὶ] οὕτω πῶς
ἐστι *Chrys.*   13 *post* λόγον] καὶ *hab. Chrys.*   16/17 γοῦν – ἔλεγεν] οὖν
ὁ προφήτης ἐκφαίνων ἔλεγε *Chrys.*   17 Σεραφεὶμ *Chrys.*

ALPHA 65   121

καὶ ταῖς δυσὶ τοὺς πόδας καὶ ταῖς δυσὶν ἐπέταντο, καὶ
20 ἐκέκραγον· Ἅγιος, ἅγιος, ἅγιος, ἀπὸ τῆς ἐκπλήξεως,
ἀπὸ τοῦ θαύματος, ἀπὸ τῆς εὐπρεπείας ἐκείνης, ἀπὸ τῆς
μεγαλοπρεπείας, ἀπὸ τῆς δόξης. Καὶ πάλιν ὁ Δαυῒδ κα-
τανοήσας αὐτὸ τοῦτο, τὸ κάλλος ἐκπλαγεὶς τῆς μακαρίας ἐκείνης φύσεως, ἔλεγεν· Περίζωσαι τὴν ῥομφαίαν
25 σου ἐπὶ τὸν μηρόν σου, δυνατέ, τῇ ὡραιότητί σου καὶ
τῷ κάλλει σου. Διατοῦτο καὶ Μωϋσῆς ἐπεθύμει πολλάκις αὐτὸν ἰδεῖν, τῷ φίλτρῳ τρωθεὶς τούτῳ, καὶ τῆς
δόξης ἐκείνης. Καὶ Φίλιππος ἔλεγεν· Δεῖξον ἡμῖν τὸν
πατέρα σου καὶ ἀρκεῖ ἡμῖν. Μᾶλλον δέ, ὅσα ἂν εἴπω-
30 μεν, οὐδὲ μικρὸν καὶ ἀμυδρόν τι ἴχνος τῆς εὐπρεπείας
ἐκείνης παραστῆσαι δυνησόμεθα. Ἀλλὰ τὰς εὐεργεσίας
βούλει καταλέξομεν; Ἀλλ'οὐδὲ ταύτας λόγος παραστῆσαι δυνήσεται. Διατοῦτο καὶ Παῦλος ἔλεγεν· Χάρις δὲ
τῷ θεῷ ἐπὶ τῇ ἀνεκδιηγήτῳ αὐτοῦ δωρεᾷ. Καὶ πάλιν· Ἃ
35 ὀφθαλμὸς οὐκ εἶδε καὶ οὓς οὐκ ἤκουσε καὶ ἐπὶ καρδίαν

Font.   24/26   Ps. 44, 4   26/27   cf. Ex. 33, 13   28/29   Io. 14, 8
         33/34   II Cor. 9, 15   34/37   I Cor. 2, 9

Mss.   *AT CDEFHKQ*

Crit.   19 ἐπέτοντο *Q,* ἐπέτανται *C*   20 ἔκραγον *FH*   21/22 εὐπρεπείας –
μεγαλοπρεπείας] μεγαλοπρεπείας ἐκείνης *DEFHKQ*   22/26 Καὶ – σου]
om. DEFHKQ   26 μωσῆς *DEKQ*   ἐπιθυμεῖ *FH*   27 ἰδεῖν αὐτὸν
DEFHKQ   καὶ] *om. Q*   28 ἐκείνης] ἡττηθείς *K*   Φίλιππος] φίλιπ-
πον *C,* ὁ *praem. DEFHKQ*   29 σου] *om. DEFHKQ*   30 μικρὸν] τί *add.*
TQ (τι *Q*)   ἀμῖδρὸν *Q*   τι] *om. Q*   32 βούλη *A E*   καταλέξωμεν *F*
Ἀλλ'] *om. EK*   οὐδὲ] β' *praem.* *E*^(*in marg.*)   32/33 λόγος – δυνήσεται] λόγω
παραστῆσαι δυνησόμεθα *A DEKQ,* παραστῆσαι δυνησόμεθα *FH*   33 Δια-
τοῦτο] καὶ *praem. T C,* διὰ γὰρ τοῦτο *FHQ*   καὶ] γὰρ *add. DEK, om. Q*
παῦλον *C*   35/37 καὶ² – αὐτόν] καὶ τὰ λοιπὰ *DEFHKQ*

Comp.   19 καὶ¹ – δυσὶ] ταῖς δὲ δυσὶ κατεκάλυπτον *Chrys.*   καὶ² – ἐπέταντο]
ταῖς δὲ δυσὶν ἐπέτοντο *Chrys.*   20 ἐκέκραγον] ἔκραζον *Chrys.*
21/22 ἀπὸ³ – μεγαλοπρεπείας] *non hab. Chrys.*   23 *post* κάλλος] καὶ
τὴν δόξαν *hab. Chrys.*   28 *post* ἐκείνης] ἐρῶν *hab. Chrys.*   *ante* Καὶ]
Διὰ τοῦτο *hab. Chrys.*   29 σου] *non hab. Chrys.*   30 καὶ] οὐδὲ *Chrys.*
τι ἴχνος] ἴχνος τι *Chrys.*   32 βούλη καταλέξωμεν *Chrys.*   33 καὶ] ὁ
Chrys.   34 θεῷ] Κυρίῳ *Chrys.*

122 FLORILEGIVM COISLINIANVM

ἀνθρώπου οὐκ ἀνέβη, ἃ ἡτοίμασεν ὁ θεὸς τοῖς ἀγαπῶ-
σιν αὐτόν. Ἀλλὰ καὶ τὸ φίλτρον ὅπερ εἰς ἡμᾶς ἐπεδεί-
ξατο, ποῖος παραστήσει λόγος; Τοῦτο γοῦν ἐκπληττό-
μενος Ἰωάννης ἔλεγεν· Οὕτω γὰρ ἠγάπησεν ὁ θεὸς τὸν
40 κόσμον, ὅτι τὸν Υἱὸν αὐτοῦ τὸν μονογενῆ ἔδωκεν ὑπὲρ
ἡμῶν. Εἰ δὲ βούλει ἀκοῦσαι αὐτοῦ τῶν ῥημάτων, καὶ
τὸν πόθον μαθεῖν, ἄκουσον τί φησὶ διὰ τοῦ προφήτου·
Μὴ ἐπιλήσεται γυνὴ τοῦ ἐλεῆσαι τὰ ἔκγονα τῆς κοιλίας
αὐτῆς; Εἰ δὲ καὶ ἐπιλάθοιτο γυνή, ἀλλ'ἐγὼ οὐκ ἐπιλή-
45 σομαί σοι, διὰ τούτου τὸν ἔρωτα ὃν περὶ τῆς σωτηρίας
τῆς ἡμετέρας ἔχει φύσεως δηλῶν.

66 Τοῦ αὐτοῦ

Ἡ τῆς ἀγάπης φύσις κόρον οὐκ οἶδεν, ἀλλὰ ἀεὶ τῶν
ἀγαπωμένων ἀπολαύουσα, πρὸς μείζονα αἴρεται φλό-

Font. 39/41 Io. 3, 16   43/45 Is. 49, 15   45/46 = Io. Chrys., Exp. in Ps., PG
55, 161, 26-27   66.1/7 = Io. Chrys., De dec. mil. tal., PG 51, 17, 23-30

Mss. *AT CDEFHKQ*   66 *AT C*

Tit. 66 Τοῦ αὐτοῦ] *om. C*

Crit. 37 Ἀλλά] γ' *praem.* E^in marg.   καὶ] *om.* F^p.corr. H   37/38 ἐνεδείξατο T
39 Ἰωάννης] ὁ *praem.* TC^a.corr. DEK, *om. FH*   γὰρ] *om. DEFHKQ*
40 ὅτι] ὥστε FQ   41 βούλη E   ἀκοῦσαι] *om. FH*   41/42 ἀκοῦσαι –
πόθον] καὶ ἐκ τῶν αὐτοῦ ῥημάτων τὸν πόθον αὐτοῦ Q   42 πόθον] τόπον F
43 τοῦ ἐλεῆσαι] *post* αὐτῆς (*l. 41*) *trsp.* Q   ἔγγονα T F   44/45 ἐπιλή-
σομαί] ἐπιλάθωμαι H^ut uid.   45 σοι] σου DEFHK   διατοῦτο A   τὴν
σωτηρίαν EK   66.1 ἀλλ' C

Comp. 36 *ante* ἀνθρώπου] τοῦ *hab. Chrys.*   37 *post* αὐτόν] *complura hab. Chrys.*
(*161, 2-5; cf. Rom. 11, 33*)   καὶ] *non hab. Chrys.*   ὅπερ εἰς] ὃ περὶ *Chrys.*
39 *ante* Ἰωάννης] ὁ *hab. Chrys.*   40/41 ὑπὲρ ἡμῶν] *non hab. Chrys.*
41 *post* βούλει] καὶ *hab. Chrys.*   43 τοῦ] τοῦ παιδίου αὐτῆς τοῦ μὴ *Is.*
44 *post* ἐπιλάθοιτο] ταῦτα *hab. Chrys. et Is.*   45 σοι] σου *Chrys. et Is.*
διὰ τούτου] ἵνα ἡμῖν δηλώσῃ *Chrys.*   45/46 σωτηρίας – δηλῶν] ἡμετέρας
σωτηρίας ἔχει *Chrys.*   66.1 *post* Ἡ] γὰρ *hab. Chrys.*   ἀλλά] ἀλλ' *Chrys.*
et Sacr. Par.

Ind. 66.1/7 = Sacr. Par., PG 95, 1200, 18-24

ALPHA 65 – 67

γα. Τοῦτο καὶ ὁ ταύτης τρόφιμος Παῦλος ἔλεγεν· Μηδενὶ μηδὲν ὀφείλοντες, εἰ μὴ τὸ ἀλλήλους ἀγαπᾶν·
5 τοῦτο γὰρ μόνον τὸ ὄφλημα ἀεὶ μὲν καταβάλλεται, οὐδέποτε δὲ ἀποδίδοται. Ἐνταῦθα τὸ διηνεκῶς ὀφείλειν,
καλὸν καὶ ἐπαίνων ἄξιον.

67   Τοῦ αὐτοῦ

Τοῦτο τῶν ἐρώντων ἔθος ἐστίν, μὴ κατέχειν σιγῇ τὸν
ἔρωτα, ἀλλ'εἰς τοὺς πλησίον ἐκφέρειν καὶ λέγειν ὅτι
φιλοῦσιν· θερμὸν γάρ τι πρᾶγμα τῆς ἀγάπης ἡ φύσις,
καὶ σιγῆσαι οὐκ ἂν ἀνάσχοιτο ἡ ψυχή. Καὶ διατοῦτο
5 καὶ Παῦλος ἔλεγεν Κορινθίοις φιλῶν· Τὸ στόμα μου
ἀνέῳγε πρὸς ὑμᾶς, ὦ Κορίνθιοι· τουτέστιν, στέγειν καὶ
κατέχειν σιγῇ τὴν ἀγάπην οὐ δύναμαι, ἀλλὰ διαπαντὸς
ὑμᾶς, καὶ πανταχοῦ, καὶ ἐπὶ τῆς διανοίας, καὶ ἐπὶ τῆς
γλώττης περιφέρω. Καὶ ὁ μακάριος πάλιν Δαυΐδ, οὕτω

Font.   3/4 Rom. 13, 8   67.1/50 = Io. Chrys., Exp. in Ps., PG 55, 159, 20 – 160, 19
5/6 II Cor. 6, 11

Mss.   AT C   67 AT CDEFHKQ

Tit.   67 Τοῦ αὐτοῦ] om. Q

Crit.   3 Παῦλος] om. T   4 ἀγαπᾶν ἀλλήλους T   6 ὀφείλεις T   67.1 ἐνών-
των (sic) T   ἔθος ἐστίν] ἐστὶν ἔθος C, ἐστὶ τὸ ἔθος DEFHK, ἐστὶ τὸ πάθος
Q   2 τοὺς] τοῦ D^(ut uid.)FH, τὸν Q   3 πρᾶγμα] om. Q   4 Καὶ] om. CK
5 κορινθίους CEK   φιλεῖν C   6 ὦ] om. T   7 διαπαντὸς] διὰ πάντας
CD, διὰ παντ() FH   8 καὶ¹] om. EK   9 πάλιν] om. TDEFHKQ

Comp.   3 Τοῦτο – Παῦλος] Καὶ τοῦτο ὁ τῆς ἀγάπης τρόφιμος Παῦλος εἰδὼς Chrys.,
Καὶ τοῦτο ὁ ταύτης τρόφιμος εἰδὼς Παῦλος Sacr. Par.   4 ὀφείλε-
τε Chrys., Sacr. Par. et Rom.   ἀγαπᾶν ἀλλήλους Chrys. et Sacr. Par.
5 μόνον] non hab. Sacr. Par.   6 ὀφείλειν] ὀφλεῖν Sacr. Par.   67.1 Τοῦτο]
Τοιοῦτον Chrys.   ἔθος ἐστίν] τὸ ἔθος Chrys.   4 σιγῆσαι – ἀνάσχοιτο]
σιγῇ στέγειν αὐτὴν οὐκ ἂν ἀνέχοιτο Chrys.   Καὶ] non hab. Chrys.
5 μου] ἡμῶν Chrys., II Cor.   6 ὦ] non hab. Chrys., II Cor.   7 σιγῇ κατέχειν Chrys.   9 Καὶ – οὕτω] Οὕτω καὶ ὁ μακάριος οὗτος Chrys.

124 FLORILEGIVM COISLINIANVM

10 φιλῶν τὸν θεὸν καὶ μαινόμενος ἐν τῷ φιλεῖν, οὐκ ἀνέ-
χεται σιγᾶν, ἀλλὰ ποτὲ μὲν φησίν· Ὃν τρόπον ἐπιποθεῖ
ἡ ἔλαφος ἐπὶ τὰς πηγὰς τῶν ὑδάτων, οὕτως ἐπιποθεῖ ἡ
ψυχή μου πρὸς σέ, ὁ θεός· ποτὲ δέ· Ὁ θεός, ὁ θεός μου,
πρὸς σὲ ὀρθρίζω· ἐδίψησέ σε ἡ ψυχή μου ὡς γῆ ἄβατος
15 καὶ ἄνυδρος. Οὕτω γὰρ ἕτερος τῶν ἑρμηνευτῶν εἶπεν.
Ἐπειδὴ γὰρ λόγῳ παραστῆσαι τὸν ἔρωτα οὐκ ἰσχύει,
περιέρχεται ζητῶν ὑπόδειγμα, ἵνα κἂν οὕτω τὸ φίλτρον ἡμῖν ἐνδείξηται, καὶ κοινωνοὺς ποιήσῃ τοῦ ἔρω-
τος. Πειθώμεθα τοίνυν αὐτῷ, καὶ μάθετε οὕτως ἐρᾶν.
20 Καὶ μή μοι λεγέτω τίς ὅτι· Καὶ πῶς δύναμαι φιλεῖν τὸν
θεὸν ὃν οὐ βλέπω; Καὶ γὰρ πολλοὺς οὐχ'ὁρῶντες φι-
λοῦμεν, οἷον τοὺς ἐν ἀποδημίᾳ φίλους ὄντας ἡμῖν, παῖ-
δας καὶ πατέρας καὶ συγγενεῖς καὶ οἰκείους· καὶ οὐδὲν
κώλυμα γίνεται τὸ μὴ ὁρᾶν, ἀλλ'αὐτὸ δὴ τοῦτο μάλιστα
25 ἐκκαίει τὸ φίλτρον, αὔξει τὸν πόθον. Διατοῦτο καὶ περὶ
Μωϋσέως ὁ Παῦλος ἔλεγεν, ὅτι καταλιπὼν πλοῦτον,
καὶ βασιλείας περιφάνειαν, καὶ τὴν ἄλλην ἅπασαν λαμπρότητα τὴν ἐν Αἰγύπτῳ, εἵλετο μετὰ τῶν Ἰουδαίων
κακουχεῖσθαι, εἶτα τὴν αἰτίαν διδάσκων, προσέθηκε·

Font. **11/13** Ps. 41, 2   **13/15** Ps. 62, 2   **25/31** cf. Heb. 11, 25-27

Mss. *AT CDEFHKQ*

Crit. **10** φιλεῖν] ἔρωτι *DEFHKQ*   **11** φησίν] φασὶν *H*   **15/19** Οὕτω – ἐρᾶν]
om. DEFHKQ   **17** παρέρχεται *C*   **18** ποιήσει *AT*   **19** μάθομεν
C   **20** τίς] *sic acc. codd., etsi indefinitum*   ὅτι Καὶ] ὅτι *T, om. DEFHKQ*
22/23 παῖδας] τὲ *add. E*   **23/31** καὶ³ – ἐκράτησεν] *om. DEFHKQ*
24 ὁρᾶν] ἐρᾶν *C*   **26** μωυσεος *(sine acc.) T*   **27/28** λαμπρότητα]
λαμπρὰν *A* *C*ᵃ·ᶜᵒʳʳ· *(λαμπρότητα sec. m.)*

Comp. **10** μαινόμενος] καιόμενος *Chrys.*   **14** σε] σοι *Ps.*   **14/15** ὡς – ἄνυ-
δρος] ποσαπλῶς σοι ἡ σάρξ μου ἐν γῇ ἐρήμῳ καὶ ἀβάτῳ καὶ ἀνύδρῳ *Ps.*
15 *post* ἄνυδρος] καὶ ἔρημος *hab. Chrys.*   **19** μάθωμεν *Chrys.*   **20** ὅτι]
non hab. Chrys.   **22/23** *ante* παῖδας] ἢ *hab. Chrys.*   **23** καὶ²] ἢ *Chrys.*
24 γίνεται κώλυμα *Chrys.*   τὸ] ἐκ τοῦ *Chrys.*   **26** ὁ – ἔλεγεν] λέγων ὁ
Παῦλος *Chrys.*   *post* καταλιπὼν] θησαυροὺς καὶ *hab. Chrys.*   **29** *post*
αἰτίαν] ἡμᾶς *hab. Chrys.*   **29/30** προσέθηκε – θεὸν] ὅτι δὴ ταῦτα πάντα
ἐποίει διὰ τὸν Θεόν, προσέθηκε *Chrys.*

ALPHA 67   125

30 πάντα δὲ ταῦτα ἐποίει διὰ τὸν θεόν· τὸν γὰρ ἀόρατον
ὡς ὁρῶν ἐκράτησεν. Οὐχ᾽ὁρᾷς τὸν θεόν, ἀλλ᾽ὁρᾷς αὐτοῦ
τὰ δημιουργήματα, οὐρανὸν καὶ γῆν καὶ θάλατταν, ὁρᾷς
αὐτοῦ τὰ ἔργα. Ὁ δὲ φιλῶν, κἂν ἔργον ἴδῃ τοῦ φιλου-
μένου, κἂν ὑποδήματα, κἂν ἱμάτιον, κἂν ὁτιοῦν ἕτε-
35 ρον, διαθερμαίνεται. Οὐχ᾽ὁρᾷς τὸν θεόν, ἀλλ᾽ὁρᾷς αὐτοῦ
τοὺς οἰκέτας, τοὺς φίλους, τοὺς ἁγίους ἄνδρας λέγω
καὶ παρρησίαν ἔχοντας. Θεράπευσον ἐκείνους, καὶ ἕξεις
τοῦ πόθου παραμυθίαν οὐ τὴν τυχοῦσαν· καὶ γὰρ ἐπ᾽ἀν-
δρῶν, οὐχὶ τοὺς φίλους ἡμῶν μόνον, ἀλλὰ καὶ τοὺς
40 ὑπ᾽ἐκείνων φιλουμένους φιλεῖν εἰώθαμεν. Κἂν εἴπῃ τίς
τῶν ἐρωμένων τῶν ἡμετέρων, ὅτι· Τὸν δεῖνα φιλῶ, κἂν
ἐκεῖνος τί πάθῃ χρηστόν, ἐγὼ τῆς εὐεργεσίας ἀπολαύειν
νομίζω· καὶ πάντα ποιοῦμεν καὶ πραγματευόμεθα, καὶ
καθάπερ αὐτὸν τὸν ἐρώμενον ὁρῶντες, οὕτω πᾶσαν
45 σπουδὴν ἐπιδείξασθαι περὶ ἐκεῖνον ἐπειγόμεθα. Τοῦτο
ἔξεστι καὶ ἐπὶ τοῦ Χριστοῦ κατορθῶσαι νῦν. Εἶπεν ὅτι·
Τοὺς πένητας φιλῶ· κἂν οὗτοι τί πάθωσιν ἀγαθόν, ὡς
αὐτὸς ἀπολελαυκώς, οὕτως ἀποδίδωμι τὴν ἀμοιβήν·

Font.   34 cf. Cant. 7, 2   47/48 cf. Mt. 19, 21

Mss.   *AT CDEFHKQ*

Crit.   31 ἐκράτησεν] ἐκαρτέρησεν *T*   31/35 Οὐχ᾽ – διαθερμαίνεται] *om. D*
31 Οὐχ᾽] ἀλλ᾽ *praem. Q*   32 οὐρανὸν – θάλατταν] *om. DEFHKQ*
θάλασσαν *T*   34/35 κἂν³ – ἕτερον] *om. DEFHKQ*   36 τοὺς φίλους]
om. DEFHKQ   38 παραμυθίαν] τὴν *praem. FH*   39 οὐχὶ] οὐ *FH*
μόνον ἡμῶν *FH*   40 εἴπῃς *H^{ut uid.}*   τίς] *sic acc. codd., etsi indefinitum*
42 τί] *sic acc. codd., etsi indefinitum*   ἀπολαύειν] ἀπολάβειν *A*   43 καὶ¹]
om. T EKQ   44 τὸν] *om. A*   45 σπουδαίως *C*   46 Χριστοῦ] καὶ
θεοῦ *add. Q*   νῦν *D*   εἶπας *E*   47 φιλῶ τοὺς πένητας *Q*   τί] *sic*
acc. codd., etsi indefinitum   48 οὕτως] ὅτως (*sic*) *T*   ἀποδίδωσι *Q*

Comp.   31 ἐκράτησεν] ἐκαρτέρει *Chrys.*, ἐκαρτέρησεν *Heb.*   31/32 αὐτοῦ – δη-
μιουργήματα] τὰ δημιουργήματα, ὁρᾷς αὐτοῦ τὰ ἔργα *Chrys.*   34 ὑπό-
δημα *Chrys.*   37 *post* ἐκείνους] νῦν *hab. Chrys.*   38/39 ἀνδρῶν] ἀνθρώπων *Chrys.*   43 καὶ¹] *non hab. Chrys.*   43/44 καὶ καθάπερ] ὥσπερ
Chrys.   45 σπουδὴν – ἐπειγόμεθα] περὶ ἐκεῖνον ἐπιδείξασθαι σπουδήν
Chrys.   45/46 Τοῦτο ἔξεστι] Ἔξεστι τοῦτο *Chrys.*   48 *post* ἀμοιβήν]
complura hab. Chrys. (l. 13-17)

126 FLORILEGIVM COISLINIANVM

Πεινῶντα γάρ με εἴδετέ φησι καὶ ἐθρέψατε, καὶ διψῶν-
50 τα καὶ ἐποτίσατε, καὶ γυμνὸν καὶ περιεβάλετε.

ΚΗ'

Περὶ ἀγαθοεργίας καὶ ὅτι οὐ δεῖ ἀποδιδόναι κακὸν ἀντὶ κακοῦ

68 Παροιμιῶν

Ἐὰν πεινᾷ ὁ ἐχθρός σου, ψώμιζε αὐτόν· ἐὰν διψᾷ, πό-
τιζε αὐτόν. Τοῦτο γὰρ ποιῶν ἄνθρακας σωρεύσεις ἐπὶ
τὴν κεφαλὴν αὐτοῦ, καὶ Κύριος ἀνταποδώσει σοι ἀγαθά. Μὴ εἴπῃς· Ὃν τρόπον ἐχρήσατό μοι χρήσομαι αὐτῷ,
5 ἀλλ'ὑπόμεινον τὸν Κύριον, ἵνα σοι βοηθήσῃ.

69 Ἐκ τῆς πρὸς Ῥωμαίους Παύλου ἐπιστολῆς

Μηδενὶ κακὸν ἀντὶ κακοῦ ἀποδιδόντες, προνοούμενοι

Font. **49/50** cf. Mt. 25, 35-36 **68.1/4** = Prou. 25, 21-22, Rom. 12, 21
4 = Prou. 24, 29 **5** = Prou. 20, 9c **69.1/2** = Rom. 12, 17

Mss. *AT CDEFHKQ* **68** *A C* **69** *A C*

Tit. Περὶ – κακοῦ] cf. Sacr. Par., PG 95, 1136, 33-39 (Περὶ ἀγαθοεργίας· καὶ ὅτι
χρὴ τὸ ἀγαθὸν πρὸς πάντας ποιεῖν· καὶ ὅτι χρὴ τὰ βάρη τοῦ πλησίον φέρειν,
καὶ μὴ μνησικακεῖν, ἀλλὰ ἀντιλαμβάνεσθαι αὐτοῦ, καὶ ἐλέγχειν, μὴ ἀποδιδόναι κακὸν ἀντὶ κακοῦ) **69** 'Εκ] om. A

Crit. **49** φησι] om. *DEFHK* **49/50** καὶ¹ – περιεβάλετε] καὶ τὰ ἑξῆς *DEFHKQ*
50 καὶ²] om. *C^{ut uid.}*

Comp. **49** γάρ με] με γὰρ Chrys. καὶ²] non hab. Chrys. **50** καὶ²] non hab.
Chrys. **68.2** post ἄνθρακας] πυρὸς hab. Prou. **3** καὶ] ὁ δὲ Prou.
5 ἀλλὰ Prou.

Ind. **68.1/4** = Sacr. Par., PG 95, 1137, 23-26 **4/5** = Sacr. Par., PG 95, 1137, 18-20
69.1/3 = Sacr. Par., PG 95, 1141, 3-6

ALPHA 67 – 72

καλὰ ἐνώπιον τῶν ἀνθρώπων. Μὴ νικῶ ὑπὸ τοῦ κακοῦ,
ἀλλὰ νίκα ἐν τῷ ἀγαθῷ τὸ κακόν.

70 Ἐκ τῆς Πέτρου ἐπιστολῆς

Μὴ ἀποδιδόντα κακὸν ἀντὶ κακοῦ, μὴ λοιδορίαν ἀντὶ
λοιδορίας, τοὐναντίον δὲ εὐλογοῦντες, ὅτι εἰς τοῦτο
ἐκλήθητε, ἵνα εὐλογίαν κληρονομήσητε.

71 Ἐκ τοῦ κατὰ Ἰωάννην

Μὴ μιμοῦ τὸ κακόν, ἀλλὰ τὸ ἀγαθόν. Ὁ ἀγαθοποιῶν ἐκ
τοῦ θεοῦ ἐστίν· ὁ δὲ κακοποιῶν, οὐχ ἑώρακε τὸν θεόν.

72 Νείλου

Εἰ βούλει ὑπὸ τοῦ θεοῦ βασιλεύεσθαι, μὴ βούλου ἁμαρτάνειν. Εἰ δὲ ἁμαρτάνεις, πῶς βασιλευθήσῃ ὑπὸ τοῦ
θεοῦ;

Font. 2/3 = Rom. 12, 21   70.1/3 = I Petr. 3, 9   71.1/2 = III Io. 11
72.1/3 locum non inueni nisi in flor.

Mss. 70 *A C*   71 *A C*   72 *A C*

Crit. 70.1 ἀποδιδόντες *C*   72.1 βούλῃ *A*   2 βασιλευθείσῃ *A C^{a.corr.}*

Comp. 70.1 ἀποδιδόντες *Ep. Petri et Sacr. Par.*   μὴ] ἢ *Ep. Petri*   72.1 βούλου]
βούλει *Sacr. Par.*   2 βασιλεύσῃ *Sacr. Par.*

Ind. 2/3 = Ps.-Max., Loc. comm. 1, 2, /2 (p. 7); Io. Georg., Sent., 646
70.1/3 = Sacr. Par., PG 95, 1141, 28-30   71.1/2 Μὴ – θεόν = Sacr. Par.,
PG 95, 1141, 31-33   1/2 Ὁ – θεόν = Ps.-Max., Loc. comm. 8, 2, /2 (p. 185)
72.1/3 = Sacr. Par., PG 95, 1169, 46-48 (Philonis)

128 FLORILEGIVM COISLINIANVM

ΚΘ′

Περὶ ἀποκαταστάσεως

73   Μαξίμου μοναχοῦ

Τρεῖς ἀποκαταστάσεις οἶδεν ἡ ἐκκλησία· μίαν μὲν τὴν
ἑκάστου κατὰ τὸν τῆς ἀρετῆς λόγον, ἐν ᾗ ἀποκαθίστα-
ται τὸν ἐπ'αὐτῷ λόγον τῆς ἀρετῆς ἐκπληρώσας· δευτέραν δὲ τὸ τῆς ὅλης φύσεως ἐν τῇ ἀναστάσει, τὴν εἰς
5 ἀφθαρσίαν καὶ ἀθανασίαν ἀποκατάστασιν· τρίτην δέ, ᾗ
καὶ μάλιστα κατακέχρηται ἐν τοῖς ἑαυτοῦ λόγοις ὁ Νύσης Γρηγόριος· ἔστιν αὕτη ἡ τῶν ψυχικῶν δυνάμεων
τῇ ἁμαρτίᾳ ὑποπεσουσῶν εἰς ὅπερ ἐκτίσθησαν πάλιν
ἀποκατάστασις. Δεῖ γὰρ ὥσπερ τὴν ὅλην φύσιν ἐν τῇ
10 ἀναστάσει τὴν τῆς σαρκὸς ἀφθαρσίαν χρόνῳ ἐλπιζομένων ἀπολαβεῖν, καὶ οὕτως τὰς παρατραπείσας τῆς ψυχῆς δυνάμεις τῇ παραστάσει τῶν αἰώνων ἀποβαλεῖν
τὰς ἐντεθείσας αὐτῇ τῆς κακίας μνήμας, καὶ περάσα-
σαν τοὺς πάντας αἰῶνας, καὶ μὴ εὑρίσκουσαν στάσιν,
15 εἰς τὸν θεὸν ἐλθεῖν, τὸν μὴ ἔχοντα πέρας· καὶ οὕτως, τῇ

Font.   **73.1/18** = Max. Conf., Quaest. et dub., 19, 5-12 = I, 13, 5-12 (p. 18)

Mss.   73 *AT CDEFHKQ*

Tit.   **ΚΘ′**] κη′ *T,* κζ′ *DEFH,* λζ′ *K, om. Q*   73 Μαξίμου μοναχοῦ] μαξίμου *DEFHK*

Crit.   **73.2** κατὰ] *om. Q*   3 ἀρετῆς] αὐτῆς *FH*   3/4 δεύτερον *FH*   4 τὸ] τὴν *EKQ ut expectaueris, om. T*   φύσεως ὅλης *FH*   5 καὶ ἀθανα-σίαν] καὶ ἀθανασίας *F, om. A*   τρίτη *Q*   ᾗ *A,* ᾗ *HK*   7 ἔστιν] ἔστιν *C,* ἔστιν *D,* ἥτις ἐστὶν *EK,* καὶ *praem. F*   8 ἐκτίστησαν (*sic*) *Q*   10/11 ἐλπιζομένῳ *FH, forsan recte,* ἐλπιζομένην *T EKQ*   11 καὶ] *om. EKQ^{p.corr.}*   παρατραπήσας *AT*   τῆς] *om. Q*   12 παρατάσει *Q*   ἀπολαβεῖν *DQ*   13 μνήμας] μνήμης *F,* ἀποβαλλοῦσαν *add. Q*

Comp.   **73.4** τὸ] τὴν *Max. (non hab. V^{a.corr.} OBLD)*   5 τρίτη *Max. (R Z C OBLD = Coisl.)*   10/11 ἐλπιζομένῳ *Max.* (ἐλπιζομένην *B L D*)   11 οὕτως καὶ *Max.*   12 παρατάσει *Max.*

ALPHA 73 – 74   129

ἐπιγνώσει οὐ τῇ μεθέξει τῶν ἀγαθῶν, ἀπολαβεῖν τὰς δυνάμεις, καὶ εἰς τὸ ἀρχαῖον ἀποκατασταθῆναι καὶ δειχθῆναι τὸν δημιουργὸν ἀναίτιον τῆς ἁμαρτίας.

Λ'

Πῶς νοητέον τὸ Πᾶν ἄρσεν διανοῖγον μήτραν;

74   Ἀμφιλοχίου

Πᾶσα φύσις παρθένου πρῶτον ἐκ συνουσίας ἀνδρὸς διανοίγεται, ἡ μήτρα καὶ ὕστερον τίκτει. Ἐπὶ δὲ τοῦ σωτῆρος ἡμῶν οὐχ᾽οὕτως, ἀλλὰ χωρὶς συνουσίας αὐτὸς διανοίξας τὴν μήτραν τῆς παρθένου, ἀφθάρτως προῆλθεν,
5   ὥστε τὸ Πᾶν ἄρσεν διανοῖγον μήτραν, ἅγιον τῷ Κυρίῳ κληθήσεται, εἰς τὸν Κύριον μόνον τὴν ἀναφορὰν κέκτηται. Μὴ γὰρ ὁ Κάϊν ἅγιος, ὁ ἐν βεβηλότητι τὸ ζῆν ἀπορρήξας, ἐπειδὴ πάντως οὗτος τῆς μητρικῆς μήτρας ἔξαρ-

---

Font.   **74.**1/37 = Amph., In occ. dom., 49-81   **5/6** Lc. 2, 23   **7/9** cf. Gen. 4, 1-14

Mss.   *AT CDEFHKQ*   **74** *AT CDEFHQ*

Tit.   **Λ'**] κθ' *T*, κη' *DEFH*, *om. Q*   Πᾶν – μήτραν] = Lc. 2, 23   ἄρσεν – μήτραν] διανοῖγον μήτραν ἄρσεν *DFHQ*, ἄγ(ιον) τῷ κυρίῳ κληθήσεται *add. E*   **74** Ἀμφιλοχίου] ἐπισκόπου ἰκονίου *add. F*, ἀρχίππου *T*, *om. Q*

Crit.   **74.**1/2 Πᾶσα φύσις παρθένου, πρῶτον ἐκ συνουσίας ἀνδρὸς διανοίγεται ἡ μήτρα, καὶ ὕστερον τίκτει *sic interpunx. codd.*   **1** Πᾶσα – παρθένου] πάσης παρθένου *Q*   παρθένων *C*   **1/2** ἀνοίγεται *Q*   **2** ἡ μήτρα] τὴν μήτραν *E*, μήτρα *A^{a.corr.}Q*   **4** τῆς – ἀφθάρτως] τῆς παρθένου, ἀφράστως *C*, ἀφράστως *DEFH*, *om. Q*   **7** τὸ ζῆν] τοῦ ζῆν *D*, τὴν γῆν *(sic) A*   **8** πάντως οὗτος] παντὸς οὗτος *T FHQ*, *om. E*   **8/9** ἔξαρχος] ἐξ ἀρχῆς *CE*, *ante* τῆς μητρικῆς *trsp. FH*

Comp.   **17** ἀποκαταστῆναι *Max.*   **74.**2 ὕστερον] εἰθ᾽οὕτως *Amph.* (ω² [-Μ²] = *Coisl.*)   **4** ἀφθάρτως] ἀφράστως *Amph.* (*VP²TKMOR* = *Coisl.*, *U* ἄφθαρτος)   **6/7** τὴν – κέκτηται] ἀναφέρεται *Amph.*   **7** γὰρ] ἄρα *Amph.*   **8** πάντως] πρὸ πάντων *Amph.*

130   FLORILEGIVM COISLINIANVM

χος γέγονεν; Μὴ ἄρα ὁ Ῥουβὴμ ἄγιος, ὁ τὴν πατρικὴν

10 κοίτην ὑβρίσας καὶ κατάρας ἀπόφασιν ἀναζέσας, ἐπειδὴ τῆς πολυγόνου κοιλίας τῆς Λείας πρῶτος ἐξελήλυθε;
Μὴ ἄρα Ἡσαῦ ἄγιος, ὁ πολέμιος καὶ πολέμου καὶ μάχης
κληρονόμος, ἐπειδὴ πρῶτος ἐξέπεσεν; Οὐδεὶς τούτων
ἄγιος, πάντες οὗτοι ἐν ἐπιτιμίοις. Ἐξ ὧν δείκνυται ὅτι

15 εἰς τὸν Κύριον μόνον τὴν ἀναφορὰν ἔχει τὸ Πᾶν ἄρσεν
διανοῖγον μήτραν, ἄγιον τῷ Κυρίῳ κληθήσεται, κατὰ τὸν
Γαβριὴλ τὸν εἰρηκότα πρὸς τὴν παρθένον· Πνεῦμα ἅγιον ἐπελεύσεται ἐπὶ σέ, καὶ δύναμις ὑψίστου ἐπισκιάσει
σοι, διὸ καὶ τὸ γεννώμενον ἅγιον κληθήσεται υἱὸς θεοῦ.

20   Ἔστι δὲ πάντως εἰπεῖν τινὰ τῶν ἀντιλεγόντων· εἰ εἰς
τὸν Κύριον τὴν ἀναφορὰν ἔχει τὸ Πᾶν ἄρσεν διανοῖγον
μήτραν, οὐκ ἔμεινεν ἡ παρθένος παρθένος· ἐφώνησε
γὰρ ἡ γραφὴ ὅτι Πᾶν ἄρσεν διανοῖγον μήτραν· ἀνέῳκτο πάντως ἡ παρθενικὴ μήτρα, εἰ εἰς τὸν Κύριον τὴν

25 ἀναφορὰν κέκτηται. Ἀλλ'ἄκουε συνετῶς· πρὸς μὲν τὴν

Font.   **9/11** cf. Gen. 35, 22   **12/13** cf. Gen. 25, 25-34   **15/16** cf. supra
l. 5/6   **17/19** Lc. 1, 35   **21/22** cf. supra l. 5/6   **23** cf. supra l. 5/6

Mss.   *AT CDEFHQ*

Crit.   **9/13** Μὴ – ἐξέπεσεν] *om. DEFHQ*   **9** ἄρα *T*   **10** ἀποφάσει *T*
11 πρῶτος] πρῶτον *C, om. T*   **12** καὶ²] *om. T*   **13** πρῶτον *C* ἐξέ-
πεσεν] ἐξελήλυθεν *T* τούτων] *om. DEFHQ*   **14** οὗτοι] *om. DEFHQ*
15 τὸν] *om. T*   **15/16** ἄρσεν – κληθήσεται] ἄρσεν διανοῖγον μήτραν *DEFH,*
om. Q   **17** τὸν] *om. Q*   **19** γενώμενον *A FQ*   θεοῦ] πᾶν δὲ, ὅτι ἐν
αὐτῷ πᾶν τὸ μῦστήριον *add. Q*   **21/23** τὸ – μήτραν] τὸ πᾶν ἄρσεν διανοῖγον μήτραν *DEFH, om. Q*   **23** ἡ γραφὴ] *om. C*   **23/24** ἀνέωκται *Q*
24/25 εἰ – Ἀλλ'] πρὸς ὃν ἐροῦμεν· καὶ πῶς ἐν τῷ Ἰεζεκιὴλ γέγραπται,
ὅτι ἔδειξέ μοι κύριος, πύλην κεκλεισμένην καὶ τὰ ἑξῆς· πλὴν *Q (cf. infra
75.12/14), om. DEFH*   **25** ἄκουε] οὖν *add. DEFH* μὲν] γὰρ *add. FH*

Comp.   **9/11** Μὴ – ἐξελήλυθε] *post* ἐξέπεσεν *(l. 13) hab. Amph. (TU = Coisl.)*
10/11 *post* ἐπειδὴ] καὶ οὗτος *hab. Amph.*   **11** Λίας *Amph.* ἐξελήλυ-
θε] ἐξῆλθεν *Amph.*   **12** *ante* Ἡσαῦ] ὁ *hab. Amph.* πολέμου – μάχης]
μαχαίρας *Amph.*   **13** *post* ἐπειδὴ] καὶ οὗτος τῆς μητρικῆς νηδύος *hab.*
Amph.   **15** μόνον] *non hab. Amph. (EPUv = Coisl.)*   **20** εἰ] ὅτι εἰ τοίνυν
Amph.   **22** *post* μήτραν] ἅγιον τῷ κυρίῳ κληθήσεται *(Lc. 2, 23) hab. Amph.*
25 Ἀλλ'] *non hab. Amph. (Τδ²υ = Coisl.)*

ALPHA 74 – 75

παρθενικὴν φύσιν οὐδ'ὅλως αἱ παρθενικαὶ πύλαι ἠνεῴχθησαν βουλήσει τοῦ ἀρτίως κυοφορηθέντος, κατὰ τὸ
φάσκον περὶ αὐτοῦ ῥητόν· Αὕτη ἡ πύλη τοῦ Κυρίου, καὶ
εἰσελεύσεται καὶ ἐξελεύσεται καὶ ἔσται ἡ πύλη κεκλει-
30 σμένη. Ὡς πρὸς τὴν παρθενικὴν τοίνυν φύσιν οὐδ'ὅλως
ἠνεῴχθησαν αἱ παρθενικαὶ πύλαι· ὡς δὲ πρὸς τὴν δύναμιν τοῦ τεχθέντος δεσπότου οὐδὲν τὸ παρεμποδί-
ζον, οὐδὲν τὸ παρενοχλοῦν· πάντα τῷ Κυρίῳ ἠνέῳκτο.
Ὅθεν καὶ αἱ ἄνω ὑπέρτεραι δυνάμεις ταῖς κάτω παρεγ-
35 γυῶσαι ἐκέκραγον λέγουσαι· Ἄρατε πύλας, οἱ ἄρχοντες
ὑμῶν, καὶ ἐπάρθητε, πύλαι αἰώνιοι, καὶ εἰσελεύσεται ὁ
βασιλεὺς τῆς δόξης.

*75   Λεοντίου Δαμασκηνοῦ πρεσβυτέρου

Βλέπε μοι τὸν ἱεροφάντην Μωϋσέα δηλοῦντα τὸ ἄφραστον μυστήριον τῆς γεννήσεως τοῦ Χριστοῦ· φησὶ
γὰρ ὅτι Πᾶν πρωτότοκον διανοῖγον μήτραν ἅγιον τῷ
Κυρίῳ κληθήσεται. Συλλόγισαι οὖν καὶ βλέπε ὅτι οὐκ
5 ἐνδέχεται διανοιγῆναι μήτραν πρὸ γάμου· γαμεῖται

Font.   28/30 Ez. 44, 2   35/37 Ps. 23, 7   75.1/28 locum non inueni; ed.
Leont. Dam., fr. 1   3/4 immo Lc. 2, 23; cf. Ex. 13, 2. 12. 15; Num. 3, 12;
8, 16

Mss.   AT CDEFHQ   75 AT CDEFHQ

Tit.   75 Λεοντίου – πρεσβυτέρου] om. Q

Crit.   26/27 ἀνεῴχθησαν Q   27/31 κατὰ – πύλαι] om. DEFHQ   33 ἀνέῳκτο
EQ, ἠνέῳκται FH   34/37 Ὅθεν – δόξης] om. DEFHQ   35 ἐκέκραγον
λέγουσαι] om. A   75.1/22 Βλέπε – κἀγώ] om. Q, sed scripsit εἰ δὲ θέλεις
καὶ ἑτέροις ὑποδείγμασι πιστωθῆναι τὸ μυστήριον, εἰπέ μοι, πῶς εἰσῆλθεν
ὁ χριστὸς κτλ. (vide. infra, l. 21/26)   1 μωσέα DE   δηλοῦν A Cᵃ·ᶜᵒʳʳ·
FHᵃ·ᶜᵒʳʳ·   2 φησὶν E   3 γὰρ] om. E   4 βλέπε] ἴδε E   5 ἀνοιγῆναι FH

Comp.   32 post δεσπότου] οὐδὲν κέκλεισται τῷ κυρίῳ, ἀλλὰ πάντα ἠνέῳκται hab.
Amph.   33 ἠνέῳκται Amph.   34 ὑπέρτατοι Amph. (ω² = Coisl.)
35 κεκράγασι Amph. (ω² = Coisl.)   36 καὶ¹ – αἰώνιοι] non hab. Amph.
(EAVPTUSv = Coisl.)

132   FLORILEGIVM COISLINIANVM

γὰρ γυνή, καὶ ὁ ἀνὴρ διανοίγει τὴν μήτραν, καὶ τότε
γεννᾶται τὸ βρέφος. Ἡ δὲ θεοτόκος οὐχ'οὕτως· μόνον
γὰρ ὅτι ἐγέννησεν οἴδαμεν, τὸ δὲ πῶς οὐκ οἴδαμεν·
ἀνὴρ γὰρ οὐχ'ὡμίλησεν αὐτῇ, καὶ Χριστὸς ἐγεννήθη ἐξ
10 αὐτῆς. Λέγει γὰρ αὐτὴν ἡ γραφὴ καὶ γεννήσασαν καὶ
κεκλεισμένην· *Διήνοιξε γὰρ μήτραν ὁ Χριστὸς μόνος,
γεννηθεὶς καὶ μὴ λύσας τὴν παρθενίαν.* Καὶ ἐν μὲν τῷ
Ἰεζεκιὴλ γέγραπται ὅτι *Ἔδειξέ μοι Κύριος πύλην κεκλεισμένην, καὶ Κύριος εἰσῆλθε δι'αὐτῆς καὶ ἐξῆλθε,*
15 *καὶ αὕτη ἦν κεκλεισμένη.* Μωϋσῆς δὲ λέγει· *Πᾶν πρωτότοκον διανοῖγον μήτραν ἅγιον τῷ Κυρίῳ κληθήσεται·*
ἅγιος γὰρ ἁγίων Ἰησοῦς. Πάλιν δὲ εἴρηται ὅτι ἐν αὐτῷ
πᾶν τὸ μυστήριον. Παιδίον οὖν ἐγεννήθη ὁ Κύριος καὶ
ἐξῆλθεν ἐκ μήτρας ὡς οὐκ οἴδαμεν· μόνος γὰρ αὐτὸς ὁ
20 διανοίξας μήτραν καὶ μὴ λύσας τῆς ἁγνείας αὐτῆς τὰ
κλεῖθρα οἶδε τὸ μυστήριον. Εἰ δέ μοι εἴποι τίς· Πῶς ἐγ-
χωρεῖ τοῦτο γενέσθαι; ἐρῶ αὐτῷ κἀγώ· Πῶς εἰσῆλθεν
ὁ Χριστὸς εἰς τοὺς μαθητὰς αὐτοῦ τῶν θυρῶν κεκλει-
σμένων; Εἰ δὲ πάλιν ἀμφιβάλλει ἄλλος, ἀντερῶ καὶ
25 αὐτῷ· Πῶς ἐξῆλθεν ἐκ τοῦ τάφου ὁ Χριστὸς ἐσφραγι-
σμένου τοῦ τάφου; Ἀκατάληπτος οὖν ἡ γέννησις αὐτοῦ
οὐχ' ἡμῖν μόνοις, ἀλλὰ καὶ προφήταις καὶ ἀγγέλοις καὶ
ἀρχαγγέλοις.

Font.   8 cf. Lc. 2, 7; Mt. 1, 25; Gal. 4, 4   9 cf. Lc. 1, 34   10 cf. supra l. 8
11 cf. infra l. 13/15   cf. supra l. 3   13/15 cf. Ez. 44, 1-3   15/16 cf. supra
l. 3/4   17 cf. Dan. 9, 24; Clem. Alex., Strom., 1, 21, 126, 2, 1-2; Hipp.,
Comm. in Dan. 4, 32, 3, 1 – 4, 2   17/18 cf. Col. 1, 19; 2, 9 (ἐν αὐτῷ
[...] πᾶν τὸ [...]) et Col. 1, 26 (μυστήριον); Eph. 3, 9   20 cf. supra l. 3
22/24 cf. Io. 20, 19. 26   25/26 cf. Mt. 27, 66 – 28, 10

Mss.   *AT CDEFHQ*

Crit.   6 γυνή] ἡ *praem. FH*   διανοίγοι *T,* ἀνοίγει *FH*   τὴν] *om. FH*
10/11 καὶ κεκλεισμένην] κεκλεισμένην (*sic*) *A*   10 καὶ²] *om.* D
11 μόνος ὁ χριστὸς *DEFH*   14/15 καὶ¹ – κεκλεισμένη] *om. DE*
15 μωσῆς *DEFH*   17 Πάλιν] πᾶν *CDEFH*   εἴρηκεν *T*   20 ἁγνείας]
ἁγίας *DE*   αὐτῆς] παρθένου *E*   23 εἰς] πρὸς *D*   24 καὶ] *om. FH*
25 ὁ Χριστὸς] *post* ἐξῆλθεν *trsp. FH*   26 τοῦ τάφου] ὄντως *D,* τυγχά-
νοντος *Q*   27 μόνον *E*

ALPHA 75 – 76   133

ΛΑ΄

Περὶ τῆς ἀπογραφῆς τῆς γενομένης ἐπὶ Αὐγούστου Καίσαρος

76   Τοῦ Χρυσοστόμου

Ἐξῆλθε δόγμα παρὰ Καίσαρος Αὐγούστου ἀπογράφεσθαι πᾶσαν τὴν οἰκουμένην· αὕτη ἡ ἀπογραφὴ πρώτη
ἐγένετο ἡγεμονεύοντος τῆς Συρίας Κυρηνίου. Καὶ ἐπο-
ρεύοντο ἀπογράφεσθαι, ἕκαστος εἰς τὴν ἰδίαν πόλιν.
5   Οὐδὲ γὰρ οἴκοθεν οὐδὲ ἀφ'ἑαυτοῦ ὁ Αὔγουστος τὸ
δόγμα τοῦτο ἐξέπεμψεν, ἀλλὰ τοῦ θεοῦ κινοῦντος
αὐτοῦ τὴν ψυχήν, ἵνα καὶ ἄκων ὑπηρετήσῃ τῇ τοῦ μονογενοῦς παρουσίᾳ. Καὶ τί τοῦτο συντελεῖ πρὸς τὴν
οἰκονομίαν φησὶ ταύτην; Οὐ μικρὸν οὐδὲ τὸ τυχόν,
10   ἀγαπητέ, ἀλλὰ καὶ σφόδρα μέγα, καὶ τῶν ἀναγκαίων
καὶ σπουδαζομένων ἕν. Ποῖον δὴ τοῦτο; Ἡ Γαλιλαία
χώρα τίς ἐστιν ἐν Παλαιστίνῃ, ἡ δὲ Ναζαρὲτ πόλις τῆς
Γαλιλαίας· πάλιν ἡ Ἰουδαία χώρα τίς ἐστι παρὰ τῶν
ἐγχωρίων οὕτω καλουμένη, ἡ δὲ Βηθλεὲμ πόλις τῆς
15   Ἰουδαίας. Τὸν δὲ Χριστὸν οἱ προφῆται ἔλεγον ἅπαντες

Font.   **76.1/4** = Io. Chrys., In diem nat., PG 49, 352, 43-47; Lc. 2, 1-3   **5/59** = Io.
Chrys., In diem nat., PG 49, 353, 19 – 354, 22   **6** cf. supra l. 1

Mss.   **76** AT CDEFH

Tit.   **ΛΑ΄**] λ' T, κθ' DEFH   γεναμένης A C   **76** Τοῦ Χρυσοστόμου] om. C

Crit.   **76.3/4** ἐπορεύετο T   **5/6** τὸ – τοῦτο] τὸ τοιοῦτον δόγμα E   **7** ἄκων]
ἄκον A D   **8** συντελεῖ] post φησὶ trsp. FH   **10** ἀγαπητοί FH
11 σπουδαζομένων] τῶν praem. E   **12** τίς] τί H   **13** ἡ] om. DE
14 καλούμενον (sic) H   **15** δὲ] γὰρ E   ἔλεγον] post Χριστὸν trsp. FH

Comp.   **76.5** Οὐδὲ] Οὐ Chrys.   ἀφ'] παρ' Chrys.   post ἑαυτοῦ] τότε hab. Chrys.
7 ὑπηρετήσηται Chrys.   **9** ταύτην φησίν Chrys.   **12** Ναζαρὲθ Chrys.
15 ἔλεγον] προὔλεγον Chrys.

134   FLORILEGIVM COISLINIANVM

οὐκ ἀπὸ Ναζαρέτ, ἀλλ'ἀπὸ τῆς Βηθλεὲμ ἥξειν καὶ ἐκεῖ
τεχθήσεσθαι. Οὕτω γὰρ γέγραπται· Καὶ σὺ Βηθλεὲμ
οὐδαμῶς ἐλαχίστη εἶ ἐν τοῖς ἡγεμόσιν Ἰούδα· ἐκ σοῦ
γάρ μοι ἐξελεύσεται ἡγούμενος, ὅστις ποιμανεῖ τὸν
20 λαόν μου τὸν Ἰσραήλ. Καὶ οἱ Ἰουδαῖοι οἱ τότε παρὰ τοῦ
Ἡρώδου ἐρωτώμενοι ποῦ ὁ Χριστὸς γεννᾶται, ταύτην
εἶπον αὐτῷ τὴν μαρτυρίαν. Διατοῦτο καὶ Ναθαναὴλ εἰ-
πόντος πρὸς Φίλιππον· Ἐκ Ναζαρὲτ δύναταί τι ἀγαθὸν
εἶναι;, ἐπειδὴ ἐκεῖνος ἔλεγεν· Ἰησοῦν τὸν ἀπὸ Ναζαρὲτ
25 εὑρήκαμεν, φησὶν ὁ Χριστός· Ἴδε ἀληθῶς Ἰσραηλίτης
ἐν ᾧ δόλος οὐκ ἔστιν. Τίνος ἕνεκεν αὐτὸν ἐπῄνεσεν;
Ἐπειδὴ οὐ συνηρπάγη τῇ ἐπαγγελίᾳ τοῦ Φιλίππου,
ἀλλ'ᾔδει σαφῶς καὶ ἀκριβῶς ὅτι οὐκ ἐκ Ναζαρὲτ οὐδὲ ἐν
τῇ Γαλιλαίᾳ τὸν Χριστὸν δεῖ τεχθῆναι, ἀλλ'ἐν Ἰουδαίᾳ
30 καὶ τῇ Βηθλεέμ, ὅπερ οὖν καὶ ἐγένετο. Ἐπεὶ οὖν ὁ μὲν
Φίλιππος τοῦτο ἠγνόησεν, ὁ δὲ Ναθαναὴλ νομομαθῶς
ἀπεκρίνατο κατὰ τὴν ἄνωθεν περὶ αὐτοῦ προφητείαν
εἰρημένην ὅτι <οὐκ> ἐκ Ναζαρὲτ ἥξει. Διατοῦτο φη-

Font.   **17/20** Mt. 2, 6; cf. Mich. 5, 1. 3   **23/24** Io. 1, 46   **24/25** Io. 1, 45
         25/26 Io. 1, 47   **32/33** cf. supra l. 17/20

Mss.   *AT CDEFH*

Crit.   **16** Ναζαρέτ] τῆς *praem.* E   καὶ] *om.* T   **19** ὅστις] ὃς FH   **20** οἱ²]
         om. FH   **22** Ναθαναὴλ] ὁ *praem.* A   **23** Φίλιππον] τὸν *praem.* FH
         27 Ἐπειδὴ] ὅτι E   **28** οὐκ] οὔτε T FH   οὐδ' T   **30** μὲν] *om.* E
         33 οὐκ] *scripsi cum FH et fonte, om. cett.*

Comp.   **16** Ναζαρέτ] τῆς Ναζαρὲθ *Chrys.*   **17** *post* Βηθλεέμ] γῆ Ἰούδα *hab. Chrys.*
         et Mt.   **19** μοι] *non hab. Chrys. et Mt.*   **22** *ante* Ναθαναὴλ] τοῦ *hab.*
         Chrys.   **23** *ante* Φίλιππον] τὸν *hab. Chrys.*   **23/24** Ἐκ – εἶναι] *post*
         εὑρήκαμεν *(l. 25) hab. Chrys.*   **23** Ναζαρὲθ *Chrys.*   **24** Ναζαρὲθ
         Chrys.   **25** φησὶν – Χριστός] ὁ Χριστὸς περὶ αὐτοῦ φησιν *Chrys.*
         26 Τίνος] Καὶ τίνος, φησίν *Chrys.*   **27** ἀπαγγελίᾳ *Chrys.*   **28** ἐκ Ναζαρὲτ]
         ἐν Ναζαρὲθ *Chrys.*   οὐδὲ] οὔτε *Chrys.*   **29** τὸν – δεῖ] ἔδει τὸν Χρι-
         στὸν *Chrys.*   *ante* Ἰουδαίᾳ] τῇ *hab. Chrys.*   **30** *ante* τῇ] ἐν *hab. Chrys.*
         31 νομομαθῶς] ἅτε νομομαθὴς ὢν *Chrys.*   **32** *ante* κατὰ] τὰ *hab.*
         Chrys.   περὶ αὐτοῦ] *non hab. Chrys.*   **33** εἰρημένην ὅτι] εἰρημένα, εἰ-
         δώς, ὅτι οὐκ *Chrys.*   Ναζαρὲθ *Chrys.*   *post* ἥξει] ὁ Χριστός *hab. Chrys.*
         33/34 φησὶν] καὶ *Chrys.*

ALPHA 76   135

σὶν ὁ Χριστός· Ἴδε ἀληθῶς Ἰσραηλίτης ἐν ᾧ δόλος οὐκ
35 ἔστιν. Διατοῦτο καί τινες τῶν Ἰουδαίων ἔλεγον πρὸς
τὸν Νικόδημον· Ἐρώτησον καὶ ἴδε ὅτι ἐκ τῆς Γαλιλαίας
προφήτης οὐκ ἐγήγερται. Καὶ πάλιν ἀλλαχοῦ· Οὐκ ἀπὸ
Βηθλεὲμ τῆς κώμης ὅπου ἦν Δαυῒδ ὁ Χριστὸς ἔρχεται;
Καὶ κοινὴ πάντων ψῆφος ἦν, ὅτι πάντως ἐκεῖθεν αὐτὸν
40 δεῖ παραγενέσθαι, οὐκ ἀπὸ τῆς Γαλιλαίας.

Ἐπεὶ οὖν ὁ Ἰωσὴφ καὶ ἡ Μαρία τῆς Βηθλεὲμ ὄντες
πολῖται, ἐκείνην ἀφέντες ἐν τῇ Ναζαρὲτ τὸν βίον αὐτῶν
κατεστήσαντο, κἀκεῖ διέτριβον, οἷα δὴ πολλὰ συμβαί-
νειν εἰκὸς ἐπὶ πολλῶν ἀνθρώπων, τὰς μὲν πόλεις ὅθεν
45 ἐγένοντο καταλιμπανόντων, ἐπ'ἄλλαις δέ, ἐν αἷς οὐκ
ἔφυσαν παρὰ τὴν ἀρχήν, διατριβόντων, ἔδει δὲ τὸν Χριστὸν ἐν Βηθλεὲμ τεχθῆναι, ἐξῆλθε δόγμα καὶ ἄκοντας
αὐτοὺς συνωθοῦν εἰς τὴν πόλιν· ὁ γὰρ νόμος ὁ κελεύων
ἕκαστον εἰς τὴν ἰδίαν ἀπογράφεσθαι πατρίδα, ἠνάγκα-
50 ζεν αὐτοὺς ἐκεῖθεν ἀνίστασθαι, ἀπὸ τῆς Ναζαρέτ, καὶ
ἔρχεσθαι εἰς τὴν Βηθλεὲμ ὥστε ἀπογράφεσθαι. Τοῦτο
οὖν αἰνιττόμενος ὁ εὐαγγελιστής, ἔλεγεν· Ἀνέβη δὲ καὶ

Font.   34/35   cf. supra, l. 25/26   36/37   Io. 7, 52   37/38   Io. 7, 42
47   cf. supra l. 1   52/59   Lc. 2, 4-7

Mss.   AT CDEFH

Crit.   34/35 ἐν – ἔστιν] om. DFH   37 προφήτης] post ὅτι trsp. A   38 ἦν]
om. H   Δαυῒδ] ὁ praem. T   ἔρχεται ὁ χριστὸς C   39 ἐκεῖθεν αὐτὸν]
αὐτὸν ἐκεῖθεν αὐτὸν (sic) FH   40 δεῖ] post ὅτι trsp. E   41 ὁ] om. DE
Βηθλεὲμ ὄντες] πόλεως Βηθλεὲμ ἦσαν FH   43 κατέστησαν F   δι-
ατρίβον T   δή] δεῖ A CD, om. FH   45 ἐπ'] ἐν FH   ἐν] om. FH
47 ἐμ βιβλεὲμ (sic) τεχθῆναι A, ἐμ βιθλεὲμ τεχθῆναι D, ἐν βηθλεὲμ γεννηθῆ-
ναι FH   48 συνόθουν D, συνώθουν FH   51 ἔρχεται T   εἰς] πρὸς FH

Comp.   34 post Ἰσραηλίτης] φησὶν hab. Chrys.   36 Ἐρώτησον] Ἐρεύνησον Chrys.
et Io.   36/37 προφήτης ἐκ τῆς Γαλιλαίας Chrys.   38 ἔρχεται ὁ Χριστὸς Chrys.   42 Ναζαρὲθ Chrys.   45 ἐπ'] ἐν Chrys.   46 ἐφύησαν
Chrys.   47 ante δόγμα] τὸ hab. Chrys.   48 post πόλιν] ἐκείνην, τοῦ Θεοῦ
οὕτως οἰκονομοῦντος hab. Chrys.   50 ἐκεῖθεν αὐτοὺς Chrys.   Να-
ζαρέτ] Ναζαρὲθ λέγω Chrys.   52 οὖν] γοῦν αὐτὸ Chrys.   post αἰνιττό-
μενος] καὶ hab. Chrys.

136 FLORILEGIVM COISLINIANVM

Ἰωσὴφ ἀπὸ τῆς Γαλιλαίας ἐκ πόλεως Ναζαρὲτ εἰς
τὴν Ἰουδαίαν εἰς πόλιν Δαυΐδ, ἥτις καλεῖται Βη-
55 θλεέμ, διὰ τὸ εἶναι αὐτὸν ἐξ οἴκου καὶ πατριᾶς Δαυΐδ,
ἀπογράφεσθαι σὺν Μαριὰμ τῇ μεμνηστευμένῃ αὐτῷ,
οὔσῃ ἐγκύῳ. Καὶ ἐγένετο ἐν τῷ εἶναι αὐτοὺς ἐκεῖ, ἐπλή-
σθησαν αἱ ἡμέραι τοῦ τεκεῖν αὐτήν, καὶ ἔτεκεν τὸν υἱὸν
αὐτῆς τὸν πρωτότοκον.
60 Ὅθεν δῆλον ὅτι κατὰ τὴν πρώτην ἀπογραφὴν ἐτέ-
χθη. Καὶ τοῖς χαρτῴοις τοῖς δημοσίᾳ κειμένοις ἐπὶ τῆς
Ῥώμης ἔξεστιν ἐντυγχάνοντα καὶ τὸν καιρὸν τῆς ἀπο-
γραφῆς μαθόντα ἀκριβῶς εἰδέναι.

ΛΒ'

Περὶ τῶν ἀκρίδων ὧν ἤσθιεν ὁ Βαπτιστής

*77 Ἀθανασίου Ἀλεξανδρείας
Ἐκ τῆς ἑρμηνείας τοῦ κατὰ Ματθαῖον εὐαγγελίου

Εἶχεν δὲ ὁ Ἰωάννης τὸ ἔνδυμα ἀπὸ τριχῶν καμήλου,

Font.   60/63 = Io. Chrys., In diem nat., PG 49, 353, 5-9   77.1/21 locum non
inueni   1/4 cf. Mt. 3, 4

Mss.   77 AT CDEFH

Tit.   ΛΒ'] λα' T, λ' DEFH   77 Ἀθανασίου] ἀθανάσιος A   Ἐκ – εὐαγγελίου]
τῆς ἑρμηνείας τοῦ κατὰ ματθαῖον εὐαγγελίου λόγος γ' A^{ut uid.}, ἐκ τῆς τοῦ
κατὰ ματθαῖον εὐαγγελίου ἑρμηνείας F, om. T

Crit.   54 εἰς²] om. F^{a.corr.} H (F hab. sup. l.)   55 πατρίδος C   56 ἀπογράψασθαι
E   σὺν] συμ (sine acc.) A C   αὐτῷ] γυναικὶ add. DE   57/59 Καὶ –
πρωτότοκον] om. DEFH   60 δηλονότι FH   61 χαρτίοις D   τῆς]
τοῖς T   62 ἐντυγχάνοντα] ἐντυγχάνοντας T, τὸν praem. FH   63 μαθόν-
τας T   77.1 ὁ] om. D   ἔνδυμα] αὐτοῦ add. T

Comp.   53 ante Ἰωσὴφ] ὁ hab. Chrys.   Ναζαρὲθ Chrys. et Lc.   56 ἐμνηστευ-
μένη Lc.   post αὐτῷ] γυναικὶ hab. Chrys.   57 Καὶ ἐγένετο] Ἐγένετο
δὲ Lc.   61 χαρτῴοις] ἀρχαίοις Chrys.   post κειμένοις] κώδιξιν hab.
Chrys.   62 ἐντυχόντα Chrys.   63 post εἰδέναι] τὸν βουλόμενον hab.
Chrys.   77.1 Εἶχεν – Ἰωάννης] Αὐτὸς δὲ ὁ Ἰωάννης εἶχεν Mt.   post
ἔνδυμα] αὐτοῦ hab. Mt.

ALPHA 76 – 77 137

τὸν τρόπον ὀρθόν, πάγιον βλέποντα εἰς τὸ ὕψος καὶ
τὰς ἐπουρανίους μονάς, ζώνην περὶ τὴν ὀσφύν, σωφροσύνην περὶ τὴν ψυχήν· ἐσθίων ἀκρίδας, οὐ τὰς ἐμψυ-
5 χωμένας, ἀλλὰ χλόην οὕτω προσαγορευομένην. Ὅτι δὲ
ἀκρὶς ὑπάρχει βοτάνη, ἔστι ῥαδίως τοὺς πάντας πληρο-
φορηθῆναι, λέγοντος τοῦ μὲν Δαυῒδ ἐν Ψαλμοῖς· Ἐξε-
τινάχθην ὡσεὶ ἀκρίδες – οὐ γὰρ Ἐδιώχθην ὡσεὶ ἀκρίς,
ἀλλ᾽ Ἐτινάχθην ὡς ἀκρίς –, ἀντὶ τοῦ ὡς αὕτη ἡ βοτάνη
10 βίᾳ τινάσσεται, οὕτω κἀγὼ μετὰ βίας πολλῆς ἀπεκι-
νήθην ἀπὸ τῶν ἐμῶν, ὑπὸ τῶν φιλεχθρῶν καὶ τοῦ ζη-
τοῦντος Σαοὺλ θανατῶσαι τὴν ψυχήν μου. Τὸν δὲ Ἐκ-
κλησιαστὴν εἰπεῖν· Ἀνθήσει τὸ ἀμύγδαλον καὶ παχυνθῇ
ἡ ἀκρὶς καὶ διασκεδασθήσεται ἡ κάππαρις. Ὥσπερ οὖν
15 τὸ ἀμύγδαλον οὐκ ἔστιν σὰρξ πτηνοῦ, ἡ δὲ κάππαρις βοτάνη καὶ οὐδὲν ἕτερον, οὕτως δῆλον καὶ ἡ ἀκρὶς ὑπάρχει βοτάνη ἐν πεδίῳ καὶ ἐν λειμῶνι αὐξανομένη. Εἰ δὲ
ἄρτον οὐκ ἤσθιεν ὁ μακάριος Ἰωάννης, πολλῷ μᾶλλον
κρεῶν οὐκ ἀπεγεύετο· τοῦ δὲ μέλιτος μετελάμβανεν,
20 ἐπεὶ ἀσκητικόν ἐστι τὸ βρῶμα· ἦσαν δὲ καὶ οἱ λόγοι τῆς
καρυκείας αὐτοῦ μέλιτι ἐοικότες.

Font.   5/6 cf. Athan., Fragm. in Matth., PG 27, 1365, 41; Isid. Pel., Ep., 1, 132, PG
78, 269, 33-34   7/8 Ps. 108, 23   11/12 cf. II Regn. 22, 1; Ps. 17, 1
13/14 Eccl. 12, 5; cf. Athan., Fragm. in Matth., PG 27, 1365, 42-43
16/17 cf. Athan., Fragm. in Matth., PG 27, 1365, 41   19/21 cf. Athan.,
Fragm. in Matth., PG 27, 1365, 43-45   19 cf. Mt. 3, 4

Mss.   AT CDEFH

Crit.   3 ζώνην] δερματίνην (cf. Mt. 3, 4) add. E   6 ἀκρὶς] ἡ praem. E   8 ὡσεὶ¹]
ὡς C   8/9 οὐ – ἀκρίς] om. Cᵃ·ᶜᵒʳʳ· (suppl. in marg.)   ὡσεὶ²] ὡς F
9 ἀλλ᾽ – ἀκρίς] om. A Eᵃ·ᶜᵒʳʳ· (suppl. in marg.)   ἐξετεινάχθην T
ὡσεὶ T E   Ὡς αὕτη] ὡσαύτη A DF, αὕτη E   10 μετὰ – πολλῆς]
βία πολλῇ E   11 τῶν²] om. H   φιλεχθρῶν (sic) A   τοῦ] om. H
12/13 Τὸν – εἰπεῖν] τοῦ δὲ ἐκκλησιαστοῦ βοῶντος E   13 ἀμίγδαλον E
παχυνθήσεται E   14 κάπαρις ATE   15 ἀμίγδαλον E   κάπαρις TE
17 δὲ] δ᾽ DEFH   19 ἐγεύετο FH

Comp.   3 post ζώνην] δερματινὴν hab. Mt.   post ὀσφύν] αὐτοῦ hab. Mt.   13 ἀνθήσῃ Eccl.   14 διασκεδασθῇ Eccl.

138 FLORILEGIVM COISLINIANVM

ΛΓ'

Περὶ τοῦ Ἴσθι εὐνοῶν τῷ ἀντιδίκῳ σου

78 Τοῦ Χρυσοστόμου

Ἄκουσον τοῦ Κυρίου λέγοντος· Ἴσθι εὐνοῶν τῷ ἀντιδίκῳ σου, ἕως ὅτου εἶ ἐν τῇ ὁδῷ μετ'αὐτοῦ. Καλὸν μὲν
οὖν καθάπαξ, καὶ πρὸς τοὺς φιλοπραγμοσύνης ἐρῶν-
τας, ἵνα μὴ δίκαις φιλονεικότερον ἐγγυμνάζωσιν·
5 βέλτιον γὰρ καὶ ἐν δίκαις προλαβεῖν φιλικαῖς διαλύσε-
σι τὸ τῆς δίκης ἄδηλον τέλος, ἢ ταῖς ἐλπίσι τῆς νίκης
ἐρειδομένους, ἀδήλῳ καταπιστεῦσαι πελάγει.
Καὶ μετὰ ταῦτα. Ὅμως οὐ δοκεῖ μοι μόνον περὶ χρημάτων ὁ λόγος ἔχειν. Τί τὸ αἴτιον; Ἴσθι εὐνοῶν τῷ
10 ἀντιδίκῳ σου ταχύ, ἕως ὅτου εἶ ἐν τῇ ὁδῷ μετ'αὐτοῦ.
Αὕτη ἡ προσθήκη δίδωσί μοι τί καὶ μεῖζον ἐννοεῖν. Εἰ
γὰρ περὶ χρηματικῶν δικῶν μόνον ὁ λόγος ἦν, ἢ τῶν
ἐγκληματικῶν τῶν αἰσθητῶν ἔλεγε, διατί προσετίθει·

Font. **78.**1/7 = Ps.-Io. Chrys., De paen., PG 59, 759, 29-36   1/2 Mt. 5, 25
8/59 = Ps.-Io. Chrys., De paen., PG 59, 759, 57 - 760, 32   9/10 cf. supra
l. 1/2

Mss. **78** AT CDEFH

Tit. **ΛΓ'**] λβ' T, λα' DEFH   Ἴσθι - σου] = Mt. 5, 25   ἀντιδίκῳ] ἀδίκῳ E
78 Τοῦ Χρυσοστόμου] Ἰωάννου praem. A, χρυσοστόμου F, om. C

Crit. **78.**2 εἶ] ἢ T C (ἢ C)   3 καθάπαξ] τὸ ῥητὸν add. E   4 ἐγγυμνάζουσιν
FH (-σι H)   7 πελάγει καταπιστεῦσαι E   8 μετὰ ταῦτα] μετὰ τοῦτο
A, μετ'ὀλίγα T, om. DEFH   μόνον] μόνος C   10 εἶ] ἢ AT CD (ἢ C)
11 τί] sic acc. codd., etsi indefinitum   12 ὁ λόγος μόνον T   τῶν] περὶ
praem. FH   13 τῶν] τῶ (sic) T   προσετέθη A

Comp. **78.**1 λέγοντος] κράζοντος Ps.-Chrys.   ante Ἴσθι] Σήμερον hab. Ps.-Chrys.
2 ὅτου] οὗ Ps.-Chrys.   μετ'αὐτοῦ ἐν τῇ ὁδῷ Ps.-Chrys. et Mt.   3 post
οὖν] καὶ hab. Ps.-Chrys.   4 μὴ] μηδὲ Ps.-Chrys.   δίκαις Ps.-Chrys.
7 ἐπερειδομένους Ps.-Chrys.   9 ἔχειν - αἴτιον] ἔχειν τὸ αἴτιον Ps.-Chrys.
post Ἴσθι] φησὶν hab. Ps.-Chrys.   12 ἦν] non hab. Ps.-Chrys.   13 ἐγκληματικῶν - αἰσθητῶν] ἐγκλημάτων τῶν ἀναισθήτων Ps.-Chrys.

ALPHA 78   139

Ἕως ὅτου εἶ ἐν τῇ ὁδῷ μετ'αὐτοῦ; Τίς γὰρ ἀντίδικος
15 συνοδεύειν ἀντιδίκῳ καταδέχεται; Τίς κοινωνεῖ τῆς
ὁδοιπορίας, μὴ κοινωνῶν τῆς γνώμης; Οὐ δέδοικε καὶ
γραμματείων κλοπήν, καὶ μαρτύρων διαφθοράν, καὶ
τὰς <κατὰ τὰς> λεωφόρους ἐπιβουλάς; Οὐκοῦν ὀφεί-
λομεν εὑρεῖν ἀντίδικον τὸν ἀεὶ συνοδεύοντα, οὗ τὴν
20 συνοδίαν καὶ σφόδρα φυλαττόμενοι φεύγειν οὐ δυνά-
μεθα, καὶ τοῦτον νοῆσαι τὸν ἀντίδικον, ᾧ προσήκει
μετ'εὐνοίας προσφέρεσθαι. Τίς οὖν ἄρα ἐστὶν ὁ ἀντίδικος;
Ἐὰν ἀκριβῶς ἐξετάσῃς, τὸ σῶμα τῆς σαρκός· οὗτος
ἀντίδικός ἐστι τοῦ ἐν σοὶ πνεύματος. Καὶ ἵνα μὴ νομί-
25 σῃς ἐμὸν εἶναι τὸν λόγον, Παῦλος κυρωσάτω τὸ ῥηθέν·
Ἡ σὰρξ ἐπιθυμεῖ κατὰ τοῦ πνεύματος, τὸ δὲ πνεῦμα
κατὰ τῆς σαρκός· ταῦτα δὲ ἀντίκεινται ἀλλήλοις. Καὶ
οὐ Μανιχαίων εἰσάγω λόγον, οὐδὲ ἄλλον λέγω σώματος δημιουργὸν καὶ ἄλλον ψυχῆς, ἀλλ'Ἡ σὰρξ ἐπιθυ-
30 μεῖ, τῇ ἡδονῇ συμβούλῳ χρωμένη· τὸ πνεῦμα κατὰ τῆς
σαρκός, ταῖς μελλούσαις ἐλπίσιν ἐπερειδόμενον. Ἀντίκεινται ἀλλήλοις ἐπιθυμία σαρκὸς καὶ ἐπιθυμία βασιλείας οὐρανῶν. Οὗτός ἐστιν ὁ ἀντίδικος, καὶ ἑκόντος

Font.   **14** cf. supra l. 2   **26/27** Gal. 5, 17   **29/30** cf. supra l. 26/27
31/33 cf. supra, l. 26/27

Mss.   *AT CDEFH*

Crit.   **14** εἶ] ἢ *A CD* (ἢ *C*)   **17** διαφθοράν] διαφοράν *T E^{a.corr.}*   **18** κατὰ τὰς]
scripsi cum fonte, om. codd.   λεωφόρους] ἐκ τῆς λεωφόρου *E*
18/19 ὀφείλωμεν *C*   **21** τοῦτο *D*   **21/22** μετ'εὐνοίας] μετανοίας *D^{ut uid.}*,
μετ'εὐμενείας *H*   **22** ἄρα *A CE*   **24/26** Καὶ – πνεύματος] *om. T*
27 ἀλλήλοις ἀντίκεινται *T*   **29** ἀλλ'] ἀλ' (*sic*) *A*   **29/30** ἐπιθυμεῖ] τὰ τῆς
σαρκὸς *add. T*   **31/32** Ἀντίκεινται] οὖν *add. F*   **33** ἐστιν] *om. CDEFH*

Comp.   **15** ἀντιδίκῳ συνοδεύειν *Ps.-Chrys.*   **17** γραμμάτων *Ps.-Chrys.*
20 συνοδείαν (*sic*) *Ps.-Chrys.*   φυγεῖν *Ps.-Chrys.*   **21** ἐννοῆσαι *Ps.-Chrys.*
22 ἄρα – ὁ] ἀκριβής ἐστιν *Ps.-Chrys.*   **23** σαρκός] ψυχῆς *Ps.-Chrys.*
24/25 νομίσῃς] νοήσῃς *Ps.-Chrys.*   **26** τὸ δὲ] καὶ τὸ *Ps.-Chrys.*
27 ἀντίκεινται] ἀντίκειται *Ps.-Chrys.*   **29** καὶ– ψυχῆς] *non hab. Ps.-Chrys.*
29/30 *post* ἐπιθυμεῖ] κατὰ τοῦ πνεύματος *hab. Ps.-Chrys.*   **30** *post* τὸ] δὲ
hab. Ps.-Chrys.   **32** σαρκὸς] κόσμου *Ps.-Chrys.*   **33** *ante* οὐρανῶν] τῶν
hab. Ps.-Chrys.   *ante* καὶ] ὁ *hab. Ps.-Chrys.*

140 FLORILEGIVM COISLINIANVM

σου καὶ ἄκοντός σου συνοδεύων· ὁδὸς γὰρ ἐστὶν ὁ βίος.
35 Ἡ ψυχὴ τὴν ἰδίαν εἰκόνα σπεύδει μιμεῖσθαι, ἡ σάρξ
ἐπὶ τὸν χοῦν καταρρεῖ· Ταῦτα δὲ ἀντίκεινται ἀλλήλοις.
Τούτῳ τῷ ἀντιδίκῳ σου ἴσθι εὐνοῶν. Καὶ πότε; Ἕως
ὅτου εἶ ἐν τῇ ὁδῷ μετ᾽αὐτοῦ, ἕως ἐν τούτῳ τυγχάνεις
τῷ βίῳ· ἐὰν γὰρ ἡ ὁδὸς τελεσθῇ, οὐκέτι σοι μετανοίας
40 καιρός, ὅτι οὐκ ἔστιν ἐν τῷ θανάτῳ ὁ μνημονεύων σοι·
ἐν δὲ τῷ Ἅδῃ τίς ἐξομολογήσεταί σοι; Τούτῳ οὖν τῷ
ἀντιδίκῳ ἴσθι εὐνοῶν. Οὐκ εἶπε Χαριζόμενος, ἀλλ᾽Εὐ-
νοῶν. Μὴ τὸ ἡδὺ ποιήσῃς τῷ ἀντιδίκῳ σου, ἀλλ᾽ὡς εὔ-
νους ἀπὸ τῆς ἡδονῆς εἰς τὴν μετάνοιαν ἀνακάλεσαι. Οὐ
45 κελεύει σε ὡς ὀψοποιὸν χρήσασθαι τῷ σώματι, πάντα
τὰ ἐξ ἡδονῆς ζητοῦντι, ἀλλ᾽ὡς ἰατρόν. Ἰατρὸς γὰρ πολλάκις καὶ πικρὸν κιρνᾷ, καὶ τέμνει, καὶ καίει, καὶ πρὸς
τὸ λυπεῖν καὶ μισθοὺς λαμβάνει. Εἰ γὰρ καὶ μικρὸν λυ-
πεῖ τὴν αἴσθησιν, ἀλλὰ καὶ σκοπὸς ὑγείας τῷ θεραπεύον-
50 τι. Μήποτέ σε παραδῷ ὁ ἀντίδικος τῷ μέλλοντι κριτῇ,
καὶ ὁ κριτὴς τῷ ὑπηρέτῃ, ταῖς τιμωρητικαῖς δηλαδὴ

Font. 36 cf. supra, l. 27   37 cf. supra l. 1/2   37/38 cf. supra l. 2
40/41 Ps. 6, 6   41/42 cf. supra l. 1/2   50 cf. supra l. 1/2

Mss. *AT CDEFH*

Crit. 34 σου²] *om. E*   συνοδεύει *FH*   ἐστὶν] ἡμῶν *E*   38 ὅτου] ὅτε *C*
εἶ] ἢ *AT CD*   τυγχάνῃς *AT*   40/41 ὅτι– σοι] *om. DEFH*   40 σοι]
σου *T C*   42 ἀντιδίκῳ] σου *add. T*   45 πάντα] καὶ *praem. T*   46 ἰα-
τρόν] ἰητρόν *DEFH*   47 κερνᾷ *T*   47/48 καὶ⁴ – λαμβάνει] *om. DEFH*
48 τὸ] τῷ *T*   49/50 θεραπεύοντι] γίνεται *add. E*

Comp. 34 σου¹⁺²] *non hab. Ps.-Chrys.*   ἐστὶν] *non hab. Ps.-Chrys.*   38 μετ᾽αὐτοῦ
ἐν τῇ ὁδῷ *Ps.-Chrys. et Mt.*   39 σοι] *non hab. Ps.-Chrys.*   40 σοι] σου
Ps.-Chrys. et Ps.   41/42 τῷ² – εὐνοῶν] ἴσθι τῷ ἀντιδίκῳ σου εὐνοῶν
Ps.-Chrys.; cf. ἴσθι εὐνοῶν τῷ ἀντιδίκῳ σου *Mt.*   45 ὀψοποιῷ *Ps.-Chrys.*
46 ζητοῦντι] ποιοῦντα *Ps.-Chrys.*   ἰατρῷ *Ps.-Chrys.*   47/48 πρὸς –
καὶ¹] προσλυπῶν *Ps.-Chrys.*   48 μισθὸν *Ps.-Chrys.*   49 καὶ] *non hab.*
Ps.-Chrys.   ὑγιείας *Ps.-Chrys.*   49/50 θεραπευομένῳ *Ps.-Chrys.*
50 *post* ἀντίδικος] τῷ κριτῇ *hab. Ps.-Chrys.*   μέλλοντι] *nonhab. Mt.*
post κριτῇ] *complura hab. Ps.-Chrys. (l. 22-24)*   51 καὶ] *non hab. Ps.-Chrys.*

ALPHA 78 – 79   141

δυνάμεσιν, εἰς φυλακὴν βληθήσῃ εἰς τὸ σκότος τὸ ἐξώτερον. Φοβερὸς ὁ τόπος· Οὐ μὴ ἐξέλθῃς ἐκεῖθεν ἕως οὗ
ἀποδῷς τὸν ἔσχατον κοδράντην. Ἐὰν πρὸ τοῦ θανάτου
55 διαλύσῃς τὸ χρέος, λέλυται· ἐὰν ὀφείλων ἀπέλθῃς, καὶ
τὸ ἐγκατάλειμμα τῶν ἐλαχίστων ὀφλημάτων ἀπαιτη-
θήσῃ. Τί ἐστι τὸν ἔσχατον κοδράντην; Ὅτι ἐνθύμιον
ἀνθρώπου ἐξομολογήσεταί σοι, καὶ ἐγκατάλειμμα ἐν-
θυμίου ἑορτάσει σοι.

ΛΔ'

Περὶ τοῦ μὴ ἀναθεματίζειν ἄνθρωπον πιστόν

79   Τοῦ Χρυσοστόμου
Λόγος οὗ ἡ ἀρχή· Πρώην περὶ ἀκαταλήπτου

Φέρε δὴ καὶ περὶ ἀναθέματος ὑμῖν τὰ εἰκότα διαλεχθέντες, καὶ δείξαντες τὴν δύναμιν τούτου τοῦ μὴ δὲ νο-
μιζομένου κακοῦ, παύσωμεν ἐξ αὐτοῦ τὰ ἀχαλίνωτα
στόματα, τὴν νόσον τὴν ὡς ἔτυχε τῶν κεχρημένων
5 ὑμῖν ἐκκαλύπτοντες. Εἰς τοσαύτην γὰρ κακίαν ἤλα-

Font. 52/53 cf. Mt. 8, 12   53/54 Mt. 5, 26   56 cf. infra l. 57/59   57 cf.
supra l. 53/54   57/59 Ps. 75, 11   79.1/9 = Io. Chrys., De anathem., PG
48, 946, 1-11

Mss.   79 AT CDEFHK

Tit.   ΛΔ'] λγ' T, λβ' D, λη' K, om. EFH   μή] om. C^{a.corr.}   79 Τοῦ Χρυσοστόμου]
om. E   Λόγος – ἀρχή] οὗ ἡ ἀρχὴ H, om. T EFK   Πρώην – ἀκατα-
λήπτου] om. T EK; cf. PG 48, 945, 1: Πρώην μὲν περὶ ἀκαταλήπτου ...

Crit. 52 εἰς¹] καὶ praem. T EFH, ut expectaueris   ἐμβληθήσῃ H   55 λέλυ-
σαι DFH   79.1 ἀναθεματισμοῦ C   ὑμῖν] post διαλεχθέντες trsp. E
2 μὴ δὲ] μηδὲν T   3 ἐξ αὐτοῦ] om. E^{a.corr.} (suppl. in marg.)   5 ὑμῖν] ὑμῶν
EK   5/10 Εἰς– ταῦτα] om. DEFHK

Comp. 52 ante εἰς¹] καὶ hab. Ps.-Chrys.   56 ὀφλημάτων] ὀφειλημάτων Ps.-Chrys.
79.2 μὴ δὲ] μηδενὸς Chrys.   4 τὴν²] τῶν Chrys.   τῶν] αὐτῷ Chrys.
5 κακίαν] καχεξίαν Chrys.

142   FLORILEGIVM COISLINIANVM

σε τὰ ἡμέτερα, ὅτι καὶ ἐσχάτως ἔχοντες, ἀγνοοῦμεν
τὰ χείρονα τῶν παθῶν ὑπερβαίνοντες, ὥστε τὴν προ-
φητικὴν φωνὴν εἰς ἡμᾶς πληρωθῆναι, ὅτι· Οὐκ ἔστιν
μάλαγμα ἐπιθεῖναι οὔτε ἔλαιον οὔτε καταδέσμους.
10   Καὶ μετὰ ταῦτα. Θεωρῶ γὰρ ἀεὶ ἄνδρας προϊόντας,
μὴ λογισμὸν πεπαιδευμένως ἐκ τῆς θείας γραφῆς κε-
κτημένους, καὶ τὰ λοιπὰ ἐρυθριῶν σιωπῶ, μεμηνότας
καὶ ἐρεσχελοῦντας, μὴ εἰδότας μὴ δ'ἃ λέγουσιν, μήτε
περὶ τίνων διαβεβαιοῦνται, αὐτὸ τοῦτο δογματίζειν
15   ἀμαθῶς μόνον τολμῶντας, ὡς γελᾶσθαι τὰ ἡμέτερα
παρὰ τῶν τῆς πίστεως ἀλλοτρίων.
Καὶ μετὰ ταῦτα. Πῶς σὺ τολμᾷς τοιαῦτα φθέγξα-
σθαι; Εἰπὲ γάρ μοι, τί ἐστι τοῦτο ὃ λέγεις ἀνάθεμα;
Ἆρα ὃ λέγεις ἐπίστασαι; Τί φῄς; Ἔγνως τούτου τὴν
20   δύναμιν; Καίτοιγε ἐν τῇ θεοπνεύστῳ γραφῇ εὑρήσεις
ἐπὶ τῆς Ἱεριχὼ τοῦτο λεγόμενον· Καὶ ἀναθεματιεῖς πᾶσαν τὴν πόλιν Κυρίῳ τῷ θεῷ σου· καὶ παρ'ἡμῖν ἄχρι
τῆς σήμερον, κοινὴ συνήθεια παρὰ πᾶσι κεκράτηκεν· Ὁ
δεῖνα τόδε πεποιηκώς, τὸ ἀνάθεμα εἰς τόνδε τὸν τόπον

Font.   8/9 Is. 1, 6   10/16 = Io. Chrys., De anathem., PG 48, 947, 1-9
13/14 I Tim. 1, 7   17/75 = Io. Chrys., De anathem., PG 48, 948, 10 – 949, 47
21/22 cf. Ios. 6, 17

Mss.   AT CDEFH

Crit.   6 ἔχοντα C   8 πληρωθῇ C^{a.corr.}   9 ἐπιθῆναι AT   10 μετὰ ταῦτα]
μετ'ὀλίγα T   11 πεπαιδευμένον EK, πεπαιδευμένας FH   12 ἐρυ-
θριωσιῶ (sic) σιωπᾶν D, ἐρυθριῶ σιωπᾶν EFHK   13 εἰδότες D
15 τολμῶντας μόνον EK   17 Καὶ – ταῦτα] καὶ μετ'ὀλίγα T, om. DEFHK
17/18 Πῶς – φθέγξασθαι] om. DEFHK   18 μοι γὰρ D   23 συνηθεία
E^{p.corr.}   24 τόδε] τότε C   24/25 εἰς – ἀνάθεμα] om. DEK

Comp.   7 ante ὑπερβαίνοντες] μὴ hab. Chrys.   10 ἀεὶ] non hab. Chrys.   προϊ-
ὼν Chrys.   11 μὴ] μήτε Chrys.   πεπαιδεύμενον Chrys.   11/12 post
κεκτημένους] μήτε δὲ αὐτῆς ὅλως τι τῆς Γραφῆς ἐπισταμένους hab. Chrys.
12 λοιπὰ] πολλὰ Chrys.   13 μὴ δ'] μήτε Chrys. et I Tim.   15 post τολ-
μῶντας] καὶ ἀναθεματίζειν ἅπερ οὐκ ἴσασιν hab. Chrys.   17/18 φθέγγεσθαι Chrys.   19 Ἆρα] Ὅρα Chrys.   τὴν] non hab. Chrys.   23 post
σήμερον] ἡμέρας hab. Chrys.

ALPHA 79   143

25   ἀνήγαγεν. Ἆρα τοῦτό ἐστι τὸ ἀνάθεμα; Καίτοιγε τοῦτο
     ὡς περί τινος ἀγαθοῦ λέλεκται, τὸ ἀναθέσθαι θεῷ. Τί
     οὖν ἐστι τοῦτο ὃ λέγεις ἀνάθεμα, ἀλλ'ὅτι ἀνατιθέσθω
     οὗτος τῷ διαβόλῳ, καὶ μηκέτι χώραν σωτηρίας ἐχέτω,
     γινέσθω ἀλλότριος τοῦ Χριστοῦ. Καὶ τίς εἶ σύ; Ταῦτα
30   τῆς σῆς ἐξουσίας, ἢ τῆς μεγάλης δυνάμεως; Τότε γὰρ
     καθίσει ὁ βασιλεύς, καὶ στήσει τὰ μὲν πρόβατα ἐκ δε-
     ξιῶν, τὰ δὲ ἐρίφια ἐξ εὐωνύμων. Τί οὖν τῆς τοσαύτης
     ἐπελάβου ἀξίας, ἧς τὸ κοινὸν μόνον τῶν ἀποστόλων
     ἠξίωτο, καὶ οἱ κατὰ πᾶσαν ἀκρίβειαν τούτων ὡς ἀλη-
35   θῶς γεγονότες διάδοχοι πλήρεις χάριτος καὶ δυνάμεως;
     Καὶ μὴν ἐκεῖνοι τὴν ἐντολὴν ἀκριβῶς φυλάξαντες, ὡς
     Τὸν ὀφθαλμὸν τὸν δεξιὸν ἐξορύττοντες, οὕτως τοὺς
     αἱρετικοὺς ἔξω τῆς ἐκκλησίας ἐξέβαλον, ὅπερ ἔνδειξιν
     ἔχει τῆς μεγάλης αὐτῶν συμπαθείας καὶ ἀλγηδόνος, ὡς
40   ἐπικαιρίου μέλους γεγενημένης ἀποκοπῆς. Διατοῦτο
     γὰρ καὶ Δεξιὸν ὀφθαλμὸν τοῦτον ἐκάλεσεν ὁ Χριστός,
     τὴν ὑπὲρ τῶν ἀποβαλλομένων συμπάθειαν ἐνδεικνύ-
     μενος. Ὅθεν καὶ ἐν τούτῳ ὡς καὶ ἐν πᾶσιν ἀκρίβειαν
     ἔχοντες, τὰς μὲν αἱρέσεις διήλεγξαν καὶ ἀπεβάλοντο,
45   οὐδενὶ δὲ τούτων τῶν αἱρετικῶν ταύτην τὴν ἐπιτιμίαν

Font.   30/31 cf. Mt. 25, 31   31/32 Mt. 25, 33   35 Act. 6, 8   37 cf. Mt. 5, 29
        41 cf. supra l. 37

Mss.   AT CDEFH

Crit.   26 περί] παρά FH   τὸ] τῷ DF^{a. uel p.corr.}   27 οὖν] om. FH   29 γενέσθω
        EK   30 σῆς] om. C   31 καθήσει FH   34 καὶ οἱ] scripsi cum DEFHK
        et fonte, οἳ καὶ AT C   39 μεγάλης] μεγίστης A   40 ἐπὶ καιρίου EFHK
        41 τοῦτο DEK   42/43 ἐπιδεικνύμενος FH   44 διήλλεγξαν T

Comp.   25 ἐπήγαγεν Chrys.   post Ἆρα] γε hab. Chrys.   27 τοῦτο] non hab.
        Chrys.   ἀναθέσθω Chrys.   28 τῷ] non hab. Chrys.   29 γενέσθω
        Chrys.   ante τοῦ] ἀπὸ hab. Chrys.   ταύτης Chrys.   30 ἢ] καὶ Chrys.
        31 ὁ βασιλεύς] Υἱὸς τοῦ Θεοῦ Chrys.   34 ἠξίωται Chrys.   38 ἀπέβα-
        λον Chrys.   40 γενομένης Chrys.   41 ἀπεκάλεσεν Chrys.   42 ὑπὲρ]
        παρὰ Chrys.   ἀποβαλόντων Chrys.   43 ἐν²] non hab. Chrys.   44 ὑπὲρ]
        44 διήλεγχον Chrys.   ἀπέβαλλον Chrys.   45 τούτων] non hab. Chrys.
        τὴν] non hab. Chrys.

144 FLORILEGIVM COISLINIANVM

προσῆγον. Τοιγαροῦν ὁ ἀπόστολος, ἐν δυσὶ μόνοις τόποις, ἐξ ἀνάγκης τὴν φωνὴν ταύτην φαίνεται εἰπών·
οὐχ̓ὁριστικῷ δὲ προσώπῳ ταύτην προσήγαγεν, ἐν μὲν
τῇ πρὸς Κορινθίους εἰπών· Εἴ τις οὐ φιλεῖ τὸν Κύριον
50 ἡμῶν Ἰησοῦν Χριστόν, ἤτω ἀνάθεμα, καὶ Εἴ τις ὑμᾶς
εὐαγγελίζεται παῤὃ παρελάβετε, ἀνάθεμα ἔστω. Τί οὖν
ὧν μηδεὶς τῶν εἰληφότων τὴν ἐξουσίαν πεποίηκεν, εἰ
μὴ μόνος ὃς ἔλαβεν, σὺ τολμᾷς ταῦτα ποιεῖν, τὰ ἐναν-
τία τοῦ δεσποτικοῦ θανάτου, καὶ προλαμβάνεις τὴν
55 κρίσιν τοῦ βασιλέως; Τὸ γὰρ ἀνάθεμα παντελῶς τοῦ
Χριστοῦ ἀποκόπτει.

Δίδαξον, ἐν πραότητι παιδεύων τοὺς ἀντιδιατιθεμέ-
νους, μήποτε δῷ αὐτοῖς ὁ θεὸς ἐλθεῖν εἰς ἐπίγνωσιν
ἀληθείας, ἐκ τῆς τοῦ διαβόλου παγίδος ἐζωγρημένους
60 εἰς τὸ ἐκείνου θέλημα. Ἐπέκτεινον τῆς ἀγάπης τὴν σαγήνην, ἵνα μὴ τὸ χωλὸν ἐκτραπῇ, ἰαθῇ δὲ μᾶλλον. Δεῖξον ὅτι ἐκ πολλῆς διαθέσεως τὸ οἰκεῖον ἀγαθὸν βούλει
ποιῆσαι κοινόν. Κᾂν μὲν βουληθῇ δέξασθαι τοῦτο ὁ τὴν
πλάνην ὑποδεξάμενος ἄνθρωπος, κατὰ τὴν τοῦ προ-

Font. **49/50** I Cor. 16, 22 **50/51** Gal. 1, 9 **57/60** II Tim. 2, 25-26

Mss. *AT CDEFH (DEFHK* usque ad ἀποκόπτει, 79.56)

Crit. **46** προσήγαγον *C* **48** εἰσήγαγεν *FH* **50** ἤτω] εἴτω *AT Cᵖ·ᶜᵒʳʳ· D* (εἶ τῶ *A*)
51 παρελάβεται *AT D* **52** ὦν] ὃ *EK* ἐξουσίαν] ταύτην *add. EK*
54 προλαμβάνει *T D* **62** βούλει] βούλη *A*

Comp. **47** τὴν φωνὴν ταύτην ἐξ ἀνάγκης *Chrys.* **48** προσήγαγεν] ἐπήγαγεν
Chrys. **50** ἤτω] ἔστω *Chrys. (I Cor. = Coisl.)* **51/52** Τί – ὦν] Τί οὖν;
ὃ *Chrys.* **52** *post* ἐξουσίαν] τοῦτο *hab. Chrys.* **52/53** εἰ – ἔλαβεν]
ἢ ἀποφήνασθαι τετόλμηκε *Chrys.* **53** τὰ] *non hab. Chrys.* **54** *post*
θανάτου] διαπραττόμενος *hab. Chrys.* **54/55** τοῦ βασιλέως τὴν κρίσιν
Chrys. **55** *post* βασιλέως] *complura (PG 48, 948, 53 – 949, 9) hab. Chrys.*
56 *post* ἀποκόπτει] *complura (PG 48, 949, 10-21) hab. Chrys.* **58** ἐλθεῖν]
μετάνοιαν *Chrys. et II Tim.* **59** *post* ἀληθείας] καὶ ἀνανήψωσιν *hab. Chrys.*
ἐζωγρημένοι *Chrys.* **60** τὸ] *non hab. Chrys.* Ἔκτεινον *Chrys.*
60/61 τὴν τῆς ἀγάπης σαγήνην *Chrys.* **62** ὅτιπερ *Chrys.* **63** *post* κοι-
νόν] *complura (PG 48, 949, 29-33) hab. Chrys.* τοῦτο δέξασθαι *Chrys.*

ALPHA 79 – 80

65 φήτου φωνήν· Ἐκεῖνος ζήσεται, καὶ σὺ τὴν ψυχήν σου
ῥύσῃ· εἰ δὲ μὴ βούληται τοῦτο, ἀλλ'ἐμμένει φιλονει-
κῶν, ὅπως ἂν μὴ ὑπεύθυνος γένῃ, διαμάρτυραι μόνον
μετὰ μακροθυμίας καὶ χρηστότητος, ἵνα μὴ τὴν ψυχὴν
αὐτοῦ ἐκ χειρός σου ἐκζητήσῃ ὁ θεός, μὴ μισῶν, μὴ
70 ἀποστρεφόμενος, μὴ διώκων, ἀλλὰ τὴν ἀγάπην δεικνὺς
εἰλικρινῆ καὶ ἀληθῆ πρὸς αὐτόν. Ταύτην κέρδησον, κἂν
μηδὲν ἕτερον ὠφεληθῇ· αὕτη μεγάλη ὠφέλεια, τοῦτο
μέγα κέρδος, τὸ ἀγαπᾶν καὶ δεῖξαι τὴν Χριστοῦ μαθη-
τείαν. Ἐν τούτῳ γάρ φησι γνώσονται πάντες, ὅτι ἐμοὶ
75 μαθηταί ἐστέ, ἐὰν ἀγαπᾶτε ἀλλήλους.

ΛΕ'

Περὶ ἀνδρῶν ἀσεβῶν καὶ περὶ αἱρετικῶν, ὅτι δεῖ
χωρίζεσθαι ἀπ'αὐτῶν

80 Δαυΐδ

Μακάριος ἀνὴρ ὃς οὐκ ἐπορεύθη ἐν βουλῇ ἀσεβῶν, καὶ

Font. **65/66** Ez. 3, 21   **68/69** cf. Gen. 9, 5   **74/75** Io. 13, 35   **80.1/3** = Ps. 1, 1

Mss. *AT C*   **80** *AT CDEFHK*

Tit. **ΛΕ'**] λδ' *AT,* λγ' *DE,* λθ' *K, om. FH*   Περὶ – αὐτῶν] *cf. Sacr. Par., PG 95,
1148, 42-44 (*Περὶ ἀσεβῶν, καὶ ἁμαρτωλῶν, καὶ κακῶν, καὶ μοχθηρῶν ἀνδρῶν, καὶ ἀδίκων, καὶ παρανόμων*)   δεῖ] δὴ *C*   **80** Δαυΐδ] *om. H*

Crit. **71** κέρδισον *AT*   **72** ὠφέλεια] ἡ *praem. T*   **73** μέγα] μέγιστον *AT*
74/75 ἐμοὶ μαθηταί] μαθηταί μου *C*   **80.1/3** καὶ – ἐκάθισεν] καὶ τὰ λοιπά *C, om. DEFHK*

Comp. **65** *ante* ζήσεται] ζωῆ *hab. Chrys.*   **66** βούλεται *Chrys.*   τοῦτο] *non hab.
Chrys.*   **67** διαμαρτύρου *Chrys.*   **69** θεός] κριτής *Chrys.*   **70** ἐπι-
δεικνὺς *Chrys.*   **71** κέρδανον *Chrys.*   **72** ὠφελῆς *Chrys.*   **73** ἀγα-
πῆσαι *Chrys.*   δεῖξαι] διδάξαι *Chrys.*   *ante* Χριστοῦ] τοῦ *hab. Chrys.*
74 πάντες] *non hab. Chrys. et Io.*   **75** ἀγαπᾶτε ἀλλήλους] ἀγάπην ἔχητε ἐν
ἀλλήλοις *Chrys. et Io.*

Ind. **80.1/2** = Sacr. Par., PG 95, 1233, 40-41

146   FLORILEGIVM COISLINIANVM

ἐν ὁδῷ ἁμαρτωλῶν οὐκ ἔστη, καὶ ἐπὶ καθέδραν λοιμῶν
οὐκ ἐκάθισεν.
   Ἐμίσησα ἐκκλησίαν πονηρευομένων, καὶ μετὰ ἀσε-
5 βῶν οὐ μὴ καθίσω.
   Μὴ παραζήλου ἐν πονηρευομένοις, μὴ δὲ ζήλου τοὺς
ποιοῦντας τὴν ἀνομίαν· ὅτι ὡσεὶ χόρτος ταχὺ ἀποξηρανθήσονται, καὶ ὡσεὶ λάχανα χλόης ταχὺ ἀποπεσοῦν-
ται.

81   Παροιμιῶν

Υἱέ, μή σε πλανήσωσιν ἄνδρες ἀσεβεῖς, μὴ δὲ πορευθῇς
ἐν ὁδῷ μετ'αὐτῶν, ἔκκλινον δὲ τὸν πόδα σου ἀπὸ τῶν
τρίβων αὐτῶν· εἰς κακίαν γὰρ τρέχουσιν.
   Μὴ ζηλώσῃς ὁδοὺς παρανόμων· ἐν ᾧ ἂν τόπῳ στρα-
5 τοπεδεύσωσιν, μὴ ἐπέλθῃς ἐκεῖ· ὁδοὺς ἀσεβῶν μὴ ἐπέλθῃς.

Font.   **4/5** = Ps. 25, 5   **6/9** = Ps. 36, 1-2   **81.1** = Prou. 1, 10   **1/3** = Prou.
1, 15-16   **4/6** = Prou. 4, 14-15

Mss.   *AT CDEFHK*   **81** *AT CDEFHK* (*DEFHK* usque ad αὐτῶν, 81.2)

Tit.   **81** Παροιμιῶν] σολομῶντος *F, om. H*

Crit.   **2** καθέδραν] καθέδρα *A*   **3** ἐκάθησεν *T*   **4/5** καὶ – καθίσω] *om.*
DEFHK   **5** καθήσω *C*ᵃ·ᶜᵒʳʳ·   **6/9** μὴ – ἀποπεσοῦνται] *om. DEFHK*
7/9 ὅτι – ἀποπεσοῦνται] *om. C*   **8/9** ἀποπεσοῦνται] ἀποξηρανθήσονται
(*cf. l. 7/8) T*   **81.1** πλανήσουσιν *E*   ἀσεβεῖς ἄνδρες *K*

Comp.   **81.2** ἀπὸ] ἐκ *Prou. et Sacr. Par.*   **3** εἰς – γὰρ] οἱ γὰρ πόδες αὐτῶν εἰς
κακίαν *Prou., Sacr. Par., Loc. comm. et Corp. Par.*   **4** Μὴ] μηδὲ *Prou.*
5 *post* ἐκεῖ] ἔκκλινον δὲ (δὲ *non hab. Sacr. Par.)* ἀπ'αὐτῶν καὶ παράλλα-
ξον. Οὐ γὰρ μὴ ὑπνώσωσιν, ἐὰν μὴ κακοποιήσωσιν *add. Prou. et Sacr. Par.*
5/6 ὁδοὺς – ἐπέλθῃς] *ante* Μὴ ζηλώσῃς (*l. 4) hab. Prou.*   *post* ἐπέλθῃς]
μηδὲ ζητήσῃς ὁδοὺς παρανόμων (*Prou. 4, 14) hab. Sacr. Par.*

Ind.   **6/7** = Sacr. Par., PG 95, 1585, 10-11   **7/9** = Sacr. Par., PG 95, 1129, 57-58
81.1/8 = Sacr. Par., PG 96, 353, 3-13   **1/3** = Ps.-Max., Loc. comm. 1, 4, /4
(p. 8); Corp. Par., 1, 415

ALPHA 80 – 84

Τρίβολοι καὶ παγίδες ἐν ὁδοῖς σκολιαῖς· ὁ δὲ φυλάττων τὴν ἑαυτοῦ ψυχὴν φεύξεται ἀπ'αὐτῶν.

82 Ἡσαΐου

Ἀπέχου ἀπὸ κακοῦ καὶ ἀδίκου, καὶ οὐ φοβηθήσῃ, καὶ τρόμος οὐκ ἐγγιεῖ σοι.

83 Σιράχ

Ὁ ἁπτόμενος πίσσης μολυνθήσεται, καὶ ὁ κοινωνῶν ὑπερηφάνῳ, ὁμοιωθήσεται αὐτῷ.

84 Παύλου τοῦ ἀποστόλου
Ἐκ τῆς πρὸς Κορινθίους ἐπιστολῆς

Ἐάν τις ἀδελφὸς ὀνομαζόμενος ἢ πόρνος, ἢ πλεονέκτης, ἢ εἰδωλολάτρης, ἢ λοίδορος, ἢ μέθυσος, ἢ ἅρπαξ,

Font. 7/8 = Prou. 22, 5   82.1/2 = Is. 54, 14   83.1/2 = Sir. 13, 1
84.1/3 = I Cor. 5, 11

Mss. *AT C*   82 *AT C*   83 *AT CDEFHK*   84 *AT CDEFHK*

Tit. 83 Σιράχ] τοῦ *praem. H, om.* D   84 Παύλου τοῦ ἀποστόλου] παύλου ἀποστόλου *A C,* τοῦ ἀπο(στόλου) *F, om.* T *DEHK*   Ἐκ – ἐπιστολῆς] τῆς πρὸς κορινθίους *A C,* πρὸς κορινθίους *T, om. DEFHK*

Crit. 7 Τρίβολοι] *scripsi cum fonte (Prou. et Sacr. Par.),* τρίβοι *codd.*   ἐν] *om. AT*
ὁδοῖσκολιαῖς *(sic)* T   82.1 φοβηθήσει *C,* φοβηθῆς *A,* φοβηθεὶς *T*
83.1 πίσης *D*   84.1 ἀδελφὸς] ἢ *add. D,* ἢ *add. FH*   ἢ¹] ἤ *E*

Comp. 7/8 φυλάσσων *Prou.*   8 φεύξεται ἀπ'] ἀφέξεται *Prou.,* ἀφέξεται ἀπ' *Sacr.*
Par.   82.1 κακοῦ καὶ] *non hab. Is. et Sacr. Par.*   84.1/2 πόρνος – πλεονέκτης] πλεονέκτης, ἢ πόρνος *Sacr. Par.*

Ind. 82.1/2 = Sacr. Par., PG 96, 353, 23-24; Ps.-Max., Loc. comm. 7*, 7, ms. F
(p. 182)   83.1/2 = Sacr. Par., PG 96, 353, 25-26   84.1/5 = Sacr. Par.,
PG 96, 353, 34-39

148 FLORILEGIVM COISLINIANVM

τῷ τοιούτῳ μὴ δὲ συνεσθίειν. Παρακαλοῦμεν ὑμᾶς,
ἀδελφοί, ἐν ὀνόματι Κυρίου στέλλεσθαι ὑμᾶς ἀπὸ παν-
5 τὸς ἀδελφοῦ ἀτάκτως περιπατοῦντος.

85   Τοῦ Χρυσοστόμου
       Ἐκ τῆς ἑρμηνείας τῆς πρὸς Ἑβραίους

Πείθεσθε τοῖς ἡγουμένοις ὑμῶν καὶ ὑπείκετε. Τί οὖν,
φησίν, ἐὰν πονηρὸς ᾖ, πειθόμεθα; Πονηρὸς πῶς λέγεις;
Εἰ μὲν πίστεως ἕνεκεν, φεῦγε αὐτὸν καὶ παραίτησαι,
μὴ μόνον ἐὰν ἄνθρωπος ᾖ, ἀλλὰ κἂν ἄγγελος ἐξ οὐρα-
5 νοῦ κατιών.

86   Τοῦ αὐτοῦ

Ἀκούσατε πάντες οἱ τοῖς αἱρετικοῖς συνεσθίοντες, ὀδυ-
νηρὰν ἀπόφασιν, ὅτι τοῦ θεοῦ ἐχθροί ἐστε. Οὐδὲ γὰρ ὁ
τοῖς ἐχθροῖς τοῦ βασιλέως συμφιλιάζων δύναται τοῦ
βασιλέως φίλος εἶναι, ἀλλ᾽οὐδὲ ζωῆς ἀξιοῦται, ἀλλὰ
5 σὺν τοῖς ἐχθροῖς ἀπόλλυται, καὶ τὰ χείρονα ὑπομένει.

Font. **3/5** = II Thes. 3, 6   **85.1/5** = Io. Chrys., In ep. ad Heb., PG 63, 231, 50-55
1 Heb. 13, 17   **4/5** Gal. 1, 8   **86.1/5** = Io. Chrys., De pseudoproph., PG
59, 557, 70 – 558, 5

Mss.   *AT CDEFHK*   **85** *AT CDEFHK*   **86** *AT CDEFHK*

Tit.   **85** Τοῦ] *om. F*   Ἐκ – Ἑβραίους] τῆς ἑρμηνείας τῆς πρὸς ἑβραίους *A C*,
ἐκ τῆς πρὸς ἑβραίους ἑρμηνείας *T, om. DEFH*   **86** Τοῦ αὐτοῦ] τοῦ χρυσοστόμου *C, om. DEFHK*

Crit.   **4** ἀδελφοί] *om. DEFHK*   στέλλεσθε *EF*   ὑμᾶς] *om. EK*   **5** περιπα-
τοῦντες *C*   **85.2** φησίν] *om. DEFHK*   ᾖ] φησὶ *add. DEK*   **3** ἕνεκα
EK   **86.2** τοῦ] *om. T*   **3** συμφυλάξων *T*

Comp.   **3** Παρακαλοῦμεν ὑμᾶς] Παραγγέλλομεν δὲ (δὲ *non hab. Sacr. Par.*) ὑμῖν *II
Thes. et Sacr. Par.*   **4** Κυρίου] τοῦ Κυρίου ἡμῶν (ἡμῶν *non hab. Sacr. Par.*)
Ἰησοῦ Χριστοῦ *II Thes. et Sacr. Par.*   **85.2** ἐὰν] ὅταν *Chrys.*   πειθόμε-
θα] καὶ μὴ πειθώμεθα *Chrys.*   **4** ἐὰν] ἂν *Chrys.*   **86.2** θεοῦ] Χριστοῦ
Chrys.   **5** ἀπολεῖται *Chrys.*

ALPHA 84 – 87   149

Ἀκούσατε ὀρθόδοξοι καὶ τοῖς αἱρετικοῖς μὴ συγκαταβαίνετε, μὴ ἐν βρώμασιν, ἢ ἐν πόματι, ἢ φιλίας σχέσει,
ἢ ἀγάπῃ. Ὁ γὰρ ἐν τούτοις ἀπατώμενος καὶ συγκατα-
βαίνων αὐτοῖς, ἀλλότριον ἑαυτὸν τῆς καθολικῆς ἐκκλη-
10 σίας καθίστησιν. Ὁ δὲ ἀληθὴς καὶ ἄδολος μαθητὴς τοῦ
Χριστοῦ μετὰ παρρησίας κράζει· Εἴ τις ὑμᾶς εὐαγγελίζεται παρ'ὃ παρελάβετε, ἀνάθεμα.

87   Τοῦ ἁγίου Ἰγνατίου
             Ἐκ τῆς πρὸς Σμυρναίους ἐπιστολῆς

Προφυλάσσω ὑμᾶς ἀπὸ τῶν θηρίων τῶν ἀνθρωπομόρ-
φων αἱρετικῶν, οὓς οὐ μόνον οὐ δεῖ ὑμᾶς παραδέχε-
σθαι, ἀλλ'εἰ δυνατὸν μὴ δὲ συναντᾶν, μόνον προσεύχε-
σθαι περὶ αὐτῶν, ἐάν πως μετανοήσωσι.

Font. 6/7 (Ἀκούσατε – συγκαταβαίνετε) = Io. Chrys., De pseudoproph., PG 59,
559, 16-17   7/12 = Io. Chrys., De pseudoproph., PG 59, 563, 56-62
11/12 Gal. 1, 9   87.1/4 = Ignat., Ad Smyrn., 4, 1, 2-5

Mss.   AT CDEFHK   87 AT C

Tit.   87 πρὸς Σμυρναίους] προσμυρναίους (sic) A

Crit. 6 ὀρθόδοξοι] οἱ praem. FK   7 ἐν¹] ἐμ A   πόμασιν T FHK   12 παρελάβεται A, παρελάβομεν C   ἀνάθεμα] ἔστω add. DEK   87.3/4 προ-
σεύχεσθε T   4 ἐὰν πῶς C

Comp. 6 ante ὀρθόδοξοι] οἱ hab. Chrys.   7 πόμασιν Chrys.   φιλίας] φιλίᾳ ἢ
Chrys.   8 post ἀγάπῃ] ἢ εἰρήνη hab. Chrys.   9/10 καθίστησι τῆς καθο-
λικῆς Ἐκκλησίας Chrys.   10 ἀληθινὸς Chrys.   11 Χριστοῦ] θεοῦ Chrys.
12 post ἀνάθεμα] ἔστω hab. Chrys. et Gal.   87.1 post Προφυλάσσω] δὲ hab.
Ignat.   2 αἱρετικῶν] non hab. Ignat.   οὓς – ὑμᾶς] δεῖ ὑμᾶς μὴ Ignat. et
Theod.   3 post μόνον] δὲ hab. Ignat.   4 περὶ] ὑπὲρ Ignat.

.nd.   87.1/3 Προφυλάσσω – συναντᾶν = Theod. Stud., Paru. Cat., 127, 51-52

150   FLORILEGIVM COISLINIANVM

88   Τοῦ αὐτοῦ
     Ἐκ τῆς πρὸς Ἐφεσίους ἐπιστολῆς

Μὴ πλανᾶσθε, ἀδελφοί μου. Εἴ τις σχίζοντι ἀπὸ τῆς
ἀληθείας ἀκολουθεῖ, βασιλείαν θεοῦ οὐ κληρονομήσει·
καὶ εἴ τις οὐκ ἀφίσταται ἀπὸ τοῦ ψευδολόγου κήρυκος,
εἰς γέενναν κατακριθήσεται· οὔτε γὰρ εὐσεβῶν ἀφί-
5 στασθαι δεῖ, οὔτε δυσσεβῶν συγκεῖσθαι χρή.

89   Ἀθανασίου Ἀλεξανδρείας
     Ἐκ τῆς πρὸς μονάζοντας ἐπιστολῆς

Ὅταν γάρ τινες ὑμᾶς τοὺς ἐν Χριστῷ πιστοὺς θεωρή-
σαντες μετ'αὐτῶν συνευχομένους καὶ κοινωνοῦντας,
πάντως ὑπονοήσαντες ἀδιάφορον εἶναι τὸ τοιοῦτον,
εἰς τὸν τῆς ἀσεβείας ἐμπεσοῦνται βόρβορον. Ἵν'οὖν μὴ
5 τοῦτο γένηται, θελήσατε, ἀγαπητοί, τοὺς μὲν φανερῶς
φρονοῦντας τὰ τῆς ἀσεβείας ἀποστρέφεσθαι, τοὺς δὲ
νομίζοντας τὰ Ἀρείου μὴ φρονεῖν, κοινωνοῦντας δὲ
μετὰ τῶν ἀσεβῶν φυλάττεσθαι· καὶ μάλιστα ὧν τὸ
φρόνημα ἀποστρεφόμεθα, τούτους ἀπὸ τῆς κοινωνίας
10 προσήκει φεύγειν. Εἰ δέ τις προσποιεῖται μὲν ὁμολο-

Font.   **88.1/5** = Ps.-Ignat., Ad Philadelph., 3, 3 (ed. Diekamp, p. 172, 13-17)
         1 I Cor. 6, 9   **2** I Cor. 6, 10   **89.1/17** = Athan., Ep. ad mon., PG 26,
         1188, 13-30

Mss.   **88** *AT CDEFHK*   **89** *AT C*

Tit.   **88** Τοῦ αὐτοῦ] ἰγνατίου τοῦ θεοφόρου *DEFK, om. H*   Ἐκ – ἐπιστολῆς]
         ἐκ τῆς πρὸς ἐφεσίου *(sic)* ἐπιστολῆς *AT, om. FH*   **89** μονάζοντας] μονα-
         ζόντων *C*

Crit.   **88.1** σχίζοντι] σε *add. D*   **5** δυσεβῶν *AT F,* δυσσεβέσι *EK*   **89.4** μὴ]
         om. T   **9** τούτων *Tᵖᶜᵒʳʳ·* (τοῦτον *a. corr., sic acc.*)

Comp.   **88.1** Μὴ – μου] ἀδελφοί, μὴ πλανᾶσθε *Ps.-Ignat.*   **3** ἀπὸ] *non hab.*
         Ps.-Ignat.   **5** δεῖ] χρὴ *Ps.-Ignat.*   δυσσεβέσιν *Ps-Ignat.*   χρή] δεῖ
         Ps.-Ignat.   **89.2** συνευχομένους] συνερχομένους *Ath.; cum eis pariter orare*
         Vetus interpretatio (PG 26, 1187-1188, 6). Vide Fernández, *A Correction,* p. 7

ALPHA 88 – 91

γεῖν ὀρθὴν πίστιν, φαίνεται δὲ κοινωνῶν ἐκείνοις, τὸν
τοιοῦτον προτρέψασθε ἀπέχεσθαι τῆς τοιαύτης συνη-
θείας· καὶ ἐὰν μὲν ἐπαγγέλληται, ἔχετε τὸν τοιοῦτον
ὡς ἀδελφόν, ἐὰν δὲ φιλονείκως ἐπιμένῃ, τὸν τοιοῦτον
15 παραιτεῖσθε. Οὕτω γὰρ διατελοῦντες, καθαρὰν τὴν πίστιν διατηρήσετε, κἀκεῖνοι βλέποντες ὑμᾶς, ὠφεληθή-
σονται.

90   Ἐκ τῶν Διατάξεων τῶν ἀποστόλων

Φεύγετε τὰς κοινωνίας τῶν ἀκαθάρτων αἱρετικῶν, καὶ
τῆς πρὸς αὐτοὺς φιλίας ἀλλότριοι τυγχάνετε. Περὶ γὰρ
αὐτῶν ὁ προφήτης Ἡσαΐας ἔλεγεν· Οὐκ ἔστι λέγειν
χαίρειν τοῖς ἀσεβέσι, λέγει Κύριος.

91   Βασιλείου Καισαρείας

Τὸν μὲν ἀσπασμὸν τοῦτον, δηλονότι τὸν κοινόν, ἐπ'οὐδενὸς ὁ Κύριος ἀπηγόρευσεν, εἰπών· Ἐὰν ἀσπάσησθε
τοὺς φίλους ὑμῶν μόνον, τί περισσὸν ποιεῖτε; Οὐχὶ καὶ
οἱ ἐθνικοὶ τοῦτο ποιοῦσιν; Περὶ δὲ τοῦ συνεσθίειν, ἔχο-

Font.   **90.**1/4 = Const. apost., 6, 18, 42-45   3/4 Is. 48, 22; 57, 21   **91.**1/7 = Bas.
Caes., Asc. magn. breu., PG 31, 1165, 39-46 (= idem, Canon 96, ed. Joannou,
p. 198, 15 – 199, 1)   2/4 Mt. 5, 47

Mss.   *AT C*   **90** *AT CDEFHK*   **91** *AT CDEFHK*

Tit.   **90** Διατάξεων τῶν ἀποστόλων] ἀποστολικῶν διατάξεων *T*, διατάξεων τῶν
ἁγίων ἀποστόλων *F*   **91** Βασιλείου Καισαρείας] βασιλείου *T*, τοῦ ἁγίου
βασιλείου *F*

Crit.   **12** προστρέψασθαι *AT*   **13** ἐπαγγέλλεται *AT* (-έλε- *A*)   **14** φιλονίκως *A*
90.1 ἀκαθάρτων] *om. C*   **91.**1 δῆλον ὅτι *D*   **2** ἀπηγόρευσεν ὁ κύριος
FH   Ἐὰν] κἂν *T*   **3** ποιεῖτε *D*

Comp.   **90.**1 *post* Φεύγετε] οὖν *hab. Const.*   τὰς] τῆς *Const.* (τὰς *yz*)   τῶν –
αἱρετικῶν] αὐτῶν *Const.*   **2** φιλίας] εἰρήνης *Const.*   2/3 αὐτῶν γὰρ
Const.   **3** Ἡσαΐας ἔλεγεν] ἀπεφήνατο λέγων ὅτι *Const.*   λέγειν] *non
hab. Const. et Is.*   **91.**4 τοῦτο] οὕτω *Bas. (Ascet.)*, τὸ αὐτὸ *Mt.*

152   FLORILEGIVM COISLINIANVM

5   μὲν παραγγελίαν τοῦ Ἀποστόλου, ἐπὶ τίνων χρὴ παραι-
τεῖσθαι, εἰπόντος· Ἔγραψα ὑμῖν μὴ συναναμίγνυσθαι
πόρνοις.

ΛϚ'

Πόσαι ἀρεταὶ τοῖς ἄρχουσιν πρέπουσιν;

92   Ἀθανασίου

Προηγουμένως μὲν ἀρεταὶ τοῖς ἄρχουσιν πρέπουσι καὶ
ἁρμόζουσι, τὸ συμπαθητικὸν καὶ φιλάνθρωπον, τὰ καὶ
θεῷ ὑπάρχοντα· εἶτα τὸ ἀμνησίκακον, τὸ ἀόργητον, τὸ
ἀπροσωπόληπτον, τὸ ἀδωροδόκητον, καὶ πρὸ πάντων
5   τὸ μὴ εὐχερῶς μὴ δὲ ἀνεξετάστως διαβολαῖς καὶ λοιδορίαις πείθεσθαι. Ἀπὸ γὰρ λογοπειθείας πολλοὺς φό-
νους ποιοῦσιν ἀδίκως, ὡσαύτως καὶ ἐξ ἀσπλαγχνίας,
ὁμοίως καὶ ἀπὸ μνησικακίας, ὥσπερ καὶ ἀπὸ θυμοῦ καὶ
ἀπὸ δωροδοκίας. Ἐκεῖνος τοίνυν θεῷ ἄρχων εὐάρεστός
10 ἐστιν, ὁ μηδὲν τῶν τοιούτων παθῶν ἑαυτῷ κτώμενος.

Font.   6/7 I Cor. 5, 9   92.1/10 = Ps.-Athan., Quaest. ad Ant., PG 28, 673, 45 –
676, 6

Mss.   AT CDEFHK   92 AT CDEFHK

Tit.   ΛϚ'] λε' T, λδ' DEF, μ' K, om. H   ποῖαι T   Πόσαι – πρέπουσιν] cf.
Ps.-Athan., Quaest. ad Ant., PG 28, 673, 45-46: Ποῖαι πλεῖστον πάντων ἀρεταὶ
τοῖς ἄρχουσι πρέπουσί τε καὶ ἁρμόζουσιν;   92 Ἀθανασίου] ἀλεξανδρείας
add. EF, om. CH

Crit.   5 τοῦ Ἀποστόλου] παρὰ praem. F   92.5 μὴ δὲ] μηδ' DEFHK   6 λογο-
πειθίας AT EFHK

Comp.   5/6 post παραιτεῖσθαι] τοῦτο hab. Bas. (Ascet. et Canon)   6 post ὑμῖν] (ἡμίν
Canon) ἐν τῇ ἐπιστολῇ hab. Bas. (Ascet. et Canon) et I Cor.   92.1 μὲν] non
hab. Ps.-Athan.   1/2 ἀρεταὶ – ἁρμόζουσι] ante Προηγουμένως hab.
Ps.-Athan.   καὶ] τε καὶ Ps.-Athan.   3 τὸ²] καὶ Ps.-Athan.   τὸ³] καὶ
Ps.-Athan.   4 τὸ] καὶ Ps.-Athan.   7 ποιοῦσιν ἀδίκως] ἀδίκους ποιοῦσιν
Ps.-Athan.   8 ὥσπερ – θυμοῦ] ἀπέχεσθαι Ps.-Athan.   9/10 θεῷ – ἐστιν]
ἐστὶν ἄρχων θεῷ εὐάρεστος Ps.-Athan.   10 ἑαυτῷ] non hab. Ps.-Athan.

ALPHA 91 – 93　　　153

ΛΖ'

Περὶ τοῦ Ἅδου

93 Ἰωσήππου
Ἐκ τοῦ λόγου τοῦ ἐπιγεγραμμένου κατὰ
Πλάτωνος περὶ τῆς τοῦ παντὸς αἰτίας

Περὶ Ἅδου ἐν ᾧ συνέχονται ψυχαὶ ἀδίκων τὲ καὶ δικαίων, ἀναγκαῖον εἰπεῖν· Ὁ Ἅδης τόπος ἐστὶν ἐν τῇ κτίσει
ἀκατασκεύαστος, χωρίον ὑπόγειον ἐν ᾧ φῶς κόσμου
οὐκ ἐπιλάμπει. Φωτὸς τοίνυν ἐν τούτῳ τῷ χωρίῳ μὴ
5 καταλάμποντος, ἀνάγκη σκότος διηνεκῶς τυγχάνειν ἐν
τούτῳ τῷ χωρίῳ, ὃ ὡς φρούριον ἀπενεμήθη ψυχαῖς,
ἐφ'ᾧ κατεστάθησαν ἄγγελοι φρουροί, πρὸς τὰς ἑκάστου
πράξεις διανέμοντες τάς τε τῶν τρόπων προσκαίρους
κολάσεις. Ἐν τούτῳ δὲ τῷ τόπῳ ἀφώρισταί τις λίμνη
10 πυρὸς ἀσβέστου, ἐν ᾧ μὲν οὐδέπω τινὰ καταρερίφθαι
εἰλήφαμεν, ἐσκευάσθαι δὲ εἰς τὴν προωρισμένην ἡμέ-

Font.　　93.1/37 locum non inueni nisi in flor.　　9/10 cf. Apoc. 20, 14

Mss.　　93 AT CDEFHR

Tit.　　ΛΖ'] λϛ' T, λε' DEF, μα' R, om. A H　　93 Ἰωσήππου] ἰωσήπου ἑβραίου F,
δαμασκηνοῦ R, om. DEH　　Ἐκ – αἰτίας] om. DEHR

Crit.　　93.1 Ἅδου] τοῦ praem. E　　ψυχαὶ] αἱ praem. E　　3 ὑπόγαιον R
4 οὐκ ἐπιλάμπει] οὐ λάμπει R　　5/6 τυγχάνειν – χωρίῳ] ὑπάρχειν· τοῦτο
τὸ χωρίον E　　5 ἐν] om. A　　6 ὃ] om. E　　8 τε] om. E　　9 τις] τινα D
τις λίμνη] λιμνή τις R^{a.corr.}, λιμναί τινες R^{p.corr.}　　10 πυρὸς] om. H　　κατερρί-
φθαι CR, κατερίφθαι D, ἐρρίφθαι E　　11 ἐσκεύασται R, παρεσκεύασται E

Comp.　　93.1 post Περὶ] δὲ hab. Sacr. Par.　　ante ψυχαὶ] αἱ hab. Sacr. Par.
1/2 δικαίων τε καὶ ἀδίκων Sacr. Par.　　5/6 ἐν – ὃ] τοῦτο τὸ χωρίον Sacr.
Par.　　8 τε] non hab. Sacr. Par.　　τρόπων] τόπων Sacr. Par.　　9 τόπῳ]
χωρίῳ τόπος Sacr. Par.　　λίμνης Sacr. Par.　　11 ὑπειλήφαμεν Sacr. Par.

Ind.　　93.1/37 = Sacr. Par., ed. HOLL, Fragmente, fr. 353, 1-35, p. 137-139 (Hippolytus,
De uniuerso) (= Sacr. Par., Par. Rupef., PG 96, 541, 25 – 544, 32)

154 FLORILEGIVM COISLINIANVM

ραν τοῦ θεοῦ, ἐν ᾗ δικαίας κρίσεως ἀπόφασις μία πᾶσιν
ἀξίως προσενεχθείη, καὶ οἱ μὲν ἄδικοι καὶ θεῷ ἀπειθήσαντες, τά τε μάταια ἔργα χειρῶν ἀνθρώπων, κατε-
15 σκευασμένα εἴδωλα ὡς θεὸν τιμήσαντες, ταύτης τῆς
ἀϊδίου κολάσεως ὡς αἴτιοι μιασμάτων γενόμενοι προ-
κριθῶσιν, οἱ δὲ δίκαιοι τῆς ἀφθάρτου καὶ ἀνεκλείπτου
βασιλείας τύχωσιν· οἳ ἐν τῷ Ἅδῃ μὲν συνέχονται,
ἀλλ'οὐ τῷ αὐτῷ τόπῳ, ᾧ καὶ οἱ δίκαιοι. Μία γὰρ εἰς τοῦτο
20 τὸ χωρίον κάθοδος, οὗ τῆς πύλης ἐφεστῶτα ἀρχάγγελον ἅμα στρατιᾷ πεπιστεύκαμεν· ἣν πύλην διελθόντες
οἱ καταγόμενοι ὑπὸ τῶν ἐπὶ τὰς ψυχὰς τεταγμένων
ἀγγέλων, οὐ μιᾷ ὁδῷ πορεύονται, ἀλλ'οἱ μὲν δίκαιοι
εἰς δεξιὰ φωταγωγούμενοι, καὶ ὑπὸ τῶν ἐφεστώτων
25 κατὰ τόπον ἀγγέλων ὑμνούμενοι, ἄγονται εἰς χωρίον
φωτεινόν, ἐν ᾧ οἱ ἀπ'ἀρχῆς δίκαιοι πολιτεύονται,
οὐχ'ὑπ'ἀνάγκης κρατούμενοι, ἀλλὰ τῆς τῶν ὁρωμένων
ἀγαθῆς θέας ἀπολαύοντες, καὶ τῇ τῶν ἑκάστοτε καινῶν
ὁρωμένων προσδοκίᾳ ἡδόμενοι, κἀκεῖνα τούτων βελ-
30 τίονα ἡγούμενοι· οἷς ὁ τόπος οὐ καματηφόρος γίνεται,
οὐ καύσων, οὐ κρύος, οὐ τρίβολος ἐν αὐτοῖς, ἀλλ'ἡ τῶν
πατέρων δικαίων τε ὁρωμένη ὄψις πάντοτε, διαμενόν-
των τὴν μετὰ τοῦτο τὸ χωρίον ἀνάπαυσιν καὶ αἰωνίαν

Mss.   ATCDEFHR

Crit.   **13** μὲν] *om. T*   **15** θεῶ *R*   **18** οἳ] καὶ *praem. D*   **18/19** οὐ τῷ]
οὐκ ἐν τῶ *DEFH*   **19** δίκαιοι] ἄδικοι *DEFH*   **19/23** Μία – δίκαιοι]
om. R   **19/23** Μία – πορεύονται] *om. DEFH*   **24/25** καὶ – ὑμνούμε-
νοι] *om. T*   **24** ὑπὸ] ὑπὲρ *F*   **25** ἀγγέλων κατὰ τόπον *F*, κατὰ τόπον
ἀγγέλων κατὰ τόπον (*sic*) *H*   **26/27** ὑπ'] ὑπὸ *DEFHR*   **27/28** ὁρωμένων ἀγαθῆς] ἀγαθῶν καὶ ὁρωμένων *DEFHR*   **28/35** καὶ – Ἀβραάμ]
om. DEFHR   **28** τῇ] τῆς *A C*

Comp.   **12** *ante* τοῦ] παρὰ *hab. Sacr. Par.*   **13** προσενεχθῇ *Sacr. Par.*   **18** *post*
Ἅδῃ] νῦν *hab. Sacr. Par.*   **19** ᾧ καὶ] ὡς *Sacr. Par.*   **20** τῇ πύλῃ *Sacr. Par.*
23 ἀγγέλων] *non hab. Sacr. Par.*   **28** ἀγαθῶν *Sacr. Par.*   θέας] θεωρίας ἀεὶ *Sacr. Par.*   **30** οἷς] οὗ *Sacr. Par.*   **31** αὐτοῖς] αὐτῷ *Sacr. Par.*
32 τε] *non hab. Sacr. Par.*   **32/33** διαμενόντων] μειδιᾷ ἀναμενόντων *Sacr.
Par.*

ALPHA 93 – 95

βίωσιν ἐν οὐρανῷ. Τοῦτον δὲ ὀνόματι κλήζομεν κόλπον
35 Ἀβραάμ. Οἱ δὲ ἄδικοι ἀριστερὰ ἕλκονται ὑπὸ ἀγγέλων
ἀκολάστων, οὐκέτι ἑκουσίως πορευόμενοι, ἀλλὰ μετὰ
βίας ὠθούμενοι.

94   Τοῦ Χρυσοστόμου

Περὶ τοῦ Ἅδου, οὐκ ἔστιν ἓν τὸ λεγόμενον, ἀλλὰ διπλοῦν
τὸ νοούμενον. Ἔστι γὰρ σκοτεινὰ χωρία, ἀλλ᾽ ὁραθῆναι
πολλάκις δύνανται, λύχνου καὶ φωτὸς εἰσαχθέντος
ἐκεῖ. Τὸ δὲ τοῦ Ἅδου χωρίον, ζοφωδέστατόν ἐστιν καὶ
5 σκοτῶδες, καὶ οὐδέποτε φωτὸς ἐδέξατο φαῦσιν, ἕως οὗ
κατῆλθεν αὐτὸς ὁ τῆς δικαιοσύνης ἥλιος ἐκεῖ.

*95   Λεοντίου Δαμασκηνοῦ

Ἅδης ἐστὶ σκοτεινόν τι καὶ κατώγαιον χωρίον, ψυχῶν
ἐν ἁμαρτίαις ἀποθανουσῶν κολαστήριον.

Font.   34/35 cf. Lc. 16, 22   **94.1/6** = Io. Chrys., De coem., PG 49, 395, 32-39
6 Mal. 3, 20   **95.1/2** locum non inueni; ed. Leont. Dam., fr. 2

Mss.   **94** *AT CDEFHR*   **95** *AT CDEFHR*

Tit.   **94** Τοῦ Χρυσοστόμου] χρυσοστόμου *F, om. HR*

Crit.   **35** ἀβραάμ *T*   **94.2** σκοτεινοχωρία *AT* (-νω- *A*)   ὁραθῆναι] *scripsi cum*
DEFHR et fonte, ὁράθη *A,* ὠράθη *T,* ὁρᾶσθαι *C*   **3** δύναντος *AT,* δύναται *R*
6 αὐτὸς] *om. A*   **95.1** κατώγεον *E,* κατάγαιον *R*

Comp.   **34** ἀναβίωσιν *Sacr. Par.*   Τοῦτον – κλήζομεν] Τούτῳ δὲ ὄνομα κικλήσκο-
μεν *Sacr. Par.*   **35** *ante* ἀριστερὰ] εἰς *hab. Sacr. Par.*   **36** ἀκολάστων]
κολαστῶν *Sacr. Par.*   **37** ὠθούμενοι] ὡς δέσμιοι ἑλκόμενοι *Sacr. Par.*
94.1 Περὶ – λεγόμενον] Εἰ καὶ τὸ λεγόμενον ἓν *Chrys.*   **4** ἐκεῖ – δὲ] ἐκεῖνο
δὲ *Chrys.*   *ante* χωρίον] τὸ *hab. Chrys.*   **4/5** ἐστιν – σκοτῶδες] ἦν καὶ
ἀτερπὲς *Chrys.*   **5** φαῦσιν] φύσιν· διὰ τοῦτο σκοτεινοὺς, ἀοράτους εἶπεν
αὐτούς· καὶ γὰρ ὄντως σκοτεινοὶ ἦσαν *Chrys.*   **6** αὐτὸς] *non hab. Chrys.*
ἐκεῖ] *non hab. Chrys.*

156 FLORILEGIVM COISLINIANVM

ΛΗ′

Περὶ ὧν σέσωκεν ἐν Ἅδῃ Χριστὸς κατελθών

96 Ἐπιφανίου Κύπρου

Τί οὖν; Πάντας ἁπλῶς ἐν Ἅδῃ σώζει Χριστὸς κατελθών; Οὔμενουν, ἀλλὰ κἀκεῖ πιστεύσαντας.

97 Τοῦ ἀποστόλου Πέτρου Καθολικῆς ἐπιστολῆς

Εἰς τοῦτο γὰρ καὶ νεκροῖς εὐηγγελίσθη, ἵνα κριθῶσι μὲν κατὰ ἄνθρωπον σαρκί, ζῶσι δὲ κατὰ θεὸν πνεύματι.

Ἑρμηνεία Μαξίμου μοναχοῦ
Ἔθος ἐστὶ τῇ θείᾳ γραφῇ τοὺς χρόνους μεταλλάσσειν
5 καὶ εἰς ἀλλήλους μετεκλαμβάνειν, τὸν μέλλοντα ὡς παρῳχηκότα, καὶ τὸν παρῳχηκότα ὡς μέλλοντα, καὶ τὸν ἐνεστῶτα εἰς τὸν πρὸ αὐτοῦ καὶ μετ᾽αὐτὸν χρόνον

Font. **96**.1/2 = Ps.-Epiph., Hom. in diu., PG 43, 440, 53-54   **97**.1/2 = Max. Conf., Quaest. ad Thal., 7, 2-3; I Petr. 4, 6   4/27 = Max. Conf., Quaest. ad Thal., 7, 5-27

Mss.   **96** *AT CDEFHR*   **97** *AT CDEFHR*

Tit.   **ΛΗ′**] λς′ *DEFH*, μγ′ *R, om. T*   σέσωκεν] ἔσωσεν *T*   **96** Ἐπιφανίου] *om. E*   **97** Τοῦ – ἐπιστολῆς] τοῦ ἀποστόλου καθολικῆς ἐπιστολῆς *T*, τοῦ ἀποστόλου πέτρου *D*, τοῦ ἁγίου ἀποστόλου πέτρου *F*, πέτρου τοῦ ἀποστόλου *H*, πέτρου ἀποστόλου *R, om. CE*

Crit.   **96**.1 ἐν ἅδῃ ἁπλῶς *R*   2 πιστεύσαντας] τοὺς *praem. T DEFHR, ut expectaueris*   **97**.1 νεκρὸς *D*   2 μὲν] ἤδη *add. E*   ἄνθρωπον] τὸν *praem. T*   3 Ἑρμηνεία – μοναχοῦ] ἑρμηνεία μαξίμου *E*, μαξίμου ἑρμηνεία *DH*, τοῦ ἁγίου μαξίμου *F*, μαξίμου *R*, μδ′ *add. R^(in marg.)*   4 ἔστι *A*   καταλλάσσειν *C*   5 εἰς] *om. FH*   7 μετ᾽αὐτὸν] μετ᾽ αὐτὸ *D*, μετὰ τὸν *R*

Comp.   **96**.1/2 ἐν – κατελθών] σώζει ἐπιφανεὶς ἐν ᾅδῃ θεός *Ps.-Epiph.*   2 Οὔμενουν] Οὐχὶ *Ps.-Epiph.*   *ante* πιστεύσαντας] τοὺς *hab. Ps.-Epiph.*   **97**.2 ἀνθρώπους *I Petr.*   4 θείᾳ] *non hab. Max.*   5 *ante* τὸν] καὶ *hab. Max.*

ALPHA 96 – 97 157

ἐκφωνεῖν, ὡς ἔστι δῆλον τοῖς ταύτης πεπειραμένοις.
Φασὶν οὖν τινὲς νεκροὺς ἐνταῦθα λέγειν τὴν γραφὴν
10 τοὺς πρὸ τῆς ἐπιδημίας Χριστοῦ τελειωθέντας ἀνθρώπους, οἷον τοὺς ἐν τῷ κατακλυσμῷ, τοὺς ἐν τῷ χρόνῳ
τῆς πυργοποιΐας, τοὺς ἐν Σοδόμοις, τοὺς ἐν Αἰγύπτῳ,
καὶ τοὺς ἄλλους τοὺς κατὰ διαφόρους καιρούς τε καὶ
τρόπους τὴν πολύτροπον δίκην καὶ τὰς ἐξαισίους ἐπα-
15 γωγὰς τῶν θείων κριμάτων δεξαμένους· οἵτινες
οὐχ ὑπὲρ ἀγνοίας θεοῦ τοσοῦτον ὅσον τῆς εἰς ἀλλήλους
παροινίας τὴν δίκην ἔδωκαν, οἷς εὐηγγελίσθαι λέγει
τὸ μέγα τῆς σωτηρίας κήρυγμα, κριθεῖσιν ἤδη κατὰ
ἄνθρωπον σαρκί, τουτέστιν ἀπολαβοῦσι τῶν εἰς ἀλλή-
20 λους ἐγκλημάτων τὴν δίκην διὰ τῆς ἐν σαρκὶ ζωῆς, ἵνα
ζήσωσι κατὰ θεὸν πνεύματι, τουτέστι ψυχῇ δεχόμενοι,
κατὰ τὸν Ἅδην ὄντες, τῆς θεογνωσίας τὸ κήρυγμα, διὰ
τὸ καὶ νεκροὺς σῶσαι κατελθόντος εἰς Ἅδην τοῦ σωτῆρος πιστεύσαντας. Ὑπὲρ δὲ τοῦ νοηθῆναι τὸν τόπον,
25 οὕτως ἐκλάβωμεν. Εἰς τοῦτο γὰρ καὶ νεκροῖς εὐηγγελίσθη, κριθεῖσιν κατὰ ἄνθρωπον σαρκί, ἵνα ζήσωσιν κατὰ
θεὸν πνεύματι.

Font. 11 cf. Gen. 6, 1 – 8, 22   11/12 cf. Gen. 11, 1-9   12 cf. Gen. 18, 16 – 19, 28
cf. Ex. 8, 1 – 10, 21   17/21 cf. supra, l. 1/2   25/27 cf. supra,
l. 1/2

Mss. AT CDEFHR

Crit. 8 ὥς ἐστι A   δῆλα DR   9 τινὲς] om. FH   10 πρὸ] πρὸς D   Χρι-
στοῦ] τοῦ praem. ER   13 τε] om. R   17 εὐηγγελίσθη F   18/19
ἄνθρωποι T   20/21 ζήσωσι] ζῶσι R   21 δεχομένους FHR   22
κατὰ – κήρυγμα] iter. Tª.corr.   23 τὸ] τοῦ E   ἄδην E   τοῦ] om. E
24 πιστεύσαντες EH, πιστεύσαντ() F   νοηθέντος FH   25 οὕτως
ἐκλάβωμεν] post πνεύματι (l. 26) trsp. E   νεκροὺς T   26 κριθεῖσιν]
ἤδη add. E

Comp. 8 αὐτῆς Max.   9 λέγειν ἐνταῦθα Max.   10 ante Χριστοῦ] τοῦ hab.
Max.   17 ἔδωκαν] ἔτισαν Max.   18/19 σαρκὶ κατὰ ἄνθρωπον Max.
23 τὸ] τοῦ Max.   τοῦ] non hab. Max.   24 πιστεύσαντες Max.

158 FLORILEGIVM COISLINIANVM

*98 Ἀθανασίου Ἀλεξανδρείας
Ἐκ τῆς ἑρμηνείας τοῦ ψαλτηρίου

Κείμενον
Αἰνεῖτε τὸν Κύριον ἐκ τῆς γῆς, δράκοντες καὶ πᾶσαι
ἄβυσσοι.

Ἑρμηνεία
5 Παρακελευσάμενον τὸ Πνεῦμα τὸ ἅγιον τοῖς οὐρανίοις
τάγμασιν αἰνεῖν τὸν Κύριον, μεταφέρει τὸν λόγον καὶ
τοῖς ἐπιγείοις παρακελευόμενον. Τριῶν δὲ ὄντων ταγμάτων, ἐπουρανίων καὶ ἐπιγείων καὶ καταχθονίων,
τῶν καμπτόντων γόνυ τῷ Ἰησοῦ, τὰ μὲν οὐράνια διὰ
10 τῶν προειρημένων ἐπὶ τὸν ὕμνον κέκληνται, τὰ δε ἐπί-
γεια διὰ τοῦ εἰπεῖν· Ἄρχοντες καὶ πάντες κριταὶ γῆς·
νεανίσκοι καὶ παρθένοι. Πρὶν δὲ τούτων μνήμην ποιήσασθαι, ἐπὶ τὰ καταχθόνια τρέπεται, ἃ διὰ τῶν δρακόν-
των καὶ τῶν ἀβύσσων σημαίνεται. Καὶ αὐταὶ γὰρ αἱ
15 πάλαι τῶν γιγάντων ἐκείνων ψυχαί, τῶν ἀπειθησάν-
των ποτὲ καὶ πολεμησάντων θεῷ, αἳ διὰ τῶν δρακόν-
των σημαίνονται, καὶ μὴν καὶ τὸ ἄλλο πᾶν πλῆθος τῆς

Font.   98.2/3 = Athan., Fragm. uar., PG 26, 1256, 17-18; Ps. 148, 7
5/26 = Athan., Fragm. uar., PG 26, 1256, 19-41   8/9 cf. Phil. 2, 10
11/12 Ps. 148, 11-12   15/16 cf. Gen. 6, 4

Mss.   98 AT CDEFHR

Tit.   98 Ἀθανασίου Ἀλεξανδρείας] τοῦ ἁγίου praem. F, om. HR   Ἐκ – ψαλτη-
ρίου] om. DEFHR

Crit.   98.1/26 fr. 98 post fr. 99 trsp. DEFHR   1 Κείμενον] om. T DEFHR
4 Ἑρμηνεία] om. DEFHR   5 παρακελευόμενον AT   5/7 Παρακελευσάμενον – δὲ] τριῶν DEFHR   7 παρακελεύομεν C   8 καὶ¹] om. DEFH
12 νεανίσκοι – παρθένοι] om. DEFHR   13/14 ἃ σημαίνεται] om. E^{a.corr.}
(suppl. in marg.)   14/17 Καὶ – σημαίνονται] om. D^{a.corr.} (suppl. in marg.)
14 αὗται R   17 πλῆθος πᾶν FH

Comp.   98.5 οὐρανίοις] ἐν οὐρανοῖς Athan.   6 καὶ] non hab. Athan.   8 καὶ¹]
non hab. Athan. (hab. Phil.)   10 κέκληνται] τρέπονται Athan.
12/13 ποιῆσαι Athan.

ALPHA 98 – 99

οἰκουμένης, τὸ ἐν ταῖς προτέραις μὲν ὑπάρξαν γενεαῖς,
κατασχεθὲν δὲ θανάτῳ, κάμπτουσι γόνυ, ἅτε ἐλευθερω-
20 θεῖσαι ὑπ'αὐτοῦ· Εἴρηκε γὰρ τοῖς ἐν δεσμοῖς, ἐξέλθετε.
Διὸ καὶ αὗται ἐπὶ τὸν ὕμνον καλοῦνται σὺν τοῖς ἄρχουσιν αὐτῶν γενομένοις καὶ μεγάλοις ἀνθρώποις. Ὅτι δὲ
οἱ ποτὲ ἀπειθήσαντες καὶ ἀντάραντες θεῷ ἠλευθερώθη-
σαν, ὁ Πέτρος ἠνίξατο ἐν Καθολικαῖς εἰπών· Ἐν ᾧ καὶ
25 τοῖς ἐν Ἅδου πνεύμασι πορευθεὶς ἐκήρυξεν, ἀπειθήσασι
ποτέ.

99 Τοῦ Χρυσοστόμου

Ὥσπερ οὖν βασιλεύς τις λήσταρχον εὑρὼν κατακρα-
τοῦντα πόλεις, ἁρπάζοντα πανταχόθεν, εἰς τὰ σπήλαια
καταδυόμενον, ἀποτιθέμενον ἐκεῖ τὸν πλοῦτον, δήσας
μὲν τὸν λήσταρχον, ἐκεῖνον μὲν τιμωρίᾳ παραδίδω-
5 σιν, τὸν δὲ θησαυρὸν αὐτοῦ μεταφέρει εἰς τὰ ταμιεῖα
τὰ βασιλικά, οὕτω καὶ ὁ Χριστὸς ἐποίησεν· ἔδησε τὸν

Font. **19** Eph. 3, 14; Phil. 2, 10 **20** Is. 49, 9 **24/26** I Petr. 3, 19-20
99.1/12 = Io. Chrys., De coem., PG 49, 395, 49 – 396, 2

Mss. **99** AT CDEFHR

Tit. **99** Τοῦ Χρυσοστόμου] χρυσοστόμου F, ἄλλως R, om. C

Crit. **18** πρώταις R **19/20** ἐλευθερωθῆσαι (sic) A, ἐλευθερωθοῦν C, ἐλευθερωθέντες DEFHR **20** ἐν] om. F ἐξέλθατε A **23** θεῷ] τῶ praem. R
23/24 ἠλευθέρωνται DEFHR, forsan recte **25** ᾅδου E **99.1** οὖν] om.
DEFHR τις] τίς A, om. CDEFHR **3** ἐκεῖ] om. R **3/5** δήσας –
παραδίδωσιν] om. R **4** μὲν¹] om. E

Comp. **19/20** ἐλεθερωθεῖσαι ὑπ'] ἐλευθερωθέντες ἀπ' Athan. **20** ἐξέλθετε] καὶ
τοῖς ἐν τῷ σκότει κτλ. Athan. **22** γινομένοις Athan. **23/24** ἠλευθέρωνται Athan. **99.1** τις] non hab. Chrys. **1/2** κατακρατοῦντα]
κατατρέχοντα τὰς Chrys. **2** πανταχόθεν] πάντοθεν, καὶ Chrys. **3**
ante ἀποτιθέμενον] καὶ hab. Chrys. **4** μὲν¹] non hab. Chrys. τιμωρίᾳ]
κολάσει Chrys. **6** ἔδησε] non hab. Chrys.

Ind. **99.1/12** Athan., De amul., PG 26, 1320, 29-40

160 FLORILEGIVM COISLINIANVM

λήσταρχον καὶ τὸν δεσμοφύλακα Διάβολον καὶ τὸν θάνατον καὶ τὸν πλοῦτον αὐτοῦ, ἅπαν τῶν ἀνθρώπων τὸ
γένος, μετήγαγεν εἰς τὰ ταμιεῖα τὰ βασιλικά. Διατοῦτο
10 καὶ Παῦλος βοᾷ, λέγων ὅτι ἐλυτρώσατο ἡμᾶς ἐκ τοῦ
σκότους καὶ μετήγαγεν εἰς τὴν βασιλείαν τοῦ υἱοῦ τῆς
ἀγάπης αὐτοῦ.

ΛΘ'

Περὶ τοῦ Ἀντιχρίστου

100 Κυρίλλου Ἱεροσολύμων

Ἔρχεται δὲ ὁ Ἀντίχριστος οὕτως, ὅταν πληρωθῶσιν οἱ
καιροὶ τῆς Ῥωμαίων βασιλείας, καὶ πλησιάζει λοιπὸν
τὰ τῆς τοῦ κόσμου συντελείας. Δέκα μὲν ὁμοῦ Ῥωμαίων ἐγείρονται βασιλεῖς, ἐν διαφόροις μὲν ἴσως τόποις,
5 κατὰ δὲ τὸν αὐτὸν βασιλεύοντες καιρόν. Μετὰ δὲ τούτους, ἑνδέκατος ὁ Ἀντίχριστος, ἐκ τῆς μαγικῆς κακο-
τεχνίας τὴν Ῥωμαϊκὴν ἐξουσίαν ἁρπάσας. Τρεῖς μὲν

Font.   10/12 Col. 1, 13   100.1/21 = Cyr. Hier., Cat. ad illum., 15, 12, 1-19

Mss.   100 *AT CDEFHKR*

Tit.   ΛΘ'] λη' *T*, λζ' *DEF*, μα' *K*, ξα' *R*, *om. H*   Περὶ – Ἀντιχρίστου] *cf. Sacr.*
Par., PG 96, 525, 27-28 (Περὶ ἡμέρας ἐσχάτης, καὶ τοῦ Ἀντιχρίστου)
100 Κυρίλλου Ἱεροσολύμων] κυρίλλου *K*, *om. C*

Crit.   8 ἅπαν τῶν] ἁπάντων *T*, ἅπαν τὸ τῶν *E*   τὸ] *om. E*   9 βασιλικά] δε-
σποτικὰ *CDHR*   100.2 πλησιάζῃ *E*   3 τοῦ] *om. DR*   3/4 ἐγείρονται ῥωμαίων *FH*   5 καιρὸν βασιλεύοντες *E*   6 ἑνδέκατος] ια' *C*
ὁ Ἀντίχριστος] *om. FH*   τῆς] *om. EK*

Comp.   7 Διάβολον] τὸν διάβολον ὁμοῦ *Chrys.*   7/8 *post* θάνατον] διὰ τοῦ θανάτου
αὐτοῦ δήσας *hab. Chrys.*   8 αὐτοῦ] πάντα *Chrys.*, αὐτῶν *Athan.*   ἅπαν
τῶν] ἁπάντων *Athan.*, τῶν *Chrys.*   *post* ἀνθρώπων] λέγω *hab. Chrys.*
9 Διατοῦτο] Τοῦτο *Chrys.*   10 βοᾷ] δηλοῖ *Chrys.*   *ante* τοῦ] τῆς
ἐξουσίας *hab. Chrys. et Col.*   11 μετήγαγεν] μετέστησεν *Chrys. et Col.*
11/12 τοῦ – αὐτοῦ] αὐτοῦ τῆς ἀγάπης *Chrys.*   100.1 *post* ὁ] προειρημένος
hab. Cyr.   οὗτος *Cyr.*

ALPHA 99 – 101

τῶν πρὸ αὐτοῦ βασιλευόντων ταπεινώσει, τοὺς ἑπτὰ δὲ
τοὺς ὑπολειπομένους ὑφ'ἑαυτὸν ἔχων, πρῶτον μὲν ἐπι-
10 είκειαν, ὡσανεὶ λόγιός τις καὶ συνετός, σωφροσύνην τε
καὶ φιλανθρωπίαν ὑποκρίνεται, σημείοις τε καὶ τέρα-
σι τοῖς ἐκ μαγικῆς ἀπάτης ψευδέσιν Ἰουδαίους ὡσανεὶ
Χριστὸς ὁ προσδοκώμενος ἀπατήσας, παντοίοις ὕστερον ἀπανθρωπίας καὶ παρανομίας ἐπιγραφήσεται κα-
15 κοῖς, ὡς πάντας ὑπερβαλέσθαι τοὺς πρὸ αὐτοῦ γενομένους ἀδίκους καὶ ἀσεβεῖς, φονικὴν καὶ ἀποτομωτάτην
καὶ ἀνηλεῆ καὶ ποικίλην κατὰ πάντων μέν, ἐξαιρέτως
δὲ καθ'ἡμῶν τῶν χριστιανῶν τὴν ὁρμὴν ἔχων. Ἐπὶ τρία
δὲ ἔτη καὶ μῆνας ἓξ τὰ τοιαῦτα τολμήσας, ὑπὸ τῆς δευ-
20 τέρας ἐξ οὐρανῶν ἐνδόξου παρουσίας τοῦ Κυρίου ἡμῶν
Ἰησοῦ Χριστοῦ καταργηθήσεται.

Μ'

Περὶ τῆς τριημέρου Χριστοῦ ἀναστάσεως

*101 Ἕκτῃ ὥρᾳ τῆς παρασκευῆς ἐσταυρώθη ὁ Κύριος. Ἀπὸ
ταύτης ἕως θ', σκότος ἐγένετο· τοῦτο νύκτα μοι νόησον.

Font. **101.**1/6 locum non inueni   1/2 cf. Mt. 27, 45; Io. 19, 14 et loc. par.

Mss. *AT CDEFHKR*   **101** *AT CDEFHK*

Tit. **Μ'**] λθ' *T,* λη' *DEF,* μβ' *K, om. H*   Περὶ – ἀναστάσεως] *cf. Mt. 12, 40; 27,
40. 63; Mc. 15, 29*   Χριστοῦ] *om. E*   **101** Ἕκτῃ] χρυσοστόμου *praem. F*

Crit. 8 ἑπτὰ] ζ' *A H*   9 ἑαυτῶν *A*   12 τοῖς ἐκ] τῆς *FH*   15 ὡς] ὥστε *R*
ὑπερβαλλέσθαι *(sic acc.) F*   15/16 γεναμένους *A*   16 καὶ¹] *om. R*
καὶ²] *om. T R*   19/20 δευτέρας] β' *H*   **101.**2 ἐνάτης *T,* ἐννάτης *EFK*
μοι νύκτα *EFH*

Comp. 8 βασιλευόντων] βασιλευσάντων *Cyr. (mm, Roe.* = *Coisl.)*   9 ὑπολει-
πομένους] ἐπιλοίπους *Cyr.*   πρῶτον] τὰ πρῶτα *Cyr.*   11 τε] δὲ *Cyr.*
18 ὁρμὴν] διάνοιαν *Cyr.*   19 *post* ἔτη] μόνα *hab. Cyr.*   20/21 Κυρίου –
καταργηθήσεται] τοῦ μονογενοῦς υἱοῦ θεοῦ καταργεῖται, τοῦ κυρίου καὶ
σωτῆρος ἡμῶν Ἰησοῦ Χριστοῦ τοῦ ἀληθοῦ *Cyr.*

162 FLORILEGIVM COISLINIANVM

Ἀπὸ θ' φῶς, τοὔμπαλιν ἡμέραν. Ἡ νὺξ αὖθις τῆς παρασκευῆς, τὸ σάββατον πάλιν ἡμέρα· ἡ νὺξ τοῦ σαββάτου
5 ὁ τῆς κυριακῆς ὄρθρος, κατὰ τὸν εὐαγγελιστὴν λέγον-
τα· Τῇ ἐπιφωσκούσῃ εἰς μίαν τῶν σαββάτων.

102   Γρηγορίου Νύσης

Ὁ πάντα κατὰ τὴν δεσποτικὴν αὐθεντείαν οἰκονομῶν,
οὐκ ἀναμένει τὴν ἐκ τῆς προδοσίας ἀνάγκην καὶ τὴν
ληστρικὴν τῶν Ἰουδαίων ἔφοδον καὶ τὴν τοῦ Πιλάτου
παράνομον κρίσιν, ὥστε τὴν ἐκείνοις κακίαν ἀρχηγὸν
5 καὶ αἰτίαν τῆς κοινῆς τῶν ἀνθρώπων σωτηρίας γενέσθαι, ἀλλὰ προλαμβάνει τῇ οἰκονομίᾳ τὴν ἔφοδον, καὶ
τὸν ἄρρητον τῆς ἱερουργίας τρόπον καὶ τοῖς ἀνθρώποις
ἀόρατον, ἑαυτὸν προσήνεγκε προσφορὰν καὶ θυσίαν
ὑπὲρ ἡμῶν, ὁ ἱερεὺς ἅμα καὶ ἀμνὸς τοῦ θεοῦ ὁ αἴρων
10 τὴν ἁμαρτίαν τοῦ κόσμου. Πότε δὲ τοῦτο; Ὅτε βρωτὸν
αὐτοῦ τὸ σῶμα καὶ πότιμον τὸ αἷμα τοῖς συνοῦσιν ἐποί-
ησε· παντὶ γὰρ τοῦτο δῆλόν ἐστιν, ὅτι οὐκ ἂν βρωθείη
παρὰ ἀνθρώπου πρόβατον, εἰ μὴ τῆς βρώσεως σφαγὴ
προηγήσαιτο. Ὁ τοίνυν δοὺς τοῖς μαθηταῖς αὐτοῦ τὸ
15 σῶμα εἰς βρῶσιν σαφῶς ἐνδείκνυται τὸ ἤδη τοῦ ἀμνοῦ

Font.   6 Mt. 28, 1   102.1/22 = Greg. Nyss., De trid. spat., p. 287, 7 – 288, 6
8 cf. Heb. 10, 5-14   9/10 Io. 1, 29   14/15 cf. Mt. 26, 26 et loc. par.

Mss.   AT CDEFHK   102 AT C

Crit.   3 θ'] ἐνάτης T, ἐννάτης EK   τοὔμπαλιν] τοῦτο πάλιν C   ἡμέρα CFH
3/4 Ἡ – ἡμέρα] om. Eᵃ·ᶜᵒʳʳ· (suppl. in marg.)   4 ἡμέραν AT   6 ἐπιφωσκούσῃ H   τῶν] om. EK   102.1 Ὁ] ἄλλο praem. C   1/3 αὐθεντείαν – ληστρικὴν] om. Tᵃ·ᶜᵒʳʳ· (suppl. in marg.)   1 αὐθεντίαν A   4 ἐκεί-
νοις] ἐν praem. T   7 ἱερουγίας C   11 τὸ σῶμα] om. T   καὶ – αἷμα]
om. C

Comp.   102.1 post Ὁ] γὰρ hab. Greg.   3 ἔφοδον τῶν Ἰουδαίων Greg. (ST = Coisl.)
4 ἐκείνων Greg. (X = Coisl., ἐν ἐκείνοις ETDU)   6 καὶ] κατὰ Greg.
(SEDUFG = Coisl., καὶ κατὰ XT)   10 δὲ] non hab. Greg.   11 ἑαυτοῦ
Greg.   13 ante σφαγὴ] ἡ hab. Greg.   14 αὐτοῦ τὸ] τὸ ἑαυτοῦ Greg.

ALPHA 101 - 102

τὴν θυσίαν ἐπὶ τέλει γενέσθαι· οὐ γὰρ ἂν ἦν τὸ σῶμα
τοῦ ἱερείου πρὸς ἐδωδὴν ἐπιτήδειον, εἴπερ ἔμψυχον ἦν.
Οὐκοῦν ὅτε παρέσχε τοῖς μαθηταῖς ἐμφαγεῖν τοῦ σώματος καὶ τοῦ αἵματος ἐμπιεῖν, ἤδη κατὰ τὸ λεληθὸς τῇ
20 ἐξουσίᾳ, οὕτω τὸ μυστήριον οἰκονομοῦντος ἀρρήτως τε
καὶ ἀοράτως τὸ σῶμα τέθυτο καὶ ἡ ψυχὴ ἐν ἐκείνοις ἦν,
ἐν οἷς αὐτὴν ἡ ἐξουσία τοῦ οἰκονομοῦντος ἀπέθετο.
Ἑσπέρα μὲν γὰρ ἦν, ὅτε ἐβρώθη τὸ ἱερὸν ἐκεῖνο καὶ
ἅγιον σῶμα, νὺξ δὲ τὴν ἑσπέραν ἐκείνην πρὸ τῆς πα-
25 ρασκευῆς διεδέξατο. Εἶτα ἡ τῆς παρασκευῆς ἡμέρα, τῇ
ἐπεισάκτῳ νυκτὶ διατμηθεῖσα, εἰς μίαν νύκτα καὶ εἰς
ἡμέρας δύο καταψηφίζεται. Ἐν γὰρ ταῖς τρισὶν ὥραις
ἐγένετο σκότος ἐπὶ πᾶσαν τὴν οἰκουμένην· αὕτη ἐστὶν
ἡ κατὰ τὸ μέσον τῆς ἡμέρας καινοτομηθεῖσα νύξ· τὰ δύο
30 τμήματα τῶν ἡμερῶν δι'αὐτῆς ὑπογράφουσι· τὸ μὲν
ἀπὸ τοῦ ὄρθρου ἐπὶ τὴν ἕκτην ὥραν, τὸ δὲ ἀπὸ τῆς θ'ἐπὶ
τὴν ἑσπέραν, ὥστε εἶναι μέχρι τούτου δύο νύκτας καὶ
δύο ἡμέρας. Εἶτα ἡ πρὸ τοῦ σαββάτου <νὺξ καὶ μετὰ
ταύτην ἡ τοῦ σαββάτου> ἡμέρα, ἔχεις τὰς τρεῖς νύκτας
35 καὶ τὰς τρεῖς ἡμέρας.

Font.   23/35 = Greg. Nyss., De trid. spat, p. 288, 13 - 289, 3   27/28 cf. Mt. 27, 45
et loc. par.   31/32 cf. Mt. 27, 45 et loc. par.

Mss.   AT C

Crit.   20 οἰκονομοῦντες T   23 μὲν] om. T   25 τῇ] om. T   27 δύο] β' A
29 νύξ] σάρξ T   δύο] β' C   30 ὑπογράφουσι] sic codd., ὑπογράφου-
σα expectaueris   31 θ'] ἐνάτης T   32 δύο – καὶ] om. T   δύο] β' A
33 δύο] β' A   33/34 νὺξ – σαββάτου] scripsi cum fonte, om. codd.
34 ἔχεις] ἔχει A, εἰς C

Comp.   16 ἐπὶ τέλει] ἐντελῆ Greg. (ἐν τέλει M)   γεγενῆσθαι Greg.   20 οὕτω]
τοῦ Greg.   21 ἐτέθυτο Greg.   22 ἐναπέθετο Greg. (SET = Coisl.)
24 ante πρὸ] ἡ hab. Greg.   27 Ἐν γὰρ] εἰ γὰρ τὸ σκότος ὁ θεὸς ἐκάλεσε
νύκτα, ἐν δὲ Greg.   30 αὐτῆς] ἑαυτῆς Greg.   ὑπογράφουσι] περιγρά-
φουσα Greg.   33 ἡμέρας δύο Greg.   34/35 νύκτας ... ἡμέρας] ἡμέρας
... νύκτας Greg.

164   FLORILEGIVM COISLINIANVM

ΜΑ΄

Περὶ τοῦ Εὐχόμην ἐγὼ αὐτὸς ἀνάθεμα εἶναι

103   Τοῦ ἀποστόλου πρὸς Ῥωμαίους

Ἀλήθειαν λέγω ἐν Χριστῷ, οὐ ψεύδομαι, συμμαρτυ-
ρούσης μοι τῆς συνειδήσεώς μου ἐν πνεύματι ἁγίῳ, ὅτι
λύπη μοι ἐστὶν μεγάλη καὶ ἀδιάλειπτος ὀδύνη τῇ καρ-
δίᾳ μου· εὐχόμην γὰρ ἀνάθεμα εἶναι αὐτὸς ἐγὼ ἀπὸ τοῦ
5 Χριστοῦ ὑπὲρ τῶν ἀδελφῶν μου τῶν συγγενῶν μου
κατὰ σάρκα, ὧν ἡ υἱοθεσία καὶ ἡ δόξα καὶ ἡ διαθήκη
καὶ ἡ νομοθεσία καὶ ἡ λατρεία καὶ αἱ ἐπαγγελίαι, ὧν οἱ
πατέρες καὶ ἐξ ὧν ὁ Χριστὸς τὸ κατὰ σάρκα, ὁ ὢν ἐπὶ
πάντων θεὸς εἰς τοὺς αἰῶνας, ἀμήν.

10 Ἑρμηνεία τοῦ Χρυσοστόμου
Τί λέγεις, ὦ Παῦλε; Ἀπὸ τοῦ Χριστοῦ τοῦ ποθουμένου,
οὗ μήτε βασιλεία, μήτε γέεννά σε ἐχώριζε, μήτε τὰ
ὁρώμενα, μήτε τὰ νοούμενα, μήτε ἄλλα τοσαῦτα, ἀπὸ
τούτου νῦν εὔχῃ ἀνάθεμα εἶναι; Τί γέγονε; Μὴ μεταβέ-

Font.   **103.1/9** = Rom. 9, 1-5   **11/32** = Io. Chrys., In ep. ad Rom., PG 60, 549,
      1-24   **11/12** cf. Rom. 8, 35-39

Mss.   **103** *AT CDEFHK*

Tit.   **ΜΑ΄**] μ΄ *T*, λθ΄ *DEF*, μγ΄ *K, om. H*   Εὐχόμην – εἶναι] = Rom. 9, 3   Εὐ-
      χόμην] ηὐχόμην *F*   ἐγὼ αὐτὸς] ἐγὼ αὐτὸν *C*, αὐτὸς ἐγὼ *FH*   **103** Τοῦ
      ἀποστόλου] τοῦ χρυσοστόμου *D*, τοῦ ἀποστόλου ἢ τοῦ χρυσοστόμου *F, om.*
      EHK   πρὸς Ῥωμαίους] ἐκ τῆς πρὸς ῥωμαίους ἐπιστολῆς *T, om. DEFHK*

Crit.   **103.2** μοι] *scripsi cum DEFHK et fonte*, μου *ATC*   **4** ηὐχόμην *F*   ἀνά-
      θεμα εἶναι] *post* ἐγὼ *trsp. EK*   τοῦ] *om. F*   **5** μου²] *om. EK*
      6 κατὰ] τῶν *praem. F*   **6/7** καὶ¹ – νομοθεσία] *om. T*   **7** αἱ] *om. A*
      8 ὁ¹ – σάρκα] τὸ κατὰ σάρκα χριστός *F*   **9** ἀμήν] *om. DEFHK*
      10 Ἑρμηνεία – Χρυσοστόμου] τοῦ χρυσοστόμου *K, om. DEFH*   **11** τοῦ¹]
      om. DEFH   **13** μήτε – νοούμενα] *om. A*   **14** τούτων *H*

Comp.   **103.4** ηὐχόμην *Rom.*   **6** *post* σάρκα] οἵτινές εἰσιν Ἰσραηλῖται *hab. Rom.*
      9 *post* θεὸς] εὐλογητὸς *hab. Rom.*   **12** σε] *post* βασιλεία *hab. Chrys.*

ALPHA 103

15 βλῆσαι καὶ κατέλυσας τὸν πόθον ἐκεῖνον; Οὐχί φησι,
μὴ δείσῃς· καὶ γὰρ καὶ ἐπέτεινα μᾶλλον αὐτόν. Πῶς οὖν
εὔχῃ ἀνάθεμα εἶναι, καὶ ἀλλοτρίωσιν ζητεῖς, καὶ χωρι-
σμὸν τοιοῦτον, μεθ᾽ ὃν ἕτερον οὐκ ἔστιν εὑρεῖν; Ἐπειδὴ
σφόδρα αὐτὸν φιλῶ φησί. Πῶς, εἰπέ μοι, καὶ τίνι τρό-
20 πῳ; Καὶ γὰρ αἰνίγματι τὸ πρᾶγμα ἔοικε. Μᾶλλον δέ, εἰ
δοκεῖ, πρῶτον μάθωμεν τί ποτέ ἐστι τὸ ἀνάθεμα, καὶ
τότε αὐτὸν ἐρωτήσωμεν περὶ τούτων, καὶ τὴν ἀπόρρη-
τον ταύτην καὶ παράδοξον εἰσόμεθα ἀγάπην.
    Τί οὖν ἐστι τὸ ἀνάθεμα; Ἄκουσον αὐτοῦ λέγοντος· Εἴ
25 τις οὐ φιλεῖ τὸν Κύριον ἡμῶν Ἰησοῦν Χριστόν, ἔστω
ἀνάθεμα· τουτέστι κεχωρίσθω πάντων, ἀλλότριος ἔστω
πάντων. Καθάπερ γὰρ τοῦ ἀναθέματος τοῦ ἀνατιθεμέ-
νου τῷ θεῷ οὐδεὶς ἂν τολμήσειεν οὐδὲ ἐγγὺς γενέσθαι,
οὕτως καὶ τὸν χωριζόμενον τῆς ἐκκλησίας, πάντων
30 ἀποτεμὼν καὶ ὡς πορρωτάτω ἀπάγων, τούτῳ τῷ ὀνόματι ἀπὸ τοῦ ἐναντίου καλεῖ, μετὰ πολλοῦ τοῦ φόβου
πᾶσιν ἀπαγορεύων αὐτοῦ χωρίζεσθαι καὶ ἀποπηδᾶν.
    Καὶ μετὰ ταῦτα. Καὶ οὐχ᾽ ἁπλῶς εἶπεν· Ἐβουλόμην,
ἀλλ᾽ἐπαινῶν αὐτό, φησὶν καὶ Εὐχόμην. Εἰ δὲ θορυβεῖ σε
35 ἅτε ἀσθενέστερον ὄντα ταῦτα λεγόμενα, μὴ τὸ πρᾶγμα

Font.   17 Rom. 9, 3   24/26 I Cor. 16, 22   33/38 = Io. Chrys., In ep. ad Rom.,
PG 60, 549, 34-39   34 supra l. 17

Mss.   AT CDEFHK

Crit.   16 καὶ²] om. F   ἐπέτεινα] ἐπέκεινα H^{a.corr.}   19 Πῶς] οὖν add. E
22 τούτων] τούτου T FH   25 ἔστω] ἤτω (cf. I Cor. 16, 22) EK   28 τολ-
μήσει FH, τολμήεν (sic) A   31 τοῦ²] om. D   33 Καὶ¹ – ταῦτα] καὶ
μετ᾽ὀλί-γα T, om. DEFHK   34 θορυβεῖ σε] scripsi cum DEFHK et fonte,
θορυβῆσαι AT C   35 ἅτε] εἴτε add. C   ἀσθενέστερον ὄντα] ἀσθενέ-
στερος ὢν FH

Comp.   16 αὐτὸν μᾶλλον Chrys.   19 τίνι] ποίῳ Chrys.   25 ἡμῶν – Χριστόν]
Ἰησοῦν Χριστὸν Chrys., non hab. I Cor.   28 post τολμήσειεν] ἁπλῶς ταῖς
χερσὶν ἅψασθαι hab. Chrys.   30 ἀποτέμνων Chrys.   32 ἀποχωρίζεσθαι
Chrys.   33 οὐχ᾽] οὐδὲ Chrys.   post εἶπεν] ὅτι hab. Chrys.   34 ηὐ-
χόμην Chrys. et Rom.   35 ἀσθενέστερον – ταῦτα] ἀσθενέστερα ὄντα τὰ
Chrys.   μὴ] post λογίζου hab. Chrys.

166 FLORILEGIVM COISLINIANVM

λογίζου μόνον ὅτι χωρισθῆναι ἐβούλετο, ἀλλὰ τὴν αἰτίαν δι'ἣν ἐβούλετο, καὶ τότε ὄψει αὐτοῦ τὴν ὑπερβολὴν
τῆς ἀγάπης.

Ἄν γὰρ τὴν αἰτίαν μὴ ἐξετάσωμεν, καὶ τὸν Ἠλίαν
40 ἀνδροφόνον ἐροῦμεν, καὶ τὸν Ἀβραὰμ παιδοκτόνον· καὶ
πολλὰ ἄτοπα ὁ μὴ τοῦτον τηρῶν τὸν κανόνα ὑποπτεύσειε.
Διὸ τὴν αἰτίαν πειράσομαι ποιῆσαι σαφῆ. Οὐδὲ γὰρ
ἁπλῶς ταῦτα εἴρηκεν, ἀλλ'ἐπειδὴ πάντες ἔλεγον καὶ
45 τοῦ θεοῦ κατηγόρουν, ὅτι υἱοὶ θεοῦ καταξιωθέντες
κληθῆναι, καὶ νόμον δεξάμενοι, καὶ πρὸ πάντων
αὐτὸν εἰδότες, καὶ τοσαύτης ἀπολαύσαντες δόξης, καὶ
θεραπεύσαντες αὐτὸν πρὸ τῆς οἰκουμένης ἁπάσης, καὶ
ἐπαγγελίας δεξάμενοι, καὶ πατέρων ὄντες τῶν αὐτῷ
50 φίλων, καὶ τὸ δὴ πάντων μεῖζον, καὶ προπάτορες
αὐτοῦ γενόμενοι τοῦ Χριστοῦ – τοῦτο γάρ ἐστιν,
Ἐξ ὧν ὁ Χριστὸς τὸ κατὰ σάρκα –, ἐκβέβληνται καὶ
ἠτίμωνται, ἀντεισήχθησαν δὲ ἀντ'ἐκείνων οἱ μηδέποτε

Font.   **39/42** = Io. Chrys., In ep. ad Rom., PG 60, 549, 53-59   **39/40** cf. III Reg.
18, 40   **40** cf. Gen. 22, 1-24   **43/65** = Io. Chrys., In ep. ad Rom., PG 60,
550, 21-44   **52** cf. supra, l. 8

Mss.   *AT CDEFHK*

Crit.   **36** ὅτι] τὸ *FH*   ἀλλὰ] καὶ *add. K*   **37** ὄψη *(sic spir.) A D*
40 ἀβραὰμ *EFHK*   **41** ἄτοπα] τὰ *praem. FH*   **41/42** ὑποπτεύσειε] *scripsi cum EK,* ὑποπτεύσοιεν *AT CDFH,* ὑποπτείσοιεν *(sic) D*   **43** Διὸ] καὶ
add. E   **43/44** Οὐδὲ – ἀλλ'] *om. DEFHK*   **47** καὶ²] *om. E*   **49** πα-
τέρων] πατέρες *E,* πάντων *H*   **51** τοῦτο – ἐστιν] *om. F*   **52** τὸ] *om. C*

Comp.   **36** *post* ἀλλὰ] καὶ *hab. Chrys.*   **39** τὴν – μὴ] μὴ τὰς αἰτίας *Chrys.*
40 *post* Ἀβραὰμ] οὐκ ἀνδροφόνον μόνον, ἀλλὰ καὶ *hab. Chrys.*   *post* καὶ²]
τὸν Φινεὲς δὲ καὶ τὸν Πέτρον φόνου γραφόμεθα πάλιν, καὶ οὐ περὶ τῶν ἁγίων
δὲ μόνον, ἀλλὰ καὶ περὶ τοῦ τῶν ὅλων Θεοῦ *hab. Chrys.*   **41/42** πολλὰ – ὑπο-
πτεύσειε] ὁ μὴ τηρῶν τοῦτον τὸν κανόνα, πολλὰ ἄτοπα ὑποπτεύσει *Chrys.*
43 Διὸ – αἰτίαν] *non hab. Chrys.*   σαφές *Chrys.*   **44** *post* εἴρηκεν]
ἅπερ εἴρηκεν *hab. Chrys.*   ἐπεὶ *Chrys.*   **48** ἁπάσης] *non hab. Chrys.*
49 πατέρων] πατέρες *Chrys.*   **49/50** αὐτῷ φίλων] αὐτῶν φυλῶν *Chrys.*
50 μεῖζον πάντων *Chrys.*

ALPHA 103 167

αὐτὸν ἐπιγνόντες ἄνθρωποι οἱ ἐξ ἐθνῶν. Ἐπεὶ οὖν
55 τὰ τοιαῦτα λέγοντες τὸν θεὸν ἐβλασφήμουν, ἀκούων
ταῦτα καὶ δακνόμενος ὁ Παῦλος, καὶ ὑπὲρ τῆς δόξης
ἀλγῶν τοῦ θεοῦ, ηὔξατο ἀνάθεμα εἶναι, εἴ γε δυνατὸν
ἦν, ὥστε σωθῆναι ἐκείνους, καὶ τὴν βλασφημίαν
ταύτην καταλυθῆναι, καὶ μὴ δόξαι τὸν θεὸν ἠπατηκέναι
60 τοὺς ἐκγόνους ἐκείνων, εἰς τὰς δωρεὰς ἃς ἐπηγγείλατο.
Καὶ ἵνα μάθῃς ὅτι ὑπὲρ τούτου κοπτόμενος τοῦ μὴ
δόξαι τὴν ὑπόσχεσιν τοῦ θεοῦ διαπίπτειν τὴν λέγουσαν
τῷ Ἀβραάμ· Σοὶ δώσω καὶ τῷ σπέρματί σου τὴν γῆν
ταύτην, ταῦτα ηὔχετο ὑπομεῖναι, ἐπήγαγεν· Οὐχ᾽οἷον
65 δὲ ὅτι ἐκπέπτωκεν ὁ λόγος τοῦ θεοῦ.

Font.   **57** cf. supra, l. 4   **63/64** Gen. 12, 7   **64/65** Rom. 9, 6

Mss.   *AT CDEFHK*

Crit.   **54** ἐξ] *om. K*   **56** δακνόμενος] δακρυόμενος *D*   **57** γε] *om. T*
59 δόξαι] *scripsi cum EK et fonte,* δόξαν *cett.*   **60** ἐγγόνους *T*
63 ἀβραάμ *TEFHK*   Σοὶ] σὺ *D*   **64** εὔχετο *ACD*

Comp.   **55** τὰ τοιαῦτα] ταῦτα *Chrys.*   **58** ἐκείνους σωθῆναι *Chrys.*   **60** *post*
ἐκγόνους] τοὺς *hab. Chrys.*   εἰς] οἷς *Chrys.*   ἃς] *non hab. Chrys.*
63/64 δώσω – ταύτην] δώσω τὴν γῆν ταύτην καὶ τῷ σπέρματί σου *Chrys.,*
Τῷ σπέρματί σου δώσω τὴν γῆν ταύτην *Gen.*   **64** ὑπομεῖναι] μετὰ τὸ
ταῦτα εἰπεῖν *Chrys.*

INDICES

Index Locorvm Sacrae Scriptvrae

Index Aliorvm Fontivm et Locorvm Parallelorvm

INDEX LOCORVM SACRAE SCRIPTVRAE*

Genesis

1, 1	1.29; 19.3/4. 39
1, 1-30	30.1/4
1, 3	19.5
1, 13-18	40.2/3
1, 26	5.56; 17.1; 19.1/2. 6. 24-25. 31. 46/47. 50/51. 52/53. 54; 29.460
1, 26-27	16.13; 40.3/4; 60.43
1, 27	34.3/4
1, 28	33.10/11
1, 31	40.3/4
2, 8	16.26
2, 9	20.6/7; 25.4/5
2, 15	16.26
2, 16-17	16.34/36; 24.1/3; 29.182/183. 192/193
2, 19	24.21/23
2, 25	16.31
3, 1-3	16.38
3, 1-6	4.22/23
3, 1-7	31.1/13
3, 6	16.47/48
3, 7	29.196
3, 7-8	16.52/53
3, 19	18.27/30; 29.138/139
3, 21	16.50/51
3, 23-24	16.48/49
4, 1-14	74.7/9
5, 1	60.43
6, 1 – 8, 22	97.11
6, 4	98.15/16
6, 9-10	40.9/13
7, 6-7	40.9/13
8, 21	62.71
9, 5	79.68/69
11, 1-9	97.11/12
12, 7	103.63/64
15, 2	33.14/15
18, 1	14.1. 3
18, 2	14.5. 15/16
18, 8	14.24; 15.2/3
18, 16 – 19, 28	97.12
18, 27	30.19
22, 1-24	103.40
25, 25-34	74.12/13
35, 22	74.9/11
48, 16	**10.5/6**

Exodus

3, 2-6	5.22/23
3, 10	42.26
3, 11	42.26
8, 1 – 10, 21	97.12
13, 2	75.3/4. 11
13, 12	75.3/4. 11
13, 15	75.3/4. 11
13, 21-22	42.26/27
14, 24	5.22/23
19, 18	5.22/23
20, 15	37.14
23, 20-21	**10.1/5**
33, 13	65.26/27

Leuiticus

2, 12	62.71
9, 2	62.114
9, 3	62.114
22, 22-23	62.73/75

Numeri

3, 12	75.3/4
8, 16	75.3/4
20, 17	60.97/98
24, 17	42.28/29

Deuteronomium

4, 24	5.22/23
5, 18	37.14
23, 19	62.40/41

---

* Sources that constitute the main text of the *FC* are in boldface.

INDEX LOCORVM SACRAE SCRIPTVRAE

Iosue
6, 17	79.21/22

Iudicum
6, 21	5.137; 15.6/7

II Regnorum
12, 16-18	62.95/96
22, 1	77.11/12

III Regnorum
18, 40	103.39/40
16, 29-34	57.29
20, 28-29	57.31/32

IV Regnorum
2.11	5.221

II Machabaeorum
5, 2	5.140

Psalmi
1, 1	49.4; **80.1/3**
6, 6	78.40/41
8, 6	32.29/30
17, 1	77.11/12
23, 7	74.35/37
25, 5	**80.4/5**
36, 1-2	**80.6/9**
38, 12	50.13
39, 7	62.111/112
41, 2	67.11/13
44, 4	65.24/26
48, 13	29.139/140;60.44/46
48, 21	29.139/140
50, 18	62.102/103
50, 19	62.105
62, 2	67.13/15
75.11	78.56. 57/59
90, 11-13	**11**
102, 15	48.7/8
103, 4	5.156
108, 23	77.7/8
148, 7	**98.2/3**
148, 11-12	98.11/12

Prouerbia
1, 10	**81.1**

1, 15-16	**81.1/3**
3, 25	60.20/21
4, 14-15	**81.4/6**
4, 25	35.31
6, 27	35.23/24
12, 10	29.358
20, 9	57.8/10
20, 9c	**68.5**
22, 5	**81.7/8**
23, 27	62.124
24, 27	52.3
24, 29	**68.4**
25, 21-22	**68.1/4**
26, 11	**43.1/3**

Ecclesiastes
1, 2	**47.1**
1, 12-14	47.6/13
1, 16	**47.6**
1, 16-18	**47.14/20**
2, 2	**47.20/21**
2, 4-8	**47.21/24**
2, 9	**47.6**
2, 10-11	**47.32/38**
7, 29	35.10/12
10, 4	35.40/42
12, 5	77.13/14

Canticum
7, 2	67.34

Iob
1, 21	**46.1/2**
8, 9	**46.2**
18, 12	45.4
20, 5	45.4
20, 8	48.3/4

Sapientia
5, 10	48.5
5, 11	48.4/5

Siracides
13, 1	**83**

Osee
13, 3	48.5/6

Amos
5, 23	62.65/66

INDEX LOCORVM SACRAE SCRIPTVRAE 173

Michaeas
5, 1	76.17/20. 32/33
5, 3	76.17/20. 33/33

Ioel
2, 4	5.221

Zacharias
1, 8	5.221
2, 5	5.143/144
6, 1-5	5.242
6, 2	5.221
6, 3	5.221
6, 5	5.156

Malachias
2, 13	62.52/54
3, 20	42.5/6; 94.6

Isaias
1, 6	79.8/9
1, 11	62.79/81
1, 13	62.85/86
1, 16	37.15/17
5, 23	60.23/24. 79
6, 2-3	65.17/20
9, 5	19.47/49
14, 12-15	2.16; 4.11/16
40, 6-7	**47.2/3**
47, 13-14	39.6/9
48, 22	90.3/4
49, 9	98.20
49, 15	65.43/45
54, 14	**82**
57, 21	90.3/4
58, 4-5	62.49/51
66, 3	62.44/45. 88/90

Ieremias
2, 21	35.4/6
4, 22	60.30/31. 93
5, 8	60.8/9
17, 11	60.24

Baruch
3, 36	4.4

Ezechiel
1, 4	5.156. 173. 184
1, 7	5.110/111. 184
1, 10	5.51. 202. 209. 214
1, 13	5.13
1, 14	5.11
1, 15	5.10. 237/238
1, 18	5.105
1, 26	5.192
3, 14	5.156
3, 21	79.65/66
8, 2	5.184
9, 2	5.129. 132. 140
10, 1	5.192
10, 2	5.10. 13. 237/238
10, 3-4	5.173
10, 6	5.10. 129. 237/238
10, 9	5.10. 237/238
10, 13	5.252/253
28, 17-18	4.11/16
40, 3	5.143/144. 184
44, 1-3	75.11. 13/15
44, 2	74.28/30
47, 1-12	5.237
47, 3	5.143/144

Daniel
6, 6	29.450
7, 2	5.156
(θ′) 7, 9	5.10. 15. 237/238
7, 10	5.13/14. 237; 33.1/2
8, 4	60.70
9, 24	75.17
10, 5	5.132
10, 6	5.184

Matthaeus
1, 25	75.8. 10
2, 1	42.1/3
2, 1-2	42.6/7
2, 2	42.9/10. 12
2, 3-4	42.31
2, 4-5	42.32/34
2, 4-8	42.34/38
2, 6	76.17/20. 32/33
3, 4	77.1/4. 19
3, 10	62.128/129
5, 19	62.13/14
5, 25	78.1/2. 9/10. 14. 37. 37/38. 41/42. 50
5, 26	78.53/54. 57

5, 29	79.37. 41
5, 44	60.84/85
5, 47	91.2/4
7, 19	62.128/129
8, 12	78.52/53
18, 12	13.16/18
19, 21	67.47/48
19, 24	62.10/11
22, 11-13	62.16/19
22, 23-30	32.1/10
22, 30	32.8/9
23, 23	62.34/37
25, 1-12	62.32/34
25, 31	79.30/31
25, 33	79.31/32
25, 35-36	67.49/50
26, 26	102.14/15
26,47 – 27,10	62.37/39
27, 4	57.33/34
27, 45	101.1/2; 102.27/28. 31/32
27,66 – 28,10	75.25/26
28, 1	101.6
28, 3	5.11/12

Marcus
9, 43-47	62.22/25
12, 25	32.8/9
14, 43-46	62.37/39

Lucas
1, 34	75.9
1, 35	74.17/19
2, 1	76.6. 47
2, 1-3	**76.1/4**
2, 4-7	76.52/59
2, 7	75.8. 10
2, 23	74.5/6. 15/16. 21/22. 23; 75.3/4. 11. 15/16. 20
3, 9	62.128/129
11, 42	62.34/37
15, 4-9	13.16/18
15, 10	5.262/263
16, 19-24	57.64/66
16, 19-25	54.7
16, 22	93.34/35
16, 25	57.66/67. 67/68. 68. 70. 72/73

18, 10-14	57.20/21
20, 35	32.8/9
20, 36	32.10/11
22, 47-48	62.37/39
24, 4	5.124

Iohannes
1, 1	4.1
1, 29	102.9/10
1, 45	76.24/25
1, 46	76.23/24
1, 47	76.25/26. 34/35
3, 8	5.170/171
3, 16	65.39/41
4, 35	52.4/5
5, 46	19.27/28
7, 42	76.37/38
7, 52	76.36/37
13, 35	79.74/75
14, 6	60.99
14, 8	65.28/29
18, 1-9	62.37/39
19, 14	101.1/2
20, 19	75.22/24
20, 26	75.22/24

Actus Apostolorum
6, 8	79.35
28, 3	29.450/451

Ad Romanos
6, 17	17.6
6, 20	17.6
8, 2	18.41
8, 15	60.74
8, 32	19.13
8, 35-39	103.11/12
9, 1-5	**103.1/9**
9, 3	103.17. 34. 57
9, 5	103.52
9, 6	103.64/65
12, 17	**69.1/2**
12, 20	68.1/4
12, 21	**69.2/3**
13, 8	66.3/4

I ad Corinthios
2, 9	65.34/37
3, 2	16.42/44
5, 9	91.6/7

INDEX LOCORVM SACRAE SCRIPTVRAE

5, 11	**84.1/3**
6, 9	88.1
6, 10	88.2
6, 11	67.5/6
7, 5	60.61/62
7, 33	30.31/32
7, 40	60.66
13, 12	18.7
14, 20	60.93/94
15, 47	29.137
15, 48	29.144/145
16, 22	79.49/50; 103.24/26

II ad Corinthios

5, 18	60.85/86
6, 11	67.5/6
9, 15	65.33/34
11, 2-3	31.1/3

Ad Galatas

1, 8	85.4/5
1, 9	79.50/51; 86.11/12
4, 4	75.8. 10
5, 17	78.26/27.29/30.31/33. 36

Ad Ephesios

1, 20	19.15/16
1, 21	1.18/20
2, 6	19.16/17
2, 10	18.1/2; 35.12/14; 60. 41/42. 43/44
3, 9	75.17/18
3, 14	98.19

Ad Philippenses

2, 10	98.8/9. 19

Ad Colossenses

1, 13	99.10/12
1, 16	1.18/20
1, 19	75.17/18
1, 21	60.86
1, 26	75.17/18
2, 9	75.17/18

I ad Thessalonicenses

5, 6	14.1/2

II ad Thessalonicenses

3, 6	**84.3/5**

I ad Timotheum

1, 7	79.13/14
3, 4	60.81/82
3, 12	60.81/82
5, 5	60.65

II ad Timotheum

1, 7	60.73
2, 25-26	79.57/60

Ad Hebraeos

10, 5	62.111/112
10, 5-14	102.8
11, 25-27	67.25/31
13, 4	60.11/12. 49
13, 17	85.1

Epistula Iacobi

2, 10	62.31/32
4, 14	**47.4/5**

I Petri

2, 2	16.42/44
2, 5	62.102
3, 9	**70**
3, 19-20	98.24/26
4, 6	**97.1/2**. 17/21. 25/27

III Iohannis

11	**71**

Apocalypsis

4, 3	5.192
4, 7	5.51. 202. 209. 214
6, 2	5.221
10, 1	5.173
15, 6	5.132
19, 11	5.221
20, 14	93.9/10
21, 15	5.143/144
22, 1	5.237

INDEX ALIORVM FONTIVM
ET LOCORVM PARALLELORVM*

Amph., *In occ. dom.*
Amphilochius Iconiensis, *Oratio in occursum domini* [*CPG* 3232], ed.
C. DATEMA, *Amphilochii Iconiensis Opera* (*CCSG* 3), Turnhout – Leuven, 1978,
p. 37-73.
  49-81   **74**

Anast. Sin., *Quaest. et resp.*
Anastasius Sinaita, *Quaestiones et responsiones* [*CPG* 7746], ed. M. RICHARD –
J. A. MUNITIZ, *Anastasii Sinaitae Quaestiones et Responsiones* (*CCSG* 59), Turnhout – Leuven, 2006.
  80, 8-13   4.18/20

Anast. Sin., *Viae dux*
Anastasius Sinaita, *Viae dux* [*CPG* 7745], ed. K.-H. UTHEMANN, *Anastasii
Sinaitae Viae dux* (*CCSG* 8), Turnhout – Leuven, 1981.
  IV, 8 – 36 (p. 82-83) **4**

Ps.-Ant. Mel., *Loc. comm.*
Ps.-Antonius Melissa, *Loci communes, PG* 136, 765-1244.
  1084, 14-15 [*CPG* 2564. 7] **8**
  1084, 17-18   9

Athan., *De amul.*
Athanasius Alexandrinus, *De amuletis, PG* 26, 1320-1324.
  1320, 29-40   99

Athan., *Ep. ad mon.*
Athanasius Alexandrinus, *Epistula ad monachos* [*CPG* 2108], *PG* 26, 1185-
1188 (cf. FERNÁNDEZ, *A Correction*).
  1188, 13-30   **89**

Athan., *Fragm. ined.*
Athanasius Alexandrinus, *Fragmenta inedita duo in Matthaeum*, ed.
T. FERNÁNDEZ, *Dos fragmentos inéditos de Atanasio de Alejandría*, in *Erytheia*
32 (2011), [p. 79-93] p. 92-93.
  *fr. I   **42**
  *fr. II   **40**

*Athan., *Fragm. in Matth.*
Athanasius Alexandrinus, *Fragmenta in Matthaeum* (= *Scholia in Matthaeum*) [*CPG* 2141. 7], *PG* 27, 1364-1389.
  1364, 15-18   **40.1/4**

---

 * Sources that constitute the main text of the *FC* are in boldface; references
preceded by an asterisk are attested only or predominantly in the *FC*.

INDEX ALIORVM FONTIVM ET LOCORVM PARALLELORVM   177

1365, 41	**77.5/6. 16/17**
1365, 42-43	**77.13/14**
1365, 43-45	**77.19/21**

*Athan., *Fragm. uar.*

Athanasius Alexandrinus, *Fragmenta uaria* (= *Scholia in Matthaeum*) [*CPG* 2141. 7], *PG* 26, 1252-1257.

1256, 17-18	**98.2/3**
1256, 19-41	**98.5/26**

Ps.-Athan., *Quaest. ad Ant.*

Ps.-Athanasius Alexandrinus, *Quaestiones ad Antiochum ducem* [*CPG* 2257], *PG* 28, 597-700.

601, 46-50	**13.16/18**
616, 24-41	**13.1/15**
629, 30-36	**34**
673, 45 – 676, 6	**92**

Ps.-Athan., *Test. e script.*

Ps.-Athanasius Alexandrinus, *Testimonia e scriptura* [*CPG* 2240], *PG* 28, 29-80.

77, 19-35	**13.1/15**

Bas. Caes., *Asc. magn. breu.*

Basilius Caesariensis, *Asceticon magnum siue Quaestiones* (*Regulae breuius tractatae*) [*CPG* 2875], *PG* 31, 1052-1305.

1165, 39-46	**91**

Bas. Caes., *Canon 96*

Basilius Caesariensis, *Canon 96* [*CPG* 2901. 5], ed. P.-P. JOANNOU, in *Discipline générale antique (IV-IXe s.)*, II. *Les canons des Pères Grecs (Lettres Canoniques)* (*Pontificia commissione per la redazione del codice di diritto canonico orientale* 9), Grottaferrata – Roma, 1963, p. 198-199.

198, 15 – 199, 1	**91**

Bas. Caes., *Hom. in Hex.*

Basilius Caesariensis, *Homiliae in Hexaemeron* [*CPG* 2835], ed. E. AMAND DE MENDIETA – S. Y. RUDBERG, *Basilius von Caesarea. Homilien zum Hexaemeron* (*GCS* N. F. 2), Berlin, 1997.

1, 5 (p. 8, 17 – 9, 16)	**1.5/28**
1, 5 (p. 10, 4-8)	**1.29/34**

Bas. Caes., *Hom. super Ps.*

Basilius Caesariensis, *Homiliae super Psalmos* [*CPG* 2836], *PG* 29, 209-493.

221, 20-29	**49**
364, 15-21	**6**

Bas. Caes., *In ebr.*

Basilius Caesariensis, *In ebriosos* [*CPG* 2858], *PG* 31, 444-464.

445, 5-9	**44**

178   INDEX ALIORVM FONTIVM ET LOCORVM PARALLELORVM

Ps.-Caesarius, *Quaest. et resp.*
   Ps.-Caesarius. *Quaestiones et responsiones* [*CPG* 7482], ed. R. Riedinger,
Pseudo-Kaisarios. Die Erotapokriseis (*GCS* 58), Berlin, 1989.
   60, 6-7 (p. 53)   3

Cat. in Gen.
   Catena in Genesim [*CPG* C 1], ed. F. Petit, *La chaîne sur la Genèse*, 4 vols.
(*Traditio exegetica graeca* 1-4), Lovanii, 1991-1996.
   1069, ad Gen. 18, 8, l. 4   14.24
   1069, ad Gen. 18, 8, l. 4-5   15.2/3
   1070, ad Gen. 18, 8, l. 3-4   14.16/17
   1074, ad Gen. 18, 8, l. 1-5   **15.3/7**

Clem. Alex., *Strom.*
   Clemens Alexandrinus, *Stromata* [*CPG* 1377], ed. L. Früchtel –
O. Stählin – U. Treu, *Clemens Alexandrinus. Stromata* (*GCS* 52 [15], 17),
Berlin, 1960-1970.
   1, 21, 126, 2, 1-2   75.17/18
   2, 19, 101, 3, 1 – 102, 1, 4   **63**

Ps.-Clem. Rom., *Hom.*
   Ps.-Clemens Romanus, *Homiliae* [*CPG* 1015. 4], ed. B. Rehm – J. Irmscher – F. Paschke, *Die Pseudoklementinen*, I. *Homilien* (*GCS* 42), Berlin,
1969.
   10, 3, 3, 2 – 10, 4, 2, 2 (p. 143)   17

Const. apost.
   Constitutiones apostolorum [*CPG* 1730], ed. B. M. Metzger, *Les constitu-
tions apostoliques*, 3 vols. (*SC* 320, 329, 336), Paris, 1985-1987.
   6, 18, 42-45   **90**
   8, 47, 17-19   60.56/58

Corp. Par.
   Corpus Parisinum, ed. D. M. Searby, *The Corpus Parisinum. A Critical
Edition of the Greek Text with Commentary and English Translation. A Medi-
eval Anthology of Greek Texts from the Pre-Socratics to the Church Fathers, 600
B.C. – 700 A.D.*, 2 vols., Lewinston NY, 2007.
   1, 38   **6.3/6**
   1, 40   **44**
   1, 265   **9**
   1, 415   **81.1/3**
   1, 429   **43**

Cyr. Alex., *Contra Iul.*
   Cyrillus Alexandrinus, *Contra Iulianum imperatorem* [*CPG* 5233], ed.
C. Riedweg, *Kyrill von Alexandrien. Werke*, I. *"Gegen Julian." Buch 1-5* (*GCS*
N. F. 20), Berlin, 2016.
   3, 23, 17-25   **25**
   3, 24, 1 – 25, 14   **18**

INDEX ALIORVM FONTIVM ET LOCORVM PARALLELORVM   179

Cyr. Hier., *Cat. ad illum.*
  Cyrillus Hierosolymitanus, *Catecheses ad illuminandos* [*CPG* 3585. 2], ed.
W. C. REISCHL – J. RUPP, *Cyrilli Hierosolymarum archiepiscopi opera quae super-sunt omnia*, 2 vols., München, 1848-1860 (repr. 1967).

2, 1, 1 – 3, 16	**35**
4, 18, 2-9	**28**
4, 18, 9-17	**39**
4, 21, 1-9	**27**
15, 12, 1-19	**100**

Did. Caec., *Comm. in Iob*
  Didymus Caecus, *Commentarii in Iob* [*CPG* 2553. 1], ed. D. HAGEDORN –
U. HAGEDORN – L. KOENEN, *Didymos der Blinde. Kommentar zu Hiob (Tura-Papyrus)*, IV. 1 (*Papyrologische Texte und Abhandlungen* 33, 1), Bonn, 1985.

375, 1-3	**8**
375, 28-31	**8**

Ps.-Dion., *De coel. hier.*
  Ps.-Dionysius Areopagita, *De coelesti hierarchia* [*CPG* 6600], ed. G. HEIL,
in G. HEIL – A. M. RITTER, *Corpus Dionysiacum*, II. *Ps.-Dionysius Areopagita. De coelesti hierarchia. De ecclesiastica hierarchia. De mystica theologia. Epistulae* (*PTS* 36), Berlin, 1991, p. 7-59.

6, 2 (p. 26, 11 – 27, 3)	**12**
15, 1 (p. 50, 13 – 51, 1)	**5.1/6**
15, 2-9 (p. 51, 22 – 59, 7)	**5.7/247**

Ps.-Dion., *De diu. nom.*
  Ps.-Dionysius Areopagita, *De diuinis nominibus* [*CPG* 6602], ed. B. R.
SUCHLA, *Corpus Dionysiacum*, I. *Pseudo-Dionysius Areopagita. De divinis nomi-nibus* (*PTS* 33), Berlin, 1990.

8, 7 (p. 204, 14)	**60.78/79**

Ps.-Epiph., *Hom. in diu.*
  Ps.-Epiphanius Constantiensis, *Homilia in diuini corporis sepulturam* [*CPG* 3768], *PG* 43, 440-464.

440, 53-54	**96**

Euag., *De oct. spir. mal.*
  Euagrius Ponticus (sub nomine Nili Ancyrani), *De octo spiritibus malitiae* [*CPG* 2451], *PG* 79, 1145-1164.

1156, 12-15	**62.42/46**

Euag., *Schol in Prou.*
  Euagrius Ponticus, *Scholia in Proverbia* [*CPG* 2456], ed. P. GÉHIN, *Évagre le Pontique. Scholies aux Proverbes* (*SC* 340), Paris, 1987.

189, 2-3	**9**

Greg. Naz, *Carm. mor.*
  Gregorius Nazianzenus, *Carmina moralia* [*CPG* 3035], *PG* 37, 521-968.

15, 133-134 (775, 13 – 776, 1)	**51**

180 INDEX ALIORVM FONTIVM ET LOCORVM PARALLELORVM

Greg. Naz., *Or.*
Gregorius Nazianzenus, *Orationes* [*CPG* 3010]

Oratio 7, In laudem Caesarii fratris, ed. M.-A. CALVET-SEBASTI, *Grégoire de Nazianze. Discours 6-12* (*SC* 405), Paris, 1995, p. 180-244.
19, 1, 1-9   **48**

Oratio 38, In theophania, ed. C. MORESCHINI, in C. MORESCHINI – P. GAL-LAY, *Grégoire de Nazianze. Discours 38-41* (*SC* 358), Paris, 1990, p. 104-148.
9, 1 – 10, 11   **2**
11, 1 – 12, 30   **16**

Oratio 44, In nouam Dominicam, PG 36, 608-621.
612, 9-18   **20**

Oratio 45, In Sanctum Pascha, PG 36, 624-663.
629, 7-40   **2**
631, 48 – 633, 17   **16**

Greg. Nyss., *De hom. opif.*
Gregorius Nyssenus, *De hominis opificio* [*CPG* 3154], ed. L. SELS, *Gregory of Nyssa. De hominis opificio. The Fourteenth-Century Slavonic Translation. A Critical Edition with Greek Parallel and Commentary* (*Bausteine zur Slavischen Philologie und Kulturgeschichte* N. F. Reihe B: Editionen 21), Köln, 2009.
151, 12 – 152, 13 (= *PG* 44, 149, 23-39)   **23**
204, 11 – 205, 21 (= *PG* 44, 188, 28 –
189, 13)   **32**

Greg. Nyss., *De trid. spat.*
Gregorius Nyssenus, *De tridui inter mortem et resurrectionem domini nostri Iesu Christi spatio* [*CPG* 3175], ed. E. GEBHARDT, in G. HEIL et al., *Gregorii Nysseni Sermones,* I (*Gregorii Nysseni Opera* 9, 1), Leiden, 1967, p. 273-306.
p. 287, 7 – 288, 6   **102.1/22**
p. 288, 13 – 289, 3   **102.23/35**

Greg. Nyss., *Vit. Moys.*
Gregorius Nyssenus, *De Vita Moysis* [*CPG* 3159], ed. H. MUSURILLO, *Gregorii Nysseni De Vita Moysis* (*Gregorii Nysseni Opera* 7, 1), Leiden, 1964.
2, 45, 3 – 46, 8   **7**

Hipp., *Comm. in Dan.*
Hippolytus Romanus, *Commentarii in Danielem* [*CPG* 1873], ed. G. N. BONWETSCH, *Hippolyt. Werke,* I. 1. *Kommentar zu Daniel. Zweite, vollständig veränderte Auflage von* M. RICHARD (*GCS* N. F. 7), Berlin, 2000.
4, 32, 3, 1 – 4, 2   75.17

Ignat., *Ad Smyrn.*
Ignatius Antiochenus, *Epistula ad Smyrnaeos* [*CPG* 1025. 6], ed. P. T. CAMELOT, *Ignace d'Antioche. Polycarpe de Smyrne. Lettres. Martyre de Polycarpe* (*SC* 10), Paris, 1969, p. 132-144.
4, 1, 2-5   **87**

INDEX ALIORVM FONTIVM ET LOCORVM PARALLELORVM   181

Ps.-Ignat., *Ad Philadelph.*
   Ps.-Ignatius Antiochenus, *Epistula ad Philadelphienses* [*CPG* 1026], ed.
F. Diekamp – F. X. Funk, *Patres apostolici*, II. *Clementis Romani Epistulae
de virginitate eiusdemque Martyrium Epistulae Pseudoignatii Ignatii Martyria
Fragmenta Polycarpiana Polycarpi Vita*, Tubingae, 1913, p. 168-190.
   3, 3 (p. 172, 13-17)   **88**

Io. Chrys., *De anathem.*
   Iohannes Chrysostomus, *De anathemate* [*CPG* 3430], *PG* 48, 945-952.
   946, 1-11   **79.1/9**
   947, 1-9   **79.10/16**
   948, 10 – 949, 47   **79.17/75**

Io. Chrys., *De coem.*
   Iohannes Chrysostomus, *De coemeterio et de cruce* [*CPG* 4337], *PG* 49,
393-398.
   395, 32-39   **94**
   395, 49 – 396, 2   **99**

Io. Chrys., *De dec. mil. tal.*
   Iohannes Chrysostomus, *De decem millium talentorum debitore* [*CPG*
4368], *PG* 51, 17*-30.
   17, 23-30   **66**

Io. Chry., *De Laz.*
   Iohannes Chrysostomus, *De Lazaro* [*CPG* 4329], *PG* 48, 963-1064.
   997, 51-54   **54.1/4**
   997, 61 – 998, 3   **54.4/7**
   998, 46-51   **54.7/12**
   1003, 44-59   **55**
   1003, 59 – 1004, 6   **54.12/20**
   1030, 27-54   **56.1/22**
   1031, 13-35   **56.23/43**
   1031, 31-32   **56.22/23**
   1041, 9-18   **57.1/10**
   1041, 39 – 1042, 27   **57.10/44**
   1042, 51 – 1044, 15   **57.44/83**

Io. Chrys., *De perf. carit.*
   Iohannes Chrysostomus, *De perfecta caritate* [*CPG* 4556], *PG* 56, 279-290.
   282, 33 – 283, 6   **41**

Io. Chrys., *De pseudoproph.*
   Iohannes Chrysostomus, *De pseudoprophetis* [*CPG* 4583], *PG* 59, 553-568.
   557, 70 – 558, 5   **86.1/5**
   559, 16-17   **86.6/7**
   563, 56-62   **86.7/12**

Io. Chrys., *De uirg.*
   Iohannes Chrysostomus, *De uirginitate* [*CPG* 4313], ed. H. Musurillo –
B. Grillet, *Jean Chrysostome. La virginité* (*SC* 125), Paris, 1966.
   14, 31-44   **30.1/14**

182   INDEX ALIORVM FONTIVM ET LOCORVM PARALLELORVM

14, 52-67	**30.15/32**
14, 74-75	**33.7/8**
14, 77-82	**33.1/6**
15, 2-13	**33.8/20**
17, 68-75	**33.21/28**

Io. Chrys., *Exp. in Ps.*
Iohannes Chrysostomus, *Expositiones in Psalmos* [*CPG* 4413], *PG* 55, 35-498.

159, 20 – 160, 19	**67**
160, 22 – 161, 14	**65.1/45**
161, 26-27	**65.45/46**

Io. Chrys., *In diem nat.*
Iohannes Chrysostomus, *In diem natalem* [*CPG* 4334], *PG* 49, 351-362.

352, 43-47	**76.1/4**
353, 5-9	**76.60/63**
353, 19 – 354, 22	**76.5/59**

Io. Chrys., *In ep. ad Heb.*
Iohannes Chrysostomus, *In epistulam ad Hebraeos* [*CPG* 4440], *PG* 63, 9-236.

231, 50-55	**85**

Io. Chrys., *In ep. ad Rom.*
Iohannes Chrysostomus, *In epistulam ad Romanos* [*CPG* 4427], *PG* 60, 391-682.

549, 1-24	**103.11/32**
549, 34-39	**103.33/38**
549, 53-59	**103.39/42**
550, 21-44	**103.43/65**

Io. Chrys., *In euang. dict.*
Iohannes Chrysostomus, *In euangelii dictum et de uirginitate* [*CPG* 4702], *PG* 64, 37-44.

39, 58-62	**45**

Io. Chrys., *In Eutrop.*
Iohannes Chrysostomus, *In Eutropium* [*CPG* 4392], *PG* 52, 391-396.

393, 12-18	**53**

Io. Chrys., *Serm. in Gen.*
Iohannes Chrysostomus, *Sermones in Genesim* [*CPG* 4410], ed. L. BROTTIER, *Jean Chrysostome. Sermons sur la Genèse* (*SC* 433), Paris, 1998.

2, 47-70	**19.1/23**
2, 70-78	**21**
2, 79-101	**19.24/46**
2, 113-122	**19.46/54**
6, 49-66	**24.1/16**
6, 77-83	**24.16/23**

INDEX ALIORVM FONTIVM ET LOCORVM PARALLELORVM   183

Ps.-Io. Chrys., *De paen.*
Iohannes Chrysostomus, *De paenitentia* [*CPG* 4614], *PG* 59, 757-766.
| 759, 29-36 | **78.1/7** |
| 759, 57 – 760, 32 | **78.8/59** |

Ps.-Io. Chrys., *In Ps. 92*
Ps.-Iohannes Chrysostomus, *In Psalmum 92* [*CPG* 4548], *PG* 55, 611-616.
| 615, 29 – 616, 5 | **31** |

Ps.-Io. Chrys., *Suff. tibi grat.*
Ps.-Iohannes Chrysostomus, *In illud: Sufficit tibi gratia mea* [*CPG* 4576], *PG* 59, 507-516.
| 508, 42 – 509, 19 | **22** |

Ps.-Io. Chrys., *Ver. frustr. cont.*
Ps.-Iohannes Chrysostomus, *In illud: Verumtamen frustra conturbatur* [*CPG* 4543], *PG* 55, 559-564.
| 559, 20-38 | **50** |

Io. Dam., *Exp. fid.*
Iohannes Damascenus, *Expositio Fidei* [*CPG* 8043], ed. P. B. KOTTER, *Die Schriften des Johannes von Damaskos*, II (*PTS* 12), Berlin, 1973, p. 3-239.
| 17, 66-74 | **12** |

Ps.-Io. Dam., *Sacr. Par.*
See *Sacr. Par.*

Io. Georg., *Sent.*
Sententiae a Ioanne Georgide Monacho collectae, ed. P. ODORICO, *Il prato e l'ape. Il sapere sentenzioso del monaco Giovanni* (*WBS* 17), Wien, 1986, p. 119-255.
| 646 | 69.2/3 |

Isid. Pel., *Ep.*
Isidiorus Pelusiota, *Epistulae* [*CPG* 5557], *PG* 78, 177-1645.
| 1, 132 (269, 33-34) | 77.5/6 |

Leont. Dam.
Leontius Damascenus, *Fragmenta*, ed. T. FERNÁNDEZ, *Un auteur inconnu dans le* Florilège Coislin *: Léonce de Damas*, SE 47 (2008), [p. 209-221] p. 218-220.
| *fr. 1 | **75** |
| *fr. 2 | **95** |

Marc. Bethl.
Marcianus Bethleemita, *Fragmenta* [*CPG* 3898], ed. M. KOHLBACHER, *Unpublizierte Fragmente des Markianos von Bethleem*, in M. KOHLBACHER – M. LESINSKI (ed.), *Horizonte der Christenheit. Festschrift für Friedrich Heyer zu seinem 85. Geburtstag* (*OIKONOMIA. Quellen und Studien zur orthodoxen Theologie* 34), Erlangen, 1994, [p. 137-166] p. 158-159.
| CPG 3898. 1 | **37** |

184 INDEX ALIORVM FONTIVM ET LOCORVM PARALLELORVM

Max. Conf., *Quaest. ad Thal.*
Maximus Confessor, *Quaestiones ad Thalassium* [*CPG* 7688], ed. C. LAGA
– C. STEEL, *Maximi Confessoris Quaestiones ad Thalassium*, 2 vols. (*CCSG* 7 &
22), Turnhout – Leuven, 1980-1990.

7, 2-3	**97.1/2**
7, 5-27	**97.4/27**
55, 201-218	**58**

Max. Conf., *Quaest. et dub.*
Maximus Confessor, *Quaestiones et dubia* [*CPG* 7689], ed. J. H. DECLERCK,
Maximi Confessoris Quaestiones et dubia (*CCSG* 10), Turnhout – Leuven, 1982.

19, 5-21 = I, 13, 5-21 (p. 18)	**73**
I, 1, 2-8 (p. 137)	**61**
I, 5, 2-7 (p. 140)	**36**

Ps.-Max. Conf., *De quat. card. uirt.*
Ps.-Maximus Confessor, *De quatuor cardinalibus uirtutibus*, ed. B. ROOSEN
– P. VAN DEUN, Ἀρετὴν εἰ ἔχοις πάνθ'ἕξεις. *Byzantine Virtue Speculation:
a Case Study*, in G. PARTOENS – G. ROSKAM – T. VAN HOUDT (ed.), *Virtutis
Imago: Studies on the Conceptualisation and Transformation of an Ancient Ideal*
(*Collection d'Études Classiques* 19), Leuven, 2004, [p. 397-422] p. 415-422.

*415-422	**60**

Ps.-Max. Conf., *Loc. comm.*
Ps.-Maximus Confessor, *Loci communes* [*CPG* 7718], ed. S. IHM, *Ps.-Maximus Confessor. Erste kritische Edition einer Redaktion des sacro-profanen Florilegiums* Loci communes (*Palingenesia* 73), Stuttgart, 2001.

1, 2, /2 (p. 7)	69.2/3
1, 4, /4 (p. 8)	81.1/3
7*, 17, ms. *F* (p. 182)	82.1/2
7*, 17, ms. *F* (p. 183)	50.7/12
8, 2, /2 (p. 185)	71.1-2
25, 4, /4 (p. 557)	43
25, 6, /6 (p. 558)	44
26, 8, /8 (p. 573)	6.3/6
48, -, /55, 18 (p. 807)	26.7/13
51, -, /58, -, /6a (p. 832)	20.5/6
66, -, /37, 9c, ms. *F* (p. 973)	64
70, 19, /41, 21 (p. 1028)	52.1/2

Nem. Em., *De nat. hom.*
Nemesius Emesenus, *De natura hominis* [*CPG* 3550], ed. M. MORANI,
Nemesii Emeseni De natura hominis (*BSGRT*), Leipzig, 1987.

c. 1 (p. 1, 1 – 16, 6)	**29**

Nil. Anc., *De uirt.*
Nilus Ancyranus, *Fragmentum de uirtute*, ed. T. FERNÁNDEZ, *Un fragmento inédito sobre la virtud, atribuido a Nilo de Ancira*, in *Bizantinistica* 12
(2010), [p. 201-214] p. 210-213.

*fr.	**62**

INDEX ALIORVM FONTIVM ET LOCORVM PARALLELORVM   185

Nil. Anc., *Ep.*
   Nilus Ancyranus, *Epistulae* [*CPG* 6043], *PG* 79, 81-581.
      3, 298 (532, 4-17)   62.11/12

Plat., *Tim.*
   Plato, *Timaeus*, ed. J. BURNET, *Platonis opera*, IV (*OCT*), Oxford, 1902.
      41 b 2-7   18.23/27

Quaest. et resp. sen.
   Quaestiones et responsa senum de tentationibus, ed. J.-C. GUY, *Un dialogue monastique inédit, Revue d'ascétique et de mystique* 33 (1957), [p. 171-188] p. 177-182
      qu. 19   **38**

Sacr. Par.
   Ps.-Iohannes Damascenus, *Sacra Parallela* [*CPG* 8056. 2. 1], *PG* 95, 1040-1588; *PG* 96, 9-441.

PG 95, 1097, 21-25	10
1097, 35-36	**8**
1097, 38-39	**9**
1113, 47-50	46
1116, 13	47.1
1116, 31-33	47.2/3
1117, 11-12	47.4/5
1117, 40-49	49
1124, 14-22	48
1125, 3-5	**51**
1128, 30-35	53
1129, 57-58	80.7/9
1132, 3-25	50
1133, 44 – 1136, 2	**52**
1137, 18-20	68.4/5
1137, 23-26	68.1/4
1141, 3-6	69
1141, 28-30	70
1141, 31-33	71
1160, 21-27	6
1169, 46-48	**72**
1172, 31-33	43
1173, 32-35	44
1200, 18-24	66
1201, 41-49	63
1204, 11-15	**64**
1233, 40-41	80.1/2
1281, 32-38	1.23/28
1509, 10-15	50.7/12
1585, 10-11	80.6/7
PG 96, 353, 3-13	81
353, 23-24	82

186 INDEX ALIORVM FONTIVM ET LOCORVM PARALLELORVM

353, 25-26	83
353, 34-39	84
405, 28-36	63

Sacr. Par., ed. HOLL, *Fragmente*
Ps.-Iohannes Damascenus, *Sacra Parallela* [*CPG* 8056. 3. b], ed. K. HOLL, *Fragmente vornicänischer Kirchenväter aus den Sacra Parallela* (*TU* 20/2), Leipzig, 1899.

fr. 10, p. 7	17
fr. 14, p. 8	**26.7/13**
fr. 26, p. 13-14	**26.1/6**
fr. 353, 1-35, p. 137-139	**93**

Sacr. Par., *Par. Rupef.*
Ps.-Iohannes Damascenus, *Sacra Parallela, Florilegium Rupefucaldinum* (= *Parallela Rupefucaldina*) [*CPG* 8056. 2. 2], *PG* 96, 441-544.

541, 25 – 544, 32	**93**

Sacr. Par., Vat. gr. 1553
Vaticanus graecus 1553, apud M. HEIMGARTNER, *Pseudojustin. Über die Auferstehung: Text und Studie* (*PTS* 54), Berlin, 2001, p. 249.

39$^{r\text{-}v}$	16.1/20
39^{v}	16.23/25

Schol. in Max. Conf.
Scholia in Maximum Confessorem; see Max. Conf., *Quaest. ad Thal.*

55, 157-169	**59**

Theod. Stud., *Paru. Cat.*
Theodorus Studita, *Parua Catechesis*, ed E. AUVRAY, *Theodori Studitis Parva Catechesis*, Paris, 1891.

127, 51-52	87.1/3

Unpublished fragments:

*Ἀθανασίου Ἀλεξανδρείας, Ἐκ τῆς ἑρμηνείας τοῦ κατὰ Ματθαῖον εὐαγγελίου (λόγος γ' add. ms. *A*) 77
*Τοῦ Χρυσοστόμου **14**
*Anonymus, inc. Ἕκτῃ ὥρᾳ τῆς παρασκευῆς ἐσταυρώθη ὁ Κύριος **101**

CONSPECTVS MATERIAE

Foreword   VII
Sigla and Bibliographical Abbreviations   IX

Introduction   XXI
    I. Genre and Compiler   XXIV
    II. The *Sacra Parallela*   XXVII

Manuscript Tradition   XXXIII
    I. Main Manuscripts   XXXIII
    II. Fragmentary Manuscripts   LXI
    III. Minor Fragmentary Manuscripts   LXVIII
    IV. Other Manuscripts   LXX

Relationship of the Manuscripts   LXXV
    I. Apographs   LXXVI
    II. The Short Recension (Γ)   LXXXVI
    III. *C* and Γ (Δ)   XCVII
    IV. Manuscripts *AT*   XCVIII
    V. *Adiaphorae lectiones*   CI
    VI. The Mixed Recension. Manuscript *R*   CII
    VII. Minor Fragmentary Manuscripts   CV

Titles and Attributions   CX

Corruptions and Dubious Readings   CXIX

Ratio edendi   CXXXII
    I. Apparatuses   CXXXII
    II. Grammar and Orthography   CXXXIV

Florilegium Coislinianum, Alpha   1
    Conspectus siglorum   2

Indices
    Index locorum Sacrae Scripturae   171
    Index aliorum fontium et locorum parallelorum .   176

CORPVS CHRISTIANORVM
SERIES GRAECA

ONOMASTICON

Acindynus, *uide* Gregorius Acindynus
Alexander monachus Cyprius 26
Amphilochius Iconiensis 3
Anastasius Apocrisiarius 39
Anastasius Bibliothecarius 39
Anastasius Sinaita 8 12 59
Andronicus Camaterus 75
Anonymus auctor Theognosiae 14
Anonymus dialogus cum Iudaeis 30
Athanasii Athonitae Vitae 9
Basilius Minimus 46
Catena Hauniensis in Ecclesiasten 24
Catena trium Patrum in Ecclesiasten 11
Catenae graecae in Genesim et Exodum 2
  15
Christophorus Mitylenaeus 74
Diodorus Tarsensis 6
Etymologicum Symeonis 79
Eustathius Antiochenus 51
Eustathius monachus 19
Eustratius presbyter 25 60
Florilegium Coislinianum 66
Gregorius Acindynus 31
Ps. Gregorius Agrigentinus 56
Gregorius Nazianzenus 20 27 28 34 36
  37 38 41 42 43 44 45 46 47 49 50 52
  53 57 58 61 64 65 73 77 78 85 86
Ps. Gregorius Nyssenus 56
Gregorius presbyter 44
Hagiographica Cypria 26
Hagiographica inedita decem 21

Homerocentones 62
Iacobus monachus 68
Iohannes Caesariensis 1
Iohannes Cantacuzenus 16
Iohannes Chrysostomus 70
Ps. Iohannes Chrysostomus 4
Iohannes Scottus Eriugena 7 18 22
Iosephus Racendyta 80
Leo VI imperator 63
Leontius presbyter Constantinopolita-
  nus 17
Marcus monachus 72
Maximus Confessor 7 10 18 22 23 39
  40 48 69 89
Mercurius Grammaticus 87
Metrophanes Smyrnaeus 14 56
Nicephorus Blemmydes 13 80
Nicephorus patriarcha Constantinopo-
  litanus 33 41
Ps. Nonnus 27 50
Pamphilus Theologus 19
Petrus Callinicensis 29 32 35 54
Procopius Gazaeus 4 67
Scripta saeculi VII *uitam Maximi Confes-*
  soris illustrantia 39
Theodorus Dexius 55
Theodorus Metochita 83
Theodorus Spudaeus 39
Theognostus 5
Theologica varia inedita saeculi XIV 76
Titus Bostrensis 82

November 2018